CHINA
YESTERDAY AND TODAY

DUKE K'UNG, LINEAL DESCENDANT OF CONFUCIUS IN SEVENTY-SIXTH
GENERATION.

CHINA

YESTERDAY AND TO-DAY

BY

EDWARD THOMAS WILLIAMS

Agassiz Professor of Oriental Languages and Literature, University of California; Formerly American Chargé d'Affaires, at Peking, China; Recently Chief of the Division of Far Eastern Affairs, Department of State.

FIFTH EDITION, REVISED

NEW YORK
THOMAS Y. CROWELL COMPANY
PUBLISHERS

Printed in the United States of America

TO

MY WIFE

𝕽𝖔𝖘𝖊 𝕾𝖎𝖈𝖐𝖑𝖊𝖗 𝖂𝖎𝖑𝖑𝖎𝖆𝖒𝖘

WHOSE ENCOURAGEMENT AND ASSISTANCE

HAVE MADE POSSIBLE THE PRODUCTION OF THIS VOLUME

IT IS AFFECTIONATELY

INSCRIBED

"And I may tell you that in acquiring this knowledge he spent in those various parts of the World good six-and-twenty years."

—*Prologue to the Book of Ser Marco Polo.*

PREFACE TO THE FIRST EDITION

Our interest in a foreign land fastens itself chiefly upon those features in which it differs from our own. When the writer first went to China he was told by Chinese acquaintances that all foreigners looked alike. He replied that to him all Chinese were so alike that it was with difficulty that he could tell one from another. In both cases, of course, it was the peculiarities of physiognomy and costume, shared in the main by all those of one nationality, that attracted the notice of men of the other nationality. The Chinese, however, are more uniform than Europeans in color and facial features, although there is considerable difference between the people of the northern and those of the southern provinces in physiognomy.

To most people in the Western World China is a faraway land of such strange customs that one is inclined to believe very readily tales told concerning its inhabitants that have no real foundation in fact. But we do rightly think of it as a land of mighty, walled cities, of lofty pagodas, of quaint, curved temple roofs, resting upon brilliantly colored bracket cornices, of curious costumes and strange products;—precious silks and satins, fragrant teas, beautiful porcelains and lacquered wares. We may think of it, too, as a sort of topsy-turvydom, where one's surname comes first and personal name last, where your friend when he meets you shakes his own hand rather than yours, where left, not right, is the side of honor, where one begins to read at the back of the book and at the right side rather than the left side of the page and finds the foot-notes at the top of the page. It is a land where dessert comes first at the feast and soup last, where the male man dresses in silk

and satin gowns of brilliant hues, and where, until the
recent revolution, all men wore their hair in long braids,
and the highest officials decorated their hats with peacock
plumes and tassels, had strings of beads about their necks
and carried fans in their hands, while on the other hand
many women were seen on the streets in jacket and trousers.

These peculiarities of costume and custom and others
that might be mentioned were universal features of Chinese
civilization until the revolution of 1911.

Since that time China has been undergoing a great
change. Architecture and dress are becoming Europeanized,
and social conditions are in flux. When you receive a
Chinese gentleman's card to-day you can not tell in many
cases whether the first or the last character represents his
surname. Some adhere to the old custom and others have
adopted the Western style. An old gentleman of conservative tastes will remove his spectacles when he talks with you
and will shake his own hands in salutation, but a young
man of progressive spirit will stare at you through his
glasses and hold out his hand to take yours in greeting.

Not all change is progress, but for good or ill, China is
changing. The social and political transformation that is
taking place is the result of a struggle between two great
civilizations, those of the East and the West. The author
has endeavored to show that these two civilizations had a
common origin. In their development, however, they took
divergent courses. After ages of separation they have met.
To-day in the Orient they strive together for mastery. To
describe this struggle, it has seemed advisable to review
briefly the history of the intercourse between China and the
West. The contest during the past century has for China
been a losing one. The West has won victory after victory,
but the end is not yet. The effects of the struggle have become most noticeable during the past thirty years, and the
events of these years have therefore been given more detailed consideration in this volume.

The writer lived in China before the tendency to change
became marked. He witnessed the downfall of the Manchu

Dynasty and the establishment of the Republic, and saw initiated the great reforms which have wrought such havoc with old-time manners and conditions. This volume is the outgrowth of his experiences and observations in thirty-five years of close association with Chinese affairs, supplemented by such research as a very busy life would permit. The aim kept constantly in view in preparing the book has been to describe the China of the past and the present, the China of yesterday as contrasted with the China of to-day.

It is impossible for men not to err, and the author cannot hope to have entirely escaped all mistakes. There may be instances in which he has unintentionally described as universal certain customs which were known only in the regions with which he is familiar, and there may be other cases in which the changes that have taken place are much greater or less than as described.

For the translations from the Chinese he holds himself responsible unless otherwise acknowledged. But he has not hesitated to avail himself of the assistance given by the work already done by others. He gladly acknowledges his debt to the monumental work of Dr. Legge in his translation of the Chinese Classics. The beautiful translation which Professor Soothill has given of the Analects of Confucius, and especially the valuable collection of notes in the commentary accompanying it, have been of great service. Acknowledgment is made also of assistance derived from the French translation of the *Shih Chi* by the late Edouard Chavannes, and of the French translations of Buddhist and Taoist works by Père Wieger. Other acknowledgments are made in place.

E. T. W.

BERKELEY, CALIFORNIA,
  January 13, 1923.

PREFACE TO THE SECOND EDITION

The author desires to express his grateful appreciation of the reception given to his work by the public. Since a new edition has become necessary, he has endeavored to increase the usefulness of the book by carefully revising the whole and adding new material to cover the recent course of events.

The startling changes that have taken place during the past three years in the internal condition of China and in her international relations call for especial notice. The section dealing with "Present Conditions in China" has been entirely re-written. The discussion of the Opium Problem has been extended to include a review of the two conferences at Geneva in 1924 and 1925. The pressing demands of the Chinese in relation to Tariff Autonomy and the Abolition of Extraterritoriality have made it necessary to report rather fully the two conferences at Peking in 1925 and 1926 dealing with these questions. The growing influence of Russia both at Peking and at Canton have made it desirable to review Russian activities in China since 1920.

One entirely new chapter has been added. This deals with Chinese Art. In the preparation of this chapter the author has become indebted to those who have been qualified to write with more authority on Oriental Art. An appreciation of the Art of China may perhaps lead us to a better understanding of Chinese civilization. With that understanding there will come improved relations.

E. T. W.

Jan., 1927.

NOTE TO THE THIRD EDITION

A chapter on Chinese Literature has been added to the fifth printing.

E. T. W.

April, 1928.

x

PREFACE TO THE FOURTH EDITION

The author, having been informed by his publishers of their intention to undertake a sixth printing of this work, has, at their suggestion, very carefully revised the volume, making what is believed to be a more logical arrangement of the chapters and bringing the historical record down to the close of the year 1928.

Acknowledgment is gratefully made to those who have called attention to errors over-looked in proof-reading and others who have intimated that a guide to the pronunciation of Chinese names would increase the usefulness of the book. Such a key to the method of transliterating Chinese characters is now provided.

The present condition of affairs in China seems to make especially appropriate and necessary a new edition of a volume that professes to describe the China of to-day. Now that the greater part of that land has been restored to comparative peace after seventeen years of civil strife, opportunity is afforded for a new estimate of the importance of the changes that have followed one another with kaleidoscopic rapidity during that period.

Whether the peace recently achieved is to be permanent or merely prove a breathing spell to be followed by further struggle, in either case the events of 1928 must be looked upon as epoch-making in character. An entirely new form of government has been adopted, whose trial will be watched by the world with great interest. The capital has been removed from Peking to Nanking. At the latter city, freed from the repressive influences of tradition and from the ultra conservative atmosphere of a monarchical capital and aristocratic estates, the new government will breathe the more freely and undertake with energy and enthusiasm the experiments which they have already proposed for the amelioration of social conditions and the creation of an educated electorate to which at some future date the exercise of self-government may be entrusted.

Already the Ministry of Foreign Affairs at Nanking has made a very successful beginning in its endeavors to recover tariff autonomy and to remove the crushing incubus of jurisdiction by foreign states over their citizens and subjects in China. It is quite evident that the China of to-day is more than ever unlike the China of yesterday. It is incumbent upon us therefore to enquire what influences have wrought so powerfully of late in a land so wedded to the past as to make possible the thorough uprooting of ancient institutions.

Whether the present form of government is to continue for a brief or for a long period one can not foretell. Who can say what the China of to-morrow will be? The leaders of to-day are young men for the most part. They are men of Western education and of liberal sentiments. They are not without political experience and they have shown themselves to be not only men of action, but also of vision. They are capable of forming great plans: are they capable of executing them? Doubtless they know their own people and can judge of their willingness to be led by the group of energetic young men that hold the reins of power. One may be disposed to question the wisdom of the present organization, but it is not possible to question the practical wisdom of the Chinese people as a whole. They are a patient people, lovers of peace, and rather disposed to "bear the ills they have than fly to others they know not of." In the end they will work out their own salvation. Whatever the future may have in store for China as a state, we may rest assured that to the people of China it will bring in the years to come as so often in the centuries that are past a restoration of unity and a consecration of their remarkable talents to the arts of peace.

China with her vast resources and her industrious population can not escape the destiny of becoming a great nation. She must yet wield an influence like that which was hers in the eighth century when all Asia visited her capital, an influence not inferior to that which she exerted in the thirteenth when Marco Polo wrote of the glory and wisdom of the Grand Khan. Indeed a greater mission awaits her, for she must now take a worthy place in the counsels of the world and contribute of her wisdom to the solution of the social and industrial problems that exercise the thoughts of men. The author hopes that this revised edition of his work may help its readers to a just appreciation of China and her great people.

E. T. WILLIAMS.

Berkeley, California,
December 12, 1928.

PREFACE TO THE FIFTH EDITION

Since the Fourth Edition of this work appeared great changes have taken place in China. The China of Yesterday, it is true, remains unchanged, in the unchangeable past, but the China of Today is in a state of unstable equilibrium. The kaleidoscopic shifting of social, economic and political forces produces a rapid succession of pictures, none of which seems to us to represent the enduring form of the new Chinese state.

A temporary peace between the warring factions was obtained in 1928 by the coalition of the army of Chiang Kai-shek with the forces of Yen Hsi-shan and Feng Yü-hsiang, and, after the removal of the capital to Nanking, there was a period of great legislative activity on the part of the Kuo Min Tang. By the promulgation of new laws and ordinances it sought to prepare for the recovery by China of jurisdiction over alien residents as well as to readjust the nation to modern world conditions.

The peace, however, as just intimated, was but temporary. Every year since 1928 has seen some form of civil strife. Factional chiefs, north, south and center, have struggled for preeminence, and the seeds sown by Dr. Sun's Russian advisers has produced the expected crop of Communism.

Added to the tragedy of civil war is the more awful disaster of the floods of 1931 in the Yangtze, the Yellow and the Huai Rivers, bringing sorrow to forty millions of people in sixteen provinces by its wide-spread destruction of life and property. In the spring of 1932 silver suddenly depreciated to an alarming extent, reducing the value of the national currency in the markets of the world.

External problems have been no less important. New treaties have been negotiated that have restored to China her tariff autonomy and a large number of foreign states have surrendered the extraterritorial jurisdiction formerly enjoyed by them. But these encouraging events have been over-shadowed by the aggression of Japan.

Geographical changes, too, have taken place since 1928. Five new provinces have been created,—four of them carved out of Inner Mongolia and one out of eastern Tibet. A number of old place names have had to give way to new. So many of these changes have been made that a new map of China in 1932 has been prepared.

It is incumbent upon me to record here my appreciation of the assistance received from the suggestions and criticisms of friends. Thanks are especially due to the Honorable C. T. Wang for official publications, among them the excellent work of Dr. Tyau, "Two Years of Nationalist China." To the Honorable Julean Arnold I am indebted for "China Through the American Window" with its valuable statistics, and to him as well as the U. S. Department of Commerce I am under obligation for the "China Monthly Trade Report." The courtesy of the publishers of the *Chinese Nation* in supplying important information is also much appreciated, as is the kindness of Dr. Kiang Kang-hu for his suggestions.

The reception that has been given CHINA YESTERDAY AND TODAY is very gratifying. It is my hope that the revision now made will add to the usefulness of the book.   E. T. WILLIAMS.

Berkeley, July 1, 1932.

CONTENTS

LIST OF ILLUSTRATIONS

xxi

PAGE

PRONUNCIATION OF CHINESE NAMES

There are several systems of transliterating Chinese words. That which is commonly employed by Americans and English is the system of Sir Thomas Wade. It is that adopted in this volume. There are, however, some exceptions. All names whose spelling has become generally adopted throughout the world are retained in those accepted forms. Such are Peking, Hankow, Canton, Chiang Kaishek, Sun Yat-sen and many others.

The system by which the sounds of other words are represented is briefly as follows:

Of the vowels:

a has the sound of a in *father*, as *Chang, Antung.*

e, the sound of that letter in *end*, but is sometimes lengthened, approaching the long a. For the first sound we have *Chengtu*, for the second, *Yenchou.*

i, as in *machine*, when it is a final, as in *Hsi-an*, for it must be remembered that each syllable is a word in Chinese. When found elsewhere than at the end of a syllable it is short as in *sing;* thus we have *Tingchou.*

o, long as in *spoke*. *Honan* and *P'oyang* are examples.

u, is long, having the sound of *oo* when at the end of a syllable, as in *P'u-k'ou*, commonly written Pukow, but has the sound of u in *full* elsewhere, as in *Shantung.*

Of the diphthongs:

ai, has the sound of i in *nice*, as *T'aip'ing.*

ao, is like ou in *bound*, as *Paoting, Ch'aochou.*

ou, has the sound of ou in *soul*, as *Tungchou* or *Haik'ou.*

ie, is like ie in the French, *bien* as in *T'iehling, Weihsien* or *Fengt'ien*, resembles long a.

ei, resembles ei in *their*, as *Wei Hai Wei.*

ua, is like wa in English, as in *wall*. *Huang Ho, Tuan-fang Kuangtung*, all illustrate the sound.

ui, is near to oo-e, but also approaches the sound of ey in *whey*. *Anhui, Weihui, Suining*, are examples.

iu, like ieu in *lieutenant*, as *Kiukiang* or *Liuchou.*

ü, like u in French *elu*, but somewhat shorter before a, e or n, as *Yünnan, Yüan Shih-k'ai.*

xxiii

Of the consonants:

ch, without the aspirate resembles an English j, as in *James.*
Examples: *Chang Tso-lin, Chengchou.*

ch', with aspirate same as ch in *church.* Examples: *Ch'angp-ing, Ch'uchou.*

h, is same as in English, but

hs, indicates a sound difficult for Americans and English, since the aspirate precedes the sibilant in pronunciation.

k, without the aspirate is hard like a hard g as in *gong.*

k', with aspirate is like English k. Thus k in *Yangtze Kiang* is pronounced very nearly as if spelled Giang with the initial g hard as in *go.* But k in *K'aifeng* is just as in the English word, *keep.*

p, unaspirated is very near to the English b. But

p', aspirated is like the English p. Thus *Paoshan* is pronounced very like *Baoshan.* But *P'oyang* is pronounced just as it would be in English without the apostrophe following the p.

t, unaspirated resembles English d, but with the apostrophe following it is like the English t. So *Shantung* is pronounced as though spelled Shandung, or very nearly so, while *T'aiyüan* has an initial t that is as plainly aspirated as in the English word, too.

j, as used in the transliteration of Chinese deserves explanation. In central China ports there are places whose dialects have an initial sound like the French j, but these words in the Mandarin begin with a sound which can scarcely be distinguished from an English r. Thus the word *jen,* meaning "man," in Peking and Nanking to ordinary ears appears to be *ren.* So *Juchou* in Honan is pronounced very like Ruchou, and *Jaochou* in Kiangsi, as though the initial sound were that of an r.

CHINA YESTERDAY AND TO-DAY

CHAPTER I

WHAT IS CHINA?

God hath made of one blood all nations of men to dwell on all the face of the earth, and hath determined the times before appointed and the bounds of their habitation.—St. Paul.

> God gave all men all earth to love,
> But since our hearts are small,
> Decreed for each one spot should prove
> Beloved over all.
>
> —Kipling.

What is China? The question was asked at the Conference on Limitation of Armament held in Washington in 1921–1922. It was not answered. An attempt to do so would probably have provoked a controversy.

The Nine-Power Treaty, signed at that Conference, in its first article stipulates that the powers other than China shall respect the sovereignty, the independence and the territorial and administrative integrity of China. But what does that mean?

TERRITORIAL BOUNDARIES

Does it, for instance, require the eight powers concerned to respect China's claim to sovereignty in Tibet? Does it mean that these powers recognize Tibet as an integral part of China? The question is important, for, although Tibet has belonged to China for many centuries, during recent years both Russia and Great Britain have maneuvred for position to control the future of this forbidding land, which a British writer describes as "rich in gold . . . enormously rich, possibly richer than any other country in the world."[1]

TIBET

In 1912 the British Government objected to the provision of the Chinese constitution which gives Tibet representatives in the Parliament at Peking. Objection was made also by the same Power to China's proposal to send a small military force to Lhasa to protect the Chinese Resident there. Warning was given that, should troops be sent as proposed, Great Britain would withhold from the new Republic of China the recognition which it was then asking.

In 1913, at the request of Great Britain, a conference was held at Simla to consider the relations of the three countries —Great Britain, China and Tibet.

The British delegation drew up a treaty which proposed to divide Tibet into two parts—Outer Tibet, adjoining India, and Inner Tibet, bordering on China. The former was to be autonomous under a shadowy suzerainty of China, and it was further provided that in case of difficulties arising between autonomous Tibet and China, the questions at issue should be referred to Great Britain for equitable adjustment. This proposed treaty would thus have put Great Britain in the position of protector of Tibet. It is interesting to recall that it was by similar arrangements that the British Government came gradually into control of Northern India. Sikkim, Nepaul and Bhutan, once tributaries of China, are now under British control. In 1913, however, China refused to sign the proposed treaty; Tibet was willing to accept it. The question therefore remains unsettled: Is China sovereign in Tibet?

OUTER MONGOLIA

In 1911 Russia encouraged Outer Mongolia to declare its independence of China, although it had been a part of the empire since A.D. 1691. Under this encouragement ad-

[1] Holdich, "Tibet the Mysterious," p. 329.

vantage was taken of the revolution in progress in China to establish an independent Mongol government under the rulership of the Hutukhtu of Urga, who was elected Emperor and crowned in December, 1911.

Subsequently by a tripartite convention signed in 1915, the suzerainty of China and the autonomy of Outer Mongolia were acknowledged, and Russia was given a voice in the settlement of questions affecting the foreign relations of the country.

After the disappearance of the Tsarist régime in Russia, China reasserted her authority and compelled the Hutukhtu, in 1919, to rescind his declaration of autonomy. He yielded only under pressure of the military occupation of his capital. When Urga was attacked and captured in Feb. 1921 by a Russian force commanded by Ungern von Sternberg, a reactionary leader, the Mongols gave him support. Japan, which was believed to be anxious to see a conservative buffer state between Korea and Siberia, was also popularly credited with giving assistance to Ungern, and was reported to have offered a loan to the Hutukhtu, if a non-communistic government should be maintained by him.

After a few weeks, however, Ungern was overthrown by the army of the Far Eastern Republic, and Urga was turned over to the troops of the Union of Russian Socialist Soviet Republics, which set up there the Peoples' Revolutionary Government.

The red army was withdrawn in the spring of 1925, but a Soviet form of government is still maintained and Russian influence predominates.

MANCHURIA

When the war between Russia and Japan came to an end in 1905, the Treaty of Portsmouth stipulated that both powers were to evacuate Manchuria completely and simultaneously, except the leased territory of Liaotung. The two powers were also to restore entirely and completely to the exclusive administration of China all portions of Manchuria then in occupation or control of Japanese or Russian troops, except the leased territory just mentioned.[2] The two powers also engaged to exploit their respective railways in Manchuria exclusively for commercial and industrial purposes.[3] Again in the treaty of July 30, 1907, these same governments recognized the independence and territorial integrity of the Empire of China and the principle of equal opportunity there for the commerce and industry of all nations.[4]

Yet in the secret treaties of 1907, 1910 and 1912 they delimited their respective spheres of special interest in Manchuria and Mongolia, and each agreed not to interfere in the consolidation and future development of the special interests of the other in the spheres mentioned.[5]

Furthermore in 1915, by the treaties of May 25, Japan after landing troops and issuing an ultimatum, obtained special privileges in South Manchuria and Eastern Inner Mongolia.

[2] Treaty of Portsmouth, Article III.

[3] Treaty of Portsmouth, Article VII.

[4] Treaty between Japan and Russia, July 30, 1907, Article II.

[5] See Treaty of 1910, Article III. The secret treaty of 1907 defined the boundaries between Russian and Japanese spheres of special interest by a succession of straight lines, which began at the Russian-Korean frontier, continued via Hunchun northwestward to the north end of Lake Porteng (also written Pilteng—Chinese name Nan Hu), thence northwest by west to Hsiu Hsin Chan (Chinese Hsin Ch'eng), near Petuna, thence down the Sungari River to the mouth of the Nonni, thence along the course of this river up to the mouth of the Tola River, and thence up the Tola to the crossing of the 122 meridian east of Greenwich. The treaty of 1912 extended the line from this point along the course of the Hulunchuerh and the Mushihsha to the watershed that divides the Mushihsha from the Haldatai, about the point where the boundary of the Amur Province crosses the 119 meridian, and from that point along the boundary of the Amur Province to the boundary between Inner and Outer Mongolia, thence southwestward along the boundary between Inner and Outer Mongolia to its intersection with the meridian of Peking (116° 27′ E.) and thence along this meridian to the boundary of the Province of Chihli.

Russia recognized Japan's special interests in the territory of Inner Mongolia east of this meridian, and Japan recognized Russia's special interests, not only in Outer Mongolia, but in Inner Mongolia west of the meridian of Peking. This arrangement assigned to Japan for exploitation all that region of Inner Mongolia and Manchuria in which she had planned to build the Ssu-p'ing-k'ai—T'aonan and the T'aonan—Jehol railway lines. The Ssu-p'ing-k'ai—T'aonan Line has since been extended to Tsitsihar. There are branches, westward to Tungliao and southward to Tahushan.

At the recent Washington Conference Japan withdrew certain of the Twenty-one Demands of 1915 which had been reserved for further consideration, and agreed that the option which had been obtained on loans for railway building in Eastern Inner Mongolia and South Manchuria, and on other loans secured upon taxes in the regions mentioned should be "thrown open to the joint activity of the international consortium recently organized." She also surrendered the preference obtained in the appointment of advisers to the Chinese Government in South Manchuria. But Japan refused to rescind the whole of the Twenty-one Demands as requested by China. Baron Shidehara said:

> If it should once be recognized that rights solemnly granted by treaty may be revoked at any time on the ground that they were conceded against the spontaneous will of the grantor, an exceedingly dangerous precedent will be established, with far-reaching consequences upon the stability of the existing international relations in Asia, in Europe and everywhere.

To this Mr. Wang Chung-Hui replied that—

> A still more dangerous precedent will be established, with consequences upon the stability of international relations which can not be estimated, if without rebuke or protest from the Powers, one nation can obtain from a friendly, but in a military sense weaker neighbor, and under circumstances such as attended the negotiations and signing of the treaties of 1915, valuable concessions which were not in satisfaction of pending controversies, and for which no *quid pro quo* was offered.

It was through the Twenty-one demands of 1915 that Japan compelled China against her will to cancel her right to redeem the South Manchuria Railway in 1939, as provided in the original contract. It was by means of the treaties of May 25, 1915, extorted from China in connection with the Twenty-one demands, that Japan was enabled to extend her lease of the Liaotung Peninsula from 25 years to 99 years. The twenty-five-year period would have terminated in 1923. By means of these same treaties the leases of the South Manchurian and Mukden-Antung Railways were also extended to 99-year periods.

In view of all these facts what is to be said of the status

of Manchuria? With large bodies of Japanese troops stationed in various parts of Manchuria, and with Japanese police forces in the Chientao district and elsewhere, to what extent does the Nine-Power Treaty guarantee Chinese administrative integrity in Manchuria?

The future will answer the questions raised. For the present we can accept no other boundaries for China than those existing under the Manchu Government at the time of its overthrow in 1912, and we must continue to regard Tibet, Mongolia, and Manchuria, therefore, as wholly within the territory of the Chinese Republic.

FORMER EXTENT OF DOMINION

It will not be amiss in passing to recall the former extent of China's dominion, and note the gradual loss of empire during the past four hundred years.

For a long time China was the dominant power in Asia. Her influence extended as far west as Aden, whose Sultan paid tribute to her. Nepaul, Sikkim and Bhutan, in northern India, were among her dependencies. Ceylon, Malacca, Burmah and Siam, Cambodia, Cochin China and Tonquin, all recognized her overlordship. The Sultan of Sulu sent tribute. The Loochoos and Korea were dependencies. Her boundaries in Central Asia touched the borders of Persia, and the valleys of the Amur and the Ussuri, on the northeast, also were hers.

To-day Aden, Ceylon, Sikkim, Bhutan, Nepaul, Malacca and Burmah all belong to the British Empire, which also has established a colony at Hongkong, once a part of China. Siam is independent. Cambodia, Cochin China, Annam and Tonquin form French Indo China, and France also has a lease to Kuangchouwan in the Province of Kuangtung. The Sulu Archipelago long ago passed under the rule of Spain, and by Spain was ceded to the United States. The Loochoos and Korea were taken by Japan, which has also annexed Formosa and the Pescadores and leased a portion of the Liaotung Peninsula. Russia has occupied a great part of Central Asia that once bowed to the sway of

Peking, and has also extended her boundaries to the banks of the Amur and annexed the Siberian Maritime Province east of the Ussuri and reaching to the borders of Korea.

Thus the great empire of China has been gradually eaten away at the fringes.

PRESENT DAY CHINA

But what remains to China still leaves her in extent of territory one of the greatest countries of the world, in latitude reaching from 19° north, in the island of Hainan, to 53° north in Manchuria, and in longitude extending from 72° east, in Turkestan, to 134° east at the mouth of the Ussuri River. It covers an area of more than four million square miles, and contains a population of some four hundred millions of people.

It is not an empire made up of scattered islands or colonies, far distant one from another, but a compact continental area covering nearly all of south-eastern Asia, cut off by the vast mountain masses of Tibet and the deserts of Turkestan and Mongolia from the rest of the continent, and protected on the east and south by the waters of the sea.

It was practically within these boundaries, through many centuries, that China developed her independent civilization, isolated from all but the most casual contact with the West. That remarkable civilization she imposed upon the lesser states with whom intercourse was possible. Siam, Annam, Japan and Korea all derived their arts and institutions from her, and the less civilized Manchus, Mongols, Turkis and Tibetans also were her pupils. Holding "dominion over palm and pine," with every variety of soil and climate, her agricultural products were more varied than those of any other land, and, equally rich in animal and mineral resources, she had raw materials for every kind of manufacture and has given the world some of its most important industries.

It was customary under the Manchu régime to speak of China as including the "Eighteen Provinces" and the de-

pendencies. The provinces had organized county, pre-
fectual and provincial governments; the dependencies were
ruled through native princes under the control of the Ministry of Dependencies at Peking and its representatives,
the Military Governors, in various districts, and the Residents in Tibet and Outer Mongolia. But in 1878 Turkestan
was converted into a nineteenth province called Hsin-
kiang, or "the New Dominion," and in 1907 Manchuria
was organized into three more provinces, making twenty-
two in all. Since the republic was established six new
provinces have been created, four out of Inner Mongolia
and two out of eastern Tibet. The four Mongolian are
Jehol (now added to Manchuria), Chahar, Suiyuan and
Ninghsia. The two from Tibetan territory are Ch'ing Hai
(or Kokonor) and Hsik'ang. To-day, then, China consists
of twenty-eight organized provinces and the dependencies;
Tibet and Outer Mongolia.

In the old Eighteen Provinces the population is almost
wholly Chinese, but there are several tribes of aborigines
in the southern and south-western provinces. In Turkestan
and all the dependencies the Chinese are in the minority.
In the four provinces of Manchuria there is a mixture of
races, but the Chinese out-number all the others added
together.

Of the dependencies, Tibet, with the exception of a few
valleys, is cold, sterile and inhospitable. It is sparsely
populated. The people are ignorant, superstitious and poor.
Although a Chinese Resident at Lhasa represents this Government there the country is ruled in fact by a theocratic
government with a dual head. The Dalai Lama wields the
political power and the Panshen Lama the ecclesiastical.

Ch'inghai, or Kokonor, once a part of Tibet, is inhabited by twenty-nine tribes of nomads, whose chief industry is grazing. They are ruled by native princes under
the supervision of a Chinese Governor at Sining in Kansu.

Inner and Outer Mongolia are also inhabited by nomads,
descendants of those hordes which, under Genghis Khan and
his successors over-ran all Asia and south-eastern Europe.
Inner Mongolia has much fertile land which is being colo-

nized by the Chinese. Outer Mongolia also, on the border of Siberia, has fertile valleys.

Inner Mongolia extends northward to the great desert plateau which forms the greater part of Outer Mongolia, and which lies at an elevation of over 4000 feet above the level of the sea. The climate is bitterly cold in winter, but on summer days the heat is intense. The proximity of this Gobi desert, and that of Taklamakan in Turkestan, to the northern tier of provinces in China is probably responsible for some of the peculiarities of the climate there, particularly for the periodical recurrence of drought and famine. One of the striking features of the climate is the occurrence of dust storms which, especially in March and April, sweep down from the desert and cover all north China with a deposit of loess, stifling man and beast and making travel all but impossible. Taken altogether Inner and Outer Mongolia cover an area of 1,272,000 square miles, and have a population of about two millions.

The Mongol tribes are engaged in raising cattle, horses, camels, sheep and goats. Camel's hair, goat's hair, sheep's wool, with hides and skins are the principal articles of export. There are valuable mines in Mongolia, but they have not been developed to any great extent.

At present (1928), Outer Mongolia, by the treaty with Russia of May 31, 1924, was restored to the suzerainty of China, but appears to be still practically under the domination of Moscow. But normally the people, whether in Inner or Outer Mongolia, are subject to the orders of their chieftains or princes, and these in turn, with all their subjects, look up with reverence to the Hutukhtu at Urga, the chief ecclesiastic of the country and the third in rank in the Lama Church. Chinese sovereignty is represented by the military governors stationed at various points, and more especially by the Resident at Urga.[6]

A conference held in the summer of 1930 between representatives of the Central Government and the Mongol Banners agreed upon various administrative and social reforms designed to win Mongol support for the Nationalist cause.

[6] The Hutukhtu died in May, 1924. No successor had yet been appointed in 1931.

TURKESTAN

Chinese Turkestan, or the "New Dominion," as it is now called, lies on the north-western frontier of China, and covers an area of 550,000 square miles, mostly desert. It has a population of more than two millions, partly Chinese and partly Turki, with a number of Sarts and Hindus also. These are found chiefly in the oases of the Tarim Valley. The Tarim River, 1250 miles long, is fed by the snows of the Hindu Kush, and supplies the water needed for the irrigation of the fields around Kashgar, Yarkand, Khotan and other towns. It flows eastward, decreasing in volume as it goes, and finally loses itself in the marshes of Lob Nor. The Pamirs and the Karakorum Mountains form a barrier on the west. The Tienshan range, extending almost in a direct line east and west, divides the region into two sections. North of the range is the valley of the Ili River, flowing westward into Lake Balkash in Russian Central Asia. Kuldja, once occupied by Russia during the revolt of Yakub Beg (1866–77), and returned to China in 1881, lies near the Russian border. Ili is celebrated for its ponies.

Other cities of Turkestan are Kuchen and Hami. The ancient route of overland travel between the East and West passes through the province by the valley of the Tarim, and crosses the Pamirs over a pass which is at an elevation of more than 14,000 feet.

Wherever cultivation is possible the province produces abundant crops of grain, cotton and fruits. All the domestic animals are reared in considerable numbers. Fields of lucerne furnish rich pasture. The region is noted, too, for its minerals, particularly the white or "mutton-fat" jade, so highly prized by the Chinese. Silk culture and rug-making are important industries of the province.

From ancient times the inhabitants have been a source of trouble to the Chinese, for this was the home of the Hsiung Nu who often invaded China or pillaged the caravans trading with the West. They are identified by some with the Huns of similar characteristics who carried terror to Europe in the Middle Ages, and also with the barbarous Scythians of whom Herodotus wrote. To-day they are Mohammedans in religion, and being of a different race from the Chinese, toward whom they have an inherited antipathy, they are sometimes guilty of plotting against the government. During the World War they were stirred to unrest by German and Turkish propaganda, but were not induced to rise. Yang-Tsen-hua, the Military Governor of the province, was credited with the preservation of peace there after 1911. On July 7, 1928, however, he was treacherously murdered. Following this a rebellion broke out, which in the autumn of 1928 was accompanied by horrible massacres.

MANCHURIA

The "Four Eastern Provinces," as Manchuria is known to the Chinese, now include Jehol, a portion of Inner Mongolia. Thus enlarged Manchuria has an area of some 448,957 square miles, and a population of about 32,000,000, found chiefly in the southernmost province, Liaoning (formerly Shengking) and the central province, Kirin. The whole region was once an independent kingdom, the home of the Manchus who conquered China in A.D. 1644. It has as its natural boundaries the Hsingan Mountains on the west, the Amur River on the north, the Long White Mountain and the Yalu River on the east, and the sea on the south. Six great rivers furnish channels of communication along its frontiers or give access to the interior; the Amur, the Ussuri, the Sungari and its tributary, the Nonni, the Yalu and the Liao.

For two hundred years after the conquest of China the Manchus discouraged immigration into northern and central Manchuria, and held the vast forests there as hunting grounds for the Court. The northern province is still but sparsely settled, although the region is one of rich soil and bracing climate. The mineral resources of Manchuria are also considerable and are but slightly developed. Gold is found in the north and coal and iron in the southern part. Wheat, the soja bean, tobacco and millet are among the best crops, and beans, pongee skins and furs among the chief exports.

This rich, undeveloped region has for years past been

coveted by Russia and Japan. There are about 200,000 Japanese resident there, and perhaps a million Koreans. The railways in the south are leased to Japan and operated by Japanese. Those in the north were under Russian control until the Great War threw Russia into disorder. Since 1930 they have been operated under joint management of Russia and China, but there are matters relating to them that have yet to be adjusted.

CHINA PROPER

The Eighteen Provinces which are the real home of the Chinese people have an area of more than a million and a half square miles and a population of about 370,000,000.

Three great rivers divide the country naturally into three sections; the Yellow, the Yangtze and the West Rivers.

NORTHERN PROVINCES

The Huang Ho or Yellow River touches eight provinces in its course. Its turbid waters carry enormous quantities of silt, which is deposited in the lower channel where the current grows sluggish. Thus the bed of the river is constantly rising and in places is above the level of the fields, which are protected by dykes. These are frequently broken in times of flood, and thus the river has come to be known as "China's Sorrow." Except in its northern bend and for some miles above its mouth the stream is not fit for navigation. The whole valley is one that from ancient times has been afflicted alternately by flood and drought. History records many floods since the days of Yü the Great, who is said to have reclaimed the fields from the overflowing waters in 2205 B.C. and many droughts have brought famine to the people since T'ang the Completer in 1761 B.C., after seven years of crop failure, proposed to offer himself as a victim to appease the wrath of God, so it is believed, and thus brought the long-desired rains. The famine of 1920-21 is reported to have destroyed eight million lives. Floods in 1931 wrought great damage.

The Yellow River rises in the mountains of Tibet at an elevation of more than 13,000 feet, within but a few miles of the source of the Yangtze. Its upper course is a crooked one. It crosses Kansu Province in a channel obstructed by huge rocks and descends rapidly in a series of cascades, leaving the province at an elevation of but 3000 feet above sea level, when it enters the Ordos country. Thus far its course has been through a wild region, sparsely inhabited, mountainous, and covered with forests. Leaving the Ordos country in the new province of Suiyüan, the Yellow River bends toward the south, flowing between the provinces of Shensi and Shansi. When it reaches the southwestern corner of Shansi it is joined by the Wei, coming from the west, and thus increased in volume turns eastward across Honan and then northeastward across Shantung.

The province of Shansi contains some of the largest deposits of coal and iron in the world.

Shantung, where the river finds its mouth, is the Holy Land of China, the birth-place and burial place of two of its greatest teachers, Confucius and Mencius, and the province which holds the sacred Mount T'ai.

This is the province on whose coast Kiaochow Bay is located, once leased to Germany, captured during the War by the Japanese, and returned to China by the treaty signed at Washington in February, 1922. On the northern shore of the Shantung Peninsula is the harbor of Weihai-wei, leased to Great Britain in 1898 for as long a period as Russia should hold Port Arthur and Dalny. At the Washington Conference, 1921-22, Great Britain agreed to return the territory to China. The rendition was made on October 1, 1930.

This province, too, has valuable mineral deposits; coal, iron and gold. Chihli,[7] its neighbor on the north, is rich in coal, and holds within its borders the former capital, Peking, and the principal port of north China, Tientsin. The capital of China during the greater part of its history

---

[7] The Nationalist Government has changed the name of this province to Hopei (north of the Ho), corresponding to that of its neighbor, Honan (south of the Ho). This change was made because the name, Chihli, signifies ''directly governed,'' implying that it contains the seat of government.

has been located in the Yellow River Valley, sometimes at Heianfu in Shensi, at other times at Loyang or at K'aifengfu in Honan, and several times at Peking as in recent times.[8] Along the northern frontier of China Proper the Great Wall extends from Shanhaikuan on the sea coast to Chiayükuan on the border of Turkestan, some 1300 miles to the west.

The agricultural products of this part of China are those that are common in the North Temperate Zone; wheat, bar1ey, oats, millet and maize, beans in great variety, hemp and jute, apricots, apples, cherries, grapes, peaches, pears and persimmons. Cotton and silk are also produced. The pongees of Shantung are well known. Railways connect Peking with Hankow and Nanking in central China and with Mukden in Manchuria. Tsinanfu on the line between Peking and Nanking is the capital of Shantung and is connected by rail with Tsingtao, the port formerly leased to Germany.

THE YANGTZE VALLEY

The valley of the Yangtze Kiang is the real heart of China. This river, one of the greatest in the world, rises at an elevation of some 16,000 feet above sea level, and in the first 900 miles of its course falls nearly 14,000 feet. It is 3200 miles long and drains an area of not less than 700,000 square miles. This area is divided among seven provinces. The river has many large tributaries and the whole valley is rich in soil, salubrious in climate, and contains a population of some two hundred millions, that is to say, one-half of the population of the entire country. The valley is the most important part of the Republic, both agriculturally and commercially. Its mineral resources are very important. Iron, coal and antimony are those most developed.

It has between 25 and 30 cities each which has a population of over a hundred thousand, and numerous other cit-

[8] The names, Peking and Nanking, meaning northern and southern capitals, are popular designations of those cities, but they have other designations, more often used in literature and in political documents. Nanking has not been the capital since A.D. 1421, yet it has been known popularly by that name. It could have done no harm to allow Peking for historical reasons to remain Peking. But the Nationalist government after the removal of the capital, changed the name to Peip'ing, signifying ''Northern Peace.''

ies and towns that approach that limit. Its industries are varied and interesting, and its trade attracts the merchant fleets of the seven seas.

Its principal crops are rice and cotton, but wheat and maize also are planted. The mulberry supplies food for the silk-worm. Ginger and indigo are produced in large quantities, and several varieties of citrus fruits are added to those which its orchards have in common with the northern region.

Shanghai is the greatest port, having a population of over a million inhabitants. Other cities open to foreign residence are Ningpo, Hangchow and Soochow, Nanking, several times the capital of China, Hankow, the center of the tea trade, Hanyang, the site of iron furnaces and rolling mills, and Chungking, the chief port of Szechuen Province. The gorges of the Yangtze below Chungking afford some of the most awe-inspiring scenery in the world.

There are 225,000 miles of canals in China, of which most are found in the Yangtze Valley. The Grand Canal, whose beginnings were undertaken in the Sixth Century B.C. but whose completion dates from the close of the Thirteenth Century A.D. connects Hangchow with Tientsin.

Railways now give communication between Shanghai and Nanking, Nanking and Peip'ing, Kiukiang and Nanchang, and between Hankow and Peip'ing. Others are planned and in part under construction.

THE SOUTHERN PROVINCES

The West River does not compare in length with the Yellow River nor in volume and navigability with the Yangtze, nevertheless its waters, taken with those of its tributaries, may be said to concern all the remaining provinces of China Proper except Fukien, which cut off by a mountain barrier from the Yangtze region and having only coast communication with the south, may be said to be isolated. Its affiliations, however, are with the south rather than with central China, and it is best considered therefore in the group of Southern Provinces.

The West River rises in the province of Yunnan and flows across Kuangsi into Kuangtung, where it is joined by the North and East Rivers to form the estuary of Canton, or the Bocca Tigris. Canton is the oldest and best known sea-port of China, and has been engaged in foreign trade since the Third Century A.D. It is still the chief entrepôt for commerce with the south, and the waters of the rivers named, give access, not only to the two Kuang Provinces but to Yunnan and Kueichou as well. A canal connects one of the tributaries of the West River with the head waters of the Siang, in Hunan Province, and thus affords communication with the Yangtze.

These five southern provinces constitute a well-defined region distinct from the rest of China. They are all mountainous and rich in mineral deposits. They have a subtropical climate and corresponding flora and fauna. The inhabitants in large part are non-Chinese aborigines, and the Chinese speak a variety of dialects and for the most part do not understand the mandarin, which is the official language. The agricultural products of the region are abundant and varied. All the grains are grown but rice is perhaps the most common. Beans, hemp, cotton, tobacco, indigo, sugar cane and tea, ginger, cassia and peanuts are all produced. Silk is common. Wild silk is produced in Kueichou. The caribou, sheep and goats are among the domestic animals. Poultry and fish are raised in great numbers.

FUKIEN

Fukien, as already stated, is cut off from easy communication with the rest of China, and its people have therefore developed in seclusion, having many customs peculiar to themselves. The population is dense and the prevailing poverty has forced many to emigrate. Most of the Chinese in the Philippines are from this province. Foochow, its capital, was formerly one of the principal tea ports of China, but has lost much of its trade.

KUANGTUNG

Kuangtung Province, whose name has been given by Europeans in the form of ''Canton'' to its chief city, was the first province visited by European vessels; and for a long period of years the port, Kuangchoufu, which we call "Canton," was the only city open to foreign trade. The Canton delta is a broad, fertile plain, crossed in many directions by a net-work of water-ways. It is densely populated and contains a number of large cities: Canton with over a million, Fatshan with five hundred thousand, Shiklung with a hundred thousand, Huichou, Chaoching, Samshui, Kongmoon, Kowloon and others of lesser importance.

Canton is connected by rail with Fatshan and Samshui and by another line with the British port, Kowloon, which is opposite the island of Hongkong and belongs to that colony. A trunk line is being built northwards from Canton which will eventually connect with the railway under construction from Hankow southward. When completed this will afford rail communication with Peking.

The Cantonese are an energetic and progressive people, and in temperament, speech and customs differ widely from the people of the north. This probably has had much to do with the bitter political strife between Canton and Peip'ing.

On the right of the mouth of the Canton Estuary, just opposite Hongkong, is the peninsula of Macao, now a Portuguese colony. It was occupied by them, with China's consent, in 1557, and rent was paid to China for its use until 1849, when Portugal attempted to assert her sovereignty there. China did not acknowledge Portuguese ownership, however, until 1887.

Since 1898 the French have held a lease upon Kuangchouwan, in the province of Kuangtung, but nothing of consequence has been done by them to develop the region. At the Conference in Washington during the winter of 1921–22 the question of the return of this leased territory to China was raised, and it was intimated that France would give favorable consideration to the proposal.

Off the coast of Kuangtung lies the interesting island, Hainan. Two tribes of aborigines occupy the central portion of the island. The Chinese live chiefly along the coast. The fauna and flora are tropical.

There are many aborigines also on the mainland in Kuangtung, but more in the adjoining province of Kuangsi, where two-thirds of the population are non-Chinese.

THE THREE SOUTH-WESTERN PROVINCES

Kuangsi, Kueichou and Yunnan are all very mountainous, sparsely settled, and rich in minerals, but very backward in social conditions. The mineral resources are largely undeveloped. Gold, silver and antimony are found in Kuangsi; iron, coal, quicksilver, copper and zinc in Kueichou; tin and lead, zinc, copper and coal in Yunnan. The tin and copper mines of Yunnan have been worked to a considerable extent by native methods. In Kueichou and Yunnan development has been hindered by lack of communications. Transportation has been very difficult in the past. Yunnan now has a railway connecting its capital with Hanoi in Indo China.

All three south-western provinces have suffered much from rebellion, due in part to the fact that so large a part of the population is non-Chinese. In Kueichou three-fourths belong to the Miao tribes. Yunnan has a large element of Mohammedans. They rose in rebellion in 1856, and kept up the struggle against the Chinese until 1872. Ten millions of people were said to have perished during the war.

Eternal snows cover the mountains in the western part of Yunnan. The province is watered by several large rivers. The branches of the Irawaddy cross the western border. The Salween flows across the province in deep gorges. The Mekong for 500 miles has cut its way through a canyon that is from 2000 to 3000 feet deep. Its banks are covered in many places with dense forests. The Yangtze forms a part of the northern boundary of the province. The West River rises in the eastern part, and the Red River flows across the southern border into Indo China.

MOUNTAIN SYSTEMS

The mountain ranges of China, which have so much to do with determining its physical characteristics and its climatic conditions, stretch out over eastern Asia like the fingers of a mighty hand. That hand, weighing heavily upon the center of the continent, is the huge mass of lofty table-lands and towering peaks which we know as Tibet. It is the largest and highest group of mountains in the world.[9] The plateau of Tibet varies in elevation from 13,000 to over 16,000 feet above sea level, but the summits of the Kunlun Range on the northern border rise to over 20,000 feet, and the Karakoram Mountains on the northwest to more than 28,000, while Mount Everest in the Himalaya on the southern frontier reaches to 29,000 feet above the sea. The northwestern part of the plateau has no drainage channel to lower levels. The rivers that flow into it from surrounding mountains deposit their waters in numerous lakes that have been formed there. But in the east and south are deep and fertile valleys drained by the head waters of the greatest rivers of Asia. These valleys fall to an elevation of 11,000 feet. In them most of the inhabitants of Tibet find their homes.

The Altai System.—A single range of mountains in China is often called by different names in different localities. Thus the western end of the Kunlun Range where it bends to the northwest is called the Karakoram Mountains. Further to the north it becomes the Pamirs, and the Pamirs pass into the Tienshan.

These three—the Karakoram, the Pamirs and the Tienshan, form the western boundary of Chinese Turkestan. Over the Karakoram range there is a pass at an elevation of 18,500 feet, by which communication is maintained between Yarkand in Chinese Turkestan and Ladak in Kashmir. The highest peaks of the Pamirs attain an elevation of 26,000 feet. There is a pass over the mountains 14,200 feet above sea level at Shishiklik. From the northern extremity of the Pamirs the Tienshan extends north-eastwards and divides into two main branches. The northern branch, or Tienshan Pei Lu, has a northeast-southwest direction. Its highest peak, Tengri Khan, has an elevation of over 23,000 feet. This range connects with the Tannuola Mountains and the Altai Range, which constitute the northwestern border of Mongolia. The Altai Mountains do

[9] Richard's Comprehensive Geography of China, p. 539.

not rise above 11,000 feet. They stretch across Siberia to the northeast in the Yablonoi Mountains, which form the northern water-shed of the Amur Valley.

The Tienshan Nan Lu.—This southern branch of the Tienshan Range has an east and west direction. It divides Chinese Turkestan into two great basins. The highest peaks reach an altitude of 25,000 feet and are covered with glaciers. Eastwards the range declines gradually and connects with the great central plateau of Mongolia, which has an elevation of about 5000 feet.

The Altyn Tagh.—The Kunlun Range, as it stretches eastward, splits into several chains. The northernmost is known as the Altyn Tagh. It maintains an altitude of about 14,000 feet. Where it approaches the pan-handle of Kansu Province it is called the Nanshan, or "Southern Mountains," and to Europeans is known as the Humboldt Mountains. There it holds in the embrace of two parallel ridges the great lake called Koko Nor, or Ch'ing Hai, which has an elevation of 10,000 feet. Bending southeastwards in parallel chains, one of which is called the Richtofen Mountains by Europeans, it expands in a tangled mass of mountains over Kansu and Shensi. The principal range strikes northeastwards along the course of the Yellow River to the Ordos Plateau, where it unites with the Alashan Range, 10,000 feet in elevation. These mountains deflect the Yellow River to the east, and after a short distance the channel is bent towards the south by the expansion of the mountains in the Shansi Plateau, which varies in height from 6500 to 11,000 feet. From Shansi eastward the range is known as the Inshan. The Alashan and the Inshan form the southern boundary of Mongolia. Eastwards the Inshan continues into the Great Hsingan Mountains, which, bending to the northeast, form the boundary between Mongolia and Manchuria and reach an elevation of about 7000 feet. A spur of this range known as the Little Hsingan separates the valley of the Amur from that of the Nonni. Further to the east a long range parallel with the Great Hsingan is called the Ever White Mountains. It extends from the southern extremity of the Liaotung Peninsula, through the

PURPLE CLOUD MONASTERY, WESTERN HILLS.

SUNKEN ROAD AND CAMELS.

eastern part of Manchuria to the junction of the Ussuri with the Amur. Its highest peak is about 8500 feet above sea level.

The Ch'inling.—Where the Altyn Tagh leaves the eastern Kunlun, another range breaks off towards the southeast in several parallel chains, known by various names in different places. By Europeans it is called the Marco Polo Mountains. To the Chinese it is known as the Ch'inling and the Hsich'ing Mountains. The elevation falls as the mountains stretch eastwards. The highest peaks reach to 13,000 feet, but the range averages about 6500. It forms the natural boundary between Tibet and the Province of Kokonor, or Ch'inghai, and it forms the water-shed between the sources of the Yellow River and the Yangtze. Bending to the east as it approaches the southeast corner of Tibet, it divides into two principal chains. The northern chain, or Pei Ling, separates the Wei River valley from that of the Han, and where the Wei empties into the Yellow River it forces the latter to make another sharp bend, this time towards the east. As the mountains strike across Honan Province the parallel spurs, running east and west, are called successively from north to south Huashan, Funiushan, Huailungshan and Huaiyangshan. These spurs fall gradually in elevation until as low ranges of hills they lose themselves in the great plain. But eastwards beyond the great plain the mountains of Shantung lift themselves, the greatest of which is Mount T'ai, with an elevation of 5060 feet. The southern chain of the Ch'inling is called the Kiulung in the eastern part and the Minling in the west. It separates the valley of the Han from that of the Yangtze and forms the natural northern boundary of Szechuen Province. It has an elevation of from 8000 to 11,000 feet. It stretches southeastwards into Hupei Province and loses itself in the Lake Plain.

The Nanling.—Where the Ch'inling mountains, in several parallel chains, reach the northeastern corner of Tibet they send off a number of branches toward the south. These lofty mountains, called by various Tibetan names, are known to Europeans as the Snowy Mountains and also as the Szechuen Alps. They maintain generally a north and south direction, and rise to 16,000 and 19,000 feet above sea level. The various chains are separated by deep gorges, and severally divide from one another the head waters of the Irawaddy, the Salween, the Mekong, the Yangtze, the Yalung and the Min. They stretch across Szechuen to the south and southeast, and spread out over Yunnan, Kueichow and Kuangsi, forming the water-shed between the Yangtze and the West River. North of the latter they form the Nanling, or Southern Range, with an elevation of between 5000 and 6000 feet, which separates the provinces of Kuangsi and Kuangtung from those lying to the north of them. Continuing eastwards this range unites with the Ta Yü Ling, 5000 feet in height, which, running parallel to the coast, forms the boundary between Fukien and Kiangsi. Further north, in Chekiang, a branch bends towards the east and ends in the sea in the Chusan Archipelago.[10]

SACRED MOUNTAINS

Mention ought to be made of the sacred mountains of China. To the Confucianist these are five: T'ai Shan in Shantung, Hang Shan in Shansi, Sung Shan in Honan, Hua Shan in Shensi, and Heng Shan in Hunan. But in the opinion of most Chinese Wu T'ai Shan in Shansi and Omei in Szechuen are equal in sanctity to any. These two are shrines for Buddhist pilgrims.

THE RIVERS

The mountain chains have determined the flow of the waters, and these have gathered in three great valleys in China Proper and in three others in Manchuria.

---

[10] For more detailed information concerning the mountain systems consult Richard's ''Comprehensive Geography of China'' and Stanford's ''Compendium of Geography, Asia.'' For geological features, Richtofen's ''China,'' Pumpelly's ''Geological Researches in China,'' ''Explorations in Turkestan,'' and the Carnegie Researches in China under Willis, Blackwelder and Sargent.

The Yellow River, 2700 miles long, drains the northern provinces, winding in a tortuous course through the northwest and crossing the great plain to the Gulf of Chihli. It is of slight use for navigation, and in its lower reaches it frequently overflows its banks and causes great distress.

The Yangtze Kiang crosses central China from west to east, and after a flow of 3200 miles enters the Eastern Sea near Shanghai. Its principal tributaries are the Yalung, the Min, the Ch'ung and the Kialing, in Szechuen, the Siang in Hunan, the Han in Hupei, and the Kan in Kiangsi. It is one of the noblest rivers of the world, navigable for over 1500 miles, and its valley is one of the richest and most populous.

In the south the West River is the principal water-way. It rises in eastern Yunnan and flows in two branches across Kuangsi Province. These two branches unite a short distance above Wuchow, from which point to the sea it is navigable for steamers. In its upper portion it flows through sandstone valleys and is obstructed by rapids. The scenery in this region is very picturesque. Near Canton its waters mingle with those of the North and East Rivers to form the Pearl River, in whose rich alluvial plain Canton is situated. The Red River, the Mekong and Salween in the southwest, the Huai and Ch'ient'ang Kiang in central China, and the Pei Ho in Chihli are also of some importance.

In Manchuria the Amur, navigable for 1500 miles, and its chief affluent, the Sungari with its tributary, the Nonni, drain Heilungkiang and Kirin Provinces. The Sungari is navigable to Kirin, about 600 miles, and the Nonni another 150 miles above its junction with the Sungari. In the southwest the Shara Muren, or Liao River, which empties into the Gulf of Chihli below Newchwang, is navigable for steamers 30 miles above its mouth, and for native boats throughout its course. In the southeast the Yalu, a beautiful stream, forms the boundary between Manchuria and Korea. It is navigable only in its lower reaches. The Tumen, which empties into Possiet Bay north of Korea, and the Ussuri, a tributary of the Amur on the northeastern boundary of Manchuria, are rivers of less importance.

THE COAST LINE

The coast of China extends in a rude quadrant from the mouth of the Yalu (Latitude 40 N.—Longitude 125 E.) to the border of Indo China (Latitude 21° 30' N.—Longitude 108° E.) a distance roughly of 2100 miles. The coast, however, has many indentations, which, included in the measurements, make the coast line about 5000 miles. The northern coast is very generally of an alluvial character, excepting that of Shantung. The southern is granitic in formation. The best bays with deepest water are found in the latter region. There are two considerable promontories, those of Shantung in the north and Leichou in the south. Leichou, with the great island of Hainan adjacent to it, is of about the same area as the Shantung Peninsula. There are five large gulfs, or bays; Korea Bay at the mouth of the Yalu, the Gulf of Liaotung at the mouth of the Liao, the Gulf of Chihli (or Peichihli) at the mouth of the Hai Ho, Hangchow Bay at the mouth of the Ch'ient'ang Kiang, and the Gulf of Tonking behind the Leichou Peninsula.

There are many islands along the coast of China, the most important of which are the Miao Tao north of Shantung; the island of Tsungming, formed within the last five hundred years by deposits of the Yangtze; Saddle Rocks and the Chusan Archipelago, near Ningpo; The Loochoos, Formosa and the Pescadores, belonging to Japan; Hongkong, belonging to Great Britain, and Hainan, south of Leichou.

THE PLAINS

Taken as a whole the country must be considered very mountainous, but there are several important plains. Chief of these is the great plain formed by the alluvial deposits of the Yellow River. On the north this merges with that of Chihli Province, deposited anciently in large part around an old mouth of the Yellow River, and in part by the Pei

Ho and other affluents of the Hai Ho. Behind the promontory of Shantung the Yellow River Plain merges to the south with that formed in the delta of the Yangtze. Taken together these three plains constitute the richest agricultural region of China. Another important plain, whose soil is no less rich but whose extent is much smaller, is that found in the delta of the Pearl River around Canton. West of Hankow is another great plain, that of Hupei, some 4000 square miles in extent, interlaced with lakes and canals.

Still farther up the Yangtze, in the province of Szechuen, is the fertile plain of Chengtu, containing some 2000 square miles, shut in on all sides by lofty mountains, through whose rocky barriers the Yangtze has worn its way. Its irrigation system, which dates from the third century B.C., is one of the marvels of early engineering skill. It has made the plain of Chengtu one of the most populous and prosperous regions of China. It is estimated that five millions of people occupy this small plain.

LAKES

China is abundantly supplied with lakes, both fresh water and salt. The great fresh water lakes are in the Yangtze Valley; Tungting in Hunan, Poyang in Kiangsi, Ch'ao in Anhui, Hungtse, partly in Kiangsu and partly in Anhui, and T'ai Hu in Kiangsu. There are two fresh water lakes of considerable size in Yunnan; Erh Hai and Tien Hu. In Tibet, Ch'inghai, Turkestan and Mongolia there are numerous lakes, some of them of large extent, whose waters, having no outlet, have become brackish. In Mongolia, however, there is one great fresh water lake, the Koso Gol, which is the source of the Selenga River.

DESERTS

There are two great deserts in China; the Gobi and the Taklamakan, or Tarim. The former covers a large part of Mongolia and extends into eastern Turkestan. The latter is practically an extension of the former into western

Chinese Turkestan. To the Chinese the Taklamakan is also known as the "Desert of Moving Sands." [11] This expressive term well describes the chief characteristic of this desolate region, where whole towns, abandoned twenty centuries ago, have been buried under the waves of this great sea of sand. This desert is the dry basin of an ancient sea. It is surrounded on all sides by lofty mountains that rise into the regions of eternal snow. The basin itself has an elevation of 3000 to 4000 feet above sea level, but in the northeastern part of Turkestan there are depressions which sink to sea level and possibly still lower. These depressions, however, are included in the region called by the name of the Gobi Desert. This is the lowest portion of the Mongolian tableland, which is a rocky waste averaging 2500 to 3000 feet above sea level. It is not entirely destitute of vegetation, however, since grass springs up in its southeastern part in the spring. These desert regions on the northwestern borders of China have had great influence upon its climate, as already said.

CLIMATE

China extends over many degrees of latitude and longitude, and varies greatly in the elevation of different regions. Its climate varies accordingly. In the far south we find a moist, tropical climate; in the north a dryer atmosphere, with a short, hot summer and a longer and fairly cold winter, and on the snow-clad peaks an arctic temperature. There are, however, two well-marked seasons, summer and winter. A brief spring and a more prolonged autumn separate these.

Along the coast and to a lesser degree in the interior the climate is governed by the monsoons.[12] In the spring and summer the air over the elevated table-land of Mongolia and over the deserts of Turkestan becomes heated, and rises, causing an inflow from the south. This spring wind

[11] Legge's translation of the Shu King. Sacred Books of the East, Vol. II, p. 76.

[12] See China Year Book 1921–22, p. 80; and Richard's "Comprehensive Geography," p. 14.

brings with it moisture from the sea. The rains advance from south to north with the advancing season, but fall more abundantly in the south.

In the winter the Mongolian table-land and the deserts of northwest China quickly become cooled, and this cold air rushes down into the lower levels and lower latitudes. These northern and northwestern winds bring with them at times great clouds of yellow dust, which settles over north China in the formation known as the loess. It is found in greatest quantity in the mountainous regions of Shensi and on the table-land of Shansi, but also in lesser amounts covering the higher levels of the great plain in Honan and Chihli and in considerable quantity in Shantung. The winds at times blow with great force and bear this finely comminuted dust as far south as the banks of the Yangtze.

FLOOD AND FAMINE

The history of China discloses the fact that from antiquity to the present time China has frequently suffered from flood and drought. Both have created famine conditions and caused great loss of life. In the twenty-third century B.C., according to the *Shu King*, the floods of the Yellow River were so extensive as to be represented as "assailing the heavens," and as "embracing the hills and topping the great heights." [13] The Great Yü, it is said, occupied nine years in his work of creating channels for the superfluous waters. In 1766 B.C., we are told in the same work, there was a great drought which lasted until 1761 B.C.—seven years. It was so severe that, as related above, the sovereign is reported to have decided to offer himself as a sacrifice to Heaven to remove the awful calamity. While he was praying, it is said, the rains came and put an end to the drought.

Alexander Hosie, of the British Consular Service in China, made a careful study of droughts in China from A.D. 620 to 1643, a period of 1023 years, [14] during which

[13] See Legge's translation of the Shu King, Sacred Books of the East, Vol. III, pp. 34-35.
[14] Journal of China Branch Royal Asiatic Society, Vol. XII, N. S. p. 51.

he found that Chinese histories recorded 583 years in which drought had occurred. That would mean one every two years or less. But these droughts did not occur every time in the same provinces. Some years one region was affected; at other times other regions. It is impossible at present to say that these droughts have occurred at regular intervals in any one district, but there seems some reason to suspect that this is the case. A degree of drought often occurs which does not result in entire destruction of the crops. In such cases no real famine occurs. We find, however, that from A.D. 801 to 1643, that is to say during 842 years, there were 214 severe droughts, which would imply that one occurred every four years or oftener. But these, too, occurred in different sections of the country. There would seem to be an alternation in northern China of flood and drought. In 1877 and 1878 there was a great famine in Shantung and adjoining provinces. Ten years later—1887—there was an awful flood in the Yellow River, which affected the same region. In 1892-94 a great famine visited the same region. Five years later—1898—there were great floods in this same Yellow River Valley. Other floods visited the region in 1905-6, 1910-11, and in 1917. More recently drought and famine visited that region in 1920–21. This record is too incomplete and covers too brief a period to allow us to deduce any rule, but the matter is one well worth investigation. An examination of the Chinese historical records, which are very detailed, would enable us to determine the facts with respect to any one chosen region—the Yellow River Valley for instance.

Ellsworth Huntington in his "Pulse of Asia," and in a more recent volume, "Climatic Changes," prepared in collaboration with Stephen Sargent Visher, has called attention to the periodicity of certain climatic changes.[15] Some of these occur in brief cycles that may be measured in years. Others are measured in decades, some in centuries, and others still in millions of years. It is evident, therefore, that, should these recurring droughts and floods be found to come in regular cycles, the aridity or humidity

[15] Op. cit. Chapter V and elsewhere.

would be emphasized or modified and the period be lengthened or shortened by the approach to the beginning or end of other cycles of greater length. At present central Asia is suffering from excessive aridity. Six hundred years ago, in the 14th century, that region was far more humid than to-day. The Caspian Sea stood thirty-seven feet above its present level.[16]

The authors just quoted appear to believe that one of the most important factors in producing these periodic changes is the influence of the sun upon our atmosphere. They say:

A detailed study has led to the conclusion that cyclonic storms are influenced by the electrical action of the sun. Such action appears to be most intense in sunspots, but apparently pertains also to other disturbed areas in the sun's atmosphere. A study of sunspots suggests that their true periodicity is almost if not exactly identical with that of the orbital revolution of Jupiter, 11.8 years. Other investigations show numerous remarkable coincidences between sunspots and the orbital revolution of the other planets, including especially Saturn and Mercury. This seems to indicate that there is some truth in the hypothesis that sunspots and other related disturbances of the solar atmosphere owe their periodicity to the varying effects of the planets as they approach and recede from the sun in their eccentric orbits and as they combine or oppose their effects according to their relative positions.[17]

It is to be remembered, however, that not all parts of the earth are affected in the same way by the electrical action of the sun. The authors of climatic changes say:

With the change in storminess there naturally goes a change in rainfall. Not all parts of the world, however, have increased storminess and more abundant rainfall when sunspots are numerous. Some parts change in the opposite way.[18]

If this hypothesis is confirmed by further investigation we may expect to find some relation between the periodical disturbances of the sun's atmosphere and the occurrence of drought and floods in China.

[16] Ibid, p. 104.
[17] Ibid, p. 243.
[18] Ibid, p. 53.

But, this speculation aside, there are other factors of the problem whose influence is more easily measured. It has been pointed out that the rapid rise of temperature in the high lands of Mongolia and the desert regions of central Asia causes the air over those places to rise and the cooler air of the south to flow in. If then for any reason this rise of temperature is not so great the wind from the south will be weak, and the moisture with which it is laden may be deposited almost entirely in the southern provinces and thus create a want of rain in the north. Huntington and Visher, discussing the famines in India in the fourteenth and eighteenth centuries, say:

These Indian famines were apparently due to weak summer monsoons caused presumably by the failure of central Asia to warm up as much as usual. The heavier snowfall, and the greater cloudiness of the summer there, which probably accompanied increased storminess, may have been the reason.

In 1920 when there was a drought in the Yellow River Valley the floods in central China were so severe as to cause destruction of life and property in those provinces. Another factor which possibly contributes to the severity of drought is the occurrence of the dust storms in the early spring months. The dust which settles over the northern provinces is equivalent to a top dressing, and when water is plentiful adds to the fertility of the soil, but the loess formed by this dust is very porous. Water sinks through it very rapidly, and should the rains fail or be less than usual the very dryness of the deposited dust may perhaps increase the disastrous effect of the drought.

A great deal has been written about the deforestation of China. The hills for the most part are barren, save for the crop of coarse grass and brush-wood which is cut every year by the fuel gatherers. This destruction of forests has been regarded as one of the causes of drought and flood. Doubtless this has been a factor in the problem, but we cannot overlook the fact that drought and flood occurred in the earliest history of China, when forests still covered the mountains, and that they have occurred at intervals ever since. I have already referred to the tradition of a flood in the twenty-third century B.C., and a famine in the eighteenth century B.C. In the year 544 B.C. a treaty signed by a number of Chinese princes stipulated in its fifth article that mutual succor should be given in time of famine.[19] This would imply a frequent occurrence of such calamities. Yet at that time these princes maintained each in his own dominions forests for hunting grounds.

The suffering from famine can be greatly reduced by the improvement of communications in China. The difficulty and expense of transporting grain from one part of the country to another has greatly increased the distress.

[19] See Martin's ''Lore of Cathay,'' p. 441.

CHAPTER II

THE BEGINNINGS OF CHINA

Beyond the Northwestern Sea, west of the Red River, is the Kingdom of the Forefathers, who lived on grain. . . . Still westward are the Wangmu Mountains, a vast range, where the Kingdom of Wu is located, whose people feed upon the eggs of the wild phœnix and drink sweet dew. Their every wish is gratified as soon as uttered.
—The Shan Hai King.

The vast area, which has just been described, covers many degrees of latitude and longitude, as has been said. It contains the loftiest mountains in the world and some of the most extensive plains. It is a land of great deserts and of fertile valleys, and one of great variety in soil and climate. In it also dwell many races of people. The dominant race, and the race that outnumbers all the others, put together, is the Chinese.

The Chinese, however, were not the earliest inhabitants of China. Neither did they originate as a people in the land after which they are called. Their origin has been a subject of speculation by various writers. The weight of evidence seems to favor the opinion that they had their beginning in central Asia, and that they came into the upper valley of the Yellow River about the beginning of the third millennium B.C.

CAUSE OF MIGRATION

The cause of their migration from their ancient home in all probability was the progressive desiccation of that region. At the close of the last glacial epoch, as Professor Pumpelly has reminded us,[1] the northern coast of Asia was covered by the ice cap. Central Asia was a region of

[1] "Explorations in Turkestan," 1904, Carnegie Institute, Washington, D. C., p. xxiv.

great inland seas and of a moist climate. There are six great basins, covering altogether the greater part of a region measuring three thousand miles east and west by sixteen hundred north and south, extending from the western border of Manchuria to the western end of the Black Sea.[2] During the glacial period these basins were filled with water, and at that time the straits of the Bosphorus did not exist. There was no outlet to the ocean. Upon the shores of these seas there developed the earliest civilization of which man has any knowledge. The region was entirely cut off from the rest of the world. City states apparently were founded whose inhabitants attained to a high degree of culture. In certain mounds of central Asia some of the remains of this ancient civilization have been found.

PUMPELLY'S EXPLORATION

In 1903 and again in 1904 Professor Raphael Pumpelly visited the oases of Merv and Anau. At the latter place, near Askabad, excavations were made at two sites. In the shafts that were sunk important cultural remains were found in various strata, the lowest of which is dated by Pumpelly as belonging to the ninth millennium B.C.[3], that is to say, 2000 years earlier than any remains found in Egypt or Babylonia. It appears from the discoveries made that the inhabitants, even at the date represented by the lowest layer of the mounds examined, were already cultivators of the soil and were growing wheat and barley, that they lived in houses of sun-dried brick, that they hunted wild animals, and that during the eighth millennium B.C. they domesticated the ox, pig and sheep. Before the fifth millennium B.C. they had added the dog, the camel and the goat.[4] By comparison with the results of explorations in other parts of the world it was deduced that these animals were the progenitors of those later introduced into western Asia and into Europe. In other words it seems most prob-

[2] Ellsworth Huntington, "The Pulse of Asia," p. 356.
[3] Pumpelly, op. cit., p. 57.
[4] Ibid., pp. 38, 39, 51, and 50.

able that in the region of central Asia, rather than elsewhere, we must look for the cradle of civilization.

The domestication of animals led to a differentiation in the peoples of central Asia. Some became shepherds and, as pasture lands were needed, these men moved about with their flocks and herds, while the cultivators of the soil remained in the towns around which their cultivated fields were found.

Numerous mounds remain in central Asia still unexplored. Their examination will doubtless shed much more light upon the early history of our race. Professor Pumpelly expressed the opinion that the oases of central Asia are the fountain of western Asiatic culture. He might have added with equal confidence that they are also the fountain of eastern Asiatic culture.

DESICCATION OF CENTRAL ASIA

As the ice cap melted and receded in northern Asia the climate gradually changed. It became dryer. This does not appear to have been an uninterrupted process. There were periods of glacial expansion followed by periods of recession.[5] There were periods of moisture and abundant vegetation followed by periods of comparative aridity. Evaporation proceeded more rapidly than precipitation or inflow of water. This was due in part, it seems, to the fact that the rain-laden clouds that blow up from the Indian Ocean strike against the loftiest mountains of the world and deposit their moisture chiefly on their southern slopes.[6]

Thus the region of these great mediterranean seas of central Asia became more and more arid. The seas themselves gradually decreased in volume. The process is still going on. Lake Balkash is much smaller than in the 18th century; thousands of square miles once covered with water have become dry land. Lob Nor, in Chinese Turkestan, has very considerably decreased within the memory of men still living; the lake has become in great part merely a

[5] Ibid., pp. 57–60.
[6] Ibid., p. 3.

marsh. The soil of Turkestan has become so brackish in many places that Chinese peasants who were cultivating it in 1890 have been compelled to remove to other districts.[7] Numerous cities in Chinese Turkestan that were busy centers of life and trade two thousand years ago are to-day buried beneath the drifting sand. Sir Aurel Stein, in his three expeditions to that region, has uncovered a few of these ancient places that in the third century of the Christian era were still peopled and prosperous.[8]

The great climatic changes which have converted the once fertile and peopled regions of central Asia into windswept deserts of moving sands are in all probability the real causes of the migrations, eastward and westward that have taken place.

THE SUMERIANS

Jastrow, in his "Civilization of Babylonia and Assyria," says that the Sumerians very possibly entered the Euphrates Valley from the mountainous regions east or northeast of Babylonia.[9] He asks "Who were the Sumerians?" and answers thus:

> We know that they were not Semites; their features as depicted on the monuments reveal a Turanian type, but the term, Turanian, is too vague to furnish a definite clue.

It is not improbable then that the climatic changes that were taking place in central Asia, and which were causing the ancient seats of civilization to be abandoned, may have been the direct or indirect cause of the migration of the Sumerians into the Euphrates Valley.

Jastrow tells us, moreover, that the Sumerians brought with them a higher form of civilization than they found in their new home, and that they imposed it upon the inhabitants there whom they subdued. The Sumerian written language became the language of the conquered and the origin of the cuneiform writing.[10]

7 Ellsworth Huntington, "Pulse of Asia," pp. 219, 266, 267.
8 "The Sand Buried Ruins of Khotan," p. 405.
9 Op. cit., 106 and 107.
10 "Hebrew and Babylonian Traditions," pp. 9 and 10.

CHINESE AND SUMERIAN

Professor C. J. Ball, of Oxford, has pointed out that the earliest form of this writing was ideographic, and in his work "Chinese and Sumerian," he gives a list of 108 ideograms in Sumerian with which he identifies certain old Chinese characters. He publishes, too, a vocabulary of more than a thousand words from the Sumerian which he shows to be substantially identical in sound and meaning with their Chinese equivalents. We are not to conclude from this that Chinese and Sumerian are identical, neither are we necessarily to infer that one borrowed from the other, but merely that the two languages are derived from a common source. That source would seem to be found in central Asia.

CHINESE EMIGRANTS

About the beginning of the third millennium B.C. a period of excessive aridity began in central Asia, driving many of the more adventurous spirits to seek new homes in less sterile regions. It was at this time that Hsüan-yüan (the name of Huangti, or "the Yellow Emperor"), is believed to have led the first band of emigrants towards China, stopping for a time, it would seem, at the Red River in Northern Kansu. Subsequently he appears to have removed some three hundred miles toward the south-east, where Ch'inchou, on the head waters of the Wei River in eastern Kansu, is associated with his name. Hsüanhua-fu, 125 miles northwest of Peking, also claims to have been his capital, which would indicate a further removal eastwards.

These pioneers were followed by others at different times. Some of these seem to have followed the Yellow River to its northern bend and pressed eastward to Hsüanhua and then southward to Pingyang, in Shansi, which is the traditional site of Yao's capital. Others settled south of the Yellow River, east of the great bend, some in the valley of the Wei near the modern city of Hsian, and others still in the northern part of Shensi.

THE CHINESE ARE TOWNSMEN

Professor Pumpelly has stated that the inhabitants of the oases of central Asia became divided into city dwellers and nomad herdsmen. It is significant that there is no evidence that the Chinese ever passed through the pastoral stage of social evolution. Like the city dwellers on the oasis of Anau, who had learned to cultivate the cereals although still living in the town, so the Chinese through all their history, so far as it is available, have been represented as cultivators of the soil, but also as living in villages and towns, and this is a striking characteristic of Chinese agricultural life to-day. The farmers build their houses in villages, around which their fields are located. Isolated farm houses are rare. This will help us to understand the references in Mencius and elsewhere to the practice of having the city, i.e., the inhabited portion, surrounded by uninhabited fields (chiao), these surrounded by the pastures for the domestic animals and these again by the wilds.[11] The "Royal Regulations" of the Li Ki tell us that in ancient China there were nine provinces, each containing 210 states. These states were held in fief and were of various sizes according to the rank of the ruler. They were, of course, city states, each with its allotment of agricultural land, pasturage and woodland. What was not so allotted was reserved as imperial, or public property.[12]

TESTIMONY OF THE ANCIENT RECORDS

The most ancient traditions of the Chinese reach back into the third millennium, B.C. and would seem to show that even at that early date the Chinese had a well organized social and political system. The Book of History begins with the reign of Yao, 2356 B.C. If we accept the view generally held that Yao's capital was in Shansi, we must agree that the Chinese, if they came from any other region into the Yellow River Valley,

[11] Mencius, Bk. 1, Part 1, Ch. 4. See Legge's footnote.
[12] Li Ki, Bk. III, Sect. 1:8.

must have brought a high degree of civilization with them. There is nowhere any evidence of their having in Chinese territory lived under stone-age conditions. They were already acquainted with the use of metals. The Ruler had a Minister of Works, a Minister of Instruction, a Minister of Crime, and a Director of Religion. They had a very respectable body of astronomical knowledge. One of the principal functions of government was to arrange the calendar, which required a careful determination of the solstices and equinoxes. They had also an elaborate ritual for the worship of God, the forces of nature, the spirits of the great dead and their own ancestors. There were three rituals; one for the worship of the Spirits of Heaven, including Shang Ti (i.e., the Supreme Being), another for the Spirits of Earth, and a third for the worship of the Spirits of Men. In another chapter I shall call attention to the resemblance between portions of their ritual and that used by the Hebrews. This does not mean that they borrowed from the Hebrews, but that both systems probably have a common origin—an origin in central Asian culture.

The ancient Chinese of the time of Yao and Shun had also a system of music and a great variety of musical instruments.

Others have called attention to the identity of a great body of astronomical lore possessed in common by the Chinese and Chaldeans; the use of a cycle of 60, of a decimal system, a musical scale, a system of astrology based upon acquaintance with five planets, five elements, five correlated colors, and a belief in the harmonies of numbers, as well as a multitude of other customs. They had a common family law and were both worshipers of their ancestors.

The possession of a common culture does not, of course, prove consanguinity, and in fact there is no relationship with Chaldeans to be established. The theory of a western origin of Chinese civilization has been discredited by attempts to prove that the Chinese are Aryan, as one writer has done, or, as another has affirmed, that the Yellow Emperor came with a band of emigrants from Elam to

China, and that these founders of the Chinese State did not belong to the Yellow Race but had blue eyes that were wanting in obliqueness.

OBJECTIONS TO THE THEORY OF A WESTERN ORIGIN FOR THE CHINESE

Dr. Frederic Hirth, in his article on China in the Eleventh Edition of the Encyclopedia Britannica,[13] objects to the theory that there is any connection between the Chinese and the people of western Asia, because the human eye is always represented by the Chinese as obliquely placed. He says:

In a pair of eyes as shown in the most ancient pictorial or sculptural representations in the West, the four corners may be connected by a horizontal straight line, whereas lines drawn through the eye of one of the oldest Chinese hieroglyphics cross each other at a sharp angle. This does not speak for racial consanguinity any more than the well-known curled heads and bearded faces of Assyrian sculptures as compared to the straight-haired and almost beardless Chinese.

These objections by Professor Hirth were particularly directed, however, against the curious theory, already noticed, that the Chinese forefathers had come to China from the region of Elam in Chaldea. His article was written apparently before the discovery that the Sumerians were of a different race from the Accadians of the Mesopotamian region. L. W. King, in his History of Sumer and Accad, says of the Sumerians:

The racial affinity of the Sumerians is problematical. The *obliquely-set eyes* of figures in early relief suggested the theory of a Mongol origin and the Chinese origin of Sumerian roots and the cuneiform character.[14]

This reference to the *obliquely-set eyes* at least removes Dr. Hirth's objection to any connection between the peoples of eastern and western Asia. Mr. King says the theory of Chinese origin of the Sumerian roots and cuneiform char-

[13] Op. cit., Vol. VI, p. 191.
[14] See ''A History of Sumer and Accad,'' London, 1910, p. 54.

acters is "too improbable to need refutation." It is not claimed, however, that the discoveries of Professor Ball show that the Sumerian writing was derived from China or that Chinese writing was derived from Sumerian, but rather that both had a common origin. Similarly the fact that Sumerians had obliquely-set eyes does not prove that Sumerians were Chinese, but does indicate a possible racial affinity and common origin.

The late Rev. John Ross, in his "Origin of the Chinese People," held to the theory that the Chinese originated in China and that their civilization was indigenous. Professor Hirth and Professor Giles agree with that opinion. The principal reason advanced for it is that Chinese history contains no record of a migration from other regions, and seems to assume that the earliest events of which it takes note occurred in the Valley of the Yellow River. But the fact that Chinese history says nothing of a migration from other regions into China is at best but negative evidence, and it must be admitted that in this instance it can have little weight, seeing that the earliest records that are contemporary with the events which they record date from a period a thousand years after the time of the supposed migration.

Dr. L. Wieger, a French scholar, tries to establish a southern origin for the Chinese, and one of the reasons given for such a theory is that the earliest ideograms of the Chinese language betray an acquaintance with the tropics. But it may be said in reply that we do not know which ideograms were in existence 3000 years B.C. Moreover the oldest known ideograms contain pictures, not only of tropical animals and plants, but of others that are known only in the colder regions of the north. They include such animals as the ox, sheep, goat, horse, dog, pig, deer, rat, toad, fish, tortoise, hare, cobra, rhinoceros, elephant, dragon, unicorn and tiger. Among plants mentioned are the willow, apple, melon, clover, wheat, bamboo, grass, hemp, flax, and millet. These are temperate rather than tropical plants. The inscriptions, moreover, date from about 1100 B.C. and the written language was in existence long before that date.

CHINESE TRADITIONS

Despite the contrary opinion expressed by such sino-
logues as Hirth, Ross and Giles, it can be affirmed that
Chinese traditions do indicate a western origin for the
Chinese people. Some of these traditions are preserved
in a work called the Shan Hai King or "Classic of the
Mountains and Seas," a sort of geography of China and
neighboring countries. It has been discredited because
of the many marvels recorded in it. This work, possibly, dates from the third century B.C., for it is evidently
referred to by the great historian Ssu-ma Ch'ien, who lived
in the following century. But it was a work which had apparently been in existence some time when he wrote, and we
may well believe that it is much older than the third century B.C. Wylie thinks it is at least as old as the Chou
Dynasty and perhaps older. The Chou Dynasty began in
1122 B.C. The "Family Sayings," an apocryphal work
which preserves many stories of the early life of Confucius,
refers to the Shan King or "Classic of Mountains" as having been written under the Shang Dynasty (1766-1122
B.C.), and the "Shan King" is believed to be the original
of the Shan Hai King. Ssu-ma Ch'ien would not accept
its statements, because it mentioned so many strange things.
Some of these are held by certain critics to be interpolations by Taoist writers of the fourth century A.D.

Considering the period in which it was written, it is not
remarkable that it contains many strange tales and substitutes fancy for fact. We have all doubtless seen copies of
ancient maps of the world representing the outlying regions as peopled with terrible monsters. In the Middle
Ages men believed that the southern ocean was steaming
hot and impassable, and that the southern regions of the
earth were inhabited by salamanders. They told strange
tales, too, of the Magnetic Mountain which would draw the
nails out of ships and so wreck them. Columbus met
with much opposition from his sailors who had heard
frightful tales of these outermost limits of the world and
who dreading the terrors of the unknown seas, feared they

would never be able to return to their homes.[15] Fiske says: "In maps made in the 15th and 16th centuries, in such places as we should label 'Unexplored Regions,' there were commonly depicted uncouth shapes of 'Gorgons and Hydras and Chimaeras dire,' furnishing eloquent testimony to the feeling with which the unknown was regarded."

Ancient Chinese geographers were quite as human as those of two thousand years later in Europe. The greater their ignorance of a region the more bizarre the description that was given of it. If, then, we refuse all credit to works that deal with gnomes and fairies, with demons and strange monsters, we shall be compelled to dispense with many works that, despite their failing, can afford valuable information.

The Shan Hai King is fairly accurate in its accounts of the regions nearest to the capital of ancient China. Its description of plants and animals is superficial; the author loves to note the medicinal properties of plants and he exaggerates the mineral resources of most places mentioned. But nothing bizarre is recorded until the writer attempts to describe regions a thousand miles or more from the capital. Of these distant places he probably knew only from travelers' tales or ancient fables and traditions. He places vast iron fields very accurately in Shansi or northern Honan, but apparently is mistaken as to supplies of copper in that region.

Routes of travel are discussed under four general heads. (1) The mountains (of which there were five that guarded the empire, one in each quarter—north, east, south and west—and one in the center); (2) the regions within the four seas by which China was believed to be bounded; (3) the region without, or beyond, the seas, and (4) the Great Desert.

THE WESTERN MOUNTAINS

Except the central region, that guarded by the central mountain and which, of course, was most densely peopled and best known, the region to which most space is given

---

[15] For some of these curious conceptions see Fiske's "Discovery of America," Vol. I, Ch. 4.

is the West. Four routes across the region of the Western
Mountains are described, and three other chapters deal with
the western region within and beyond the seas and with
the Great Desert of the north-west.

Although these chapters are not free from marvels the
accounts which they give of the western borders of China
and the region adjoining it on the north-west agree very
well with the facts. In its description of southern Shensi
the work mentions certain rivers as flowing north into the
Wei, and notes the water-shed that divides them from those
flowing south into the Han. The first route carries one to
the Koko Nor. The second route follows for some distance
the northern side of the valley of the Wei. The third leads
to the head waters of the Yellow River, notes the Tien Shan,
and farther west finds the desert of moving sands, that is
to say, the Taklamakan. It rightly describes some of the
streams as losing themselves in the sand and others as
flowing into a reedy marsh. It mentions this region very
correctly as the chief source of jade, and properly places
the Kunlun Mountains to the south and south-west of it.
The fourth route takes one farther north among white
wolves and white foxes, the pine and the cypress, and ends
in a fabled mountain, Yen-tzu, where the sun sets in a cave.

It is difficult to identify some of the plants and animals
from the descriptions given, but those that can be identified
are, generally speaking, placed in their proper localities.
The golden pheasant in southern Shensi, the yak, musk
deer, monkey, rhinoceros and elk in the vicinity of Tibet.
The rhinoceros does not exist in China now, but it was
found there in ancient times. The wolves and white foxes
and the wild sheep are placed in the north and north-west.

Three seas are mentioned in this western region; the
Western Sea, identified by the Chinese with Koko Nor, and
the North-western and South-western Seas, which may be
variously identified. The vast desert with its shifting sands
and brackish lakes is undoubtedly that of Chinese Turkestan.

Beyond the South-western Sea, the author tells us there
is a burning mountain, and at the base of the Kunlun

Mountains the Weak Water has its source. What volcano is intended is unknown, as none now exists in that region. The Weak Water by some is thought to be a lake, by others a river. The Chinese commentator says of it that the water is too weak to support a goose feather.

FABLE AND SUPERSTITION

Mingled with the facts are many fancies derived, perhaps, from a too fertile imagination, and possibly in part from misunderstood traditions or from ancient fables. A pheasant is seen with a human face. Birds are described which have but one eye and one wing each, so that they fly in pairs, one supporting another. Similar birds, called "love birds," are said by fable to have carried the love letters that passed between the Emperor Wu of the Han Dynasty and the Fairy Queen. In one region, we are told, there is a wild beast called a *chiao,* which looks like a dog but has panther markings and horns like an ox and barks like a dog. To see one is a good omen, since it betokens great prosperity. We read of a flying reptile with six feet and four wings whose advent is a fore-runner of drought. Another strange animal has the head of a man and the body of a tiger.

On the Kunlun Mountains the Fairy Queen lives in a beautiful garden. Her subjects feast on phœnix eggs and drink sweet dew. Their every wish, once uttered, is immediately gratified.

In the midst of the desert is a kingdom of women who worship their female ancestors, and somewhat farther on a kingdom of husbands. Just north of the kingdom of women is a land whose inhabitants live for eight hundred years and are not considered old. They have human heads but serpent bodies. That is a heavenly land, where the female phœnix sings and her mate dances in accompaniment. Even the wild beasts live in peaceful flocks, and the people drink the sweet dew and eat the eggs of the phœnix.

In that distant region one must not shoot an arrow toward the West, for there is the mound, or grave, of

Huang Ti, the "Yellow Emperor." Not far away is another land of very tall men, and beyond them the kingdom of white men, whose hair hangs down their backs and who ride the *fei huang*, an animal that looks like a fox, but has horns and lives for 2000 years.

Here we seem to find an echo of stories told by Herodotus of the swift-riding Scyths, who are descended from a princess with a human head but a serpent body. He, too, as well as other ancient writers, described a kingdom of women in this region of central Asia.

Pindar tells us of the Hyperboreans, who live to a fabulous age in a northern land, even to the age of a thousand years—a happy people in a beautiful country, where they feed on fragrant herbs and drink ambrosial dew.

But it is in the description of the spirits that inhabit the mountains, the wilderness and the desert that fancy runs riot. There are those with human head and dragon's body, which is a rather common description of the ancient heroes of China. Many of them are so represented on the sculptures of Shantung. Others are represented as having a human head but with the body of a horse, tiger stripes and with wings like a bird.

Some are evil spirits, others are harmless. Of the latter we are told of one that looks like an ox but has two heads, eight feet, a horse's tail and a voice that sounds like the whirring of beetles' wings. In the desert of moving sands the spirits have the appearance of men but with panther tails. In one of the western mountains is a wicked demon named *Lilun*, which will at once remind us of the Hebrew tradition of Lilith, who also dwelt in the wilderness.[16]

Because of the marvels which it records and the bizarre creatures which it describes many writers, Chinese and European, have refused to give any consideration to the statements of the Shan Hai King. But we really ought not to be surprised that such tales are preserved in it. Herodotus tells us of men with goats' feet, as well as of ants as large as foxes which guard the gold in the eastern deserts. He quotes Skylax as authority for the story of

[16] See the Hebrew text of Isaiah xxxiv:14.

men with ears so large that they rolled up in them when they went to sleep.

This habit of filling the unknown wilds with strange and savage creatures of terrible mien seems to be one that was common to primitive men. Numerous examples will occur to readers of classical literature and to students of anthropology. The centaur, half man half horse, Scylla with her twelve feet and six necks and mouths, the griffons that guard the gold in India, huge birds large as wolves, with feathers black and red but with claws like those of a lion, are instances of such fables, found in our classics.

As for the demons and hobgoblins that fill the desert and waste places, classical and Biblical literature, as well as the folk-lore of all lands, record this as the common belief of men. Yet we do not on that account refuse to profit by the writings of the ancients.

Fa Hsien, a Buddhist monk, crossed the Taklamakan Desert in A.D. 399, and speaks of it as inhabited by evil demons,[17] yet we give much credit to Fa Hsien's account of his visit to India. Hsüang Chuang, another Buddhist monk, crossed the same desert of shifting sands twice in the seventh century, and tells how he "encountered all sorts of demon shapes and strange goblins."[18] Marco Polo, in the thirteenth century, also crossed this desert, and repeats the story of wicked spirits that seek to lead the traveler astray.[19]

That such tales fill the Shan Hai King then is but evidence, not of its Taoistic origin in the fourth century A.D., as one writer holds, but rather of its very primitive character and very ancient origin. Indeed if the work had been produced in the fourth century A.D. it would be difficult to explain its want of more complete information concerning the countries of the south and west, for China had 600 years earlier entered into treaty relations with 36 states of central Asia, and for 300 years had been acquainted with the eastern part of the Roman Empire. For a hun-

---

17 Fa Hsien; Chap. I. See Legge's Translation, p. 12.
18 Beal's Translation, pp. 21, 22.
19 Marco Polo, Cordier's edition, Scribner, 1905, Vol. II, p. 197.

dred years sea-borne commerce had been carried on through Canton. It would have been strange then to have a book appear which showed so little knowledge of all foreign intercourse. These added to the reasons already given emphasize the early origin of the book.

VALUE OF THE SHAN HAI KING

The theory of a western origin for Chinese civilization does not rest for its chief support upon the trustworthiness of the Shan Hai King; the theory is entirely independent of such support. But the testimony of the Shan Hai King is of value because it indicates a common belief at the time the book was written that many of the earliest events of which Chinese tradition takes notice were concerned with a region beyond the Northwestern Sea and others with regions less distant beyond the Western Sea and on the borders of the Desert of Moving Sands.

In the midst of the Great Desert is the Sun-and-Moon Mountain, the axis of the sky. The gate of the heavens is there, into which the sun and moon retire.

"In a corner of the desert beyond the North-western Sea," we are told, "is the Broken Mountain." This is the north-western pillar of the sky which, a mythical tale tells us, was broken by Kungkung in his rebellion against the Emperor. His aim was said to be to let down that corner of the sky so that the waters above would flood the earth.

In the same region lived Nukua, said by tradition to have been a sister of Fushi, the inventor of numbers and the founder of the Chinese state, who established his throne in 2852 B.C. There, too, lived Shennung in 2737 B.C., worshiped to-day as the patron saint of agriculture and the first teacher of medicine. There was the kingdom of Hsüanyuan, better known as Huang Ti, i.e., the "Yellow Emperor," who ascended the throne in 2697 B.C., and there was the home of Houchi, who first taught the people to cultivate the grains.

There on the Kunlun Mountains was the home of Wangmu, generally called the Hsi Wang Mu, that is to say the Western Wang Mu, which is translated Western

Royal Mother, otherwise the Fairy Queen. Wangmu was more probably the name of a local chieftain or of a small state in the region of the Kunlun Mountains, but in transliterating the name the Chinese used the two characters, *wang* for "royal" and *mu* for "mother." Later the adjective *hsi*, meaning "west" was added, and out of this grew all the legends respecting the Fairy Queen, the Jade Palace, the lake of gems and the peach of immortality.

Even the strange and incredible tales which the Shan Hai King tells us of this north-western region bear witness to the importance which that distant country had in the estimation of the Chinese. Fancy grew busy with the race memories and shed upon the original tradition the transfiguring light of romance.

All this suggests that it is there that we should look for the childhood home of this ancient people.

MIGRATION OF HUANG TI

Other ancient records that are also tinged with romance but probably have a basis of fact tell us that King Mu, who reigned in China in the tenth century B.C., paid a visit to the western ruler Wangmu, and that, standing on an elevation in the Kunlun Mountains, he looked down upon the ruins of an ancient palace of Huang Ti. This story may be based upon a passage in the Shan Hai King which tells us that Huang Ti had a secondary capital in that region, identified by some as in the north-western part of modern Kansu. This would seem to indicate a migration of Huang Ti from his ancient home "beyond the North-western Sea."

Several places in the province of Kansu are associated with his name, and Ssu-ma Ch'ien, the Herodotus of China, locates his capital at Hsüanhuafu, about 125 miles northwest of Peking.

These facts have given rise to a belief that Huang Ti came into China from the north-west, and that he led a band of immigrants which moved gradually from place to

place until they had covered the thousands of miles that lay between their ancient home and Hsüanhuafu.

OTHER MIGRATIONS

There were many successive waves of immigration from central Asia southeastwards into China, some before the time of Huang Ti and some after that date. Three hundred and fifty years after the traditional date of his accession it is said the capital of China was located near the north bank of the Yellow River 400 miles south of Hsüanhuafu. The emperor then reigning surrendered his throne to a man named Shun, who belonged to a tribe called the *I* that had settled, according to the statements of Mencius, in what we know to-day as Shantung. This tribe may possibly have come to China before the days of Huang Ti, but the people appear to have been related to the Chinese.

During the reign of Shun, who took the throne in 2255 B.C., according to tradition, there arose a feudal lord named Shang, who had settled in the valley of the Wei in modern Shensi, about 400 miles west of Shun's capital. The Shangs also were apparently Chinese, but had come into Shensi much later than Huang Ti. Subsequently they, too, moved farther eastward and established a state in what we know to-day as Honan Province. From the last mentioned locality they attacked and overthrew the reigning house of China in 1766 B.C.

The Shangs in turn were followed in the valley of the Wei by another tribe known as the Chou. This tribe, too, had come from the north-west. They claimed connection with the same ancestors as Huang Ti, and were no doubt related to that branch of the Chinese family. Their traditions alleged descent from Houchi, the man who, according to Chinese legend, first taught the cultivation of the grains. Among his descendants was the chieftain who led his people to the region we call eastern Kansu, to the place known to-day as Ch'ingyang. From this place the tribe afterwards removed to the western part of modern Shensi, the Pinchou of to-day. There this tribe of Chous flourished for a time, but was attacked repeatedly by the Hsiungnu, ancestors of the Huns who over-ran Europe in the Middle Ages. Because of these attacks the Chous moved to the south side of the river Wei to the modern prefecture of Fenghsiang. But they were again subject to attack by the Hsiungnu and migrated again to the vicinity of the present city of Hsianfu. While located at this place they became a powerful state, and one of their chieftains organized a league of eight western tribes, which, in 1122 B.C., moved eastward and overturned the Shang Dynasty.

We have here then an example of the manner in which these movements of population were taking place. In a thousand years or more the descendants of Houchi had gradually moved south-eastward a distance of 1500 or 2000 miles. They pressed down upon the Chinese who had preceded them and eventually conquered and replaced them. They became the rulers of China for nearly 900 years of the most important formative period of their history, the period which gave to the world Lao Tzu, Confucius, Mencius, and Chuang Tzu, as well as many less noted philosophers and statesmen. This was the period, too, in which Chinese social and political institutions became fixed and definite.

The Chous, however, were also subjected to continual pressure from the northwest. They resisted more successfully than their predecessors had done, but in 249 B.C. they, and all Chinese had to yield to the domination of a new power, which had gradually grown up on the northwestern frontier, in the very region where the Chous, and still earlier the Shangs, had once established themselves. The new dynasty was known as Ch'in, from which the European world obtained the name "China." It was a short-lived dynasty, but its greatest emperor, Shih Huang Ti, subdued the Hsiungnu, built the Great Wall, and brought all south China and Annam nominally under his sway. These conquests were not permanent, however, for the Hsiungnu continued to be a thorn in the side of the Chinese for many centuries, sometimes as unwilling and turbulent vassals, sometimes as open and avowed enemies. In the south the Cantonese and Annamese for a time regained their independence, but later under the Han Dynasty, in 110 B.C., became again a part of the Chinese empire.

GROWTH OF THE CHINESE STATE

At this time the Chinese state included all of China Proper north of the Yangtze River and the coast between the mouth of the Yangtze and Canton. This advance had been a slow but steady process, and had been accompanied by the absorption of many other tribes that were already in the land when the Chinese arrived.

The earliest inhabitants of China were probably a race of small, dark-skinned, curly-headed savages, related to the Negritos or, perhaps, identical with them. They were followed by the Miao, mentioned repeatedly in the classical history of China as a people with whom the Chinese colonists had to contend. The Miao call themselves *Meng*. They perhaps are of Hindu origin and connected with the people known in Indo China as Mon Khmer.

The Miao, as they spread over the country, drove the Negritos before them. The Negritos passed into the Indo-Chinese Peninsula, where they are known as the Selon. Some of them perhaps reached the Philippines. The Miao in turn were driven southward by the Shans and other related peoples, such as the Karens and Tibeto-Burmans, and to-day are found in the mountains of south-western China and most probably also in Indo-China, where they are called the Mon Khmer.

Many other tribes of the earliest inhabitants of China were pushed south-eastwards to the coast. It is well known that along the coast from the mouth of the Yangtze River to Canton there are a great many different dialects spoken, some so unlike that the people can not understand one another. Yet all these dialects, and the languages of Indo China also, excepting those of the Negritos and Mon Khmer, are tonal languages and are related one to another.

The pressure which forced these tribes to the south-eastern coast and drove the Miao to the mountains came from the north-west. The successive waves of Chinese immigrants drove the earlier colonists to the south. These earlier colonists, such as the Shans, pushed the Miao and other tribes still further south, and the Miao drove the aboriginal Negritos out of the country.

The Shans were the progenitors of the Siamese and perhaps of the Cantonese also. Many were eventually pushed down into the Peninsula, where they subdued, and to a certain extent, displaced, the Selung or Negritos and the Mon Khmer. Others of the Shans remained in China, some of whom for a long time refused to be absorbed. They established a kingdom in south-western China about A.D. 345 which was not overthrown until the 13th Century of the Christian Era, when it was subdued by the Mongols. The Karens also remained in China until the latter part of the 8th Century A.D. when they passed into Burmah.

As a part of the same movement of peoples from north to south we have the Tibeto-Burmans migrating from eastern Tibet into Burmah. They came, so we are told, from the Tien Shan, that range of mountains which divides Chinese Turkestan into northern and southern sections. About the year 600 B.C., Sir George Scott tells us,[20] they were located in the valley of the Irawaddy, from which place they had driven out the Mon Khmer. Subsequently they themselves were forced to follow the Mon Khmer into Burmah.

A similar story is told of Cambodia, on the eastern side of the Indo-Chinese Peninsula. Colquhoun mentions six tribes that are found there, which before 215 B.C. were located in the Chinese provinces of Kuangtung and Kuangsi, and were forced out of China in two migrations.[21]

Mr. A. W. Graham in his "Handbook of Siam" says:

It is now the very generally accepted theory that, during the last few thousand years, Siam, and in fact the whole of Further India, has been subjected to periodical flooding. by successive waves of humanity, set moving by natural or social upheavals of population far to the north in Central Asia. We may imagine that the Negrito population of Siam or rather of that part of

[20] Handbook of Burmah.
[21] "Amongst the Shans," by Archibald Colquhoun, p. 46.

what now constitutes Siam which was then above the sea, leading their primitive existence through countless generations, their condition scarcely advanced beyond that of their celt-wielding forerunners, until there came down upon them one of these great waves of population which broke them up, thrust them aside into the remoter hills, all but exterminated them, and finally settled itself down in their place.

This irresistible tide of humanity was the advance down all the rivers of Further India of the tribe which constituted what is conveniently called the Mon-Annam Family, the savage ancestors of the Mon, or Talaing, the Khmer, or Cambodian, and the Annamese, civilized races of yesterday and to-day, and of a host of lesser tribes which still persist in quasi-barbarism.

Mr. H. R. Davies in a volume called ''Yunnan, the Link between India and the Yangtze,'' says:

Whatever the pure Chinese may have been five thousand years ago, it seems historically certain that the Chinese of the present day have grown up out of the gradual welding into one empire of Tartar tribes from the north and of Mon-Khmer, Shan and possibly to some extent of Tibeto-Burman races who were originally in occupation of much of the country that has grown into China.

It seems plain from these facts that the movements of population in Eastern Asia have been from north-west to south-east and from north to south, and not vice versa as some would have us believe. It is not unreasonable to suppose that the real cause of these movements was the great physical change that had taken place in central Asia, and which has caused a number of migrations both east and west, some of them in historic times, as already stated.

The Chinese as we know them to-day, then, are a mixture of a number of tribes, for the most part related, whose earliest seats were in that region of central Asia where man first became a civilized being.[22]

22 The views presented in this chapter were first set forth by the writer in a paper read before the Anthropological Society of Washington, D. C., in April, 1918, and published in the Journal of Physical Anthropology for April-June, 1918, pp. 183–211. The whole subject has been gone over anew, however, in preparation for this volume.

Since this chapter was written an important work* by Henri Maspero has appeared which advocates the autochthonous origin of Chinese civilization. He rejects the traditional accounts of early dynasties and holds that real Chinese history begins near the close of the Yin Dynasty (about 1100 B.C.) with certain kings whose names have recently been discovered in inscriptions on tortoise shell fragments anciently used in divination. The reigns of these rulers covered but a few years. From them he turns to the late years of the eighth century B.C. At that period he finds two groups of Chinese; one living in the valley of the Wei River in Shensi, the other settled in the middle and lower Yellow River regions. The latter group, he declares, was the older of the two and the Wei River settlements were those of colonists who emigrated westward from the parent group.

The colonists were in close contact with indigenous tribes of barbarians while the eastern group, long settled in their homes, were separated from non-Chinese tribes by mountains and marshes.

He regards Chinese civilization as a development of the cultures of intermingling Chinese and non-Chinese peoples. The affinities of the earliest Chinese culture he finds in southeastern Asia rather than in the northwest. The Chinese language, he says very truly, is related to the monosyllabic and tonal tongues of the Indo-Chinese Peninsula and more distantly to those of Burmah and Tibet. An agricultural civilization, a feudal political system and a land tenure sanctioned by religion connect the Chinese, he asserts, with their southern neighbors.

This relationship has been stated in this chapter also, but a different explanation from that made by M. Maspero is given for it. It does not indicate a southern or a southeastern origin for Chinese civilization. On the contrary, the preservation among the peoples of those regions of some of the most marked characteristics of the ancient Chinese, physical, linguistic and cultural, is due to the fact that the pressure of invading tribes coming from the northwest has

* La Chine Antique Liv. Prem. ch. i and ii; Paris 1927.

forced the earliest inhabitants of China to move towards the south and southeast. Thus the peoples most nearly representing the ancient Chinese are found in the southern and southeastern provinces, and some of their relatives in the Indo-Chinese Peninsula. This interpretation, as we have seen, is confirmed by Siamese and Burmese traditions. This shifting of populations from the northwest towards the south and southeast has been going on, in fact, in our own day.

Maspero points out, too, and he is undoubtedly correct, that there is no evidence of nomadism among the early Chinese. The fact has been mentioned in preceding pages and an explanation is there given of it. Maspero's brilliant chapter has painted for us a vivid word picture of the China of the eighth century B.C. He shows us an industrious population, largely devoted to agriculture living in small hamlets, surrounded by the fields that they cultivated. They were ruled by feudal lords whose castles were located in the walled towns that were their capitals. Barbarian tribes shut them in, so that, in his opinion, they could not have come from without. The argument is not convincing. Conditions existing in the eighth century B.C. cannot be said necessarily to represent the conditions of 2000 or 3000 B.C. His picture, so accurate for the eighth century, does not make impossible an original migration of the Chinese forefathers from the northwest. That migration, as we have shown, must be admitted upon other grounds.

Any theory of Chinese origins, to be acceptable, must harmonize with all the ascertained facts. Maspero ignores the well-established fact of centuries of migration of populations from the northwest across China, caused by the dessication of central Asia. These movements must have begun long before the historical period. They occasioned great changes in China during the historical period. He ignores the evidence of archæology. He gives no adequate explanation of the cultural relationship between eastern and western Asia, which can be best explained by the theory of a central point of diffusion.

CHAPTER III

THE FAMILY

Be filial and fraternal and so give weight to human relationships.
K'anghsi; ''The Sacred Edict.''

> Union with wife and child is sweet,
> Sweet as when lutes in concert blend;
> 'Tis when united brothers meet
> That mirth and concord have no end.
> The Shih King; translated by Jennings.

The social unit in China is not the individual but the family. Family solidarity is nowhere better illustrated. There are other countries where family ties are strong and where great regard is paid to kinship, but none where these characteristics are more marked or have such far-reaching effects.[1]

This statement is true, generally speaking, of all parts of China, but it is particularly in the southern provinces that the kindred are most thoroughly organized and the domination of the family—not to say its tyranny—over the individual is most pronounced.

In the south of China, due perhaps to the infrequency of invasion by alien tribes, the family seems to be more permanently attached to a single locality and the ties of kinship stronger and more extended than in the north where invasion, strife and capture have so often uprooted the family and dispersed its members.

At any rate the clans are larger and far more powerful in the south than in the north and much more disposed to tyrannize over their members and to unite in defense of the kindred.

This solidarity of the Chinese family manifests itself in all the relations of life. It is shown in the organization of

[1] An excellent discussion of the Family Law of the Chinese, by P. G. von Möllendorff, will be found in the Journal of the China Branch of the Royal Asiatic Society, N. S. vol. xxvii, No. 2, 1892–93.

the kindred. The father is the head of his own family and, under the old régime, possessed the power of life and death over his children. This power was identical with the *patria potestas* of the ancient Romans. There was no limit in the age of the son over whom this power might be exercised. Even though the children might themselves be parents and advanced in years, the father, so long as he lived, possessed this power of putting his unfilial children to death. But, although the father would not be punished for killing an unfilial child, the law presumed that in case of unfilial conduct the father would bring accusation against his child before a court, rather than take the law into his own hands. This was the practice in that ancient period, the 6th century B.C. when Confucius himself served as Chief Justice in his native state. It is said that a father brought before him a disobedient son for punishment involving the death penalty. Confucius imprisoned both father and son, and when remonstrated with by his Prince replied: "When those of an older generation fail in their duty towards their juniors, it is not right for them to ask that these juniors be put to death. This father has not taught his son to be filial." He refused to execute the law, and subsequently released both father and son.

The old penal code of the Manchus provided that if a man, upon a false accusation by a third person, put a son or grandson to death when such son or grandson was innocent of wrong doing, the person guilty of the false accusation should be punished with seventy blows of the heavy bamboo and sent into exile for a year and a half, and the parent guilty of the killing should be sentenced to sixty blows of the heavy bamboo and a year's exile within his native province. This was light punishment for murder. Apparently it was only because the murdered son or grandson was innocent of the offense charged that any punishment at all was inflicted.

Since the Republic was established a new criminal code has been adopted. The new code does not specifically affirm the possession by parents of the power of life and death over children, but it does so by implication; since it provides that one may, without committing an offence, use force in resisting an attack upon himself, except it be an attack by a lineal ascendant. In such cases he may forcibly resist only if the attack upon himself be one of excessive violence by a step-mother, or one of excessive violence upon a woman by her husband's ascendants, or an attack by an ascendant when such an ascendant is "in a state that shows apparent violation of the legal relationship."[2]

The authority of ascendants is recognized also in the provisions for increase of the prescribed penalties if the offense be one against a lineal ascendant.[3]

The solidarity of the family is recognized in the exemption from punishment of one who appropriates to his own use, or injures, property belonging either to an ascendant or a descendant, and in the leniency shown by the new code towards offenses committed against the property of other relatives.[4]

Dr. Wang Chung-hui, recently Chief Justice of China, in a pamphlet published not long since entitled "Law Reform in China," points out that the new code is based upon the Continental legal system rather than upon Anglo-American principles; because, as he says, "The Anglo-American law emphasizes the individual as against the family, while the Continental system inherits something of the Roman *familia*. The unit of Chinese society being the family, reform naturally seeks to preserve this institution and to modernize it as far as possible after the Continental idea."[5]

Under the Empire the power of the father could not be exercised upon a son in the service of the Government without the permission of the Emperor. A daughter, once married, no longer belongs to her father's house, but to that of her husband. A divorced woman, however, returns to her father. Having the power of life and death, the father

---

[2] See New Penal Code of China, Chap. II, Art. XV, and Amendment to the Code, Art I.

[3] See Chapters XX, XXVI and XXVIII.

[4] See Chapter XXXII, Articles 367, 377 and 387.

[5] Op. cit., p. 15.

could under the old Manchu code sell his children into slavery, if he so desired, but this law was modified by the Manchus themselves in 1910, to the effect that in times of distress parents might be allowed to sell their children into bondage for a term of years only, and with the right of redemption under certain circumstances.

But while no father could legally be punished for killing an unfilial son, such deeds, of course, were rare. The affection of a father for his children is sufficient in most cases to prevent his injuring them. In addition to this there is the dread of public opinion. The neighbors would frown upon a man that could be so cruel as to kill his own child.

INFANTICIDE

It is not strictly true, as just said, that parental affection would prevent the killing of a child. At least it does not apply among all classes with regard to infant children. In some parts of China infanticide has been quite common in past years among the very poor. In such cases it was the girl babies that were destroyed. The pressure of population upon subsistence was so great in some regions that one more mouth to feed meant suffering for the whole family. Another reason for the practice was that in the districts where it occurred the female population outnumbered the male because of emigration. There was, therefore, slight chance for the making of a marriage that might recompense the parents for the outlay made in the upbringing of the child. The girl is not usually looked upon as an economic asset by the family, but rather as a liability. She is to be married into another family, so that all that is spent for her is spent for the benefit of another family. Her bridal equipment, too, is a heavy burden, but this is covered in a large measure by the money payment made by the family of her prospective husband.

Infanticide, however, is not so common now as it was some years ago. Public opinion frowns upon it.

It was not often that a boy was exposed by his parents,

for he would grow up to labor for the family and increase its wealth, and he would carry on the line and keep up the sacrifices to the ancestors. Once, however, I had the experience of rescuing a baby boy whom I found in a coffin at the gate of a cemetery in Nanking. The coffin lid had been put on, but, as I passed I thought I heard a sound from the inside. I opened the coffin and found the wasted form of a little child who had long been ill. I carried him to a hospital, where he was cared for, but he died some three days later.

Under the old code of the Manchus it was forbidden to expose a child over three years of age, but this very prohibition shocks one, for it implied that children under three years of age might legally be exposed. Some mitigation of this practice was brought about by Buddhist teaching, which forbids the taking of any life, and by Buddhist charity which provided foundling asylums for children whom their parents could not support. In some districts where the Christian missionaries have labored they have done much, both by teaching and by charity, to prevent such a sacrifice of child life.

Although the father had the power of life and death over his children, if he were himself a younger son, he was subject to the commands of his elder brother, who assumed the headship of the family upon the death of the parents.

INHERITANCE

Sometimes the family property remains undivided for several generations. One finds grandparents, parents, sons and grandsons and their several families all living in one home. The home, in such a case, is a group of buildings gathered around several courts. Among the well-to-do each husband and wife will have a house and court for themselves and their children, but enclosed within the same compound as the other brothers, and cousins. You can sometimes find a whole village consisting almost entirely of but one clan. The names of such villages often indicate this, as the "Wang Chia Ts'un," or village of the Wang family; the "Cheng Chia Tun," or the hamlet of the Cheng family; the "Yang Chia Tien," or the farmstead of the Yang family. When the property is divided, the sons, whether by the principal wife or by a concubine, all inherit the fathers' estate, share and share alike. In the case of the death of a son leaving children, these children divide equally among them the share that would have fallen to their father. Thus it happens that many farms in China have become divided into minute portions, sometimes so small that a single portion is no longer sufficient for the support of a family. Although the property is divided among the sons, the widow holds a certain right of administration and has a claim to a sum sufficient to pay her funeral expenses. A concubine, however, has no claim upon the estate.

In practice, it seems that as long as the mother lives her children do not deprive her of the right to live in the old home, and even the concubines are cared for out of respect to the father. Filial piety will not allow less than this to be done.

Even a son by adoption enjoys the same rights as a son by blood. As long as a male heir exists, no female heir has any claim upon the estate. It is to be noted, too, that even the property brought by a wife at the time of her marriage remains in the possession of the husband, although the marriage may have been dissolved.

So strict is the law with regard to the equal division of the property among all the sons that a case is on record in which the will of the father leaving to the eldest son a larger share than given to the others was set aside by the court, and the property equally divided, although the contesting claimant was the son of a concubine. Customary law is not the same in all districts, however, for in some the eldest son obtains a double portion, because responsible for the upkeep of the worship in the ancestral temple.

The guardianship of infants is the duty of the next of kin, but a wife will continue the guardianship exercised by her husband, if the latter should die. If, however, the wife desires to be relieved of this a guardian will be appointed by the blood relatives, and relatives by marriage have no voice in the matter.

The wealthy clans maintain large ancestral temples, in which the tablets of the deceased ancestors are preserved, and where sacrifices are offered to their spirits at stated intervals, particularly at the winter solstice.

Clan meetings are held in these temples, in which the spirits of the dead may be presumed to participate, although unseen. The whole family in heaven and on earth may be considered as reunited. At such meetings important matters pertaining to the clan are discussed and settled in family council, for, while the father may possess arbitrary power over his children, the head of the clan does not ordinarily exercise such autocratic power over the clan. He consults with the members of the clan. In the clan council all families of the clan are on an equality. If a man has been guilty of unfilial conduct or done something to bring discredit upon the clan, the assembled members of the clan may decide to punish him by removing his name from the register, thus depriving him of all right to participate in the inheritance of his family. They may even condemn him to death and execute the sentence. A case occurred a few years ago in which a man was expelled from the clan for becoming a Christian. The Government does not interfere in such matters. Indeed the law itself provides for the punishment of unfilial conduct. This reminds us of the Law of Moses which punished with death any one who should curse his father or mother. (Exodus xxi: 17.)

The Manchu Government not only did not interfere with the punishment by a clan of its members, but it was even compelled to tolerate war by one clan upon another. In southern China, where, as I have said, the clans are stronger than in the north and more compactly organized, one often heard of clan feuds, which reminded him of the mountaineer feuds of eastern Kentucky. The clans are so powerful in their own districts that the Government in the past has not been able to put an end to such private wars.

VICARIOUS PUNISHMENT

The solidarity of the family is shown, furthermore, by the responsibility admitted by the clan or family for the deeds of any one of its members. If a man owes a debt, it is not canceled by his death and the seizure of all his property; his relatives can be called upon to pay the balance due. If a debtor absconds, some member of his family may be arrested and imprisoned in his stead, for imprisonment for debt has not yet been abolished in China. And once in prison, a man does not get out until, as the Scripture says, he has paid the "uttermost farthing." This responsibility of a family for the conduct of its members was strongly insisted upon by the old Penal Code of the Manchus, which however was a slight improvement on that of the Ming Dynasty that preceded it. The Manchu Code was revised by Edict of the old Empress Dowager in 1905, and vicarious punishment for the most part abolished, but only in respect of criminal offenses. Under that old code a serious crime committed by a man automatically involved in punishment all his own family and his paternal relatives to the third degree. If a man were convicted of treason, for instance, he himself was put to death by the slow process of slicing. His father, his grandfather, his brothers, his father's brothers and their sons, as well as his own sons, if over sixteen years of age, were all put to death. His sons or his uncles' sons under sixteen years of age were sold into slavery (after castration), and his wife, mother, paternal grandmother, paternal aunts, and his own unmarried and unbetrothed daughters were also sold as slaves.[6]

Although this severe punishment of a man's relatives shocks us, it was but little more cruel than that which prevailed under British law so late as the early part of the last century. High treason in Great Britain was then punished by attainder of blood and property, which made the criminal an outlaw, deprived him of the right to inherit or transmit property, and thus involved his family in the

---

[6] Ta Ch'ing Lü Li, Vol. XXIII; Section on Rebellion, fol. i.

punishment. In addition to this the guilty man was hanged, but before he was dead was cut down, placed upon a wattle mat, dragged to a cross-road and there disemboweled, beheaded, dismembered and the four quarters suspended, one at each corner of the roads.[7]

In 1901 the American Government, when settling the "Boxer" troubles interceded for the relatives of Chang Yin-huang, who had been accused of plotting against the Manchu Government while he was Chinese Minister at Washington. The Minister was put to death while being sent into exile, his sentence having been commuted at the request of the American Government. Despite the promise to spare his life he was treacherously murdered. His property had been seized and his sons were in serious danger, when advantage was taken of the settlement of the "Boxer" claims to rescue them from the threatened punishment.

INDIVIDUALISM

Now, while Chinese law looks upon the family as the social unit, modern Western civilization emphasizes the importance of the individual—asserts his rights and points out his duties. It is all a part of the general progress of democratic ideas. The contact between the East and the West, which has produced so many serious effects in China, has brought these two systems into conflict.

In a democracy men must learn to think for themselves, if their system of government is to be a success. The Chinese classics, themselves, recognize that self-control is the root of good government, for the Chung Yung says: "He that would rule the state must first learn to govern his own family, and he that would govern his family must first learn to control himself." But while there were a great many democratic principles approved in theory in China before the advent of the European, it was the coming of the Western man that stirred them into activity.

[7] Blackstone, Book IV: Sec. 91 and Sec. 429.

The Christian missionary, especially, emphasized the responsibility of the individual for his own conduct, and the worth of the individual soul. He insisted that each man should do what he believed to be right, whether his family approved or not, that

> No man can save his brother's soul,
> Or pay his brother's debt,

as Matthew Arnold has said. Such teaching, as the Scripture declares, tended to set "the mother against the daughter and the mother-in-law against the daughter-in-law, and to make a man's foes those of his own household." The missionary refused to excuse a man because he followed the faith of his fathers or obeyed the injunctions of his clan. This was one cause of the hostility of the Chinese to the missionary. We must, I think, admit the advantage of this individualism in the long run to the progress of the race. Progress is impossible under the rule of the dead hand. It is only by breaking away from the traditions of our fathers that we can improve upon our fathers. This is true of ourselves as well as of the Chinese. We ought to remember our fathers with reverence and be grateful for all that they did, but our real loyalty is best shown, not by literal adherence to their doctrines or exact imitation of their practices, but by devotion to the truth. This is the only guiding star. He that discovers a new truth lights a new star in the firmament to guide men through the night of ignorance. The backward look is fatal to progress. He that puts his hand to the plough and looks back will plough a very crooked furrow. Under the old régime in China a man looked back with reverence to the beliefs and practices of his ancestors and dared not change from them. Ancestor worship confirmed and emphasized this tendency. With the introduction of a new religion and of democratic ideals, the power of tradition was weakened and the tyranny of the family was lessened. This, however, has led to a moral crisis in China.

ANCESTOR WORSHIP AND MORALS

Filial piety is the strongest sentiment experienced by the Chinese. The worship of his ancestors is his religion. The acceptance of their faith and the observance of the rites as enjoined by them is held to be a solemn duty. The ethical teaching received from them is his moral law. This filial piety, then, affords the strongest sanction of the moral law of which he has any knowledge. Take away his reverence for his ancestors and what is there to bind him to moral living? The family solidarity meant and still means to most Chinese moral living.

We know, of course, that ethical standards find their sanction not in the teachings of any ancestor, nor in the regulations of any clan. Neither do they find it in the teachings of any book of ethics. They are broad based upon the law of our being—proved by the experience of a thousand generations, for moral precepts have a natural sanction. The ordinary Chinese, however, does not know this. Therefore, some Chinese statesmen have feared the introduction of Western education and Western political ideas.

The Viceroy Chang Chih-tung, when he collaborated with the Minister of Education, Chang Po-hsi, in preparing the regulations for the Public School System introduced in 1904, emphasized the importance of insisting upon the observance in the schools of the Confucian religion, for "otherwise," he said, "the morals of the students would deteriorate."

We have heard similar statements from our own pessimistic prophets, who have feared the teaching of certain sciences in our schools, lest the foundations of faith should be shaken. Professor Goldwin Smith some years ago in the Atlantic Monthly foretold a coming moral interregnum because of the effect of the evolutionary philosophy upon religious belief, but it has not materialized.

In a somewhat similar frame of mind, the late Liang Ch'i-ch'ao, the foremost scholar of China, deprecated the growth of individualism among his people because of the weaken-

RETURNING FROM FUNERAL.

TABLET TOWER, PRIVATE CEMETERY.

ing of the family bonds which he thought essential to the morals of the rising generation.

In the long run, however, these things correct themselves. There is no real safety except in following the truth. "Ye shall know the truth and the truth shall make you free," is a declaration of wide application. It is never safe to bottle up the truth; there is danger of an explosion. If you try to persuade young people not to investigate certain branches of learning, lest their faith be shaken, you at once sow doubt as to the value of a faith that can be shaken. The better way is to show that moral precepts do not rest upon any insecure foundation, but are grounded in nature and the eternal.

So, while there are young Chinese with lax morals who have lost confidence in the wisdom of their fathers, the remedy is in making them see that the requirements of the moral law are essential to the existence of society. Moral precepts are binding, not because my father said so, nor because some sacred book says so, but the sacred book says so and my fathers said so, because the experience of the race had found that they were binding.

This acceptance of the family as the social unit and the habit of submitting for a hundred generations and more to the authority of the clan, has had, of course, some very noticeable effects upon the character, the customs and the political ideals of the race.

For one thing, it has bred in the Chinese a great respect for authority, a tendency to obey those in power. As a rule the Chinese, wherever you find them, are quiet, orderly and law-abiding.

For another thing, it has fostered in them an undue reverence for the past, and made the Chinese the most conservative of all races, the race most unwilling to change. When I first went to China I tried to rent a house. The owner desired to have the money that the rent would bring him, but was doubtful of the propriety of renting to a foreigner. He consulted his ancestors by casting lots in the hall before the tablets of his fathers. The lot was unfavorable and he, therefore, refused to let me have the house. So the dead were still ruling the living. This reverence has been an obstacle to all progress. It has not only opposed religious propaganda, but sanitation, plague prevention, and all educational and political reform. Happily now this conservatism is breaking down because family solidarity is being given up.

FAMILY GOVERNMENT AND DEMOCRACY

The recognition of family unity and authority would seem at first sight to encourage the adoption of a monarchical and autocratic form of government. To a certain extent this is true, and the family has been made the pattern of government. The Emperor stood to his people *in loco parentis*. The people were regarded as his children and taught to reverence and obey him. The *patria potestas* was his. He could do as he liked with his children, and they ought not to murmur. The local mandarin, too, the representative of the Emperor, was called the *"fu-mu-kuan,"* that is to say, the father-mother-official.

This tendency towards autocracy, however, was greatly modified by another feature of family government, the clan council. The head of the clan was not an autocrat. All heads of families in the clan participated in the discussion and decision. The custom of meeting together to discuss clan affairs, the practice of settling these affairs themselves without appeal to the State, and the tendency even to ignore and over-ride the political authorities by executing judgment upon an offender and by waging private war— all this tended to produce in the family as a unit a feeling of independence and a capacity for self-government.

This tendency towards democratic feeling and action seems to have been stronger than that towards submission to autocracy, for it is in the south where the family is most thoroughly organized and the clans most powerful that we find democratic sentiment most generally nourished and expressed. In the north, moreover, where family sentiment is weaker, we see a willingness to submit to autocratic rule. This is not difficult to explain. In the south of China the individual submitted to the rule of his own clan, and was trained to look upon the authority of his clan as superior to that of the State whenever there was conflict between them. But he also participated in the councils of the clan, and he thus became a ready believer in popular government.

In the north the authority of the father was admitted, but there was less family consultation, fewer well organized clans, and consequently less experience in settling matters among themselves. Moreover the willingness to submit to the control of a monarch was daily inculcated by the nearness of the Imperial Court and the experience of its power and dread of its tyranny. The pomp of the court, too, bred an admiration for monarchical forms. There are other reasons for the differences between the people of the north and the south of China, of which mention will be made hereafter. This difference in regard to the organization and authority of the family ought to be borne in mind when we have our attention called to the present struggle in China between the extreme liberals at Canton and the conservatives in the north.

Bertha Phillpotts, in her "Kindred and Clan," says of the clan in Europe: "Where adhesive kindreds persist into the later Middle Ages, there the peasant or townsman tends to be free. Where, on the other hand, the solidarity of the kindred disappears early, there the liberty of the individual suffers and seignorial rights make their appearance."[8] This statement is equally true of the history of the clan in China.

RELATIONSHIP

Relationship is frequently defined in terms of the mourning regulations. This is the practice in the old Penal Code.

The nearest of kin are those for whom the heaviest mourning is worn, and nearness is measured by gradations

[8] Op. cit., p. 254.

in mourning. For one's father a man wears until after the funeral a dress of coarse sackcloth with frayed edges. This degree of mourning is called *Chan Shuai*. For such relatives one continues to mourn for three years. For one's mother a man wears second mourning. Until after burial this consists of a sackcloth less coarse than first mourning, and the garments have finshed edges. This is called *Ch'i Shuai*. Relatives of the third degree are those for whom the mourning is worn nine months. The next nearest are those for whom mourning is worn five months, and the fifth degree of relationship is expressed by the term for fifth degree mourning, that for three months.

Relatives of the same surname are regarded as of far greater importance than those of another name, and reckoned correspondingly closer of kin. The Chinese language is rich in terms defining relationship; there are different names for relatives on the mother's side from those applied to corresponding relatives on the father's side, and relationship through a daughter is unlike that through a son.

The Chinese recognize three social ties as of the greatest importance; those between ruler and subject, between husband and wife, and between father and son. These are at times increased to five by the addition of two more; those between older and younger brothers and between friend and friend. Friendship is frequently sealed by a blood covenant. By pricking a finger a drop of blood is contributed by each friend to a cup of wine, of which both then partake. The obligations of such friends are like those of relatives by blood. A passage in the Li Ki says: "With the slayer of one's father a man should not live under the same sky; on meeting the slayer of one's brother one should not have to go back for his sword to avenge the killing; with the murderer of a friend one ought not to live in the same state." [9]

The Sacred Edict of K'ang hsi gives great importance to the relationship between brothers. It is second only to that between father and son. "Brothers," we are told, "can not be treated as different persons: they are of one flesh

[9] Li Ki, Bk. I Ch'ü Li 1:27.

and blood, just like hands and feet." The commentator complains that men are apt to love their wives more than their brothers, and says: "But if your wife dies you can get another; if your brother dies how can he be replaced?" The duty of obedience to an older brother becomes at times, no doubt, very irksome, as to us it appears very unjust; and when several sons are living with their wives and children in the same compound, a tyrannical older brother with his arrogant wife must be the cause of much unhappiness. The solidarity of the family in primitive society no doubt had its advantages, but greater freedom for the individual and a separate home for each husband and wife undoubtedly means greater happiness for the greater number.

A new law on Family Relationships passed its second reading in the Legislative Court on December 2, 1930,* but does not appear to have received final approval. The proposed law retains the old system of family organization and urges the duty of maintenance of relatives in real distress, but seeks to modify responsibility and promote individual independence. The new law, if adopted, will also place male and female heirs exactly upon the same footing.

* *Chinese Affairs*, Dec. 15, 1930.

CHAPTER IV

MARRIAGE AND THE STATUS OF WOMAN

But happy they! The happiest of their kind!
Whom gentler stars unite and in one fate
Their hearts, their fortunes and their beings blend.
Thomson.

The woman followed the man. In youth she obeyed her father and brother. Married, she obeyed her husband, and, after the death of her husband, she obeyed her son.
Li Ki, xi:38.

The family being the social unit in China, marriage as the foundation of the family has always from the most ancient times been treated by the Chinese with all the seriousness which its importance demands. The marriage state for them has always been one to be entered into only with due formality and with the observance of religious rites.

RELIGIOUS SANCTION

In the Li Ki, which is the Chinese Leviticus, dating in its present form from the second century A.D. but containing a record of ceremonies observed from before the time of Confucius, we are told that "the marriage ceremony is the root of all ceremony." [1]

In antiquity, it is said, the proposal of marriage was received by the young woman's father in the ancestral temple.[2] The spirits of his ancestors were witnesses of the solemn betrothal. "As for the marriage rite," says the Hun I, "it secured the affectionate union of two families. Looking back, it sought to keep up the worship of ancestors; looking forward, it aimed to continue the line of descendants." [3]

[1] Li Ki, Book xliv, Hun I or "Meaning of Marriage."
[2] Ibid.
[3] Ibid.

To-day some of the young people of China, under the impression that what is old is useless, are rejecting the ceremonies of their fathers and trying to make marriage a purely legal relation. But this is perhaps merely a passing phase in the modernization or Westernization of the country. The masses of the people still adhere to the traditions of their ancestors and to the ceremonies of Confucianism. Betrothal and marriage for most Chinese are not only matters of formal contract duly witnessed, as they have always been, but solemn ceremonies to which Heaven and Earth and the spirits of ancestors are called to bear witness. Marriage, indeed, is represented as foreshadowed by the "Union of Heaven and Earth," which "has given birth to the myriad creatures of the world." [4]

MONOGAMY AND CONCUBINAGE

Marriage is not compulsory in China as men have sometimes tried to make it in other lands, but celibacy is frowned upon, just as it was in the Mosaic legislation.[5] Old maids are rarely seen and, if a young man is unmarried it is usually due to poverty.

Monogamy is the rule, but bigamy has been legalized in the past under certain circumstances, and concubinage is tolerated. Even polyandry is known in at least two regions.

Generally speaking, in China a man has but one wife, but he may have many concubines, as many as he cares to support. Even the revised Penal Code does not forbid concubinage. But, while the practice is still tolerated, it is falling more and more under the ban of public opinion.

Under the Empire the Emperor had one wife, the Empress, but he usually had also a secondary consort, four ladies of the third rank, and many of lower grades. The

---

4 Li Ki, Vol. V. Book XI, Chiao T'e Sheng, or Sacrifices at Suburban Altars.

5 A quaint discussion of this is given in an old work, "The Antiquities of the Hebrew Republick," by Tho. Lewis, M.A. LONDON. Printed for Sam. Illidge under Serle's Gate, Lincoln's Inn, New Square; and John Hooke, at the Flower-de-Luce, over against St. Dunstan's Church in Fleet St.

Emperor Kuanghsü, who died in 1908, had one wife, the Empress Lungyü, who died in 1913. But he had also two concubines—two sisters—daughters of a Grand Secretary and women of considerable education, who exerted great influence over the young Emperor and sympathized with his liberal views and his plans for a reform of the government. The body of one was found in a well in one of the palace court-yards after the flight of the Court in 1900. She was said to have been drowned by order of the Empress Dowager. The sister, who was a pleasant little lady, was seen at all the Court entertainments to which, after the settlement of the Boxer troubles, the ladies of the diplomatic corps were invited.

The Great Empress Dowager, who conducted the Government at the time of the Boxer rising, entered the palace at first as a concubine, but after the birth of her son, the only son of the Emperor Hsienfeng, she was raised to the rank of "Western Empress," that is to say Secondary Consort. The principal wife occupied the Eastern Palace, the east in court etiquette being the side of honor.

In practice, except among the nobility and the rich, concubinage is not common. If practiced by the ordinary man it is usually because his wife is childless, and because children are needed to keep up the worship of ancestors.

It sometimes happens that a childless wife will herself provide her husband with a concubine, just as, our own Bible tells us, was done by Sarah in order to provide her husband, Abraham, with a son.

The concubine in China has a legal status and is, therefore, duly protected. Her children are all reckoned as the children of the principal wife. The principal wife they call "mother," and not the woman who gave them birth. The latter takes an inferior place in the household as the servant of the wife.

The concubine is usually selected, however, by the husband himself. Formerly, while slavery was tolerated, she was frequently chosen from a lot of slave girls educated by their masters for this purpose. They were taught to read and write, to play upon some musical instrument, and generally to make themselves attractive in appearance and manners. Every evening in the Foochow Road, Shanghai, one could see these girls carried in their sedan chairs, or sometimes upon the shoulders of a servant, going from one tea house to another to sing and play and to chat with the young men gathered in these places.

If a man wanted to entertain his friends at dinner under the old régime, he did not invite them to meet his wife and daughters. They were kept secluded. He would give a dinner at a restaurant and provide for each guest a young girl, engaged from one of these slave masters, to chat with him or to play the lute and sing. They were not prostitutes and had to be treated with respect. It was only with such young women that a young man in the old days could get acquainted. Young ladies of good family were kept secluded except among the very poor.

A young man's wife was chosen for him by his parents to please themselves. His concubine he chose himself to please himself. A very just requirement of the law is that a man who seduces a girl and begets a child out of wedlock, must marry her if he be unmarried, and if he be married must make her his concubine. The child in any case is his legitimate child.

Concubinage, of course, makes for disorder in the household. It is degrading to the unfortunate women whom it condemns to lives of drudgery, and it is a fruitful source of jealousy and strife. It is not always so, however, among the very wealthy. I recall the instance of a Chinese official some years ago at Shanghai, who provided a beautiful home for his wife in the foreign settlement, but had at his official residence a brilliant woman as his concubine, who was also his secretary and kept his accounts. She was a woman of middle age. In addition he had two younger women also as concubines, one of whom was mother to the only child on the premises. The secretary managed the official home and was waited upon by the younger women as though she were their mother, while all three were mothers to the baby, who was being petted and spoiled. Such exceptions, however, attract attention because they are in striking contrast with the rule. The system to-day is recognized as evil by the most enlightened opinion in China, and is one that is being abandoned.

Not only do the children of concubines call the principal wife the mother, they must wear full mourning for her when she dies, that is for three years (by custom reduced to 27 months) if they are sons or unmarried daughters. They are not permitted to wear such mourning for their natural mother.

All children, whether of wife or concubine, stand upon an equality as regards inheritance. If the wife, however, should have a son, he will become the head of the household after his father's death, even though he may have an older brother who is the son of a concubine.

LAWFUL BIGAMY

I have said that under certain circumstances bigamy is legalized. The circumstances are those which require a man to keep up a double *sacra.*

The present boy Emperor, Hsüant'ung, who, although he has no empire is still permitted to retain his title, was the adopted son of the late Emperor Kuanghsü, but also made adopted son and heir of the former Emperor T'ungchih, cousin of Kuanghsü. T'ungchih died childless. It becomes necessary, therefore, for this heir to provide two lines of descendants, one for T'ungchih, the other for Kuanghsü. Hence, it was agreed that when he should reach marriageable age he should take two wives and maintain two households of equal rank. He was married in December, 1922, and Peking despatches in the autumn of 1923, in reporting a mutiny among the eunuchs of the palace, stated that in consequence thereof the young Emperor with his *two* wives had gone for a visit to the home of his father.

POLYANDRY

Polyandry is practiced in Tibet and in two districts of Fukien Province. In both regions the custom is due to poverty. A woman becomes the wife of all the brothers of one family. The wife remains at home in charge of whatever little property there may be, while her husbands take turns in living with her, and in turn go abroad to increase the earnings of the family. The practice keeps down the birth-rate, and so reduces the pressure of population upon subsistence.

BETROTHAL

Marriages are generally arranged by the parents of the young people, whose wishes are not at all considered. The first step is betrothal. This is brought about by a broker, usually an old woman, who is engaged by one family or the other, generally by the family of the groom. But sometimes, being a professional match-maker, she is on the lookout for suitable alliances and herself offers her services. In some cases among the very poor, parents arrange a betrothal while their children are still infants, and even before they are born, pledging themselves that if one have a son and the other a daughter they shall be married. I knew very well in Nanking a family with one son, which adopted for him a wife while both were babies, and brought up the little girl in the home with her future husband. They played together as brother and sister while they were children, and later the girl was sent to one mission school and the boy to another. After they had completed the course of study they were married.

If a broker is employed, the parents of the principals generally manage to get a glimpse of their future son-in-law or daughter-in-law, as the case may be, and sometimes the principals also succeed in getting a look at the future husband or wife. The young man, of course, is easily seen, unless he lives at a great distance from the young lady's home, for he is often on the street. He does not find it so easy to get a view of his fiancée, for under the old régime young ladies were seldom seen walking on the street. This is still the rule. When they go out on rare occasions, they ride in a cart (in north China) or a sedan chair and are accompanied by a chaperon. Brokers are not at all scrupulous, and many tales are told of the deceptions which they practice in order to bring about a marriage contract and secure their fees. At the ports where Western influences are strong and foreign manners are in vogue, and in missionary circles, where many of the old customs are taboo, there are marriages arranged by methods more like those which obtain in Europe, and once in a while a young man and a young woman will enter into an engagement quite on the American plan, without waiting for parents or brokers. Sometimes they elope and are married secretly in order to escape the unions which have been arranged for them by their parents. Generally speaking, however, the old-time methods and customs still prevail.

The marriage contract is an exchange of red cards on which the names of the principals, of their parents, the brokers, and the horoscope of the prospective bride and groom are written, that of the groom on one, that of the bride on the other. A picture of a dragon is printed on one side of the groom's card, and of a phœnix on that of the bride. Each card is accompanied by a needle threaded with a red thread. These red cords are sometimes used to tie together the wine-cups out of which they drink in the wedding ceremony, but at other times they are used in the dress of bride and groom.

The contract is a very formal document and is protected by the courts. It cannot be broken without the payment of damages by the party at fault. A money payment is provided for by the family of the groom to that of the bride. This is not to be looked upon, however, as the price of the bride, so much as a compensation to her family for the loss of her services, and in practice the money returns to the family of the groom in the outfit of the bride which accompanies her to her new home.

THE HOROSCOPE AND THE WEDDING DAY

After the betrothal is made the family of the groom sends presents to the bride and her family, including bracelet and ring and two fish, and the bride's family return a present of artificial flowers, vermicelli, bread and cakes. Everything sent has some good-luck significance, and the customs vary somewhat from province to province. The vermicelli, for instance, signifies long life. We have, of course, our own superstitions, and even though we may be no longer superstitious, we keep up these customs. So the Chinese also keep up their old customs.

The Chinese Almanac, formerly prepared by the Government College at Peking, marked the lucky days in the calendar, but while these are ordinarily lucky they may not be so for every individual. The wedding day is selected about three months in advance; it must, of course, be on a lucky day in the calendar, but also one of these days which will be lucky for the pair to be married and for their parents. Therefore, it is necessary to send for a fortune teller. He must consult the horoscope of the bride and groom. This is indicated, in the case of each, by eight characters, which tell the year, the month, the day and the hour of birth—one pair of characters for each period. If the astrologer be a first-class one he will take into consideration the 28 constellations, the 60 cycle stars, the 12 constellations of the zodiac, and the 129 lucky and unlucky stars.

The characters which tell the year, month, day and hour of one's birth are those of the ten stems and twelve branches, which are capable of 60 combinations, that is to say one for each year of the cycle, for a "cycle of Cathay" is only 60 years long. The ten stems correspond to certain of the five elements and also to the five planets, and the twelve branches to the twelve hours of the day (for in old China each hour is twice the length of ours), and to the twelve signs of the Zodiac, as well as to certain animals and to certain directions. The ten stems and twelve branches are as follows:

The Ten Stems:

Chia	corresponds to	wood	and to	Jupiter.
Yi	"	"	"	"	"
Ping	"	"	fire	"	"	Mars.
Ting	"	"	"	"	"	"
Mou	"	"	earth,	"	"	Saturn.
Chi	"	"	"	"	"	"
Keng	"	"	metal	"	"	Venus.
Hsin	"	"	"	"	"	"
Jen	"	"	water	"	"	Mercury.
Kuei	"	"	"	"	"	"

The Twelve Branches:

Tzu	corresponds to	Aries, rat, North.
Ch'ou	"	"	Taurus, Ox, N.N.E.
Yin	"	"	Gemini, Tiger, N.E.E.
Mao	"	"	Cancer, Hare, E.
Ch'en	"	"	Leo, Dragon, E.S.E.
Ssu	"	"	Virgo, Serpent, S.E.S.
Wu	"	"	Libra, Horse, S.
Wei	"	"	Scorpio, Sheep, S.S.W.
Shen	"	"	Saggitarius, Monkey, S.W.W.
Yu	"	"	Capricornus, Cock, W.
Hsü	"	"	Aquarius, Dog, W.N.W.
Hai	"	"	Pisces, Boar, N.W.N.

The hour corresponding to *Tzu* is 11 p.m. to 1 a.m. The constellation is Aries and the animal the rat. The year 1922, for instance, is *Jen-Hsü*, the sign is Aquarius, the planet is Mercury and the animal the dog. You can see what a fine chance there is for a man with an imaginative mind to invent an interesting fortune for the happy pair.

THE WEDDING CEREMONY

A month before the wedding the groom's family sends presents again, among which are cakes, fruit, five kinds of silk for the bride's trousseau, wine, the money payment, and a gander and goose—emblems of the happy pair. I remember once meeting such a procession of gifts. The pair of geese were naturally pure white but had been dyed red, because white is the color of mourning and red that of happiness. We may laugh at the use of the geese, but after all a pair of geese is not a bad emblem of conjugal fidelity, for the gander selects one goose as his mate, to whom he pays special attention and whom he never exchanges for another favorite. Anciently the groom himself carried a wild goose to the home of the young lady as a present to her parents. A cock and a hen are also sent. They do not seem so appropriate. The family of the bride retains the silk, money and cakes, but returns one jar of wine and the female animals, keeping the gander and cock.

The bride's family also sends a pair of candles and candle-sticks, and in the old days sent also a pair of satin boots and a mandarin's cap for the groom, as well as material for his wedding coat.

The cakes sent by the groom are distributed by the bride among her friends, as an invitation to the wedding.

Two or three days before the wedding the bride sends to the family of the groom a list of the articles of furniture which she will contribute to the new home. This announcement is to indicate to the groom's family how many carriers there will be, so that there will be for each one a present of money, bright coins with good-luck emblems pasted on them.

The bride has had to consult the astrologers and sooth-sayers a great many times before she has prepared her trousseau, but at last the lucky day and hour arrive. The groom sends a sedan chair covered with red cloth or silk beautifully embroidered. This is carried by four men. She is clothed in red silks and satins with a red veil over her face. She weeps and wails and struggles with those who would tear her from her home but finally she is carried by main force to the chair and locked in it. The curtains are down and no one can see her. Fire-crackers are set off in great quantity and a band of music begins to play as her escort leads her away. The music and fire-crackers keep her company all the way. Two lighted lanterns head the procession bearing the name in large letters of the groom's family. These are followed by another pair of lanterns bearing the name of the bride's family. Then come a red umbrella, some lighted torches and the groom's friends, among them a mandarin if possible. There are ragged urchins carrying boards with titles, if any, of the groom. When a short distance has been traveled the lanterns from the bride's family and her friends turn back. No member of her family attends the wedding, but she frequently takes an old servant with her.

On arrival at the groom's home the chair is set down, and the master of ceremonies bids all lookers-on who were not born under the proper sign to go away lest ill luck happen. An old lady engaged for the occasion comes out to open the chair and lead the bride in. She walks on red carpet and enters the house, where her husband meets her and escorts her to her room. After going out for a few moments he returns and pretends to lift her veil. They sit down side by side, each trying to sit upon a portion of the other's garment. The one succeeding in so doing, it is said, will rule the house.

They then go out into the court under the sky and kotow to Heaven and Earth, then into the main hall to worship the groom's ancestors. They complete the service by drinking from the cups of wine tied together with a red cord. Anciently two halves of a melon were used instead of cups, and this is still the practice in some places.

The bride and groom then return to their room to receive their friends. She is severely criticized as to looks, size of her feet, clothing, etc., but she must show no trace of emotion, neither pleasure nor anger. The feasting follows, which lasts two days. On the third day she visits her mother and introduces her husband.

Thereafter she devotes herself to the comfort of her parents-in-law, and is subject to the commands of her husband and her father-in-law. Happy is she if she be the wife of the eldest son, otherwise her sisters-in-law may make her life far from pleasant.

If she should become the mother of a son the whole house will rejoice, and red eggs will be sent to the neighbors to notify them of the event. If a daughter is born there is less rejoicing theoretically, but in real life a baby is a baby, and dear to parents and grandparents, whether girl or boy.

STATUS OF WOMAN

The Book of Odes, however, gives a very lowly place to the daughter of the house. A poem believed to have been written in the eighth century B.C. contains the following lines:

> He then shall have a son
> To sleep upon a couch,
> To wear a costly dress
> And play with toys of jade;
> Imperious, too, his cry;
> His pinafore of red; The house's lord he'll be.
>
> A daughter too he'll have
> To sleep upon the floor,
> A napkin for her gown,
> A potsherd for her toy.
> No choice is hers to make
> Save choose the food and drink
> And spare her parents pain.[6]

In theory the woman is inferior to the man and subject to the three obediences; in childhood subject to her father or elder brother, in marriage to her husband, in old age to her son. But in practice, women in China are quite as influential in the home as they are in other lands. Some years ago in company with a friend, I was traveling in Central China. It was a hot summer's day, and at noon when we reached a village we went into a tea-house to rest and have luncheon. The villagers, who had never seen Europeans before, came crowding into the tea-house until it was almost impossible to move. They put many questions to us; what were our "honorable names" and "exalted

6 Shih King, Minor Odes, v:18.

ages,'' how many sons had we, and why did my friend were brass in his teeth. At last one man said, ''In your honorable country the woman is the head of the family, is she not?'' My friend replied that it depended upon circumstances, that, if the woman had more sense than the man she would rule the house. An old man standing by who was rather deaf leaned over the table with his mouth open listening to the conversation. When he heard this statement he straightened up with a sigh and said, ''Well, it's just the same in our unworthy country.''

The most disagreeable feature of married life for the women, no doubt, is that custom requires the wife to live with her parents-in-law and serve them. The Book of Rites says that a wife should serve her parents-in-law as she served her own father and mother. She should rise at cockcrow, dress herself, and then visit the room of her parents-in-law and ask after their comfort, assist them in making their toilet, and then bring them their breakfast.

It often happens that the life of the young bride is made very unhappy by the ill temper of her husband's parents, the arbitrary demands they make upon her, and by the tyranny of her sisters-in-law, particularly the wives of her husband's elder brothers, who outrank her in the home. Her chief solace lies in the hope of some day becoming herself a mother-in-law.

DIVORCE

A woman may not seek a divorce from her husband, no matter what his offenses may be, but a man can divorce his wife for any one of nine causes; (1) if the marriage contract contains false statements, (2) barrenness, (3) sensuality, (4) want of filial piety, (5) loquacity, (6) jealousy, (7) incurable disease, (8) leaving the home without the husband's permission, (9) beating her husband. Divorce may also take place by mutual consent. If she were unfaithful, the husband, under the old régime, might kill both the wife and her paramour, should he surprise them *in flagrante delicto.* If the husband did not kill her he could sell her as a concubine.

Except in the case of infidelity, the husband cannot divorce his wife, no matter what her faults, if she shall have kept the three years' mourning for the husband's parents, or if her husband was poor at the time of marriage and has since grown rich. The divorced woman returns to her father's house or, if that should be impossible, becomes *sui juris.*

IMPEDIMENTS TO MARRIAGE

Besides the natural disqualifications for marriage, other recognized impediments are insanity or other disease, deafness or dumbness, and possession of the same surname. Having the surname does not necessarily prove relationship, for there are very few surnames in China, but the possession of the same name is regarded as proof of membership in the same clan. Marriage with cousins of a different surname is not forbidden unless they be of a generation above or below.

Marriage is not permitted during the period of mourning. There is no impediment to marriage with a deceased wife's sister, as exists in some Christian countries, but marriage of a deceased brother's widow, allowable among many peoples [7] was punishable with death under the old penal code.[8]

WIDOWS

It is considered bad form for a widow to marry a second time, but a well-known proverb says, "If heaven wants to rain or your mother marry again you can't prevent it."

[7] Compare the Jewish Levirate, Deut. xxv:5. The Mongols also practiced it in Polo's time, but it was not only a brother who could take the widow of a deceased brother; the son also could take his father's wives, his own mother excepted. Cordier, Marco Polo, Vol. 1, p. 253.

[8] *Ta Ch'ing Lü Li:* X: *Hu Li Hun Yin*—Marriage with a Concubine of a Relative.

Most widows, however, prefer to remain widows, and the number of honorary portals erected to the memory of those who have been thus faithful shows in what esteem the practice is held. Some girls refuse to marry if their affianced dies before marriage. A rather remarkable case came to my knowledge in Peking. The daughter of a Grand Secretary was engaged to the son of another high official. The young man died before the wedding could be celebrated. The young lady not only mourned for him as for a husband, but refused to take food and, in spite of the efforts of her family to prevent it, actually starved herself to death. Yet she was but slightly acquainted with the young man, if she really knew him at all.

WOMEN OF THE CONVENTS

The women of China, like those of most lands, are usually very religious. Although they participate as far as allowed in the worship of ancestors they do not find in these services all the satisfaction that their spiritual nature demands. Confucianism is essentially a man's religion. Most of the women turn to Buddhism, especially to the cult of Kwanyin, the Goddess of Mercy. Many keep images in their homes, before which they recite their beads. They observe fast days, and upon occasion visit the temples to pray or make pilgrimages to famous shrines.

It is not surprising, therefore, to find that some young women give up all plans for marriage, separate from their families, shave their heads and put on the grey robes of the Buddhist nun.

Some of the convents are endowed with small pieces of land, which supply in part the living of the sisterhood, and for the rest they depend upon the charity of the lay worshipers who receive instruction from them. Some maintain orphan asylums and thus provide homes for abandoned children.

As a rule the nuns appear to be sincere and devout. While many monks are found who are victims of the opium habit and grosser vices, it is rarely that one learns of an authenticated case of opium smoking or immoral conduct in the convents.

Chinese, of course, have their tales of immoral conduct, but they appear to be born of a prurient imagination rather than founded on fact. An old Chinese proverb says, ''The door of the monastery always opens toward the convent.'' A rather pretty tale is that of a monk on one side of a mountain valley who used to carry water from a spring at the foot of the hill. There he met a nun who came from the convent on the other side of the valley. As they met day by day they became acquainted. Acquaintance ripened into friendship and friendship into love, so that one day they decided to leave their orders and return to the world and be married. A well-known bit of sculpture represents the monk with his boots in his teeth, carrying his sweetheart nun on his back through the waters of a river that had to be forded.

Not only do young women take the vows of Buddhist nuns, but many widows when they can arrange their family affairs so as to permit it, renounce the world and enter the cloister.

During my residence in Nanking there was living in a convent near the West Gate the widow of the Taiping rebel chieftain. After the suppression of the rebellion and the suicide of her husband she fled to the convent for safety and found a refuge there for the remainder of her life.

CHAPTER V

THE FARMER

Give careful attention to farming and sericulture that there may
be sufficient food and clothing.—Sacred Edict of K'anghsi.

> For him light labor spread her wholesome store,
> Just gave what life required, but gave no more:
> His best companions, innocence and health,
> And his best riches, ignorance of wealth,
>
> Goldsmith.

Theoretically, agriculture is held in high honor among
the Chinese. Every spring, under the old régime, the
Emperor was expected to offer sacrifices to the Patron Saint
of Agriculture in the temple at Peking dedicated to that
worthy. He was also expected to guide the plow with his
own hands until he had turned eight furrows in the Sacred
Field. This he did to show to the whole empire his respect
for the farmer's calling, upon which all classes depend for
food and raiment.

In every county town, too, the local officials at the
appointed season used to repair to the temple of the
farmer's saint for the observance of similar ceremonies.
The sacrifices offered consisted of a goat or a bullock. The
great K'anghsi, in his Sacred Edict, urged the importance
of agriculture, and his son, Yungcheng, in his amplification
of that edict, devoted a whole chapter to the encouragement
of husbandry, exhorting the farmer not to forsake "the
good old calling for the multiplied profits of commerce."
He reminded them that in the olden time emperors, themselves, plowed the fields and that empresses reared the silk
worm.

THE FARMER'S PATRON SAINT

Mencius points out that Shun, the mythical emperor who
is supposed to have reigned about 2255 B.C., rose from

among the channeled fields to the control of the empire. An earlier emperor, Shennung, is deified and worshiped as the first teacher of agriculture. Not far from the author's home in China there was a temple dedicated to the "Three Emperors." These three famous worthies were Fuhsi, Shennung and Huang Ti, all mythical personages, supposed to have reigned from 2852 to 2597 B.C. The temple was very commonplace in appearance, but one of the images in the main hall was rather remarkable. It was that of a primitive man. His only article of apparel was an apron of leaves. This was reputed to be an image of Shennung. He is said to have been conceived miraculously and born of a virgin Princess. To-day he is honored by the Chinese as the Patron of Agriculture. All this is in keeping with the fact that the Chinese are essentially an agricultural people. They divide mankind into four classes, as is indicated by a common phrase in constant use, which runs "Scholars, farmers, mechanics, merchants." An old proverb, however, gives the first place, not to the scholar but to the farmer, "First the farmer, the scholar second." But, nothwithstanding the high esteem in which their calling is theoretically held, the farmers are in reality, perhaps, the least prosperous class in the country. The establishment of the republic has not improved their condition. They are as near the brink of misery as they were half a century ago.

POVERTY OF THE PEASANTS

I remember riding late one autumn over the old highway which was built by Hungwu from Nanking to Fengyang. We were some forty miles beyond Nanking, approaching a low range of mountains known as the Kwan Shan. My attention was directed to a number of people whom we passed, each carrying a bundle of clothes and trudging homeward from the neighboring city of Ch'uchou. The sight of a traveler with his clothes tied up in a bundle and carried over his shoulder is not a rare one. But these country people, as I learned to my surprise, were carrying their clothes home from the pawn-shops, where they had been deposited earlier in the year to raise money for the purchase of seed for the spring planting. They had had a bad season the previous year, followed by a hard winter, and had exhausted their resources. This year they had had better fortune and so were able to recover their winter garments before the cold weather set in. This custom of depositing clothes with the pawn-shops is not, however, an uncommon one, either in country or city. Furs and silks are stored in them during the hot season and receive much better care than they would otherwise obtain. Valuable goods are thus preserved, too, against destruction by fire or loss by burglary. So extensive and important, indeed, is this business that in some parts of China the prosperity of the city is measured by the number of its pawn-shops. For the common people they serve as banks. The peasants whom we passed upon the highway had no valuable furs or silks to deposit, and were carrying simply their ordinary winter wadded clothing. Each had raised a small loan upon which he had paid interest at the exorbitant rate of 2 per cent a month. One could only shudder at the thought of the possible consequences had there been another bad harvest. This incident revealed in a very startling manner the true condition of the agricultural classes in that region, and helped one to understand how easily the failure of a single harvest might precipitate wide-spread distress. It serves, too, to explain in a measure how it is that in a country of such splendid natural resources a careful and experienced observer could estimate that three millions of people die annually in China from lack of proper sustenance.

THE COUNTRY VILLAGE

The farmer, as a rule, lives with his neighbors in a little village. Rarely does one see a farm-house by itself. Life and property are more safe where neighbors congregate. The Chinese are a sociable people, and enjoy the opportunities given in village life for gossip with one another. There is advantage for the children, too, who are enabled to attend the village school which is made possible by this combina-

tion of families. The school is often held in the temple
which has been erected by self-levied taxes for the worship
of some local deity and as a shelter for the ancestral tablets.

These farm villages are often composed almost wholly
of members of one family, descendants of a common ancestor, in which case the village usually bears the family
name, as the "Wang-Family-Village," or the "Li-Family-
Village," a custom which recalls the similar one among our
own ancestors, who left their names upon the hamlets and
towns of England, its "wicks," "hams," "tuns" and
"steads," as Greene has pointed out. Thus we have such
place names as "Kes-wick," "Green-wich," "Bucking-
ham," "Harring-ton," and "Hamp-stead," in all of which
the suffix carries the general meaning of "Village," corresponding to the Chinese *tien, tun, hsiang, ts'un* and *chuang,*
also used as suffixes in such combinations as those given
above.

The writer had occasion one summer day, in company
with a friend, to visit a typical farm village among the hills
south-east of Nanking. It was late in the afternoon when
we turned from the highway, or what passed for such, into
a narrow path that led up a rather lonely valley. After
winding about for a mile or more, we came upon a little
hamlet of five or six hundred people, known as She-ts'un,
or the "She Village." It was harvest time and nearly all
the able-bodied men and women were busy in the surrounding fields, cutting the wheat with rude sickles, or more
properly, bill-hooks. Our advent took the old women and
children by surprise, and the latter fled from us in fright.
It was some time before we could find anyone who would
dare to talk with "foreign devils," but presently Mr. She,
himself, the head of the clan and the chief man of the
village, heard of our predicament and came to our assistance. He was an educated gentleman, some forty years of
age, and showed himself exceedingly polite. His dress and
manners indicated that he was no farmer, though he lived
among farmers. His soft white hands had probably never
done a stroke of manual labor in his life. He was indeed
the village school-master as well as the principal land-owner

of the district. He led us to the village temple, which served as a shelter not only for gods but for guests, though the latter were certainly few and far between. We were soon made very comfortable except for the multitude of fleas and mosquitoes. There was no monk in charge, for it was not a Buddhist or Taoist temple, but the old man who served as sexton soon came in, and proved to be as interesting as he was loquacious, which is saying a great deal. He had no vegetarian vows or Buddhist prejudices to interfere with his preparation of a fine dinner of fresh pork and other dainties, to which, with our hungry stomachs, we did full justice. When the meal was over, Mr. She came in with other villagers, and we chatted with them far into the night. The next day we had an opportunity of inspecting the place more carefully. Mr. She invited us to his home, an extensive pile of buildings constructed of brick, and consisting of the usual succession of halls and courts. There was an air of comfort and ease about the place. It was well furnished, and the crowd of women, children and servants that came in to stare at us indicated that there was no waste room. The family of Mr. She's younger brother shared the home, according to Chinese custom. We found the village school in session in the guest-hall. Our host had traveled considerably in central China and had lived for a time in Hankow, where he had met many Europeans and had lost many of his prejudices. Yet he seemed quite contented in the village home, and well he might be; he lived as a lord of the manor might have lived among his retainers in the Middle Ages in Europe. Most of the villagers were his tenants. Their homes, too, were well-built houses of brick with tile roofs. The lanes that wound among them, however, were narrow and crooked. There were no shops in the place, but one of the farmers acted as butcher, when needed, and sold meat and a few other necessaries to his neighbors. On the whole the people seemed well fed and clothed, contented and happy. As a rule, however, the tenant farmers in the region about Nanking do not appear to be so comfortable or prosperous as those in She-ts'un. The country has never entirely recovered from the ravages of the Taiping Rebellion, and this fact in some measure accounts for the unsightly appearance of many of the villages in central China. But in northern Kiangsu, there are large districts that were never visited by the armies, and many of the villages and farmsteads in that region present a very prosperous appearance. The houses are in good repair, the ancient temples are well preserved, and there is the grateful sight here and there of broad-spreading shade trees. The soil for the most part is very rich and the numerous canals, which the low level of the land makes possible, afford an easy means of communication which is wanting in many parts of China.

A MODEL FARM

In this region one sees not a few isolated farm-houses. While traveling through the district in a Chinese house-boat the writer was invited to visit the home of a Mr. Liu, a wealthy farmer who owned some two hundred English acres, an unusually large holding for the Chinese. The buildings of the farmstead were arranged around a large court, some seventy-five feet long by about sixty feet wide. They were all of brick and apparently much more substantial than the ordinary Chinese structure. The roofs were partly of tile and partly of neatly trimmed thatch. A fine garden, containing box and orange trees, was surrounded by an ornamental wall, the upper part of which was made of open work in green glazed tile. The stables were a pattern of neatness and the horses, mules and buffaloes were sleek and well fed. There was a large granary stored with wheat and containing effective machinery of good native workmanship for threshing, fanning and grinding. These machines were worked by mule power. The fields were irrigated by the usual Chinese pump, an endless chain of square wooden paddles working in a box trough, through which the water was drawn from the canal up into the irrigating ditches. Power was supplied by a good-natured, lazy looking buffalo, blindfolded and tramping round and round in a picturesque thatched shelter-house, thus turning a large horizontal wheel whose wooden cogs fitted into those on the shaft of the pump. The fertile fields produced abundant harvests of wheat, barley, cotton, and rice. There was some silk culture in the neighborhood but conducted on a small scale only. Mr. Liu was blessed with a large family and gave employment to a great many servants, male and female. On the whole it was a very attractive home. The great mansion, embowered in trees and dominating the broad acres of the smiling plain, the patriarchal character of the household and its easy-going manners, the contentment expressed in the very faces of the dumb brutes, and the restful picture of abundance and health, all contributed to make a very pleasant impression, which was only heightened by the involuntary recollection of less happy scenes to be witnessed in neighboring districts. Not far away a quiet grove of pines, surrounded by a strong wall, gave shelter to the family graves, amidst which rose the ancestral temple. There at the prescribed seasons sacrifices were offered to the spirits of the departed.

LAND TENURE

In this part of Kiangsu Province, that is, north of the Yangtze River, there are many large estates. One family, it is said, owns 400,000 *mou*, i.e., 66,666 acres; another 300,000 mou and others still possess from 40,000 to 70,000 *mou*. There are some temples in the same region which own from 3000 to 5000 *mou*. In this district, therefore, tenant farmers outnumber those who cultivate their own land. From seventy to eighty per cent, it is estimated, are renters. In the southern half of the province just the opposite conditions prevail. There, we are assured, nine-tenths own the land that they cultivate. These figures are taken from the report of the China Branch of the Royal Asiatic Society on "Land Tenure in China and the Condition of the Rural Population."[1]

[1] Journal of the China Branch, R. A. S., 1888, vol. xxiii, pp. 59-143.

Easy access to land promotes independence and the division of land into small holdings favors social equality. Large holdings, on the other hand, with dependent tenantry promote class distinctions and political dependence. The difference between north and south China in regard to land tenure and the size of holdings has no doubt had much to do with the difference between them in political ideals, for democratic sentiment is much stronger in the south than in the north.

From the report just mentioned we learn that there are many farms of one hundred acres and not a few of two hundred in Manchuria. A smaller number will be found containing as much as five hundred. In the provinces of Hopei (i.e. Chihli) and Shantung, in North China, there are farms containing 10,000 *mou*. But, taking China as a whole, large holdings are rare. The average for Hopei Province is given by Rev. Timothy Richard as eighty *mou*, i.e., 12.12 acres. The same authority gives thirty *mou* (5 acres) as the average for Shantung.[2] The late E. L. Oxenham, Esq., while serving as British Consul at Chinkiang, gave the average for the rich province of Kiangsu as twenty *mou* (3⅓ acres). Further inland the holdings are still smaller. So far as the above-mentioned report shows, the majority of the farmers of China cultivate their own land. One of the most noted exceptions to this general rule of farmers cultivating their own land is found in the populous region about Swatow, where three-fourths of the farmers are tenants. In Hopei the proportion of those owning their farms is given as seventy per cent, in Shantung as sixty per cent, in Hupeh thirty, and in the northwestern provinces generally about seventy. From such figures one is rather led to expect a very prosperous condition among the peasantry, but the real situation is quite disappointing. So far as my own observation goes, the ordinary farm-house in central and northern China is but a rude hovel of beaten earth, thatched with straw. The living room is also the granary. A cheap table, two or three trestles for seats, the baby's cradle and the agricul-

2 Ibid.

tural implements make up most of the furniture. In the cotton-raising districts there may be also a rude spinning wheel and a loom, or, if the family be engaged in silk-culture, there will be the simple machinery used in preparing the silk for the market. Cleanliness is unknown. Pigs and fowls run in and out of the house at will, and a donkey or water-buffalo may be tethered in the lean-to adjoining it.

TAXATION

The lack of prosperity can not be charged altogether to the land tax, for although higher as a rule than we are accustomed to in the United States, it is not enough of itself to discourage agriculture. It has been estimated as averaging for all China about one-twentieth or one-thirtieth of the gross produce. When the Manchu Dynasty obtained control of the empire, a solemn promise was given that the land tax should not be increased. It is levied partly in money and partly in kind, but the grain tax is commuted for a payment in money. It varies greatly in different districts. The Chinese tax was formerly levied only on land listed as agricultural, and the most valuable of all, city land, was not taxed at all, except where, by growth of a city, land anciently listed as agricultural has become encroached upon, for "once taxed, always taxed," is the rule in this conservative country. New legislation is now changing this—municipal taxes are to be levied on houses and lands. In the immediate vicinity of Shanghai an acre of land, still used for farming purposes, paid $5.00 Mex., i.e., about $2.50 U.S., per annum a few years ago. This acre was then worth $600.00 U.S. Rev. John Ross, in 1887, reported the tax in Manchuria as about one shilling per acre, the land being worth about $150.00 Mex., or $75.00 U.S. per acre. In Shantung it is said to average $0.205 U.S. per acre, and in Hopei $0.21 to $1.66 per acre.

But in reality the land tax in Hopei varies from $0.032 to $0.51 an acre in silver, plus a grain tax which varies from 1.09 quarts to 1.36 pecks of rice, and from 1.07 quarts to 4.37 quarts of beans per acre. Mulberry orchards are taxed $0.007 an acre.

In calculating the value of the grain tax in money the collector does not consider the market price; the reduction is made at an artificial rate fixed by statute. A few years ago this was estimated to be about $0.155 a bushel, whereas the actual value of the grain would be about a dollar a bushel.

We must not think, however, that the farmer really commutes the grain tax at the rate stipulated in the statute. Both the money tax and the grain tax are calculated in taels of silver, but a tael is merely a Chinese ounce; there is no such coin, and this must be reduced to its equivalent in copper cash, the money of the people, or, in many places to-day, to its value in copper cents. The number of cents in a tael varies from day to day, but the tax collector does not make the exchange at the market rate; he makes it at a rate more favorable to the government. Formerly in addition he would demand certain fees, such as meltage, expense of collection and other such charges, originally irregular but legalized by long usage. In 1923 the taxes were converted at a fixed rate of $2.30 (Chinese silver) to the tael.

The grain tax, moreover, is manipulated to the advantage of the collector by being calculated by weight, although levied in measures of capacity, and the difference between local and official standards of weights and measures makes it easy to increase the revenue.

Thus it happens that, although the land tax was definitely fixed by the Manchus in 1713 at a rate not to be changed, yet by the manipulation of exchange and the other practices mentioned, the sum actually paid now by the farmer in copper money is two or three times as much as was paid then. A tael of silver paid in taxes in 1713 meant, moreover, a great deal more to the peasant than it does to-day.

Before the setting up of the republic the revenue from the land tax was claimed by the central government; to-day it is proposed to reserve all but a fraction for local uses. The general lack of prosperity among the agricultural classes cannot be charged, therefore, entirely to heavy taxation of the land nor to high rents, but rather to the more important fact that the farmer gets almost nothing in return for his taxes. He is dependent almost entirely upon himself and his neighbors for the protection of his property, and there are no roads for the transportation of his produce to market. In central China, except in those fortunate districts where there are water-ways, nearly all farm products are carried to town upon the shoulders of the farmer himself. Sometimes the wheel-barrow or the pack donkey is called into service. In the north and in some parts of the west there are rude carts, but it makes one's heart ache to see the dumb brutes straining to draw their heavy loads through dust or mire in which the wheels sink to the hub. In addition to these drawbacks there are the heavy likin duties to be paid at many barriers and the octroi duties at every city gate. Returning to his home, the farmer must pay duties again on all that he brings from the city. There is thus but little inducement to trade, and what trade there is is driven to seek roundabout ways to avoid more or less of the taxation.

METHODS OF CULTIVATION

Millenniums of experience have taught the Chinese farmer many valuable lessons in agriculture. His farm is very carefully tilled. His fields are divided into narrow beds, affording a certain amount of surface drainage. Wheat is sown in rows and carefully hoed; the rice is set out by hand in the flooded fields whose soil has first been thoroughly prepared. On hill-sides these rice fields are terraced, and water, admitted from above, is allowed to run slowly from one terrace to the next below. It is a strange sight to behold men and women wading in mire above their knees setting out the young shoots, which they do very deftly and regularly. Rain does not stop the work; a thatched coat of straw, which gives the wearer a very picturesque appearance, affords all the protection needed. On the plains water is pumped into the fields from canals or rivers, sometimes by buffalo power, as described above, but very often by human labor. In the latter case three or four women or as many men work at one pump. Leaning on a stout rail for support they turn the pump with their feet, and, keeping time with a lively song or a noisy gong, they make a very cheerful picture. Great attention is given to fertilizing, and in this the Chinese are perhaps wiser than many Western farmers. No night-soil is allowed to drain away into the creeks and rivers to poison the drinking water, but is carefully preserved, both in city and country, and carried daily to the farms where, after proper decomposition, it is scattered over the fields. The complaint of waste which Victor Hugo makes against the Parisians in *Les Miserables* can not be applied to the Chinese. It must be admitted, however, that, no matter how praiseworthy in this respect their economy may be, the result will perhaps appear to the Western man as hardly compensating for the daily pollution of the air, so utterly at variance with all the associations of beauty and healthfulness which the thought of the country-side brings to his mind.

Gardens are kept in use all the year round in the latitude of Shanghai and further south. Even farm lands often bear three crops a year, yet the soil is not exhausted. The Chinese understand in a measure the need for a rotation of crops, but there is of course no really scientific farming, as, indeed, there can not be where science is a thing unknown. Proper care is not taken in the selection of seed and there is therefore a constant tendency to degenerate. Wheat is often troubled with fungus growths, and there is said to be considerable suffering from ergotism on this account in the north, where wheat is eaten more commonly than rice.

PRODUCTS

Fruits are grown in great variety, as would be expected in a land of such widely varying soil and climate. There is, however, much room for improvement in quality. No proper effort is made to protect the fruit from injury by insects. American fruit trees have been introduced into

Shantung and some other provinces, but it is very difficult
to induce the Chinese to take care of them or to refrain
from pulling the fruit before it is ripe, according to their
old-time custom. Among the many kinds of fruit to be
found are oranges, lemons, bananas, pineapples, pumeloes,
mangoes and lichis in the south, while further north there
are loquats, plums, apricots, peaches, pears, apples, cherries,
grapes, pomegranates, persimmons and others. Among the
fruit trees none perhaps is more highly esteemed by the
Chinese than the peach, whose beautiful blossoms symbolize
the bride, as orange blossoms do with us, and whose fruit is
the emblem of immortality. There are many legends connected with it, and its twigs are supposed to possess magical
powers. It is the flat peach, more particularly, that is
identified with the fruit of the ''Fairy Peach Tree,'' growing in the garden of the Fairy Queen on the Kunlun Mountains, of which, if a man eat, he shall live forever. Many
peach trees are cultivated for the blossoms only. They are
in great demand during the season, and the road from
Shanghai to the Lunghua Pagoda at such times is crowded
with carriages, jinrickshas and wheel-barrows, carrying
pleasure-seekers into the country to see the peach orchards.

Of field crops the most important are rice, tea, cotton,
beans, rape, millet, sesamum, tobacco, ginger, indigo, hemp,
wheat, maize, buckwheat, peanuts, and formerly the poppy.
The last-mentioned is still grown in some places in spite of
laws to the contrary. The cotton plant appears to have
been introduced into China about A.D. 1000,[3] though cotton
cloth was known much earlier through intercourse with
central and western Asia. The cultivation of the plant,
however, did not spread rapidly, owing to the opposition of
the silk growers. But in time silk and linen had to give way
and cotton became, as it remains to-day, the most common
material for clothing. Its cheapness made it particularly
acceptable to the poorer classes. The supply of home-

[3] Journal of the China Branch of the Royal Asiatic Society, New
Series, Vol. XXV, No. 1, containing E. Bretschneider's ''Botanicon
Sinicum,'' under 388, note referring to W. F. Mayer's ''Notes and
Queries on China and Japan.''

grown cotton, however, is not now equal to the demand.
It was not without reason that the silk growers feared the
introduction of cotton, for, as a result, the silk industry
declined for a long period and nearly disappeared. It was
not until the development of trade with Europe had created
a demand in that quarter for these rich fabrics that the
industry revived.

Cotton is grown in small patches only; there are no large
plantations. In many cases it is picked, ginned, spun and
woven by the growers, being raised simply for the use of
the family. The plant is small, however, and the staple
short. Efforts are being made to improve the quality by the
introduction of American seed.

Silk culture is common to all the provinces. The silks,
satins and velvets of Hangchow, Soochow and Nanking are
particularly in demand, and formerly factories were maintained in these cities for the express purpose of manufacturing these goods for the Imperial Court. As one travels
on the canals of Kiangsu Province and through the northern
part of Chekiang, he sees everywhere along the banks extensive orchards of mulberry trees. They appear stunted,
which is due to the fact that they are kept constantly
pruned. The tree is usually the wild mulberry improved
by a graft of the cultivated variety. Careful attention to
the trees is necessary to secure a good quality of silk. The
leaves are not picked until the fifth year, after which they
are gathered regularly. The longest lived trees are said to
reach the age of fifty years.

SERICULTURE

In southern Kiangsu a large part of the farmers are
engaged in silk culture. Every spring they purchase a
supply of eggs, hatch and rear the worms, and either have
the silk reeled at home or, as is often done since the introduction of steam filatures, sell the cocoons to these establishments. There is a noticeable difference between the
cocoons of the male and the female, and as soon as the

moths make their escape the Chinese take them in charge and pair them. Their life is very brief. The female lives but five or six days, takes no food but lays innumerable eggs. These are secured by confining her on a piece of paper or cloth under a sieve. A sheet of paper a foot square, covered with eggs, sells in the interior for some two hundred cash, i.e., about fifteen cents. The women often carry the eggs on their persons, the warmth of the body serving to hasten the process of hatching. When the worms first appear they look like small black ants, and are called ants, indeed. After two days they turn to a brown color and in five to a yellowish white. The worms are kept in shallow trays and are fed at first on chopped mulberry leaves. After a few days the chopping is unnecessary. Great care is needed in feeding them; it must not be neglected even at night. It gives one an uncanny feeling in the quiet hours to hear the clicking sound which they make as they devour their food. Throughout the whole period of their growth the Chinese insist on keeping the house very quiet. Strangers are unwelcome, lest some unusual sight or sound should cause the worms to intermit their feeding. Four times during their brief life they molt their skin. The first occasion is on the fifth day. The worm erects itself and falls asleep. For two days it remains in a state of stupor, and shuffles off its skin, after which it arouses itself and continues its feeding. In another five days it is prepared for its second moulting, and thus it continues, alternately eating and moulting at regular intervals until it has completed its fourth change of skin. Then it is removed to a small sheaf of cut straw where it proceeds to spin its cocoon, a process which occupies another five days. When it has thus wrapped itself in its silken robes, it falls into the long sleep, from which, if it wake at all, it will come forth in ten days as a beautiful white-winged moth. Formerly the cocoons were either reeled before the ten days period was completed or the pupa was killed by steaming. Now, in regions near the steam filatures, the Chinese, taught by foreigners, have learned how to accomplish the same end by heating the cocoons in ovens. This process does **not** injure the silk as steaming is apt to do. There is still much room for improvement in the care of the worms. Every year from twenty to forty per cent die before attaining their growth. Sometimes, indeed, the loss is as high as sixty per cent. A more scientific treatment would prevent such a great waste. As it is, when leaves are high priced, the growers under-feed the worms. This not only lessens the quantity of silk, but injures its quality and damages the breed as well.

The ramie is a valuable textile plant grown in many parts of China. The inner bark supplies a fiber which is used in the manufacture of the celebrated grass-cloth. A coarser kind of grass-cloth is made from the *ko*,[4] a plant of the dolichos tribe. There are many varieties of hemp, which are cultivated, sometimes for the oil which is expressed from the seed, but also for the fiber. From the finer kinds linen cloth is woven; ropes and bags are made from the coarser varieties. Jute is also grown, and another plant, whose bark is used in the manufacture of ropes and matting is the coir palm, which is quite common in central China.

THE OPIUM POPPY

In a "Historical Note on the Poppy in China," by Rev. J. Edkins, D.D., published by the Imperial Maritime Customs in 1889, we are told that tobacco was probably introduced into China from the Philippines about A.D. 1620. The Spaniards probably brought it to the latter place from America. Prohibitory edicts were issued by the Chinese emperors against the cultivation of the plant, but in spite of these its use spread rapidly and to-day it is grown in all parts of the empire. After the leaf is prepared it is smoked in a pipe, either a small brass bowl with long bamboo stem, or, as is more often the case, in the water pipe, usually a rather artistic construction of brass. It is sometimes beautifully engraved and is commonly decorated with silk cord

4 Botanicon Sinicum; Journal of China Branch, R. A. S., Vol. XXV, No. 1, p. 208.

and tassels. By its use the smoke is made to pass through water, and is thus cooled and deprived in some measure of its nicotine. But to-day the cigarette has replaced the pipe to a large extent.

The poppy appears to have been introduced to the notice of the Chinese by Arab traders in the seventh or eighth century A.D. The poppy seeds were used by the Arabs as a medicine and became among the Chinese a very popular remedy for many diseases. Thus the plant soon became quite common throughout China. The juice of the capsule was already in use for medical purposes in the twelfth century, and in the latter part of the fifteenth century foreign opium was a common article of import in south China. It was not, however, until the habit of smoking tobacco was spread abroad that opium began to be used in the pipe. At first it was mixed with the tobacco, probably for the purpose of giving it a pleasant flavor as well as to add to its narcotic properties. In the early part of the eighteenth century the vice of opium smoking had already become so common in Formosa and at Amoy as to attract the attention of the Government, and in A.D. 1729 an edict was issued prohibiting the sale of opium and the opening of opium-smoking houses, but the import continued as before. It paid the usual duty at the custom houses and no effort seems to have been made to carry the edict into effect. At about the same time the cultivation of the opium-poppy became quite common in Yunnan,[5] and from that time on the manufacture of native opium gradually spread throughout the empire, until in 1906 effective measures began to be taken to restrict poppy planting and the use of opium.

DYE PLANTS

What is called indigo in China is prepared from a number of different plants. The true indigo plant (*indigofera tinctoria*) is found only in the southern part of the empire,[6]

[5] For these facts regarding the introduction of opium into China I am indebted to the above mentioned "Historical Note on the Poppy in China."
[6] Botanicon Sinicum, p. 212.

but other plants, notably the *polygonum tinctorium* and the *isatis indigotica,* are cultivated over a large part of the empire. In the neighborhood of Shanghai the last mentioned is quite common. In Chekiang the *strobilanthes flaccidifolius* is cultivated for this purpose. Other plants that are cultivated for dyes are the madder, safflower, and the *tzu ts'ao* or purple herb. But the introduction of aniline dyes from the West has interfered very seriously with the sale of native vegetable dyes.

Aside from the fruit trees and others that have been mentioned, there are many useful trees grown. Among them are the oak, valued not only for its wood but for the cupules of the acorn, which are used to produce a black dye, the chestnut, willow, catalpa, camphor, the paper mulberry (*Broussonetia papyrifera*) from the bark of which a strong paper is made, miscalled "leather paper," the tallow tree (*sapium sebiferum*) from which the oil is obtained for the manufacture of candles, the soap tree (*gleditschia sinensis*), from whose seeds a substitute for soap is made, the elm, from the inner bark of which a powder is prepared for the manufacture of mucilage and as an important constituent of the incense used in the temples, the walnut, arbor vitæ, the ash and the privet. A variety of the privet, the *ligustrum lucidum* or "large-leaved" privet, is the tree on which the wax insect of Szechuen is found.

INSECT WAX

Alexander Hosie, of H.B.M's. Consular Service, in his "Three Years in Western China" gives a very interesting description of the manner in which the wax is produced. The insect is found in many parts of China, but its favorite home seems to be in south-western Szechuen, in an upland valley some five thousand feet above the level of the sea. The eggs are deposited on the branches of the privet and covered with a brown scale. At the end of April carriers are sent into the valley to purchase these scales, which are done up in small paper packages, weighing about a pound apiece. Each carrier, loaded with some sixty pounds of the precious freight, hurries over the mountains to the prefecture of Chiating, some two hundred miles to the north-east. They travel only at night to avoid the heat of the day, which would hasten the development of the insects. Having reached their destination they take the scales, twenty or thirty together, and wrapping them in a large leaf of the wood-oil tree, suspend them to branches of a species of ash, the *fraxinus Chinensis.* After feeding on the leaves of the tree for thirteen days, the insects return to the branches, where the females deposit their eggs and cover them with the brown scale, and the males deposit the white wax. In a hundred days from the time the insects are fastened on the tree the deposit is complete. The branches are then cut off and as much of the wax as possible removed by hand. This is put into a pot of boiling water where the wax melts and rises to the surface. It is then skimmed off and placed in molds. A second grade of wax is prepared by throwing the branches and twigs into the pot and gathering in the same way all the wax that can be obtained from them. Formerly the wax was in great demand for coating tallow candles, as well as for sizing paper and cotton goods, but since the introduction of kerosene, the demand has greatly fallen off. The wax is also exported to foreign countries where it is used in the preparation of certain medicines.

Another important tree of western China is the *yingtzu t'ung (aleurites cordata),* from which the well-known wood-oil is produced. The tree grows to the height of fifteen feet and is beautiful and shady. It bears a small pink-white flower. The fruit looks like a green apple and contains the pits from which the oil is expressed. These are gathered in August and September. The oil is much used in the manufacture of varnish and for other purposes. Large quantities are exported every year to foreign countries.

The varnish, or lacquer tree is also a very valuable one.

THE TEA PLANT

None of China's trees or shrubs, however, are more celebrated or valuable than the tea. It seems that it was not until the sixth or seventh century of the Christian era that tea drinking became common, even in China.[7]

The plants seem to prefer a rather poor soil. They are set out at a distance of four or five feet apart and grow to a height of two and a half or three feet. The leaf is of a glossy dark green color and the blossom a waxy white. Some good tea is grown in the southern part of the province of Anhui, more in Kiangsi, Fukien and Chekiang, but most, perhaps, in Hunan and Szechuen.

Much complaint has been made by tea-traders during the past few years of the losses sustained by competition with the teas of India, Japan and Java, and many attempts have been made to induce the Chinese Government to take measures to compel a more careful cultivation of the plant and a more scientific preparation of the leaf. Efforts have been made, too, to obtain a reduction of the heavy taxation with which the trade is burdened. So far as the preparation of the leaf is concerned some progress has recently been made, and a school for that purpose has been established in Kiangsu Province.

China tea is not grown, as in India, on large plantations supplied with all the apparatus for preparing and boxing the tea. Each proprietor has but a small plot of ground, picks the leaf himself, with the aid of his family, and often carries it himself, sometimes a long distance, to market. It is, therefore, very difficult to secure uniformity in the methods of culture. The preparation, too, is carried on, in part at least, in a large number of small establishments with very unequal skill and care. There are two varieties of the tea plant, the green and the black, though it is quite possible to prepare both green and black from the same leaf. One variety, however, lends itself more readily to the preparation of green and the other of black. A third pro-

[7] Botanicon Sinicum, p. 131.

vides the Oolong. There appears to be no doubt that the Chinese tea possesses a more delicate flavor than that of India and that it is much less astringent, but the cultivation of the plant leaves much room for improvement.

The plants are raised from seed sown in moist sand. The shoots produced are set out in the second year. At three years of age the plucking of the leaves may begin, but the shrub does not attain its full growth until six or seven years of age. The average lifetime of a good plant seems to be about ten or twelve years, though some plants thirty years of age have been reported as still in use. Trenching, hoeing, pruning and the use of fertilizers are said to be needed to secure the best growth, but these processes are very much neglected by the Chinese. The first picking occurs about the middle of April and must be completed in from three to five days or the leaves are spoiled for the production of the best article. The end leaves are left in place. Two or three pluckings a year are said to be all that should be allowed, but in some cases the leaves are gathered four or five times. The second picking takes place in June and the third in August. The first chop is the finest, and there is much competition among foreign buyers to secure this. The practice unfortunately too often leads the natives to the gathering of as large a quantity as possible at the expense of quality. The growers used to pay to the Government a "hill tax" of 640 cash per picul, about fifty cents on every 133⅓ lbs. Probably this is still collected. Other taxes amount to from 20 to 35% of the value of the tea at the time of export.

One of the most interesting processes connected with tea manufacture is the preparation of brick tea. This may be witnessed in the large factories at Hankow and Kiukiang. During the season the delicate aroma from the steaming tea-dust may be detected at a considerable distance from the town.

The bamboo is also a most useful vegetable product, and small groves of it are found on nearly all farms in central China. The young shoots are a much prized and very pleasant article of food, while the full-grown plant finds a ready market for an infinite variety of purposes. The plant grows at the rate of a foot or more a day, and in central China attains the height sometimes of forty feet or more. It is said to blossom only once in a period of from thirty to sixty years.[8]

But the Chinese farmer is not content merely to cultivate the land. He lays tribute also upon the water, particularly upon the waters of the ponds, lakes and canals. Many aquatic plants are grown, some for food and others for fertilizing purposes. Among the former one of the most common as well as the most beautiful is the lotus, whose roots and seeds are both regarded as table delicacies. The seeds, stewed in a sweetened syrup, are indeed delicious eating, but the root is astringent and rather insipid. Another plant grown in marshy ground is the *pich'i*, by some called the "water-chestnut." It is the *Scirpus tuberosus*. The tuber is of the size of a chestnut and has the same general appearance, hence the name. When peeled and cooked it makes a pleasant dish, having the flavor of green corn (maize).

Much attention, too, is given to fish culture. At the proper season the farmer purchases a supply of spawn with which he stocks his ponds. Hosie, in his "Three Years in Western China," mentions a method in vogue in that part of the empire for obtaining the spawn. Bundles of reeds and grass, weighted with stones, are placed in the waters of the Yangtze. On these the fish deposit their spawn and, in that region, the ova are scattered in the flooded fields which are being prepared for the rice. The fish are hatched and after a few months they are large enough to be used. Several methods are employed for catching the fish. In the larger ponds they are caught with a seine, the larger fish only being kept for use, the smaller being tossed back to complete their growth. In the shallow creeks the fisherman uses a long bottomless basket, shaped some-

[8] Botanicon Sinicum, p. 393.

what like a truncated cone. With this in his left hand and a long bamboo pole in his right he wades into the water and strikes about with the pole until he catches sight of a darting fish, when he lunges forward and attempts to encircle it with the basket, which he thrusts into the water with the large mouth downward until it reaches the bottom. He then reaches down through the smaller opening in the top of the basket and takes the fish out with his hands. At other times he wades slowly through the water with a dip net. More common on the river banks is the sight of the large dip net attached to a stout framework of bamboo, which is alternately raised and lowered by a lever in shape somewhat like an old-fashioned well-sweep. In the numerous creeks, canals and lakes of Kiangsu cormorants are used. The owner, with perhaps a dozen of these large birds seated on the sides of his skiff, paddles out to the fishing ground where he drives the birds into the water. A long pole enables him to stir up the lazy ones, but, as a rule, they seem to require little urging, and may be seen constantly diving and returning to the surface. A ring around the throat prevents the greedy bird from devouring the catch, which is at once brought to the boat and deposited there. The cormorants appear to be well cared for, and are rewarded for a good day's work by a share of the fish.

POULTRY

Poultry raising in some parts of the country has become a special industry. The writer had the privilege a few years ago of visiting a Chinese hatchery at Soochow. The shop on the street, through which we entered, was filled with baskets of peeping chicks and ducklings, which were being offered for sale. At the rear we crossed a court and entered a dark building about thirty feet square. The walls were of earth and the roof of thatch. The only opening was the door which was kept closed by a weight suspended over a pulley, although there was more or less ventilation at the eaves. The watchman in charge was lying down at one side of the room. Six or eight furnaces of earth, hemi-spherical in shape, were placed at regular intervals and supplied with a smothered fire. On top of each furnace was a shallow covered tray containing the eggs. There was no thermometer, and the only way of determining the temperature was by the feelings of the watchman. After lying some days on the furnace the eggs were removed to a shelf, extending across the room a few feet above the furnace, where they were covered with straw. Later they were removed to a still higher shelf and in due time were hatched. The whole outfit of building and furnaces was not worth over $50.00, yet it served its purpose very well, and such hatcheries have been in use among the Chinese for no one knows how long.

AGRICULTURAL IMPLEMENTS

The farmer's tools are all of a very primitive pattern. His plow is somewhat similar to the shovel plow used by Americans for corn cultivation. It has but one handle and is usually drawn by a buffalo or an ox. The harness consists of nothing more than a rude wooden yoke and rope traces. Sometimes a mule and a cow may be seen yoked together. The smaller fields are dug by hand with a large four-pronged mattock. The grain is cut with a sickle or bill-hook, and is commonly threshed with a flail on an open threshing-floor of beaten earth. The men and women of the farm take their places in two lines, facing each other, with the unthreshed grain between them, and make lively music as the two rows of flails alternately rise and fall. The winnowing is done by tossing the grain up into the air against the wind, but this process is supplemented by the use of a fanning-mill. If the flail is not used the sheaves of grain are arranged in a circle on the threshing floor, and an ox or buffalo is made to drag a stone roller over them, moving round and round until the grains are all shaken from the stalks.

Rice is hulled in stone mortars by heavy hammers, worked either with the foot or swung by the arms. When the foot is used the stone hammer is fastened to the end of a beam, which serves as a lever. By the pressure of the foot the hammer is raised and when the foot is removed it falls by its own weight. The grain is ground in small mills, most commonly turned by mule power, though the water wheel is not unknown.

MARKET DAYS

Taken all in all the life of the ordinary Chinese peasant does not seem to the Western man to be much happier than that of his ox or mule. He is dull, ignorant and superstitious. His hard toil barely suffices to secure him needed food and coarse clothing. He marries and rears a family of children like himself. His world is the village in which he lives, and where in all probability his ancestors for a hundred generations have lived before him. His home is cheerless and squalid; he has few interests beyond his plowing, sowing and reaping; his longest journey will probably be to his county town and, if made, will afford food for thought and theme for conversation for months to come. His dialect is peculiar to his native district. He has heard vaguely of the "Eighteen Provinces" and of the "foreign devils," those outside barbarians who are said to pay tribute to the "Son of Heaven" at Peking. Some have heard that a republic has been formed, but do not know exactly what it means. The births and deaths of the village, the weddings and funerals, with the occurrence of the great annual feasts, serve to break the monotony of existence and furnish landmarks for the reckoning of time. There is another institution, however, which rivals these in importance, the village market. Here and there on the highways of travel are villages of more than ordinary size and importance. They have inns for the passing caravans with refreshment for man and beast, tea-houses for the comfort of the village idlers and gamblers and the exchange of neighborhood gossip by visiting farmers, and shops for the sale of such necessaries and luxuries as salt, matches, kerosene, sugar, candles, incense and mock money, printed

HONORARY PORTAL ON MOUNTAIN ROAD.

MARKET AT KALGAN.

cottons, soap and toilet articles. Every five days, or it may be every ten, a market or fair is held in the streets. Peasants gather from all the countryside, bringing their produce; rice, beans, fresh vegetables, pigs, poultry and eggs, and the little village assumes a busy aspect. Its one principal street is so crowded that passing caravans can scarcely make their way through.

This is the farmer's sabbath; he gets away from his hoe and the hum-drum life of the farm to talk with his fellows, to enjoy the latest scandal and to listen with bated breath to scraps of misinformation that have filtered in from the great outside world, of which he knows so little and can form no real conception; how Great Britain and Germany have been at war, how Japan is attempting to annex Siberia, or Dr. Sun marching on Peking. The fortune-teller and the quack are on hand to reap a harvest from his superstition and credulity, and the Punch and Judy show to furnish him amusement. The traveling pedlar and the peripatetic tinker make themselves more useful.

One April morning some years ago, I came into a little village in central Anhui, called "Great Willow Tree." The market was already in progress and the street was a busy scene of bargain and sale. Just outside the village gate an itinerant blacksmith had set up his kit and was mending plow-shares. As we passed through the gate and entered the village we met a caravan of pack-mules, laden with hemp-oil and making their way to Nanking. Several trains of wheel-barrows followed, carrying opium, oil, cotton, vermicelli or native medicines, i.e. herbs and roots. One barrow-man sometimes wheels as much as three hundred pounds over these rough roads. Other caravans came in during the day making the return journey, bringing cotton cloth, kerosene, matches, paper and a varied assortment of other manufactures. There were a number of Mohammedan families in the place, who had built themselves a small mosque. An old inn-keeper of this faith, with whom we had some acquaintance, hailed us in the street and insisted on carrying us off to the inn to drink tea with him and to meet the young mollah, who had lately come there to live. Meantime the marketers were busy haggling with their customers over the prices of cabbage and garlic, turnips, chickens and eggs. The shop-keepers within doors were having quite as good a day's trade as the farmers outside, and both seemed well satisfied. Tables were set by the roadside for the sale of hot tea and a cool smoke with a native hubble-bubble for those who wanted such refreshment, while the usual group of loafers were noisily settling the affairs of the universe in the tea-house. Suddenly the hum of traffic was drowned by a gong and, looking up, we saw a huge idol of fierce mien, brandishing a long sword in his upraised right hand, being carried through the crowd by four bearers. He was seated on a chair, or throne, richly carved and gaudily decorated. A rather well-to-do farmer of the neighborhood was very ill and, other remedies having failed, his family had sent to a neighboring town for this image, which was celebrated through all the country round for its powers of healing, as famous in its way as the Virgin of Lourdes or other miracle-working images of Europe. The idol was taken to the shop of the village physician, where preparations had already been made for his reception. The doctor, wearing a pair of huge tortoise-shell spectacles, sat behind a table with paper before him and a Chinese pen in his hand. The bearers, supporting the idol upon their shoulders, stood facing him. Rows of drugs in neatly labeled packages were hung upon the wall behind him. An assistant with a rod in his hand pointed to these packages one by one, saying as he did so: "Please Sir, will you have this?" If there was no response, he passed to the next and the next, until the bearers were suddenly thrust forward, which was taken as an indication that the drug was needed. Then followed the question: "Please Sir, how much will you have? Five scruples? One dram?" When the proper amount was mentioned the bearers were thrust backward. Thus the prescription was gradually compounded. At first I felt a sort of pity for the patient who would have to swallow the decoction, but later concluded that it was probably no worse a dose than such a physician would have given had he lacked the assistance of the chair-bearers. My suggestion that the idol's chair should be placed on the floor and that he should be allowed to move it himself backward and forward did not meet with approval. Gradually the crowds in the street began to disperse, and before evening the village had already assumed its wonted aspect of dullness. The farmers could be seen trudging homeward over the hills, each with a pole over his shoulder to which a pair of baskets were suspended, containing the purchases of the day. They went home sober, too, as they usually do. There was not the slightest sign of drunkenness or disorder throughout the whole day.

AGRICULTURAL DISTRESS

Among the least fortunate of the peasant classes are the farm laborers, who are hired by the day, month or year, at wages which seem to us pitifully small. They vary from three cents a day and food, at ordinary times, to five or ten cents a day with food in harvest time. When hired by the month they receive from fifty cents to a dollar and a half besides board and lodging. Annual wages vary from $7.50 to $15.00 with board. Living, as many farmers do, from hand to mouth, it takes but little misfortune to create deep distress. In the Yellow River region of Shantung an unusual rise of the water often leads to the breaking of the dykes and an overflow which drives myriads from their ruined homes to beg upon the highway. Not infrequently has the writer seen such unfortunates making their way southward in search of better luck, the head of the family pushing a wheel-barrow on which were stored the family bedding and kitchen utensils, and perched among them, perhaps, a small-footed wife and one or two children. Such a family came a few years ago to the little village of Yühotzu, in Anhui. Mr. Chang had been a small farmer and a country school teacher; and, as is often true in such cases, had succeeded in neither. At any rate he could find no pupils in Yühotzu, and he supported his

family, or rather failed to support them, by picking up
odd jobs in the neighborhood. When I first met them I
was struck by the peculiarly pathetic look in the face of
the wife. The meaning of this look was explained to me
by the neighbors somewhat in the following fashion. About
a year before my visit Mr. Chang was returning from the
next village, where he had found a day's work. It was
just after dusk, and as he passed a lonely spot on the road,
he heard the wail of a little child by the wayside, the cry
of some waif whose heartless parents had left it there to
die. But Chang had four half-starved children of his own
at home and could not stop to take pity upon the child of
another. He kept the matter to himself until the next
morning when he mentioned it to a neighbor. The neighbor's wife, a compassionate woman, rushed off at once to
the spot indicated to see if anything could be done. It
was too late; the torn clothing of the child was there, but
dogs or wolves had devoured the little unfortunate during
the night. A few weeks later one of Chang's children, a
bright little boy, was taken ill and died. His sister, who
was greatly attached to him, pined for him daily and would
go out and sit by his grave and sing a little song which
both had learned in a mission Sunday-school lately established in the village. It was a strange song from the lips
of a Chinese child, though familiar enough in Christian
lands:

There is a happy land; far, far away.

Not long after she too fell sick and died. The circumstances of the family did not improve, and finally to save
the lives of the two remaining children the father sold
them to strangers and they were carried far away. The
strange, hungry look in the mother's eyes was not hard to
be understood; her heart was broken.

As the story was told to me there was the implication
that Mr. Chang's later misfortunes were a punishment
from Heaven for his heartlessness toward the forsaken waif
whose piteous appeal he had denied. For Chinese men and

women are quite as ready as their Western cousins to interpret the ways of Providence.

I have endeavored in this chapter to give a true picture of country life in China, its lights and shadows. It is not wholly a gloomy picture, yet the shadows, perhaps, predominate. One must ever bear in mind the wide distinction to be made between those whose large estates furnish such revenues as enable them to live at ease, and the circumstances of the great majority who are but small proprietors or tenants, and whose environment from birth to death is one of sordid, comfortless poverty. Few of the latter class ever learn to read. Some obtain just enough knowledge of the characters to be able in rough fashion to set down their accounts. Their acquaintance with mathematics, if they have any, is confined to the rather curious method of using cash as counters. The coins are arranged in groups of five, and the method of reckoning is somewhat similar to that with the abacus. A badly printed calendar pasted on the wall of the hut helps them to keep track of the seasons. The calendar is illustrated with a gaudy print of an impossible cow in varigated colors of red, green, yellow and purple, and the arrangement of these colors indicates to them what the prophecies of the wise men are as to the weather of the coming year. This serves to show how simple-minded, credulous and wanting in all scientific knowledge the Chinese peasant is. He has but slight acquaintance with the government under which he lives. Its representative to him is the opium-smoking rowdy who comes to collect the taxes, and his little experience has taught him that the less he knows of the yamen the better.

To outward seeming he may appear to be utterly

> . . . dead to rapture and despair,*
> A thing that grieves not and that never hopes,
> Stolid and stunned, a brother to the ox,

yet beneath the rough exterior there beats a truly human heart. His better impulses, unfortunately, are sometimes

* Edwin Markham's *The Man With the Hoe.*

checked by fear of ghostly powers. A peasant family in the suburbs of Nanking, when they saw that the old grandmother was about to die, removed her to an out-shed lest the spirit of Death should enter the house. There she lay for weeks with no bedding but a pile of straw, until she breathed her last. Yet it is not to be understood that the family entirely neglected her or were altogether indifferent to her comfort.

Sometimes the dread of officialdom prevents the exercise of kindness. A man dying by the roadside is left unattended, for any good Samaritan who may be disposed to minister to his wants is likely to be seized and held accountable for the death, and though the accused may easily prove his innocence, he will not escape the clutches of the law without paying heavy blackmail. But, when fears and suspicions do not interfere, the hand of charity is not withheld from the needy nor the word of comfort from the bereaved. Our peasant shares all the sorrows as well as all the festivities of his native village. He takes an interest in the ailments of his neighbor and is quick to suggest remarkable remedies, mostly magical, which his experience has proved. He is hospitable to the stranger within the village gates; even the vagabond and the beggar are rarely turned from the door. Yet, once the villager's suspicions are aroused or the rumor of evil intentions circulated, his wrath is fierce, sweeping and merciless, as has been repeatedly shown in attacks upon missionaries against whom foolish charges of witchcraft have been made.

The farmer's life is not too often relieved by merrymakings, and we may be sure no such occasion will be neglected by him. He makes the wedding lively with his rough jokes, and he does not forget the congratulations and gifts due to the father of a new-born son. When a religious feast is to be celebrated he gives his humble contribution cheerfully and joins enthusiastically in the ceremonies. If he be an old man, afflicted with rheumatism or the subject of special misfortune, he and perhaps his aged consort will don the red garments of the penitent, and fall in with the noisy procession which escorts the idol on his rounds. If a younger man, he may load himself with chains or carry heavy weights hooked into his flesh, ostensibly to atone for sin and win the favor of the god, but more aften, perhaps, out of mere love of display.

The picture of the Chinese peasant's life, given above, is still correct for the greater part of China, but in some of the central and southern provinces a change is taking place. This change has been wrought by the suffering occasioned by twenty years of civil strife.

The Nationalist Government at Nanking, it is true, has sought to relieve this distress. Much legislation in aid of agriculture has been proposed;—assisted emigration from congested districts to border provinces, reclamation of waste lands, establishment of agricultural banks, permanent funds for famine relief, public granaries for surplus crops, agricultural colleges to teach scientific farming, and improved communications for the transport of farm products and farmer's requisites. But these, although commendable, are still only paper reforms.

While Dr. Sun was still alive the peasants in many districts of south China were organized into unions by his Russian advisers. These unions under the new constitution will have representation in the future parliament. In the mean time a frank report to the Government by Yang Chien declares that the distress of the peasantry in Kiangsi has driven them into the arms of the Communists. Seventy-six counties in that province are either wholly or partly governed by Communists. Adjoining provinces are also showing a similar trend. Thirty divisions of government troops were recently sent against a Communist army of three hundred thousand. The Communists have confiscated the property of the wealthy, removed boundary marks, burned title deeds and notes and abolished all taxes except that on land. Organized Communism in Yang Chien's opinion is the chief obstacle to the success of the Nationalist Party.*

* *Chinese Affairs*, July 15, 1931.

CHAPTER VI

THE VILLAGE REPUBLIC

Law is not the command of a superior to inferiors, but a declaration by the village elders of immemorial usage.

Maine; "Village Communities."

Ten households make a *pai* (tithing); each *pai* shall have a headman. Ten *pai* make a *chia;* each *chia* shall have a chief. Ten *chia* make a *pao;* each *pao* shall have a director. These heads of the *pai, chia,* and *pao* shall each be elected by the ten heads of the groups which he represents.

Ta Ch'ing Hui Tien: Bk. 17, p. 9.

I have already called attention to the fact that the family in China is the social unit. The village may very properly be called the political unit. The family grew into the clan and the clan, as already stated, frequently grew into the village, and, although the family is autocratically governed by the father, the clan is ruled by the council of the elders or heads of families. The tendency of the clan government, as has been shown, is toward democracy rather than toward autocracy.

This tendency was exemplified in the conflicts which often occurred between the clan and the local representatives of the national government. The members of the clan stood together for the protection of their ancient family rights against encroachment by the mandarins. A similar tendency was shown in Europe in the Middle Ages. Miss Phillpotts, in a work already mentioned, "Kindred and Clan in the Middle Ages," says:

We may summarize what seems to have been the tendency of the kindreds by describing it as democratic—that is to say, that in discouraging the rise of petty local chiefs they tended to keep the status of all freemen equal—but we must believe that they achieved this result by refusing opportunities to the strong as well as by protecting the weak against outside aggression.

They were not democratic in the sense that the medieval church was democratic. But though it seems that we must concede this quite considerable degree of influence to the kindreds, we must be careful to note that it implies no active organization, no conscious political aim on their part. It was achieved, as it were, anonymously, by what we may call passive resistance. We still have no right to think of the Teutonic kindreds as organizing themselves in any but a temporary manner, or as combining for aggression. A kindred can only be said to exist at the moment when it groups itself round a given kinsman, and a large proportion of this group must merge into other groups if some other individual is in need. So long as kinship was recognized through both male and female—i.e., during the whole period— these characteristics of the kindreds must have set very definite bounds to their political power.[1]

In China, however, the clan was not weakened by the recognition of the claims of maternal kindred, and, therefore, it has been both formally organized and has exerted a more permanent influence than in Europe, not often by direct political action, but indirectly by union in defense of customary rights and in resistance to new imposts by either local or national authorities.

MUTUAL RESPONSIBILITY

The permanence and strength of the clan organization was fostered, too, by the ancient practice on the part of the national government which held the members of a clan responsible for the offenses of any one of their number. Freedom and self-government always carry with them certain obligations. A clan might successfully resist the exactions by the provincial or national authorities of new imposts or new services, but, once a serious crime was committed by a member of the clan, the punishment of the clan was swift and merciless. For the system of mutual responsibility extended upwards from each individual member of the clan to the highest provincial authorities. The local authorities were responsible to the national government for the peace and good order of their districts, and the same motive that induced them to avoid antagonizing a clan,

[1] Op. cit., pp. 256, 257.

when it could be safely avoided, that is to say, the desire to avoid being called to account for the disorder that would result from a quarrel with the clan, made them equally zealous to exact the full penalty of the law when others created a disturbance of the peace. Neglect to do so would bring them under the condemnation of the national government, and render them liable themselves to severe penalties. Numerous illustrations may be given of the infliction of such penalties. In October, 1905, the American Presbyterian Mission at Lienchou, Kuangtung Province, was attacked by a mob. Several missionaries were killed and the hospital and other mission buildings burned. In punishment for the crimes committed several rioters were put to death, and the district magistrate and the commander of the local military force were removed from office never to be employed again, although they had nothing to do with the rioting. The following year, in the province of Kiangsi, a French mission was attacked with some loss of life, and not only were a number of the rioters executed but the Governor of the province, the provincial Judge and the provincial Treasurer were all removed from office.

THE TITHING

As long as a village was occupied simply by one clan, the elders of the clan were, of course, the elders of the village and responsible for its peace. But the time came in the natural growth of the village when several families, or clans, were found in its population, and a system of mutual responsibility had to be devised to cover this condition. That time came in a distant antiquity. The social organization adopted to secure the peace was that of the tithing. Under the late Manchu Dynasty, the *Ta Ch'ing Hui Tien,* or Constitutional Code of the Manchus, provided that ten families should constitute a tithing with a tithing-man at its head, that ten tithings should make a hundred with a hundred-man at its head, and that ten hundreds should make a thousand—or a *li* or *fang*—with a thousand-headman. The term *li* was used in the village and *fang* in the cities.[2]

The system, however, is much older than the Manchu Dynasty. Under the Chou Dynasty (1122-249 B.C.), and probably under those that preceded it, five families were grouped together and made mutually responsible one for another. Five of these groups, that is to say twenty-five families, constituted a *lü*. Four *lü* were combined in a hundred, and five hundreds made a *t'ang*, five *t'ang* a *chou*, and five *chou*, that is 12,500 families constituted a *hsiang* or village.[3] Each of these groups had its headman, just as in case of the later division into tithings.

Probably the group often had more or less than the number of families required by the law, but the principle which made neighbors responsible for one another remained unchanged. The attempt to introduce western theories and methods has scarcely affected village life as yet.[*]

VILLAGE ELDERS

These headmen are to-day the elders of the village and of the city ward. Theoretically they are chosen by the families concerned and appointed by the county magistrate. In some cases this is the actual practice. Through these headmen the village governs itself. One of the headmen becomes the *ti-pao*, that is to say the responsible representative of the whole village, corresponding to the post of the head of the *hsiang*. He is the mediator between the officers of the national or provincial government on the one side and the people of the village on the other side. He is held responsible for the peace and good order of the village and for the collection and payment of the taxes. In all transfers of real estate his name appears upon the title deed as surety for the legality of the transaction, without which the county magistrate will refuse to affix his seal

[2] Ta Ch'ing Hui Tien: Bks. 17 and 157.

[3] Chou Li, Vol. III.

[*] In December 1930 the Nationalist Government issued instructions to the local governments of the country to enforce registration of households and the system of mutual responsibility of the inhabitants of the villages.

or allow the deed to go to record. The same is true in the several wards into which the city is divided, for theoretically the city appears to be a group of villages enclosed by one surrounding wall. The law required the headman to be honest, to be able to read and write and to be married.

POLICE

The changes in political agencies and organization wrought by the reforms that followed the "Boxer" rising of 1900 and the revolution of 1911 have affected some branches of the government very greatly. One of these changes was the establishment, in 1905, of a national gendarmerie, or police force. But, while theoretically the police powers of the whole country are exercised by the Ministry of the Interior at Peking, in reality except in some of the principal cities the peace is maintained very much as of old, by control through the village elders and the system of mutual responsibility.

As an illustration of the measure of success attending this method of police I recall that some years before the revolution of 1911 my home was burglarized. The county authorities were informed and the Magistrate sent for the local *ti-pao* and directed him to recover the stolen goods or arrest the thieves within a certain number of days, otherwise he would be held accountable. Before the expiration of the time limit all the important articles stolen were recovered and returned to us. The *ti-pao* knew, of course, where the thieves' market was held, and articles of foreign manufacture at that time were easily detected. Had it been a native house that was robbed perhaps the *ti-pao* would have had much greater difficulty in identifying the stolen goods. On the whole, however, the method of holding the neighbors responsible for one another's conduct and the elders responsible for the village tends to check serious offenses. On the other hand, if the general sentiment is opposed to any regulation, such as that forbidding opium smoking, the probabilities are that the neighbors will shield one another. The responsibility of the *ti-pao,* as the principal elder, for the good order of the whole village makes his office anything but a sinecure.

Bearing in mind what has already been said, that there are few farmers living in detached farm-houses and that, as a rule, they congregate in villages, it will be seen that China for the most part is a land of village communities. There are 1943 district capital cities in China, and they will not average 50,000 inhabitants each, so that they contain not more than 95 millions of the 400 millions of the population, that is to say something more than one-fifth. The remaining 305 millions are the villagers. Probably three-fourths or more of the people, therefore, live in villages. You may stand on an elevation almost anywhere in the central or eastern provinces of China and count the villages in sight by the score. They are rarely more than a fraction of a mile apart on any of the principal roads. This will enable us to understand the importance of the village elders to the peace of the state.

All important villages are protected by ramparts of earth and gates that are supposed to be closed at night, but in many cases the walls and gates are allowed to fall into bad condition, and the smaller hamlets, of course, have no such protection. In times of public disorder, however, the elders will see that the walls are repaired and the gates kept closed and, if the condition be very perilous, the local train-band will be called upon to set guards and supplement the work of the village watch-men. The train-band is one of the volunteer organizations of the village which still further illustrates the independence of the village in the matter of protection. The professional soldier, in fact, is feared and disliked. A Chinese proverb says: "You don't make nails out of good iron; you don't make soldiers out of good men." The spice of the proverb is in the pun upon the word *ting,* which is used for nails and for soldiers. In reality two words are used which are entirely different when written but which are both pronounced *ting.* The proverb is not so applicable to-day as it was before the organization of the new national army. There are many countries besides China, however, in which the militia-man in times of peace is preferred by the ordinary house-holder to the professional soldier. The members of the train-band belong to the village. They are known. They are interested in preserving their neighbors' goods, and they are easily called to account for any offense committed. If brigandage is rife and the highways unsafe, the elders of neighboring villages will arrange to combine their train-band forces to patrol the roads.

BRIGANDAGE

Against a large army the village train-band, of course, is of no use, but for defense against brigands it serves very well.

In times of drought or flood, which always bring famine in their train, many poor people are driven to organize themselves into bands of robbers, which pillage the homes, and particularly the granaries, of the well-to-do. And since the national government does little or nothing to prevent flood or to correct the conditions that bring drought, these calamities occur with considerable frequency, sometimes in one region, at others in another. The highways thus become infested with robbers, and the inefficiency of the national and provincial authorities has forced the people to take the question of protection into their own hands. Caravans are protected by the payment of blackmail to the robber chieftains. These caravans, which, before the introduction of railways, were the only freight carriers on overland routes, still form the ordinary means of transport to places not on rail or water ways. Upon payment of a fixed sum by the month to the agent of the robbers the merchant is given a small flag bearing the seal of the robber chieftain, which is placed upon the leading animal of the caravan. This insures immunity from attack.

THE VILLAGE INN

Other travelers are less fortunate, but if they escape attack on the road they will be grateful for the shelter at night of the village inn and for the protection of the village guard. The village inn is nothing more than a caravansary. The wheel-barrows and carts, with their freight, are parked in the courtyard, around which are built the stables for the mules and horses. Their drivers with the barrow men sleep in the rooms adjoining the stables. Nothing but a thin partition separates them from the animals, whose munching can be heard throughout the night. The traveler carries his own bedding, which is spread out upon a few boards stretched over two trestles. The accommodations are rude, but the food is wholesome and abundant, and when one has ridden twenty or thirty miles sleep, even on a board, is sound and healthful.

In the north these village inns are usually built of beaten earth with roof of thatch or slate; in the central and southern provinces they are more attractive in appearance, being generally constructed of a grey brick with a roof of dark-colored tiles. In the north, however, instead of a bedstead composed of two trestles and a few boards there is built in one corner of the room a platform of earth covered with matting. This platform is heated, either by flues passing through it in which straw and twigs are burnt, or by a charcoal stove built in one side. The latter is often the cause of death from asphyxiation on cold winter nights.

THE NIGHT WATCHMAN

In ordinary times the village needs no other protection than that of the watchman who makes the round of the place once every watch, that is to say once every Chinese hour, which is twice as long as a western hour. The first watch is from 7 to 9 o'clock p.m. During that hour the *ta-keng-ti* walks through the village streets carrying a lantern and beating his gong, or wooden rattle, with one stroke every few paces. Between 9 and 11 he patrols again giving two strokes, and thus each watch of the night is announced, usually towards the end of the watch. It gives one a pleasant sense of security, as he turns drowsily in his bed, to hear the beating of the watch and become half conscious of the fact that someone is awake and watching over him. But it must also be an assurance to any prowling thief that the watchman is unlikely to call again before two hours are passed.

Since the villagers are chiefly engaged in agriculture, it is necessary to protect not only their homes but their fields which are situated outside the village. This is provided for by a mutual arrangement among the neighbors, who, at harvest time or when the fruit is ripening, take turns sleeping in the fields in a lodge of twigs. Such was the "lodge in a garden of cucumbers," mentioned by the prophet Isaiah.[4]

CARING FOR THE STREETS AND ROADS

The village elders must also see that the streets are lighted and the roads and bridges kept in repair. At present the lights are small kerosene lamps placed at considerable distances from one another, but formerly they were shallow cups with spouts similar in shape to the ancient Roman lamps. These contained a little bean oil in which there was placed a wick of pith that projected through the spout. These lamps were placed in a sheltered receptacle on top of a pillar of masonry. Inside the village gates the streets are paved either with cobble stones, as is common in the north, or, in central and southern China, more often with brick and flag-stones. Where carts are unknown a row of flagstones is laid down the middle of the street with a pavement of brick on either side. The flagstones serve as a track for the wheel-barrows. In places where there are stone quarries near at hand the whole street may be paved with flat stones. This was formerly the case in the vicinity of Peking. These stones wear off at the joints, which fills the road with holes and makes a journey in a

---

[4] Isa. 1:8.

springless cart over such a pavement a torture to the body and a serious injury to one's morals.

With the introduction of European carriages in recent years, and the coming now of the motor car, some improvement has been made in streets and roads in the vicinity of a few large cities. During the famine of 1920, the distribution of relief was accompanied in some places by the employment of the sufferers in the construction of good roads. But, generally speaking, the national government has done nothing of consequence to supply the country with roads, and the villagers do only what is absolutely indispensable in the repairing of the roads outside the village gates. Now and then, however, they are aided by the generosity of some well-to-do resident who repairs a bridge or builds a mile or more of good roadway to secure credit with his gods and the permission of the elders to erect a monument to himself by the roadside, recording his good deed.

If a widow of the village has remained faithful to the memory of her husband throughout a long period of years to the day of her death, the elders will obtain contributions from the villagers and erect to her memory an honorary gateway of stone built across the street near her late home, and inscribe thereon a tribute to her virtue.

THE VILLAGE COURT

Should a quarrel occur in the village, the law courts of the district will not be used to settle it except as a last resort. A Chinese proverb says:

> The doors of the Magistrate's court open wide,
> But right that is moneyless does better outside.

The villager has a wholesome fear of getting into the clutches of the yamen runners, those underlings who squeeze plaintiff and defendant alike upon pretext that fees are required for this service and that, so that the scripture is fulfilled which saith:

Agree with thine adversary quickly whiles thou art in the way with him, lest at any time the adversary deliver thee to the judge and the judge deliver thee to the officer and thou be cast into prison. Verily I say unto thee, thou shalt by no means come out thence till thou hast paid the uttermost farthing.[5]

The village elders, therefore, use their good offices to reconcile the disputants and earn for themselves the reward of the peace-makers. They hear the complaint and the defense, the rejoinder and the sur-rejoinder. They find a middle ground on which the parties to the quarrel may meet. The law-suit is avoided: the ill-feeling is removed, the principals and their relatives are reconciled, and the whole village participates in the feast with which the event is celebrated. The house of the complainant is decorated with red hangings, and the neighbor against whom complaint was made brings great bunches of fire-crackers attached to a pole and sets them off in the gateway. Thus full atonement is made for the alleged injury or affront and everybody is happy.

THE TEA HOUSE

The village tea house is an institution that deserves a word. It is the club, the newspaper, the vaudeville of the village, and its saloon. Usually it is a restaurant as well as a tea house. In the early morning many of the men of the village will have their breakfast there, rice congee or steamed meat dumplings and plenty of tea. The tea is served in covered cups. A few leaves are placed in the cup, boiling water is poured over them and the cup is covered. This preserves the flavor in the tea. When the drinker takes a sip he pushes the cover a little to one side. Sometimes an extra cup is provided into which the liquid is poured after it has acquired sufficient strength, and the cup with the tea leaves is filled again with boiling water. The old men of the village gather day by day in the tea house to gossip and to smoke and to read or listen to the

5 Matt. v:25, 26.

reading of the news, and there the loafers come to gamble. At irregular intervals the proprietor will engage a public story-teller to entertain his patrons, who pay merely for the tea they drink. Many of the illiterate get their history from the theater and the public story-teller. He is an experienced elocutionist. Sometimes he is a ventriloquist as well. He recites rather than reads. Sometimes it is a tale from the novel called "The Three Kingdoms" that he tells. Or it may be "The Dream of the Red Chamber," or more probably one of the stories from the *Shui Hu,* a collection of tales of gallant robbers who were champions of the people against their oppressors—stories that remind one of Robin Hood and his Merrie Men. The story-teller sits behind a table on a platform and imitates the voice and manner of the various characters in his tale—the grand air and commanding tones of the mandarin, the shrill voice of the virago, the soft utterances of the shy maiden or the querulous tremolo of the decrepit grandsire. He mimics the sound of the watchman's rattle and the twittering of the birds at dawn, and, as he unfolds the plot, he is encouraged now and then by a shout or grunt of approval from his auditors. They nevertheless keep up their conversation with one another, making a bargain over the tea-cups or discussing the latest rumors. A pair of old cronies to whom the story is more than a twice-told tale have perhaps retired to a corner to play chess. It may be that a group of noisy youths in another corner are staking, each a string of cash, in a game of "Sparrows," the game at one time so popular in the United States as *ma jongg.* At Peking it is called *ma ch'iao,* which is the name of the bird we call a sparrow. The story-teller is not disturbed by any of these things; his story runs on without interruption and without any loss of eloquence on the part of the reciter.

It is especially upon market days that the tea house is made so attractive, for the peasants bring in their produce from the fields, and people from neighboring hamlets and villages also are present. The village market, which has already been described in another chapter, is also under the supervision of the elders. To assist the peasants in remembering the date of a market it is generally held upon the days of the moon that have a certain figure in the units place, as for instance on all *three* and *eight* days, i.e., the third, eighth, thirteenth, eighteenth, twenty-third and twenty-eighth; or on all *four* and *nine* days, i.e., the fourth, ninth, fourteenth, nineteenth, twenty-fourth and twenty-ninth. The elders of neighboring villages arrange the dates of the markets so that no two villages will have markets the same day.

THE VILLAGE TEMPLE

The elders must attend also to the upkeep of the village temple, provide a care-taker and see that the offerings are made at the proper times. In some villages there are fields set aside for the support of the temple worship, i.e., commons, the produce or rent of which belongs to the community.

These temples are sometimes dedicated to one divinity, sometimes to another. It may be to a Taoist deity or a Buddhist saint. In some cases it is dedicated to the *San Chiao*, i.e., the "Three Religions," Confucianism, Buddhism and Taoism. The ordinary Chinese is a liberal minded man. "All religions are the same," he says. "They all exhort men to do good." I remember well such a temple called the *San Shan An*, or the "Abbey of the Three Mountains." Located, as the abbey was, in a valley in sight of three mountains, the name was very appropriate, but it probably was intended to have a double significance, since "The mountain" or "The mountain gate" is a common synonym for "the monastery." Over the portico and on the pillars that supported it were appropriate mottoes teaching the unity of the human race and the common faith that underlies all differences of religion.

In most villages there will be a temple to the *T'u Ti Lao Yeh*, or the deity of the locality. The Chinese divide the underworld into provinces, counties and townships corresponding to the divisions of China, so that each village is supposed to have its counterpart in the world of shadows, and the shadowy village to have its *ti-pao* just as the one on earth has. The *T'u Ti Lao Yeh* is the ghostly *ti-pao*. When a man dies he goes to his own place, and it is the duty of the family to notify the *T'u Ti Lao Yeh* of his coming. This deity is supposed to look after the welfare also of his community in the upper world. If there are good crops and corresponding comfort in the home, the god is rewarded by offerings of incense and candles, but if otherwise the Chinese are not unwilling at times to treat the image of their deity with considerable disrespect. I recall a visitation of locusts many years ago in central China, which spared the garden of a poor widow. She showed her gratitude by incense and candles offered at the shrine of the *T'u Ti Lao Yeh* of the district. The next day a second swarm of locusts appeared and devoured all her growing vegetables. Then in her wrath she went to the shrine and, shaking her fist at the idol she cursed the god for his neglect. Small shrines to this deity are often seen in the fields or along the highways. The written character for sun appears sometimes in one gable of the little building and that for the moon in the other. Frequently instead of these you find the *yin yang* symbol, i.e. the circle divided by a curved line into two portions, one white the other black. On the face of the shrine a common motto is "Ask and ye shall receive."

The village temple is not only a temple but the town hall as well, where public meetings of the villagers are held. It is also commonly used for the ancestral tablets of those families too poor to maintain a proper ancestral hall. Coffins are frequently stored in it, both those which are bought against the day of death by the well-to-do householder who wants to be fully prepared to die, and those of the dead, which are guarded by the care-taker or the monk in charge until a lucky site for the grave and a lucky day for burial have been selected by the local soothsayers.

Where all the people of a village are worshipers in these temples there is no difficulty in laying assessments for their upkeep, but when a family has become converted to Christianity it will refuse to pay the assessments, and this at once creates trouble. To the idolater the refusal of the Christian seems but a subterfuge to escape taxation, and the convert in his zeal often adds fuel to the flame of discontent by ridiculing the mud gods and their worshipers. The Chinese have been accustomed in many places, however, to the presence of Mohammedans, who also refuse to support the worship of images, and it has always been possible to arrange a compromise by which the non-worshiper contributes an extra sum for some other public enterprise in lieu of the temple assessment.

More serious trouble occurs when the villages of different faiths fall to fighting one with another. Such conflicts have unfortunately taken place between Roman Catholic and Protestant converts. The origin of the feud is sometimes unknown to the missionary, who has been unconsciously made a party to an ancient quarrel. Some years ago a well-known British missionary escaped the toils of such a plot by his extreme caution. He was visited one day by the elders of a village in which some Christian work had been done. The elders informed him that the whole village desired to become Christian. That seemed so remarkable that the missionary made an investigation and discovered that the village had a feud with another village in the same neighborhood which had a large number of Roman Catholics in its population. The elders of the first village had decided that if they should all become Protestants they might claim that they were being persecuted for their faith's sake, and so obtain the protection of the British Government. The American Legation at Peking has had to report a number of quarrels between Protestants and Roman Catholics in which its good offices were sought by the missionaries. The author was sent by the American Minister one winter to investigate such a quarrel which had involved a number of villages in the province of Chihli. It was discovered that some crops had been destroyed, some animals killed, a few houses burned, grain carried off and a number of people injured. Old grudges and personal animosities, rather than religious differences, seemed to be the real sources of trouble.

THE GUEST HOUSE

On this journey acquaintance was made with the village guest house, which was found to be a very beneficent institution. The village inn is not always clean and lacks many comforts and all privacy. The guest house was well built and provided with fuel, food and servants. It gave us the warmth, quiet and rest that were most desirable after a weary ride of ten miles in a sedan on a bitter winter's day. The guest house was built by the village as a place for the entertainment of officials or other visitors who had to pass that way, and was a credit to the elders who had initiated the enterprise.

THE VILLAGE SCHOOL

The elders must also provide a school for the children of the village. If possible a local scholar is engaged as teacher. The small pittance which is his salary is obtained by assessment upon those families whose children attend the school.

An edict of the late Empress Dowager, Tzuhsi, in 1905, adopted a public school system for the whole country, and directed that an examination should be made of community temples which, if found suitable, were to be taken for village school-houses, unless other provision could be made by any village concerned. This would not, of course, require the removal of the idols, but, as a matter of history it is worth recording that in not a few instances the idols were taken out and thrown into the rubbish heap to make room for pupils and teacher. The curriculum, too, was determined by edict. The school system adopted provided for a lower and an upper primary school in every village, and required every village of 100 families or more to maintain at least one primary school. These schools were to teach arithmetic and geography, history and elementary science, as well as reading and writing. But it was still impossible to find the number of teachers needed who were qualified to teach all these branches. Under the old system, which made education largely a private interest, and which required of the pupil nothing but the ability to read and write Chinese and to expound the classics in order to obtain entrance to the civil service, the teacher as a rule knew nothing else. A district magistrate, who was, of course, a graduate, once asked me: "Is it true that the world is round?" I assured him that it was but he shook his head in doubt.

Since the adoption of the public school system some villages have diverted for the support of the village school the funds the proceeds of which have in the past been used for the village theater.

THE THEATER

The theater is not, as one might imagine, a public hall, provided with seats for the spectators and a stage and dressing room for the players. Sometimes there is no building at all, but merely a temporary platform made for the occasion. At best there is a covered stage with dressing rooms. This is built at the foot of a hill, so that the villagers can seat themselves on the hillside and look down towards the stage. Sometimes it is placed in front of a Buddhist monastery, and the play becomes a part of the festival in honor of the Buddha or the Buddhist saints that are worshiped there. The plays are thus given in the open air and are free to all comers. The players are paid by the elders, who either use the proceeds of a fund devoted to this purpose or raise the necessary money by private subscriptions.

The actors theoretically form one of the despised classes in China. Under the old régime they and their descendants for three generations were not allowed to enter the examinations for the civil service. They were classed with beggars, barbers, butchers and chair-bearers, who, because of the menial services performed or, in the case of butchers, because they were familiar with the sight of blood, were regarded as unfit to hold office.

There were always ways of removing the handicap, however, if one were eager to enter the service, for he could be adopted as a son by someone who was free from the disqualification.

The drama in China found its highest development during the Mongol Dynasty (A.D. 1260–1368). The plays are mostly of a historical character, but the amusing farce is not lacking. As a rule the tone is highly moral, but there are exceptions. The lessons of filial piety and loyalty are emphasized and virtue always finds its due reward.

TAKING THE CENSUS

One of the most important duties of the elders is the taking of the census. This is supposed to be reported every fifth year to the Ministry of Finance at the capital. A blank form is posted at the door of every house, and the number of males and females in the household, including the servants, is written plainly on the card. This is open to inspection by anyone interested so that, if a false return is made, the neighbors may be able to report it. In the smaller villages, of course, the elders know every one and can themselves check the returns: in the large villages the tithing-man certainly will know the facts. In the early years of the Manchu Dynasty there was a poll tax levied, and the returns were therefore of considerable importance. This subsequently was combined with the land tax. In those days there was a disposition, no doubt, to conceal the real number of adult males in a household, but no such inducement exists to-day. Among the Manchus, however, as long as the dynasty lasted, there was a temptation to pad the returns in order to draw the pensions which were paid to every Manchu male. I was told by a Manchu at the time of the Revolution in 1912 that the names of many persons long dead were still carried on the rolls of some of the banners. This seems quite credible.

COLLECTING TAXES

The land tax assessed upon the cultivated fields, the reed tax—a small payment made by those who cut the reeds from the public lands in the marshes along the foreshore of certain rivers—the salt tax, the excise on distilled liquors and tobacco, and the likin* collected along the highways and water-ways on goods in transit—all these have to be paid by the villagers. The proceeds formerly were reserved for the provincial and national treasuries. This is no longer true; a percentage of the receipts belongs to the village, in addition to which it is permitted to levy and collect all taxes formerly allowed for its support.

It will be seen, then, that the village is a self-governing community, a little republic which has existed for ages, formerly in the midst of an empire and to-day as part of a larger republic, the State. Thus the village, as well as the clan, has given the people experience in self-government, and helped in their preparation for the establishment of representative institutions.

* Likin was nominally abolished December 15, 1930, but the authority of the central government is not everywhere respected.

CHAPTER VII

THE CITY

The cities are full of pride,
  Challenging, each to each—
This from her mountainside,
  That from her burthened beach.
  .   .   .
And the men that breed from them
  They traffic up and down,
But cling to their cities' hem
  As a child to the mother's gown.
                              Kipling.

In China the word most commonly used as the equivalent of "city" is *ch'eng*. Strictly speaking the word means "a city wall" or "rampart," and it is applied as a rule only to those towns which are surrounded by a substantial brick wall and a moat. The place of lowest rank that may be called a city is the *hsien*, the capital of a county. Any town which is the seat of government of an officer of the rank of a county magistrate or above it may be called a *ch'eng*. There are market towns and villages in China which are larger and of greater commercial importance than some cities, but it is political importance that gives a place the rank of a city.

CLASSIFICATION OF CITIES

By an enactment in June 1930 certain cities of special importance were placed under the direct control of the central government and others under the jurisdiction of the province in which they are located. Generally speaking the cities of a million or more inhabitants are included in the first class, but there are exceptions. In the second class, as a rule, are cities of two hundred thousand inhabitants but less than a million provided they have revenues of a fixed amount.

In the first class are Nanking, Shanghai, Hankow, Tsing-tao, and Tientsin. But Peip'ing and Canton, probably for political reasons, are put in the second class.

To place the municipal governments of the large and important cities under the direct control of the central government may possibly do away with the graft of local bosses and lessen the danger from mob violence, but such increase of the power of the national administration is likely to be resisted in a land where local autonomy is so highly prized.

The arrangement above described is still but an experiment. It has not yet been generally adopted.

THE WALLS

These great walls of grey brick, sometimes with projecting bastions, always with crenellated parapets, give the cities of China a picturesque appearance. They rise from 25 to 60 feet in the air and are weather-worn and often over-grown here and there with vines and shrubbery.

They have a core of earth, and in the days when they were built they were a strong defense against besieging forces. Even to-day, if furnished with modern artillery and properly manned they could give an attacking army a great deal of trouble.

The gates are closed at night. When the watchman makes his round about nine o'clock the gate-keeper swings one of the pair of great doors into place and lights a stick of incense. As long as the incense burns the other door is left ajar for late comers, but when the incense is burned out the gate is locked and cannot be opened until day-break, except in obedience to official orders.

While living in the foreign settlement at Shanghai I was invited to attend the service in the Confucian Temple, which is within the native city. The service is held about three or four o'clock in the morning. To enter the city at such an hour was impossible without a pass. The Taotai sent me a gate tally. It was a polished piece of wood about 15 inches long on which there appeared one-half of an inscription which could not be read until the counterpart of the tally was placed alongside, for the inscription had been written over the joint. When the two parts were joined the inscription proved to be a permit to open the city gate. At three o'clock in the morning I presented it at the West Gate and, after a brief delay, was admitted.

To the skillful climber the walls are not such an obstacle as they appear to be to the ordinary man. At the time of the "Boxer" Rising in 1900, when the American army of relief reached the city of Peip'ing where the foreign Legations were besieged, an American drummer boy clambered up one corner of the wall of the outer city. Each course of brick is set in about a half inch from the edge of the course below it, thus giving the wall a slight incline away from the perpendicular. The storms of centuries had also worn holes here and there in the bricks. With one man up the ascent of others was made easier, and the little squad of men, although under fire, were able to get down on the inside and open a gate and admit the army.

The various foreign governments keep legation guards at Peip'ing. That of the United States is composed of marines and numbers usually between two and three hundred. It was a common practice in the years 1911–13 for the officers of this guard to call for volunteers to scale the city wall which bounds the American Legation grounds on the south. It is fifty feet high, yet as many as forty men would respond and accomplish the feat very successfully and expeditiously.

At present there is a disposition among the Chinese to destroy the old city walls. This is unfortunate. The first place to lose its walls was Tientsin, a city of some 700,000 inhabitants. The destruction of its wall was a penalty imposed by the allied governments because of Tientsin's participation in the "Boxer" attacks upon Europeans and Americans. The people of Tientsin and the officers of the national government resisted the demand for a long time, and only consented under compulsion, for the loss of the walls was regarded at that time as a disgrace to the city. The walls were torn down in 1903, and the débris was used to fill up the moat. On the site of wall and moat a beautiful, wide boulevard with a street car line was constructed. This was so attractive that other cities began to imitate. Shanghai and Canton took the lead in so doing. In the case of these two cities the destruction of the walls is probably an improvement to sanitary conditions, for the streets are narrow and the locations are low and damp. The removal of the walls has let in air and sunlight. But for most places the destruction of the walls would lessen the attractiveness of the city and be of no compensating advantage, either to sanitation or to transport. To destroy such walls as those of Peip'ing or Nanking, of Wuchang, Chengtu, or a hundred other places that might be named, would be a crime. It is encouraging to see the Chinese people showing a progressive spirit, but mere imitation of the West is not necessarily progress.

GENERAL APPEARANCE OF CITIES

Seen from the top of a city wall the Chinese city, as a rule, does not present a very interesting appearance. The prospect is one of dark grey gabled roofs covering grey brick buildings. Here and there will be seen an open space overgrown with grass and weeds.

Most houses are of one story; a few have two stories; fewer have three. The monotony of the view is broken only by the trees that rise above the garden walls, or by an occasional pagoda. There are some exceptions to this rule of a drab and uninviting appearance. The northwestern part of Nanking, for instance, consists very largely of rolling hills, devoted to temples, bamboo groves and market gardens. This is due chiefly to the fact that when the founder of the Ming Dynasty made it his capital (A.D. 1368), he extended the city wall on the north and west so as to enclose a larger area. The remains of the old wall and moat can still be seen. The wall of Nanking thus became the longest in the empire, having a circuit of about 26 miles, the territory that was added in this way to the city was never closely built over and retains a rural appearance.

Peip'ing is unlike all other cities. Not only are the walls more massive; they are strengthened by enormous bastions, and protected at the corners and at the gates by towers that rise 100 feet in the air. As one approaches the city from any side and beholds these lofty towers, the bastions and parapets, he can not but be impressed by its appearance. And when one stands upon the wall he finds a very attractive prospect. He looks down upon four cities, each enclosed by its own wall. In the center are the yellow roofs of the palaces, shining like gold in the sunlight. Enclosing these palaces is a grey brick wall some forty feet in height. Outside of this is the Imperial City, surrounded by what the Chinese call a "purple wall." Within the Imperial City are the lakes of the Western Park, the President's palace, the Marble Bridge, the Finger Pagoda, the Prospect Hill, and many beautiful temples and other public buildings. Surrounding the Imperial City is the Tartar City, enclosed by a wall fourteen and a half miles in circuit, fifty feet in height, and fifty in thickness at the top. Within this enclosure are the homes of the people, shops and temples, the Drum Tower and the beautiful Bell Tower, the White Dagoba, the Twin Pagodas, several lamaseries, princely palaces, the foreign legations and the mission churches with their spires.

On the south you look over into the "Chinese City" and catch a view of the blue-tiled tower of the Temple of Heaven, and, over in the south-west, the pagoda of the Tien Ning Monastery, which was built in the sixth century A.D. In the distance rise the hills which extend in a horseshoe curve around the city on the west, north and east, and give to the plain of Peip'ing, in the eyes of the geomantic expert, its assurance of happiness and prosperity.

THE STREETS

The principal thoroughfares of Peip'ing are broad avenues a hundred feet or more in width, that cross one another at right angles. The lanes, 20 to 40 feet in width, are also for the most part quite regular, but there are some exceptions.

Generally speaking, in the northern part of China the streets of a city are wide and unpaved, but Peip'ing and a few other places have macadamized the principal streets. In central and southern China the city streets are crooked and much narrower than in the north. They are from ten to fifteen feet in width and are paved with brick and stone. The shop fronts are usually open, exposing the whole interior. In the summer time the business streets are shaded by mats that rest on poles stretching from one side of the street to the other, and giving it the appearance of a bazaar. Like most old-world cities, those of China grew up at a time when sanitary science was unknown. Peip'ing has a system of sewers which was constructed in the Ming period (A.D. 1368–1644), but they are not water-tight, and were evidently intended originally merely to carry off surface water from the streets into the city moat. There are gutters for this purpose under the pavements of southern towns. Night-soil is carried by coolies in open buckets from city closets out into the country, where it is mixed by the farmers with wood ashes and used as a fertilizer.

The city is districted by chance, each district taking its name from some local landmark, such as the Three Honorary Gateways, the Confucian Temple, the West Water Gate, the Drum Tower East or the Drum Tower West, the Temple of Ancient Worthies, or the Sweet Water Fountain. The streets of each district are named without regard to the names existing in other parts of the city, so that you are likely to find names duplicated. The same street, too, will have different names in different districts. Such confusion exists, it is true, in other countries than China. The origin of most of the street names is lost in obscurity. They have been named from circumstances that no longer exist. We have in Peip'ing: Sheep-Pen Lane, Linen Thread Lane, and Filial Piety Alley, although there is now no sheep pen to be found and linen thread is not made in the place indicated. Neither do we know whose filial piety is commemorated. The true name of Legation Street is "Alley of the Tributaries," which is reminiscent of the days when Korean, Loochooan and Annamite, Siamese and Burmese foregathered in the hostelries there, and when European embassies were placed in the same category and the kotow was demanded of their chiefs.

The "Mouth of the Lamp Market" means nothing to the residents of that place to-day. At various places along the principal avenues in Peking, and in the open spaces of some other cities, ornamental gate-ways are erected. They are usually of wood and richly decorated with red lacquer and gold. Upon them in gilded characters there is inscribed on one side of the street such a sentiment as "Walk in Charity," and on the opposite side of the street "Tread the path of righteousness." On one gate-way will appear; "Support the civil authorities," on its companion; "Assist the military." The panels of one exhort us to "Make daily improvement," those of its counterpart to obtain "Monthly advancement."

HOMES

One sees nothing from the street of the beauty of a Chinese home. When you leave the business quarter and turn down a lane, you are shut in by high brick walls on either side of the way. There are rarely any windows to be seen. The only openings, as a rule, are the gate-ways, through which you catch a glimpse of a screen or the brick wall of an inner court. On the lintel of the gate-way a motto is posted. It may be: "The Five Happinesses come from Heaven," or "Chiang T'ai Kung is here; we do not fear a hundred devils." The "Five Happinesses" are Children, Official Emoluments, Long Life, Wealth, and Pleasure. Chiang T'ai Kung was an ancient worthy who canonized so many men, even his enemies, that to-day he is regarded as a maker of gods and therefore more powerful than demons. On the gates of the house are other mottoes. One of the most common is: "Blessing for the State, Happiness for the Family, Long Life for the Individual, Abundance for the Year.'' The servants' quarters and often the kitchen also are next to the street. When you pass through the gate you are met by the gate-man, who takes your card and escorts you from the front court into a second. This is frequently bordered on three sides by a corridor. Sometimes there are rooms upon the right and left. Generally the reception hall is directly in front of you on the opposite side of the court as you enter. If possible, this, the principal hall of the house, faces the south. It will never open to the north if that can be avoided, for that is the side of darkness. Three large door-ways, each closed by a pair of doors, occupy the middle of the façade. The upper half of the whole front, including the doors, is of lattice work, sometimes beautifully carved. Formerly the lattices were covered with paper or ground shells; to-day they are frequently glazed. The roofs are curved and covered with dark tiles in roll and pan fashion. The cornices are painted in bright colors.

The walls of the interior are covered with interesting scrolls. On the side opposite the entrance is the raised dais for the seat of honor. It is covered with cushions and divided into two parts by a low tea table. When one enters he takes a chair near the door. When the host enters he will invite him to ''come up higher,'' and will place him on his left on the dais. Often the partitions between the rooms are of precious wood richly carved; sometimes they are of grille work backed by bright-colored silk. The sandal-wood used in the palaces is sometimes inlaid with cloisonné. In the homes of the wealthy there are cabinets stored with rare pieces of porcelain, ancient bronzes, and carved lacquer. On some of the walls will be seen celebrated paintings. The floors are covered with rich rugs of silk or camel's hair. Blackwood screens, embroidered hangings and other articles of beauty bear witness to the taste of the owner.

Behind the main hall is another court with the private quarters of the host and his family. Other courts open on the right and left, and if he be a wealthy man there will be extensive gardens with rockeries, ponds of water, picturesque bridges, dwarfed trees and beautiful flowers. Here you will also find pleasant pavilions where, if you are an intimate friend, you will be invited to smoke and drink tea.

RECREATION GROUNDS

Public gardens, parks and recreation grounds are conspicuous by their absence. Only in recent years, under the influence of Western example, a few parks have been opened to the public, and here and there a zoological garden. Peip'ing is rich in temple grounds that can be used for this purpose. One public park with an interesting museum has been opened in the court of the She Chi T'an, that is the "Altar to the Guardian Spirits of the Land and Harvests."

In all large cities there will be found certain open spaces where the crowds love to gather for holiday making. The *Liu-li Ch'ang*, or "Crystal Market," in Peking is a popular resort of this kind. The open plaza between the Temple of Heaven and the Temple of Agriculture is another. The bank of the canal near the Confucian Temple in Nanking is also a noted meeting place. Fashionable tea houses are located there. Hangchow is fortunate in having outside its walls the West Lake, which is a beautiful sheet of water surrounded by picturesque hills. Tea houses and temples are built upon its shores and pleasure barges float on its waters. In many towns the City Temple is a gathering place of merry-makers. In Soochow it is also an art gallery. Exhibition for sale is made there of the work of present-day painters, much of it of a very high order.

THE CITY TEMPLE

The City Temple is dedicated to the tutelary guardian of the place. There is a representation in the temple of the ten wards of hell, each with its presiding judge passing sentence upon evil doers. Around the judge are gathered his lictors, the devils who execute the sentences passed.

The images are frequently of life size. The tortures of the damned vary in each ward. Some are being sawn asunder, others are being pounded to a jelly in a mortar. Some are made to embrace a red-hot cylinder. Others are being flayed. Some, after punishment, are being transformed into animals to be re-born for a period of probation. The hardening and brutalizing effect of these representations can be imagined. Perhaps they are responsible in part for the devilish cruelties that have been inflicted by Chinese mobs upon foreign missionaries.

Buddhism is responsible for the introduction into China of the doctrine of hell and for the belief in transmigration. The Buddhist ruler of hell is known as Yama. The name is adopted by the Chinese, who call him *Yen-lo Wang,* or King *Yen-lo.* He is the Radamanthus who presides over the hell in the City Temple. It is to him that the village *Tu Ti Lao Yeh* must report the death of each subject in his district.

The City Temple is adorned with many fine mottoes and exhortations to virtue, such as,

> Gambling is near to robbery;
> Adultery is next to murder.

or,

> Heaven sees; earth sees; the gods see; the devils see; don't say "Nobody sees."

In spite of such exhortations, and the sculptured representations of the terrible punishments that await the sinner, I saw on one visit a group of loafers gambling on the pavement of the temple, under the outstretched arm of a fiendish looking image that was intended to frighten men from their wicked ways.

STREET SIGHTS AND SOUNDS

The shop signs generally hang perpendicularly, and, as they are suspended at right angles to the shop front, so that they can be easily read by persons passing up and down the street, they are often an inconvenience in a narrow street to the man who is riding, for he may strike his head in attempting to pass under them.

The proprietors of a shop do not often place their names upon the sign-board. The shop has a name of its own which it will retain through all changes of ownership. "Concord Hall" is a restaurant. The Shop of the "Precious Tree" is that of a dealer in teas. "Continuous Happiness Shop" provides the sedan and other paraphernalia for weddings. The "Balcony of the Drunken Moon" is a café. "Peace and Prosperity" is the sign of a pawn shop. The "Fountain of Luxury" merely sells stockings. The "Golden Cow" sells needles, and the sign of the "Black Monkey" is that of a felt cap maker.

Many trades and callings have symbols which for the illiterate are better than flowery names. A couple of small hoops suspended with fringes hanging to them is the sign of a restaurant. A gourd with two bulbs joined by a narrow neck is the sign of a drug store, and is perhaps the origin of the bulbous bottles with colored water which our own druggists use, for the gourd of old was a bottle and still is so used in interior places in China. A pair of gilded posts set in stone bases, one on either side of the doorway, is used in Peip'ing to announce a bank. A representation of a string of cash, carved in wood and gilded, tells of an exchange shop. A shallow drum of brass is the sign of an oil dealer, and many other dealers have the hat, or shoe, or other article that is for sale, pictured upon the sign-board, just as western dealers do.

The sounds of a city street are always an interesting study. In China they are unlike those at home. The pedlar of embroidery thread, of needles and tape, has a hand drum which he swings as he walks, and which is beaten by two little balls attached to the drum by cords. The blind fortune-teller has a small disc of brass which is struck by an ivory mallet. The peripatetic barber is fast disappearing since the head is no longer shaved. He carries a pole on his shoulder, from one end of which is suspended a stool and the barber kit, and from the other a light stand and toilet articles. He announces his coming by beating an iron triangle. The vender of water chestnuts cries "Mai-pi-tzu-o," prolonging the *o* sound, and the bread man calls, "Mai-man-t'ou," "Buy rolls," also prolonging the final syllable. The monk who is soliciting subscriptions with which to build a monastery carries on his back a picture of one of his saints, and walks the street with solemn tread and an immobile countenance, beating the while a wooden "fish-head," as the emblematic article is called. A humble traveler riding a donkey finds the stirrups short and his knees well up toward his chin. The donkey-boy runs behind and beats the donkey, which plunges through the crowd jingling a string of sleighbells, while the boy yells: "*Shengkou lai la,*" "An animal is coming."

A band playing mournful strains of music leads a funeral procession. The coffin is hidden under a richly embroidered covering. It rests upon a bier carried by twenty-four or thirty-six men. A number of ragamuffins, hired for the occasion, carry emblems before it and boards, each having an honorary title which may or may not have belonged to the deceased. A paper cock perhaps is perched upon the coffin. It is a good luck emblem and betokens many male descendants to keep up the rites of ancestor worship. A sedan chair follows with the tablet of the deceased. Sometimes a portrait of the dead man is also carried in a chair. The chief mourners, clothed in sackcloth, follow behind the coffin; others in white garments ride in their chairs or carts. Fire crackers frighten away the evil spirits, and at intervals the procession pauses while a table with offerings of food is set out to refresh the soul of the dead on his journey to the tomb.

Or it may be a band is heard playing a livelier tune. Pipe and cymbal and drum announce the approach of the red bridal chair, escorted by the bridegroom's friends. The bride, hidden from view in the locked sedan, is borne to her future husband whom perhaps she has never seen.

Another sound, more common in the days gone by than it is to-day, is that of a great gong announcing the coming of a high official. His green chair with a pewter knob on top is carried swiftly through the streets by four bearers. Lictors in red jackets and black caps, each decorated with a red cock's feather, run in advance carrying boards that have inscribed on them the great man's titles. Secretaries ride behind on horseback. And, as the gong is sounded, the runners cry out, "The great man is coming."

STREET LIGHTING

The streets are very poorly lighted in most cities. There is an oil lamp here and there, but if a man goes out after dark it is really necessary to carry his own lantern. This is made of bamboo splints, or sometimes of wire and covered with paper. His name in Chinese, cut out of red paper, is pasted on the lantern so that it is easily read by a watchman or anyone else passing in the street. If one is riding in a sedan chair he will have two big globe lanterns carried by servants in front of the chair-bearers so that they may avoid stumbling.

A number of cities near the coast have now installed electric lighting plants, so that conditions in them have much improved in this respect. Where good roads have been built the motor car with its brilliant lights has replaced the sedan chair and the paper lantern.

THE WATER SUPPLY

The city dwellers still depend in most places upon wells and pools for their supply of water. That such water is often polluted can not be denied. Doubtless the practice of drinking tea made with boiling water accounts for the fact that the mortality is not greater. Chinese rarely drink cold water. During many years of our residence in Peking we were daily supplied with water brought in wooden tubs on wheel-barrows. This came from certain "sweet-water wells," as they are called. Most of the wells in Peip'ing supply a brackish water which is good neither for drinking nor cooking. About the year 1910 water works were built by the government, the supply being found in the hills north-west of the city. This enterprise has been of great benefit to the people. A few other cities in the eastern part of the country have also established water works.

OTHER PUBLIC UTILITIES

Much remains to be done in bringing to the cities of China the material comforts of modern civilization. Telephones have been introduced in a number of places and street railways in a few. Motor omnibuses might be used to advantage in northern towns where there are wide macadamized streets. Electric inter-urban railways would be a blessing to the city and the village, and, judging from the success of the city trams, and the ordinary railways, they ought to be a profitable investment.

VOLUNTEER ASSOCIATIONS

Many matters that are usually left to the government in other countries are managed by the Chinese through voluntary associations of the citizens. They organize volunteer fire companies, as used to be common once in our own country. The equipment is generally antiquated and not very effective. The engine is a small force pump in a tub which is carried on the shoulders of men. The hose is slender and the stream small and weak. The companies have their captains, who transmit their orders to the fire-men by signals. There are also towers with watchmen to give alarm in case of fire.

This condition of affairs has in recent years been improved in some of the larger and more progressive cities. Under the influence of the example given by European communities in China, these cities have purchased foreign fire apparatus and have fire departments similar to our own, but such places are few. The temples to the god of fire still exist and superstition in many places supplants reason in fire prevention.

While I was living in Nanking some years ago a serious fire broke out near the South Gate which did great damage. The authorities consulted a geomancer to learn the cause.

A CITY WELL, PEIPING.

BELL TOWER, PEIPING.

He studied the situation and reported that the buildings in the southern part of the city were too high, and that this caused the influence of the south, the region of heat, to overpower that of the north. He recommended that a pagoda on top of one of the hills in the northern part of the city should be built higher. This was done. The pagoda was torn down and re-built considerably higher than before.

MUNICIPAL GOVERNMENT

The city, as has already been said, is in reality a collection of villages, for the several wards have their tithings and hundreds with their elders and tipao. These elders are as jealous of their prerogatives as those in the isolated villages. They are prompt to resent any encroachment upon their rights. Sales of real estate cannot be made without their approval, and any attempt upon the part of the officials to interfere with customary privileges will be resisted and generally prevented. The wards are often separated one from another by gates that are closed at night, and each ward maintains its own watchman who goes the rounds with lantern and rattle or gong, just as in the villages. There is also a head office of the tithings which exercises general supervision over the whole city.

The importance of the ward elders and of the voluntary associations of the people is overshadowed, however, by the near presence of high officials of various departments of the government, with their yamens and their numerous subordinates, and by the uniformed national police and the military.

THE COUNTY MAGISTRATE

The *Hsien*, or County Magistrate, is in some respects the most important officer in the government. He levies and collects the taxes. He is the Recorder of Deeds, the County Superintendent of Education and the Commissioner of Industry. He is the County Treasurer, the head of the local militia and the police. He is the Coroner and the

Administrator of Poor Relief, the Commissioner of Public Works and the Judge of both the civil and criminal courts, and he is the Mayor of the city or, if more than one county is represented in the city, Mayor of the borough.

In 1905 the criminal code was revised, and new courts were organized separate from the administrative branch of the government. Because of this, the judicial functions of the County Magistrate have been curtailed in some places. It has been impossible, however, to establish the new courts everywhere; there is a lack of qualified judges. The old administrative courts therefore are still very largely in use. The post of County Magistrate, then, under the republic, as under the empire, remains the principal unit of public administration. In this yamen are gathered all branches, both of the municipal and the county government. The elders of the city wards and the country village alike report to it. Regulations adopted in 1929 provide for provincial conferences once a year of county Magistrates to discuss administrative problems. Each Magistrate likewise is to confer twice a year with his subordinates and make periodical visits of inspection.

Under the Manchu régime no magistrate could serve in his native province. The object of this was to prevent partiality and injustice. Family solidarity is so marked in China, family loyalty so much stronger than loyalty to the state, and the influence of friendship and acquaintance so great, that it was felt most improbable that any magistrate would be able or willing to sacrifice the interests of relatives and friends for the sake of justice. For this reason the Board of Civil Office sent men to posts where they were strangers. The incumbent would take his secretaries with him, but the numerous clerks and lictors were natives of the district where they served. When the Magistrate arrived at his new home he found himself, therefore, among strangers, whose speech in many cases he could not understand, and dependent upon subordinates who belonged to the community and had in most cases inherited their offices from their ancestors. These under-paid underlings lived by their wits and were notoriously corrupt. They held the magistrate to a great extent in their power. They were his eyes and ears and could make or mar any case that came before him. Hence these yamen subordinates were pilloried as universally corrupt and insatiable in their demands for "squeeze." I have used the past tense in describing the character of these yamen underlings, but thus far the establishment of the Republic does not seem to have improved conditions very much. A man is no longer debarred from holding office in his own province, and the change will probably be beneficial on the whole, for in a land where provincialism is as strong as it is in China the native is more apt than the stranger to consider the welfare of the people of his district. Two things have been responsible in the past for much of the corruption in the county governments of China. The first is the fact that prior to the revolution the salaries, where any were paid, were wholly inadequate. In some posts no salaries at all were paid; the incumbent lived upon the fees which he was allowed for services plus the squeeze which he could extort, added to the bribes that were offered to him. The second cause was the practice of making the subordinate posts in a yamen a private possession, bought originally by some ancestor who had left the office to be inherited by his descendants. Without regard to character or qualifications a man was, and in many cases still is retained in an office, where he is a dangerous parasite, simply because his great-grandfather paid for the post. There can be no efficient service where public office is regarded as private property.

Under the old régime even the Magistrate himself received no proper salary. Nominally it was about $150 a year. In addition he was allowed a payment from the "Nourishing Honesty Fund." In the case of the Viceroy at Nanking, ruler of three provinces, the allowance from this fund amounted to about $350 a year. This was popularly considered as given to prevent dishonesty. In fact, the extra allowance for the County Magistrate never passed into his hands at all. The funds were retained in the hands of the Provincial Treasurer to cover possible fines and defalcations, and it was because of this, no doubt, that it was given the name "Nourishing Honesty Fund." It was, in fact, an insurance fund.

The Magistrate, out of the taxes collected, had to pay all the expenses of the county government. A fixed minimum was sent to the Provincial Treasury to be forwarded to the capital. The balance the Magistrate regarded as his own perquisite. In other words the taxes were simply farmed out.

Under the Republic the principle has been adopted of paying adequate salaries and requiring all collections to be considered as public monies, of which proper account is to be made. But the theory does not appear to have been put into practice generally. Until the country is restored to peace most of the projected reforms will remain merely projects.

TAX COLLECTION

The County Yamen is divided into bureaux corresponding to the several functions which the Magistrate exercises. I have in a previous chapter discussed the amount of the land tax. Although originally payable partly in money and partly in grain, it is in fact all paid in money. But the amount is to be determined by the acreage and character of the grain sown, hence there is an annual inspection by the yamen of the land under its jurisdiction. The runners are sent out to assess the tax. They meet the village elders and discuss the matter over the tea-cups in the village tea house. After much wrangling, and probably some bribing and squeezing, the amount is fixed and the tax bills are made out. Part is payable in the spring and the balance in the autumn. In case of drought and a short crop there will be an effort made by the elders to have the tax reduced. The Magistrate will also appeal to the Governor and the Governor to the national government to have the tax remitted. If the situation is really serious the tax will almost certainly have to be remitted, because payment will be impossible. If the situation is not very serious the representations of the Magistrate may secure a remission, but the tax will probably be collected nevertheless, in whole or in part, by the county yamen, and swell the perquisites of the officers there.

There are other taxes also to be collected by the County Magistrate. There are various licenses required, such as those for conducting a pawn-shop or operating a distillery. There are excise taxes on distilled liquors and tobacco, taxes on transfers of real estate, and a variety of miscellaneous charges.

THE CORONER

An important but disagreeable duty of the Magistrate is that pertaining to the office of coroner. There are some curious superstitions connected with the discharge of this duty.

While I was serving as assessor in the Mixed Court at Shanghai some years since, it became my duty to attend an inquest upon the body of a man found dead in the street. The County Magistrate conducted the inquest. A yamen runner sponged the body with vinegar and warm water to discover whether there were any marks of violence. This runner assured me very earnestly that if the body was that of a murdered man the eyes of the corpse would open while this examination was being made. There was no mark of violence and the dead man did not open his eyes. At an inquest held by another magistrate I was interested to find that at its conclusion the official purified himself by stepping over a fire of burning artemisia. This was to keep the spirit of death from clinging to his gown and accompanying him to his home.

Under the Manchu Dynasty the Magistrates were supplied by the Government with a Coroner's Guide, known as the *Hsi Yüan Lu*, much of which was incorporated in the Penal Code. In 1907 I had occasion to translate portions of this work for a paper on "Witchcraft in the Chinese Penal Code," which was subsequently published in the *Journal* of the China Branch of the Royal Asiatic Society.[1] Some extracts from this translation will be appropriate here.

[7] Vol. XXXVIII, 1907, pp. 61-96.

To identify the bones of a deceased parent, when there is doubt upon the subject, we are told to proceed as follows:

Drop a little of the child's blood upon the supposed bones of the parent. If the bones be really those of a parent the blood will soak in, but if otherwise it will not do so. Care must be taken, however, that the bones be not washed in brackish water, lest in that case the blood and bones refuse to unite, even though they be related. Elder and younger brothers have a common origin, and may prove their relationship by dropping a little of the blood of each in a vessel of water. If the persons concerned be really brothers the drops of blood will flow together. But if by any chance vinegar or salt be mixed with the water, the union will take place, even though there be no relationship. Some say that husbands and wives may establish the fact of such relationship by the blood and water test; others say that the blood and bone test cannot be made to apply to such a relationship, so that there is some room for doubt upon this point. If, however, the vessel of water be too large, or the quantity of water too great, the drops of blood, being too widely separated, may not unite; and if an interval elapse between the dropping of one person's blood and that of the other, there will be a difference of temperature in the two drops which may prevent their union.

This test was employed as lately as November 25, 1882.

More remarkable is the method prescribed by the *Hsi Yüan Lu* for the discovery of the location and character of wounds on a body which has already been entirely destroyed, or of which but a few odd bones remain. This method is referred to and described a number of times in the work just mentioned. In one case the grave was opened and but a few bones were found. These were taken out and a hot fire made in the grave pit. Sesamum seed was then thrown in and scattered about. The grave was covered over for an hour, and afterwards the sesamum seed was swept out with a broom. But some of the seed clung to the soil, and on examination it was found that there was outlined by it, on the bottom of the grave, the image of the dead man. A clot of the sesamum seed was found at a spot corresponding to the navel. The remainder of the seed was then taken out and another fire built in the pit. Some dregs of grain from a still were mixed with water and thrown in. The fire was then increased in intensity and later some hot vinegar was poured in. A new table, lacquered with gold lacquer, was then placed top down over the grave and left there for a few moments. When it was taken off there was found outlined on its surface the image of the dead man, and just over the navel was the mark of a stab, an oblique wound 1.3 inches in length, a mortal wound inflicted by a wooden instrument.

The following method is prescribed in the same work for determining the guilt or innocence of a wife and her alleged paramour who have been killed by the husband, as the old code permitted:

Take a water jar and fill it with water, one half from the river and the other half from the well. This is called "yin-yang" water. Take a stick and stir the water into a swiftly whirling eddy. Then take the heads of the decapitated corpses of the man and woman and place them without delay in the water. If the pair were really guilty, the heads will turn nose to nose; but, if they were innocent, they will turn back to back, one above and the other below in the jar.

It is not to be assumed. of course, that all officials believed in the efficacy of these prescriptions, but the fact that such a work was officially regarded as authoritative up to the year 1905 is a very significant one.

PUBLIC CHARITIES

Of the five Chinese virtues, mercy or benevolence is placed first. Under the influence of the Christian religion the West has done far more to relieve suffering than the older East, but China has not been entirely wanting in charitable institutions. Some of these are voluntary associations of the people. There are societies for the free distribution of medicine. Buddhist monasteries sometimes open such dispensaries. But the want of a knowledge of medicine, or even of hygiene, renders them of little use. I saw a chart in one of these monasteries which pretended to describe the human anatomy, but it represented organs and ducts which have never existed in any human being. It reminded me of the professor who wrote a treatise on the camel. Never having seen a camel, he evolved one out of his inner consciousness. The severe laws that have in the past provided punishment for the dissection of a dead body are no doubt responsible for much of the ignorance of medical science that has prevailed in China.

The Buddhists also support foundling asylums. Other charitable institutions are those which provide free coffins and graves for the poor, free vaccination, free schools for manual training, free ferries and monthly doles to indigent widows.

Official charities include orphan asylums, homes for widows, homes for the aged, homes for cripples, and rice kitchens. These so-called homes are very cheerless institutions—a group of buildings with the simplest sort of furniture, cheap clothing, and a little rice each day, barely enough to keep one alive. The inmates of the old-folks' home at Nanking used to sit outside the gate and beg of passersby. A Buddhist orphanage is apt to be a more comfortable place than one under official management, but both are liable to show a high death rate, because they lack trained nurses who understand infant feeding. A Chinese physician, a lady who had been educated abroad, told me what difficulties she had with careless and untrained servants, in her endeavors to secure clean surroundings and healthful food for the children in an official orphanage under her care.

One of the most common forms of relief given by government officials is that of cooked rice distributed to the destitute during the winter months. When floods or drought have destroyed the peasant's grain many of them, who are without reserves of food, will take their families to the suburbs of the county town or some other large city where relief can be expected. In Nanking there were large stores of rice kept in the official granaries. Rice was the principal article of tribute sent by the Viceroyalty to the Court at Peking. Some of this rice was retained for distribution in times of distress.

I have a very vivid recollection of a bitter winter at Nanking. There had been unusual falls of snow and much suffering among the poor. Outside the West Gate was an encampment of refugees driven there by the floods in the Huai River which had destroyed their homes. For two miles this camp extended along the bank of a creek that formed the city moat on that side. The number of these sufferers was given as thirty thousand, but allowing for exaggeration it may be put down as not less than ten thousand. The tents were made of reed mats. Each mat, eight feet square, was bent into the form of an arch and the sides pinned to the ground. Another mat closed one end. The front was either wholly or partially open. Under one of these wretched shelters a whole family would be huddled together. There were mothers with nursing children, half-starved boys and girls, and grey-headed old men and women. Many were bare-footed except for straw sandals. The daily dole was eleven ounces of coarse rice. That it was only partially hulled made it, perhaps, a more wholesome diet.

The County Magistrate went down one day to visit the camp to see if anything more could be done for the people. They rushed upon him so furiously in their eagerness to get his assistance that his sedan was torn to pieces, and he barely escaped with his life. A native Christian went down on behalf of the missionaries, and when his purpose to give relief was learned they were like wild beasts as they struggled one with another to reach him. He, too, had his clothing torn from him and had to be rescued by soldiers, who carried him to the home of one of the missionaries. An excited mob of some hundreds followed him, and when they were denied entrance to the mission compound they began stoning the house.

Organized official relief of distress has been aided in the past few years by the American Red Cross and other foreign societies, so that better order and more comfort than were found in early days has been maintained among the sufferers. The self-respect of the peasants has been saved, too, by giving them work to do, and paying them wages with which to buy their supplies of grain. The women and girls have been employed in making clothing or weaving hair nets for the foreign market, and the able-bodied men set to building good roads.

This improvement in the administration of public charity has affected the management of orphanages and other refuges for the afflicted and needy, so that to-day many of them maintain workshops where simple trades are taught, and the inmates enabled to earn, in part at least, their support.

ADMINISTRATIVE COURTS

The City Hall and County Court House in China do not remind you of anything that you have ever seen in any other country. It is a collection of large, barn-like buildings of brick, with curved roofs of tile. They are placed one behind the other, with spacious courts between. Smaller buildings at the sides of the court-yards sometimes connect these large halls one with another.

Along the kerbing of the side-walk in front of the main entrance a screen is built, usually of brick. In the days of the empire there was painted on the inside of the screen a representation of a huge blue dragon about to swallow a red sun. The Chinese have a keen sense of humor. In reply to my query as to the meaning of this picture a Chinese friend said: ''Anciently there were ten suns in the sky. The dragon swallowed nine, but he left one. This picture is intended to remind the magistrate that when he collects the revenues of his district, he should leave at least one-tenth for the Emperor.''

But the dragon is no longer a popular symbol in China. It was the emblem of autocratic power, of brute force. It suggested that distant age when ''Dragons of the prime tare each other in their slime.'' Those huge saurians have disappeared from the earth, as autocratic power is also doomed to disappear. To-day the people are sovereign in China, and the dragon banner has been replaced by the new republican flag an emblem of hope for the Republic and a promise of prosperity to its citizens.

But the screen still stands in front of the entrance to the yamen. The word *"ya-men"* means "The door to the official tent." Set back a few paces from the street this great door-way is closed by two huge doors, 15 to 20 feet high, that swing on pivots. They are decorated with pictures of the door gods, one with a light face that watches by day, and one with a dark face that stands guard at night. This principal entrance is usually closed except when high officials enter or leave. A smaller door is available for ordinary service.

In a great chamber at the rear of the principal courtyard is the hall of justice. There the Magistrate, in the time of the Empire, sat in his official dress to administer the law. His gown of silk or satin was richly embroidered with the insignia of his office. Around his neck was suspended his string of court beads. On the crown of his hat was the button that indicated his rank, and, if he had been decorated, there was attached to the base of the button the peacock plume or the blue feather.

The republican official has discarded all this finery, and discharges the duties of his office in ordinary European dress.

Under the Empire a man obtained office through his knowledge of the classics and his literary talent. He may have known but little of the laws of his country. But at his side, or within call, he had a law secretary who knew the statutes and the precedents. By aid of this assistant he was able to give judgment, which, however, in capital cases, had to be confirmed by the Department of Justice at Peking.

Where the new courts have been established efforts are made to-day to place men in them as judges who have been trained in the law.

Prior to 1905, in criminal cases both the accused and the witnesses were liable to torture. No one could be subjected to the severe penalties of the law unless he confessed his guilt, and the torture was designed to persuade him to make confession. Beating with a heavy bamboo paddle, hanging by the thumbs with the toes barely touching the ground, and kneeling on chains, were some of the simplest methods of torture.

The use of torture was abolished by imperial edict in 1905, except that it was still allowed in capital cases where the Magistrate was convinced of the guilt of the accused and the latter refused to confess. Under the Republic all such torture is forbidden.

THE PRISON

In one court-yard of the yamen, in the old days, the county jail was located. It was usually vile and insanitary in the highest degree. While I was serving as American Assessor in the Mixed Court at Shanghai, I passed several times a week through the jail court-yard there. The two wards, one for men, the other for women, were next to the street and near the entrance to the yamen, but the wall along the street was a dead wall except for one small dust-covered window in the women's ward, far up out of their reach. This ward was about 25 feet square. Except for the brief glimpse of sunlight given through the window just mentioned, the only light for the inmates came from a hall-way that opened through a narrow door-way into the court-yard. The hall was cut off from the rest of the room by a barred partition. Fortunately women prisoners were few, but sometimes they brought young children with them. All the women and children occupied this room together. They brought with them their bedding, which was unrolled and laid upon the floor at night and gathered up into a bundle again the next morning. The men's ward was about 50 by 25 feet. It was better ventilated, for the whole north side was open, except for a stockade of heavy poles arranged about three or four inches apart, firmly fixed in the pavement and attached above to the roof timbers. The floor was of brick and quite damp. A urinal occupied one corner. There was no privacy, and in the winter there was no fire and no shelter from the winds. I have seen as many as 30 men at one time shut up in this pen. Prisoners supplied themselves with bedding, and for a tip to the guard their families would be permitted to bring them food. Otherwise they had to get on with prison fare, which was frugal and unsavory. The prisoners were not allowed to go out for exercise and were given no work.

But with the reforms that came after the Boxer Rising this prison disappeared, and has been replaced by a modern building with all necessary sanitary arrangements. In Peking the convicts are taken out to work at cleaning the streets or repairing the roads. In Tientsin they are employed in work-shops and provided with a night school.

CHAPTER VIII

THE CRAFTSMAN

The fifth officer is called Chief of Manufacturers. He orders the making up of the eight materials. The sixth officer is called the Chief of Trade; he provides for an abundant circulation of goods and money.—The Chou Li (1122-249 B.C.) *

Great economic changes have taken place in China during the past thirty years and especially since the revolution of 1911. In many places machinery is gradually replacing handicraft. In the large open ports where Europeans live in considerable numbers they have organized joint stock companies and have built great factories in which Western machinery driven by steam power has been in operation for many years. More recently Chinese capitalists have followed the example set, and have successfully entered into competition with the foreigner.

The Nationalist Government in June 1931 adopted measures providing for the organization of a National Economic Council to carry out the stipulations of the new constitution relating to industrial improvement.

INDUSTRIAL REVOLUTION

The new enterprises of the past three decades have already done much to break up cottage industries in certain lines, and have attracted many enterprising and ambitious laborers to the treaty ports. Wages have risen, the standard of living has improved and apprenticeship to the old trades is losing its appeal. Women and girls find employment in the mills, and thus the ancient seclusion of women is being abandoned and family restraints are loosened.

These changes, however, are limited as yet to small districts. Over the greater part of China it is still proper to use the term ''manufacture'' in its original sense, for

* The genuineness of the *Chou Li* is doubted by some critics.

in most places raw materials are still worked up by hand into articles of use and ornament. Tools are used, but they are primitive and crude, and such machinery as has been invented is simple. The motive power is the human hand or foot, the water-wheel or the strength of the ox or mule. Steam and electricity in these inland towns are all but unknown.

The conditions of manufacturing industry in such places are substantially the same as prevailed in Europe before the invention of the steam engine. The great change which the application of steam and the wonderful progress of mechanical invention have wrought during the past century in the manufacturing communities of the West has scarcely begun.

The craftsman's home, as a rule, is still his work-shop. His capital is small, his apprentices and journeymen are limited in number, and the former are generally bound to him for a term of years and are inmates of his own house.

Although China possesses a hundred roller flour mills, one has but to visit almost any native city to see wheat still ground by ox-power, and the flour bolted by primitive machinery worked by the miller himself, who, standing on a balanced lever, one foot on either side of the support, presses alternately on one end and then on the other to shake the sieve to and fro. So, too, the old-fashioned wedge press is still used for expressing oil. Rice is hulled by heavy hammers in stone mortars, and cotton is prepared for spinning by the rude native gin and the great twanging bow, and is spun on a distaff and woven in ancient looms that Marco Polo might have seen in his journeyings in the thirteenth century, although the same work is done by the most improved machinery in many of the open ports.

LOCAL CRAFTS

Each district in China is noted for some one or more articles, in the manufacture of which its people show expert skill or artistic taste. Peip'ing, which has gathered within its walls craftsmen from many parts of the country, is especially distinguished for its rugs, its cloisonné and enameled ware, its jade polishing and its lacquer carving. Of less importance but equally interesting is its manufacture of artificial flowers and imitation butterflies, dragon-flies, cicadas and other insects, in which the workmen show great skill.

RUG MAKING

The rug industry has sprung up quite naturally, since Peip'ing is near the border of Mongolia, where great herds of sheep and camels supply the material of which they are made.

The workman draws his design on a small piece of paper, and colors it with water colors of the shade that he intends to use. This is fastened to one of the upright poles ot his loom. An outline is sometimes drawn on the cords of the warp, which is stretched between an upper and lower roller. The yarns are tied around the cords of the warp, clipped with shears, and beaten down into place with a smooth stick or an iron fork. The workman often trusts to his eye to determine how much of each color is to be used and just where it is to be placed to carry out the design.

Formerly the dyes were native vegetable dyes and the colors were fast, but the foreign demand for rugs has grown apace, and the import of chemical dyes has been encouraged by their cheapness, with the result that much harm has been done to the business. During the late war the import of foreign dyes fell off of necessity and the production of native dyes revived.

Peip'ing embroideries, too, are known the world over, but the best, perhaps, are brought there from Shansi, the neighboring province on the west.

CLOISONNÉ

Cloisonné was introduced into China from Constantinople, probably in the thirteenth century, when not a few adventurous travelers passed to and fro between Peip'ing and the Hellespont. At that time the Mongols, who subdued nearly all Asia, gave peace to the eastern world and protected the routes of travel and trade.[1]

There are a number of shops in Peip'ing where excellent work is done. The proprietors are very courteous and you have but to express a desire to witness the process of making cloisonné to be conducted to the rooms in which the men are at work. A copper vase is being beaten into shape by one. Another is outlining the arabesque pattern upon the surface of a bowl. A third is soldering the wires along the lines of the pattern on some other vessel. The colors are being ground and made into a paste. The little cells are filled with appropriate colors, and when the vessel is ready for firing it is taken out into the court-yard and placed in a brazier of glowing charcoal, which is kept at a white heat by the use of fans in the hands of the workers until the colors have fused and fastened themselves upon the copper. The process must be repeated until every cell is completely filled, when the surface is polished with pumice and the copper lines are gilded. The whole establishment is housed in a cottage of five or six rooms.

CARVED LACQUER

Not far away from one of these cloisonné shops you will find another unpretentious building in which a small group of workmen with their graving tools in hand are carving lacquered trays and jewel boxes. The wooden trays are first covered with the lacquer, black inside and red or olive without, and when the surface is sufficiently hardened the delicate pattern drawn on thin paper is fastened upon it, and the graver carves out in low relief the ornamental tracery or scene to be depicted.

JADE CUTTING

The jade cutter uses a sharp steel wheel, which is turned alternately forward and backward by means of a strap attached to a treadle. The workman holds the precious

[1] See Bushell's "Chinese Art," Vol. II, pp. 73-74.

stone firmly against the cutting edge. Water drips upon
the point of contact to cool the steel, and a handful of wet
jade dust is pressed into the cutting to assist the process.
Glass and crystal cutting are also common, and the painting of minature scenes on the interior of snuff bottles is
an art for the practice of which a patient attention to
detail especially fits the Chinese.

Bronze making in China is of great antiquity. The
modern work seems to be of poor quality. The brass work
of the Ming Dynasty (1368–1644) is highly prized, but
equally good work appears to be done by the brass-smiths
of to-day.

BRASS WORKERS

Not only in Peip'ing but in any large city you can watch
the workmen beating the brass vessels into shape or deco-
rating them with a graver's tool. Scroll work, floral and
geometrical designs, and inscriptions of Chinese poetry in
ornamental characters form his themes. The furnace blown
by a bellows, worked by an apprentice is visible from the
street, throwing out its tints of green and purple. On
the shelves of the shop the attractive wares are displayed,
among them the foot-stoves with perforated covers. In
these brass vessels a glowing ball of charcoal burned in
wood ashes will serve to keep my lady's feet warm when
she journeys in her sedan. An ink-stone encased in a brass
box supplies her husband with the palette on which to
prepare the ink for his official despatches. And there is
the brass water pipe, too, for the tobacco with which he
comforts himself between sentences. The manufacture of
these pipes is a special branch of the brass-smith's trade.
An oval box divided into two compartments forms the
principal feature of the pipe. One compartment is for the
tobacco supply, the other for water. The top of the water
compartment connects with a long curved stem, also of
brass. The bowl is movable and ends at the bottom in a
slender projection which fits into an opening in the top
of the water compartment. The projection extends beneath the surface of the water. There are receptacles, too,

for tapers and various little implements used in cleaning the pipe. The bowl does not hold more than a thimbleful of tobacco, which is consumed in one or two inhalations. The taper is of brown paper saturated with salt-petre and burns very slowly. Held close to the lips it is blown into a flame by a quick in-drawing of the breath. The tobacco is lighted and the smoke is drawn through the water with a bubbling sound. With one breath it is discharged from the mouth at the same time that the flame of the taper is extinguished. The bowl is then removed and the ashes thrown out by blowing through the lower end, after which it is replaced, another pinch of tobacco inserted, and the operations just described are repeated.

SHANTUNG WARES

The province of Shantung is noted for its strawbraid and its pongees. The former is exported in large quantities for the manufacture of hats. The latter is made from the cocoons of the wild silk-worm which feeds upon oak leaves. The word "pongee" is a corruption of the Chinese words meaning "natural color," and was applied to these silks because formerly they could not be dyed. In recent years German chemists have taught the Chinese how to treat the silk so as to enable it to take the dye.

LACE-MAKING

Besides these two products Chefoo, in Shantung, is celebrated for its laces. The manufacture of lace was introduced into China by the missionaries. An Italian convent at Hankow appears to have been the first to teach the art, and the silk lace made there soon acquired a well-deserved reputation for beauty. Protestant missions followed with the introduction of cotton and linen laces. These are made not only in Chefoo, but at Soochow, Amoy and Swatow as well. The last-mentioned port is celebrated, too, for its grass cloth, a sort of linen made from the fiber of the ramie (*Boehmeria Nivea*).[2] The women and girls in the

2 Botanicon Sinicum, 391.

mission schools have been taught to make drawn work of this grass cloth. The *ch'u,* or ramie, is a perennial which produces two or three crops of stalks each year and will last five or six years. Arnold states that the best comes from Kiangsi Province.[3] The cloth woven on native looms is rather uneven in texture; a better variety is made on power looms.

PORCELAIN

Kiangsi Province is better known to the world for another product, for it is at Chingtechen, in that province, that the finest porcelain is made, the ware to which China has given her own name.

These potteries are located about seventy-five miles southeast of Kiukiang, and extend some distance along the Ch'ang River, which flows into the Poyang Lake from the east. The place began to attract attention early in the seventh century A.D. when a potter working there produced a green ware called "Pottery Jade." True porcelain does not appear to have been made, however, until the time of the Ming Dynasty (A.D. 1368–1644), when the clay from a range of hills known as the *Kao Lin,* or "High Range," began to be used in the manufacture. At any rate the ware made previous to the time just mentioned, in so far as available specimens show, did not differ in character from the pottery made during the Sung period,[4] which was not a true porcelain.

The potter's wheel has been at work in China from very early times. It was evidently known to Chuang Tzu, the Philosopher, who lived in the fourth century B.C., and who says: "Therefore the holy man reconciles positive and negative and finds satisfaction in the heavenly potters' wheel." The import of the passage is that God moulds the affairs of the world as the potter does the vessel on

[3] Commercial Handbook of China, Vol. 2, p. 286.
[4] For a description of the wares of the Sung period see "Keramic Wares of the Sung Dynasty," by Rose Sickler Williams, in a volume on "Chinese, Corean and Japanese Potteries," published by the Japan Society, New York, 1914.

the wheel. The revolving sky, the succession of day and night and of summer and winter, bringing with them the blessings and calamities of the year, suggest the movement of a potter's wheel and the vessels made thereon, "some to honor and some to dishonor." The specimens found of the pottery of the Han Dynasty (206 B.C. to A.D. 220) show the mark of the wheel, according to Laufer, who made a collection of such vessels in China, in 1901–04, for the American Museum of Natural History.[5]

Some writers ascribe the invention of porcelain to the Han period, but there is no evidence to show that the wares of that and succeeding dynasties, to the close of the Sung, were true porcelain.

During the Ming Dynasty and throughout the period of the Manchu rule Chingtechen was famous for its beautiful productions. For a time there were as many as 500 kilns in operation there, but during the Taiping Rebellion (1851–66) the whole region was laid waste, and the industry has never since that time regained its former importance. During the Manchu Dynasty the best products of the kilns were reserved for the Imperial Court. Certain patterns were exclusively used for this purpose. It was always possible, however, to buy at Kiukiang so-called defective or rejected pieces of imperial ware, for the officers in charge could always find excuse for rejecting a certain number of pieces, which were, of course, disposed of to the trade at a good profit.

The range of hills known as Kao Lin has given its name throughout the world to the clay of which the porcelains to-day are made, and the art of making porcelain has become a fine art in many countries of the world, but it is to China that the credit is due for its invention.

In 1928 there were but 104 kilns in operation at Chingtechen, and of these 30 only were in use the whole year; the remainder gave employment in the summer. Each kiln employed from 100 to 200 men. Some effort has been made since the establishment of the republic to develop a foreign trade for the old imperial potteries by adopting patterns

[5] "Chinese Pottery of the Han Dynasty," p. 8.

better suited than the Chinese to the uses of the European and American dinner table. This effort is meeting with success. At present the trade amounts to some $250,000 a year.

There are many other districts in China that make Chinaware, but it is generally of a coarser variety than that produced at Chingtechen.

A very attractive ware of terra cotta is manufactured at Ihsinghsien, in Kiangsu Province.

Kiukiang, the principal river port of Kiangsi Province, is celebrated for two things, the manufacture of silver ware and the preparation of tea.

The most attractive patterns used for the beaten silver are the dragon and the bamboo. Good wishes expressed in Chinese characters are also used for ornament, and some vessels are decorated with scenes from well-known plays or illustrating ancient legends.

TEA FIRING

During the tea-firing season the atmosphere of Kiukiang is permeated with a fragrant aroma that floats out from the factories. But this is still more noticeable perhaps, at Hankow, which is the great tea port of central China. There are located the largest factories for the manufacture of brick tea, which is so much in demand in Russia. The tea dust is steamed and put into moulds, which are placed in hydraulic presses. The solid cakes thus formed have the shape of bricks, from which circumstance the name "brick tea" takes its origin. In the old days when traffic with Russia was almost wholly by caravan across Mongolia the tea bricks formed a good part of the cargo. The compact character and convenient shape of the cakes made it possible to transport considerable quantities of tea in small space.

Foochow used to be one of the great tea ports but has lost a large part of its trade. It is in Fukien Province, of which Foochow is the chief port, that the Oolong teas are grown. These are so-called from a range of hills known

as the *Wu-lung,* or "Mist Dragon," Mountains. To-day
Foochow is distinguished for its paper mills. The best
paper is made from bamboo pulp.

FANS AND INK

Hangchow, in Chekiang, is the city which exports the
largest number of fans. Anhui Province is noted as furnishing the best Chinese ink. It is made of lamp-black
produced by burning wood oil or other vegetable oils. The
lamp-black is mixed with glue and scented with various
perfumes. The small bars, after being hardened and dried,
are decorated in gold-leaf with floral designs or inscribed
with poetical sentiments. Men who can afford it sometimes
have their own names or seals stamped upon them in gold.

PEWTER WARE

Hankow is the principal port for the shipment of wood
oil. For pewter ware Ningpo is noted, but it is made in
many other places as well. I used to stroll through the
narrow lanes of old Shanghai to study the processes of
Chinese manufacture, and saw the pewterer there at work.
Few homes are without specimens of his handicraft, such
as tea-pots, candle-stands, wine pitchers and incense
burners.

CANDLE MAKING

I had an opportunity, too, of watching the candle makers
at their work. The oil expressed from the berries of the
tallow tree is most commonly used, but beef fat is employed
to some extent. The candle-wick is composed of a stem
of a common reed—the *Arundo Phragmites*—around which
the pith of a rush—the *Scirpus Scapularis,* or the *Juncus
Effusus*—is carefully and closely wrapped. A number of
these fastened to a light stick are dipped into the jar of
hot oil and then hung up to dry. The operation is repeated until the candle has acquired the proper size. Those
of the best quality are then coated with insect wax and are
commonly dyed red. White candles are also used, but

never on any ceremonial occasions of a joyful character, for white is the color of mourning and such white candles are used at funerals. The stem, which forms the inner part of the wick, projects at the lower end of the candle, the end by which it was suspended, and is used for fastening it upon the candle-stick, for Chinese candle-sticks do not have a socket into which the candle is thrust, as with us, but a sharp spike on which the candle is impaled. Western candles are being imported in great quantity, and with them the foreign candle-stick also, but the sale of the candles would probably be hastened if they were colored red.

On another street an incense manufacturer was beating into a proper consistency the dough-like mass of pulverized barks and gums from which the "joss-sticks" are made. On sieve-like screens before his door the finished sticks were drying in the sun, to take their place later on the shelves of the shop in attractive packages wrapped in red paper and decorated with gilt.

BEAN CURD

I stopped at a neighboring door to watch a great, lazy-looking water-buffalo turning a heavy mill-stone grinding beans. In a shop down the street the bean flour was being cooked, mixed with a little ground gypsum and turmeric to curdle it. The cooked paste, wrapped in cloths, was placed in a cheese press from which, after it should be properly solidified, it would be taken, cut into small cakes and exposed for sale. It is the cheese of the Chinese and a very popular article of diet, rightly so, indeed, in a land where meat is too dear a luxury to be the daily food of the poor. There are several varieties of this bean-curd; one known as the "stinking bean-curd" rivals the choicest cheeses of Europe in odor. At an oil-mill another variety of beans was being ground and pressed for its oil. The refuse finds a ready sale for fertilizing purposes. Vegetable oils are in great demand in China for culinary and other domestic purposes, animal fats not being abundant enough to supply the need. Besides beans, cotton-seed, rape-seed, peanuts a variety of tea, or camellia seed, hemp-seed, sesamum, seed of the castor-oil plant and the nuts of the wood-oil tree are all used for this purpose. The oils of the cotton, rape, beans, hemp and peanut are all used in cooking, and the bean and rape-seed oils are also used for lamps. The lamp of the poor man is merely a shallow cup with a spout at one side, like the classic lamp of ancient Rome. A piece of rush pith is placed in it for a wick. The soja bean is used for making soy, the common sauce of the rich and poor alike. It is said to have suggested to the English the manufacture of their Worcestershire and other sauces.

JEWELRY

It was interesting to watch a jeweler cutting the beautiful feathers of the ''Turquoise'' king-fisher into small bits and mounting these in various patterns on cheap brass brooches and ear-rings. The finished work had the appearance of blue enamel, and the jewelry is very popular among the poorer Chinese women. More delicate work of this sort is done on the Island of Hainan, where the feathers are mounted on silver, making a very attractive combination.

Other shops devoted themselves to silver-work, and others still to stringing pearls and precious stones and weaving them into elaborate head-dresses of various patterns. Some took the shape of butterflies and others of flowers. Gold, too, is used in considerable quantity for jewelry; it is not coined at all.

FIRE-CRACKERS

Fire-crackers are an indispensable article in every Chinese home. They are used on nearly all ceremonial occasions: when the bride starts for her husband's home, at funerals, when starting on a journey, on all religious festivals and other holidays, at the settlement of any quarrel and on any occasion when bad luck is to be averted or evil spirits frightened away. The process of manufacture may be observed in almost any native city, but Canton, perhaps, supplies the greatest quantity. Several sheets of paper cut to the proper size are laid on the red wrapper. One end of the latter projects a little and is moistened with paste. A small iron rod, not unlike a knitting needle, is rolled in at the other ¢nd of the pile, and with one stroke of a smooth wooden trowel having a handle like a plane the rolling operation is completed. For the larger kinds a short, heavy, curved plank is suspended in a stout framework just far enough above the table to catch the cracker and roll it up. These shells are fastened in bundles and set on end for the process of filling with powder. One end is stopped with a little clay. The fuse is inserted at the other end with the aid of an awl. An interesting variety is known as the "Twice-sounding cracker," a combination of rocket and cracker. To make these the larger shells are divided into two chambers by a wall of clay through which a fuse is passed. Both chambers are filled with powder and a second fuse is thrust into the side of the lower chamber. When this is lighted the explosion in this chamber throws the cracker high into the air where the second charge explodes.

Canton is celebrated for its decoration of pottery. The best ware is brought over the mountains from Chingtechen, in Kiangsi, in an unfinished state. At Canton the decoration is put on and the pieces are re-fired. The Cantonese matting goes into all parts of the world, and their carvings of black wood and of ivory are exquisitely beautiful.

THE WHEEL-BARROW

The presence of the foreigner has introduced into Shanghai a number of entirely new industries, such as the manufacture of foreign boots and shoes and other Western clothing, stove casting, safe making, ricksha and carriage building; yet even in the European settlements the old still holds its place in competition with the new. Beside the carriage maker the wheelwright builds his barrow, the only carriage possible on the narrow roads of central China. The wheel is some three feet in diameter with felloes four inches wide. The tire is not whole, but consists of sections each fastened on with rivets. The hub is solid. A wooden axle driven firmly into each end of the hub revolves in and supports the frame-work of the barrow. Oil is rarely used when the barrow-man has passed beyond the jurisdiction of a foreign policeman, for the creaking of a long caravan of heavily laden wheel-barrows is music indeed to the weary traveler's ear. The wheel is near the middle of the barrow and divides it into two parts, an open frame-work of wood serving to protect the clothing of the passenger or the wrappings of the freight from injury. Passengers ride sidewise, back to back, as in an Irish jaunting car, and rope stirrups serve to support their feet. A strap fastened to the handles passes over the shoulders of the barrow-man and helps him to lift and guide his load. In some parts of the country two pairs of handles are provided and two men are employed on each barrow, one pulling and the other pushing. A single man often conveys as much as four or five hundred pounds over the uneven roads of China for the magnificent sum of twenty-five cents a day.

SILK

Silk is made in every province of China. In Nanking it was estimated that there were before the revolution more than ten thousand looms engaged in weaving silks, satins and velvets, employing some thirty thousand men. Several hundred looms belonged to the imperial factories which supplied the Court at Peking with these precious fabrics. As many as twenty thousand pieces of satin have been sent in a single year overland from Nanking to Peking. Some of the imperial patterns were forbidden entirely to the common people, chiefly certain damasks and pongees. To-day the cocoons are generally sold to the steam filatures, but formerly the silk was reeled from the cocoons by experts, who went from one farm-house to another and put up their temporary furnaces of clay or old brick in the door-yard. This is still true in interior districts. In the thin iron kettles which are set in these furnaces they boil the cocoons to dissolve the glue and loosen the silk. It is very important that the water should be perfectly clean and to this end it is frequently purified beforehand by putting shell-fish in it which consume the impurities. With a piece of bamboo in his hand, one end of which is split so as to form a sort of coarse brush, the reeler gathers up from the boiling water four or five filaments of silk, which he reels off together very quickly on a rude wheel worked by hand or foot. From five to seven filaments twisted together are said to form the best thread. From twenty-five to forty ounces of silk are reeled in a single day by one man, whose wages amount to about two cents an ounce. The pupa is often used for food and by some is considered a delicacy. It is reckoned that each catty of cocoons will produce one and three-tenths taels of silk. A tael is equal to one and one-third ounces avoirdupois. The wild cocoons cannot be reeled in the same way as those which are the product of human care, but are washed in lye water and spun like cotton.

DYES

After the silk is reeled it is sold to dealers who dispose of it to the weavers. Before being woven, however, it is sent to the dyer, who is well skilled in the art of coloring and has a great variety of dye-stuffs at his command. As noted above the dye industry of the Chinese was revived during the late war. The most common color for clothing is blue. Black is seen, though less frequently, for work-a-day wear, but on holidays and ceremonial occasions the most brilliant combinations are seen. The bridal dress is red. White is reserved for mourning, though the deepest mourning is expressed by wearing unbleached sack-cloth. Buddhist monks and nuns confine themselves to grey or saffron. Yellow formerly was reserved for the imperial

family. This was the distinctive color of the Manchu
Dynasty, but it has not always held the preeminence. Some
of the earlier dynasties chose other colors for the Court
dress; during the Han period—206 B.C. to A.D. 220—it
was carnation.

For blue the most common native dye-stuffs are the
Chinese woad (*Isatis Indigofera*), dyer's knot-weed (*Polygonum tinctorium*), and true indigo; for the various shades
of red, Chinese madder (*Rubia cordifolia*), safflower and
Tibetan red (*Crocus sativus*) are used; for green the ox-plum, or buck-thorn, (*Rhamnus parvifolius*) yields its
bark; for yellow, sumac (*Rhus cotinus*), turmeric and gamboge are employed; for purple, the purple plant (*Lithosperum erythrorhizon*), and for black the cupules of the
acorn, both of oak and chestnut-oak. Besides these are
many imported dyes, chief among which are logwood and
sapanwood.

WEAVING

The weaving is done, for the most part, in the homes
of the workmen. The imperial factory at Nanking, however, formerly consisted of an extensive pile of barn-like
brick buildings, separated by courts and alley-ways, each
containing ten or a dozen looms. The windows were grated
with wooden bars which in winter were covered with paper.
The floor was of brick or of beaten earth. Three men were
employed at each loom, one for the warp, one for the pattern, and one to weave. Each loom contained a piece of
heavy satin, or silk brocade of richest colors; gold or blue
or scarlet, or it might be a damask of variegated hues, pink
and turquoise woven together in various patterns being a
favorite combination. Floral designs were common, and
another popular figure was that of the character *shou,*
"long life." The same patterns are used from generation
to generation; there appears to be no desire to cater to
the changeable tastes of the West. As is the case with
government employees generally the world over, the workmen are not too diligent, and one of them assured me that

two feet of brocaded silk was a very good day's work. Ordinary weavers, however, who are paid by the piece, make a much better showing; a master and his two apprentices will weave from five to ten yards of ordinary silk in a day.

China gave silk to the world, but through lack of intelligent direction and cooperation she has fallen far to the rear in production. The nations that were her pupils are now her teachers. Want of selection and care in breeding, want of judgment in feeding, want of proper machines for reeling and weaving—these failings have made China's silk less desirable than that of other countries.

In 1870 China produced about one-half of the world's silk. According to Julean Arnold, the American Commercial Attaché, it constituted 40 per cent of China's export trade at that period. The proportion has gradually declined so that in 1930 it amounted to no more than 16 per cent.

The trade has passed in good degree to Japan, whose government has been very active in eradicating disease of silk worms and has taught the producers to employ scientific methods. The present Nationalist Government of China is now following this example. Measures have been taken to get rid of diseased worms and schools of sericulture have been opened to train the people. A bureau of inspection and testing has been established at Shanghai, where exports are required to conform to standard in quality and weight.

The export of home-reeled silk is steadily decreasing and that from the steam filatures is increasing.

In this as in other industries, no doubt, the cottage must eventually give way to the factory, but the change will come slowly. The China Year Book for 1925 reports more than 356 silk filatures in China, with not less than 118,000 spindles. They have undoubtedly increased rapidly within a few years past. But the weaving is still done for the most part on hand looms, and, even though the cocoons may be taken to the filatures, the weavers will continue for a long time to do their work at home.

COTTON

The situation is akin to that in the manufacture of cotton. Cotton spinning mills have been in existence in China for several decades, and have rapidly increased in number during the past twenty years. It is interesting in this connection to remember that when our trade with China began, in 1784, one of the chief commodities brought from China was cotton piece goods—the nankeens of which our great grandmothers were so fond. It was the invention of the cotton gin and the application of steam to the loom that made us exporters, rather than importers, of cotton goods. Now we have carried our machinery to China, and the former mistress of the trade, with her patient workers and low wages, may yet recover her ancient position. She may at least be able to supply her own needs at a price with which we can never compete.

In Shanghai alone there are over a million spindles producing cotton yarn. In Hankow there are 116,000 spindles and 90,000 at Tientsin, but very few of these mills do any weaving. There are 3500 looms in Shanghai mills and 600 in Hankow. In all China there are 127 cotton mills with more than three million spindles.* Generally speaking, however, the mills produce yarn rather than cloth, and leave the weaving to the hand-looms in the cottages. Commenting on the use of the hand-looms Julean Arnold, the American Commercial Attaché at Peking, in his Commercial Handbook of China (1919) says: "The hand-loom in industry is so firmly established and so widespread in China that it is doubtful whether it will be seriously affected for some time to come by the competition of foreign cotton goods." [6]

Among the reasons assigned for this judgment is the common practice among farmers of buying yarn to work up into coarse cloth during the dull season of the year.

* Statistics for 1930 are: For all China 127 mills, of which 81 are owned by Chinese, 43 by Japanese and 3 by British. Spindles number 3,969,552. Operatives (four cities only) 150,636. Value of total output, Taels 31,980,246, equivalent to U. S. $14,710,913 at the average rate of exchange for the year.

[6] Op. cit., Vol. II, p. 355.

Many homes thus supply their own clothing. The use of the hand loom in small Chinese factories is also a growing custom, for less capital is required for such than would be required in a factory employing power looms. But the increase in the number of these small factories of 50 to 100 looms indicates a movement away from cottage industry. In time the small hand-loom factories will be forced to surrender to the more economical power-loom and huge mills with their thousands of operatives.

THE STEAM ENGINE

The Chinese government began to use steam-driven machinery over sixty years ago in the government arsenals, but no encouragement was given to its general introduction in private manufacturing.

The fear of economic disturbance, of social unrest, and accompanying disorders and riots had something to do, no doubt, with this attitude, but the want of company laws that would encourage coöperation by subscriptions of capital for large industrial undertakings no doubt was a contributing cause.

The sewing machine and the portable ginning machine, however, were exceptions to the general rule. They very easily found acceptance with the people. Far in the interior you will find many small shops using the "iron tailor" as the sewing machine is called in Chinese slang.

Gradually, however, the Europeans at the ports in their own enterprises introduced the steam engine and trained Chinese operatives in the use of machinery. Steamers appeared on inland waters, and accustomed the natives to the sight of the "fire dragon." Nevertheless, the use of steam-driven machinery in manufacture and transportation "upset the rice bowl" of many a poor laborer and created considerable ill feeling. When the Boxer rising occurred, in 1900, the first foreign invention that was attacked was the railway which had deprived the boatmen on the Pei Ho of the business of transporting freight from

Tientsin to Peking. The rails were torn up and the shops at Fengtai were set on fire. Such outbreaks have occurred in other countries upon the sudden introduction of labor-saving machinery.

But it is beginning to be realized now that steam and electricity cheapen production and so benefit all; that, while one form of industry is displaced, new openings are created, and the total amount of employment is increased. This brings greater diversification of industry and lessens the pressure of competition in any one line. It has in fact already brought about an increase of wages in the districts where Western machinery has been introduced, and thus has been accompanied by an improvement in the standard of living.

EVIL EFFECTS OF WESTERN INVENTIONS

Two ill effects are to be noted, however, as resulting from the introduction of foreign machinery in manufacturing in China. One is the displacement of the artist by the artisan; the other the bringing of the cheap labor of China into competition with the highly-paid labor of the West, in the production of those goods in the manufacture of which the West has heretofore enjoyed a monopoly. In the long run this will mean the transfer of capital from the West to the East, and the enforced idleness of some of our own operatives whose services will no longer be needed because our export trade will have fallen off.

As to the first-mentioned evil, while it may be admitted that the displacement of hand-made goods by a standardized machine-made product brings the greatest good to the greatest number, one cannot but regret the loss of the more beautiful artistic product of brain and hand. It has been suggested by a recent writer [7] that the curse of the machine can be neutralized by the employment of artists as designers and giving them credit for the design—that the beauty of an industrial object is not lessened by its repro-

[7] "Industrial Art and the Craftsman," by Matlack Price, in Arts and Decorations, Jan., 1922.

duction, and though a thousand copies may be made it is still beautiful.

It is unreasonable, however, that the process of adopting foreign inventions should be carried so far as to destroy native culture altogether, and make the fashions of the West the only standard of good taste. Why should the whole world be forced to wear a sacque coat and a bowler hat? Why should the graceful gown of the Chinese with its bright colors give place to the dull greys, browns and blacks and the ugly shapes of European dress? Why must the whole world be reduced to the dead level of uniformity! The charm of the world—the pleasure of living—is increased by variety. When the Creator made the forest he did not say "Go to, let us make a tree" and then create a pine only and declare: "This is a tree; let all trees be like it"; but He made an almost infinite variety of arboreal forms. The customs and manners of men also become the more attractive if variety is preserved.

It is to be hoped that the present craze in China for the adoption of everything Western will subside, and a reaction set in for the preservation of at least a remnant of the old civilization. It is surprising to note how even many missionaries, although they owe their religion to Asia, identify Christian civilization with the customs of Europe —with European dress, manners, architecture and the mechanical contrivances of the West.

But St. Paul didn't wear a frock coat and silk hat. Socrates and Cicero in their dress approached more nearly to that of the old-fashioned mandarin than to that of the modern gilt-edged diplomat.

As to the second evil, the bringing of American labor into competition with the underpaid labor of China, the hope of the world would seem to be, not in a leveling down of Western standards to those prevailing among the workmen of the Orient, but in the raising of the standards of the East, so as to equalize as far as possible the happiness of all races.

But at present the great difference in the level of wages East and West tends to induce a flow of capital to the East, despite the relative inefficiency of the cheaper labor. That labor, however much lacking in experience with machinery, can be used very profitably in the production of many articles. This is shown by the growth of industries of a foreign type in China. Among these are the silk filatures already mentioned. There are also many cotton mills with over three million spindles and some seven thousand looms, producing each year a million bales of yarn and over two million pieces of cotton cloth.

There are 135 flour mills of foreign type, 48 tanneries, 114 match factories and sixteen paper mills. Besides these there are smelting furnaces, rolling mills, ship yards, brick and cement works, chemical dye works, breweries, egg albumen factories, canneries for fruits, vegetables and meats, glass works, cigarette factories and manufactories of electrical supplies. This list is far from exhaustive, but will give one an idea of the wide range of foreign industries that have been undertaken.

MUNICIPAL IMPROVEMENT

In addition to these must be mentioned municipal utilities, such as electric lighting, water works, gas works, telephones and street railways. There are over 200 cities supplied with electric light, a convenience unknown outside of the Shanghai foreign settlements when the writer went to China in 1887.

It must not be understood that these industries of foreign type are all financed by Europeans and Americans. That was true only at the start, but Chinese capitalists soon found it profitable to buy shares in these foreign companies, and during the past fifteen years have established not a few concerns that are wholly Chinese.

Not many years ago a visit was made to a sleepy little city called T'ungchou, situated about 70 miles from Shanghai on the north bank of the Yangtze River. There was no wharf or steamer landing. The steamer paused in midstream and we leaped into a small native boat and were rowed ashore, where we scrambled up the mud bank and then hired a wheel-barrow, which carried us two or three miles over an unpaved path to the city gate.

The city was surrounded by a brick wall and moat, and a walk through its streets showed it to be wholly mediæval in character, without the slightest sign of any desire for Western innovations. But T'ungchou is in the midst of one of the best cotton growing districts of China, the district that made the nankeens, once so much in demand in our own country.

To-day, under the guiding genius of Chang Ch'ien, that sleepy little city has been converted into a great hive of industry. Great cotton spinning and weaving mills have been erected there. Modern roads have been built, and the company of which Mr. Chang was founder has its own steamers and steamer landing, while the town is supplied with electric light, telephones and all the conveniences and inconveniences of modern civilization. The company maintains offices in Shanghai and New York and does a thriving business.

Another enterprising Chinese capitalist is building a similar industrial city at Chengchou, in Honan, one of the central provinces of China. These facts indicate the direction in which industrial life in China is moving.

CHAPTER IX

THE GUILDS

There were in this city (Hangchow) twelve guilds of the different crafts and each guild had 12,000 houses in the occupation of its workmen.—The Book of Ser Marco Polo.

In the quiet, quaintly-named streets, in town-mead and market-place, in the lord's mill beside the stream, in the bell that swung out its summons to the crowded borough-mote, in merchant-gild and church-gild and craft-gild, lay the life of Englishmen who were doing more than knight or baron to make England what she is.

Green's History of the English People.

Attention has been called in discussing the land tenure of China to the fact that the holdings, as a rule, are small, and that this promotes independence and social equality.

I have spoken also of the influence of the clan organization as favoring democracy, and of the existence of tithings and village elders as giving a degree of self-government.

There is another institution which may also be said to have aided in preparing the way for the establishment of a republic, that is the guild. What the guilds of the Middle Ages were to Europe, that the guilds have been from a still more ancient time to China. The boroughs of England were protected in their ancient privileges by the guilds formed among the townsmen, and in China, too, the old-time customs and rights of the people have been jealously guarded by similar organizations.

The origin of these associations is lost in the mists of antiquity. No doubt the claims which some make as to origin during the Chou Dynasty (1122–249 B.C.) are impossible of acceptance, but it is true, according to the *Chou Li* (the ordinances of the Chou Dynasty) that in that ancient period, during the existence of the city states, the people were divided into nine classes and each class placed under a leader for the discharge of its duties. The fifth class was engaged in manufacturing. The sixth, under the direction of the Chief of Trade, attended to the transport and distribution of goods. The seventh class, composed of women, engaged in the weaving of silk and linen. We do not know how far this theoretical division of labor was carried out in practice, but conceivably these arrangements may have led to the formation of guilds. In any case we know this, that the guilds of China throughout the ages have been the nurseries of independence and a check upon the tyranny of officialdom.

In so far as organizations of craftsmen are concerned, the guilds of Europe have been supplanted by trades unions, but the trades unions lack some important features of the ancient guilds. The latter were associations of all who were engaged in a given trade; the master who supplied the capital and the craftsmen and apprentices who were employed by him. Capital and labor were united for mutual assistance and protection. In the modern world organized capital, in huge corporations, is separated from the organized labor of the unions, and is often hostile to it.

Dr. Sun's introduction of Russian advisers in 1923 led to the organization of unions among artisans and farmers. These unions have no affiliation with the guilds. The Russian advisers seized the opportunity to fill the agricultural and industrial workers with a bitter hatred of landlords and capitalist employers and thus created a feeling of hostility between employers and employees that had scarcely existed before that time in China. After the split in the Nationalist Party in 1927, many of the labor unions attached themselves to the Communist movement.

The Nationalist Government is sincerely interested in the welfare of the manual toilers in field and factory. It aims to reconcile the interests of capital and labor, but does not design to make the labor unions take the place of the guilds.

Chinese guilds are of four kinds; the craft guild, the merchant guild, the community guild and the provincial guild.

THE CRAFT GUILDS

The craft guilds are local only. They are limited to one craft in one town. The carpenters' guild of Soochow has nothing to do with the carpenters' guild of Shanghai. There is no provincial union of carpenters, much less any approach to a national guild of carpenters. A similar condition exists in other trades.

The organization of these guilds varies somewhat from place to place, but they all possess certain features in common. The membership usually includes all the followers of a particular craft, masters as well as workmen, within the district concerned. No craftsman, in fact, can afford to remain outside the order. He would be ostracized, and in some cases might suffer bodily harm. The members are not always drawn, however, from the citizens of the place in which the guild is located. In some instances the guild is formed entirely of men from some other city, and often from some other province. Thus the fish-hook makers of Wenchow are all from Foochow. The guild rules will not permit the admission of any man from any other place than Foochow. The needle makers of Wenchow are all from T'aichou, in Chekiang, or from the province of Kiangsu. The gold-beaters of Wenchow all come from the neighboring city of Ningpo.[1]

The regulations of the guilds are difficult to obtain. There is much secrecy observed in all the transactions of the craft guilds. Although I formed the acquaintance of a good many artisans, and obtained much information from them relating to their crafts, every effort to obtain copies of the guild regulations was a failure. A number of features of these organizations, however, have become known.

The members of the guild are all on a footing of equality in so far as guild matters are concerned. Each has a voice in the selection of the officers and in determining the regulations. The control is democratic. A managing committee

[1] These instances are given by Morse in his ''Guilds of China,'' but quoted from Macgowan's monograph on that subject, p. 181.

is elected annually by the members. This often consists of twelve persons, each one of whom serves as chairman and general manager of the guild for one month. Sometimes the committee is much smaller. The carpenters of Wenchow have a committee of five to manage the guild. The millers of the same city some years ago organized a guild of sixteen flour mills located there. The sixteen proprietors elected a committee of four, but arranged the election so that each one of the sixteen would serve on the committee in regular rotation.[2]

Often there is also elected a treasurer to serve one year. Those that are well supplied with funds employ a paid secretary, who must be a graduate so that he can better represent the interests of the guilds in the courts, whenever that becomes necessary. Some guilds also employ a chaplain, who attends to the religious services in honor of the patron saint and reads masses for the dead. On the fête day of the saint there is sometimes a pageant. More often there is a feast at the guild hall, followed by a theatrical entertainment. All guilds have their religious features, for they are dedicated to some saint or deity under whose protection they rest. The poorest are accustomed to meet in the city temple, which is always open to any citizen. Such a use of the building would naturally call for certain offerings of incense and candles on the altars. The mediæval guilds of Europe, also, all had their patron saints. The shoe-makers had St. Crispin, the tailors St. John the Baptist. So in China the carpenters and masons have Lu Pan. He was a well-known artisan of the State of Lu in the days of Confucius. Mencius speaks of him. He was said to be so skillful that he made a miracle-working image which brought a drought upon the neighboring state of Wu. This was done to punish the men of Wu who had murdered the father of Lu Pan. The story tells us that the drought lasted three years, and was brought to an end by Lu Pan after the people of Wu had petitioned him and paid him a good sum of money. The image had one hand outstretched towards the state of Wu. When Lu Pan

---

[2] These two instances are recorded by Macgowan.

would end the drought and bring the desired rain he cut
off the offending hand.

Many Chinese crafts place themeslves under the protection of the God of War, others under that of Kuanyin,
the Goddess of Mercy. Some worship the Queen of Heaven,
that is to say the Moon, whose birthday comes at the time
of the harvest moon in September. The druggists of Wenchow have Huat'ou, the God of Medicine, for their patron
deity.

Some of the guilds are very wealthy. The income is derived usually from an entrance fee, from fines and from
certain taxes on the trade. The fishmongers of Ningpo
make a deposit of $3000 on being admitted to membership.[3]
This is a guarantee against breach of the regulations. They
also pay an annual tax whose amount depends upon the
number of boats engaged in fishing. This is one of the very
wealthy guilds. The druggists of Ningpo are said to have
an income of $500,000 [4] a year. Part of this is probably
derived from invested funds.

The guilds fix the standard of weights and measures for
the craft. Although the Government has adopted a uniform system of weights and measures, it has not found
acceptance outside official transactions.* Each craft has its
own, and the confusion that exists is astonishing to a
stranger. The unit of weight is the *chin,* or catty. The
word *chin* literally translated means "a hatchet." By
treaty it is fixed as the equivalent of one and one-third
pounds avoirdupois, or 21.33 ounces, but this agreement
does not affect domestic transactions. The weight varies
in the several trades from 4 ounces avoirdupois for tea in
Peip'ing and 16 ounces for fruit at Ningpo, to 18.55 for oil
at Nanking and 20 for metals at Canton to 28 for coal
in Honan. The *chin* is divided as our pound is into 16
parts, which the Chinese call *liang,* but which are better
known as taels. This is one of the few instances in which
the Chinese depart from the decimal system in their tables
of weights and measures. One hundred *chin,* or catties,

3 Morse, op. cit., 14.
4 Ibid.
* For new standards of weight and measure see the Appendix.

are called a *tan*, or picul. The picul, of course, varies with
the sort of *chin* that is used.

The unit measure of capacity is the *tou*, or peck. In
Nanking for rice it contains 558.3 cubic inches. In Shanghai for rice 728.6, but for beans only 655.4 cubic inches.
In Ningpo a *tou* of rice measures 565 cubic inches, but in
Swatow 768.8. Ten *tou* make a *shih*, or stone, which in
Nanking rice would weigh 180.40 lbs. av., considerably
more than a *stone* in English weight. A half-*shih*, or
5 *tou*, is known as a *hu*, and a tenth of a *tou* is a *sheng*,
which is a near approach to our pint, 34.66 cu. in. The
smallest *sheng* contains nearly 31 cu. in., the largest about
95. The Government, under the Manchu régime, kept a
standard *hu* in the yamens with which to measure the
tribute rice. County magistrates paying the tribute rice
were compelled to send their measures to the yamen to
be tested, and their capacity was recorded. Theoretically
the *tou* is divided into quadrillionth parts by a decimal
system of measures descending through the *sheng, ko, shao,*
etc., to the *ho*.

The linear unit is the *ch'ih*, or foot, which is divided into
ten *ts'un*, or inches. The foot is fixed by treaty at 14.1
inches English, but in common practice its length depends
upon locality and upon the calling. In Shantung, in the
city of Linch'ingchou, a foot in brick-work is 11.15 inches,
in land measure 12.2 inches, and in measuring cloth it is
23.75 inches. In the neighboring city of Tsinan the land
measure is a foot of 14.55 inches and the cloth measure one
of 21.4 inches. In Nanking the tailor's foot is 13.75 inches,
while the carpenter's is 12.5 inches.

The guilds also regulate wages and determine the number
of apprentices which a master may take. Some years
ago the members of the gold-beaters' guild of Soochow
killed one of their fellows for taking more apprentices than
the rules permitted.[5] The apprentice pays for the privilege of learning the trade. He is bound to the master for
a period of years and during that period he receives no
wages, but he is given quarters and board in his master's

5 Macgowan, p. 182.

home. After his apprenticeship he is required in some cases to serve his master for another period for wages. In some guilds, according to Macgowan, no master is allowed any apprentices except sons and nephews. Although the journeymen are members of the guild they do at times strike to force the masters to raise wages. In some crafts the city is districted, and a member of the guild is forbidden to take a contract outside his own district. This, of course, lessens competition.

The introduction of foreign machinery, driven by steam or electricity, has greatly injured handicrafts that are thus brought into competition with machine manufacture. The cheap production of the factory may be less artistic than the hand-made article, but cheapness wins with the masses. Apprenticeship in certain lines has therefore become undesirable, and the guilds of such trades are naturally losing power. Trade unionism has not entirely supplanted the guild in China, but the large combinations of capital that are investing in factories are separating the master from the workmen, and are beginning to bring about in China the formation of provincial and national unions of laborers, as has been done in other lands, and array capital and labor in opposing camps.

THE MERCHANT GUILDS

It is difficult to draw the line between the craft guilds and the merchant guilds. They are organized on the same general plan. Moreover, many craftsmen are also merchants. They maintain their small establishments with their own capital, and open shops in which they retail their own manufactures. This, of course, was once true in the West also. Many merchants, too, whose prime business is to distribute goods, are also engaged in manufacturing. The tea merchant, for example, in the wholesale trade is generally engaged also in firing and packing the tea.

But the general distinction between the craft guild and the merchant guild is clear. One is engaged in production, the other in distribution. One is a combination of artisans whose capital is small or who work for wages; the other

is a combination of traders whose capital is sufficient for
large commercial ventures.

The artisan guilds, as a rule, are too poor to afford guild
halls. They meet in temples. There are exceptions but
they are few. On the other hand the merchants who form
a guild generally build beautiful and costly guild halls.

The Bankers' Guild of Shanghai has one of the most
attractive of these halls to be found anywhere in China.
A façade of grey tiles, unglazed but planed, is surmounted
by a highly ornamental roof with dragons on the upturned
corners. A pair of stone lions guards the entrance. A
triple gate-way opens into a court-yard. A series of large
buildings separated by courts constitutes the guild hall.
There is a shrine dedicated to the God of Wealth, with
an image of that worthy deity, and a theater for the presentation of the plays that are frequently given. The council
room of the guild is richly furnished with carved blackwood, and all the appointments are in keeping.

In the matter of membership the merchant guilds appear
to be quite unlike the craft guilds. In many of the former
admission to the guild is limited to one representative of
each firm. The object of this provision seems to be to
prevent any one firm from acquiring too much power in
the guild. Since all are competitors in the same line of
trade this is an important provision.

Each of the merchant guilds regulates the trade with
which it is concerned. The guild determines standards of
quality, fixes and enforces penalties for adulteration or
other violation of the rules, establishes rates of commission,
methods of payment, forms of bills of lading, rates of exchange, and determines other matters in which there is a
common interest.

As in Europe during the Middle Ages some guilds were
authorized to hold court and settle disputes among their
members, so in China, although without express authoriza-
tion by the Government, the guilds attempt to settle all
such difficulties. Some guilds forbid their members to
bring suit in an official court against a fellow member.
Violation of this rule will deprive the offender of the sup-

port of the guild in any subsequent trouble. In some cases a heavy fine is inflicted for such offense. It may even cause expulsion from the guild.

If a reputable member of the guild becomes involved in a suit at law or is prosecuted by the Government the guild will come to his assistance and go surety for him. But if a member is found guilty of a serious offense the guild will arrest him and deliver him to the authorities.

Although most of the merchant guilds are like the craft guilds in having a merely local character, there are some which exercise a wider control. The Shanghai guilds, for instance, which control the trade in tea and silk at that port, are in a position to dictate the policy of the guilds in other localities which have to do with trade in those articles, for they are in close association with the foreign buyers and have intimate acquaintance with the conditions of the export trade. It is the Bankers' Guild, however, which exercises the widest control. It is the only one which exercises anything like a national influence.

For centuries past the bankers of China have been drawn almost wholly from the province of Shansi. It is a curious feature of business life in China that certain districts have secured a monopoly of certain occupations. Thus all the clerks in the yamens of China are drawn as a rule from Shaohsingfu in Kiangsu Province. All the eunuchs of the Peking palaces during the Manchu régime came from Hochienfu, Chihli, and Shansi has long enjoyed a monopoly of banking. The Bankers' Guild has a branch in every important city, and thus it is possible to buy bills of exchange on any part of the country. The guild fixes rates of discount and interest and determines the exchange between the various currencies of the country. That is a matter of serious importance in trade and travel, for the currencies are too numerous to catalogue. In some parts of the Republic the Hongkong dollar is the standard coin, minted by the British Crown Colony of Hongkong. In Shanghai the common currency is the Mexican dollar. In Anhui Province it is the old Carolus dollar of Spain. In Tientsin it is the Chinese dollar. Formerly the money of the people was the brass cash, a circular coin with a square hole in the center. These coins were strung on strings of straw, in hundreds or thousands. A thousand was commonly called a *tiao*. But in reality the string of a hundred contained but 98, and in some cases but 95. There were two strings of 95 each in a *tiao*, so that a *tiao* really numbered 974.

In 1892 a Mexican dollar at Shanghai exchanged for 1050 cash. In 1897 it brought but 900. The price of copper had risen in the meantime and the value of silver had fallen. In 1919 a Chinese silver dollar brought 1300 cash. This was due chiefly, no doubt, to the rise in the value of silver brought about by the Great War.

Some years ago, owing to the rise in the price of copper, the Chinese Government ceased the coinage of cash and minted one-cent pieces instead. These, however, were token coins, and the people of China are not accustomed to the use of such coins. They passed for a while at 100 to the Chinese or the Mexican dollar, but when the Government refused to receive 100 in payment of a dollar in taxes, the quotations fell, so that in 1925 a silver dollar brought about 130 copper cents.[5a]

But, while the brass cash and the copper cent are the coins most used by the people, in all large transactions prices are reckoned in taels. The tael is not a coin, but a weight of silver—that is to say a *liang*, or Chinese ounce of silver. But, as already pointed out, the *liang* varies in actual weight everywhere, and in the valuation of a *liang* of silver it is necessary not only to know the real weight, but the pureness of the silver as well. There are frequently several kinds of taels used in the same city, and in going from place to place the varieties are multitudinous.

I have a table of the weight and fineness of 91 different taels. They vary in weight from 520 to 583.3 grains, and in fineness from 900 to 1000. The customs tael, which exists only in imagination, is known as the Haikwan tael, and is 1000 fine and weighs 583.3 grains. But in paying

---

[5a] The China Year Book, 1923, says depreciation of cent caused dollar to vary from 169 to 203 cents in 1922.

duties, one pays in local taels, and as the local tael is merely bar silver, or sycee, the payment is usually made in dollars. Hence, the duty in Customs taels must be reduced to its equivalent in local taels, and that to its equivalent in Chinese dollars. Thus China is the paradise of money changers, and in other days the angel that stood guard over that paradise was the Shansi Bankers' Guild. Formerly the power was much greater than to-day. It could control the financial policy of the Government. But in these latter days the heavy foreign indebtedness, the establishment in China of powerful foreign banks, and the creation of rival Chinese institutions, have curtailed to a considerable degree the power of Shansi.

As an illustration of the control over financial transactions exercised by the Bankers' Guild I quote a few of the rules of the guild in Wuhu.[6]

1. Sycee must be changed into dollars at the rate posted; otherwise a fine of Tls. 100 will be imposed.
2. Shanghai drafts must be sold at the posted rate, and for 10 days after sight or 12 days after date. Violation of this rule entails a fine of Tls. 100.

. . . .

5. Members of the guild must attend its meetings held on the 15th of each moon to fix rates. Anyone who adopts another rate will be fined Tls. 100.
6. No drafts may be ante-dated or post-dated.
7. A deposit of Tls. 100 must be made by members to cover possible fines.
8. If the member should be fined, another deposit of Tls. 100 will be required.
9. Informers will receive one-half of the fine.

PROVINCIAL GUILDS

The name "Provincial Guild" inaccurately describes the character of the third sort of guilds. They are associations of men from the same province who are living away from home, and generally in a province of which they

6 Decennial reports of the Chinese Maritime Customs, 1882-91, p. 289.

are not natives. Sometimes, however, the membership is restricted to men who have come from the same city or from a common prefecture. The attachment to home is very strong in a Chinese. I have known men in Peking, who were born in that city and whose ancestors for two or three generations had resided there, who, nevertheless, spoke of themselves as belonging to distant provinces. "What is your native province?" you will ask such a man, and he may reply: "Kiangsi, but it is 500 years since my family left there."

It is readily understood, then, that when men of the same province meet in a city, far distant from their home and where they are engaged in business, they will be drawn one toward another. This tendency is strengthened by the differences of dialect which make it so difficult for Chinese of different regions to communicate with each other.

The provincial guilds usually build attractive guild houses which are in the nature of clubs. There the members congregate and discuss common interests. Visitors from home are introduced and enjoy the privileges of the club. There are rooms to be rented to such visitors at low rates. There is a kitchen, a dining-room, and a *chef* who is familiar with the preparation of home dishes. There are rooms for games, sometimes a theater, and usually a hall for public meetings.

The guild stands sponsor for its members or for fellow provincials, properly introduced, and it also exercises a wholesome restraint over them by threatening to withdraw support if the practices of a firm or an individual are contrary to the rules. The influence of the guild, too, is used to promote the political advancement of expectant or substantive officials from the province or district represented. When such an official takes office in the town where the guild is located, he is expected to make a handsome contribution to the funds of the guild, and he in turn is hospitably entertained by the guild.

These guilds are also benevolent societies. They provide relief for their fellow provincials who may be in distress, and they have a cemetery where the remains of those who die away from home may be buried until opportunity offers to send the remains to the distant family grave plot. If such fellow townsmen died unprovided with funds, the guild will bear the expense of the funeral and the cost of shipping the body home.

These provincial guilds are organized on much the same plan as the craft guilds. The members elect annually a committee of managers, each one of whom serves for a time as president. There is a paid secretary who must be a graduate, and who is the active representative of the guild. Funds are raised usually by a light tax on the trade of the members. For example, the Ningpo Guild at Wenchow has a committeeman from each of the important trades conducted by the members, and charges $2.00 per thousand on the value of cargo, except cotton and dried fish. The cotton pays $0.20 a bale of 120 catties, and the dried fish 44 cash a package. Members not receiving cargo pay from 300 to 1000 cash a month, according to the amount of their business. The Hanyang Guild at Ichang levies a tax on trade, and also collects 300 cash from each junk for each trip made. Working men pay 30 cash a month and clerks 2 per cent of their salaries.[7]

In Chungking eight guilds, representing as many different provinces, are associated together in one general guild for mutual protection and assistance. They maintain a fire department, a volunteer military company, adjust cases in bankruptcy, raise relief funds, and support an orphanage and other charitable institutions.[8]

COMMUNITY GUILDS

There are two places in China where the guild assumes charge of the municipal administration, in addition to the oversight of trade. These are Swatow, in Kuangtung Province, and Newchwang, in Shengking. That in Newchwang is called "The Great Guild of Newchwang," and that at

7 Decennial Reports of Chinese Maritime Customs, 1882-91, p. 158.
8 Decennial Reports of Maritime Customs, p. 119.

Swatow is the "Swatow Guild." The latter is composed of representatives from six counties and is divided into two sections, each covering three counties. Each section has 24 representatives. Two of these from each section serve in turn for one month, one as accountant, the other as treasurer, the four together constituting for that month the managing committee. The guild acts as a municipal government, as a board of trade, and a chamber of commerce. It has tremendous power. It levies taxes, maintains a fire brigade, determines standards of weights and measures, rates of commission and settling days, and penalizes all violation of the ordinances. Among the taxes upon which it depends in part for its revenue are fees for the entrance and clearance of all steamers and sailing vessels owned or chartered by members of the guild. Other taxes are levied on cargo, either a specific or an ad valorem duty. There are license fees for commission merchants and fines for various offenses. In addition to these sources of revenue there is considerable income from rents of property belonging to the guild. All bankrupts are boycotted. No Swatow agent is permitted to act for an outside firm which refuses to pay its indebtedness to a local firm, and no outside firm may have more than one agent in Swatow. Its patron deity is the "Queen of Heaven," i.e., the Moon. Members who fail to participate in the celebration of her birthday, which comes at the time of the Harvest Moon, are fined 10,000 fire-crackers.

Sometimes the decrees of the guild are unwritten. Word is passed around and united action follows, as in the case of an attempt by the provincial government to collect a new tax in 1890. The tax collector not only failed to collect, he could not even find a house to serve as an office. He soon abandoned the task and left the port.[9]

The Swatow Guild is unique in that it attempts to control the trade of Swatow with other ports of China at which Swatow men are doing business. This is done through branch guilds opened in those ports.[10]

[9] Decennial Reports of Maritime Customs, p. 537.
[10] Morse, op. cit., 54.

The Great Guild at Newchwang is similar to that at Swatow, but exercises less extensive control. It is also divided into two sections, one for the eastern, the other for the western part of the port. Each section annually elects a president and vice president, and these four make the managing committee. As a municipal government the guild looks after the upkeep of streets and roads, builds and maintains toll bridges, cares for drains and reservoirs, controls the commons, supports charitable institutions and administers poor relief.

As a commercial association it establishes rules for conducting the grain market, which is one of the chief interests of the port. It also controls the money market, which is open only to members of the guild and visitors properly introduced. The latter, however, are not permitted to enter into any transactions there. It regulates exchange and commission rates and fixes the standard for silver sycee and the rules and charges for smelting and assaying silver. Its revenues are derived from annual dues, taxes on trading operations, and the bridge tolls already mentioned. Protection to the business of the members is secured by requiring all bankers and brokers to collect 2 per cent on all monies passing through their hands which belong to travellers or non-members.

Penalities are provided for non-observance of these rules.[11]

THE GUILD AND THE GOVERNMENT

The tendency of the guilds to cultivate in their members a spirit of independence is well shown in the numerous contests between them and the Government. I have already mentioned the incident at Swatow in which resistance was made to an unusual tax. Many other illustrations may be given. During the last decade of the nineteenth century I was living in Nanking. The Viceroy had just established a mint for the coinage of silver dollars. They were nominally of the same weight and fineness as the Mexican dollar;

[11] Decennial Reports of I. M. Customs, p. 35.

in reality there was a slight difference. The Viceroy issued a proclamation requiring the public to accept them at a certain valuation in the brass cash. The bankers and exchange shops protested that they were not worth that price. The Viceroy insisted and threatened punishment. The guilds took action. The following day every bank and exchange shop in Nanking closed its doors. This lasted for three days, after which the Viceroy accepted the bank's rate. The Ningpo Guild at Shanghai maintains a guild hall and a cemetery. In 1898, while I was living in that city, the Municipal Council of the French Settlement decided, for sanitary reasons, to remove the cemetery, which was already entirely surrounded by the city. This action was in violation of an agreement made in 1878, in which the French Government had promised not to disturb the graves. The Ningpo Guild at once took action. Merchants, bankers, artisans, servants—all quit work. The police were on hand in force. The foreign volunteers were called out; blue-jackets were landed from foreign men-of-war in the harbor. But at the first attempt to touch the cemetery a riot broke out. Twenty Chinese were killed, but the guild triumphed. The cemetery is still undisturbed.

I remember, too, very well the wheel-barrow riot of 1897. The Municipal Council of the International Settlement had decided to increase the license for wheel-barrows from 400 to 600 cash a month, i.e., from $0.20 to $0.30 in American money. The Chinese wheel-barrow has a wheel about three feet in diameter. It is set in a framework which prevents contact with the packages being carried. These barrows are numerous and are used for carrying merchandise through the settlements, particularly between the warehouses and the vessels. They are used also for passenger carriage among factory hands and other laborers. The tire of the wheel is very narrow, and the vehicle is responsible for much of the wear and tear of the streets.

The Municipal Council, composed of British and American merchants, had voted the increase in the license fee without consulting the wheel-barrow guild. A riot resulted. The police, volunteers, blue-jackets from the foreign men-of-war, were all unable to bring the wheel-barrow men to submission. After several days wrangling the Council rescinded the action. Three months later, after consultation with the heads of the guild, the barrow-men agreed to pay the increased tax.

One of the most interesting exhibitions of the power of the guilds was given during the revolution of 1911 which brought about the overthrow of the Manchu Dynasty. The immediate cause of the revolution was a dispute between the people of the province of Szechuen and the central government as to the building of a railway in that province. A company had been organized by the people themselves and work had been begun, but the president of the company appointed by the Peking authorities had misappropriated a large part of the funds. The work stopped. The Ministry of Communications at Peking decided to take over the enterprise, and for this purpose arranged for a large foreign loan. The people demanded the return of the money subscribed and paid in. The Government offered shares in the railway to the amount of the funds expended and in hand, but excluding the amount misappropriated. The people held public meetings and vented their anger. They declared that the Peking Government was responsible for the loss, and demanded shares to the full amount of the original capital. The Prince Regent stubbornly resisted. The Szechuen Guild at Peking met in a number of stormy sessions. They waited repeatedly upon the Prince and tried to obtain a reversal of his decision. They were in constant telegraphic communication with the provincial capital, and were fully informed of the situation there. In the end the people triumphed and the Government was overthrown.

The guilds of China are not organized under charters from the Government, but the Government has always recognized their power and has usually been careful to avoid open conflict. Conflict, as we have seen, has usually resulted in defeat for the Government.

The guilds, as already stated, have their own courts, and the members, as a rule, avoid the official courts. Sometimes.

however, it is impossible to do this. Outside parties bring suits against guild members before the government officials, and these members must appear, just as other citizens do. In the past, however, the government courts have usually decided such cases in harmony with the regulations of the guild concerned.

While living in Shanghai it was my duty for two years to serve as American Assessor in the Mixed Court there, and in the various civil suits that were brought before the court it was the rule to consult the regulations of the guild concerned. It has been asserted that China has no commercial code of law. In so far as legislation by the government is concerned, this was quite true under the Manchu Dynasty. The *Ta Ch'ing Hui Tien* may be considered as a constitutional compilation rather than anything else, and the *Ta Ch'ing Lü Li* was the penal code. But the lack of imperial legislation in regard to commercial matters was due to the fact that the guilds supplied the needed laws. Civil suits were decided by the officials in accordance with the practice of the locality concerned, and this was nothing more than the practice sanctioned by the guilds.

Thus it appears that the guilds have not only been a training school in independence and self-government, but have also been one of the important sources of Chinese law. The clan council, the practice as to land tenure, the village elders and the guild have together formed a strong quadrilateral in defense of popular liberty. The democratic tendencies of these institutions have done much to prepare the people for the introduction of a republican form of government.

CHAPTER X

THE CALENDAR AND ITS FESTIVALS

The purple palace announces the new moon;
The yellow way (the ecliptic) opens a path for the sun.
Chinese Proverb.

Under the heavens there are no unending feasts.—Chinese Proverb.

Every nation has its festivals, its seasons of recreation
and holiday-making. China does not lack them. On the
contrary, since it is a very old country, it is well supplied
with them. In the Western world we have the weekly
sabbath, not identical with the Jewish, but derived from
it and from the earlier Chaldean.

The Chinese formerly had no weekly day of rest,* but
the seven-day period has been known to them from very
ancient times. One of their oldest books, the Yi King, or
"Book of Changes," speaks of it, saying: "The seventh
day returns again." It is a period which was anciently
observed, too, in the funeral rites. Special sacrifices were
made to the dead every seventh day after death for seven
weeks, that is to say, for a sabbath of weeks.

But while the Chinese did not observe a weekly sabbath,
they had quite a number of holidays. If they belonged
to the wealthy or well-to-do classes, they would close their
shops for a whole month at the Chinese New Year. If they
could not afford to do that, they would rest not less than
three days, and many prolonged the vacation to ten or
fifteen days. Other holidays that are still observed are the
Fifth Moon and Eighth Moon feasts, when three days are
allowed for the celebration of each festival.

* On December 30, 1929 a law was promulgated giving factory
workers a right to rest on one day in seven in addition to an allowance of eight other rest-days annually. These eight rest-days are
given in the Appendix.

The celebration of the New Year has been somewhat affected by the adoption in 1912 of the Western Calendar. Before that action had been taken, the Chinese calendar was a lunar one, and the celebration of the beginning of a new year is still reserved by most Chinese for the begining of the year according to the old calendar.

THE COLLEGE OF ASTRONOMY

Under the old régime the calendar was fixed each year by the College of Astronomy, perhaps more properly called the College of Astrology. The first quotation at the head of this chapter refers to this, for the College of Astronomy was under the control of the Imperial Palace, the "Purple Palace," and new moons were announced by the flying of flags. The College of Astronomy was a department of the government which had existed from very ancient times. The offices of the college were located near the south-eastern corner of the Tartar City of Peip'ing. There the observatory still stands, with the quadrant, the stellar sphere, and other instruments presented by Louis XIV of France. Alongside the tower still older instruments formerly were housed which date from the Sung Dynasty (A.D. 960–1127). All these instruments were carried off by the French and Germans after the relief of the Legations at the time of the "Boxer" troubles. The French government, however, would not permit the instruments to be unloaded in France, but returned them immediately to Peking. The older instruments, taken to Potsdam by the Germans, were placed on exhibition there until the close of the Great World War, when the treaty of peace provided for their restoration to China.

One of these ancient bronze instruments was used to determine the solstices. A beam of sun-light was allowed to fall upon a graduated scale, and by this means the advance of the sun towards the north and its retreat towards the south were noted. The College took note, too, of the entrance of the sun into the constellation of Aquarius. The

first new moon after that date was the beginning of the
new year. This caused the new year to commence sometimes as early as the 21st of January. It was never later
than the 19th of February.

A curious discrepancy is observable between the comparative calendars (Chinese and Western) used by the
Chinese in the United States and those prepared for use
in China. The new year's day of the lunar calendar arrives
in the United States one day ahead of schedule. This is
due to the fact that the first Chinese coolies who arrived
in America were ignorant of the fact that when one travels
eastward around the earth he gains a day. They did not
repeat the day in which they crossed the 180th meridian,
as the Europeans and Americans on shipboard did. Thus
when they arrived in San Francisco they were one day in
advance of the local calendar, and they have continued
ever since to reckon time accordingly.

THE ALMANAC

Inasmuch as twelve lunar months do not correspond with
the period of the earth's revolution around the sun, it became necessary to adjust the lunar to the solar year by
adding at times an extra month. This thirteenth month
was added sometimes near the beginning of the year, sometimes at other seasons. The addition was made where the
least disturbance would be given to the operations of the
farmer, who had learned to plow and sow at times indicated
by the almanac. This official almanac was, therefore, a
document of very great importance, and was very carefully prepared. Not only was the time of the insertion
of an intercalary month to be determined, but the dates
had to be fixed for all the important sacrifices offered by
the State. Anniversaries of the death of important members of the imperial house were recorded, for such days
were tabu for public business. Other unlucky days, too,
were marked, as were also the lucky ones. It was a matter
of importance for everyone to know what days would

be fortunate or unfortunate for the great affairs of life, especially if these affairs were "red" or "white," i.e., had to do with marriages or funerals. For the common people many cheap almanacs* were prepared by astrologers and soothsayers in which predictions of the weather were made. For the man who could not read the Chinese script the character of the new year as already said [1] was indicated by the colors of a variegated cow printed on the front page. The "Purple Cow" was a real institution in "Old China." If a splotch of purple was found on the cow's shoulder that would indicate one sort of year, while red or yellow there or elsewhere would mean something else. Thus the wetness or dryness of the year, its heat and cold, snow and frost were foretold. But, perhaps, the Chinese peasant put no more trust in the almanac than our fathers did when they planted potatoes during "the dark of the moon" or consulted the signs of the zodiac in the treatment of disease. Zadkiel's Almanac is still studied by multitudes in Europe.

ECLIPSES

The College of Astronomy also calculated correctly the coming of eclipses of the sun and moon, and set down in the almanac exactly the hour and minute when either of these heavenly bodies would enter and leave the shadow. In accordance with the prediction made, the Board of Rites, which no longer exists, used to arrange for a special service at its yamen, for rescuing the sun from the dragon or the moon from the dog that was seeking to devour it. Of course, the Minister of Rites and the members of the Board of Rites did not really believe that the dragon and dog were attacking the sun or moon, and probably nine-tenths of the people did not share in the ancient superstition; but they observed the custom of beating drums and gongs and making a great noise to frighten the dragon, just as we

* The Nationalist Government has forbidden the issue of such almanacs and banned the celebration of the lunar calendar new year. It stipulates also that all documents to be held legal must bear a Western calendar date. (*Chinese Affairs*, Oct. 15, 1929.)

[1] See Chap. V.

to-day, at Christmas or Eastertide, observe many customs of our forefathers which have lost their original significance.

In 1902 I had the good fortune to attend a service at the yamen of the Board of Rites during an eclipse of the sun. In the great court-yard of the yamen a number of young men and boys, engaged for the purpose, were making an unearthly din with gongs and drums. On a terrace in front of the main hall an altar had been erected, on which incense was burning. Various officers of the Board were in attendance clothed in full regalia—heavily embroidered robes, coral buttons and peacocks' plumes on their hats, strings of court beads around their necks and jade pendants hanging from their girdles. At stated intervals one of them would attend at the altar and reverently kotow, facing the darkening disc of the sun.

A high official, when asked why these ancient ceremonies were continued, replied that the people expected them and would be offended if they were neglected. Perhaps he gave the people too little credit for intelligence, for the neglect of these and other ceremonies of a far more important character, since the establishment of the Republic, has disturbed very little the peace of mind of the Chinese peasant.

CELEBRATION OF NEW YEAR'S DAY

First in time and importance among the festivals is the celebration of the arrival of the new year. That celebration begins one week before the end of the old year. On the 23d of the Twelfth Moon, which in the lunar calendar has but thirty days, each family gathers in the kitchen to worship the Kitchen God, whose image is pasted on the kitchen chimney. On that night he is said to return to heaven, to report to the Ruler of the world the conduct of each member of the household during the year that is drawing to a close.

The mouth of the image is smeared with molasses to indicate the desire of the family that he shall report nothing but good of them. The paper on which the gaudily-colored picture of the Kitchen God is printed is then taken down from the chimney and carried out into the principal court-yard of the home. There it is sometimes placed in a miniature sedan chair made of reeds and paper, which is set on fire. Or, if the palanquin be omitted, the paper image in any case is burned, and in his chariot of fire the guardian of the household ascends on high. One week later on the 30th of the Moon, the last day of the dying year, the family assembles once more in the kitchen to welcome the return of the god. The bursting of strings of fire-crackers proclaims the joy of the household. A new pic-ture is pasted upon the chimney above the kitchen range, the God of the Furnace—or Kitchen—is installed again in the care of the home, and all is in readiness for the beginning of a happy new year.

In the absence of any accurate knowledge of hygiene and in the want of sanitary regulations, perhaps the superstitions of the people with respect to the kitchen range have served a good purpose. The Book of Rewards and Punish-ments, one of the Taoist scriptures, is very specific in its prohibitions regarding conduct in sight of the range. No unseemly act is to be allowed in the presence of the Spirit of the Furnace. One is forbidden to sharpen a knife upon the range. No one must spit toward the altar of the Kitchen God. One must not wash his face or hands in the kitchen, and for a woman to comb her hair in sight of the range is unpardonable.

The origin of this reverence for the furnace and its deity, on whose altar the food of the family is prepared, is lost in the obscurity of antiquity. The worship was common in the days of Confucius, when a well-known proverb said: "It is better to worship the god of the kitchen than the god of the hall." The proverb had a cynical use. It im-plied that one by courting the good-will of underlings could obtain more than by appeals to the superior authori-ties. When an officer, who thought himself more powerful than his lord asked Confucius about the proverb, the Sage at once denounced it saying: "It is not true, for he who

offends against Heaven has no one to whom he can pray";
by which he meant that no mediators or intercessors are
powerful enough to change the purposes of Him who is
perfect in wisdom and justice, "with whom there is not
even the shadow of a turning." But it is interesting to
note that even in the sixth century B.C. the Chinese used
the Kitchen God to intercede for them with the Supreme
Being.

The last night of the old year according to the lunar
calendar is called "*San-shih Wan Shang*," i.e., the "Night
of the Thirtieth." It is a busy time in every Chinese
city. This was particularly true under the old régime,
because all debts must be paid off before the new year
dawns or one loses face. Men have been known, in fact, to
steal in order to pay their debts, rather than begin the new
year with a *loss of reputation*.

Through the dark, dismal streets of an old-fashioned
Chinese city, on the last night of the year, you may see
the paper lanterns hurrying to and fro, carried by their
owners intent on settling their accounts. The shop-keepers
are busy with their books. Belated purchases are being
made for the coming festival. The noise of bursting fire-
crackers is heard everywhere, and it will be long after
midnight before the town settles down to the accustomed
quiet of the dark.

In strong contrast to this noise and bustle is the sabbath-
like stillness of the new year's morning. Every house and
shop is closed. Scarcely anyone is seen upon the street.
This first day is devoted to the family. Everyone wears
his best clothes and goes to the principal hall of the house
to worship the parents and grandparents. Incense is
burned to the deceased ancestors, and all give themselves
up to feasting and drinking and the joy of a family reunion.
Plenty of food and fuel must be on hand for not less than
three days' consumption, for it is impossible to buy anything outside. The well-to-do lay in enough provisions
for a month.

On the third day a few pedlars will be seen selling toys
and confectionery, and jugglers will appear on street

corners and in temple courts to amuse the crowd and gather in a few cash. The humblest citizen will go out to call upon his friends, leaving upon each one a great red card bearing his name and new year congratulations. This red card is giving place to the small white one among those who have studied abroad or who are becoming fond of Western ways. The white card is conventional, to be sure, but it is commonplace and uninteresting in comparison with the red, which is peculiar to the country and carries with it the color of joy.

It seems probable that the Western custom of making a round of calls upon New Year's day is really derived from that of China, one that was introduced by merchants and mariners who traded in the Far East.

THE LANTERN FESTIVAL

After the first few days of the new year business houses begin to open, but public offices in the old days remained closed until the 15th of the First Moon, and normal life does not return until after that date. That is the time of the Lantern Festival. Like the Roman Lupercalia, it is a festival of light, celebrating the lengthening of the day and the returning light of spring. The celebration is not so interesting in the north as it is in the southern part of the country. Peip'ing merely hangs out lanterns before the doors of the homes; but in the vicinity of Shanghai many a village will erect a tall pole, or flag-staff, to the top of which are attached long strings of lanterns that are drawn out at equal distances, making a cone-shaped tent of light around the pole. The peasants arrange processions, too, of men and boys carrying lanterns of every conceivable shape, some representing birds or other animals, some mythical creatures and others merely geo-metrical figures. The bearers are often dressed in costume. Boys on stilts that are hidden under long robes stalk along like giants. Many wear grotesque masques. The most striking lantern is the dragon, often 50 or 60 feet in length, borne by a dozen or more men whose bodies, except their legs, are concealed in the dragon. As this wriggling creature winds its way through the town it seems like a living monster.

This feast of the first full moon of the new year was formerly a very important one in the State Calendar, for it was about that time that the Emperor used to visit the covered altar in the Temple of Heaven to pray for a good harvest. But this service will be described in another chapter.

THE CH'ING MING

Eastertide is an important time in the Christian Church Calendar. It is with us a time when we remember in an especial manner our dead, and endeavor to strengthen our hope of immortality. At about the same season the Chinese celebrate the Ch'ing Ming, the fifth of the solar periods, when the sun is in Aries. It falls about the beginning of April. During this period the Chinese visit the graves of their ancestors and put them in repair. When this has been done and the family burial ground is in perfect order offerings of food and wine are made to the spirits of the dead. This service of communion with those who have passed into the unseen world combines in some degree the sentiments expressed in our Easter observances and our Decoration Day exercises. Most Christian missionaries object to any participation by their Chinese converts in the worship of the dead, but the reverence shown is very like that which we show at the graves of those whom we love, and the offerings of rice and spirits scarcely mean any more than our offerings of flowers. In fact, in some Christian countries offerings of food are placed upon the graves on All Souls Eve. The Jesuit missionaries in the seventeenth century tolerated ancestor worship among Chinese Christians, and when the practice was criticised by other orders the Emperor K'angshi was asked whether or not the worship was of the same sort as that paid to the Supreme Being. He replied that it was not. The Catholic missionaries who opposed the practice then appealed to the Pope, who decided that the worship of ancestors was incompatible with the worship of God. The Jesuits were recalled from Peking and were replaced by the Lazarists. The influence once exercised by Ricci, Schaal and Verbiest over the Court at Peking was never recovered, and the Emperor, who had been favorably impressed by them, became thereafter suspicious of the aims of the missionaries and hostile rather than favorable.

There are many broad-minded men among the missionaries to-day who would be glad to see the Ch'ing Ming celebration not only tolerated by the Church but transformed into a Christian festival, just as the Easter of our ancestors, once a heathen festival, was consecrated to the celebration of the Resurrection.

THE DRAGON BOAT FESTIVAL

The next feast of importance in the Chinese calendar is that of the Fifth Moon, the Dragon Boat Festival. According to tradition this festival celebrates the patriotism of Ch'ü Yuan, a Minister of the State of Ch'u during the Chou Dynasty, who repeatedly urged upon his king a course of reform which the monarch refused to take. In protest the minister committed suicide by drowning himself in the Tungting Lake, included within the boundaries of modern Hunan Province. In Foochow five days are given to the feast; in central and northern China three days are devoted —the fourth, fifth and sixth of the Moon; but it is the fifth of the Fifth Moon that is the great day of the feast. This is one of the settling days in China. Accounts are supposed to be settled at New Year, on the fifth of the Fifth Moon, and on the fifteenth of the Eighth Moon.

At the beginning of the Fifth Moon every house, as a rule, has a bundle of artemisia and sweet flag suspended at the door-way. These aromatic plants are said to keep away evil spirits. The particular connection with Ch'ü Yuan does not appear to be known. Perhaps the custom is only incidentally associated with the festival, for it is a custom of the Chinese to burn dried aromatic plants during the summer to keep off mosquitoes. It is worth noting, however, that as the festival originated in the search with boats for the body of the drowned statesman, the association with death would naturally suggest the use of aromatic plants to keep off the evil spirits of death. At inquests in central China, as already related, the magistrate after completing the examination steps over burning artemisia, or some other aromatic plant, to purify himself and keep the evil spirit from following him to his home.

The principal exercise in celebration of this feast is the racing of the dragon boats. These graceful boats are long and narrow and end at the bows in a dragon's head. Imitating the boatmen that searched for the body of Ch'ü Yuan, the young men engage in swift racing on the lakes, rivers and canals, and the winning crews receive prizes for their skill.

THE HERD BOY AND WEAVER MAID

The Seventh Moon is distinguished by two popular festivals—one of ancient, unknown origin, the other a Buddhistic feast. The ancient folk tale relates to two stars, one on either side the Milky Way, which the Chinese call the Heavenly River. The stars are in Aquila and Vega and are said to be, the first a herd boy, the second a weaver girl. The story is a pretty one. It forms the theme of many a painting and is often illustrated in embroideries.

The weaver maid was the daughter of the Sun God. He thought she was too closely confined by her work and decided to give her in marriage to the herd boy. But after her marriage her character entirely changed. She became idle and foolish and neglected her duties. The Sun God was wroth and determined to separate her from her husband. He directed a flock of magpies to make a bridge with their wings across the Heavenly River, and sent the herd boy to the other side of the stream. They were forbidden to meet except once a year. On the Seventh of the

Seventh Moon the magpies flock together again and make a bridge, over which the weaver maid lightly runs to meet her husband. One day only can she spend with him, after which she must return to her work. But if there should be rain on the Seventh day of the Seventh Moon she will be unable to see her husband until another year has passed, for the River of Heaven is brimming full, and even one drop more of water will cause it to overflow and sweep away the bridge. Therefore, the maidens and wives of China pray for clear skies on the night of the Seventh of the Seventh Moon. They make offerings of watermelons and other fruits, of vegetables also and cakes. They burn incense and pray for skill in needle-work.

The Heavenly River, or Milky Way, according to Chinese mythology, is the source of the Yellow River. A mighty rebel against one of the ancient mythical rulers of China butted his head against the north-western pillar of the sky and broke it down. This allowed the River of Heaven to enter the earth. In the second century B.C. a famous Chinese explorer, Chang Ch'ien, reached the head waters of the Yellow River. The story tellers enlarged upon his exploit by combining his real achievement with the ancient folk tale. They tell us that Chang Ch'ien sailed many days upon the bosom of the mighty stream until he arrived at a place where he found a boy on one side of the stream herding cattle, and on the other side a young woman weaving cloth. He enquired the name of the place, whereupon the young woman handed him her shuttle and told him to carry it to Chün Pi'ng at the Chinese capital. Chün Pi'ng was a celebrated astronomer. He at once recognized the shuttle as belonging to the Weaver Maid, and asked Chang the date of his visit at the place where she lived. On learning the date he looked up his records and discovered that, sure enough, at that very time he saw a strange star come between the Herd Boy and Weaver Maid. Thus there could no longer be any doubt about the Yellow River's origin being in the Milky Way.

ALL SOULS FESTIVAL

There is, however, a more important festival in the Seventh Moon. This is the Buddhist feast of All Souls, or more properly the Feast for Hungry Ghosts. It begins on the 15th day of the Seventh Moon and lasts until the 30th. Throughout this period offerings are made to the dead, but particularly to the unhappy dead, those known as the "orphaned spirits," that is to say, those who have no living descendants to keep up the sacrifices to them. The offerings frequently are imitations, made in paper, of money, garments, houses, horses, servants and other useful articles. The images are burned and the dead are supposed to obtain the ethereal counterparts of the objects offered. On the warm summer nights of this season one may watch the burning offerings floating down the river—offerings made to the spirits of those who have been drowned.

There is a great celebration of the festival at the monastery of *Ch'ing Liang Shan,* or "Clear Cool Mountain," a hill within the walls of the city of Nanking, but among the bamboo groves and gardens of the northern part of the city, far away from the busy streets. This monastery is dedicated to *Ti Tsang,* the ruler of Hades. More than one story probably is combined in the account given of his life.

In his first incarnation he was a maiden who was much disturbed by her mother's unbelief. By filial piety she was enabled to rescue her mother from the pangs of hell. In a later re-birth the maiden became a Prince of Siam. Historically such a prince is said to have come to *Chiu Hua Shan,* a mountain in the province of Anhui, not far from Nanking. He led such a holy life as a monk that after his death he was identified with Ti Tsang, and is said to have charge of the world of the dead.

During the last fifteen days of the Seventh Moon the people come in crowds from all quarters to worship at the Clear Cool Mountain. At the foot of the mountain a fair is held. All sorts of notions, toys and curios are offered for sale, while jugglers and mountebanks amuse and enter-

tain the pilgrims for the few cash which they can collect
from them. Some of these pilgrims have come scores of
miles, bowing in prayer and striking their foreheads in
the dust at every second or third step of the long journey,
in fulfillment of a vow made, perhaps, to save a sick parent.
The most devout carry their rosaries and count their beads
incessantly. Some come to seek cure for themselves or
for others. The air of the temple is heavy with the odor
of incense and the smoke of thousands of candles offered
upon the altar before the huge bronze image of Ti Tsang.
The face of the idol, like that of the Buddha, is placid and
benignant.

The worshiper as he enters the temple first makes an
offering of money, which is thrown into a huge chest. He
then lights candles and bundles of incense sticks, which are
placed upon the altar. Not until his offerings are made
does he kneel, kotow and pray. Arising from his knees
he takes from the altar a vase of sortilege rods, which he
shakes gently as he faces the idol. When one rod projects
beyond the others or falls to the ground he seizes it and
hands it to a monk, who examines the number which it
bears and opens a drawer that has the same number. A
slip of paper taken from the drawer will have printed
upon it the answer to the prayer. These answers are
frequently in rhyme, and tell the worshiper what the
prospect of recovery is and what must be done to obtain
a healing. Some are so superstitious that after obtaining
the oracular response they burn it, drop the ashes in a
cup of tea, and drink the whole for good luck.

But the main purpose of the festival, as already said, is
to relieve the orphaned spirits. A deep-toned bell is tolled
once or twice a minute. It has a very musical sound and
can be heard at a great distance, above the noise of the
city streets. Like all Buddhist bells it is struck by a
wooden beam, so that the harsh, clanging sound of western
bells is lacking. As long as the sound can be heard, it is
said the souls in torment have surcease of pain.

On the 30th day of the month, the last great day of the
feast, which is All Souls Day, the spirits of the dead are

believed to enjoy a holiday. They are released from their prisons for that one day and freed from pain.

The 15th day of the Eighth Moon is another feast day. This is the Eighth Moon Festival, which, as already said, is one of the settling days of the year. The Chinese, so to speak, have but three quarters in the year, that is to say, they settle accounts three times in the year instead of quarterly. The 15th day of the Eighth Moon is the day of the full moon, and it is the time of the Harvest Moon, which rises immediately after sunset and seems to prolong the day. This is called the Moon's Birthday. The day before and that following it are usually included in the celebration. The Moon is the object of worship at this festival. She is the Queen of Heaven to whom the women offer moon cakes. The moon cake usually has a crescent on its surface. Some support a small pagoda, while others have an image of the rabbit that is said to inhabit the moon. According to Chinese legend it is a rabbit pounding the drug of immortality, and not a man's face, that we see in the moon. The Chinese, however, do have another legend of a lady in the moon. She, too, is sometimes represented on this festive occasion. According to the tale that is told she was the beautiful wife of an ancient worthy who was given the elixir of immortality by the fairy queen. The wife stole the elixir and drank it, in punishment for which she was transformed into a frog and translated to the moon, where she may still be seen.

The feast is marked by out-door enjoyment and general holiday making. Fairs are held at which toys are sold, particularly small pagodas made of clay and highly colored. At Foochow and in the vicinity dolls are offered for sale. Parents who have had a child born during the preceding twelve months buy a doll to represent it. The child's name is written upon it, and thereafter it is used in various idolatrous ceremonies to represent the child. If the child dies before maturity (sixteen years of age) the doll is buried with it in the grave.

In many parts of China at this season the Bushel Mother is worshiped. This is a female said to reside in the constellation of the Great Bear. This is known to the Chinese as the "Measure," or "Bushel," just as we often speak of it as the "Great Dipper." As is well known there are seven stars in the constellation. Flags bearing the seven stars properly arranged to represent the constellation are flown from tea houses during the festival.

THE NINTH MOON FEAST

The Ninth Moon also has its festival, which falls on the 9th day of the month. This is the festival of "Going up on a high place." It originated, it is said, in some great calamity, the details of which appear to be forgotten. An ancient seer had warning of it in advance. He went to the hills to spend the day and so escaped. In memory of this, and to avoid any calamity that may be threatening, the people betake themselves to the top of a hill or go up on the city wall. In some places the day is given largely to kite-flying.

THE BIRTHDAY OF THE REPUBLIC

Since the revolution of 1911 a new holiday has been added to the calendar, the 10th of October, the anniversary of the revolt at Wuch'ang, headed by Li Yuan-hung and his troops. This anniversary is kept according to the Western calendar, which was formally adopted by the Republic. The celebration has a patriotic character—the flying of flags, processions with bands of music, public meetings with speech making, and in some places exhibitions of relics of the revolution and pictures of its leaders. At the celebration in Peking in 1912 and 1913 the edict of abdication, on yellow satin, sealed with the seal of the Empress Lung Yü, who issued it, was placed on exhibition under a richly decorated canopy erected before the principal entrance to the Imperial City.

One of the most important festivals of the year falls in the Eleventh Moon according to the old lunar calendar. This is the feast of the winter solstice, held on the longest night in the year. It is interesting to note how wide-spread among many races and nations is the observance of a festival at this season. Our own Christmas, which falls at this time, is undoubtedly a transformation of a much older festival observed by the Romans, as well as by the Teutonic tribes and the Britons. The encroachment of the night upon the day, in the season of frost and snow and all the chilliness and gloom of dying nature, must have very early attracted the attention of men, so that the cessation of that encroachment of darkness would become an occasion for rejoicing.

In China the spirit world is the land of darkness. The ghostly powers are more active in the dark. The spirits of the dead are worshiped as dwelling in the north, on the side of darkness. This season of the winter solstice became, therefore, long, long ago, a time consecrated in an especial manner to the worship of the dead. At this season of the year the ancestors are worshiped, not at the grave but in the ancestral temple, or in the principal hall of the house where the tablets are kept on the family altar. This is the great family festival of the year. The wandering sons return, if possible, to the home of their fathers. There is a joyous re-union. On this long night the members of the household gather in the hall, where a rich feast of smoking viands is spread before the altar. Chairs for the deceased ancestors are placed on the north side of the table. The living head of the family, supported by his wife and children, stands reverently on the south side facing the north, with the table between himself and the ancestral tablets. Falling upon his knees three times he kotows, striking his head thrice with each kneeling, in worship of the dear departed, and as if inviting them to share in the feast. The family then all stand reverently for a few moments, while the ancestral spirits are supposed to partake of the ethereal portions of the feast. Thus the whole family in heaven and on earth are re-united.

Under the imperial régime this was a time, too, for the most solemn service in the worship of the Most High, but this subject will be treated in another chapter.

CHAPTER XI

CONFUCIUS AND HIS TEACHING

Hence the sage forms a ternion with Heaven and Earth, and stands side by side with spiritual beings, in order to the right ordering of government.—Li Ki, translated by Legge.

The Master said: ''A transmitter and not an originator, a believer in and lover of antiquity, I venture to compare myself with our ancient worthy P'eng.''

Analects of Confucius, Soothill's Translation.

Confucius was born in 551 B.C. at the town of Ch'üfu [1] in what is to-day the province of Shantung. At that time the district was included in the state of Lu, which was a dukedom. The name, Confucius, is a Latinized form of the Chinese words, *K'ung Fu-tzu*, i.e., ''the teacher, K'ung.'' K'ung was his surname. His personal name was Ch'iu. He was also called Chung-ni, for a Chinese usually has several names—his ''milk-name,'' or baby name, his school-name, and his name given on coming of age. For distinguished men, servants of the State, there is also a posthumous name.

The family of Confucius originally lived in the state of Sung, which joined Lu on the west and occupied a region which to-day is partly embraced within the province of Shantung and partly in Honan. One of his ancestors in Sung, named K'ung Chia, had a beautiful wife who was coveted by a powerful minister of state. The husband, K'ung Chia, was murdered and an attempt was made to abduct the wife. She, however, resisted and committed suicide. Because of this outrage, the family removed from Sung and settled in Lu.

The father of Confucius was a noted military leader and a man of courage and of great physical strength. It is

[1] Not to be confounded with *Chefoo* in the same province.

related of him that once when attacking a city some of
his followers were led by a ruse to enter the open gate of
the town and would have been entrapped there. But, just
as the warden was about to drop the portcullis, the father
of the sage caught it with both hands and upheld it until
all his men had escaped. This Chinese Samson was an
old man, 70 years of age, when Confucius was born. The
mother was a young woman, a second wife. The first wife
had had nine daughters, but no sons. A concubine had
borne a son, but he was a cripple. The birth of the boy,
Confucius, was therefore, an occasion of great rejoicing.

The Confucian books, as a rule, are free from tales of
the marvelous, but some uncanonical works give account
of certain miraculous occurrences that are said to have
attended the entrance of Confucius into the world. These
tales no doubt were invented by over-zealous disciples, who
wanted to make their teacher the equal of others concerning
whom such stories were told. Before the birth of the Sage,
we are informed, a spirit appeared to the young wife and
announced to her that she was to become the mother of
a great teacher. About the same time a unicorn was led
into her presence by five aged men. Around its horn she
fastened a ribbon. Long years afterward, so the story
runs, when Confucius was an old man, the unicorn was
captured by hunters with the ribbon still clinging to its
horn. When Confucius saw it he realized that its appearance presaged his death, and he wept. According to other
accounts his birth was signalized by the appearance of
angels in the sky and the sounds of sweet music.

A work known as "The Chia Yü," or "Family Traditions," gives us a few interesting details of his early life.
His father died when he was but three years old, and, like
his greatest disciple, Mencius, he was brought up by a
widowed mother. She passed away when he was twenty-
two years of age. Of her he was naturally very fond. It
is remarkable that, according to the Li Ki, he did not know
where his father was buried. He made enquiries, and,
taking up the remains, interred them in the same grave
with his mother. A storm arose just as the burial was

completed and washed away the mound. This deeply affected the young man, who felt that he must have been at fault in some way in the construction of the grave. As a child he showed a great fondness for religious exercises. He loved to play at conducting the temple services and making the offerings required. He was a bright student, and made such rapid progress that at twenty-two years he already had a reputation as a scholar and had gathered a band of earnest students around him. In his old age, when reviewing his career, he said:

At fifteen I was bent on learning;
At thirty I stood fast;
At forty I had no doubts;
At fifty I knew the will of God;
At sixty my ear was open to the truth;
At seventy I could follow my desires without transgressing the "square" (i.e. the bounds of right).[2]

In this he recalled his early zeal in the pursuit of knowledge. He was married at nineteen, and at twenty was the father of his only son, Li. The name *Li,* "a carp," was given the son, it is thought, in order to perpetuate the memory of the then reigning Duke, who sent a present of a carp at the time of the child's birth. This is probable, for Confucius at the time was in the employ of the ruler, as steward of his estate. We know very little about the wife of Confucius. She was a young lady from the state of Sung. The marriage, like that of the great Greek teacher, Socrates, does not appear to have been a happy one. Tradition says that Confucius divorced his wife, but the belief rests upon an obscure passage in the Li Ki,[3] or "Book of Rites," which is capable of quite a different interpretation. It is recorded of him, however, that a year after his wife's death, when his son still kept up the formal wailing for his mother, Confucius rebuked him for his excessive grief.[4] This incident and others related of him would seem to indicate that Confucius was a great stickler

2 Analects II:4.
3 Li Ki; T'an Kung, Section I, part I:4.
4 Ibid., Section I, part I:28.

for form, an unimaginative and an unsympathetic literalist, who placed the letter above the spirit of the regulations. If so, one would feel a good deal of sympathy with the wife who had had to live so many years with such a pedantic worshiper of conventions.

But we are scarcely justified in making such an estimate of his character. A man of that sort would hardly have attracted to himself such a group of devoted disciples as Confucius had, or have been able to hold their affection and loyalty as he did, through years of apparent failure and misfortune. His tastes, too, would indicate a companionable spirit. He was fond of music and played well on the lute. He had faith in the salutary influence of good music upon the human character. Shakespeare's lines would have delighted him:

> The man that hath no music in his soul,
> And is not moved by concord of sweet sounds,
> Is fit for treason, strategems and spoils;
> Let no such man be trusted.

He studied music under a celebrated master, and when in after years he visited the state of Ch'i, and heard the *Shao,* it is said he knew not the taste of meat for three months, and exclaimed "I never imagined there could be such music as this." [5] He said to his disciples: "A man's character is formed by the Odes, developed by the Rites, and perfected by Music.[6] And on another occasion he said: "When you enter a state you can know what the people have been taught. . . . If they are large-hearted and generous, bland and honest, they have been taught from the Book of Music." [7]

Confucius was an earnest student and he was also an accomplished musician, but this is not all. He was not indifferent to the pleasures of out-door life. He was fond of archery. This was one of the accomplishments of a gentleman in his day. It was one of the six arts considered

[5] Analects VII:13.
[6] Analects VIII:8.
[7] Li Ki XXIII:1 (Legge).

essential to a liberal education. The tournaments were conducted with a great deal of ceremony. A chivalrous bearing towards competitors was cultivated. The shooting was accompanied by music, and one could discharge his arrow only when the proper note was sounded.[8] It was the teaching of the day that archery was a test of character. He kept a stable, too, which implies a measure of out-door life. In fact, he was fond of horses and dogs, which would indicate that he was something other than a student, that he was, in fact, a natural man among men. A touching incident is told of his fondness for his dog, that, when the animal died, he had the body wrapped in the silk covering of an old umbrella to keep the earth from touching it when he laid it away in a carefully prepared grave. He was also a good sportsman, for we are told that he never used a net in fishing, but a line only, and that he never shot at a bird while it was at rest.[9]

All these things indicate that Confucius must have been a very likable human being. The very tenacity with which he clung to old forms was perhaps but a manifestation of a dominant trait of his character—a trait more particularly shown in his young manhood—that of a courageous adherence to his convictions: "To see the right and not do it," said he, "that is cowardice." It was, no doubt, his keen perception of the moral principle underlying any question of conduct, and his resolute insistence upon an effort to realize his ideals, that won the admiration of his followers and bound them to him.

HIS VISIT TO THE CAPITAL

In 518 B.C. a prominent citizen of the town, dying, directed that his young son should be placed under the tutelage of Confucius, who was then thirty-three years of age. This boy had a chum who came with him to school, and who one day heard the teacher express an ardent desire to visit the national capital, in order that he might witness

8 Li Ki XLIII.
9 Analects VII:26.

the service in the royal temple and make enquiries of Lao
Tzu and others concerning the ritual. The chum reported
the incident to the reigning duke, and the duke at once
provided the means for such a visit. Confucius accepted
the generous offer, and made what was then a long and
difficult journey to Loyang, on the southern bank of the
Yellow River in north-western Honan. Even to-day, if
made in a cart over the rough roads of China, such a
journey would require ten or twelve days. In Confucius'
time certainly it needed no less.

In those days for a Chinese in a distant state to visit
the capital was as great an event in his life as it used to
be in the United States for an American to make a tour
of Europe. At Loyang, where many heroes of his race
had lived and died, he saw the ancient palaces and temples.
He visited the great park of the Temple of Heaven in the
suburbs. From childhood he had taken delight in the
splendid pageantry of the ritual prescribed by the national
religion. But up to the time of this visit what he had
seen had been but the lesser rites observed in the ducal
temple or in the worship of his ancestors. Never before
had he seen an altar erected to Shang Ti, the Most High,
and he doubtless looked with a thrill of awe upon the
vessels of the sanctuary which perhaps had been used by
King Wu, the founder of the Chou Dynasty, perhaps by
T'ang the Completer, the earlier hero of the House of
Shang. He saw in the palaces the portraits of the great
sovereigns of whose deeds he had read in his youth, and
he must have felt a pang of sorrow when he looked upon
the decaying city and the neglected court and realized that
the House of Chou was doomed.

He called upon Li Erh, or Lao Tan, as he is also called,
the unintentional founder of Taoism, a man who was as
far removed in his sentiments and sympathies from the
modern Taoist monk as Spinoza from Madame Blavatsky.
Li Erh is known to the world generally as Lao Tzu, the
"Old Philosopher." He was custodian of the archives,
or "Keeper of the Rolls," as one might call him, in the
ancient capital of China. Confucius was a born anti-

quarian. He called himself "a lover of the ancients."
He knew that Lao Tzu could explain to him many passages
in the sacred books, and enable him to understand better
than he had understood how certain requirements of the
ritual were to be fulfilled. But Lao Tzu was too near to
the court and temple, too familiar with the ceremonies
and with the frailties of kings, to be greatly impressed,
either by the pagentry of the one or the personality of the
other. To Confucius' enquiries he is reported by Ssu-ma
Ch'ien, the great historian, to have replied as follows:

> Those about whom you enquire have mouldered with their bones
> into dust. Nothing but their words remain. When the hour of
> the great man has struck he rises to leadership, but before his
> time has come he is hampered in all that he attempts. I have
> heard that the successful merchant carefully conceals his wealth
> and acts as though he had nothing—that the great man, though
> abounding in achievements, is simple in his manners and appear-
> ance. Get rid of your pride and your many ambitions, your
> affectations and your extravagant aims. Your character gains
> nothing from all these. This is my advice to you.

The language probably is colored, if not invented, by some
Taoist author, for the Taoists have not loved Confucius.
Ssu-ma Ch'ien records the alleged conversation, but by
his phraseology casts doubt upon the authenticity of the
report. Lao Tzu undoubtedly was curt, and if he was
caustic in his comments they would not be altogether out
of harmony with his style shown in the Tao Te King. But
regardless of the manner in which he received Confucius.
the latter was deeply impressed, according to the reports
that have been transmitted. He said to his disciples:

> The birds—I know they can fly; the fishes—I know they can
> swim; the wild beasts—I know they can run. The runner may
> be caught by a trap, the swimmer may be taken with a line,
> and the flyer may be shot by an arrow. But, as for the dragon,
> I am unable to know how he rises on the winds and the clouds
> to the sky. To-day I have seen Lao Tzu; he is like the dragon.[10]

If we accept the report of this interview as substantially
correct, we may explain Lao Tzu's attitude towards Con-

[10] Ssu-ma Ch'ien, Shih Chi, chap. 63, Lao Tzu Chuan.

fucius by recalling that Confucius was full of the enthusiasm of youth, that he was making his first long journey from home, and that he was deeply interested in the sights of the capital and the places of historic interest. All seemed very wonderful to him. He doubtless showed great eagerness in his questioning, and he may have been voluble in expressing his own opinions upon certain points. We may remember, too, that Lao Tzu was old, that he had lost his illusions, if he ever had any, and that he was a quietist. He thought the world too much governed and very badly governed. He says in the Tao Te King: "They who know don't talk; they who talk don't know." He disliked the busybody reformer who thought he could correct the faults of the world by new rules and laws. He said:

The people are difficult to govern because too much learnedness is employed. To govern the state with learnedness is the spoiling of the state. To avoid the use of learnedness in government, that is the happiness of the state.

He urged a "back to nature" movement. He wanted to promote the return of the people to the simple life, to go back to the use of the knotted cords instead of writing, to have men live and die in their native villages, content with their surroundings and unacquainted with the people even in the nearest neighboring state. His ideal man was one free from many desires, one who was not learned and who did not prize things difficult to obtain. He would let things alone and allow nature to pursue her own course. His most striking utterances are in paradoxical form, and his criticisms of the world of his day were almost vitriolic in their sarcasm. Thus he says:

When the great *Tao* is forgotten, then we have virtue and justice. Learnedness and cleverness appear, then we have much hypocrisy. It is when family relations are inharmonious that we hear of filial piety and affection. The government is confused and disorderly, and then we talk of loyalty and fidelity.

Abjure holiness and cast away learnedness, and the people will benefit a hundred fold. Abjure mercy and cast away justice, and the people will revive their filial piety and fraternal affection. Abjure your cleverness and cast away your profit, and robbery and thieving will disappear.[11]

Are the people starving? Because their rulers consume too many taxes therefore they starve. Are the people difficult to govern? Because their rulers are busy about it, therefore they are difficult to govern. Do the people think lightly of death? Because of their intense desire for real life, therefore they make light of death.[12]

So, if this eager young school-master from one of the distant provinces began to talk to Lao Tzu learnedly about the ancient worthies, and perhaps expound theories for the amelioration of the condition of the world, it would not have been unnatural for Lao Tzu to look upon the stranger as too inquisitive, and make an attempt to puncture what may have seemed to him a bubble of self-complacency colored with iridescent dreams. He might then advise the young man not to be so well satisfied with himself and to give up his extravagant aims. According to the Book of Rites, Confucius in later years occasionally referred to other conversations with Lao Tzu, in which he had obtained information of various requirements in the ceremonial regulations.

The visit to the capital undoubtedly enhanced the reputation of Confucius in his home town. It is said that his following considerably increased thereafter. But he was not popular with all classes. To a good many people he seemed to be a visionary, too unpractical for a work-a-day world; and he was too stern a moralist to suit the careless nobles who ruled the land. It will help us to understand the situation to call to mind the disturbed political condition of the empire.

CONDITION OF THE EMPIRE

The Chou Dynasty was established in 1122 B.C. The founder, King Wu, made the rather natural mistake of

11 Tao Te King, 18 and 19.
12 Ibid., 75.

dividing the empire among his near relatives, who were bound together in a feudal system for the support of the crown. During the first two or three generations the system worked very well; the rulers of the various states, all related by blood to the head of the Kingdom, were loyal to him and maintained friendly relations one with another. But as the centuries passed, the tie of blood grew weaker. The Middle Kingdom, in which the capital was located, was one of the smaller states. Trusting to the support of its vassals its own military forces were insignificant. The outlying states had room to expand and gradually grew large, prosperous and powerful. Those on the frontiers, exposed to raids by barbarous tribes of alien peoples, grew more and more experienced in war, and became militaristic and aggressive in their character. New states sprang up on the borders, ruled by chieftains who were not related to the Sovereign. The authority of the King gradually waned as the strength of his vassals increased. The most powerful of the latter assumed the title of King. Their allegiance to the head of the empire became formal only. Since he was the representative of the eldest branch of the house of Chou they paid him honor. His authority became religious rather than political in character. In the time of Confucius the great states had become practically independent. They made war upon one another without regard to the will of the Chou monarch, and entered into treaties with each other as though they were entirely separate and each sovereign within its own boundaries. A situation existed not altogether unlike that which was seen in Europe after the downfall of the Roman Empire, when the former vassals of the Emperor became sovereigns of independent states.

One of the frontier states, that of Ch'in, in the northwest, whose ruler was not related to the Chous, finally in 256 B.C. overturned the Chou Dynasty, swallowed up the territories of all the states, and established a new empire.

But in the days of Confucius this event was still more than two centuries in the future. Confucius mourned over the weakness of the central government, and constantly condemned the assumption by feudal princes of titles, honors and functions belonging only to the king.

It is interesting to remember that the civilization of China was carried into Japan, and that the Confucian classics became the Bible of Japan. The saints and heroes of the Chou Dynasty became the saints and heroes admired by the Japanese, and so long years afterward, in the 19th century A.D., we find in feudal Japan a state of affairs very similar to that which existed in China in the days of Confucius—the Mikado secluded, reigning but not ruling, a divinity regarded with religious veneration by the multitude, but the puppet of designing ministers and feudal lords, who made war one upon another.

The misgovernment and oppression which afflicted China in the days of Confucius stirred the indignation of that young reformer. While traveling with some of his disciples along an unfrequented road one day he came upon a woman weeping by a grave. He sent one of his disciples to offer condolence. The disciple said: ''You weep as if you had suffered many sorrows.'' She replied: ''It is true. My father-in-law was killed here by a tiger. Later my husband was also killed here by a tiger, and now my son has died in the same way.'' The Master asked her: ''Why don't you leave the place?'' She replied: ''There is no oppressive government here.'' Then said Confucius to his disciples: ''Remember, my little children; oppressive government is more terrible than tigers.'' [13]

This incident probably happened when Confucius was leaving his native state to go into exile. There was civil war in the state of Lu. The legitimate ruler had been dethroned, and had fled to the neighboring state of Ch'i. Confucius, who was a stickler for legitimacy, followed the duke. While living in the state of Ch'i its ruler offered him the revenues of a small district, which would suffice for his support. Confucius declined. To his disciples he said: ''A gentleman will not receive payment except for service given, and although I have offered the duke advice he has not acted upon it.'' His fastidiousness in this

[13] Book of Rites, T'an Kung, Sec. II, part 3:10, Legge.

regard was somewhat moderated in later years, for we
learn that, when traveling in the state of Wei some twenty
years later, the duke of that state gave him a stipend of
60,000 measures of grain for his support, which he accepted
although the ruler of Wei was notoriously corrupt.

HIS OFFICIAL CAREER

Confucius remained in Ch'i about eight years, and upon
his return to his native state lived quietly occupied with
his researches until the year 501 B.C., when at fifty-one
years of age he accepted an appointment as governor of
Chungtu. He now had opportunity to put his theory of
government to the test. Thus far he had been looked upon
as a visionary.

The ruler of Ch'i had found pleasure in his conversation
during his sojourn in that state, and had been disposed
to employ him, but had been dissuaded by his minister, who
showed a contempt for the acedemic theories of a mere
student who lacked practical experience. One cannot avoid
a feeling that the minister was not altogether wrong when
Confucius' theories are considered. He held that a virtuous ruler could reform a state by force of his example,
that the people would imitate him spontaneously and flock
to his standard, "as the grass bows when the wind blows."
He said: "He who rules by his virtuous character is like
the polar star, which rests in its place while all the other
stars revolve about it." [14] On another occasion he declared:

If you guide the people by rules and correct them by penalties,
they will evade them and lose their sense of shame; but, if you
guide them by a virtuous example and correct them by your own
piety, they will keep their sense of shame and, moreover, imitate
your example. [15]

We cannot deny the influence of a good example, but we
can scarcely accept it as a ruling principle of political

[14] Analects II:1.
[15] Ibid., II:3.

science, and there can be no doubt that Confucius over-emphasized its importance. When asked upon one occasion for a definition of government, he replied with a pun:

> *Cheng?* (government)—that is *cheng* (uprightness). If you, as leader, are upright, who will dare not to be upright![16]

On another occasion he said:

> When the ruler is pious, none among the people will dare to be irreverent. When the ruler loves justice, none among the people will dare to be otherwise. When the ruler loves good faith, none among the people will dare not to keep faith. When the ruler is of such sort, the people of the four quarters will flock to him with their children strapped upon their backs.[17]

In explanation of Confucius' theory, however, it must be stated that by a "virtuous example" he did not refer alone to the private character of the ruler; he included the right conduct of government. The word, *te*, which he employed, and which is translated "virtue," is that which is used in the title of Lao Tzu's work, the Tao Te King, and which there means the practical exemplification of the *Tao*, or "teaching." Confucius undoubtedly used the word in a similar sense. When he spoke of a "virtuous example" he did not refer so much to the negative virtues—the absence of vice—as he did to the active virtues. Of these the Chinese count six: "Wisdom, humanity, holiness, justice, moderation, and conciliation." Thus, taken in the sense in which Confucius meant his teaching to be taken, the ruler who governed by a virtuous example was one who governed wisely, with a due regard for human rights, who did not neglect the national altars, who was always just, but not unduly severe, and who sought peace rather than strife. Such a monarch would deserve to win the confidence and obedience of his subjects. That this was the meaning of the Sage is shown in numerous sayings uttered by him upon the art of government. When asked by one of his disciples about the proper administration of government

[16] Ibid., XII:17.
[17] Analects XIII:4.

he explained that it consisted, among other things, in promoting those enterprises on which the people depended for their gains, yet without wasteful expenditure of the revenues, and in using the corvee—which was common in those days—only upon works of real necessity, and then without interfering with the peasants' agricultural occupations. He pointed out, too, that a ruler should not become so filled with a sense of his own dignity as to neglect his duties, no matter how unimportant they might seem, and that he should not be guilty of putting men to death for violation of law, who had never been taught their duty under the law.[18]

On his journey to the state of Wei he commented on the rapid growth of the population. A disciple asked him saying: "Now that the people are so numerous what should be done for them?" He answered: "Enrich them." "What then?" was the next query. "Educate them," he said.[19] Thus he recognized the welfare of the people as the supreme duty of the state; and it is noteworthy that he made their material prosperity first in the order of importance. As modifying this opinion another conversation may be quoted in which he declared that the essentials of good government were "sufficient food, sufficient military force, and the confidence of the people." When asked which should be given up, in case all these could not be obtained, he replied: "The military." If two of the three had to be abandoned he declared that the next thing to be surrendered should be "sufficient food," "for," said he, "men have always had to die, but without faith no people can stand."[20]

His disciples, looking back to the brief term of his public service in the state of Lu, thought that they found his theories confirmed by this practical experience, for they reported that he made rules for the support of the living and the worship of the dead, that old and young had food suited to their needs, the relations of the sexes were care-

18 Ibid., XX:2.
19 Analects XIII:9.
20 Ibid., XII:7.

fully regulated, and such good order was maintained that anything lost upon the road was never wrongfully appropriated, and all fraud and cheating disappeared. The duke, astonished by the results, is said to have asked whether the same method of government might be applied to the whole dukedom, and Confucius is reported as replying: "Certainly, not only to the state but to the whole empire." Not long afterwards the duke appointed Confucius Minister of Justice, and crime rapidly diminished. It became unnecessary to apply the penal code. It must be admitted, however, that his theory as to the influence of example was not fully confirmed by his experience, for his own filial piety, in accordance with that theory, ought to have made impossible in his jurisdiction such a case of grossly unfilial conduct as has been mentioned in an earlier chapter, one that was brought before him for judgment. A father demanded the death penalty for his unruly son. This was the punishment provided by law. Confucius refused to put the son to death, and imprisoned both the disobedient son and the complaining father. The duke objected, but the judge declared: "If seniors neglect their duty and yet demand that their juniors be put to death, it is not just. This father has never taught his son to be filial."

In 496 B.C. he became Prime Minister of his native state, and it seems probable that it was during his exercise of this office that he served as Master of Ceremonies at an interview between the Duke of Lu and the Duke of Ch'i, for the negotiation of a treaty. A plot had been formed for the kidnaping of the ruler of Lu. Confucius discovered it and prevented its execution. Then he skillfully made such good use of the incident that he obtained an advantageous treaty of alliance and a retrocession of territory that had been taken from Lu.

His accession to this high post in his native state is represented by his disciples as having aroused the envy and fears of the Duke of Ch'i. The latter, we are informed, thereupon resorted to an unworthy strategem to win the Duke of Lu from his attachment to the Sage. A present of eighty beautiful chorus girls and 120 thoroughbred horses was sent to the ruler of Lu. He accepted them, and was soon so absorbed in pleasure as to neglect the duties of state. This discouraged Confucius. He felt that he could no longer exercise a good influence, and accordingly resigned.

HIS EXILE

For five years he had served his prince in various capacities and with considerable success, but five years was a brief period and his influence must have been slight after all, if a girl and a horse could cause such a sudden and complete disregard of his advice, and such utter neglect of the administration as is represented. Sadly and reluctantly he left his native land and went abroad, in the hope of finding elsewhere a ruler who would accept his theories of government, and bring in the reforms that would cure the crying ills of the time.

For thirteen years he wandered in this self-imposed exile. He visited various states, was received with honor in some, but failed to find that acceptance for his principles which he sought. He visited the state of Wei a number of times, and seems to have had a liking for its ruler. At one time he accepted a stipend from him, as already said, although he was not appointed to any office. But the courtiers were jealous of him and, after ten months, he left Wei for Sung. He was attacked on the way to the latter place, and after some delay changed his mind and returned to Wei. There he found his position embarrassing, because he had to ride behind the duke and the beautiful but notorious woman who was his consort. The people were amused by what they called "virtue following in the train of vice," and the humiliation was more than the sage could endure. He departed again, in 494, and this time, after some adventures and delays, reached Ch'en. In two years, however, he returned again to Wei. On this journey he was taken captive by some enemies, who made him take a solemn oath that he would not proceed to Wei. He took the oath, but as soon as he was free violated it and went on to Wei. Some of his followers were astonished by such disregard of his plighted word, for Confucius had taught them to "hold sincerity and good faith as ruling principles." [21] Confucius, however, justified his action on the ground that the oath was extorted from him by force and was not binding. These years of adversity and wandering had wrought considerable change in the man who, in his youth, had shown such rigid adherence to lofty principles. The Duke of Wei was growing old, but he was as little inclined as ever to adopt Confucius' advice. He was kind to him but did not employ him.

Discouraged by repeated failure, the great teacher was almost disposed to accept an invitation from the leader of a rebellion in an adjoining state. He was dissuaded by a disciple, who pointed out the inconsistency of such action in one who had been such a staunch supporter of legitimacy. Subsequently Confucius proposed to visit the state of Chin, but he discovered that a revolution was going on there and came back to Wei. He then removed to Ch'en and from there to Ts'ai. From the latter place he went to Ye, a territory that had revolted from the state of Ch'u. Confucius would have taken office under the rebel leader, but found no more willingness there than elsewhere to accept his teaching. He went back to Ts'ai, where he remained three years, after which he accepted an invitation to Ch'u, one of the three most powerful states in China, then struggling for the mastery. The ruler of Ch'u would have employed him but was dissuaded by courtiers, and the wanderer, now sixty-three years of age, returned to Wei, where he found the grandson of his former patron engaged in rebellion against his own father. Confucius was invited to accept a position in his service, but he could not bring himself to support a son in rebellion against his father, the legitimate ruler of the state, so he went into retirement. After some five or six years spent in this seclusion in Wei, a messenger arrived from his native state of Lu, inviting him to return. He accepted the invitation, but even in his

[21] Analects XII:10.

home state he found the government conducted upon principles which he could not endorse. Nor did the ruler show
any desire to serve the cause of righteousness and promote
the welfare of the people.

The career of Confucius to all appearance had been a
failure—a great failure. Well did he say: "I have never
seen a man who loved virtue as much as he loved beauty."
And on another occasion: "I have never been able to see
a holy man; could I see a noble one I should be content.
I have never been able to find a good man; could I find
a constant one it would be enough."

But the years of wandering had not been altogether
fruitless. It was during these years of adversity that he
gave to the few faithful disciples who followed him much
of the teaching which has made him one of the great moral
leaders of the race. These disciples treasured every word
that fell from his lips, and, so great was their veneration
for him, that even his little mannerisms were noted as
worthy of record. We are gravely informed that he never
stood in the gate-way of the palace nor stepped upon the
door-sill; that at audiences his robe, front and back, hung
straight, and that he moved with his arms outstretched like
a bird flying; that he didn't wear purple facings nor
use red, even in undress, that his night-shirt was half as
long again as his body, that he liked fine rice and wanted
his meat minced; that his only limit in wine was to stop
short of confusion, and that he would not eat without
ginger.[22] We can forgive this careful record of trivialities
for the sake of the picture which it gives us of the man,
so punctilious and yet so human. He was "amiable but
dignified," we are told, "strict but not severe, polite but
at ease." We are told, too, that if a friend died in need
he would say: "I'll attend to his funeral," and that
"when he heard a good song he would ask to have it repeated and would himself join in the melody." With all
modesty, too, he disclaimed being a sage, and declared that
while he might have some literary ability he had not yet

[22] See Analects X.

attained to the living of the ideal life.[23] Among note-worthy sayings which fell from his lips, other than those already mentioned, I quote these:

Have no friends not equal to yourself.[24]

If you have faults, do not fear to abandon them.[25]

Sorrow not that men do not know you, but sorrow that you do not know men.[26]

Hear the truth in the morning, and in the evening you can die without regret.[27]

The princely man thinks of virtue; the mean man of gain.[28]

Do not unto others what you do not like done unto yourself.[29]

We know not life; how can we know death![30]

Rotten wood can't be carved, and a dung wall ought not to be whitewashed.[31]

Formerly I listened to men's words and took their actions for granted; now I listen to their words, but I also watch their conduct.[32]

He who knows not the will of God can not be a princely man. He who knows not the Rites has nothing with which to shape his character.[33]

The princely man is catholic, not narrow; the small-minded man is narrow, not catholic.[34]

Only the humane man can love men or hate them.[35]

The princely man aims to be cautious in speech but prompt in action.[36]

Those who know are free from doubt. The humane are free from sorrow; the courageous, from fear.[37]

Over-passing is like coming short (of the mark).[38]

Self-denial and piety—these are virtue.[39]

Who takes no thought for the future has sorrow at the door.[40]

HIS LITERARY WORK

After Confucius in his old age had returned to Lu he gave himself up to study and to literary work. This work was not that of an author, but rather of an editor. He

23 Ibid., VII and X.
24 Ibid., I:8.
25 Ibid., I:8.
26 Ibid., I:16.
27 Ibid., IV:8.
28 Ibid., IV:11.
29 Ibid., XII:2.
30 Ibid., XI:11.
31 Ibid., V:9.

32 Ibid., V:9.
33 Ibid., XX:3.
34 Ibid., II:14.
35 Ibid., IV:3.
36 Ibid., IV:24.
37 Ibid., IX:28.
38 Ibid., XI:15.
39 Ibid., XII:1.
40 Ibid., XV:11.

said of himself: "I am not a creator but a transmitter, one who has faith in the ancients and loves them."[41]

Ssu-ma Ch'ien, from whose biography of Confucius much of this chapter has been drawn,[42] tells us that the Sage made a careful study of the rites of the Three Dynasties (i.e. the Hsia, the Shang and the Chou), and that he classified the subjects treated and grouped the passages under their proper headings. He says, moreover, that he wrote an introduction to the Shu King, or Canon of History, and placed the historical fragments of which the work is composed in their proper order, beginning with the times of Yao and Shun, and coming down to the period of Duke Wu of Ch'in (i.e. 2357–621 B.C.). He notes, too, that he made a selection from the more than three thousand odes then extant, and that he suppressed those which he did not consider useful in the rites or animated by the proper spirit. There are apparently some references in the Analects to his work on the Rites. He is reported as saying that he could talk of the rites of the Hsia and the Yin Dynasties, but that he could not obtain sufficient confirmation of his opinions from the houses of Ch'i and Sung —the heirs of these two dynasties. He is quoted in another passage as referring to the correction that had been made in the music of the ritual after his return home. As is well known the tyrant of the Ch'in Dynasty attempted to destroy the Confucian books in 213 B.C. But four years later he was dead, and in 202 the new dynasty of Han arose. In the mean time many scholars had preserved portions of the ancient literature. The Li Ki or Book of Rites, as we have it to-day, perhaps contains most of the collection made by Confucius, but also contains other documents, so that it is not identical with the Rites, as edited by him. In its present form it dates from the second century of our era.

Ssu-ma Ch'ien, quoting from a distinguished scholar, a descendant of Confucius, assures us that Confucius, in edit-

---

41 Ibid., VII:1.
42 For accounts in English of the life of Confucius see Soothill's Analects, Introduction II, or Douglas' "Confucianism and Taouism."

ing the ancient historical records, arranged them in one hundred books. The present Shu King, or Canon of History, contains but fifty-nine, even when we count the sections of books as separate documents.

The Odes as we possess them are probably identical with the collection made by Confucius, but we cannot help wishing that he had possessed more of that love of the ancients, which he professed to feel, so that every fragment of ancient literature could have been preserved, and not merely those that supported his opinions as to ancient practice, or measured up to his ethical standard.

The work which he regarded most highly, and by which he declared that he would be judged, is the Ch'un Ch'iu, or Annals, compiled just before his death, and drawn chiefly, it is believed, from the official records of the state of Lu. When one reads this work he cannot but wonder what it was in it that gave satisfaction to Confucius. It is a bare chronicle of events covering a period of 242 years. Dr. Legge, in his Prolegomena, says truly that it is

Without the slightest tincture of literary ability in the composition, or the slightest indication of judicial opinion on the part of the writer.

It is nothing but the syllabus of a book. Without the commentary of Tso Ch'iu-ming it would be an arid literary desert, a valley of dry bones. Tso alone has breathed upon these bones and clothed them with flesh and made them live. He gives details of the events to which a bare allusion is made by Confucius, and by his anecdotes adds color and flavor to the record. The commentary is the thing worth reading; the Annals are but chapter headings. One wonders, whether, after all, the Ch'un Ch'iu is anything more than the outline of the work, which the Master did not live to complete, but which the extravagant admiration of the disciples for the Master have induced them to accept as the work itself. If it is by the Annals that Confucius is to be judged, as he declared, the judgment cannot be a favorable one. Not only is there shown an utter absence of literary ability—an entire lack of that trenchant criticism of men and events which one finds in his conversations with his disciples, or with the princes of his day—there is no expression of praise or blame, such as would be expected from the great moral teacher of his race. Dr. Legge goes much farther than this in his severe criticism of the work. He accuses Confucius of deliberately misrepresenting the history of the period covered, by concealing some of the facts and distorting others. He declares that Confucius "had no reverence for truth in history," that he "shrank from looking the truth fairly in the face," and that "he had more sympathy with power than with weakness, and would overlook wickedness and oppression in authority rather than resentment and revenge in men who were suffering from them." [43]   Dr. Legge supports his indictment by numerous quotations. Such a falsification of history as is charged would be the more remarkable in view of the praise given by Confucius to the historiographers who would leave a blank in the record rather than record an inaccurate statement.[44]   In fact, the historiographers of China to this day are distinguished for their faithful record of events as they occur, and instances can be given in which they have suffered death rather than change the entry made.

For myself I am disposed to accept the judgment of a few Chinese writers, that the text of the Annals which we have is not the text of the work compiled by Confucius.

HIS DEATH AND CANONIZATION

In the year 479 B.C. when Confucius was seventy-two years of age, he was seen walking slowly to and fro muttering to himself these words:

> Mt. T'ai must crumble;
> The great beam will break;
> The wise man, too, will wither away.

[43] Chinese Classics V. Part I Prolegomena, Section V.
[44] Analects XV:25.

DISTANT VIEW OF MOUNT TAI, SHANTUNG. THE MOST SACRED MOUNTAIN IN CHINA.

TOMB OF CONFUCIUS.

One of his younger disciples, Tzu Kung, was with him at
the time, and saw that his old master was ill. Tzu Kung's
surname was Tuan-mu. His personal name was Tzu. By
this last he was familiarly called by Confucius. As he
came in the Master said: "Tzu, why are you late? I had
a dream last night. I dreamt that I waś sitting in the hall
between the pillars with funeral offerings before me. No
wise monarch comes to power. There is no one who wants
me for a teacher. My time to die has come." He was
right; in a week he had passed away. It was the 11th day
of the Fourth Moon in the year 479 B.C.

He was buried outside the north gate of Ch'üfu, where
his grave may still be seen. A number of his disciples kept
watch at the side of his tomb for three years. Tzu Kung
remained there for six years. The site of his hut is pointed
out to-day to the traveler who visits the grave. The Duke
of Lu, who found no use for the advice of Confucius while
he lived, mourned for him when he was dead. In China,
as in the West, men neglect the prophets while they live,
but build magnificent monuments to them after they are
dead. Thus Duke Ai built a temple to the memory of
Confucius, and directed that sacrifices should be offered to
his spirit four times a year. From that day to this, except
during the brief period when Confucianists were being persecuted in the third century B.C., he has been publicly worshiped. At first this honor was done him only in his
native state. But in 195 B.C. the founder of the Han
Dynasty visited his grave and made an offering of an ox
in sacrifice. In A.D. 57 the worship was introduced into
the colleges of the empire. In A. D. 609 he was worshiped
in temples specially erected for that purpose and dedicated
to him. At the time of the overthrow of the Manchus in
1912 there were not less than 1500 temples in China set
apart for this worship.

Until the year 1906 the Manchu code provided that the
sacrifices to Confucius should be of the second grade, that
is to say one degree lower than those offered to the Most
High. But in 1906 the Empress Dowager, Tzuhsi, issued
an edict raising Confucius to the first rank in the Chinese

pantheon, and ordering the same honors paid to him that were paid to the Supreme God. This edict possibly was due to the desire to make the great teacher of the East equal in rank with the great teacher of the West, who in the mission schools was held to be one with God and to be worshiped as God. This desire was strengthened by the fears expressed by the commissioners who drew up the new public school system, as already related, a fear that the national religion might lose its hold upon the students in the schools who were to take up the study of Western science and foreign languages. Because of this fear they had urged that the students be required to attend the services of their ancestral religion. The increased honor paid to the Sage, it was no doubt believed, would increase the reverence of the young for him. This plan to strengthen the established faith included also the creation at Ch'üfu, the ancient home of Confucius, of a school to be devoted to the study of the Confucian classics, the sacred literature of China, so that there might never be lacking those who could expound the teachings of these books. An edict to this effect was promulgated at the same time as that raising the rank of the Sage in the pantheon.

When Duke K'ung, the lineal descendant of Confucius in the 76th generation, read these edicts, he asked permission to visit Peking and pay his respects to Her Imperial Majesty, the Empress Dowager. He came, and at the audience granted him he expressed his gratitude for the high honor done to his ancestor, but he also asked that the school to be established at Ch'üfu might be made, not simply a school for the study of China's sacred books, but also a school for teaching foreign languages, western science, international law, and political economy. His request, of course, was not granted, for the original intention of the Empress Dowager was to make the ancient home of Confucius a center of conservative influences to counteract the feared tendencies of the new learning.

The author had the privilege of two interviews with the Duke during this visit, and found him to be a rather handsome man, in the prime of life, physically fit and mentally alert. He enquired about the mission schools in China and showed keen interest in Western education.

Before the plans for a classical school at Ch'üfu could be carried out the Empress Dowager died. A little later the revolution swept the Manchus out of power, and inaugurated a period of irreligion not unlike that which accompanied the French revolution. The sacrifices at the state altars in Peking and in the provinces were neglected. The temples were abandoned; their courts were overgrown with weeds. The sacred inclosure of the Temple of Heaven was opened to the populace. Ribald inscriptions were scrawled upon the walls. The altar to the Most High was desecrated by the erection upon it of booths for the sale of food and cigarettes. The Temple to the Earth was converted into barracks, and the Temple of Agriculture became a public park and a show ground for jugglers and acrobats. After a few months, however, there came a reaction. A society was organized to urge the re-establishment of Confucianism as the religion of the state. A great national convention was held at Ch'üfu in September, 1913. Officially it met on the 24th day of the Eighth Moon of the 2464th year of Confucius. The 27th of the Moon was observed as the birthday of the Sage. The convention lasted one week, and met in the Confucian Temple. Duke Yen attended. The autumn sacrifices to Confucius were offered that year in Peking and in some of the provincial capitals. President Yuan Shik-k'ai attempted to re-establish the ancient national religion, and make it the religion of the Republic, but after his death the modernists had their way.

Not long after the meeting of the national Confucian convention at Ch'üfu I had an opportunity of visiting that ancient town. The railway now passes within six miles of it. A Chinese cart carried us over the old road so often trodden by the feet of the Sage, and not far from the station we forded the River Wen, the old boundary between the states of Lu and Ch'i. We entered the town by the North Gate and, on reaching the Drum Tower in

* The Nationalist Government in 1928 issued instructions to all local authorities to preserve in good condition the temples to Confucius in their districts.

the center of the place, we turned toward the west. Not far away we found the temple, the most beautiful of all the temples in China erected to the memory of the great teacher. There is the usual succession of buildings and spacious courts. The buildings are roofed with yellow glazed tiles; the walls are covered with vermilion stucco. The pillars along the corridors, instead of being teak covered with red lacquer, as is customary in other temples, are of marble, carved with entwining dragons. Behind the principal hall, separated from it by a court, there is a smaller hall in which is preserved a series of tablets depicting important incidents in the life of Confucius as recorded in the Chia Yü or Family Traditions.

A small pavilion in one of the courts covers a stone monument, whose inscription tells us that it is erected on the site of a favorite apricot tree, under which the teacher loved to sit. The home of Duke Yen adjoins the temple grounds. Outside the north gate, about half a mile distant, is the entrance to the cemetery. It is beautifully shaded with numerous trees, and the path to the tomb passes over a stone bridge which spans the little stream known as the Chu. The way is bordered by stone images of lions, horses and men. A little shrine near the tomb shelters the altar and the tablet that bears his posthumous title. Duke Yen was engaged there, when we arrived, offering special sacrifices in behalf of the President.

The grave itself is a simple mound marked by a plain stone. Around it are gathered the graves of innumerable descendants. In the great imperial cemeteries near Peking we had seen the huge mounds and magnificent mausolea that made the resting places of once mighty but forgotten monarchs. The "Uncrowned King" needs no such imposing structure to guard his grave or preserve his dust from desecration. In the hearts of four hundred millions of living men his memory is enshrined, and the pathway to his grave will be worn by the pilgrim feet of a thousand generations yet unborn. For virtue is mightier than valor, and the teacher of righteousness than the conqueror of a thousand cities.

CHAPTER XII

CONFUCIANISM IN THE HOME

The services of love and reverence to parents when alive, and those of grief and sorrow to them when dead:—these completely discharge the fundamental duty of living men.

The Hsiao King, translated by Legge.

Under the Manchu Dynasty the Chinese Government officially recognized three religions: the *Ju Chiao*, the *Shih Chiao* and the *Tao Chiao*. The last-mentioned is Taoism. The term, *Shih Chiao*, is one applied to Buddhism. The words, *Ju Chiao*, mean "the Religion of the Learned." Sometimes it is called *Ta Chiao*, or "the Great Religion," and not infrequently it is known as the *K'ung Chiao*, or "Confucian Religion." This is the name by which it is generally known among Americans and Europeans.

There is no foundation in truth for the statement sometimes heard that "Confucianism is not a religion, but a system of ethics." The author of the statement may have meant that Confucius was a teacher of ethics and not the founder of a religion. It is true that he did not found a religion, but "Confucianism" is the generally accepted name of the religion practiced by Confucius, the religion whose sacred books were edited by Confucius and his disciples, and the religion in which Confucius himself is one of the principal objects of worship.

It is not true even that Confucius taught only a system of ethics. Even as a child, as we have seen, he was deeply interested in the sacrificial ritual of the national religion, and the Analects, which report his conversations with his disciples, give evidence of the frequency with which he urged the importance of the *li*, that is to say, the "rites." The primary meaning of this word, *li*, is "religious worship." We are told in the Analects that the things about

249

which he most often spoke were the Odes, the Book of History, and the observance of the Rites. The Odes, the Book of History and the Rites are three of the sacred books of the Chinese. It is unfortunate that one of the earliest translations of the Li Ki, or "Record of Rites" renders the title of the work by the words: "A Collection of Treaties on the Rules of Propriety or Ceremonial Usages." Dr. Legge, the translator, used the phrase, "Rules of Propriety," as the equivalent of *li* in his translation of the Analects of Confucius as well as in that of the Li Ki. Now, not only is the primary meaning of the word, *li*, "religious worship," the book, itself, the Li Ki, which Dr. Legge calls "A Collection of Treatises on the Rules of Propriety," deals with religious rites. It describes those employed in the worship of God and the worship of ancestors, the ceremonies observed in the capping of a young man when he comes of age, and those employed in the solemnization of marriage, as well as with the funeral rites and the observances during the period of mourning—all of a deeply religious character. It treats also of the ceremonies at Court and those used in the intercourse of states, together with those of the tournament and the banquet; of social intercourse among friends, as well as those employed in the home, in the relations of husband and wife, of parents and children.

Of the forty-six books that make up the present Li Ki far more than half have to do with rites that are of a distinctly religious character, and the remainder, which deal with social and political functions, are none the less of a serious sort. The ancients did not make such distinctions as are common to-day between the religious and the secular. The ceremonies attending social and political functions also had a sacred character. When Confucius said that without the *li* a man had nothing upon which to stand, that is, to keep himself upright,[1] he was not referring to some code of etiquette, mere rules of politeness; he undoubtedly had in mind the whole body of rules and ceremonies which regulated a man's life. The collection which he had in

[1] Analects XX:3 and elsewhere.

mind was not identical with that known to-day as the Li Ki, but it was essentially the same, and to characterize it by such a colorless term as "Rules of Propriety" is as incongruous as it would be to call the book of Leviticus a treatise on dietetics, because a chapter is devoted to a description of the meats that may and may not be eaten.

Confucius on all occasions emphasized the importance of filial piety and, when asked what he meant by it, explained it as consisting of a devotion to living parents according to the Rites, a burial of them when dead according to the prescribed ritual, and the worship of them after death according to the ritual.[2] He spoke of himself as a man of prayer: "I have been praying for a long time."[3] It is said of him that "He sacrificed to the spirits as if realizing their presence,"[4] and that he did not regard worship by proxy as real worship, saying: "If I am not present at the sacrifices, it is just as though I had not sacrificed."[5] To Confucius, too, is ascribed the statement in the Li Ki that "The highest expression of worship is shown in the suburban sacrifice to God, and the highest expression of human affection in the offerings in the ancestral temple."[6] In the Classic of Filial Piety we have the teaching of Confucius upon this subject as transmitted to us by his disciples, and we cannot read that brief treatise without realizing that the Master was an earnest teacher of that which is above all else the religion of the Chinese—the honoring of parents while they live and worship of them after their death.

THE SACRED BOOKS

To know what the Confucian Religion is we must study its sacred books. These are commonly referred to as the "Four Books" and the "Five Classics." The Four Books are (1) the Analects, that is to say the sayings of Con-

[2] Ibid., II:5.
[3] Ibid., VII:34.
[4] Ibid., III:12.
[5] Ibid., III:12.
[6] Li Ki, Book VIII, Section II:18.

fucius as collected by his disciples; (2) the Great Learning, a treatise written probably by Tseng Tzu, a disciple of Confucius; (3) The Doctrine of the Mean, by Tzu Ssu, a grandson of the Sage, and (4) the works of Mencius.

The Five Classics are (1) The Book of Changes, or Yi King, used in divination; (2) The Shu King, or Book of History; (3) the Collection of Poetry, or Shih King; (4) the Li Ki, or Book of Rites, and (5) the Ch'un Ch'iu, or Annals.

Another arrangement makes thirteen in all instead of nine. This is done by including two other collections of Annals and two other collections of Rites, also an ancient dictionary and the work known as the Classic of Filial Piety. The Doctrine of the Mean and the Great Learning in that case are not counted, as they are included in the Book of Rites.

Of the Five Classics, the Book of Changes is a treatise on the sixty-four hexagrams formed by the permutations of six whole and six broken lines. The Book of History contains fragments of ancient history, and may be likened to the historical books of the Old Testament. The Collection of Poetry contains a number of religious pieces, and may be likened to the Psalms, although there are none of the Odes that approach in lofty aspiration the best of the psalms. The Annals remind one of the Books of Chronicles.

The Four Books belong to a later age than the Five Classics, and therefore may be said to occupy in the Confucian literature a place not altogether unlike that of the New Testament in our Bible, that is to say, the Analects report the discourses of Confucius and the other three works contain the teachings of the greatest of his disciples. But one has only to read these books to realize how unlike the Christian and Confucian Bibles are, either as literature or as food for the soul.

The Chinese also have their apocryphal books. Among these may be mentioned the Chia Yü, or "Family Traditions," from which have been derived much of the information given by Ssu-ma Ch'ien in his Life of Confucius. The sacred books of China also have had their lower and higher critics, and their numerous commentators. The most influential of the commentators was Chu Fu Tzu,* who lived in the Twelfth century of the Christian era, and was an advocate of a system of philosophy. His views still prevail with most Chinese scholars, and are chiefly responsible for their attitude toward things religious.

PRIVATE WORHIP

Confucianism has its private as well as its public worship. Of the individual and the family it requires the worship of ancestors with definite rites at certain times, the worship of Heaven and Earth on special occasions, and sometimes the worship of Confucius and the canonized teachers.

At the solemnization of marriage Heaven and Earth are called upon to bear witness to the covenant by which, as Confucius said, "Two families are united in affection to provide descendants who will keep up the sacrifices to Heaven and Earth and to ancestors." [7] A red rug is spread in the principal court of the bride-groom's home, and upon it the man and the woman kneel together and offer incense to the dual powers of nature, Heaven and Earth, and prostrate themselves in worship. On other occasions, as the sacred books provide, they must offer sacrifice (1) to the Genius of the Hall, i.e., the living room of the house, (2) to the God of the Furnace, i.e., the spirit that presides over the kitchen, so important to the health of the family, (3) to the God of the Door, that is the guardian against the entrance of evil influences, to-day represented by the door-goods, one with a light face who watches over the house in the daytime, and the other with a dark face to protect it at night; (4) to the God of the Soil, i.e., the deity of the locality in which the home is placed, and (5) to the Spirit of the Well, whose waters are so essential to health and comfort. The five sacrifices to the spirits of the home mentioned in the classics are

[7] Li Ki XXIV:10.
* Vide infra; pp. 403 and 404.

probably these. But Confucianists may, and commonly do, worship many other so-called deities. The God of Wealth is a popular one, and the occupation of the householder will probably lead him to worship the saint who presides over his trade. Formerly when a young boy started to school he had to learn to bow to the tablet of Confucius, and if he prepared to enter the examinations for the Civil Service, he would worship the God of Literature. Military students would make offerings to Kuan Wu Ti, the God of War, or to *Yo Fei,* one of the canonized warriors of China.

But the religion, which above everything else is the religion of the family, sacred and authoritative, is the religion of Filial Piety, the service of living parents and the worship of dead ancestors. The worship of the dead begins immediately after the decease. For the first seven weeks, as a rule, the services are continuous and very elaborate, but the customs vary in different parts of the country, and vary also according to the wealth or poverty of the family and according to its social standing. The worship consists of prostrations and prayers, the lighting of candles and burning of incense together with offerings of food and of spirituous liquors, and the burning of paper images of servants, of domestic animals, clothing, furniture and money. Anciently wives and concubines, men and women servants, horses and other animals, themselves, and not their images, were actually buried with the dead. Clothing and food were put in the tomb, together with jewelry and other articles of great value. In some instances the home, or a part of it, appears to have been abandoned and set aside for the worship of the dead.

Indeed some of these practices have continued to recent times. At several imperial funerals in the reign of the Ming Dynasty (A.D. 1368–1644) ; and at the burial of one of the wives of the Emperor Shunchih of the Manchu Dynasty, in the seventeenth century, living men and women, servants and concubines of the dead, were buried with them. When the great Viceroy, Li Hung Chang, died in 1901, his home in Peip'ing was entirely abandoned after the

funeral services, and was converted into a temple where his
spirit is worshiped to this day.

During the period devoted to the funeral services in the
home, there are morning and evening sacrifices before the
coffin, which may be considered as a continuation of the
service due the master or mistress of the household while
they were still living. They still partake of the meals of
the family. When the time for the interment arrives offerings of food and drink, libations of liquor, and the burning
of incense and of paper images accompany the coffin. There
are often repeated pauses of the funeral procession, during which offerings are made along the route to the grave,
and a sacrificial meal is set out at the tomb after burial.
By a special service at the grave the soul of the dead is
believed to be induced to attach itself to the spirit tablet,
by which it is conveyed back to the home. The tablet is
placed in the principal hall, and sacrifice is then offered
again for the repose of the soul. The ancient rule was
that the tablet should be conveyed the next day to the
ancestral temple, if there was such a building, and sacrifice
offered again.

Special sacrifices are offered at the first and second anniversaries of the death of parents, and at the end of the
mourning period. The tablet is a piece of wood about
twelve or fifteen inches long and two or three inches wide,
upon which are inscribed the posthumous name of the dead
and his titles, if he should have any. The eldest member
of the oldest generation is usually the priest of the family,
and will see that the worship of the ancestors is properly
observed, but all members of the family may, and commonly do, participate in the worship. It is considered very
important that the representative of the family shall have
a wife to take part in the worship. If there is no ancestral
temple the tablet is kept on the family altar in the home.
This is usually the main hall of the house, but sometimes
there is a room set aside as a chapel, or shrine, in which
the tablets and sacrificial vessels are kept.

ANCESTRAL TEMPLES

Some wealthy families maintain an ancestral temple, surrounded by a sacred field whose produce is used to support the service. Others have the temple without the field. In some instances there is a temple erected in the family, or clan, cemetery. The spirit tablets of deceased ancestors of many generations are kept in these temples, arranged on shelves in the form of steps. All ancestors of the same generation are placed on the same step, or shelf, the lowest shelf being occupied by those of the latest generation that has passed away, that is to say, by the tablets of those most nearly related to the living. The very poor have a little shrine on a shelf in the principal room of the home. Even the boatmen, whose families live with them on their boats, have a shrine in the cabin. Some families place their tablets on the altar of a Buddhist or Taoist shrine and pay their worship there. The ancestral temples of the nobles and of the imperial family are very imposing. The T'ai Miao in Peip'ing, devoted to the worship of the ancestors of the Manchu Emperors, is located just outside the South Gate of the Forbidden City, in a grove of cypress trees. There are also beautiful temples in the imperial cemeteries known as the Eastern and Western Tombs. In the latter the great sacrificial hall of the temple at the tomb of Yungcheng, in the arrangement of its furniture and in its services, is not unlike the Holy Place of the Jewish Temple. On a marble terrace which rises five or six feet above the pavement of the court an oblong hall is built. Its brick walls are covered with vermilion stucco. The roof is of glazed tiles of golden color, supported by bracket cornices decorated in the five colors. This hall is about 150 feet long east and west by 75 feet north and south. The entrance is on the south side. The floor in the interior is of grey tile; the ceiling is made of panels of dark green, relieved by lines of black, white and red surrounding the double dragon in gold. Great pillars of teak covered with red lacquer and gold support the heavy beams. The windows are covered

with red lattices delicately carved. As you enter you see
upon the threshold the altar of incense. In the middle of
the chamber is a table spread with shew-bread, which is
changed every new moon and every full moon. On the
north side is an altar for the offerings of fruit, vegetables
and wine. Before it are trusses upon which, at the new
moon and full moon, there are placed the bodies of slain
beasts; oxen, sheep and swine. Behind the altar are two
throne chairs, in which at the time of sacrifice the tablets
of the dead emperor and his consort are placed. These
chairs are placed just in front of a richly embroidered curtain, which separates this holy place from a dark chamber
behind it. In it is kept the spirit tablet, which is brought
out only at the time of sacrifice. I was not allowed to
enter this dark chamber, but at the time when the American
army handed back the Forbidden City to the Chinese Government, it was my good fortune to be a member of the
committee appointed to inspect the T'ai Miao, or Temple
of Imperial Ancestors in Peking, to see that all was in
order. On that occasion we entered the dark chamber, which
corresponds to the Most Holy Place, and found on the right
side an ark, or box, overlaid with gold lacquer, in which,
wrapped in cloth of gold, were ten tables of stone. These
were of green jade, engraved upon which, in deeply incised
characters of gold, was a eulogy of the dead monarch to
which this chapel belonged. At the northern end of the
chamber was a gilded shrine before which there hung a
curtain of cloth of gold, and behind it in the shrine was
the spirit tablet. It also was gilded, and upon it was the
posthumous name of the dead monarch. The great building in which this chamber was found was divided by partitions into chapels, all opening into a corridor which extended east and west along the south side of the building.
Each chapel contained, next to the corridor, a chamber or
"holy place" furnished with an altar of incense and with
the flag and official umbrella of the dead monarch, and
behind this chamber, on the north side, the dark chamber
which I have just described.

The great sacrificial hall at this temple is a separate

building, south of that just described, and facing the main entrance, which is an imposing gate-way on the south side of the inclosure. On the east and west sides of the spacious court, in front of the sacrificial hall, are chapels dedicated to the great statesmen and warriors of the dynasty.

These arrangements, of course, are much more elaborate than those allowed to the common people. The sumptuary laws of the Manchu Dynasty prescribed very carefully the dress and architecture, and the ceremonies to be employed by the various classes of subjects. The Li Ki, too, defined the rites of the Royal Temple and those allowed in the worship of ancestors to the several ranks of the nobility, and to the common people. Confucius blamed the princes of his day very severely for their usurpation of paraphernalia and ceremonies reserved for the King.

Very religious families will make offerings of incense and food every day, others at the new moon and full moon. Anciently there was a special service at the first new moon of each quarter and at the end of the calendar year. There were also offerings of first fruits. Those who adhere strictly to the rites as prescribed in the sacred books no doubt still observe these ancient customs. The most important services to-day in this worship of ancestors are the sacrifices at the grave in the spring during the period known as the *Ch'ing Ming,* and those in the home or ancestral temple at the winter solstice.

RITES AT THE GRAVE

The *Ch'ing Ming* is one of the twenty-four solar periods into which the year is divided by the Chinese, and extends from the 1st to the 15th of the Third Moon of the lunar calendar. The period falls, therefore, between the last week in March and the middle of April, just about the time of our Eastertide. The origin of this annual sacrifice at the grave is unknown. The ancients apparently seldom made offerings at the grave after the burial rites had been completed. One looks in vain through the Li Ki and other ancient works for any regulations touching this subject.

There are abundant references to sacrifices in the ancestral temple and some notices of sacrifices at the tomb at the time of burial, but the only reference I have found to offerings at the grave at stated periods after burial is one in which Confucius explains that in the absence of the eldest son by the principal wife, his brother by a concubine may offer the sacrifices and that, in such a case, the brother will erect an altar at the grave and make the offerings there at the proper seasons.[8]

A passage in the Chou Li states that at all sacrifices at the grave the officer in charge of the graves serves as impersonator of the dead,[9] but there is nothing to indicate that such sacrifices were made at any time except, to the god of the locality when the grave was marked out, and, at the time of interment, to the dead. It is difficult to understand why Confucius is represented as teaching that a younger son by a concubine, representing the heir at a sacrifice, should make the sacrifice at the grave rather than at the home.

But there can be no doubt that in the early ages sacrifices at the grave were rare, for when the mother of Confucius died and he desired to bury her in the same grave with his father, as I have already said, he had to make enquiry of others to learn where his father's grave was located.[10] His father had died when Confucius was an infant. But, if annual sacrifices at the grave were customary, he could not have escaped knowing where his father was buried, for although he had an elder brother it would have been his duty to be present at the worship. He was already twenty-two years of age when his mother died. Attempts have been made to throw doubt on the genuineness of this passage of the Li Ki, but the very fact that it shocks a Chinese to read the statement is evidence of its genuineness. Worshipers of Confucius would not have invented it.

Sacrifice at the tomb, after the burial rites were com-

8 Li Ki V:2.
9 Chou Li V: ch'un kuan 18.
10 Li Ki II, Sect. I:10.

pleted, could not have been altogether unknown, even in the days of Confucius, for the disciples built a hut alongside his grave and worshiped him there, some of them for three years, and one for six years. Ancient emperors came long distances to worship there. Mencius, too, relates a story of a shiftless man who boasted to his wife and concubine of his frequent dinings with great people, which they discovered to be eating of the offerings made by these great families upon the graves of their kindred.[11] It is true, however, that there is nothing in the account to show that these may not have been offerings made at the time of interment.

The lack in classical times of any definite ritual for sacrifice at the grave may have been due to the prevailing philosophy of that period, which considered man to be a duad, composed of an intelligent spirit which survives the body and ascends on high, which is called the *shen*, and an animal soul called the *kuei*, which goes into the grave with the body and perishes. This is the explanation ascribed to Confucius in the Li Ki.[12]. Having such a faith, it would be natural to pay attention chiefly to the *shen*, which was supposed to attach itself to the tablet, and which was worshiped in the home or in the ancestral temple. In later ages a new philosophy became prevalent, which is still held by most Chinese. Man, according to this philosophy, has three *hun*, or spirits, and seven *po*, or animal souls. The seven *po* gradually evaporate into nothingness after death, but the three *hun* survive, and it is a popular belief that one remains with the body in the grave, one is installed with the tablet on the ancestral altar, and the third goes to the realms of the dead, or Hades. With such a belief there would, of course, be developed a more definite practice for worship at the grave.

However this may be, the worship at the grave during the Ch'ing Ming Festival, which has already been described, has become an established practice regarded as of great importance. Within the two weeks known as *Ch'ing*

11 Mencius, Li Lou II:33.
12 Li Ki XXI, Sect. II:1.

APPROACH TO A PRINCE'S FAMILY CEMETERY.

BURIAL PIT, TEMPLE TO THE EARTH.

Ming, when all nature is reviving from the long, cold sleep of winter, you may see groups of Chinese, carrying baskets filled with offerings, wending their way to the open country to visit the family burying ground. There they carefully gather up the dead leaves and branches and repair the grave mounds. When all is in order they set out, either upon the ground or, more properly, upon an altar of earth or stone, a food and drink offering. This is sometimes a very elaborate feast of rice, with fish, fowl, and pork and cups of spirituous liquors. The drink offering is of spirits distilled from rice or millet. There may be also burnt offerings of paper imitation money. The dead are not believed to partake of anything but the ethereal essence of the offerings. There are prayers, too, sometimes written and burned, in which the spirits of the dear departed are asked to bestow their blessing upon the living and give the family their guardian care. There is also in the worship a recognition of the debt of the living to the dead, to whom they owe all the blessings of life.

WORSHIP AT WINTER SOLSTICE

Still more important is the service in the home or ancestral temple at the winter solstice, also mentioned in another chapter. Once it was my good fortune to be invited to attend such a service. The table spread in the principal room of the home was loaded with steaming viands. Two chairs, one for the departed grandsire and one for the sainted grandmother, were placed on the north side of the table. The family gathered reverently on the south side while the head of the household, himself well advanced in years, reverently knelt and worshiped the spirits of the dead. It was not an occasion of sadness, but rather a joyful festival, celebrating the return of the absent living from distant regions and of the absent dead from the spirit world.

OBJECTIONS TO ANCESTOR WORSHIP

All this is worship, it is true, and as a rule the missionaries, both Catholic and Protestant, frown upon it as being idolatrous. They do not permit Chinese Christians to participate in it. In the strict sense of the word, of course, it is not "idolatrous" for there is no image used at the grave, and in the temple worship is offered before the spirit tablet. Ancestor worship is a religion that was once common among nearly all races. The sentiment which prompts men to care for the graves of their dead and to seek communion with them is one which all must respect. The human heart is everywhere the same. We yearn for the society of those whom we have known and loved and who have gone from this life. All peoples, too, have memorial services in honor of the dead, and that is the essence of the Chinese worship of their ancestors.

One of the objections to the worship of the dead is the effect seen in the ultra conservatism which it cultivates. Extravagant respect for the teaching and practices of dead ancestors makes progress very difficult. The dead hand rests heavily upon the living and restrains all movement toward change, even though it be toward a betterment of conditions. The Chinese undoubtedly over-emphasize the duty of reverence for the dead. They stand with their faces to the past, and follow too much the precedents of those who have gone on before. Confucius said that the man who, for three years after his father's death, does not change from his father's ways may be counted truly filial.[13]

We should profit by the wisdom and experience of the past, but we ought to make these stepping stones to higher levels in the future. We ought to be better than our fathers. To-day there is a movement among the young in China away from the restraints of the past. Some are going too far, and abandoning the good as well as the evil of old customs. But there will come a reaction, and in the end, no doubt, the Chinese will find the *chung yung,* or the "middle path."

[13] Analects I:11.

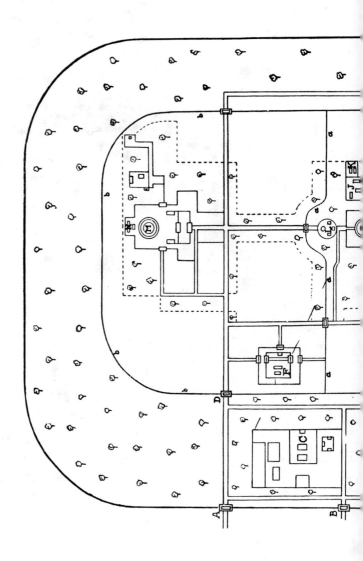

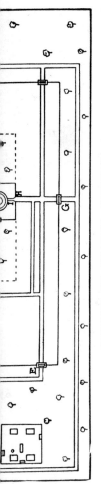

TEMPLE OF HEAVEN, PEIPING.

Scale 1 to 10,000.

EXPLANATION OF THE PLAN OF THE TEMPLE OF HEAVEN.

A=The Hsi T'ien Men,

B=The Wai Yüan Hsi Men,

C=The Ning Hsi Tien, or Hall for the rehearsal of the ceremonies, particularly by the posturers and musicians.

D=The Nei Hsi T'ien Men, the usual entrance into the northern section of the Inner Court.

E=The Kuang Li Men, the Emperor's gate of exit from the southern section of the Inner Court.

F=The Hall of Fasting.

G=The Chao Heng Men, principal entrance to the southern section of the Inner Court.

H=The Wai Wei Men, the southern gate to the outer or square court of the Altar.

I=The Nei Wei Men, the southern gate to the inner or circular court of the Altar.

J=The Treasury.

K=The Slaughter House.

L=The Huang Ch'iung Yü.

M=The Ch'i Nien Tien.

N=The Huang Ch'ien Tien.

a a a=The division wall between the northern and southern sections of the Inner Court.

b b b=The wall of the Inner Court.

CHAPTER XIII

CONFUCIANISM AS A STATE RELIGION

The sacrifice to God in the suburbs is the highest act of worship.—
Li Ki.

In the preceding chapter Confucianism has been discussed as the religion of the individual and the family; in this chapter it is proposed to consider it as once the established religion of the State. Under the republic to-day there is no established religion, but under the Manchu Dynasty and for many centuries before that period Confucianism was the state religion. Buddhism and Taoism were subsidized, but the official religion was Confucianism. Although its disestablishment makes it politically of less importance to-day than formerly, to one who is concerned with the comparative study of religions it can never cease to be of interest. Its hoary antiquity, alone, gives it a claim upon the attention of such a student.[1] The facts here presented have been obtained by a study of the Chinese texts of the classics, particularly portions of the Shu King, certain odes of the Shih King, and the teachings of the Li Ki, which is the Chinese Leviticus, and texts also of those chapters of the Ta Ch'ing Hui Tien, or "Fundamental Statutes of the Manchu Dynasty," and those of the Ta Ch'ing Lü Li, or "Penal Code of the Manchus," which deal with the subject. The Manual of the Ministry of Rites has also been examined, and has furnished details of the modern ritual. To these sources of information the author may be permitted to add his personal inspection of the

---

[1] In the Journal of the China Branch of the Royal Asiatic Society for 1913 the author published a paper upon the "State Religion of China during the Manchu Dunasty," which contains much of the information given in this chapter. The whole subject, however, is here given fresh treatment.

temples and the paraphernalia of worship, measurements and photographs taken on the ground, attendance upon the services in the Confucian temple, and visits to some of the State Altars at Peking immediately after the close of the worship, while the vessels of sacrifice and other paraphernalia were still in place.

THE STATE RELIGION

Confucianism has no order of priesthood, that is to say, there is no body of officials set apart from secular life, devoted solely to the performance of religious functions. The Emperor, in the days of the empire, was the head of the State, and officiated as the High Priest of his people at the most important sacrifices. Every civil and military officer of the government had duties to perform in connection with the state worship. In the provinces the principal civil official of the district presided over the services at the local altars and temples. His subordinates assisted, and at the worship of Confucius all the scholars of the district, who had received degrees, were expected to participate. There was, however, a Board of Rites at Peking, charged with general oversight of religion and education, and there were also a Court of Sacrificial Worship and a Board of Music, which were responsible for the details of the worship. The Imperial College of Astronomy, too, as will be seen later, had important functions to discharge in connection with the religious services.

THE BEINGS WORSHIPED

The ritual of the late dynasty divided the objects of worship into three classes. In the first rank were placed (1) the Supreme God, Shang Ti, (2) Imperial Earth, (3) the ancestors of the Emperor, and (4) the Guardian Spirits of the Soil and the Harvests. To these in 1907 the Sage Confucius was added, as has already been stated. Previously he had been placed in the second class.

In the second rank, besides Confucius—later included in the first class—there were the Sun, the Moon, Emperors and kings of preceding dynasties, the patron saint of Agriculture, the patroness of Sericulture, the Spirits of Heaven, the Spirits of Earth, and the Year Star—that is to say the planet Jupiter, by whose revolutions around the sun the Chinese lunar calendar was regulated.

In the third rank of the pantheon were placed the patron saint of Medicine, the God of War, the God of Literature, the North Star, the Eastern Peak, the tutelary deity of Peking, the God of Fire, the dragon of the Black Dragon Pool (near Peip'ing), the dragon of the Jade Fountain (near the Summer Palace) and that of the Summer Palace Lake, the God of Artillery, the God of the Soil, the patron of Mechanic Arts, the God of the Furnace, the God of the Granary, the door gods, and a host of canonized patriots whose number has increased from generation to generation.

LOCATION OF TEMPLES AND ALTARS

The most important altars and temples were, of course, located at the capital. Peip'ing is composed of four walled cities. Its heart is the Forbidden City, one mile square, within which the principal imperial palace is situated. This is surrounded by a grey brick wall with a crenellated parapet. The wall is about forty feet high and forty feet thick. It is protected by a moat which is some forty feet in width. All important buildings in China, for geomantic reasons, face the south. As one comes out of the South Gate of the Forbidden City he finds himself in the Purple, or Imperial City, two miles square and surrounded by a purple wall. On his left, the side of honor—the eastern side—is a grove of dark cypresses, within which is located the T'ai Miao, or Temple of Imperial Ancestors. On the west, i.e., the right side, he would have found in the old days a court enclosing the Altar to the Guardian Spirits of the Soil and the Harvests. This, with adjoining courts, has been converted into the Central Park by the Republic, and some of the buildings are used for a National Museum. Still moving south the observer will pass out of the South Gate of the Imperial City into the capital proper, known as the Tartar City which, as already said, is surrounded by a wall fourteen and a half miles in circuit and fifty feet high. Through the great Ch'ien Men, the principal gate on the south side of this city, the visitor passes into the southern suburb, known as the Chinese City. This formerly had no wall, but is now surrounded by a wall ten miles in circuit and about twenty-five feet wide and twenty-five feet high. On the left, in the south-eastern portion of this city, is a great enclosure containing 737 acres, which is the Temple of Heaven where Shang Ti, the Most High, was worshiped. On the right, in the south-western part of this suburb, is the Temple of Agriculture with the Field of God, an enclosure somewhat smaller than the Temple of Heaven. These two enclosures are separated by a wide plaza.

North of the Tartar City is placed the Temple of Earth. In the Eastern Suburb is the Temple to the Sun, and in the Western the Temple to the Moon. The Peip'ing temple to Confucius is in the northern part of the Tartar City, the temple to the tutelary deity of Peip'ing in its western section. The temple to the Eastern Peak is in the Eastern Suburb near the Temple to the Sun. In every county there is, or should be, a temple to Confucius and an altar to the Guardian Spirits of the Soil and Harvests. Temples to canonized patriots are found in all parts of the country.

TIMES OF WORSHIP

Under the Manchu régime the method of selecting the date upon which these various deities and saints were to be worshiped was a very elaborate one. Two years in advance, in the Tenth Moon, the lucky days of the year under consideration were to be determined by the Imperial College of Astronomy, which resorted to divination for this purpose. From this list of lucky days a date was chosen sacrifice to be offered, and these dates were sub- approval to the Ministry of Rites. The Ministry of Rites directed the Court of Sacrificial Worship to report upon the appropriateness or otherwise of the dates proposed. In the First Moon of the following year, that is to say one year in advance of that in which the sacrifices were to be offered, this religious calendar, after such revision as had been found necessary, was copied out on yellow paper and submitted to the Throne for approval. This was given in an edict, which directed the Court of Sacrifical Worship to proceed according to the proposed calendar, and also to memorialize the Throne in advance of each sacrifice, so that sufficient time might be given to the necessary preparations.

The calendar was then printed by the Ministry of Rites, and a copy sent to each and every civil and military officer in the empire, a corrected list of these being supplied by the Ministry of Civil Office and the Ministry of War. Thus these officers were fully notified, nearly a year in advance, of the date of every state sacrifice, and could govern themselves accordingly.

The season at which the most important sacrifices were to be offered was fixed by age-old custom. The Most High was to be worshiped at the Winter Solstice, the Imperial Earth at the Summer Solstice, Confucius at the Spring and Autumn Equinoxes, but the exact dates of these in any particular lunar year had to be calculated by the College of Astronomy. Prayer at the Temple of Heaven was to be made at the covered altar in the first moon of the year, on a day whose cyclical representation contained a specified character. The Guardian Spirits of the Soil and Harvests were worshiped in the midmonth of spring and the midmonth of autumn, on days determined in a similar manner.

MANNER OF WORSHIP

Worship consisted in bathing, fasting, prostrations, prayers and thanksgiving, offerings of incense, lighted candles, gems and silk, fruits, cooked meats, salted vegetables and shew-bread, libations of wine and sacrifices of

whole oxen, sheep and swine—sometimes of deer and other
game—and on certain occasions the burnt offering of a
young bullock. The presentation of the offerings was accompanied by instrumental music and posturing, or dancing, sometimes also by chanting.

All sacrifices to deities of the first grade, under the
Manchu rule, were preceded by three days of fasting; those
of the second grade by two days' fast. Due notice of the
fast was given in all yamens by closing the middle door
of the triple gate-way opening into the yamen court-yard
and the corresponding door of the main hall. A warning
notice on a red tablet was placed on a table before the
closed gate, and a second, on a yellow tablet with an inlaid
border of dragons, was put on another table in front of
the hall.

When the fast was preparatory to the solemn sacrifice
to the Most High at the winter solstice, it was announced
by the Emperor in an edict, such as the following:

On the —— day of the —— Moon of the —— year of ——,
being the Winter Solstice, WE shall reverently sacrifice to the
Great Ruler of Imperial Heaven at the Altar to Heaven, in
behalf of you, Our people.

The purity of the Ministers depends upon their hearts, their
righteousness upon the determination of each to exalt his office
lest, by neglect of his duties calamity be brought upon the State.
Be reverent. Let there be no carelessness.

On the occasion of sacrifices of the second grade the red
notice only was used. In the palace, itself, the notice was
suspended alongside a small bronze image, about two feet
in height, which was placed at the entrance to the hall of
audience.

Before beginning the fast it was necessary to bathe.
Fasting did not mean entire abstinence from food, but
from all flesh and strong-smelling vegetables, such as garlic,
leeks and onions, and from wine and all strong drink. No
criminal proceedings were to be held, no invitations to feasts
issued or accepted. There was to be no music. No enquiries after the sick were allowed, and there was to be no
mourning for the dead. One was particularly forbidden

to enter the death chamber of a woman, to sacrifice to ancestral spirits or to sweep the tombs. All association of any kind with the sick or the mourner was forbidden. These prohibitions remind one of those enforced in connection with the Hebrew sacrifices. Aaron and his sons were forbidden to drink any wine or strong drink when about to go into the tabernacle, and warned not to mourn for their dead when serving there.[2]

In the case of the great sacrifice to the Most High the Emperor and court officials kept the first two days of the fast in the imperial palace, and other officials observed it in their yamens. Officers who were sixty years of age or over were excused from keeping the fast, if they were unable to endure it, and even if they kept the fast they were not required to accompany the Emperor to the sacrifice. Their ages, however, had to be verified and entered on the record. The object of the bathing and fasting was to make oneself pure in body and heart, and worthy to come into the presence of the divinity. Special officers were appointed to visit and inspect the various yamens. Any officer found neglecting the fast was punished according to law.

On the third day of the fast, that preceding the sacrifice, the Emperor and attending ministers repaired to the Temple of Heaven, to the Hall of Fasting in that enclosure. The bronze image and warning notice were then set up in a small marble pavilion on the north-east corner of the terrace in front of the Hall of Fasting. Before leaving the palace the offerings of silk, the gems and the prayer, which were to accompany the Emperor, were carefully inspected by him in the great T'ai Ho Tien, the hall in which the most important court functions were held. The prayer was written on blue paper in vermilion ink.

SYMBOLISM

Color, form and number all played an important part in the construction of the altars, the temples and their furni-

[2] Leviticus x:6-9.

ture, and in the ceremonies connected with the worship.
The characteristic color at the Temple of Heaven is blue—
the azure of the sky. The word used to describe it, however, is one of those primitive words which may mean blue
or green. It is well known that some primitive peoples fail
to distinguish these two colors and use one word for both.
It is the color of nature—the blue of the sky and the green
of the grass. The jade emblem offered at the altar to
Heaven is called *ch'ing,* which is also used for the color
of the sky, but the gem is green. During the Ming Dynasty
the tiles on the buildings at the Temple of Heaven were
green. This was true, too, of the older temple at Nanking.
During the reign of Ch'ienlung (A.D. 1736–1796), who was
an antiquarian and a stickler for accuracy, the buildings
in Peking were reconstructed in accordance with ancient
tradition, and blue tiles were substituted for the green.
Nevertheless, on the Hall of Fasting and buildings of lesser
importance the green tiles are still to be seen. All the
sacrificial vessels used at the Temple of Heaven were blue.
The golden candlesticks were surrounded by a shelter of
blue gauze. The silk offered to God was blue. The cover-
ings of the tabernacle and of the awnings that sheltered
the walks were blue. But the lanterns were purple rather
than blue.

The circle is appropriate to Heaven and the heavenly
bodies, hence the shape of the altars and vessels used at
the Temple of Heaven was circular. Odd numbers belong
to Heaven; even to Earth. Three and nine were the numbers chiefly used at the Temple of Heaven. When Ch'ienlung ordered the three terraces of the great marble altar
there to be rebuilt, he gave strict injunction that all the
odd numbers of the nine digits should be represented in the
construction. This was done, according to the official report, by making the diameter of the topmost terrace nine
chang (90 feet) in diameter, which would represent 1×9.
The second terrace was made 15 *chang* representing the
product of 3×5, and the lowermost terrace was 21 *chang,*
the product of 3×7. Thus all the odd digits were represented. The *chang* used, however, was not the official *chang*

of the Board of Public Works, for on measuring these terraces I found that they were much smaller. The ratios, however, are substantially as required. The odd numbers are conspicuous in other features of the altar and the furniture. One circular stone forms the center of the pavement of the topmost terrace. In the first circle around it are nine stones; in the second 18; in the third 27. There are nine concentric circles, each containing a number of paving stones which is a multiple of nine. The outermost has 9 × 9, or 81 stones. Nine times nine represents perfection in Chinese philosophy. This arrangement of paving stones continues in the middle and lowermost terraces. From the topmost terrace nine steps lead to the middle terrace, and nine from that to the lowest. The same number connects the lowest with the ground. The Emperor in worship had to kneel three times and kotow nine. There were nine pieces of music in the service, nine pieces of silk were offered, and nine tabernacles were erected on the uppermost terrace. There were five pedestals on this terrace, and there were three tall masts in the outer court of the Altar, from which during service three large lanterns were suspended to cast a faint glow over the courts.

But there were some even numbers used also. The circle contains 360 degrees, in China as with us, and since the circle is appropriate to Heaven the marble balustrades around the three terraces of the Altar were made to contain 360 panels.

At the Altar to Earth yellow is the prevailing color. The soil in north China is yellow. The tiles of buildings at the Temple to the Earth are, therefore, yellow. The vessels of the sanctuary are yellow and the gem and silk offered are yellow. The prayer was written upon yellow paper. Since in the ancient belief of the Chinese the earth is square, the Altar to the Earth is square, and all the vessels used were four-sided.

The Earth represents the female element in nature. Its number is even. This number is eight. Eight pieces of silk were offered and the music consisted of eight pieces. At the Altar to the Sun the color of tiles, of silk and gem

was red. The number was seven. At the Temple to the
Moon the number was six and the color was white.

The Altar to the Guardian Spirits of the Soil and Harvests was peculiar. It had to symbolize the influences of
Heaven and Earth.   In worshiping the *She,* or Spirit of
the Soil, a yellow gem was used, but a green one for the
Spirit of the Harvest. It is described as round in its upper
part and square in the lower. The offering of silk consisted
of four pieces, an even number, and the music of an odd
number, seven. The prayer was written in black on white
paper. The altar was square, and all the five primary
colors of Chinese philosophy were employed. The top of
the altar was yellow; its east side was constructed of blue
glazed brick; the south side was of red, the west of white,
the north—the side of darkness—was of black. The walls
of the court surrounding the altar were of corresponding
colors.

Direction, posture and time all had their significance.
The Emperor, as High Priest of his people, worshiped
God at the Temple of Heaven, at the Winter Solstice at
night, facing the north. The Jewish High Priest also faced
the north when offering sacrifice on the altar of burnt
offerings.   The Emperor worshiped the Earth at the
the Summer Solstice facing the south at high noon. He
worshiped the sun on a stated morning in spring before
sunrise, facing the east, and the moon on a stated evening
in autumn after sunset, facing the west.

At the sacrifices of the first order the officials used the
ceremony of the three kneelings and nine prostrations.
The service was accompanied not only by music, but by
dancing or posturing as well. At the Altar to Heaven, and
at all sacrifices of the first rank, these posturers were
arranged in ranks of eight. There were 64 civilian posturers, carrying wands, and 64 military, armed with spears.
At the worship of Confucius only the civilians attended.
The music was furnished by an orchestra consisting of
stringed instruments, horns, drums and cymbals, musical
stones and bells. The Master of Ceremonies gave the signal
to start or stop the music. The stopper is an instrument

in the shape of a crouching tiger with erect bristles along his spine. By drawing his baton across these bristles the Master of Ceremonies created a shrieking noise, which was heard above the din of discordant instruments and was the signal to stop. The Chinese sacred music is written in the ancient pentatonic scale, but the instruments are not tuned to harmony one with another, so that the music was but a "joyful noise."

The use of gems in worship is common to many religions. We have but to recall the ephod of the Jewish High Priest, with its breast-plate of twelve precious stones, each of the twelve tribes of Israel having its own symbol. The stone in the Christian bishop's ring also has its significance. Color, too, is important in other religions as well as in Confucianism, as the Cardinal's robe and the Bishop's purple remind us. The part that number plays in architecture, and that of posture and music in worship are well known. The sacrifice of animals, accompanied by offerings of wine and incense, lighted lamps or candles, cooked food and fruits, is common to most religions.

MEANING OF SACRIFICE

The meaning of sacrifice in the Confucian religion is stated in the Li Ki, or Book of Rites. "Sacrifice is for petition, for thanksgiving, and to ward off calamity."[3] Theologians tell us that there is no idea of *expiation* in it, but merely of *propitiation*. This is doubtless true, but it is also true that all calamities in China are regarded as punishments for sins committed, and sacrifices offered to Heaven were believed to be able to appease the deity and so avoid the punishment. Probably the idea of substitution never occurred to them. The sacrifices were believed to be offerings of "sweet-smelling savor" "well pleasing to God" and to the spirits, and thus likely to win their favor. There is, however, one interesting passage in the Li Ki which ought to be mentioned: "The blood was offered be-

[3] Li Ki V:11.

cause it contained the breath"[4] (or life). This will recall a passage in Leviticus which reads: "The life of the flesh is in the blood, and I have given it to you upon the altar to make an atonement for your souls."[5] But most sacrifices offered in China are offered to ancestors, and it was customary to offer those things which were believed to have life-giving properties, in order to strengthen the feeble life of the disembodied soul. For this reason jade, or pieces of mother-of-pearl were placed between the lips of the dead, these substances being associated in Chinese belief with life. As the spirits were believed to partake of the ethereal essence of the offering, the blood, which was believed to contain the very essence of life, would be especially acceptable.

A distinction should be made, too, between the animals offered on the marble altar, whose flesh was carried away and eaten by worshipers, and that of the bullock whose body was consumed upon the altar of burnt offerings. The former was a feast of communion with the divine.

The animals offered had to be without spot or blemish. Inspection had to be made, either by the Emperor in person or by someone deputed by him, and after the inspection the ceremony of killing had to be witnessed by such person. The sacrifice to Shang Ti, the Most High, was that of a young bullock. This, according to the *Li Ki,* was the supreme act of worship: "The sacrifice to God in the suburb is the highest act of worship."[6]

In the Hebrew ritual "The bodies of those beasts, whose blood was brought into the sanctuary by the High Priest for sin" "were burned without the camp,"[7] or, in later Jewish history, outside the city gate. So the bullock sacrificed at the Temple of Heaven as a whole burnt offering to God was burned outside the city gate.

There has never been but one recognized altar to Shang Ti in China. To erect a second one was as great an act

4 Ibid.
5 Leviticus xvii:11.
6 Li Ki, V:10.
7 Hebrews xiii:11.

of treason as among the Hebrews it was to raise an altar to Jehovah anywhere else than in Jerusalem. In both cases the worship of the Supreme God was centralized at the capital.

THE TEMPLE OF HEAVEN

The Temple of Heaven is an oblong enclosure, measuring 5583 feet from north to south and 5750 feet from east to west. It contains about 737 acres. It is surrounded by a strong brick wall, which has no entrance except upon the west. The northern wall is an arc of a circle, convex toward the north, being in this respect similar to the walls built upon the north side of grave plots to ward off evil influences which may come from the side of darkness. Two gates on the west side give entrance to the outer court, which is continuous around the four sides. It was used as pasture for the flocks and herds offered in sacrifice. A beautiful bell tower stands near the entrance to the court, and walks crossing it in various directions are shaded by a species of acacia. Formerly no one was admitted to this court except the officers in charge, those participating in the worship and the slaves who cared for the flocks and herds. The bell in the campanile announced the approach of the Emperor when he came to worship. A larger building near by was used for rehearsals of the musicians and posturers who assisted at the worship.

Surrounded on all sides by this outer court is an inner court, 4000 feet long north and south by 3400 east and west. It also is protected by a high brick wall, in which there are gates on the east, west and south sides. It is shaded by a grove of cypress. This inner court is divided into two sections, a southern one for service at the open marble altar, and a northern one for the ceremonies at the covered altar. The beautiful building, erected upon the top of a triple-terraced marble altar, like the altar itself, is circular in its ground plan. The walls and carved lattices are vermilion in color, and the triple roof of blue glazed tiles is supported upon huge pillars of teak decorated with red lacquer and gold. A circular medallion in the center of the ceiling bears the emblems of the Emperor and Empress, the dragon and the phœnix. These emblems also appear carved upon the marble stairs that lead from one terrace to another. Formerly the lattices were filled with blue glass rods which shed their color over the furniture of the interior. The old building was struck by lightning in 1890, a calamity regarded even then as an omen of the approaching downfall of the Manchu Dynasty. The present building never was completed and was never used by the Emperor. After the revolution the parliamentary committee appointed to draft the new constitution of the Republic held its meetings in this sacred chamber. A covered zigzag passage connects the building with the slaughter-house and kitchen in the north-eastern corner of this section of the inner court. To the north of the altar is an enclosure containing the hall in which the tablets to God and to the assisting spirits were kept. The covered altar is called the Hall of Prayer for the Year, that is to say, the hall where prayer was made for a year of peace and plenty. The stated service was held in the First Moon, according to the old calendar, and special services were held there in time of drought or other calamity, that prayer might be made for relief of the distress. This beautiful structure, however, is not the most important part of the Temple of Heaven. The southern section of the inner court, where sacrifice was offered to the Most High upon the uncovered marble altar under the star-lit dome of the sky, was the most holy place.

Before worshiping at this altar the Emperor had to prepare himself in the Hall of Fasting, which is situated in the south-western corner of the northern section of the inner court. This is a group of green-tiled buildings surrounded by a double wall and two moats. Around the outer wall, on the four sides, there is a colonnade. Within this wall the first court was given up to the guards and servants who accompanied His Majesty. Crossing the second moat, one passed through the inner wall into the central court, where the Emperor had his private quarters, and in which,

TABLET PAVILION, IMPERIAL CEMETERY, MUKDEN.
(Now called Shenyang)

THE EMPEROR KUANGHSÜ, GOING TO WORSHIP AT
THE TEMPLE OF HEAVEN.

too, there was a campanile whose bell announced his coming and going.

The open marble altar occupied the center of the southern section of the inner court. At the time of worship heavy beams were laid upon the floor of the uppermost terrace, for the support of nine tabernacles that were constructed there. These were made of boards with tenons that fitted into sockets in the beams just mentioned. These tabernacles were lined inside with yellow satin (yellow being the color of the Manchu Dynasty), and covered on the outside with blue silk. The one on the north side sheltered the throne chair upon which was placed the tablet of the Most High. In front of the tabernacle was a table spread with offerings of fruit and cooked food, and before the table was a trencher with the offering of a whole bullock, flayed. At one side was a table with the prayer placed upon it; at the other a table with offerings of jade, silk and wine, with the wine-cup and pitcher. In the middle of the terrace were the five carved pillars. On the central one was placed the golden censer, on either side of it a golden candle-stick, and, on the outermost pair, vases with gilt flowers.

On the eastern and western sides of the terrace were the tabernacles of the imperial ancestors, four on each side. These were fitted up like that of the Most High but there were no separate tables for prayers or for the silk offerings. But one prayer was offered—that to God, and the rolls of silk were placed on the same table as those offered to the Supreme Being.

Similar tabernacles were erected on the middle terrace. There were two on the east; one for the tablet to the Sun, and the other to those of the North Star, the Five Planets, the Twenty-eight Constellations, that is, Stars of the Zodiac. Two tabernacles also were erected on the west; one for the Moon and one for the Master of the Clouds and the Spirits of the Winds, Rains and Thunder. These were the "Assisting Spirits," probably occupying the place of the "Six Assisting Spirits" mentioned in the Book of History.[8]

[8] Shu King, Canon of Shun.

A small tent was erected on the south side of the middle terrace for the use of the Emperor. Toward the four cardinal points of the compass steps led from the upper terrace to the ground, three flights of nine steps each, in each direction, and at the foot of each flight of nine steps, on the north and south, was placed a pair of huge bronze urns from which great clouds of incense ascended during the worship. A pair of urns for incense to the assisting spirits on the east side of the middle terrace was placed outside the east gate of the circular court of the altar, and another pair outside the west gate for those worshiped on that side. This circular court surrounding the white marble altar is 335 feet in diameter, and is surrounded by a red wall covered with blue tiles. There are openings toward the four cardinal points of the compass. Each opening is divided into three door-ways constructed of white marble pillars and lintels, decorated with dragons and flying clouds. The doors were covered with red lacquer and closed during worship. At the foot of the altar stairs on the south side the orchestra was arranged, and behind it the ranks of the posturers.

This circular court of the altar was surrounded by a square court 549 feet on a side, with its walls and gates. In the south-western corner of this court were three tall masts that supported huge lanterns of purple silk. In the south-eastern corner was the Altar of Burnt Offerings, constructed of green glazed tile with stairs on the east, west and south. The furnace opening was on the north. In a quadrant extending north-eastwards from this altar were eight braziers, in which the offerings of silk were consumed.

In a grove of dark cypresses outside the east gate of this court was the treasury, in which the holy vessels were stored, and the slaughter-house where the victims were killed. Outside the north gate was a temple in which the tablet to the Most High and those to the imperial ancestors and the assisting spirits were kept. The principal building was circular with red walls, and covered with a conical roof of blue tiles. Outside the south gate and on the east side of the walk there was a dressing tent for the Emperor.

The paved way from the tent to the south gate of the southern section of the great inner court, and thence by way of the outer court to the Hall of Fasting, was covered with coir matting and sheltered by a canopy of blue silk lined with yellow satin. Standards supporting lanterns of purple silk were stationed every fifteen or twenty feet.

At the winter solstice, a season of religious celebration in all lands, the most solemn service was held. Five days before the sacrifice all the animals were carefully inspected, and, at the fifth watch in the early morning of the day preceding the worship, the furniture was arranged upon the altar. At that hour the roadway from the south gate of the Imperial Palace to the Temple of Heaven was swept and covered with yellow earth. Guards were stationed along the route and ordered all houses and shops to close their doors. Blue curtains cut off the cross streets. At nine o'clock A.M. the bell and drum in the tower over the south gate of the palace announced that the Emperor was leaving for the Temple of Heaven. This was echoed at the campanile in the outer court of the temple. All trains were forbidden to enter or leave the city. A sabbath-like stillness settled over the capital. The Emperor dressed in his dragon robes, sitting in his palanquin, which was covered with yellow satin and lined with blue silk, was carried by 36 men. A herald announced his coming. All persons except the guards and attendants left the street. An incense-bearer followed the herald, and behind him were carried the imperial standard and the yellow umbrella, just preceding the imperial chair. Princes, dukes, and high ministers of state followed it and the Imperial Guard completed the retinue. Between files of kneeling soldiers it made its way to the southernmost gate on the west side of the Temple of Heaven. There all officers except those who had been excused because of age were compelled to leave their chairs, horses and carts, and enter the temple on foot. The Emperor was carried in his palanquin to the south gate of the inner court, where he, too, was compelled to leave his chair. He entered on foot through the eastern opening of this gate-way. The central door-ways and the central paths were reserved for the spirits. From the south gate he walked to the temple where the tablets were kept, and there offered incense to God and to his ancestors. He knelt three times, each time bowing his head three times to the earth, and announced that he would sacrifice to them on the following morning. He then inspected the offerings and the altar, and went to the Hall of Fasting where he spent the day in preparation.

At nightfall the lanterns and the candles in the golden candlesticks were lighted. Just before midnight the Court of Sacrificial Worship erected a temporary altar at the slaughterhouse, and, after burning incense thereon, the victims were slain. The handle of the sacrificial knife was decorated with bells. The blood was caught in a globular vessel and poured into a pit on the east side of the slaughterhouse. The hair of the victims was also burned there. The wood was arranged upon the altar of burnt offering, and one bullock laid thereon. The other offerings were placed in their proper places on the marble altar and the prayer tablet placed on its table. Three hours and a half before sunrise, the Emperor is informed that the time for worship has arrived. The bell at the Hall of Fasting announces his departure and gives warning to the officials at the altar, who, with appropriate ceremonies take the tablets from their shrines and place each one in a kiosque with a cylindrical body and a conical top, painted in black and gold. These are carried by means of rods passing through rings at the sides. The tablets are carried to the south gate of the square court of the Altar, and thence to the top of the Altar, where each is placed in its appropriate tabernacle. The Emperor follows the sacred way to the south gate of the square court of the Altar, and enters there his dressing tent. There he puts on his High Priest's robes. When all is in order he comes out of his tent and is met by ministers bearing a ewer and basin of water, in which he washes his hands, for the Emperor had to be a man of clean hands, as well as of pure heart, in order to worship God. The Jewish priests also were required to wash their hands and feet in the laver ''between the tent of the congregation and the altar, before going to the altar to minister.'' [9]

The Emperor then passes into the eastern entrance of the south gate of the square court of the Altar, and through the corresponding gate of the circular court, and ascends the Altar from the south. There he stands facing the north, the side of darkness, just as the Hebrew High Priest did at Jerusalem. It is still dark. A faint glow is shed over the courts by the light of the great lanterns. Ushers conduct the various officers to their places. The musicians stand in two ranks, one on either side of the pathway. The 64 civilian posturers, with wands and plumes, and the 64 military posturers, bearing spears and battle-axes, are also arranged, a group of both on each side of the pathway. Behind these, arranged according to rank, are the princes, dukes, marquises, earls, viscounts and barons, and the high officials of the government, rank on rank in the circular court, the square court, and outside the opened doors of the square court, all facing the north. The Master of Ceremonies announces the service for the reception of the Spirit of the Most High. The fire is lighted under the Altar of Burnt Offering, and the orchestra plays the first piece of music.

The service was divided into nine sections by nine pieces of music. The first act was to offer incense. It was accompanied by three kneelings and nine prostrations. When the Emperor kotowed and the attending ministers heard ''the sound of the cornet, flute, harp, sackbut, psaltery and all kinds of music''—''they all fell down and worshiped.'' [10] Thus the long programme was carefully carried out. The offerings of jade and silk each had its appropriate piece of music, and each offering was followed by kneeling and prostration of the whole company. But when the first libation of wine was made to the Most High it was accompanied by the dancing of the military posturers, with brandishing of spears and battle-axes.

Immediately after this first libation the whole company

[9] Exodus xxx:18 and 19.
[10] Daniel iii:7.

knelt while the prayer was read. After its reading it was placed on the Altar of the Most High. During the offerings of wine to the imperial ancestors, none but the civilian dancers took part in the posturing. After these libations, a plate of meat offerings and a cup of the drink offering were carried to the shrine of the Most High, where the Emperor, kneeling, was served by Ministers of the Court of Imperial Banquets and officers of the Guards. They handed to him first the cup of blessing, of which he took a sip, and then the tray of cooked food, which he took and raised reverently in his right hand and passed to the officers on his right. Thus symbolically he entered into communion with the Most High and with his ancestors. After the offerings had been made the prayer tablet, the silk, the incense and the wine were carried to the Altar of Burnt Offering, and to the braziers of other spirits, and burned. The services were ended and the tablets reverently restored to their shrines.

WORSHIP AT OTHER SHRINES

The services in spring at the covered altar were very similar. At the Altar to Imperial Earth in the northern suburb the sacrifices were not burned but buried. The spirits of mountains, rivers and seas were associated with the Earth in the worship.

There has been a disposition shown among some writers to describe Confucianism as a dualism because of this worship of Heaven and Earth, and the philosophical doctrine of the *Yin* and *Yang* [11] lends some support to the theory. But a more careful analysis will show that this is not the case. The prominence given in the construction of the Temple of Heaven, and in its worship, to the number, three, is not without reason. It has its origin in the Confucian triad—Heaven, Earth and Man. The three cere-

[11] The *Yin* is the female, the *Yang* the male principle. The *Yin* is the negative, the *Yang* positive. The *Yin* darkness and weakness, the *Yang* light and strength.

monies used in the worship of this triad can be traced to the earliest known period of Chinese history. The "Three ceremonies" are mentioned in the Book of History.[12] The worship of the spirits of men is shown in the ancestor worship already described, but the representative man, the Chinese ideal man, is Confucius; and the official worship of the Sage at the spring and autumn equinoxes in more than 1500 temples in China was regarded as scarcely less important than that of Heaven and Earth This cult, however, is comparatively recent. In ancient times the third ceremony was that for the worship of the imperial ancestors. This, too, was not neglected by the Manchus, as we have seen, but the worship of Confucius since the Seventh century A.D. has over-shadowed it.

The first time I ever attempted to witness the service in a Confucian temple I was mobbed, and perhaps might have been seriously injured if I had not been rescued. Another American and myself were invited by a Chinese gentleman to attend the worship at one of the large temples in Nanking. We thought it would be interesting first to visit the temple on the afternoon preceding the sacrifice, in order to study the arrangement of the furniture and see the sacrifices in place. As we entered the gateway we were seen by a crowd of idlers who did not approve of the conduct of our Chinese friends in thus leading two "foreign devils" into the holy precincts. The temple is one of the finest in the whole country. Its buildings are covered with red stucco and roofed with golden-colored tiles. The courts are spacious and paved and are surrounded with pillared cloisters. We passed from court to court, followed by an ever-increasing crowd of angry Chinese. When we reached the door of the Sacrificial Hall, on whose portico we saw arranged the instruments of the orchestra, we found that the crowd had grown dangerous. We attempted to escape through one of the cloistered ways, but found ourselves stopped by the mob, who began to beat us. When after much struggling we reached the entrance, the mob closed the gates and were punishing us. The

[12] Shu King, Canon of Shun.

Chinese friend had disappeared and we saw no way of escape, but in a few moments the friend returned with the official in charge. This kind old gentleman, in his flowing robes and mandarin's hat, parted the crowd right and left and escorted us into the street, warning the crowd at the same time not to attack us. Needless to say we did not witness the sacrifice the next morning.

Some years later at Shanghai the Taotai invited me to attend the autumn service in the temple there. About three o'clock in the morning of September 21, 1898, I arrived at the West Gate and was admitted. A palanquin with bearers was awaiting me on the inside. There was no electric light in those days in the Chinese city, and no gas, but here and there in the narrow, crooked streets the darkness was made visible by a small oil lamp. The chair-bearers were not puzzled; they knew their way over the slippery pavements with their eyes shut. After a ride of twenty or thirty minutes the temple was reached. The court was filled with the students and gentry of the district, each in his religious dress. This was a dark blue gown with light blue facings. It was belted in at the waist. The hat was similar to the Chinese dress hat of those days but had a longer spike on the top. Each worshiper carried a panache of peacock feathers and a tablet on which the hymn to Confucius was written. The orchestra contained the usual collection of stringed and wind instruments, drums and cymbals, bells and musical stones, the starter and the stopper.

The Taotai placed me at one end of the hall where I could witness the whole service. A Master of Ceremonies directed it. There was no image in the temple. The tablet to Confucius was on the altar. Before it was spread a table of fruits and cooked vegetables. In front of that, on trusses, were the bodies of a sheep and a pig. The orchestra played appropriate music, and the Taotai entered the hall kotowed, and then lighted incense upon the altar of incense just inside the doorway. The worshipers outside, arranged in ranks, bowed and waved their plumes and chanted the pean to Confucius. There were offerings likewise of wine and silk. These were made first to Confucius and then to the four principal disciples; Tseng Tzu, Yen Tzu, Tzu Ssu, and Meng Tzu. The last we know as Mencius. The altars to these disciples were at the sides of the hall. After the offering had been made upon the altar the silk and wine were carried out into the court and burned in a brazier. At the close of the service the meats were distributed to those participating in the worship, and I went to breakfast with the Taotai.

While the service was being conducted in the main hall of the temple, similar offerings were being made in two side chapels to the seventy disciples of the Master. In each of these chapels one sheep only was offered. After the decree of 1907, raising the rank of Confucius in the pantheon, it became necessary at his altars to offer a whole bullock, as well as the sacrifice of sheep and swine. The same sacrifice was made to him as to the Most High. In some Confucian temples there is a chapel behind the main hall of sacrifice, dedicated to the mother of the Sage.

One of the very interesting religious services under the old Manchu régime, but one which dates from a great antiquity, was that celebrated in the Temple of Agriculture. On a great square altar in the grove sacrifices were made to Shennung, the Patron Saint of Agriculture, and the Emperor himself plowed eight furrows in the Field of God. The plow was a light shovel plow, painted yellow, and was drawn by an ox. After the Emperor, various princes and nobles also plowed each his allotted number of furrows. In truth the field had been well plowed beforehand and the soil was as soft as that of a garden, so that the task was not a difficult one. The field was then sown with grain, which later in the year was harvested and made into flour to be used in the temple offerings. This service took place in the mid-month of spring, and was intended to be a recognition by the State of the importance of agriculture and thus an encouragement to the farmer. In every county there is an altar to the local guardian spirits of the soil and the harvests, and surrounding or adjoining it there is such a field of God, which the local authorities were accustomed to plow in the spring, in imitation of the good example of the Emperor.

ATTEMPTS TO REVIVE CONFUCIANISM

Several attempts have been made to revive Confucianism as a state religion since the establishment of the Republic, but Parliament has decided to follow the American example and make no establishment for religious worship. Opposition to Confucianism came from three quarters; from those who were indifferent to all religions, from the Christians, who are becoming a very influential element in Chinese politics, and from the Buddhists, who had organized a society to promote the establishment of their religion as that of the State.

The Confucianists were filled with fear that the disestablishment of their religion would mean the disintegration of society and the moral deterioration of the individual, but the experience of our own country is just to the contrary. Religion is less formal and more powerful when it is supported, not by state authority and subsidy, but by the free-will offerings of those who believe in it. Our country is not less religious than those which support established churches. This was pointed out in 1913 to the leaders of the Confucian Society. The reply made was that the sacrifices were too costly to be borne by private enterprise. It was suggested in rejoinder that bloody sacrifices were not necessary to worship. The example of Judaism was mentioned, which long ago gave up its sacrifices of slain beasts, yet has not lost its ethical influence. The answer was that this might do for vegetarians, but not for meat-eaters; that worship means the offering of the best that we have, and that we do not invite guests to dinner and omit the meat courses. China needs a prophet Micah to proclaim the worthlessness of forms, to teach the people that the sacrifice of "thousands of rams and tens of thousands of rivers of oil" are not needed to purchase the favor of God, but that true worship consists in the practice of justice, mercy and piety.[13]   A Chinese St. Paul is wanted to allegorize the old ritual and substitute spiritual for material offerings.

On the whole the influence of Confucianism has been beneficial. It has promoted peace and good order in society and encouraged moral living in the individual. It has allowed the widest latitude in philosophical speculation. It has never formulated an authoritative creed. It places no obstacle in the way of research nor prevents the acceptance of the conclusions of modern science. Neither has its worship been a mere matter of form. The Book of History says: "The spirits are not always favorable; they accept only the worship of the sincere."[14] Sickness, poverty, drought and war, it teaches, are sent as punishments for sin. "The ways of the Most High are not invariable; upon the good He bestows blessing a hundred fold; upon the evil He visits a hundred fold calamity."[15] It is a religion that emphasizes the five virtues: mercy, justice, piety, wisdom and honesty. It aims to strengthen the three cords of society: the tie between ruler and subject, that between parents and children, and that between husband and wife. It thus promotes peace in the State and seeks to preserve the purity of the home. Of the lofty sentiments inculcated many have already been quoted from the teachings of Confucius. To these we may add a few from the greatest of his disciples. Mencius said: "Virtue is man's restful habitation; righteousness is his straight path."[16] Mencius also combated the prevailing belief that suffering is always a punishment for sin. He said: "When God is about to call a man to some great undertaking, He first excites his resolution by bitter suffering and wearies his sinews and bones with toil. He starves his body and impoverishes him. He causes all he does to fail. Thus He

13 Micah vi:8.
14 Shu King III, T'ai Chia.
15 Shu King III: I Hsün.
16 Mencius. Book IV. Li Lou, Part I, Chap. X:2.

stimulates his mind, hardens his resolution, and supplies his deficiencies." [17] Again: "The path is at hand; we seek it afar." [18] "The great man is one who does not lose his child heart." [19] "Although one may be a wicked man, yet if he adjusts the wrong, fasts and bathes he may offer sacrifice to God." [20] "God sees as the people see; God hears as the people hear." [21] This last, however, is a quotation from the Book of History. Mencius was greater than his Master in some respects. He had more sympathy with the common people, whom he regarded as the very foundation of the State.

[17] Ibid.   Book VI.   Kao Tzu, Part II, Chap. IV:2.
[18] Ibid.   Book IV.   Li Lou, Part I, Chap. XI.
[19] Ibid.   Book IV.   Li Lou, Part II, Chap. XII.
[20] Ibid.   Book IV.   Li Lou, Part II, Chap. XXV:2.
[21] Ibid.   Book V.   Wang Chang, Part I, Chap. V:8.

CHAPTER XIV

CHINESE BUDDHISM

Earnestness is the path of nirvana; thoughtlessness the path of death.—The Dhammapada.

On New Year's day, 1914, I was in Colombo, the chief port of the Island of Ceylon. It was a brilliant day and intensely hot—too hot, indeed, to go into the sun without a sun-helmet or umbrella. The glare of the street, too, was very trying to the eyes. But we went ashore properly protected, and rode out to a celebrated Buddhist shrine, the Temple of Kelaniya, five miles from the city on the banks of the Kelani River.

As we passed through the city we stopped to admire a great banyan tree whose branches covered a circle of something like a hundred feet in diameter. Here and there a branch shot downward and entered the ground, forming a support and new source of nourishment to the spreading tree above. The whole resembled a natural colonnade. This tree is to the Buddhist a sacred emblem, the symbol of his faith, for under it—the Bodhi tree—the Master Gautama, the "Lion of the tribe of Sakya," attained to enlightenment, and, like it, his great religion has marched through Asia, putting down a new root and starting a new growth in each country which it has entered.

The ride to Kelani over the smooth roads, shaded by the dark foliage of tropical groves, was a delightful one, and the temple was particularly interesting because the earliest form of Buddhism still persists in Ceylon. We wanted to compare this shrine with those which we had seen in China and Japan.

Kelani Temple consisted of a group of unpretentious brick buildings that had been white-washed. The most prominent was a bottle-shaped dagoba of some fifty feet in diameter and perhaps a hundred feet in height. It was supposed to cover a portion of the ashes of the Buddha.

On the opposite side of the enclosure was the assembly hall, which is an open pavilion—a platform of tile sheltered by a roof supported upon numerous pillars. There were no walls. Here the monks gathered at stated seasons for instruction and conference.

The central building contained pictures of the Buddha similar to those in China and Japan, except that the halo behind the head was made to represent the flattened head of the cobra de capello, the head proper and the hood taking the appearance of a trefoil. The cobra was the protector of Buddha, and this is perhaps the origin of the halo.

In the Bodhi tree and the hooded cobra many scholars find traces of that ancient tree and serpent worship which is common to so many lands. Buddhism has always been tolerant of local superstitions, and probably adopted and re-interpreted the story of the tree and the serpent, just as our own religion has adopted and Christianized so many of the festivals of the ancient Romans and other Europeans.

When we came away from the temple we bought as souvenirs some verses of a Buddhist sutra, written, as all the earliest Indian books were, on palm leaves.

THE BUDDHIST LEGEND

The story of Buddha is well known in its general outlines, but it may be worth while to recall the principal events of his life.

He is said to have been an Indian Prince, Siddartha. His mother, Maya, a young bride, dreamed of his coming from Heaven. She miraculously conceived and bore a son, the re-incarnate Buddha. There were many marvelous manifestations at his entrance into the world. Immediately upon his birth he stood upright, took seven steps, then turned to the four quarters and said: "Now only I am

born this once to be the savior of the world.'' Forthwith
two streams of water fell from heaven upon him in baptism.
The devas sang and foretold that he would deliver the
world, and unite all kings under his sway. An old seer
came to the palace, took him in his arms, and predicted
that he would be a great teacher. When once instructed
he excelled all his teachers.[1]

He grew to manhood and at seventeen was married to
Yashodara. But he was not satisfied. The misery of the
world oppressed him. One day, accompanied by his
charioteer, he drove out the east gate of the city intending
to go to a pleasure garden. He met an old man with white
hair and crooked back, and thought with sadness of the
rapidity with which men grow old. He returned home
depressed. Another day he drove out the south gate
and met a sick man with swollen features and loathsome
eruptions. Again he returned depressed to his palace.
The third time he went out the west gate and saw a dead
man being carried to his grave, while his careless relatives
followed chatting and laughing. The horror of it all ap-
palled him. The last journey was outside the north gate,
where he met a beggar monk with bowl and staff, who
taught him to abandon the world and its pleasures.

After deciding to try the path of asceticism he forsook
his home and went to a distant spot beside a river, where
for six long years he lived in abject poverty, scarcely
eating at all. This was unsatisfactory. He arose one day,
bathed, and went to sit under a bodhi tree. There he was
tempted of the devil, but triumphed and attained to enlightenment, from which circumstance he is called the
Buddha, or ''enlightened one.'' This is the tradition as
recorded in the Chinese Buddhist scriptures. It is proper
to say that some of these stories, which remind us of the
Christian gospels, are unknown to the Southern Buddhist
tradition.

Once enlightened the Buddha began to teach. The first
truth, so he declared, is that life is sorrow. As Edwin
Arnold phrased it in his Light of Asia:

[1] Buddhism in China, by Rev. Samuel Beal, p. 74.

> The first truth is of sorrow, Be not mocked!
> Life, which ye prize, is long-drawn agony;
> Only its pains abide; its pleasures are
>   As birds that light, and fly.

The second truth is that the cause of sorrow is desire. The third is that the cure for sorrow is the suppression of desire. The fourth truth sets forth the method by which desire can be suppressed. It is an eight-fold path; right understanding, right wisdom, right speech, right action, right manner of life, right helps, right recollection, and right meditation. This eight-fold path leads to nirvana. The passage to nirvana is likened to the falling of the dew-drop into the sea. As "The dew-drop slips into the shining sea," and is swallowed up in its wide waste of waters, so the individual soul sinks into the great sea of life and becomes one with the all soul. By the method outlined one thus escapes the endless round of transmigration which binds man to the earthly life.

Early Buddhism is said to have been atheistic, because it points to no almighty over-ruling God for deliverance. In fact it teaches the superiority of the Buddha to the gods—i.e., there is a fate which even the gods cannot escape. But it is hardly fair to call Buddha an atheist, and a religion of atheism is well-nigh self-contradictory. What Buddha refused to do was to frame a theory of the origin of all things. For even a little child, when you tell him that God made all things, will ask "But who made God?" So when Gautama was asked the question as to the origin of the world he was silent. Afterwards he said: "Only a Buddha can understand this." Whatever we may think of the pessimism of Buddhism—whatever fault we may find with its cure for the miseries of the world—we must admit that in some of its teaching it has wonderfully anticipated some of the conclusions of modern science. The existence of multitudes of worlds, all controlled by fixed and immutable law, the evolution of life from the lowest to the highest orders, the relationship of each to the whole, the constant birth and destruction of worlds, a continual emerging from chaos and successive returns thereto, and the spontaneous variation which is the origin of species; in all this the modern evolutionary philosophy has been in a humble way foreshadowed.[2]

BUDDHIST ETHICS

In its ethical teaching Buddhism takes a high rank. Here are its ten commandments as commonly translated:[3]

Thou shalt not kill.
Thou shalt not steal.
Thou shalt not commit adultery.
Thou shalt not lie.
Thou shalt not drink intoxicating drink.
Thou shalt not defame.
Thou shalt not boast.
Thou shalt not be stingy.
Thou shalt not be angry.
Thou shalt not revile the three precious ones.

The Dhammapada contains a multitude of wise precepts beautifully phrased:[4]

If a man speaks or acts with an evil thought, pain follows him as the wheel follows the foot of the ox that draws the carriage.

He who wishes to put on the yellow dress without having cleansed himself from sin, who disregards also temperance and truth, he is unworthy of the yellow dress.

The thoughtless man, even if he can recite a large portion of the law, but is not a doer of it, has no share in the priesthood, but is like a cow-herd counting the cows of others.

Earnestness is the path of nirvana; thoughtlessness the path of death.

Like a beautiful flower, full of color but without scent, are the fine but fruitless words of him who does not act accordingly.

The scent of flowers does not travel against the wind, neither that of sandal-wood; but the odor of good deeds travels even against the wind.

[2] See "Three Lectures on Buddhism," by Ernest J. Eitel, pp. 65 and 66.

[3] See "Initiation into Monkhood"—infra—for ten vows taken on entering the order.

[4] Translation of Max Müller, in Sacred Books of the East, Vol. X.

Long is the night to him who is awake; long is a mile to him who is tired, long is life to the foolish who do not know the true law.

If a fool be associated with a wise man. even all his life, he will perceive the truth as little as a spoon perceives the taste of soup.

One is the road that leads to wealth, another the path that leads to nirvana.

Well-makers lead the water whither they will; fletchers bend the arrow, carpenters shape the log of wood; but wise people fashion themselves.

Even the gods envy him whose senses, like horses well broken in by the driver, have been subdued, who is free from pride and from appetite.

If one conquer in battle a thousand times a thousand men, and if another conquer himself, he is the greatest of conquerors.

Let us live happily, then, not hating those that hate us.

Let a man overcome anger by love; let him overcome evil by good; let him overcome the greedy by liberality, the liar by truth.

The man who gives himself to drinking intoxicating liquors, he, even in this world, digs up his own root.

A multitude of other sayings equally wise and beautiful may be culled from the Buddhist scriptures.

BUDDHIST PROPAGANDA

Sakyamuni, i.e., the "Sage of the Sakyas," known also as Prince Siddartha, the "perfect one," and as a religious teacher called Gautama, was born perhaps in 600 B.C. and died probably about 543 B.C.*

For many years his followers were found only in his native kingdom, but in the chaos which resulted from the invasion of Alexander the Great, Chandragupta, whom the Greeks know as Sandrokottos, a man of low birth, was enabled to establish an empire which swallowed up the rival kingdoms of India. Being an upstart, and frowned upon by the high caste Brahmins, he gave his sympathy and support to Buddhism. His grandson, Ashoka, continued the favor of the state to the new religion and established a board of foreign missions, so that Buddhism spread rapidly in all directions. About 275 B.C. it was introduced into Ceylon, and from thence it was extended to Java,

* Oriental scholars give various dates for the birth and death of the Buddha, from 744 B.C. to 477 B.C. for the birth and from 628 B.C. to 380 B. C. for the death.

Sumatra, Burmah and Siam. It also spread northwards into Cashmere, Nepaul and Central Asia. At a general council held at Pataliputra in 242 B.C. the Buddhist church split into two branches, the Northern and Southern; and after Buddhism was suppressed in India, in 178 B.C. these two schools, being without communication, developed along different lines.

The Buddhism of Ceylon, Burmah and Siam still remains much as at the beginning. Northern Buddhism, on the contrary, adopted many local superstitions and was influenced by various philosophical and religious teachings.

About 250 B.C. certain apostles of the Buddhist faith are said to have carried its teaching to north-western China, but this date is uncertain. At any rate little impression was made upon China at that time. The apostles numbered eighteen, of whom sixteen were Indians and two Chinese. They are worshiped to-day in every Buddhist temple in China. This much we know, however, that for two centuries before Christ, China was engaged in constant warfare with the tribes of Central Asia, and undoubtedly the Chinese became acquainted with Buddhism, which at that time flourished in those regions. From one of these expeditions they appear to have brought back as loot a golden image of Buddha, and there is, therefore, nothing improbable in the story that the Emperor Ming Ti dreamed one night, in A.D. 61, that this golden image came into the palace. The brother of the Emperor appears to have been favorably disposed towards Buddhism, and he persuaded the Emperor to send a deputation to bring Buddhist teachers to China. They arrived about A.D. 65 or 70 with a sandal-wood image and one sacred book.

Slowly the faith spread over the country. Oftentimes it was persecuted and all but crushed by Confucian opposition, but to-day its monasteries are found everywhere and its followers are divided among numerous sects. For besides the great schism in the Buddhist church, 242 B.C., resulting in northern and southern branches, other numerous divisions occurred. There are more than twenty sects in the southern church and not less than ten in China.

AMIDHISM

In this transfer from India to China the religion of Gautama has been greatly modified, as I have intimated. The most flourishing sect in China is that of Amidha Buddha, so different in its teaching from that of early Buddhism that some would classify it as a separate religion. Some believe that it has been influenced by Christianity, perhaps through a Persian medium.

Over and above all the Buddhas it places one who is eternal, omnipresent, perfect in virtue, and who has compassion upon the weak and erring and delivers them by his power and grace. Him even the Buddhas worship. It teaches that there is another Buddha yet to come, Maitreya, a Messiah such as was expected by the Jews and by the Zoroastrians. He will plant faith in the supreme Amitabha (Omito Fo). It teaches, too, not that one should save himself from sorrow by ascetic practices, but that he should trust in Amidha's help for his own salvation and also that he should endeavor to save others.

Instead of an unconscious nirvana it holds out the hope of immortality in a paradise of happiness in the Western Heaven. These doctrines, so foreign to early Buddhism, began to flourish about A.D. 100. This popular sect is known as the Lotus Sect, or the Pure Land Sect.

When I first went to China I made my home in a little temple of this sect in the city of Nanking known as "Thistle Abbey." It was a retired spot among the hills and bamboo groves of the northern part of the city, within the walls, but a mile or more from the city streets. Our nearest neighbors were the dead. All around us, covering the hills in every direction, were graves; some of them the tombs of the well-to-do, well kept, surrounded by walls or banks of turf and shaded by shrubs or groves of trees. Others, the graves of the poor, were neglected and overgrown with wild grass, in some instances so shallow that the dogs had torn open the coffins and scattered the bones on the hillsides. The abbey had been built by one or two wealthy families who wanted to make a pious use of their money and who desired masses said for the souls of their dead. The solitary monk in charge had little else to do save to gather rents from the lands attached to the abbey for its support. He was a good-natured, generous person but extremely weak morally. He attended to his prayers at stated hours, not only in the day but throughout the night also. His fondness for opium and his addiction to grosser forms of sin soon cost him his post.

We had a part of the temple fitted up according to European and American ideas. The brick pavements were covered with wooden flooring. The rooms were ceiled and plastered; chimneys were built, and glass replaced the paper in the window lattices. To this day the resinous odor of pine shavings at once suggest to me the fragrance of burning incense, the tinkle of the altar bell in the night watches, and brings to memory the happy experiences of those days.

THE GODDESS OF MERCY

One of the saints worshiped by this sect is Kwanyin, popularly known as the Goddess of Mercy. Some five miles north of Nanking outside the Shengtzu Men, or Gate of Divine Strategy, is a little village known as Kwanyin Men —the Gate of Kwanyin. The village is on the bank of the Yangtze River, and guards a pass through the range of hills known as the Tiger Mountain. The range is very precipitous on the river side and is full of caves, commonly known as the Twelve Caves. In one of the caves is an image of Kwanyin, but it is the likeness of a man, not a woman. This is accounted for by the belief that Kwanyin has had three incarnations—the last time as a woman. She has, therefore, three birthdays every year which are all kept by her devout worshipers. She is not a Buddha but a Bodhisatva—from choice. She declines to accept nirvana, because she has compassion upon the sinful and sorrowing and desires to save them. Therefore, she remains within the power of the wheel of change, i.e., she is subject to re-incarnation, birth and death. Her story is a beautiful one. She loved the religious life and refused to marry, although her royal father promised the throne to the husband of her choice. She entered the White Sparrow Convent and became a nun. The most menial tasks were given her to perform, but the dragons drew water for her and the wild beasts of the field carried her wood. In his anger the father burned the convent, but her prayers brought rain that extinguished the flames. She was forced to return home and was given her choice of marriage or death. She still refused to marry and was put to death. She descended into hell, but at her approach hell became a paradise of lilies. King Yama, the ruler of hell, begged her to go away so that he could make evil doers suffer. She received the gift of immortality but refused that of nirvana, and came back to earth that she might comfort the sorrowing, soothe the afflicted and deliver the sinful. Everywhere in China temples are erected in her honor. Everywhere she is loved and worshiped. Her pity, her mercy, her love, bring all the afflicted to her altar, and her rosary is recited in a thousand times ten thousand homes.[5]

One of the most common forms of the cult is that of the Kwanyin who gives sons. She is represented standing on the lotus holding a child in her arms. The desire for sons is so strong that many devout women frequent her altars in petition for this gift, and often you see the altars adorned with votive offerings, embroidered slippers for the goddess or miniature babies, little dolls dedicated to the gracious saint. There is such a striking resemblance in her image to that of the Virgin and Child that the Roman Catholic altars to Mary find ready worshipers among the Chinese, and good Abbe Huc thought the devil was imitating the true religion in order to delude souls.

Once while waiting at Kwanyin Men for the ferry to take me over the Yangtze I went into a temple and sat down to chat with the monk in charge, who kindly brought me a cup of tea. While we talked, a stranger, a boatman,

[5] From the translation of the Life of Kwanyin, Goddess of Mercy, by Rose Sickler Williams.

came in apparently in great distress. He put his offering
in the box, bought a bundle of incense (which was lighted
and put upon the altar), kotowed and prayed. Then he
drew his lot. The monk went to the corresponding drawer
and brought him the answer to his prayer. The boatman
asked him to read it. The monk said: "About what were
you praying?" He replied, "About sickness in my family.
My wife is lying very ill in the boat." "Well," said the
monk evasively, "she will get better." "But read the
answer," said the boatman. The monk flushed and sent
for the monastery cook, who could read. The cook read
it to the boatman. The portion referring to illness said,
"The person who is ill will get better if a good physician
is called." "Where shall I find a good physician?" enquired the boatman. "You can't expect the god to tell
you what to do and find a physician too," said the monk
in an angry tone.

Kwanyin is frequently represented as standing on a rock
in the midst of the sea and rescuing men and women from
the engulfing waves. This represents the sea of misery and
sin.

BODHIDHARMA

In one of the Twelve Caves, far up the mountain side,
reached by a path that is very little frequented, there is
an image of a celebrated Buddhist saint, Tamo, the first
of the Chinese patriarchs. The face and the heavy black
beard are decidedly non-Chinese. Tamo is in Sanscrit
Dharma. Bodhidharma came to China from India during
the reign of Wu Ti, the first Emperor of the Liang Dynasty,
about A.D. 526. When he arrived in Nanking, then the
capital of China, tradition says that the Emperor asked
him about Heaven and Hell. The saint replied, "I am
Heaven; you are Hell." This shocked the Emperor; but
he was such a zealous Buddhist that a few years later he
resigned his throne, like Charles V of Spain, and retired
to a monastery for the remainder of his life. The Emperor
said to Dharma, "I have all my life been building temples,

copying sacred books, and admitting new monks to take
the vows; how much merit may I be supposed to have
accumulated?" "None," said Dharma. "Why not?"
asked the Emperor. "All this," replied the saint, "is but
the insignificant effect of an imperfect cause, not complete
in itself. It is the shadow that follows the substance and
is without real existence." "Then what is real merit?"
asked the Emperor. "Purity and enlightenment, depth
and completeness; being wrapped in thought while surrounded with vacancy and stillness. Such merit cannot be
obtained by worldly means," was the reply. Dharma was
dissatisfied with his visit to Nanking and crossed the
Yangtze. Tradition says that he floated over the river
on a reed, and this has become a favorite theme of Chinese
artists. From Nanking he made his way to Loyang, near
the Yellow River, and at that time in the Kingdom of Wei.
In a monastery there he sat with his face to the wall for
nine years. When he died he was placed in a coffin, and
a few days later a disciple came to view the remains and
found the dead man with one shoe in his hands. "Whither
goest thou?" asked the disciple. "To the Western
Heaven," the dead man answered. Again a few days later
the coffin was opened and lo, the saint had disappeared.
One shoe only remained in the coffin. In popular representation he is shown carrying one shoe. The shoe left
behind was, it is said, preserved many years as a sacred
relic, but was stolen during the T'ang Dynasty and nobody
knows where it is to-day.

A little tract circulated by the monk in this cave of Tamo
contains some curious teaching which savors of Christian
influence. It condemns the Buddhist doctrine of an endless round of metempsychosis, and its theory of salvation
by abstraction, and declares that to attain salvation we
must bathe in blood. The young monk seeking instruction
is told that that which he seeks is One and no more, without form or shape, and the source of all things in heaven
and earth, and he is commanded to preach this doctrine
until it has pervaded the whole earth. He asks how to
obtain an upright disposition, and is told not to seek it out-

side himself, that it is not by ascending into heaven nor descending into the abyss, but that he must find it in his own heart.

The meditative school or sect established by Bodhidharma scorns the worship of images and the use of books and all ceremonies. In a conversation with a young monk Dharma asked him what he was studying. "The law," said the young man. "I see no law," said the patriarch. "All that's white is paper and all that's black is ink." Dharma's manner of life and scorn of culture remind one of Simon Stylites and other pillar saints who sought salvation in silent meditation in extraordinary positions.

Somewhat similar to this sect is the *Wu Wei Chiao,* or "Do Nothing Sect," which originated in the province of Shantung, where so many religious societies have had their origin. Its members are a highly moral people and total abstainers from wine and tobacco. They revere Buddha but decline to worship him. They are quietists in religious practices, have no use for images and ceremonies.

LAMAISM

Upon the introduction of Buddhism into Tibet it became very much corrupted by the incorporation of Shamanist superstitions, and this form of Buddhism is that which is prevalent in Mongolia and in North China. This sect is known as the Lama sect. The Lamaists have a very compact organization reminding us of the Roman Catholic Church. They have two popes in Tibet—one, the Dalai Lama, is the civil head of the church and ruler of Tibet; the other, the Dashilumpo Lama, is the religious chief of the system. China, including Mongolia and Tibet, is divided into districts in each of which there is a Hutukhtu. There is one in Peip'ing. The Hutukhtu in Urga, in 1911, became Emperor of independent Outer Mongolia. He died in 1924 after being deprived of his temporal power. His kingdom was seized by the Mongol People's Revolutionary Government, which acknowledges allegiance to China, but in reality is in affiliation with the Russian Soviet Republics. Altogether there are 160 of these Hutukhtus. Each one, as well as the Dalai Lama and the Dashilumpo Lama, is held to be the reincarnation of his predecessor. The method of selection may be explained by an account of the manner in which the Dalai Lama is chosen. He is regarded as the incarnation of Avaloketishvara. When he dies a search is at once made for the baby into whom his spirit has passed. Certain marks are necessary. A number of boys having such marks are found. The date of birth, their parentage, etc., are recorded. Their names, written on lots, are then placed in a golden urn, and in the presence of the Chinese Resident a lot is drawn from the urn after appropriate ceremonies. This is the true incarnate Dalai Lama. He is placed in charge of ministers who act as his representatives and as regents of Tibet, until the child has grown to manhood and come of age. The Chinese have been careful in drawing the lot to see that the child who is to rule Tibet does not belong to too powerful a family or to one hostile to Chinese policy. Usually the child of a poor family is drawn, so that the family with all its relatives will feel under obligation to the Chinese government. In Mongolia, on the other hand, the tribal chiefs have been careful to see that the office is kept in the family.

TRANSMIGRATION

The Buddhist belief in reincarnation is wide-spread in China. Some persons apparently hold it in all sincerity and others fear it may be true, while the hard-headed skeptics use it as a frame-work for amusing stories. I remember a beggar on the streets of Nanking many years ago who had lost one foot. The stump resembled a pig's foot, and the beggar used to relate that one time in a previous state of existence he had been a bad man, and on being reborn into the world he was born as a pig. He had very nearly completed his term of existence as a pig when he was brought to an untimely death by a butcher, and as his period of punishment had not yet quite expired he was born with one pig's foot.

Another instance is that of the father of a former

PRAYER WHEEL OF LAMAS.

THE RELIGIOUS DANCE, LAMA TEMPLE, PEIPING.

official in China who has had many dealings with foreigners in recent years. Mr. Sheng was born in Soochow. Previous to his birth a Buddhist monk lived in a little temple near by. When he was about to die he called his mother and said to her: "I am dying, but do not weep for me. I shall be reborn very soon in the family of Mr. Sheng. You must wait at his gate and beg a few cash from him from day to day. On the day that I am born the servants will try to drive you away, saying they are too busy to wait upon you, that the master has just had a son born to him. But do not go away. I shall cry and make a great hullabaloo. The servants will be distracted and say they do not know how to stop that baby's crying. Then you must offer to quiet the baby. At first they will not listen to you but after a time they will consent to bring you in, and when I see you I will stop crying and you shall be my nurse." The mother did as she was told. Daily she went begging at the gate of Mr. Sheng. One day the servants told her to go away—that a new baby had come to the house and they had no time for her, but she remained and presently she heard the baby crying. The servants ran hither and thither and tried in every way to quiet the child, but in vain. The old woman said she would quiet him but no one listened to her, until weary of trying everything else they brought in the beggar. At once the child stopped and the beggar became the nurse.

When the child was six or seven years of age he went out walking with his nurse, and seeing the little temple insisted on going in. The nurse took him in. The child said, "In yonder room there is a closet; let us go there." They went. He pointed to the closet and said, "On such and such a shelf I left such a book." They looked and lo! it was there.

"Master, who did sin, this man or his parents, that he was born blind?" asked the disciples of the Master. This passage indicates that even among the Jews in the time of Christ the belief in transmigration was more or less prevalent—a belief that men suffered sometimes for sins committed in a previous state of existence.

It is only in the Lamaist communities of China, however, that the doctrine of metempsychosis has serious practical results. These we have seen in the choice of rulers. The lamas are the most ignorant, and therefore, the most superstitious monks in the country. They are also the most depraved and the most unclean and ill-smelling. Even in China most of the lamas are non-Chinese, i.e., Tibetans, Mongols and Manchus.

TEMPLES AND SERVICES

One of the most famous lamaseries is the Yung Ho Kung in Peip'ing, a vast enclosure once a princely palace. It contains cells for five hundred monks and five large halls with a multitude of smaller chapels. It was the birth-place of the Emperor Ch'ienlung, who enriched it with many valuable gifts. Among them are a pair of enormous bronze lions and a beautiful censer, besides cloisonné altar-pieces, valuable rugs and rich silk hangings.

Prayer-wheels are placed here and there in the corridors, so that visitors or inmates as they pass may give them a turn, and so put several "Omito Fus" to their credit. One must be careful, too, to turn the wheel the right way, else he may undo his prayers. Some turn with the sun and some in the opposite direction. There is an image of Amidha seventy-five feet high in the main hall.

The monks, as all Buddhist monks do, carry their rosary —a string of 108 beads—which they continually finger. The most important service in a lama temple is that near the beginning of the New Year, which foreign visitors call the "Devils' Dance." It is a service to ward off all calamities during the new year. The morning is spent in chanting prayers in Sanscrit. The Hutukhtu sits cross-legged upon a throne and directs the service. A small brass hand-bell rests upon the table before him, which he rings to stop the droning chant. A tripod before the throne rests upon three imitation skulls and holds an offering of grain. The monks sit cross-legged in rows across the vast assembly hall, and at intervals the neophytes carry tea to them. When the prayers are said a procession is formed which marches to the front court, where lamas in masques dance about a triangular coffin containing an image of the devil. The masques represent the heads of horses, oxen and elks. The proctors who preserve order wear death's-head masques. The devil of dough in the coffin is threatened with a knife, a bell, a lama sceptre, and finally is cut to pieces, after which the lamas march about the monastery and the service is ended. The human skull plays an important part in the service. Such skulls are sawn asunder and the upper part used as a cup for the presentation of offerings upon the altar. One of these skulls, lined with silver, is that of a noted rebel. There is a great deal that is degrading in this service, and generally this is true of the Lamaist use of charms and incantations.

In contrast with this is the service at the T'an Che Ssu, some thirty miles west of Peip'ing in the mountains. This temple does not belong to the Lama sect but to another form of Buddhism. Here the service is also conducted in the Sanscrit tongue, but is dignified and impressive. In the old days we used to make the journey to this monastery on horse-back or in sedan-chairs; now we can travel by train to a station within five miles of the monastery. But those five miles are not easily done; one has to climb over a very steep range. On reaching the summit, however, you feel well repaid for the toilsome march, for the scenery is beautiful. You look down into a thickly wooded valley, surrounded by mountains on all sides except towards the south, where it opens into the plain. A stream of clear water ripples over the rocks down into the forest, and following this stream you are guided to the vast pile of buildings that make up the monastery. This, too, was richly endowed by the Emperor Ch'ienlung, who planted there a ginko tree, which is the Chinese substitute for the banyan. This is still growing, and while it does not produce branches that enter the ground, it does put forth many shoots from the roots which reach up into the branches.

This is one of the most beautiful of all the Buddhist monasteries, and it is here that many monks are initiated into the order. There are eighty guest rooms, and large conferences at times assemble here. Before explaining the initiation service I ought to describe the typical Buddhist temple.

The Buddhists have done much to cultivate amongst Chinese a love of natural scenery. Except in the cities, the monasteries are located usually in the most picturesque spots in the mountains. If possible a spot will be chosen beside a brook of clear running water. You cross the brook by an arched bridge of white marble. Before the entrance to the gate-house there is placed a pair of marble or bronze lions, one on either side of the door, the male on the left with his right fore paw resting on a sphere, the female on the right, her left fore paw playing with a cub that lies on its back. The lion is the emblem of Buddha, an emblem suggested, it is said, by his tribal name, Shakya. In the gate-house are the two door gods, one with a dark, the other with a light countenance; one to guard the place by night, the other by day. In the court behind the gate-house there are two towers, one containing a large bell, the other a drum to mark the watches. The Hall of the Four Mighty Ones is just across the court. They are the kings who guard the four quarters of the universe. The images of these kings are colossal; one with a blue face for the east, one with a red face for the south, one with a white face for the west, and one with a black face for the north. Each has his own emblem; a guitar, a sword, an umbrella, a serpent.

In the center of this hall is an altar upon which is placed an image of Maitreya Buddha, a fat, jolly looking deity whose appearance betokens the good time coming. Back to back with him is the image of Wei T'o, a gilded likeness of a warrior in coat of mail with drawn sword. He is the officer who carries out the orders of the Four Kings.

Behind this hall is a large court-yard, on the right and left of which are side chapels for inferior saints, one of them being usually Titsang. Facing the visitor across the court is the principal hall of the temple, which contains the high altar with images of the Three Holy Ones; the

Buddha, the Law and the Congregation, according to one tradition, but in popular estimation, a trinity—the Buddhas of the Past, Present, and Future. An altar of incense is just inside the door and before it usually there is a contribution box. Upon the altar are placed the eight sacred emblems; the conch shell, the pot of incense, the wheel of the law, the umbrella, the stupa, the pair of fishes, the net, and the banner. On the right and left are the bell and the drum and other musical instruments used in worship, and upon the altar, in Lama temples, brass lamps of melted butter—in other temples candle-sticks.

Along the east and west sides are the eighteen Lohan, or apostles of Buddhism, nine on a side, each with his own emblem. Behind the altar and separated from it by a screen is an image of Kwanyin, standing on a rock amidst the dashing waves, rescuing men and women from the sea of misery. In the larger monasteries there is also another hall for general assemblies. In some there is a hall of the Five Hundred Disciples. One such near Peking has life-sized images of these disciples, all heavily gilded.

LAY MEMBERSHIP

Although Buddhism, as originally taught, requires celibacy and forbids its disciples to engage in business, in its present form provision is made also for lay membership. Some lay persons content themselves with abstinence from flesh-eating, some with the observance of certain fast days. Others take five of the monkish vows: (1) during life-time not to kill any living creature, (2) during life-time not to steal, (3) during life-time to abstain from all sexual impurity, (4) during life-time to abstain from lying, (5) during life-time to abstain from all intoxicants. Another class of lay members adds to these five, three other vows: (6) not to seat oneself upon a broad couch or an elevated divan, (7) not to adorn oneself with flowers or to use perfumery, (8) not to associate with actors or courtesans. Before taking these vows the candidate must confess faith in the Buddha, his law, and the order, and then must make confession that in previous incarnations he has been guilty of killing, stealing, lying and impurity, and he must ask absolution for these sins.

INITIATION INTO MONKHOOD

In order to become a monk one must pass through a period of novitiate. The candidate selects a god-father, and, when brought before the chapter, asks through the master of ceremonies that he may be permitted to have his head shaven by his god-father. This done, the candidate begs to be permitted to quit his family. Consent having been given, the brother appointed to instruct him uncovers the right shoulder and arm of the novice, removes his gown, and causes him to kneel upon his right knee and raise his joined hands in supplication. In this position he recites three times this confession: "I give my faith to Buddha, to his Law and to his Order. In imitation of Buddha I quit my family. I recognize —— as my god-father. He who has come, the True One, and all the Illuminated Ones are the objects of my veneration." He then vows to observe the following ten commandments:

(1) Thou shalt not kill.
(2) Thou shalt not steal.
(3) Thou shalt not commit adultery.
(4) Thou shalt not lie.
(5) Thou shalt not drink wine.
(6) Thou shalt not adorn thyself with flowers nor use perfumes.
(7) Thou shalt not sing nor dance, nor associate with actors nor courtesans, nor visit a theater, nor listen to singing.
(8) Thou shalt not sit upon an elevated seat nor upon a broad divan.
(9) Thou shalt not eat except at permitted hours.
(10) Thou shalt not touch silver nor gold, whether as bullion or money or in the shape of jewelry.

He then passes a period of instruction and probation in preparation for initiation into monkhood. When the time for initiation arrives the candidate, in the presence of the chapter, begs his god-father to obtain for him permission to enter the order. If the god-father consents the candidate is then removed from the chapter hall, and the master of ceremonies asks the brethren present if one of them will volunteer to serve as instructor. When such an one offers himself the master of ceremonies requests the assembly to consent to his appointment. The instructor then goes out to the candidate and examines him. He first learns whether the candidate has the proper inner and outer garments and the begging bowl. These are indispensable. He then solemnly charges the candidate to answer all questions frankly and truthfully. He must satisfy the instructor that he does not hold heretical views, that he has not been guilty of impure living during his novitiate, that he has not violated any other rules of the order, that he has not chosen this calling from unworthy motives, that he is not mutilated nor a slave, that he is a free man, that he is not a refugee from justice, that he is not married, that he is not afflicted with any contagious disease, and that he is of age and has the consent of his parents. The instructor, having satisfied himself of the candidate's qualifications, returns to the assembled chapter to report, and asks permission to present the candidate for initiation. There being no objection, he calls with a loud voice: "Enter." Before the chapter the candidate is then put through another examination. The master of ceremonies announces that he has examined the candidate and found him qualified. He then calls out: "If any one has objection to his admission let him now speak. This is the first summons." He repeats the statement adding, "This is the second summons," and again closing with, "This is the third summons." The master of ceremonies then warns the candidate that there are four offenses, for any one of which he will be expelled from the order: impurity, theft, killing any living creature—even an ant, and boasting. He also notifies him that there are four fundamental requirements of monkhood: (1) he must wear clothing made of remnants or cast-off articles, (2) he must beg his food,

(3) he must be content with the shelter of a tree unless supplied with a hut or home by some benefactor, (4) he must use no medicine except that he may take as remedies sour milk, oil or honey, if these be provided by some benefactor.[6]

When a monk takes his vows they are registered one by one upon his skin by pressing the burning end of a stick of incense, either upon his scalp or upon his right arm. Some sects locate them upon the one and others upon the other.

INFLUENCE OF BUDDHISM IN CHINA

The Chinese regard for the family and the desire for descendants to keep up the sacrifices for the dead have made them slow to accept the teachings of Buddhism. For six hundred years missionaries came from India preaching the faith. Sometimes the religion received the imperial favor, but at other times it was persecuted; monasteries were confiscated, bronze bells and images melted into cash, and thousands of monks and nuns compelled to return to their homes. But in spite of all opposition the faith took hold of the hearts of the people. It supplied something which Confucianism lacked. In its modified form of Amidhism it was particularly attractive. It has had a profound influence upon Chinese civilization; upon its arts, its literature and its religions. It has filled the land with beautiful pagodas. It has taught landscape gardening and encouraged sculpture and painting. Its symbols are common in all decorative art. The lion is seen at every palace gate; the umbrella is the emblem of imperial and magisterial authority; the rosary is, or was, a part of the ceremonial dress of every high official. The swastika, the net of metempsychosis, the wheel of the law—all these and many other symbols are woven into their fabrics, carved in their wood-work, and frescoed upon their ceilings.

Buddhism has given a new phraseology to Chinese literature. It has introduced keen philosophical disputation,

6 Bouddhisme Chinois, pp. 181-183 and 193-202.

and even the indigenous religions have been compelled to borrow its doctrines and adopt some of its ceremonies. Taoism imitated it in the introduction of images, and even the proud Confucianist calls in the monks to read prayers over his dead.

Some of the Buddhist literature is very arid. One of the most popular of its treatises is the Diamond Sutra, so called apparently because of its ability to resist all attacks upon its doctrines. Yet the meat which it supplies to the hungry soul is made up of such sentiments as these:

> Anyone who has entered upon the path of the Bodhisatvas must thus frame his thought; as many beings as there are in this world of beings—with form or without form, with name or without name, or neither with nor without name—as far as any known world of beings is known—all these must be delivered by me in the perfect world of nirvana. And yet after I shall have delivered thus innumerable beings, not one single being will have been delivered. Why? If a Bodhisatva had any idea of a *being* he could not be called a Bodhisatva.[7]

That is to say, beings have no real existence. The whole argument in the book may be summed up in three statements: (1) The state of nirvana is happiness because it frees one from the misery of existence. (2) Human life and the sensuous world are deceptive phenomena. (3) Matter is non-existent; to realize this is to take the first step towards enlightenment.

But there is more attractive literature than this. Listen to the parable of the mustard seed. A poor widow had an only child that was taken ill and died. She bore the dead body about with her and tried to nurse it back to life, but in vain. Pitying friends bade her go to the Lord Buddha and ask his help. He listened sympathetically to her plea that he would restore her child to life. He said: "Yes, if you will bring me a little mustard seed." She was about to hasten away but he stopped her, adding, "You must first borrow the mustard seed from some household in which no one has ever died." She went to one neighbor after another begging a little mustard seed, saying, "The

7 Sacred Books of the East, Vol. XLIX, Part II, p. 132.

Master has promised that if I will bring it he will restore my child to life.'' They said, ''We will give you the mustard seed gladly.'' ''But,'' said she, ''I must first know whether anyone in this household has died.'' ''Ah,'' said they, ''what home has not been visited by death!'' Then her eyes were opened. She saw that she was not the only mourner in the world and came back to thank the Lord Buddha for his teaching.[8]

One of the most unfortunate influences of Buddhism has been its teaching with regard to hell. Originally it taught that there were eight hot hells and eight cold hells, or earth prisons beneath Mt. Sumeru. In China, in every town, there is at least one and oftentimes there are several representations of the ten hells of which Chinese Buddhists speak. The tortures of the damned are represented by images, sometimes of life size, picturing men and women flayed by demons, roasting on red-hot cylinders, pounded in mortars, sawn asunder, being transformed into beasts, and undergoing other indescribable sufferings. So far from deterring men from sin, these cruel representations appear to harden the hearts of those who look upon them, and to suggest to them abominable methods of tormenting the victims of their wrath in times of riot or of religious or political persecution. The Yü Li, or Precious Records, is a book of tales recounting the experiences of those who have passed to the realms of Yama and been punished for the lack of filial piety or for other sins committed in this life.

BUDDHIST CHARITIES

It has been said that Buddhism has given the world no great humane institutions, that it really does nothing to relieve the suffering of the world. It does fall far behind Christianity in this regard, but it is not true that it does nothing to relieve human suffering. It is true that it spends much energy in saving animal life. It will screen a candle to keep the moths from singeing their wings; it

[8] Edwin Arnold's ''Light of Asia,'' Bk. V.

will shrink from treading upon an ant, and it will buy fish and other living creatures in the market to set them free. But it also maintains free dispensaries for the sick, although the knowledge of anatomy and medicine is slight, and it establishes foundling asylums and schools for the young. Many of the monks, it is true, are worthless creatures, lazy, ignorant and vicious. But there are also some very sincere, devoted men among them. When one of my neighbors fell into a pond and was drowned the first man to attempt a rescue was a Buddhist monk, who threw off his clothes and jumped into the pool. He swam about treading water until he located the body. He was too late, it is true, but he brought the body ashore and did what he could. This act will be more appreciated when it is known that Chinese fear to rescue a drowning man, believing that demons drag him down. I have a friend of many years, an old Buddhist monk, in the hills near Peip'-ing, a scholarly man, and as gentle, pure and good as any man I know. I shall never forget how affected he was when he read in a Chinese newspaper of the sinking of the *Titanic*. Tears stood in his eyes as he praised the conduct of the captain and the men who went down with the ship that they might allow the women and children to be saved.

REFORMED BUDDHISM

From China Buddhism passed to Japan, where it has undergone further transformation. The newest sect there is that which meets in the Nishi Honwangji, a temple in Kioto. This sect of reformed Buddhists permits marriage and has stated services every Sunday with preaching. It maintains charities and has rites of confirmation for its lay members. I had the privilege one Sunday of attending its services. It, too, worships Amidha Buddha. Recently it has introduced its teachings into China. One of its advocates was the abbot of a monastery not far from the American Legation in Peip'ing. He used to visit us occasionally. One year he endeavored to organize a pan-religious committee, to be composed of Buddhists, Taoists, Confucianists, Mohammedans, and of Protestant and Roman Catholic Christians. His aim was to bring these different religions into mutual acquaintanceship and so put an end to strife. He failed in his endeavor but the effort did honor to his heart. He established at his own charge two schools for boys in Peking and provided teachers, not only of the Chinese language and literature but of mathematics, geography and physical sciences. He was highly educated and wrote a history of Buddhism in three countries—India, China and Japan. After the overthrow of the empire he wrote a tract pleading for the adoption of Buddhism as the state religion of the republic, holding very truthfully that Buddhism frowns upon all distinctions of rank and teaches the brotherhood of man. The last time I visited him he was stone blind. Age and over-work in a poor light, with perhaps under-nourishment, had destroyed his sight. But he was still cheerful and interested in his work. A few months later he had passed. Whither? Shall we say to nirvana, or to the happy Western Heaven? He passed—to the immortality in which he and we believe.

ATTITUDE TOWARD MILITARISM

One characteristic of his school aroused some comment. He required the pupils to have military drill. This was done to comply with the requirements of the new public school system. He desired to make his schools equal to those maintained by the state. Buddhism, it is true, is a religion of peace. It frowns upon war since it forbids all killing. Yet the Buddhist has not been any more consistent in this regard than the Christian. When the Sung Emperor was being driven south by the armies of Genghis Khan, in the 13th century, these Mongol raiders were held in check on the banks of the Yangtze by the monks of the Yüan-t'ung Monastery, who came to the aid of the Imperial Court. In 1126 the abbot of a monastery in Shansi, on the famous Wu T'ai Mountain; became a cavalry leader of great renown, through his success in drilling and leading his monks against the Tartar hordes. We have seen this same militant spirit in our own day. The Boxers were organized and drilled in Buddhist monasteries in 1900, and duped into believing themselves invulnerable because of the charms which had been given to them by the monks. If we are horrified by the outrages committed by these Boxers, we must also remember that they were not without provocation, seeing that foreigners had seized some of the finest harbors in the land and were openly discussing the partitioning of China.

Buddhism has been called the "Light of Asia," and undoubtedly it has dispelled much gloom. It has been a civilizing force. But there are black spots on the disk of the sun, and Buddhism, too, is not free from faults. It has not qualified itself to be the "Light of the World." Yet a Buddhist might retort upon us by pointing out inconsistencies in our own creed and ridiculing our pet superstitions. What is desirable is that, no matter what our faith, we should love truth above all things and be willing to acknowledge it wherever it may be found, for in that alone is progress possible. "Ye shall know the truth and the truth shall make you free"—free from the bonds of superstition. "And if the truth shall make you free ye shall be free indeed."

CHAPTER XV

TAOISM

The rewards of good and evil follow as naturally as the shadow follows the substance.—*Kang Ying P'ien.*

Taoism is both a philosophy and a religion. As a philosophy it is traced to Lao Tzu, which is by interpretation "Old Philosopher." His name was Li Erh; his *nom de plume* Li Po-yang, his posthumous name Li Tan. Li was his surname, and means Plum. According to the accepted tradition he was born in 604 B.C. near the modern city of Kueitefu, in the province of Honan. In a sketch of the life of Confucius, in another chapter, a description of Lao Tzu's character has already been given, and some of the striking sentences from his work—the Tao Te King—have been quoted. His authorship of that classic has been questioned by Professor Giles, although without sufficient reason, as I think. But whether we call the author of the book by the name Lao Tzu, or by some other cognomen, is of small consequence; the book still remains, and it is the remarkable teaching of this book, the Tao Te King, that has attracted the attention of the world.

THE TAO TE KING

It is in this book that Taoist philosophy finds its roots, just as it is in this book, also, that the religion called Taoism finds its most holy scripture. True, Lao Tzu had no thought of founding a religion, and he could have had no sympathy with the modern conglomeration of shamanism, sorcery, astrology, necromancy, demonaltry and magic which passes for a religion. Lao Tzu was a profound thinker, a political philosopher of keen insight, and an ethical teacher of very high order; but he did not pose as a saint, and it was not until 700 years after his death that he was canonized and that a temple was built for his worship.

The Tao Te King treats of two subjects, *tao* and *te*. *Tao* is the fundamental principle of the philosophy which it teaches, and *te* is the practical exemplification of the principle in conduct. *Tao* means the "way," or the "word." As a verb it means "to walk," or "to speak." *Te* implies action. It is commonly translated "virtue." It also means "energy" or "power." When one walks in the "way" the result is right conduct, or virtue.

Lao Tzu began his work with a brief, sententious discussion of the one great problem of philosophy: to discover the unity underlying all diversity, the changeless that lies behind all change, the infinite surrounding the finite, the eternal principle of the universe. This he called *Tao*. The first chapter of the Tao Te King may be translated as follows:

The way that can be trodden is not the eternal way; the name that can be named is not the unchanging name.
Or—The word that can be spoken is not the eternal word; the name that can be named is not the unchanging name.
Unnamed it was the beginning of heaven and earth; named, it became the source of all things.
As ever free from desire, it is seen as the mysterious; as ever possessed of desire, it is seen as the limited.
These two are of one origin, yet different in name.
This common origin we call the abyss. It is the abyss within the abyss, the gateway to all mystery.

This is a literal translation. A reasonable paraphrase of it in modern philosophical terms would read somewhat as follows:

The eternal principle which lies behind the phenomenal world is undefinable. Undefined, it lies at the beginning of the universe. To define it is to limit it. As the source of the whole world it is defined. It limits itself. Free from all attributes it is seen as the Absolute. Possessed of attributes it is seen as limited. These two, the Absolute and the Limited, have a common origin. Their common origin we call the abyss. It is indeed the abyss of abysses and the doorway to all mystery.

In the fourth chapter, discoursing further upon this profound principle, the *Tao,* he says:

I do not know whose son it is; I think it existed before God.

This use of *Tao* as the equivalent of the Eternal Word and the source of the visible universe led the translators of the New Testament to employ the word *tao* in translating into Chinese the Greek word *logos,* in the first chapter of the Gospel of St. John.

Some years ago, when visiting the Twelve Caves near Nanking, I found in one of the largest a ladder reaching up through a cleft in the rock. On climbing it I came out upon a natural terrace on the face of the cliff. Walking some distance along this terrace I found another ladder which led up through a trap door into a small shrine that hung upon the face of the rock. Pushing open the trap I entered, and stood before an altar erected in front of the image of a Taoist divinity. An old man with long beard and long white hair, held back from his face by a brass band over his head, came from a cave at the rear of the shrine and received me very graciously. Over a cup of tea he told me his story. He had been a soldier in the Taiping army, and when the rebellion was suppressed he had renounced the world and taken refuge in a Taoist monastery. After we had talked of many things, he left me a moment and brought from the cave a well-thumbed copy of the Chinese version of St. John's Gospel. He read the first few verses:

In the beginning was the Tao, and the Tao was with God, and the Tao was God. The same was in the beginning with God. All things were made by him; and without him not anything was made that was made.

He told me that this was just the teaching of his religion, and that he was very fond of the Gospel of St. John.

LAO TZU'S POLITICAL PHILOSOPHY

From the quotations made in an earlier chapter we might be led to think that Lao Tzu in his political theories was a philosophical anarchist. This would hardly be a fair judgment, however, for while he sought to reduce government to the minimum he did not deny that government was needed. "The holy man's method of government," he says, "is to empty the people's hearts and fill their stomachs; to weaken their desires and strengthen their bones."[1] For him the welfare of the people was the true object of government. He disliked, however, to see the people struggling for wealth and official position and taking pleasure in display. "The lust of the flesh, the lust of the eye and the pride of life," were things he condemned. "Riches, honor and pride," he said, "leave a heritage of ill fortune."[2] "Horse-racing and hunting disorder the mind, and the scramble for wealth mars the character of man."[3] He did not think, however, that matters were to be improved by legislation, for he said: "The more warnings and prohibitions there are in the world, the poorer the people become . . ." "The more laws and commands there are, the greater the number of thieves and robbers." Therefore, the holy man says: "I do nothing and men, themselves, reform. . . . I suppress desire and men, themselves, become simple in their tastes."[4]

"Do nothing," was his motto—"Do nothing, and all will be done." He loved paradox. "The Tao is ever inactive, yet there is nothing which it does not accomplish."[5]

"Whoso endeavors, fails; he who seizes, loses. The holy man does nothing, so fails in nothing. He seizes nothing, and therefore, loses nothing. He desires to be free from desire, and not to prize things that are hard to get."[6]

[1] Tao Te King, Chap. III.
[2] Tao Te King, Chap. IX.
[3] Ibid., Chap. XII.
[4] Ibid., Chap. LVII.
[5] Ibid., Chap. XXXVII.
[6] Ibid., Chap. LXIV.

Again he said: "There is no sin greater than desire; there is no misfortune greater than not to know when one has enough. There is no fault greater than greed of gain." [7] This policy of suppressing desire and allowing things to take their course, he believed to be the way of nature—the way of the Tao. He had no use for noisy busy-bodies. "A typhoon," he said, "can't last all morning; a pouring rain can't last all day." [8] His theory of "do nothing and all will be done," he illustrated by the value of vacancy. "Thirty spokes are inserted in one hub, but the wheel's usefulness depends upon the nothingness of the hole in the hub. We knead the clay to mould a vessel, but it is the nothingness of the hollow of the vessel that gives it usefulness. We build a house and cut doors and windows in the walls, but the usefulness of the house and that of doors and windows depends upon the nothingness of the space inclosed." [9] He believed in the power of a quiet example. He taught that gentleness would accomplish more than force. Real goodness he likened to water, which seeks the lowly place and benefits all sorts of creatures. [10] "There is nothing more yielding than water, but nothing can equal it in attacking the hard." . . . "Weakness conquers strength; the soft overcomes the hard." [11]

HIS ETHICS

Lao Tzu was an altruist, for he said: "The holy man keeps himself in the background, and therefore, he comes to the front. He puts self aside, and therefore, his own interests are preserved." [12] He rises to a greater height than Confucius. The latter opposed the teaching that one should return good for evil. "What, then, will you return for good?" he asked. Lao Tzu, on the other hand, said: "I am good to the good; I am also good to the bad,

[7] Ibid., Chap. XLVI.
[8] Ibid., Chap. XXIII.
[9] Ibid., Chap. XI.
[10] Ibid., Chap. VIII.
[11] Ibid., Chap. LXXVIII.
[12] Ibid., Chap. VII.

for virtue (the *Te* of his philosophy) is goodness. With
the faithful I am faithful; with the unfaithful I am also
faithful; for virtue is faithfulness.''[13] ''Requite enmity
with kindness.''[14]

He hated war. ''Even the best weapons,'' he said, ''are
unlucky instruments. . . . They are not the instruments
of the perfect man. Only when unavoidable does he use
them. He gives high place to tranquillity and quietude.
He conquers, but he does not find pleasure in it, for to
find such pleasure would be to rejoice in killing men.''[15]
Elsewhere he says: ''Where armies have encamped, there
thorns and briers spring up, and famine stalks ever in
the rear of marching hosts.''[16] ''When the world has
Tao, horses are used to haul filth, and when it is without
Tao war horses are bred in the suburbs.''[17]

By his philosophy he seeks to make men masters of
themselves. Thus he teaches as follows: ''Whoso knows
men is knowing, but he who knows himself has understanding. He who subdues others is strong, but he who conquers
self is mighty. He who knows sufficiency is rich.''[18]

But the method by which one attains this self-control
is not to be a method imposed upon one from without
by laws and commands. It is the self-determined choice
of the soul, which, knowing Tao to be the source of all
things and the only true way of life, seeks to live in
harmony with that living Word and to walk in that high
Way.

It will at once be recognized that Lao Tzu was a quietist. He would live in quiet meditation, himself, allowing
the Tao to work its own will in him and in all around
him. He would be passive—yield himself to the influence
of Tao. It could not be right, therefore, for him to strive
—''to cry or cause his voice to be heard in the street.''
Hence the Taoist, to this day, is a quiet man, not easily

13 Ibid., Chap. XLIX.
14 Ibid., Chap. LXIII.
15 Ibid., Chap. XXXI.
16 Ibid., Chap. XXX.
17 Ibid., Chap. XLVI.
18 Ibid., Chap. XXXIII.

provoked, one who refuses to engage in controversy. Strife, impatience, anger—all these destroy the peace of the soul which is the *summum bonum.* They injure the vitality of the man and shorten his life. The Taoist agrees with the Buddhist in endeavoring to suppress desire; but whereas the Buddhist looks upon desire as the cause of birth and re-birth, from which one should seek deliverance, the Taoist suppresses desire because desire frets the soul and wears out the life. The Buddhist is a pessimist and thinks life to be evil—a curse to be escaped. The Taoist loves life, believes it to be a blessing and seeks to prolong it.

From this follows the regimen of the Taoist. ''He who dies but perishes not has long life'' (that is, is immortal).[19] To attain to this, we are told, one must give careful attention to the animal soul, that *p'o* which the Li Ki tells us accompanies the body into the grave. He must also pay especial attention to the *ch'i,* the vital vapor. I quote the Old Philosopher:

Nourish and discipline the soul (p'o). Maintain unity (i.e., union of the soul and spirit). Thus you can escape dissolution. Give especial attention to the breath (ch'i) until it grows soft (impalpable), and you can become as a little child.[20]

All this, as he tells us in another place,[21] requires one to guard very carefully the quietude of his surroundings. The affairs of the world disturb him not. He sees them pass and re-pass. He sees them arise, but knows that they will return again, as the petals of a flower fall to the root of the plant.[22]

All this, of course, tends to destroy interest in the events of the day and unfit one for the duties of life. Yet many an old man in China whose passions have burned themselves out, whose ambitions have been quenched, whose endeavors have failed, turns to the quiet retreat of the Taoist monastery to seek in its discipline a method of pro-

[19] Ibid., Chap. XXXIII.
[20] Ibid., Chap. X.
[21] Ibid., Chap. XVI.
[22] Ibid., Chap. XVI.

longing his days, though it be a prolongation of a life no longer useful.

TAOISM POSSIBLY OF HINDU ORIGIN

A number of modern students of Taoism believe that it has an Indian origin. Père Wieger, a missionary of the Society of Jesus, thinks that the very terms *Tao* and *Te*, are but transliterations of two Sanscrit words, *Tat* and *Tyad;* i.e., "The First Being" and "The Others." He believes that he has found several Sanscritisms in the work.[23] There is no evidence, however, of any communication between China and India at so early a date as the time in which Lao Tzu lived. Later Chinese philosophy does owe much to India. It must be admitted, too, that the Tao Te King, in some passages, reminds one of the teaching of the Upanishads.

CHUANG TZU

The greatest of Lao Tzu's disciples was Chuang Tzu, who lived in the fourth century B.C. He was a contemporary of Mencius, but the two men do not appear to have met. Chuang Tzu was in some respects a more brilliant writer than Lao Tzu, and his style is still the delight of Chinese scholars.

Professor Giles, in publishing his translation of Chuang Tzu, asked the Rev. Aubrey Moore of Oxford, to write a note on the first seven chapters. He did so, and made a very interesting comparison between the teachings of Chuang Tzu and those of Heraclitus and Parmenides, who were probably contemporaries of Lao Tzu. There could not have been, so far as we can see, any communication between them nor between their disciples and Chuang Tzu.

Both China and Greece are indebted to India for much of their philosophical thought, but it is impossible to say how any of this debt could have been created before the sixth century B.C.

[23] Taoisme, Tome I. Introduction, p. 9, footnote.

Chuang Tzu assumed an attitude towards officialdom even more contemptuous than that of Lao Tzu. When his prince offered him the premiership, he is reported to have answered in these words those who brought the message:

> You offer me great wealth and a proud position indeed; but have you never seen a sacrificial ox? When, after being fattened up for several years, it is decked with embroidered trappings and led to the altar, would it not then willingly exchange places with some uncared for pigling? Begone! Defile me not! I had rather disport myself to my own enjoyment in the mire than be a slave to the ruler of a state. I will never take office. Thus I shall remain free to follow my own inclinations.[24]

One of the most fascinating chapters of Chuang Tzu's work is that on "The Identity of the Contraries." I quote a few paragraphs from Giles' translation:

> There is nothing which is not objective; there is nothing which is not subjective. But it is impossible to start from the objective. Only from subjective knowledge is it possible to proceed to objective knowledge. Hence it has been said: "The objective emanates from the subjective; the subjective is consequent upon the objective. This is the Alternation Theory. Nevertheless when one is born the other dies. When one is possible the other is impossible. When one is affirmative, the other is negative. Which being the case the true sage rejects all distinction of this and that. He takes his refuge in God and places himself in subjective relation with all things.
> And inasmuch as the subjective is also objective and the objective also subjective, and as the contraries under each are indistinguishably blended, does it not become impossible for us to say whether subjective and objective really exist at all? When subjective and objective are both without their correlates, that is the very axis of Tao. And when that axis passes through the center at which all infinities converge, positive and negative alike blend into an infinite One. . . .
> Therefore it is that, viewed from the standpoint of Tao, a beam and a pillar are identical. So are ugliness and beauty, greatness, wickedness, perverseness and strangeness. Separation is the same as construction. Construction is the same as destruction. . . . Only the truly intelligent understand this principle of the identity of all things. They do not view things as appre-

[24] Giles' Translation of Chuang Tzu, Introduction, p. vi.

hended by themselves, subjectively, but transfer themselves into the position of the things viewed.[25]

.   .   .   .

If there was a beginning, then there was a time before that beginning. And a time before the time which was before the time of that beginning. If there is existence, then there must have been non-existence. And, if there was a time when nothing existed, there must then have been a time before that—when even nothing did not exist. Suddenly, when, nothing came into existence, could one really say whether it belonged to the category of existence or non-existence? Even the very words I have just now uttered—I can not say whether they have really been uttered or not.[26]

.   .   .   .

How do I know that love of life is not a delusion after all? How do I know but that he who dreads to die is not as a child who has lost the way and cannot find his home? . . . Those who dream of the banquet wake to lamentation and sorrow. Those who dream of lamentation and sorrow wake to join the hunt. While they dream they do not know that they dream. Some will even interpret the very dream they are dreaming; and only when they awake do they know it was a dream. By and by comes the Great Awakening, and then we find out that this life is really a great dream. Fools think they are awake now, and flatter themselves they know if they are really princes or peasants. Confucius and you are both dreams; and I who say you are dreams—I am but a dream myself. This is a paradox. To-morrow a sage may arise to explain it; but that to-morrow will not be until ten thousand generations have gone by.[27]

.   .   .   .

Once upon a time I, Chuang Tzu, dreamt I was a butterfly, fluttering hither and thither, to all intents and purposes a butterfly. I was conscious only of following my fancies as a butterfly, and was unconscious of my individuality as a man. Suddenly I awaked, and there I lay, myself again. Now I do not know whether I was then a man dreaming I was a butterfly, or whether I am now a butterfly dreaming I am a man.[28]

[25] Ibid., pp. 17, 18 and 19.
[26] Ibid., p. 23.
[27] Giles' Translation of Chuang Tzu, pp. 29 and 30.
[28] Ibid., p. 32.

We are told that when Chuang Tzu was about to die his disciples were arranging to give him an impressive funeral. The philosopher attempted to dissuade them, saying: "With heaven and earth for my inner and outer coffin, with the sun, moon and stars as my burial regalia, and with all creation to escort me to the grave—are not my funeral paraphernalia ready to hand?" [29]

THE ELIXIR OF IMMORTALITY

After the passing of Chuang Tzu, the great idealist, Taoism began to degenerate. Men of smaller mind than Chuang Tzu could not live in the rarefied atmosphere in which he delighted. They came down to lower levels.

Forgetting the lofty ethics of Lao Tzu some of them fastened upon what he had written about caring for the animal soul and regulating the *ch'i*, or vital vapor, and sought by a regimen of mental and physical calisthenics to rejuvenate themselves. By holding the breath (which is called *ch'i*), by preserving the bodily secretions, and by suppression of desire, by retirement from the world, avoidance of all violent emotions and the cultivation of passivity, they thought to attain to immortality.

THE PHILOSOPHER'S STONE

Others gave to the Tao and its operations a physical instead of a metaphysical interpretation. They found in it the primal substance out of which all things are made. Chuang Tzu's idealism, which reconciled all contradictions in a higher unity, which identified all diversities in the all-pervading One, was transformed into the grossest sort of materialism, in accordance with which all substances were considered as modifications of the one original matter. They reasoned that as a base of all the various metals there must exist a common substance, from which any or all of them can by manipulation be produced. Thus, one might

29 Ibid., p. 434.

take a quantity of lead and, by divesting it of certain qualities, reach the primal substance, which, by the addition of other qualities, could be converted into gold. So alchemy was born. Perhaps they recalled that chapter of Lao Tzu in which he likened the Tao to water. At any rate they fastened upon mercury as the agent that could be used in the transmutation of metals. The *lien tan*, or pill of transmutation, is the original "philosopher's stone." Ignoring the Old Philosopher's condemnation of greed, his teaching that acquisitiveness is the greatest of faults, these men became absorbed in a scheme for the manufacture of gold. They made haste to get rich. Subsequently it was recalled that Tao was described as the source of life as well as of matter, and the transmutation pill was heralded as a cure for old age—the elixir of immortality. The term *lien tan*, "pill of transmutation," was accepted by later generations as the technical term to describe the hygienic and spiritual regimen still practiced by Taoists for the prolongation of life. These ideas began to find currency in the third century B.C.

THE ORIGIN OF ALCHEMY

European writers have been disposed to find the origin of alchemy among the Alexandrian Greeks, in the third century of the Christian era.[30] Western Europe is said to have derived its knowledge of the subject from the Arabs after the conquest of Spain. The teaching spread from the eleventh century onward into France and Britain.

The Arabs, no doubt, introduced the knowledge of alchemy into Europe, but they did not obtain that knowledge from the Alexandrian Greeks. The prescriptions found in Egyptian tombs relate only to certain trade secrets of jewelers, concerned with the manufacture of alloys. The Persians also were believed to have influenced the researches of the Greeks. The Persians had speculated upon the possibility of a transmutation of metals, and Ostanes

[30] Encyclopedia Britannica, Eleventh Edition, Article "Alchemy."

the Mede had a formula for the making of an elixir of immortality. Thus these two processes were associated in their introduction into Europe. Astrology influenced the experiments in Persia, as it did also in China. We now know, however, that alchemy originated, not in Egypt or Persia in the third century A.D., but 600 years earlier in China. And while we may smile at the ignorance of these early adepts, and ridicule the superstitions with which their theories were associated, we should remember, as Liebig has said, that alchemy "was never at any time anything different from chemistry."

We have seen that in China the Taoists were occupied with two problems. They sought to apply the teachings of their philosophy practically, both in the realm of psychology and in that of physics. Thus the two searches for the elixir of immortality and the pill for the transmutation of metals went on together. In imitation of the real students there arose a crowd of charlatans and fakirs who imposed upon a credulous age with tricks of legerdemain and fables of distant lands. One of these was Lu Sheng, who lived about 225 B.C. The great emperor who had overthrown the last remnants of the Chou Dynasty, who had built the Great Wall and burned the Confucian classics, was nevertheless a captive to fear and superstition. He was afraid of assassins. He shuddered at the thought of death. He fell an easy victim to the arts of Lu Sheng. The latter was an alchemist, but he had had no more success than others.

THE ISLES OF THE BLESSED

In 219 B.C. Lu Sheng told the emperor of the "Isles of the Blessed," P'englai, Fangchang, and Yingchou, which were said to lie in the ocean 70,000 *li* (23,333 miles) east of China. Living there were people who were already possessed of immortality and perfect happiness. In these islands there was growing the *chih,* a plant that cures old age and "all the ills that flesh is heir to." On one of these islands, he said, there was a mountain of jade 10,000 feet high, from whose base gushed forth the fountain of perpetual youth, the taste of whose waters was like that of sweet wine. Whoso should quaff that water would be intoxicated with delight and live forever. And so with the Philosopher's Stone and the Elixir of Immortality, there came to be associated also the legend of the Isles of the Blessed and the Fountain of Youth.

The emperor believed the fakir, and sent an expedition to search for the islands. The commander of the expedition, named Hsü, was equal to the occasion. He returned saying that he had met one of these immortals at sea, who had asked him what he was seeking, and that he had replied that he was in search of the elixir of immortality. The immortal had then told him that the gifts which the emperor had sent were too valueless for the purchase of so precious an article. "You may see the elixir," he had said, "but you may not taste it." On being asked what gifts the immortal desired he had replied, "Youths and maidens and craftsmen of all sorts." Accordingly the emperor sent Hsü to sea again, accompanied by 3000 youths and maidens. They sailed away but never returned. Some think that they colonized Japan.

CELEBRATED ALCHEMISTS

Another devotee of alchemy was Chang Liang, an intimate friend and adviser of the founder of the Han Dynasty. After the death of his patron he retired from public life and devoted himself to the study of Taoism and the search for the elixir of immortality. This he sought by fasting, by hygienic living, and by spiritual exercises, but also by the compounding and use of drugs. He failed, and died in 189 B.C.

An Chi-sheng, a druggist, is said to have succeeded in compounding the pill of immortality. But he ascended to Heaven from the White Cloud Mountain and carried the secret with him. It is discouraging to note that all those who succeeded in the search for immortality found it, just as ordinary people do, by passing into another world.

This druggist was the teacher of an apprentice, Li Shao-chün, who succeeded in winning the confidence of the great Emperor Wu of the Han Dynasty. This was about 140 B.C. Li said to the emperor: "I know how to harden snow and convert it into white silver; I know how cinnabar changes its nature and passes into yellow gold. I can rein the flying dragon and visit the ends of the earth. I can bestride the hoary crane and soar above the ninth heaven." [31]

The Emperor Wu was a great conqueror. He extended the borders of China to the southern coast and annexed the island of Hainan. He sent the great explorer, Chang Ch'ien, into central Asia and contended with Turkish tribes there. He made his influence felt as far as the frontiers of Persia. It may well have been that in this way the first knowledge of Chinese alchemy spread to the West. At the beginning of his reign Wu was an ardent Confucianist; but his mother was a firm believer in Taoism, and under her influence he became the victim of charlatans. He listened to the boastful words of Li Shao-chün, who claimed to be possessor of supernatural powers, and satisfied the emperor that he knew the secret of making gold and of living without eating and without growing old. Li urged the emperor to study alchemy, saying: "If you will apply yourself to alchemy you will convert the cinnabar into gold. When the gold is produced make of it a vessel. When you have eaten and drunken from this vessel you will be assured of great longevity. Then you may go and visit the immortals on the island of P'englai. When you have seen them, then perform the ceremonies of *feng* and *shan,* and you will never die." [32] He did as he was told. He sacrificed to the God of the Furnace and sent an expedition in search of the Isles of the Blessed. The explorers came in sight of them but were driven back by contrary winds.

Li Shao-chün died, but his patron would not believe that

[31] See Mayers' Chinese Readers Manual, under Li Shao-chün.
[32] Ch'ien Han Shu.

he was dead. "He has merely changed his form," he said.
He could find no one to tell him what the ceremonies of
feng and *shan* were. For years he yielded himself to the
influence of the alchemists, but at last in his old age, after
he had been led by the intrigues of magicians to distrust
his own son and heir and have him put to death, he confessed that he had been duped. "All they told me," he
said, "was false." He built a tower in which he sat, hop-
ing that he might have communication with the spirit of his
lost son. Upon it he inscribed these words: "I am thinking of my son; I am longing for his return."

His conquests and his superstitions made him a great
figure in Chinese history. Many marvelous tales are told
of his reign. Among them, preserved in painting and in
literature, is the story of the visit paid him by the Fairy
Queen, the Hsi Wang Mu of that ancient work, the Shan
Hai King. She is fabled to live in the Kunlun Mountains
in a palace of jade, surrounded by a wonderful garden.
There grows the peach tree, the fruit of which if one eat
he shall live forever. Like the Queen of Sheba, who had
heard of the wisdom of Solomon and came to see him, the
Queen of Fairyland had heard of the glory of Wu and
came to see him. The artists picture her approach with
her long train of fairy attendants. The story tellers relate
that these royal personages became much enamored, one
of the other, and kept up their correspondence by means
of love birds—the blue birds that fly always in pairs; one
with a wing on the right, the other with a wing on the
left, so that they thus support each other. These birds
carried the love notes to and fro.

But the awakening of Wu at the close of his reign did
not stop the search for the philosopher's stone, nor that for
the elixir of immortality. The experiments went on from
generation to generation. Prince Liu-an, who was a grandson of the founder of the Han Dynasty, lived during the
reign of the Emperor Wu and died in 122 B.C. He sought
to explain the origin of gold. "It grows in the earth,"
he said, "by a slow process, and is evolved from the immaterial principle underlying the universe, passing from one

form to another up to silver and then through silver to gold." Another alchemist held that gold was of the essence of rock. This essence after a long period becomes quicksilver. This is fluid because of lunar influence, which belongs to the principle *yin*, i.e., the negative and the female principle. It must be acted upon by the solar principle, *yang*, before it can become solid. When the change takes place it becomes gold. Cinnabar, the red sulphide of mercury, was the substance most commonly used in the experiments of the alchemists. With it many other substances were combined, such as arsenic, borax, potash and mother-of-pearl. This last was highly esteemed by the ancient Chinese as having the power of preventing dissolution. They regarded it as of the same nature as jade, and when no jade was at hand to place in the mouth of a corpse they used mother-of-pearl. Jade was the most precious of substances—more precious than gold—and some of the experiments were devoted to the production of artificial jade. It is believed by some that this led to the discovery of porcelain.

Taoism has eight celebrated magicians, usually called the "eight fairies," a popular theme of the artists. The Chinese name, *hsien*, by which they are called, is represented by a character composed of "man" and "mountain." It is the man alone on the mountain—the hermit —who by observation, discipline and meditation has acquired his knowledge of nature and its forces, and his power to work miracles. Of the eight magicians one only was a woman, Ho Sien-ku, who lived in the seventh century A.D. and who acquired immortality by eating mother-of-pearl. She traveled over the hills as though with wings, and is reported to have been seen floating in the clouds.

Chang Kuo was a more interesting character. He had a white mule which he could fold up and put in his wallet. When he wanted to use him he spurted water upon the wallet, which caused the mule to resume his proper shape. This wonderful mule could travel thousands of miles a day, and cost nothing for provender.

Equally interesting was Li T'ieh-kuai, who could sepa-

rate his spirit from his body and visit the heavenly regions.
On one occasion he went to heaven to consult Lao Tzu
and left his body in charge of a disciple, who was to keep
the *p'o,* the animal soul, alive for seven days. If the
wizard did not return on the seventh day the *p'o* was to
be allowed to disperse. The disciple carefully tended the
body and the animal soul for six days, but on that day
he received word of his mother's illness and went home.
On the evening of the seventh day Li returned from heaven
to find that his body was no longer animated. He looked
about for a refuge and saw a lame beggar about to expire.
When the beggar's spirit had departed Li's spirit took
possession, and from that time onward he dwelt in the
body of the lame beggar and walked with an iron staff, i.e.,
a *t'ieh kuai,* hence the name.

Alchemy continued to find many devotees through the
early centuries of the Christian era, and had royal patronage down to the eleventh and twelfth centuries. During
the T'ang Dynasty there was constant intercourse between
China and Persia. Nestorian Christianity was introduced
into the capital of China in A.D. 635, and about the
same time Mohammedan Arabs established a mosque at
Canton. It is easy to see, therefore, how the alchemy of
China was made known to Persia, Greece and Egypt, and
how the Arabs later became the special agents for its prop-
agation in Western Europe in the eleventh century. As
alchemy lost its hold in China it increased its power in
Europe, and there, through the great intellectual movements of the sixteenth century, it became the herald of
modern science.

TAOISM AS A RELIGION

In China, however, as early as the middle of the second
century A.D. Taoism had ceased to be a philosophy only,
and had become a religion as well. In A.D. 166 a temple
was erected to Lao Tzu. The Old Philosopher became a
god. This transformation was probably due to the growing
influence of Buddhism, which was introduced into China

in A.D. 68. The jealousy of the Taoist adepts was aroused. They gathered into one system all the ancient superstitions of China, and in imitation of Buddhism built temples and filled them with images. The old councilor, Chang Liang, already mentioned, who retired from office when the founder of the Han Dynasty died (B.C. 194), was declared to have been one of the patriarchs of the sect, and his descendant in the eighth generation (A.D. 34), Chang Tao-ling, who was declared to have lived to be 123 years of age, was proclaimed as the first pope, although he had been dead more than a hundred years when this honor was conferred. From that day to this the descendants of this Chang Tao-ling have held the headship of the sect. In A.D. 423 the emperor conferred upon the pope of that day the title of Heavenly Teacher, a title still used by his successors. In A.D. 748 the papal authority was limited to members of the family of Chang Tao-ling, and in 1016 the pope was granted a large domain in the province of Kiangsi. The White Deer Grotto, on the Dragon-Tiger Mountain, is still the papal seat. This, in fact, was the home of Chang Tao-ling, and it was here, according to tradition, that he discovered the elixir of immortality. After reaching the age of 123 years, it is said, he ascended to Heaven, bequeathing the secret to his son.

THE PANTHEON

At the head of the Taoist pantheon there is placed a supreme god, called the *Yü Huang Ta Ti,* i.e., the Gem Emperor Great God. He dwells in one of the stars of the constellation of the Great Bear, and from his throne there is believed to rule the universe. This universe is organized much as the Chinese Empire was. It is divided into provinces, prefectures, and counties. Over each of these divisions a subordinate deity presides. Every community has its presiding spirit and each family its kitchen god. These make their reports to their superiors, just as in the days of the empire the local officials did to the imperial authorities.

EVIL EFFECTS OF TAOISM

Taoism has done more than any other religion to perpetuate the harmful superstitions of the Chinese. The belief in witchcraft, the dread of the fox spirit, the use of mediums to communicate with the dead, belief in demon possession and the practice of exorcism—all these are common practices of the Taoists. The ouija board was their invention many centuries ago, and charms and amulets are their merchandise.

The Chinese ouija board is usually a table covered with sand, in which Chinese characters are drawn by a forked twig of the peach or the willow. At the point where the two branches of the fork join, a third short branch extends downwards towards the table forming a support. After sacrifice and invocation to the spirit, the operator takes hold of one prong of the twig and the questioner the other. The fork is held over the table, very much as well-seekers hold a twig of witch-hazel. Suddenly the fork bends downwards toward the table and writes in the sand. But it takes an expert to find in the scratching any resemblance to Chinese characters.

There is great fear of evil spirits among the ignorant Chinese. These are supposed to be everywhere and on the alert to do harm. Many, therefore, are the charms and amulets used for the protection of the house and the person. The Taoist pope derives a considerable revenue from the sale of cryptic monograms, which are pasted on the lintel of the front door to frighten away the evil spirits. Sometimes a screen is built at the kerb, just in front of the main entrance. It is said that evil spirits fly only in straight lines, and cannot pass around this screen to enter the door-way. Probably the curious images that often adorn the roof are also of Taoist origin.

The theory of demon possession has taken a strong hold upon the Chinese, and all the phenomena that attend such supposed possession in other lands are common also in China. The unfortunate insane are by many regarded as possessed of the devil, but they are not treated as severely as such persons were in mediaeval Europe. One of the principal occupations of the Taoist is that of an exorcist. The Taoist pope wields a sword said to have come down to him from Chang Tao-ling, a sword which all the devils fear. With this he can cast out evil spirits and rid haunted houses of the ghosts that infest them. In his temple on the Dragon-Tiger Mountain, it is said, there are numerous jars in which demons are confined, jars sealed with the papal seal, which holds in lasting imprisonment these captives of the *ex calibur*.

The fear of foxes is a wide-spread superstition. There are many were-foxes abroad, it is believed. They are said to make their dens in old cemeteries, and to derive a great deal of vitality from the remains of human beings upon which they feed. They delight to take the forms of young women, and are reported to be of ravishing beauty and very bewitching. While I was living in Nanking there was an officer in charge of the arsenal there who was reported to be very superstitious. He kept a fox skin in his room and was a worshiper of the fox spirit.

It is the influence of such superstitions as these that has made it necessary in the past for enlightened officials to please the masses by engaging in the degrading worship of reptiles and inanimate objects. I have seen a small crocodile carried through the streets of Nanking on a little platform in time of drought, while shop-keepers contributed small sums of money to the bearers, with which to purchase incense for his worship. This was supposed to be effective in producing the much-needed rain.

When the Yellow River burst its banks some years ago the great Viceroy, Li Hung-chang, was commanded by the Imperial Government to leave his capital, Tientsin, and visit a little town on the bank of the Yellow River to worship a small serpent that had escaped from the flood. This harmless creature was reverently carried to the temple, where the Viceroy was required to pray to it to cause the flood to subside.

One of the most beautiful buildings in Peip'ing is the

ENTRANCE TO THE TA KAO TIEN, WHERE THE EMPEROR PRAYED FOR RAIN.

PRIVATE CHAPEL OF EMPEROR.

Ta Kao Tien, a Taoist temple situated across the street a little to the west of the back gate of the Forbidden City. In the court-yard before the principal entrance to the temple are two pavilions in which the Taoist monks used to chant their scriptures in time of drought. Behind the main hall of the temple there is a well which played an important part in the service for bringing rain.

Many deities were implored in time of drought. High officials in the provinces and at Peking used to visit various shrines that had a reputation for miracle working, but the last resort was an appeal by the Emperor in person to the spirit of a well in the southern part of Chihli Province. An iron tablet is kept suspended in the water of this well, and thus acquires great spirituality. This tablet was carried by high officials to Peking and suspended in the well of the Ta Kao Tien. There it was worshiped by His Majesty the Emperor, and the spirit that clung to the tablet was implored to bring rain.

It will be gathered from this that any object—a tree or stone—may become animated by a spirit. Such indeed is the fetich of the savage. According to the wise man "There is nothing new under the sun." Men to-day return in their philosophies to the theories of their primitive ancestors. That animals and plants, and perhaps even the so-called inanimate objects, may be the possessors of souls, is one of the favorite theories of the German philosopher, Paulsen.

Some things, of course, are much more spiritual than others. Age adds to spiritual power. Mt. T'ai in Shantung is of great might. Its spirit is the judge before whom the dead appear, before whom all devils tremble. Thus, if one take a stone from Mt. T'ai it will carry with it some of the great power of that mountain. In all parts of China you will find stones set up, usually at the end of a lane, which bear the inscription: "A stone from Mt. T'ai dares to oppose," i.e., oppose the coming of an evil spirit. It may be that the stone never saw Mt. T'ai, but the devil does not know that.

The Chinese, however, are not the only superstitious

people in the world. Other peoples' superstitions are always amusing, but what of our own? Frequently one reads in the daily paper a brief paragraph headed "Astrological Character Builders." Many read it as an amusement—others take it seriously. Astrological almanacs are still sold in the United States. Relics of the dead are touched for healing in many lands. Palmistry and fortune-telling are profitable occupations in all our large cities. Charms and quackery are still the resort of many for protection against evil and for the cure of disease. Not long since I read on the front page of the Times, of London, the advertisement of a woman who claimed to be an expert in laying ghosts.

As long as these superstitions exist in the West it is not easy to throw stones at the Chinese. But after all alchemy is the mother of chemistry, astrology the parent of astronomy, and the *feng-shui* of China is the beginning of the science of physics. All our superstitions are stumblings toward the light.

Despite its failings Taoism has a very admirable ethical code. The Kang Yin P'ien, which is known to all Chinese, contains such beautiful sentiments as the following:

There are no gate-ways to calamity or blessing save those which men open for themselves. The recompense of good and evil follow as naturally as the shadow follows the substance.

Enter the right path; avoid the wrong path. Do not walk in the way of evil.

Be compassionate towards all creatures.

First correct yourself, and then convert others.

Have pity upon the orphaned; assist the widow; respect the aged; be kind to children.

Be grieved by the misfortunes of others and rejoice in their good luck.

Do not publish the faults of others nor praise your own goodness.

Bear insult without hatred; accept kindness as unexpected; bestow charity without seeking reward; give to men without regret.

No religion that upholds an ethical code with such precepts can be wholly false.

CHAPTER XVI

CHINESE ART

Art is the expression of the society in which it exists.
—William Morris.

All art originates in the failure of reality to satisfy man's needs.
—Hermann Bahr.

Art is the power of the imagination to transform materials,—to transfigure them.—Fenollosa.

The Chinese recognize six arts: Ceremonial, Music, Archery, Charioteering, Writing and Mathematics. This seems to leave no place for painting and sculpture. They are included, however, in the term, *shu*, translated "Writing." The ideograph is composed of two symbols; that for "pencil" and that for "speak." The symbol for pencil was originally in the form meaning "stylus." The word, *shu*, therefore means the "stylus (or pencil) speaking." Such speaking might be done either by words or by pictures. But all written words in Chinese were at first pictures of the object named or the act performed, and the Chinese written characters used to-day are all derived from pictographs.

THE EARLIEST CHINESE ART

The oldest art objects found in China at the present time are vessels of bronze used in religious worship,—vases and wine cups upon which one finds the ancient pictographs that were a part of the written language in that far away period. They are found stamped on the vessels to indicate their ownership and use. Some of them are no longer understood. Some were probably private marks. Among these pictographs are drawings of a spear, a sheaf of arrows, a boat, a bow and halberd. All these archaic symbols approach the shape of the thing designated much more nearly than the modern conventional forms of the characters do.

The written characters on these ancient vessels are entirely distinct from the themes used for decoration. The outer surface of each vase and tripod is covered with scroll work, lozenges, heart-shaped and dagger-shaped motifs, animal heads and grotesque faces. Even at that early day the Chinese showed a fondness for the grotesque and the trait still persists. The most common themes for decoration during the Shang and Chou periods were the "Thunder Scroll" and the *T'ao T'ieh* or "Ogre Head." In this last some have noted a resemblance to the faces often seen on the totem poles along our Pacific Coast. Fenollosa was of the opinion that these forms originated in the south Pacific and were introduced from that region into China and Alaska, but recent developments in the study of culture movements would seem to indicate northern or central Asia as the most likely region for their invention. It is not impossible that they may have originated independently in more than one place.

Although the Chinese written characters on the ancient bronzes mentioned were not intended for decoration, Chinese writing easily lends itself to ornamental uses. One can not enter the home of an educated Chinese without finding some highly-prized specimen of calligraphy hanging on the wall of the reception room. It may be a single character, expressing the good wishes of a friend, or, perhaps, a pair of scrolls, setting forth in well balanced sentences a friendly appreciation of the householder's virtues. Such an autograph of some distinguished poet, painter or statesman is a precious legacy to be transmitted to one's heirs. One New Year's the Empress Dowager, Tzuhsi, sent me an autographed tablet, expressing the wish that my salary might increase like the light in spring. I regret to say that her prayer did not seem to have much influence with the God of Fortune.

Among the single characters used for decorative purposes to-day are those for the five sources of happiness: Domestic

CHINESE EMBLEMS.
(See List of Illustrations.)

RUBBING FROM A STONE, Etc.
(See List of Illustrations.)

Joy, Official Position, Long Life, Wealth and Pleasure.
These are often represented by rebuses. The word, *Fu,*
for domestic happiness has exactly the same tone as the *Fu*
meaning a "Bat," and for that reason the bat has become
a common theme in decoration. A mandarin in his robes
represents *Lu,* "Official Position," *Shou* for "Long Life"
is sometimes represented by an old man with a staff, but
the character itself has 360 forms and is highly ornamental.
The smiling and corpulent God of Wealth speaks for himself and "Pleasure" is represented by a character that
doubled is often used on wedding presents. Symbolism
appears to be a characteristic of all primitive art. The
artist is a mystic. He is a seer. He looks below the surface. The painter sees colors to which the common eye is
blind. The poet interprets a common experience in words
that revive in the breast the emotions aroused by the experience although but vaguely recognized at the time by
the ordinary man. The musician catches harmonies to
which our duller ears are deaf. To the common man a
triangle is a figure of three sides, the circle a curved line
every point of which is equally distant from the center.

> The primrose by the river's brim
> A yellow primrose is to him
> And nothing more.

But to the artist the visible object is but a symbol of that
which lies deeper. To him the triangle speaks of some
Trinity, the circle of an all-perfect One, the primrose of
a dead hero and a great cause. The symbol awakens emotions that he would fain express in form, in color, in verse
or in song.

Many symbols have been used for decorative purposes
by the Chinese from very ancient times. The Classic of
History tells us that in the twenty-third century before the
Christian Era the ruler wore upon his robes twelve emblems; the sun, moon and constellations, the mountains,
the dragon and the phoenix embroidered upon the upper
garment, and the sacrificial cup, the aquatic plant, the
flame, grains of rice, the battle axe and the *fu* on the lower

robe. These emblems continued to be worn on imperial robes down to the end of the Manchu Dynasty in A.D. 1912, at the time of the establishment of the Republic. The Statutes of the Manchu Dynasty contain the following provision: [1]

The court robes of the Emperor in winter are of bright yellow, but on audience days are red. The collar and sleeves are of *shih ch'ing* (literally, "stone blue") with bands of gold and green dragons. Upon each shoulder there is embroidered a dragon erect, on the skirt, five dragons running. On the breast is a dragon erect and on the pleats, nine small dragons in front and the same number behind. The lower robe shall have two erect dragons and four running, the collar two running dragons and the sleeves each a small erect dragon. Before and behind are embroidered the twelve emblems: the sun, moon, constellations, mountains, dragon, phœnix, battle axe and fu on the upper robe, and the sacrificial cup, aquatic plant, flame, and rice on the lower garment. In the midst are the five colored clouds and on the borders the eight precious objects and the peaceful waters (i.e. representation of the waves of the sea).

As will be noted, the twelve emblems are the same as in the twenty-third century B.C. but the arrangement upon the upper and lower robes is somewhat altered. Some additional emblems are added also. While the Emperor wore the whole number of the twelve emblems, he often conferred upon his ministers the right to wear one or more of these decorations, but never more than nine. The first three on the list, representing the sun, moon and constellations, all being celestial objects, were reserved for the sole use of the Emperor, the "Son of Heaven" and vicegerent of God. The constellations were usually regarded as the twenty-eight of the zodiac, but the constellation of the Great Bear was also regarded as of importance. Its seven stars were known as the "Seven Directors," and probably these seven, consulted in the astrology of all lands, may have led to the use in the Western World of the seven-branched candlestick.

The mountains represented the kingdom. In the earliest ages there were four, located in the four quarters of the

[1] Ta Ch'ing Hui Tien T'u: No. 3.

country. In modern times a fifth has been added located near the center. The dragon, a creature of awful mien and tremendous power, represented Heaven and the authority of the divinely ordained agent of God on earth. The phoenix, originally the rukh or garuda, was pictured like a pheasant, the most beautiful of birds, and was fit representative of the most beautiful woman, the wife of the ruler. The sacrificial cup spoke of the ruler's office as high priest of his people, for he alone was permitted to worship the supreme God. To-day the aquatic plant symbolizes literary elegance, suggested perhaps by its delicate structure. The flame, so necessary in the preparation of food and the comfort of the home, has been an object of worship in many lands, and the spirit of the furnace was one of the gods of the household in the Confucian system. Rice is the principal article of diet in China, and the Ruler, to honor agriculture, plowed and sowed the land every spring as an example to his subjects. The battle axe represented the ruler's office as chief of the military forces of the state. The *fu* was an ornamental figure related to the "key" pattern of the Greeks, and probably typified the order and beauty of the social relations. The five colors of Chinese art and Chinese philosophy in which these embroideries were worked were blue (including green), red, yellow, black and white. They were regarded as the primary colors and were mentioned in the Classic of History as having special significance in the twenty-third century B.C. These five colors were and are correlated with various other quinary groups, such as the five elements,—wood, fire, earth, metal and water,—with the five planets, the five directions,—south, north, east, west and center,—with the five musical notes,—they had a pentatonic system of music,—with the five virtues,—mercy, justice, piety, wisdom and honesty,—and with the five human relationships,—those of ruler and subject, parent and child, husband and wife, brother and brother, friend and friend.

There were four creatures that the ancient Chinese regarded as having supernatural powers: the dragon, the phœnix, the unicorn and the tortoise. Two of these have been considered. The unicorn was described as having the body of the deer, the tail of an ox, and a single horn. It was said to be the incarnate essence of the five elements, to live to the age of a thousand years and to be an emblem of perfect goodness. It was the unicorn that tradition said had heralded the birth and death of Confucius. The tortoise fitly represented the triad of the ancient religion,— the upper shell the vault of heaven, the lower, the earth, and the living creature, man, who dwelt between the heaven and the earth. There were three rituals, as has been described elsewhere, for the worship of Heaven, Earth and Man. The shell of the tortoise was used in divination, and sculptured images of the creature are placed at the grave to bear the stone tablet, as being fit emblem of immortality. This may be due to the fact that the markings on the shell suggest one of the forms of the character *shou,* meaning ''Long Life.''

The tiger, as a theme for decoration, appears to have been introduced during the period of the Chou Dynasty, 1122–256 B.C. Fenollosa says that the period was one of decline in art. This can be true only of the latter part of the time. The decoration of the bronzes of the Chou Dynasty, as described in the *Hsi Ch'ing Ku Chien,* for the most part show but a natural development of the art of the Shang Dynasty that preceded. The *T'ao T'ieh* and the ''Thunder Scroll'' are still used. Various combinations of the *Fu* are found and there are dragons and sea monsters in conventional forms and wild beasts and birds treated very artistically. It is true, however, that towards the close of the dynasty the lines of some of the vessels were less graceful than before and some were over ornamented to such an extent as to offend the taste. In the later centuries of the Chou period the vassal lords became more powerful than the King. The sumptuary laws of the kingdom, which prescribed and restricted the dress, palaces, furniture and ritual of the vassals, forbidding them to imitate the royal court, were disobeyed. The vassals, calling themselves kings, were practically independent and there was great license, luxury and dissipation. In such a society it was easy for parvenues to show bad taste, and bad taste in fact was exhibited.

A RENAISSANCE

When the Prince of Ch'in overthrew the House of Chou in 256 B.C. new influences were introduced into Chinese life. This state of Ch'in was situated on the northwestern frontier of old China and inhabited by a non-Chinese people probably related to the Turks. They adopted Chinese manners, intermarried with the Chinese and in time became the ruling race. With them there came new cultural elements. Art themes derived from the north and the west began to appear. The conquest of central Asia by Alexander the Great no doubt had much to do with opening up channels of communication with the west. The Ch'in Dynasty was short-lived and disappeared in 206 B.C. but the succeeding dynasty, the Han, greatly increased China's acquaintance with central Asia and promoted intercourse with Parthia and through Parthia with Rome. The reorganization of the empire and the awakened interest in the non-Chinese world furnished a new stimulus to art production and this stimulus was reinforced by the use of new material for these products. The use of the potter's wheel was known in China certainly as early as the fourth century B.C. but under the Han Dynasty the production of pottery became an important industry. Vessels of clay began to take the place of bronze both in the home and in the temple. It is in the decoration of these clay vessels that the new art motifs were particularly made evident, though they appear also in the bronze of the period. Of the elements of this decoration Laufer says:

The whole style of this art, dominated by the conventional design of the flying gallop as its fundamental leading motive, bears such a striking resemblance to that of ancient Scytho-Siberian art that a connection between the two must be presumed almost *a priori*.[2]

Laufer refers particularly to the use of the lion as an art

[2] Berthold Laufer: Chinese Pottery of the Han Dynasty, p. 213.

motive and to the introduction of representations of bowmen shooting from horseback. The lion was unknown to
ancient China and the Chinese did not learn to ride horseback until near the close of the Chou Dynasty. The archer
on horseback, as Laufer points out, was a motive in Siberian art at an earlier date than this. Another influence
manifested in the art of this period was that of legends
that apparently had their origin during the short-lived
dynasty of Ch'in. The ruler, who called himself the First
Emperor, in the third century B.C. hearing of the Isles
of the Blessed, as the abode of immortals and possessing
a Fountain of Perpetual Youth, sent an expedition in
search of them. According to the legend there were three
of these islands; P'englai, Fangchang and Yingchou, lying
seventy thousand li to the east in the great ocean. The
Emperor failed to find them, but the tale entered into
literature and art. The three islands suggested the form
of the cover of certain censers, known as ''Hill Censers''
from the fact that these covers represent three mountains
or hills surrounded by a shallow basin in which water was
poured. The word, *Shan,* meaning ''Mountain'' or ''Hill''
is used also for ''Island.'' The motive was first worked
out in bronze, but during the Han Dynasty it found expression also in pottery. It has continued to form a theme
for the decoration of pottery and porcelain down to the
present time. The so-called ''Willow Ware'' dinner sets
of porcelain, even when manufactured in England or the
United States, still show the three Isles of the Blessed in
the bottoms of the tea cups and coffee cups.

The Emperor of the Han Dynasty who left the most
lasting impression upon Chinese culture was Wu Ti, who
lived in the second century B.C. (140–87 B.C.). He, too,
sent an expedition in search of the Isles of the Immortals
and was made the dupe of fakirs who pretended to have
discovered the ''Pill of Transmutation'' or Philosopher's
Stone that would change the baser metals into gold. He
was noted, however, for more important enterprises, such
as his military expeditions that led to the conquest of vast
regions in central Asia, the negotiation of treaties with

many nations in that part of the world and the discovery
of the source of the Yellow River. These explorations
gave rise to many romantic tales that have been preserved
in the literature and the art of the time. Among these
was one that told of a visit made by the Fairy Queen from
her supposed home in the K'unlun Mountains to the capital
of China to see the Warrior Emperor of whose glory she
had heard. Each became enamored of the other and when
she returned to her western home, communication between
the lovers was kept up by means of the ''love birds'' that
fly only in pairs and that carried missives from the capital
to the fairy palace and return. These blue birds with three
wings each are still represented on the ''Willow Ware''
porcelain. The alleged visit of the Fairy Queen stirred the
imagination of Chinese painters who pictured the Queen
with a wonderful procession of attendants.

INFLUENCE OF BUDDHISM

It was during this period of the Ch'in and Han Dynasties
that Buddhism was introduced into China. Probably as
early as the second or third centuries B.C. the worship of
the Buddha began in Chinese Turkestan, but the religion
was not brought into China Proper before the first century
of our era. The Gandhara image of the Buddha, said to
have been modelled on that of the Greek Apollo, became the
pattern of the Chinese idol of the Sakya Muni. The Buddhist monks were fond of the mountains. They established
themselves in caves and in secluded valleys. They did
much to develop in the Chinese a love of the picturesque.
In their quiet retreats, where the stranger always meets
with a hospitable welcome, many of the artists and poets
of China found shelter and in their surroundings inspiration for their work. Upon the walls of the temples and
monasteries frescoes were painted depicting scenes from the
life of the Buddha or portraying the beauty of the Buddhist paradise. There were images of the Eighteen Lohans
or Apostles of Buddhism, of the merciful Kuanyin and of
other saints. On the altars were images of the Three

Holy Ones, in the Gateway perhaps there would be seen huge idols representing the Four Kings that guard the Universes around Mount Sumeru.

The introduction of Buddhism enriched Chinese architecture by two forms, the pagoda and the stupa. These are generally very attractive in their shapes, are built of brick or stone and do much to relieve the monotony of the Chinese landscape in the Great Plain or in a Chinese city where the houses are usually of one story of grey brick and covered with dark tiles.

The Lion, the Lotus and the Swastika are three of the symbols introduced by Buddhism, although the swastika, —the cross with the bent arms—has been found in all parts of the world and may have been used in China before the Christian Era. It is the mark found upon the breast of the Buddha. The lion is the protector of Buddhism, but the Buddhist lion is entirely unlike that of Western Asia brought in during the early Han period. The Buddhist lion looks more like a Pekingese pug than the king of beasts. The lotus rising out of a muddy pool and spreading its beautiful petals over the surface of the turbid water symbolizes the power of Buddhism to transform the filth and ugliness of the world. The elephant, too, is a Buddhist emblem. It recalls the dream of Maya, the mother of the Buddha. Frequently it is seen in the decoration of an altar and the head is sometimes used to form the handle of a censer. Buddhism has also given to art eight "precious emblems," that are found as decorative themes in wood carving, on the sculptured marble, on porcelain, in etchings on silver and brass and woven into the patterns of silk and satin or ornamenting Peking and Tientsin rugs. These eight emblems are (1) the Wheel of the Law,—the law of Karma, in accordance with which the wheel of transmigration continually revolves,—(2) the Conch Shell that calls the assembly to worship, (3) the Umbrella, symbol of the Buddhist trinity,—the spike representing the Supreme One, so Lillie affirms, the canopy, the overshadowing Spirit and the handle, the Buddha,—(4) the Pall that covered the coffin of the Buddha and that reminds us of the sure approach of death, (5) the Lotus, already explained, (6) the Urn that holds the ashes of the monk after death, (7) the pair of Fishes, which possibly had an astronomical meaning, and (8) the Endless Knot or the Net of Desire in which we all are taken.

TAOIST EMBLEMS

It was the introduction of Buddhism that was responsible in good measure for the transformation of Taoism into a religion. To retain their hold on the people the Taoists imitated Buddhism by establishing monasteries, creating a pantheon and building temples. Instead of the Three Holy Ones they had the Three Pure Ones, a trinity representing Lao Tzu in three appearances. They gathered together the folk lore and the superstitions of the common people and combined the pseudo sciences of astrology and alchemy with their theology. Their pretended magic fascinated the ignorant and credulous, their ritual promised length of days and their necromancy brought consolation to the bereaved.

I have already mentioned their eight celebrated magicians. Like the Buddhists, the Taoists must have "Eight Precious Emblems." To each of the eight magicians, therefore there was assigned a symbol. These eight symbols are (1) the Fan with which Chung Li-ch'üan revived the dead, (2) the Sword of Lü Tung-pin, who slew dragons much as St. George did, (3) the Gourd carried by Li T'ieh-kuai, (4) the castanets of Ts'ao Kuo-ch'iu, (5) the Basket of Flowers carried by the witch, Lan Ts'ai-ho, (6) the Vase of Divining Rods that belonged to Chang Kuo, (7) the Flute of Han Hsiang-tzu and (8) the Lotus blossom carried by the maiden Ho Hsien-ku. Besides these the Taoists may be held responsible for the use of many symbols of longevity, such as the Pine Tree, the Stork, and the Fungus, as well as for the use of the Plum Blossom (mistakenly called hawthorn by Europeans), the Hare mixing the Elixir of Immortality in the Moon, the Raven as symbol of the Sun, and the Peach, another emblem of long life.

CONFUCIAN EMBLEMS

In the description of the Imperial robes already given mention was made of "eight precious objects" to be embroidered on the border of the garment. There is nothing in the text to determine which of the groups of eight was intended. But since neither Buddhism nor Taoism was the state religion under the Manchu Dynasty, the reference may be to another group of "Eight Precious Objects" which may be said to typify Confucian civilization. These eight are (1) a Jewel, probably representing domestic affection, by which the Chinese set great store, (2) a Coin, meaning wealth, (3) the "Lozenge of Victory," meaning official success, (4) Books, representing learning, (5) a Painting, referring to art, (6) a Musical Stone, representing music, (7) a Pair of Rhinoceros Cups, used in libations to ancestors, and (8) a Leaf of Artemisia, signifying long life. There are some other ancient emblems that are often combined with these, such as the eight trigrams and the *yin-yang* symbol of the dual forces of nature, that is to say the circle divided by a curved line into two portions, one dark, the other light.

All these various emblems in modern times have been used indiscriminately in combinations that give great variety and significance to decoration.

WOOD CARVING

In wood carving the Chinese excel, as they do also in the carving of ivory and lacquer and their work in jade and crystal. Wood carving is mentioned in the classics and in ancient times as well as to-day the homes of the rich were decorated with carved beams and rafters. In modern Peking one often sees in the palaces there the upper part of the partitions between the rooms composed of panelling that is most exquisitely carved, some times in low relief and sometimes in perforated work. A background of colored silk throws the open-work into bold relief. On the

panels carved in low relief the theme may be a landscape
or a scene from some popular legend. The perforated work
will be composed of interlacing vines combined with the
swastika or some lucky character. In ancient times images
of human beings were made of wood. These were buried
in the graves with the dead as substitutes for living servants who were in earlier periods buried with their masters.
Confucius condemned the practice of burying even the
wooden images.

SCULPTURE

It is only in recent years that we have come to know
much about stone sculpture in China. The first examples
to attract the attention of the Western World were found
in the province of Shantung and have been described by
Professor Chavannes.[3] They are bas reliefs on the walls
of shrines dedicated to the dead. In part they are pretended portraits of noted historical characters and in part
they are illustrations of scenes from Chinese history or
from ancient legends. Fuhsi and Nukua are represented
as creatures with dragon bodies and human heads. That
will recall a tale by Herodotus. Yao and Shun and other
rulers of the olden time are pictured. Confucius is por-
trayed in his celebrated meeting with Lao Tzu. Mencius
is shown as a youth being reproved by his mother for
neglect of his studies. Ching K'o who attempted the life
of the King of Ch'in is hurling his javelin at that monarch.
There is a picture, too, of Lao Lai Tzu, one of the alleged
paragons of filial piety who rolled on the floor at seventy
years of age to please his aged parents who still regarded
their son as an infant. The activities of the spirit world
are not overlooked; the God of Thunder is seen beating
his drums. Some of these reliefs remind one of similar
scenes on the walls of Assyrian temples, but inspection
shows a difference. The physiognomy of the persons represented is not Assyrian and the costumes are Chinese. The
chariots are unlike those of western Asia and the horses

[3] *La Sculpture sur Pierre en Chine.*

are of a different breed. These Shantung stones date from the first century of the Christian Era, but show no trace of foreign influence. This is true also of other sculptures discovered more recently in western China. The latter are of greater artistic value. They are cut in the round and show life and movement. One discovered by Victor Segalen in Shensi is a very spirited piece representing a war horse leaping upon a Hun who defends himself with a spear.

During the period in which north China was ruled by the Wei Dynasty (A.D. 386–532), the influence of Buddhism upon Chinese sculpture became very marked. The Northern Wei Dynasty was established by a Tartar family, the House of Toba. They made their capital in northern Shansi on the border of Mongolia. Before their invasion of China they were accustomed to worship their ancestors in caves and after their conversion to Buddhism the caves became temples for the worship of the Buddha and Buddhist saints. While their capital was in northern Shansi they worshipped in the caves of Yün Kang, near Tatungfu. There one may see hundreds of these cave temples cut in a sandstone cliff and filled with sculptured altars and images. Waley says of the work that it reminds one of late Roman rather than Greek or Indian art, and to him they seemed "the most beautiful of Chinese sculptures." [4] A friend [5] who has visited the region quite recently reports that he found these rock-hewn shrines about twelve miles northwest of Tatungfu. More than a century was consumed in this work of piety. To-day the descendants of those who wrought so well in the service of religion are engaged in the more profitable work of cutting coal mines in the neighboring hills. A portion of the face of the cliff is hidden behind a façade of blue tiles. Stairways lead from the caverns on one level to those above. In some there are statues of colossal size. One is mentioned as being fifty feet in height.

A more careful study of the place was made a few years

[4] Arthur Waley: *Introduction to the Study of Chinese Painting*, p. 123 n.

[5] Emil S. Fischer: *The Sacred Wu Tai Shan*, Shanghai, 1925.

PIECE OF TAPESTRY.
(See List of Illustrations.)

RUBBING FROM A STONE.
(See List of Illustrations.)

ago by Professor Edouard Chavannes,[6] the reproduction of whose photographs shows very clearly the details of the work. Some of the images have the broad face and rather stolid expression that one sees on the ordinary Chinese idol, but others have the slender body, narrow waist and thin face of the Hindu, with a more animated facial expression. The decoration of the shrines exhibits fine workmanship. One of these hewn out of the rock has as the upper border of the niche a representation of the eaves of a tiled roof temple. Beneath it as a cornice are three horizontal registers. The first is composed of geometrical designs. The second is remarkable in its grace and beauty. It is formed of two chains of angelic figures, right and left of the center, the curves of whose bodies and floating draperies compose a meander of scroll-like pattern. At the middle point, where the two chains approach each other, there is represented a flaming pearl. The third register is an arrangement of floral designs. The whole is exquisitely done. Other sculptures illustrate the well-known story of the enlightenment of Prince Siddartha, the Buddha.

In the year A.D. 495, the House of Toba removed its capital to the vicinity of the ancient Loyang, where another series of rock-hewn shrines was cut in the cliffs that border the river Yi, a branch of the Yellow River. The gorge is known as the *Lung Men* of "Dragon Gate." The sculptures there are better known than those at Yün Kang and have also been described by Chavannes. But the place has been visited by vandals as well as by artists and archaeologists. Chinese coolies have been hired by American and European travellers to break off the heads or arms of some of the finest statues and these fragments, mute witnesses to the barbarism of the West, have been purchased by some of our great museums. Some of the statues at Lung Men are of huge size, carved where they stand out of the solid rock of the cliff, statues of Buddhist saints and Indian gods,

---

[6] Edouard Chavannes: *Mission Archéologique dans la Chine Septentrionale.*

imperishable evidence of the inspiration of a gentle life and a heroic faith.

While the Northern Wei ruled in the Yellow River Valley, China was divided. Native dynasties were in control of the South. Buddhism was later in its arrival there than in the North. In the middle of the sixth century Wu Ti of the Liang Dynasty, like Charles V of Spain, abdicated his throne and retired to a monastery in Nanking. But it was a Buddhist monastery. The grave of this monarch, which I have often visited, is marked by a pair of winged lions that remind one of certain monuments found in western Asia. Not far away is a cave temple on the bank of the Yangtze River, in which there is a seated statue of the Buddha that measures thirty feet or more in height. Beside the entrance to the cave there is a pagoda of stone, dating from the sixth century, upon each of the eight sides of which there is sculptured a human figure of heroic size and in bold relief. During the fifth and sixth centuries Buddhist art spread eastwards into Manchuria and Korea, and from Korea into Japan. In 1913 Langdon Warner visited Peking and reported his discovery of some fine specimens of cave sculpture of the Northern Wei period in five cave chapels at Wan Fo T'ang near Ichou in Manchuria. According to Warner the stone sculptures of the Northern Wei became the models upon which the Buddhist bronzes of Japan were shaped. He reminds us that Japan has no good stone for sculpture and that Japanese artists were forced to work in bronze and in wood with a result in these earliest examples that he characterizes as "stony."[7] In China, on the contrary, bronze and stone had each its own technique and the two arts developed abreast. But in due time the Japanese mastered the art and improved upon their models.

PAINTING

Attention has been called already to the early use of colors in China for purposes of decoration. Dyeing in the

[7] Langdon Warner: *Japanese Sculpture of the Suiko Period*, p. 26.

five colors was done in the twenty-third century B.C. and robes were embroidered in these colors. They were used, too, in the decoration of palaces. The sumptuary laws forbade certain colors for this purpose to any one but the King. The commentator on the Annals of the State of Lu condemned the Marquis of that state for painting the pillars of his ancestral temple red instead of black, as required by law.

One of the earliest references to painting as a fine art is made in the account of the visit of Confucius to the royal capital where he saw the portraits of the great rulers of the Chou Dynasty. About the same time—500 B.C.—the ancestral temple of the King of Ch'u was said to be decorated with paintings of "all the marvels of Heaven and Earth, Gods, and Spirits of the hills and streams, ancient sages and wondrous doings."[8] Account is given also of certain paintings in a palace in what is now the province of Shantung, that were to be seen there in the second century before our era. Waley says: "The earliest Chinese painting which exists is perhaps to be found upon certain earthenware vases, dating from the first century onwards. Some of these are decorated only with formal ornament, others with conventionalized dragons or flowers. Two much more elaborately decorated specimens were brought to England recently. They seem to date from the third century A.D."[9]

Chinese painting had already developed its characteristic features before it was subjected to foreign influences. The oldest painting on silk now in existence is the "Admonitions" by Ku K'ai-chih, of the fourth century A.D. It is now in the British Museum where I had the pleasure of examining it not long since. It is impossible to be sure of the genuineness of any old Chinese painting, for the works of the great masters were copied and re-copied, again and again. Even the seals of the artists and of the connoisseurs who certified to genuineness were frequently forged. Nevertheless the painting in the Museum is gen-

[8] Arthur Waley: Op. Cit., p. 22.
[9] *Ibid.*, p. 38.

erally accepted as that which belonged to the Ch'ienlung collection in the eighteenth century and which was regarded at that time as a genuine work of Ku K'ai-chih.

The painting illustrates an ancient literary production of the third century of our era, ''Admonitions to the Ladies of the Court,'' written by one, Chang Hua, who gathered together old tales of virtue and heroism for the instruction and inspiration of the women in the Imperial Palace. The painting as it exists is incomplete. Part of it has crumbled and disappeared. One of the scenes represents the Lady Feng courageously attacking a bear to save the life of her husband, the Emperor Yuan of the Han Dynasty (first century B.C.). Another preserves for us the story of the beautiful Lady Pan, author of the poem, ''The Autumn Fan'' written in the first century B.C. She refused to ride abroad with her husband, the Emperor, lest the people should think that he was neglecting the duties of his office to enjoy her society. As age deprived her of her beauty she was supplanted by a younger woman This suggested the theme, ''The Autumn Fan,'' which since that time has become a synonym for the neglected wife. There is a representation, too, of the Lady Ts'ao, completing the ''History of the Early Han Dynasty,'' begun by her brother. All the themes are drawn from Chinese history unmixed with any alien legends and are treated in a thoroughly Confucian manner. Petrucci has pointed out that in this painting we have to do not with a primitive art but with one long established. The religious sentiment aroused by the advent of Buddhism had not yet apparently made its appeal to the painter. Yet within fifty years after the completion of this painting the frescoes in the Tun Huang caves of Kansu, representing Buddhist saints and demon quellers, were begun. But Ku K'ai-chih lived in the South, in the vicinity of Nanking where Buddhist influence was not felt until long after its recognition in the art of the Northwest. By the beginning of the T'ang Dynasty that influence was potent throughout the Empire. It is to be noted, however, that long before this foreign faith had exercised any moulding influence upon the art of China

Proper, the Chinese Six Canons of Art had already been formulated by Hsieh Ho in the fifth century of our era. These canons continued to be the guiding principles of the painter down to our own time. They may be stated as follows:

1. The picture should express life and action,
2. Attention should be given to the structure of the object painted,
3. One must be true to nature,'
4. Be faithful in coloring,
5. Be artistic in composition, and should
6. Conform to tradition.

The importance of these canons is easily seen. It is only the master who can give life and movement to his picture, and before one can paint the needles of the pine or the foliage of the maple he must study the structure of leaf and tree. Before he can picture the horse in motion he must know the anatomy of the horse. Truthfulness to nature and faithfulness in coloring are no denial of idealism, for the painter must look with the artist's eye. He has a vision of the pattern that nature strives to realize and he endeavors to 'fix with his brush the fleeting nuances with which the delicate touch of the Master Artist has glorified His world. The canon means that there shall be no straining after bizarre effects. It is in the composition of his picture that the greatness of an artist is revealed, but conformity to tradition would seem to hamper talent and put convention in the place of originality.

These canons could only arise among a people who had for many generations been students of art. They give evidence of reflection, of a disposition to philosophize which would be possible only where art had reached its maturity. It is wrong, therefore, to assume that China owes her art to Buddhism or any other foreign influence. But foreign intercourse and the introduction of alien cults did furnish new themes and give a new inspiration. The themes, however, were treated in Chinese fashion. The materials, the technique, the canons followed were all Chinese.

TECHNIQUE

In discussing technique, one often hears it said that the Chinese ignore perspective. Petrucci has explained to us that such an observation is due entirely to misunderstanding. One can not do better than quote in part what he has said so well: [10]

This error arises from the fact that we have confused one system of perspective with perspective as a whole. . . . The practice of drawing and painting offers the student the following problem in descriptive geometry: to represent the three dimensions of space by means of a plane surface of two dimensions. . . . European perspective, built up in the fifteenth century upon the remains of the geometric knowledge of the Greeks, is based on the monocular theory of the latter. . . . But, in assuming that the picture is viewed with the eye fixed on a single point, we put ourselves in conditions which are not those of nature. The European painter must therefore compromise with the exigencies of binocular vision, modify the abrupt fading of forms and, in fine, evade over-exact principles.

The Chinese theory of perspective he explains as follows:

Chinese perspective was formulated long before that of the Europeans and its origins are therefore different. It was evolved in an age when the method of super-imposing different registers to indicate different planes was still being practiced in bas-reliefs. The succession of planes, one above the other, when codified, led to a system that was totally different from our monocular perspective. It resulted in a perspective as seen from a height. No account is taken of the habitual height of the eye in relation to the picture. The line of the horizon is placed very high. Parallel lines, instead of joining at the horizon, remain parallel, and the different planes range one above the other in such a way that the glance embraces a vast space. Under these conditions, the picture becomes either high and narrow,—a hanging picture, —to show the successive planes, or broad in the form of a scroll, unrolling to reveal an endless panorama. These are the two forms best known under their Japanese names of Kakemono and Makimono. The Chinese terms are *Li Chou* and *Heng P'i*. But the Chinese painter must attenuate the forms where they are parallel, give a natural appearance to their position on different levels and consider the degree of their reduction demanded by the various planes. Even he must compromise with the binocular

[10] Raphael Petrucci: *Chinese Painters*, pp. 26-30.

vision and arrive at a *perspective de sentiment* which, like our own, while scientifically false, is artistically true.

To this linear perspective is added moreover an atmospheric perspective . . . by means of tone values and harmony of shading. . . . Thus they were familiar with chiaroscuro before the European painters."

It was Wang Wei, he tells us, who first established the principles of atmospheric perspective. This was in the eighth century of our era. The increasing thickness of layers of air deprives distant objects of their true coloring, substituting a bluish tinge which causes them to become indistinct. Distant objects were therefore colored blue. This contrasts with the green of grass and foliage in the foreground. Wang Wei became the originator of a school of landscape painting in which this striking use of blue and green was a distinguishing characteristic.

RIVAL SCHOOLS

Two distinct schools of painting have been developed in the Far East, one called the Southern, the other the Northern School. "South" comes before "North" in Chinese grouping of directions. These terms, "South" and "North" in relation to art schools are not used in a geographical sense, but refer to the character of the painting. To understand what is meant, one must recall a passage in the *Chung Yung,* or "Doctrine of the Mean," a treatise written, as is generally believed, by the grandson of Confucius. The passage is as follows:

To teach with gentleness and tolerance and not to avenge a wrong; that is the strength of the South, and the gentleman relies upon it. To take up arms and die without regret; that is the strength of the North, and the violent trust to it.

The meaning, therefore, of the terms, "South" and "North" as applied to painting is quite plain. The Southern School painted in subdued tones. Pictures by artists of this school are dreamy and full of poetry. The Northern School uses strong colors: it shows great firmness

and boldness in drawing and displays brilliancy, precision
and force. Sometimes the same painter was distinguished
in the use of both methods. He might live in the South
or in the North; his residence had nothing to do with the
name of the school to which he belonged. Fenollosa and,
after him, Waley and others trace the distinction between
the Southern and Northern Schools of art to a similar distinction between two divisions of the Ch'an or Zen sect of
Buddhists. There is a connection,[11] but the use of the
terms, "Southern" and "Northern" with reference to sect
of Buddhists is also to be understood in the sense explained
by Tzu Ssu in the *Chung Yung*. The Southern Ch'an sect
was devoted to quiet retirement and contemplation. It is
not surprising therefore that it was among them that the
Southern School of painting found its greatest artists.
Philosophy and Art, just as Religion and Art, go hand in
hand. The poet, the philosopher, and the artist are all
akin. They look behind the phenomenal world to find that
which inspires it. A composite of multitudinous forms
creates in their minds the ideal. "A poem," said a Chinese
artist, "is a formless picture; a picture is a form poem."
The philosopher and the artist must both be contemplative.
The Ch'an monk among the Buddhists, like St. Francis
among the Christians, was a mystic. He had no use for
images or for liturgies. He found God within. In an
earlier chapter I have told of Bodhidharma, the founder
of this sect. Many tales have gathered about his name
and the names of some of his disciples. Waley tells
the story of Tan Hsia, which has been immortalized by the
artist.[12] Tan Hsia, a monk of the Ch'an sect, was visiting
a monastery of another sect of Buddhists. Growing cold
in the night, he arose, took the wooden idol from the altar,
split it into kindling and made a fire of it, much to the

---

[11] When the Ch'an sect divided, the legitimate Patriarch remained
in the South while his rival located himself near the Court in the
North, which may have suggested the use of the terms "Northern"
and "Southern," but the continued application of these terms to
certain distinctions in philosophy and art was undoubtedly based
upon the older views as to the character of races, South and North.

[12] Arthur Waley: Op. Cit., p. 227.

horror of his hosts when they discovered the sacrilege the next morning.

But the Ch'an monk of the Southern Sect did love nature, he revelled in its beauty. In the quiet nooks of the mountains where these mystics preferred to dwell, in the dreamy atmosphere of gentleness, contentment and meditation amidst which they lived, the artist found himself at home and there he wrought those soft-toned landscapes, whose cloud-capped mountains, sylvan beauty and hazy distances so charm us that Binyon can write of them: "Chinese landscape is certainly pre-eminent in the landscapes of the world in suggesting infinite horizons, the look of mountains beyond mountains, melting away into remote sky." [13]

Sometimes the artist was tempted to illustrate by pictured parables the philosophical theories of the monk. One such during the T'ang Dynasty in a series of ten paintings illustrated man's search for truth by picturing a man in search of a stray bull. He finds its tracks and follows them. He sights the animal in the distance. He captures it and rides it home. He leads it into the stable and places it in the stall. Then, as he turns about, he finds that the stall is empty; there is no bull. [14]

Although the Southern School attained great popularity, especially in Japan the Northern School did not lack adherents. The founder of this school was Li Ssu-hsün. He painted in heavy colors, blue and green outlined in gold. It was a striking style that appealed to certain natures, but the Southern School despised it as garish and blatant. Just as the monks of the Northern Sect of the Ch'an Buddhists were patronized by the courtiers at the capital and regarded by their retiring brethren in the South as worldly-minded renegades, so the Northern School of painting was considered heretical, devoted to the showiness of the world and blind to the spiritual interpretation of life.

But the Northern School, no less than the Southern was influenced by Buddhist beliefs and Buddhist traditions.

[13] Laurence Binyon: The Flight of the Dragon, p. 79.
[14] *Ibid.*, p. 155.

Artists of both schools painted bodhisatvas, scenes from the life of the Buddha and pictures of the joys of the Buddhist Paradise. The Buddhist religion occupies a position in relation to Chinese and Japanese art quite similar to that held by Christianity in its relation to European art in the Middle Ages. Instead of the Christ and his Apostles the Buddhists have the Buddha and the Eighteen Lohan. Instead of the Madonna they worship Kuan Yin, the Goddess of Mercy, often represented as holding a child in her arms. Instead of the "Beloved Disciple," St. John, they have Ananda; instead of St. Francis, a Ti Tsan; and instead of a St. Dominic, a Nagarjuna. All of these and a host of others appear in painting and sculpture with halos about their heads just as do the saints of Christianity.

We have seen how great an influence Buddhism exerted upon Chinese sculpture from the fifth century onwards. It is even more manifest in Chinese painting. It increased from generation to generation. In the British Museum I saw a part of that wonderful collection of paintings brought from the caves of Tun Huang by Sir Aurel Stein. The caves were discovered in 1907, and, hidden behind a wall in one of them, were these paintings that had been placed there for safety in A.D. 1035. Twenty-four cases of manuscripts and five of paintings and embroideries were carried away by Sir Aurel. The paintings are on silk and for the most part date from the T'ang Dynasty (A.D. 618–907). Among the subjects treated are scenes from the life of the Buddha, the Goddess of Mercy, Kuan Yin, other Buddhist saints, and a vision of the Western Paradise.

The caves were visited subsequently by Professor Pelliot, who has published a portfolio of photographs taken there. Most interesting of these are the reproductions of the wall paintings which are believed to date from the sixth century of the Christian Era.

From the eighth to the thirteenth century painting flourished in China in great vigor. Under the T'ang Dynasty China became a mighty empire extending its sway over central Asia to the borders of Persia, holding Korea in its grasp, and reaching from Lake Baikal in Siberia to Cambodia in the Indo-Chinese Peninsula. Students from all the surrounding countries came to Changan, the capital, to attend the Imperial College. Christian missionaries, Mohammedan merchants, Zoroastrian and Manichaean emissaries had their temples there. Men from many lands and clothed in strange costumes jostled one another in the streets. Trade flourished by land and by sea. The poets of the T'ang period who won national fame were more than two thousand. Their best works collected in the eighteenth century number nearly 'fifty thousand and fill nine hundred books. The cosmopolitan atmosphere of the great capital, the activities of commerce, the controversies of rival faiths and rival philosophies are all reflected in the literature of the age. All this gave great stimulus to the artist. Most famous of all the artists of China, ancient or modern, was Wu Tao-tzu, known to the Japanese as Go Doshi, who lived in the reign of Ming Huang of this Dynasty. He painted Buddhist saints and he painted Taoist wizards, but he is credited, too, with founding a new school of landscape. It is of him that the Taoist legend speaks, saying that he painted upon the wall of Ming Huang's garden a landscape so beautiful with mountain, forest and living creatures, as to charm the beholder, and that the artist then invited the monarch to follow him into a cave in the picture. The door of the cavern opened at the clapping of his hands. The painter entered and disappeared, never to be seen again. He was not only the greatest Chinese painter, but one of the few great painters of the world. Fenollosa said of him:

There is a certain primal and universal energy in Godoshi's design which has hardly been surpassed in the whole range of the world's art. . . . His art establishes itself side by side with Phidias and Michelangelo.[15]

Wu Tao-tzu was a native of the province of Honan and was born about the beginning of the eighth century of our era. From extreme poverty he rose by the force of his own genius to a position of influence at the luxury-loving

[15] Ernest F. Fenollosa: Epochs of Chinese and Japanese Art, Vol. I, p. 131.

court of Ming Huang and through his art achieved distinction and honor while still living. In him Chinese painting reached the highest point of its development.

Contemporary with Wu Tao-tzu was Wang Wei, of whom
mention has just been made. He was noted both as a
poet and a painter. A little younger than Wang was his
pupil, Han Kan, who became celebrated as a painter of
horses. A picture by him of a boy riding a goat is to
be seen in the British Museum.

The number of distinguished painters of the T'ang
period is legion. Few of them can be noticed in this brief
chapter. Chou Fang who lived at the close of the eighth
century must be mentioned because there is in the Freer
Gallery in Washington a picture ascribed to him which is
much admired, "Listening to Music." Probably it is only
a copy, but the copyist seems to have been able to transmit
to us much of the charm of the original.

Two other noted painters of the T'ang Dynasty were
the brothers Yen, who were a century earlier than Wu
Tao-tzu. The younger, Yen Li-pen, was one of those who
took advantage of the opportunity afforded by the presence in the capital of representatives of so many peoples
to preserve by his art a record of their strange physiognomy
and foreign dress. He is supposed to have designed the
reliefs representing war horses, which were prepared for
the tomb of the Emperor T'ai Tsung, two of which are to
be seen in the Museum at Philadelphia.[16] In Kyoto one
finds some Chinese paintings claiming to be of the T'ang
period. Some of them probably are genuine.

Following the downfall of the T'ang Dynasty in 907
there was a period during which six short-lived dynasties
came in rapid succession. In this period, despite the disturbed condition of the empire, art did not lose its interest.
One great painter, Kuan T'ung, invented a new style of
landscape with human figures. Not long since a long makimono was brought to me for examination. It bore the
name of Kuan T'ung and was indorsed with the seal of

16 Arthur Waley: Op. Cit., p. 110.

the Hsüan Ho Academy, instituted by Hui Tsung of the
Sung Dynasty. It is difficult to believe that this painting
on silk so well preserved has survived the vicissitudes of a
thousand years, yet the preservation of the painting by
Ku K'ai-chih and the existence of the Stein collection are
evidence that such survival is not an impossibility. We
may say, at any rate that, if the seal of the Hsüan Ho
Academy is genuine, we have either the original of Kuan
T'ung or a Sung Dynasty copy of it.

SUNG DYNASTY PAINTERS

Some art critics regard the painting of the Sung period
as an improvement on the whole of that of the T'ang.
They would place here the point of the highest development of Chinese art. Hui Tsung of the Sung Dynasty was
a patron of painters but also an artist himself of considerable merit. He was particularly fond of painting eagles
and falcons. He established an academy of Painting and
made a large collection of the works of the most famous
artists. A catalogue of this collection published by him is
still extant. He mentions the names of two hundred and
thirty-one painters of the centuries preceding A.D. 1200 and
gives the titles of more than six thousand of their paintings. But this is a small part of the total. K'anghsi's
encyclopedia of painting fills one hundred books. There
were eight hundred celebrated painters during the Sung
period alone. The Sung period was noted for philosophical
speculation. Under the leadership of Chou Tun-i, the
brothers Ch'eng, Chang Tsai and Chu Hsi in the eleventh
and twelfth centuries, a new school of philosophy came into
existence which has dominated Chinese thought from that
time to our own day. Buddhism and Taoism had fallen
into disrepute and in the tenth century some thirty thousand monasteries had been closed. The new philosophy
sought to restore Confucianism to the position which it had
formerly held in Chinese esteem. The result was in reality
a neo-Confucianism which had but little in common with
the teachings of the ancient sage. But advocated by the

greatest thinkers of the time it had a tremendous vogue and did much to destroy the hold of Buddhist and Taoist superstitions.   Thus less attention was given to religious painting and more to nature studies.   Among the painters of the Sung Dynasty whose names stand out with prominence there are two that must be mentioned, Li Lung-mien and Mi Fei.   The former first came to note as a painter of horses, but later turned to other subjects.   It is said that he did much to revive an interest in Buddhist subjects.   Petrucci says of him:—''No matter what models he chose to follow, he always gave them a stress and a peculiar distinction.''[17]   He adds that Li Lung-mien ''challenges comparison with a facile genius like Raphael''[18]   Of Mi Fei it is said that some of his work in monochrome recalls drawings by Rembrandt.

YUAN, MING, AND CH'ING DYNASTIES

It is the fashion to speak of the deterioration of Chinese art after the fall of the Sung Dynasty, which gave way to the Mongols in 1278.   No doubt it is true that we find fewer painters of the first rank and it is also true that much of the work was lacking in originality.   There was too much conventionality.   There was a loss of simplicity in composition.   Pictures were crowded with too many objects, too much detail.   But there are not a few great artists to be found in the lists, nevertheless.   The disparagement of modern Chinese art may be due in part to the criticism of Chinese connoisseurs.   In accepting their judgment, however, one must make allowance for the national disposition to belittle the present and exalt the past.   Like some occidental pessimists, the Chinese say: ''The former days were better than these.''   It is an old trait and ingrained.   In the days of Confucius a Chinese proverb said: ''His father split fire wood; his son can't carry a lily.''

Among the best painters of the Yüan or Mongol period

17 Raphael Petrucci: Op. Cit., p. 84.
18 *Ibid.*, Op. Cit., p. 84.

PAINTING BY
CHAO MENG-FU.
(See List of Illustrations.)

PAINTING BY CHIU YING.
(See List of Illustrations.)

Chao Meng-fu is perhaps to be given first place. He was, it is true, a relative of the Sung imperial family and did some painting under that dynasty, but his greatest work was done after the overthrow of his own people and the advent of the Mongols under whom he accepted office. Since the Mongols were expert horsemen, there was a demand for pictures of horses, and Chao Meng-fu rivalled Han Kan in the talent he displayed in painting horses. One of his horse pictures is to be seen in the British Museum. Among Europeans it is for such painting that he is celebrated, but he did excellent work in other lines, especially in landscape and in human figures. He delighted to fix upon his canvas the striking traits of the many races that gathered at the Mongol court.

As an heir of the Sungs, he adhered for a time to the traditions of the Southern School of the Sung period, but, living among the Mongols, a more primitive people with a taste for more vivid coloring, his style was somewhat modified in his later work. I have a painting that bears his signature under the date corresponding to A.D. 1313. I am disposed to accept it as genuine upon the assurances of Chinese connoisseurs. It represents the celebrated poet Li Po of the T'ang Dynasty among his wine jars. The portrait of the old poet conforms to tradition. The house, the garden, the figures of the servants, the expressions upon the faces—all show the hand of a master. The striking use of blue and the touches of other more brilliant colors bear out the statement that he adopted somewhat the Northern style of painting but subdued to a degree by his inheritance from the Southern School.

There are many private and public collections of Chinese pictures in the United States and elsewhere that contain paintings by the masters of the Yüan, the Ming and the Ch'ing Dynasties. In fact most of our Chinese pictures are of these three dynasties. Even those that claim an earlier date are, in many instances, copies made in the Ming or Ch'ing periods, so that our acquaintanceship with Chinese painting is based to a great degree upon the work of these late periods. I have in my possession a

painting by Chiu Ying of the Ming period, a landscape
with human figures, whose rich coloring bears witness to
the continuing influence of the preceding Mongol period.
In its execution the artist does not appear to fall far below
the masters of earlier times.

Among the paintings in the British Museum belonging to
the three Dynasties under review I noted one representing
the ''Peach Blossom Valley,'' the title of a striking allegory
written in the fifth century by T'ao Ch'ien, which recalls
the Rasselas of Dr. Johnson. The painting dates from the
late fifteenth or early sixteenth century. Others to be seen
there whose merit can scarcely be questioned are a ''Cock
and Mallows'' of the sixteenth century, a picture of the
Taoist wizard, Chung K'uei, of the seventeenth century
and a portrait of a woman by Wang Chao-hsiang of the
eighteenth century.

Petrucci speaks of the subtle monochromes of Lu Fu of
the Ming period and of the ''trunks of old trees, bearing
hardy blossoms under the radiance of the moon'' as painted
by Wang Yüan-chang of the same dynasty.

The Chinese work, *T'ung Yin Lun Hua,* furnishes a list
of noted painters of the Manchu period, including a few
of the late Ming time who survived into the early Ch'ing.
This work with its supplement gives biographical notes of
four hundred and eighty four painters with comments upon
the style of each. Of these it mentions forty-two as deserving the rank of *Shen P'ing,* that is to say, as having
the divine afflatus. One artist of the Manchu period, Shen
Nan-p'ing, is said to have gone to Japan where he founded
a school of modern painting.

The Manchus gave encouragement to art throughout the
whole period during which they possessed the empire. The
Empress Dowager, Tzuhsi, though responsible in large
measure for the overthrow of the dynasty, was nevertheless, a discriminating patron of the fine arts and maintained
a school of painting in the palace. She was particularly
fond of floral subjects.

CHAPTER XVII

CHINESE LITERATURE

Of making many books there is no end and much study is a weariness of the flesh.—Ecclesiastes.

A nation, which, like the Chinese, has had a written language for four thousand years, we should expect to find possessed of a voluminous literature. A nation, which in its most ancient records gives evidence of a remarkably high degree of civilization, as is true of China, would be expected to have a worthy literature. In these expectations we are not disappointed. China does indeed possess a literature abundant in quantity and comparing favorably in quality with the best of the Western World.

THE WRITTEN LANGUAGE

Chinese writers, however, labor under a severe handicap: they have no alphabet, not even a syllabary. Each word has its own symbol. These symbols are built up, of course, in accordance with a system, but it is a cumbrous one. Originally each symbol was a picture of the thing which it represented, but in process of time by abbreviation and modification these pictographs have become so changed that it is difficult to see in most cases any resemblance to the things for which they stand. In the inscriptions on the bronzes of the Shang Dynasty,[1] some of the resemblances are easily detected, and in some modern characters one can still find suggestions of the ancient pictures. This is true, for instance, of the character for sheep or of that for horse, or those for tree, bow, mouth, gate, and others that might be mentioned. To represent abstract ideas was not so easy. East was indicated by a picture of the sun rising behind a tree and west by a bird on its nest. Two men, one behind the other, represented the verb, "to follow." A dot above

[1] 1766-1122 B.C.

a line indicated "above" and one below a line meant "below." Since the number, "two," was represented by two horizontal lines, there was likelihood that the word for "above" or that for "below" might be mistaken for "two," consequently to-day the dots are connected with the line by perpendicular strokes. A character which forms a part of many others of a spiritual or religious significance is composed of the ancient sign for "above" with three perpendicular strokes below it, that is to say, it represents the conception of spiritual influences,—influences descending from above. Thus, the word *li*, meaning "rite" or "religion," is composed of this ideogram annexed to a picture of an offering on an altar. The root meaning of the word then is "influences from above, obtained by sacrificial offerings." The word for "happiness," i.e. *fu*, is composed of the same ideogram annexed to symbols of "one woman and a field." A wife and a piece of land with the blessing of Heaven meant happiness.[2] A curved line coming out of the sign for "mouth" meant "to speak," and a series of lines above the character for "mouth" meant "words." A picture of the stylus above the sign for the verb "to speak" meant "a book," i.e. "the stylus speaking." The same combination was used for the verb, "to write" and at times has the significance of "history," i.e. "that which is written."

A number of these ancient symbols, representing root ideas, were modified by additional strokes or combined one with another, to form new characters. These two hundred and fourteen symbols are known as radicals and are supposed to give a clue to the meaning of the characters in which they are found, but it must be admitted that often the clue is misleading. In certain classes of characters the portion added to the radical is known as the phonetic and is supposed to give a clue to the pronunciation, but this, too, at times is an unreliable guide. The written symbol for "sea" illustrates very well this method

[2] There are other explanations of this character. The phonetic is composed of the characters for "one," "mouth" and "field." But the character, *k'ou*, "mouth," is also a classifier of women, so that the phonetic portion may be translated, "One woman and a field."

隹（惟）十又五年三月既霸丁亥，王在□□宮。□□乃友樂□山，天子□，王呼善夫□召大，賜駁□駒，大拜稽首，對揚天子丕顯休，用作朕烈考□伯盂鼎，其子子孫孫永寶用。

of forming characters. It is pronounced *yang* and has exactly the same sound and tone as the word meaning "sheep." The sign for sea, therefore, is composed of the radical, meaning "water" annexed to that for "sheep." It is the *yang* then that has to do with "water" as its root idea, that is to say, the *yang* meaning "sea."

During the period from the seventh to the third century B.C. China was in decay. The central government was weak and the states were frequently at war one with another. Learning was neglected and many of the scribes were ignorant. The written language became corrupted. A good many unauthorized forms came into use. Confucius in his day said:—"I can still remember recorders who left blank spaces in their writing . . . alas! there are no more such men."[3] Apparently he meant that when they did not know the correct form, they would leave the space blank, while in the time in which he was speaking the ignorant scribes would use a wrong character.[3a] During the third century B.C. a dictionary of authorized forms was compiled. It contained over ten thousand characters. The dictionary prepared under the reign of K'anghsi (A.D. 1662-1723) and which is still the standard dictionary of Chinese contains some forty thousand characters, but there are less than fourteen thousand of these that are of any practical use.

BOOK MAKING

In the most ancient times books were made of tablets of wood or bamboo on which the characters were cut with a stylus in perpendicular columns. These tablets were strung together with thongs passed through a hole in the end of each tablet. Some writing was done with a sort of ink on silk and leather during the latter part of the Chou period (ended 256 B.C.) and this led to the substitution of a brush for the stylus. The invention of the brush pencil is ascribed to General Meng T'ien in the third century

[3] Analects: xv, 25.

[3a] In this interpretation of a disputed passage I have followed Dr. L. Wieger, S.J., in the introduction to his work, *Chinese Characters.*

B.C. The Chinese invented paper in the first century of the Christian Era. This gave a great stimulus to literary production. Ch'in Shih Huang Ti in the third century B.C. attempted to destroy the classics, but after his death the greater part of the text was recovered and was carved upon stone in the second century of our era. By the use of paper it became possible to distribute ink rubbings of the text. As early as the eighth century of our era block prints of religious images were made and during the closing years of the T'ang Dynasty, in the ninth century, paper money and playing cards were printed. The first book printed from blocks was the Buddhist Diamond Sutra in the year A.D. 868, six hundred years before printing was introduced into Europe. Movable type were made in the eleventh century, but not of metal. Metal movable type were probably first cast in the fourteenth century a hundred years before Gutenberg's work. Books continued to be printed, however, from wooden blocks down to our own day, for it was difficult to arrange such a multitude of different characters in a manner that would permit any desired character to be easily found. It was not until the middle of the nineteenth century that a member of an American mission succeeded in having metal type cast and arranged in such a way as to make rapid type setting possible. Since that time the publication of books and newspapers has enormously increased.[4]

HISTORICAL LITERATURE

The Chinese Government from very ancient times has given attention to the recording of important events and since the second century B.C. has exercised great care for the preservation of the records. Under all dynasties there were official historiographers whose duty it was to set down in writing from day to day all events of importance affecting the nation, whether natural occurrences such as eclipses, storms or pestilence, or those of a political char-

[4] The author desires to acknowledge his indebtedness to the splendid work of the late Professor Thos. Carter: *The Invention of Printing in China.*

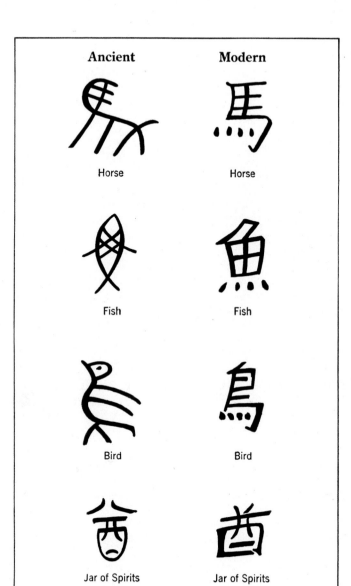

Ancient   **Modern**

Horse   Horse

Fish   Fish

Bird   Bird

Jar of Spirits   Jar of Spirits

Ancient and modern Chinese characters.

acter. Ma Tuan-lin, who wrote in the fourteenth century of our era says that "the pencil of the recorders was kept busy from the time of Huang Ti," a legendary sovereign who is supposed to have lived in the twenty-seventh century B.C. Lao Tzu tells us that the earliest records were made of knotted cords. This, we know, was true of other primitive peoples. The earliest historical records of the Chinese are preserved for us in the canonical book called the *Shu*, or "Historical Records" and in an equally ancient work, known as "the 'Bamboo Books.'" This latter, made of bamboo tablets, was found in the grave of a Prince of Wei who was buried in the year 295 B.C. The grave vault caved in in the year A.D. 279, exposing a collection of ancient writings carved on bamboo, among them this chronicle giving accounts of various historical events from the time of Huang Ti (27th century B.C.) to the year 299 B.C. These records were buried therefore some eighty-two years before the attempted destruction of the classics by the tyrant Ch'in Shih Huang Ti, in 213 B.C.

The *Shu* or *Shu King* originally contained, it is said, about one hundred documents collected by Confucius. It does not claim to be a complete nor a continuous history of ancient China, but it has preserved for us valuable documents which furnish a fragmentary record of the national life from 2357 to 627 B.C. These documents are of two kinds. The earliest were not contemporary with the events which they record, but were based upon traditions and possibly upon certain writings more ancient than themselves. They begin with the phrase, "Examining into antiquity, we find." There are four of these documents. The others claim an origin contemporary with the events described. In the year 221 B.C. the King of the state of Ch'in completed the conquest of the empire and proclaimed himself the First Emperor. He was a man of strong character and a far-seeing statesman. He realized that the weakness of the ancient monarchy was its toleration of feudalism. This he sought to destroy and supplant with a strongly centralized form of government. In this attempt he found himself opposed by the scholars who were conservative followers of Confucius. Confucius, they reasoned, had approved the feudal organization of the Chou Dynasty, therefore it must have been the best form of government. After vainly endeavoring to overcome their opposition the Emperor was advised by his Prime Minister to gather up the books that preserved the traditions of the Chou Dynasty and destroy them. The edict as said above was issued in 213 B.C. All copies of the ancient classics except those in the possession of high ministers of the state were ordered to be delivered up for burning and scholars under penalty of death were forbidden to discuss these works or quote them against the Government. Several hundred · scholars were put to death. But the tyrant died within four years and there were not a few who had dared to hide their copies of classical works. It would have been comparatively easy to recover the complete text of these books had it not been for the civil war which raged for some years after the death of Ch'in Shih Huang Ti. In that war, which overthrew the Ch'in Dynasty and established the Han, the capital with its priceless library was destroyed. The edict, however, was not as sweeping as it is sometimes represented to have been: it excepted from destruction the Yi King and other works dealing with divination and all books that treated of medicine and horticulture. The works of Mencius, who had been dead but seventy-five years, were evidently not regard as classical and were spared. In the year, 191 B.C. the Han Dynasty being in power formally repealed the edict and earnest efforts were made to recover the text of the ancient writings. Some thirty-five books of the *Shu* were recovered at once. A little later additional chapters were found in the walls of the home of Confucius' descendants together with copies of the Spring and Autumn Annals, the treatise on Filial Piety and the Analects. A third portion of the *Shu* was discovered during the first century of our era. Of the hundred books which it is claimed were originally in the *Shu* fifty-nine were thus recovered. It must be remembered, however, that there existed the possibility of error in transcribing the ancient characters which in the case of the tablets found in the home of Confucius were quite unlike those in use at the time of discovery. It must also be admitted that interpolations were possible during this period of recovery. But the great care taken in editing the text and the character of those engaged in the work incline one to accept the present *Shu King* as a genuine portion of the original collection.

CREDIBILITY OF THE RECORDS

How much confidence is to be placed in these fragments of ancient history found in the *Shu King* and the "Bamboo Books"? One must not be more credulous than the Chinese. Mencius in his day said: "It would be better not to have the *Shu* than to believe every statement in it." China has never lacked sceptical critics, higher or lower. The earliest portions of the *Shu,* as we have seen, were based upon ancient tradition, oral or written, and must be regarded as having somewhat of a legendary character. Certain marvellous occurrences recorded in the Bamboo Books may well be considered apocryphal. Yet it is remarkable in such an ancient work as the *Shu* to find so little of the marvellous. In this respect it contrasts favorably with the early records of other nations. To judge fairly the accounts which it gives of the glorious days of old, one must bear in mind the accepted Chinese philosophy of history. That philosophy may be summed up in the phrase, "Be good and you will be happy." To the Chinese historian success was evidence of the favor of Heaven and defeat was proof of wickedness in the conquered. In recording the overthrow of a dynasty, therefore, there was a strong temptation to ascribe great cruelty and viciousness to the last monarch of the fallen house and to conceal the faults of the triumphant conqueror, who, having received the mandate of Heaven to set up a new government, must have been a man after God's own heart and must therefore be represented as possessed of all the virtues. Due allowance is to be made then for this tendency in reading the character sketches of ancient tyrants and national heroes.

Natural occurrences such as the eclipse of sun or moon

and great calamities like flood or famine were considered, as they have been among Western peoples, as manifestation of the wrath of God, as warnings against evil courses or punishment for sin. But this mistaken philosophy does not make less reliable the accounts given of a great flood in the days of Yao (24th century B.C.) nor that of famine in the time of T'ang (18th century B.C.). Flood and famine have alternated in the Yellow River Valley throughout the historical period. The Chinese, like all ancient peoples, paid great attention to astronomical phenomena. Astrology was a branch of learning supported by the state, for the stars were believed, as they were also among the Hebrews, to "be for signs" and to indicate the fate of nations. Dr. Legge in his Introduction to the *Shu* expressed a willingness to accept as genuine the documents relating to the twenty-second century B.C. but was disturbed by what seemed to be an inaccuracy in dating an eclipse of the sun, account of which is given in one of these documents. The calculations of astronomers have determined the fact that there was an eclipse of the sun on the day mentioned, but that it was not visible at the place which was then the capital of China. The astrologers were expected to foretell the eclipses. In this instance there was some miscalculation for which the ruler, Chung K'ang, reprimands the officers. It may be, however, that the very fault for which he blamed them was this mistake as to the visibility of the eclipse at the capital. In other respects the astronomical data given in these very ancient writings are found to be correct. The determination of the exact dates of the equinoxes and the solstices depended upon the culmination at dusk of certain stars. Dr. Legge reminds us that the Chinese were ignorant of the precession of the equinoxes until the fourth century of our era, so that, if the documents were forgeries of a later date than that claimed for them, the backward computation of the movements of the stars would have been inaccurate. But the statements made in the documents as to the culmination of certain stars in the twenty-fourth century B.C. have been found by astronomers to be quite accurate. This fact tends to confirm the opinion of Legge and others that even

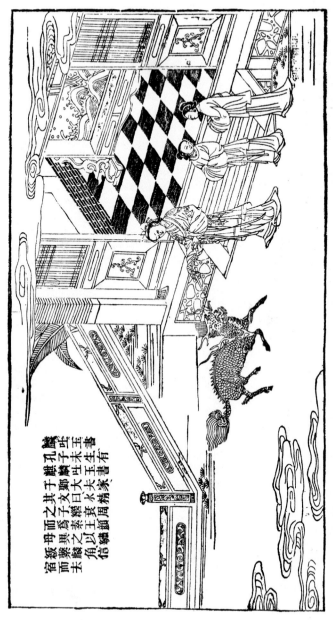

麟吐玉書

麟孔子既生而其母顏氏夢
而異之繫繡紱以麟之角信
夫孟子為素王麟為素王之文
宿緣母而子其麟子吐未生玉書有

Illustration from "Holy Foot-prints." The Unicorn visits the mother of Confucius to announce the approaching birth of her great son.

these earliest records of the Chinese are of historical value.

The "Bamboo Books" give strong support to the record in the *Shu King*. The sequence of events is the same in the two works, although the "Bamboo Books" indulge in accounts of a marvellous character unknown to the *Shu*. But there is discrepancy in the dates given of certain events in the two ancient writings. This discrepancy is greatest in the earliest records, amounting to a little more than two hundred years, and gradually decreases as one approaches modern times. The dates in the *Shu King* are older than those of the "Bamboo Books. From the year 841 B.C. the two chronologies agree. This year then is considered as the beginning of the historical period. From that date to the present source materials for Chinese history have been abundant and numerous historical works have appeared.

It is to Confucius in good degree that the Chinese owe the preservation of these very ancient writings. They are of value to us not because they teach us the names of ancient heroes and tell of the rise and fall of dynasties, but chiefly because they reveal to us the high degree of civilization which existed in the valley of the Yellow River as early as the twenty-fourth century B.C. The people had a written language. They had a pentatonic system of music and eight kinds of musical instruments. They had an elaborate ritual for the worship of God and their ancestors. They had an organized government with a monarch, a prime minister and six departments and they were acquainted with many of the arts: agriculture, mining and the manufacture of silk, linen, leather and metal goods. Their ethical ideals were noble as is indicated by the teachings of the *Shu King* quoted in an earlier chapter.[5]

OFFICIAL CHRONICLES

During the classical period, 1122 to 256 B.C., the various states into which China was divided each had its historiographers. Entry was made day by day of any event of interest to the state. These were called Spring and Au-

[5] Chapter xiii.

tumn Records, but the term, "Spring and Autumn" was intended to embrace the whole year. The most important of these chronicles is that of the state of Lu, in which Confucius lived, and which has been preserved to our day. I have already given reasons elsewhere for doubting that the text which we have is that upon which Confucius labored. It is more reasonable to suppose that it is merely a transcription of the official record used by Tso Ch'iu-ming as supplying the themes for his commentary. He, not Ssu-ma Ch'ien, should be called the Herodotus of China, for, like the Greek writer, of whom he appears to have been a contemporary, Tso shows a great fondness for anecdote. This gives a liveliness to his narrative which is rare in ancient writers. The gossip of three centuries is preserved for us here. Although he makes the chronicle of Lu his text, he does not confine himself to matters affecting the state of Lu, but brings together racy stories about persons in all parts of the kingdom. He spares neither king nor minister, neither lord nor lady, but recounts the scandals of royal and feudal courts,—the amours of princes, the intrigues of dowagers, the jealousies of wives and concubines, the struggles of rival claimants to feudal thrones, the romantic adventures of exiled nobles, the dark deeds of hired assassins, and nobler acts of chivalry and heroism. Tales of adultery and murder, of sedition and rebellion find place with those of love, loyalty and self-sacrifice. In this commentary we have a fascinating picture of life in China during the closing years of the Chou Dynasty. The work begins with the year 721 B.C. and the latest date discoverable in it is 424 B.C. It thus deals with events during a period of 297 years.[6]

SSU-MA CH'IEN

But the writing of history in China, as we to-day understand the term, history, began with Ssu-ma Ch'ien, in the second century B.C. His work, the *Shih Chi*, or "Histo-

[6] Tso's work has been translated into English by Dr. James Legge. It with the *Ch'un Ch'iu* form parts I and II of Volume V of his *Chinese Classics*.

Sculpture of second century of our era, in Shantung. Top register—a man apparently wounded, shielded from attack of enemies. Middle register—Ching K'o, 227 B.C., attempting to kill the King of Ch'in. His javelin struck a pillar and the King escaped. Third register—Two legendary sovereigns, assigned by tradition to the 29th century B.C. Fuhsi with square and Nükua with compasses. They have dragon bodies, indicative probably of semi-divine character.

rical Records," was begun indeed by his father, Ssu-ma T'an, the Chief Historiographer under the Emperor Wu Ti of the Han Dynasty (140–87 B.C.). It is to the son, however, that we owe the painstaking research and critical acumen displayed in this history of China from the earliest times to the first century B.C. Another member of the Ssu-ma family, Ssu-ma Cheng, in the eighth century A.D. prepared an introduction to the *Shih Chi*, which carries its beginning far back into the fabulous ages before the time of the "Yellow Emperor" with whose reign, Ssu-ma Ch'ien begins his work. The Shih Chi became a model for the writings of later historians. He divided his work into five sections: 1. Imperial Records, 2. Chronological Tables, 3. the "Eight Books" (i.e. eight treatises, dealing with such topics as Religion, Music, Pitch Pipes, the Calendar, Astrology, Sacrifices, Water Courses and Economics), 4. Biographical Sketches and 5. Narratives. European writers have called him the Herodotus of China, but in his careful weighing of evidence he was more like Thucydides.[7]

OTHER HISTORIANS

After the days of Ssu-ma Ch'ien every dynasty took pains to have a careful record kept of all events of political importance together with biographies of its noted men and accounts of economic conditions. Pan Ku took up the story of China where Ssu-ma Ch'ien left off and began the history of the Early Han Dynasty which was completed by his sister, the Lady Ts'ao. The Twenty-four Dynastic Histories, published in 1747 in 219 volumes, have been supplemented in recent years by the *Tung Hua Lu* and the *Tung Hua Hsü Lu* which bring the history of the nation down into the reign of the Emperor, Kuanghsü (1875–1908). Among the dynastic historians, besides those mentioned, the most noted are Ch'ien Shou (A.D. 223–297), who wrote the History of the Three Kingdoms (A.D. 220–

[7] A great part of the *Shih Chi* has been translated into French by the distinguished scholar, Edouard Chavannes. His notes are of inestimable value.

280), Ou-yang Hsiu (A.D. 1007–1072), who collaborated in writing the New History of the T'ang Dynasty. A greater genius was another member of the celebrated Ssu-ma family, Ssu-ma Kuang (A.D. 1019–1086), who wrote the "Mirror of History" covering the period, fourth century B.C. to his own time. This consisted originally of 294 books. In the century following its production it was revised and condensed by the great philosopher, Chu Hsi, who reduced it to 59 books and continued it to A.D. 960.

POETRY

We learn from the *Shu King* that in the twenty-third century B.C. an ancient ruler of China appointed a Director of Music to whom he spoke as follows:—"Poetry is the expression of earnest thought: singing is the prolonged utterance of that expression." [8] This sentiment was copied and elaborated in the Introduction to the Book of Odes:

> Poetry is the product of earnest thought. Thoughtful meditation leads to earnestness. The expression of this in words is poetry. The emotions are stirred within us and find utterance in speech. If these feelings are inexpressible in words, recourse is had to sighs and exclamations. When these are insufficient, we turn to song, and if this fails fully to express our emotions, unconsciously our hands begin to move and our feet to dance. . . . To set forth properly our success or failure, to influence Heaven and Earth and move spiritual beings there is no readier instrument than poetry.

Much of the earliest literature of China, like that of other nations, is in verse. In the worship of God and their ancestors the ancient Chinese sang hymns to the accompaniment of orchestral music. Some of these ancient hymns have been preserved. Versification aids the memory and where oral tradition was of importance verse and rhyme were commonly resorted to among all primitive peoples as effective means of transmitting the traditions accurately. Many proverbs and other wise sayings to which ancient worthies appealed were thus preserved in poetic form. Some of these are found even in the oldest

8 *Shu King*, Part II, Bk. i, Legge's translation.

parts of the *Shu King.* Shun (2255-2205 B.C.) and his Minister of Justice, Kao Yao, are represented as singing to one another about the importance of coöperation between monarch and minister. In another portion of the *Shu* the warning instruction left by the Great Yü to his descendants is set forth in verse.

The ancient Chinese had great faith in the power of poetry and music to mold the manners of men. On one occasion Confucius asked his son:—"Have you studied the Odes?" The son replied in the negative. "If you do not study the Odes," said his father, "you will have no topics for conversation."

RHYME

Rhyme is regarded by the Chinese as an essential element of poetry. This was true in the most ancient times and is still true. In the Book of Odes the stanzas, as a rule, have four lines each. Some, however, have eight. The rule is that the second and fourth lines rhyme, and, if the stanza have eight lines, the second, fourth, sixth and eighth lines have the same rhyme. Other lines need not rhyme. We sometimes meet with poems whose verses are not all of the same length, but the rule as to rhyming remains unchanged. Such irregular versification became very popular between the fourth and second centuries B.C. It was due to the influence of a poem, called *Li Sao,* written by Ch'ü Yüan, the minister of the state of Ch'u, whose suicide became the origin of the Fifth Moon festival, as told in another chapter.[9] In his allegorical poem the minister bewailed the degeneracy of the times and his loss of influence. During the T'ang Dynasty the most popular stanza was one of four lines in which the first, second and fourth lines had the same rhyme. It will be noted that this was the form of stanza used by Omar Khayyam for his quatrains. Here is a stanza from a poem of the T'ang Dynasty that will illustrate this:

[9]Chapter x.

> False men are like the flowers: the true and tried
> Are like the pines upon the mountain side.
> One wintry eve there falls a bitter frost;
> The pine trees still are green, the flowers have died.

Chinese words are all monosyllables, although some approach the dissyllable in pronunciation. This makes it impossible to preserve the Chinese meter in translation. The shortest meter has but three words, that is, three syllables, to a line. In the Book of Odes the lines have four syllables. In the second century B.C. the poet Mei Sheng wrote verses of five words each, but in the T'ang period (A.D. 618–905) the stanza with a non-rhyming third line of which mention has just been made had seven words, that is to say, seven syllables, to a line. This is still the most popular meter.

PARALLELISM

There is one characteristic in which Chinese poetry resembles that of the Hebrews, that is in the use of parallelism. In some instances the thought expressed in the first line is repeated in synonymous language in the second:

> Days and months go like the shuttle,
> Light and darkness as the arrow.

Sometimes the sentiments expressed in the two lines are in contrast:

> On the mountains are thousand-year trees;
> On the earth are no hundred-year men.

> He who knows others is clever;
> He who knows himself is enlightened.

Much proverbial philosophy has been preserved in such couplets.

In lyric poetry the parallelism takes a more subtle form. In the first part of a stanza a natural scene is depicted; in the second part a human experience is described, with which the natural scene may be said to correspond in a metaphorical way. The first poem in the Book of Odes illustrates this:

> Kua! kua! the ospreys are crying
> To mates in the mid-river marshes,
> And lovelorn our prince who is sighing
> To claim yon sweet maid as his own.

The second stanza has eight lines, the first two of which present the tangled water plants swaying in the river as typical of the conflicting emotions of the lover:

> But lo! how the mallows are tangled
> That sway in the swift-flowing current,
> And shy is yonder sweet maiden
> Whose face fills his dreams in his sleeping,
> Whom vainly he seeks in his waking.
> Distracted his waking and sleeping,
> Affection with fear ever struggling
> In endless and restless revolving.

THE CAESURA

Sir John Davis, who in 1834 was the Chief Superintendent of British trade in China, was an enthusiastic student of the Chinese language. He was perhaps the first European scholar to discover that the caesura has a fixed position in the five- and seven-word lines. In the five-word line it follows invariably the second word, while in the seven-word verse it comes after the fourth, that is to say, it always precedes the third from the last word in the line. He noted also that there are certain words in Chinese that are so closely associated together as to form what we call compound words. The caesura is never permitted to fall between two such words.

POETASTERS

There is a good deal of artificiality in the construction of a Chinese poem. Under the old imperial regime every Chinese student was required in the civil service examinations to write poems. Because of this guides were prepared which instructed the poetasters how to write in verse. The metaphors that were permissible were carefully listed and rules as to tones were prescribed. Of the four tones in Pekingese, the first is a natural and even one; the second has a rising inflection, the third a falling inflection and the fourth is quick and emphatic. These last three may be used indifferently in a verse of poetry, but they must be combined with the words of even tone in a definite order in a given line and in the succeeding line the order of even and deflected tones must be reversed. There was also a rhyming dictionary, for words that rhymed in the classical age have often in the passage of the centuries so altered their pronunciation that they no longer furnish a rhyme to the modern ear. Nevertheless reverence for the past demands that the ancient rhymes shall be preserved.

THE BOOK OF ODES

One of the canonical books of the Confucian System is the *Shih King*, or "The Odes." Tradition ascribes the collection of these poems to Confucius. It is said that out of three thousand he chose but three hundred and five. These we still possess. Collections existed, however, before his time, for it was a custom of the monarch to visit his vassals once every five years. Upon these journeys he was accompanied by his Director of Music who was required to make copies of the popular songs of each state through which they passed. It was a theory accepted then that the popular songs would reveal the character of the local government by disclosing the feelings of the people. The "Book of Odes" is more properly speaking a collection of hymns and ballads. It gives us interesting glimpses of the life of the Chinese in olden times. Four of the most ancient pieces are hymns that were used in worship. Another, dating from the twelfth century B.C., is in the nature of a prayer for the blessing of God upon the King. The vassals visited the royal court once a year, except in the fifth year when the King made his journey to the several state capitals. The vassals assisted the King in his worship in the Temple of Ancestors. At the conclusion of the service these visiting nobles sang the hymn mentioned:

Heaven protect and preserve thee!
Grant thee security,
Make thee virtuous indeed,
That happiness may be thine!
Heaven grant thee much increase
That all things be in abundance.

*   *   *   *   *

Auspicious and pure are thine offerings
And filial thy worship each season
Of ancestors, ducal and royal.
May they in response to thy service
Say! "Thine be the years ever endless."

Their spirits forever attend thee!
And shower their blessings upon thee.
So shall thy people who trust thee
Have daily their food and their raiment.
The black-haired myriads, thy people,
In virtue make thee their exemplar!

Like the moon in her glory,
Like the sun at his nooning,
Like the hills of the southland,
Never waning, never sinking,
Like the fir and the cypress—
So lasting the reign of thy children.

The Book of Odes contains also many love ballads. There
is a school of Chinese commentators who are unwilling to
believe that their great master, Confucius, could have
thought it worth while to include in the collection such
productions as mere love poems. They endeavor to explain
away these ballads by allegorical interpretation. These attempts remind us of the mystical meanings attached by
the sufis to the voluptuous quatrains of Omar Khayyam.
Thus the Chinese commentator would have us believe that
the lover in the Book of Odes is the King or, in some instances, the vassal lord, and the lady is to be regarded as
the minister of state who complains of the neglect of his
advice by his ruler. Even Christian divines, however, show
themselves equally prurient in their endeavors to interpret
the Song of Solomon, that much wived monarch, as referring to the love of Christ for his Church. We ought rather

to look with satisfaction upon these evidences of a common
human nature, shared by the greatest of the sages.

The desire of the Chinese for sons to carry on the family
name and keep up the sacrifices to ancestors is well known.
The comparative value to the family of the girl and the
boy, as judged by their standards, is indicated in these verses
also from the Book of Odes:

> He then shall have a son
> To sleep upon a couch,
> To wear a costly dress
> And play with toys of jade.
> Imperious, too, his cry.
> His pinafore of red.
> The house's lord he'll be.
>
> A daughter, too, he'll have
> To sleep upon the floor,
> A napkin for her gown,
> A potsherd for her toy.
> No choice is hers to make
> Save choose the food and drink
> And spare her parents pain.

WOMEN POETS

A celebrated poet of the second century B.C. was Ssu-
ma Hsiang-ju, who was as skillful with his lute as with
his pen. Being desperately poor, he earned a little money
by playing at a dinner given by a wealthy merchant. He
played so well that that he played himself into the affec-
tions of the merchant's daughter. The father having forbidden the marriage, the lovers eloped. They opened a wine
shop in a distant city and the bride became the bar maid.
The angry father relented after a time and brought them
home. The musician became so famous for his verses that
he was invited to Court. But success there made him for-
getful of the wife who had sacrificed all for his love. She
wrote some farewell verses that are very touching in their
tenderness and sadness, sorrowing that thenceforth their
paths had to divide and that nought but tears remained
for the wife whose husband would not be true down to
old age.

There have been not a few women whose verses have brought them renown. The Lady Pan, in the first century B.C., was a favorite of the Emperor. In time he tired of her and chose a younger woman. The discarded concubine wrote a poem known as the "Autumn Fan" that has been quoted through all the centuries since. And the phrase, "Autumn Fan" has become a synonym for the deserted wife, who is neglected just as the fan is laid aside when the warmth of summer is over.

POETS OF THE T'ANG DYNASTY

Buddhism, which was introduced into China about the year 65 of our era, influenced the poetry no less than the philosophy of the Chinese. It gave men a new outlook upon life. The thought that all living creatures are related and that transmigration from one form to another is possible, the pessimistic belief that life is sorrow and that we should strive to attain to Nirvana, and the later teaching which pictured the delights of heaven and the tortures of hell. all had a profound effect upon both art and literature. New themes, new phraseology, new metaphors began to appear. The new Taoism that appeared about the same time added its influence, encouraging the practice of necromancy and causing men to dream of an elixir of immortality and of a voyage to the Isles of the Blessed. By the time that we reach the period of the T'ang Dynasty (A.D. 618–905) we find all these elements fused in the wonderfully rich vocabulary of the muse. This period was the Golden Age of Chinese Poetry. A collection of Chinese poems of the T'ang Dynasty still extant contains nearly fifty thousand poems by some two thousand poets. The greatest of these by universal consent was Li Po or as he is sometimes called, Li T'ai-po (A.D. 701–762). He was for a time a favorite at the court of the Emperor, Hsüan Tsung, better known as Ming Huang or the "Brilliant Emperor." It was he who possessed as a concubine the most beautiful woman in all Chinese history, Yang Kuei Fei, whose every whim and caprice became the pleasure of the monarch, so that he squandered an imperial fortune upon

her. Li Po was called upon to sing the praises of this fair
lady, which he did with right good will. But he was over
fond of wine and sometimes he was too drunk to get to
bed alone on which occasions the Emperor commanded his
Chief Chamberlain to pull off the poet's boots and help him
to his couch. This was distasteful to the proud eunuch who
sought for opportunity to avenge the supposed insult. One
day the poet made a slip when he likened the beautiful
woman to the ''Flying Swallow,'' a sobriquet of a dancing
girl and courtesan of the Han Dynasty. The Chamberlain
persuaded the lady that the comparison was intended as
an insult. The white-haired poet was banished from the
palace. Subsequently he was accused, probably unjustly,
of having had a part in a conspiracy against the government. He was condemned to death, but the intercession
of friends and admirers obtained a commutation of the
sentence to banishment for life to the far southwest. This
was in 757. He journeyed very deliberately towards the
place of exile, but before reaching it shared in the general
amnesty that followed the suppression of rebellion. Many
of his poems have been translated into European languages,
but all poetry suffers in translation. He was a lover of
nature and revelled in picturesque scenes. The wine cup,
too, is a favorite theme. Beautiful women inspire his muse
and friendship is a sentiment that finds frequent expression in his verses. A strain of melancholy pervades his
work, stirred by a sense of the fleetness of time and the
vanity of living. Taoist fancies took strong hold upon him
especially in his later years. The story of his death from
drowning while attempting to embrace the reflection of the
moon in the river is a romantic one, but is wholly without
foundation. He died at the home of a relative at T'aip'ing
Fu on the Yangtze in the year 762. Here is a translation
of one of his poems: [10]

> The Yellow River's waters ceaselessly
> Flow downward to the bosom of the sea:
>   In slow content they pass their destined way,
>   Nor turn again to gladden you or me.

[10] Translation by Rose Sickler Williams.

The old man weary with the weight of years,
Views in the mirror's depth his whitening hairs,
　　Glossy at morning like the raven's wing—
Silvered at evening with a thousand cares.

And since life's morning mounts to highest noon,
And since the evening cometh sure and soon,
　　Let us now fill until they over-brim
These silver goblets that outstare the moon.

'Tis said that Heaven shapes man's destiny.
Then surely Heaven takes note of you and me,
　　And when we drink three hundred goblets round,
Heaven knows that we have feasted thankfully.

So comrades fill the cup with sparkling wine,
And pledge our friendship in a draught divine,
　　Then fill again—and drink again—nor pause
To listen to this foolish song of mine.

Full many an ancient worthy strove for fame,
Seeking in abstinence the world's acclaim:
　　The world forgets them when the rich wine flows,
And only merry topers leave a name.

Some find in gallant horses their delight,
And some in broidered robes and jewels bright.
　　All these I'd sell, were such the need, to buy
One heady cup to drink your health aright.

Li Po had several contemporaries who fell but little behind him in talent and in fame. Of the group known as the
"Eight Wizards of the Wine-cup," next to Li Po the most
celebrated was Tu Fu (A.D. 712–770). He was called the
"God of Poetry." One of his poems with a few swift
strokes paints the misery of war, in the cruel work of "The
Recruiting Sergeant." [11] Other contemporaries of Li Po
were the two friends, Meng Hao-jan, who shunned public
life and Wang Wei, the poet-painter.[12] An intimate friend
of Tu Fu was Ts'en Ts'an, the imagery of whose verses
as well as their delicate suggestiveness won him well-deserved renown. The philosophy of Buddhism and its charming legends, as well as the mysticism of Taoism and its
dreams of the spirit world attracted most of the poets of

[11] Translated by L. Cranmer-Byng in *Lute of Jade.*
[12] Vide Giles: *History of Chinese Literature,* 149.

this period, but Han Yü (768–824), although a poet of some eminence, was a better statesman and made strong protest against the official support given to Buddhist superstitions. Po Chü-i (772-846) whose verses were for a time the most popular in China and are still admired in Japan [13] was a bold official who was twice sent into banishment for opposing the Government's policies. He, too, ridiculed the pretensions of Buddhists and Taoists. Nevertheless in his poem, "The Everlasting Wrong," telling the story of the beautiful Yang Kuei Fei and her tragic death, he writes sympathetically of the attempts of the deposed emperor to communicate with the spirit of his lost favorite. He had never known Yang Kuei Fei, or her imperial lover, for he was not born until sixteen years after her murder, but his verses, relating the romantic tale were read and quoted far and wide. This long poem is the best known and most popular of his writings. Several European scholars have translated it in whole or in part.[14] Greater talent is shown perhaps in his satirical poems, attacking militarism and official incapacity.

Every dynasty since the fall of the T'ang has had its quota of poets, but there are few of outstanding merit. There was one in the Sung period (960-1278), however, whose name should be mentioned, Su Shih (1036-1101). He was a brilliant scholar, and famous both as poet and statesman. In the latter capacity he fell more than once into disfavor and his opinion of the intellectual calibre of ministers of state was expressed in the following verses: [15]

> Families when a child is born
> Want it to be intelligent.
> I through intelligence
> Having wrecked my whole life,
> Only hope the baby will prove
> Ignorant and stupid.
> Then he will crown a tranquil life
> By becoming a cabinet minister.

[13] Arthur Waley: 170 Chinese Poems, 169.
[14] H. A. Giles, Arthur Waley, Cranmer-Byng and others.
[15] Translation by Arthur Waley.

PHILOSOPHY

In the chapters on Confucianism, Taoism and Buddhism we have already become acquainted with some of the great philosophers of China and their teachings. The contents of those chapters should be borne in mind while reading this brief review of the literature of Chinese philosophy. The earliest literary remains of the Chinese,—*Shu King, Shih King, Yi King* and "Bamboo Books,"—all reveal to us certain philosophical conceptions as prevalent in the twenty-third century B.C. The world was a universe, a cosmos, a thing of order and harmony. It was regarded as one kingdom, governed by a supreme ruler, *Shang Ti,* i.e. the "Most High God." The ancient Chinese were not mono-theists, in the strict sense of the word, for they worshipped many spiritual beings, but they recognized one as supreme. The supreme God was assisted in the government of the universe by a multitude of lesser divinities presiding over the various departments of nature. These spiritual beings were divided into three classes;—those of Heaven, Earth and Man. There were three rituals provided for the wor-ship of these three classes of beings.

The government of God was not looked upon as capri-cious, but was regarded as one conducted in accordance with principles of justice. Virtue was rewarded with long life and prosperity, wickedness was punished with visita-tions of calamity, such as sickness, drought, famine, pesti-lence and war. The ancient Chinese studied the stars, too, as all primitive peoples did, seeking in celestial phenomena an index to the will of God. Eclipses, showers of me-teors, lightning, drought and flood,—all had significance. Terrestial conditions also had importance. There were four lofty mountains guarding the four quarters.

The numbers five and seven had special significance, for there were five planets and seven rectors, as the seven stars of the Great Bear were called. Thus from very early times the five planets were associated with the five elements;—water, fire, wood, metal and earth. These were correlated with the five primary colors;—blue-green, red, yellow, black and white—with the five notes of music, with the five human relationships and with other quinary groups, as already mentioned in the chapter on Chinese Art. The number seven did not find such frequent use, but it had importance in the ritual for the worship of the dead, for special sacrifices were offered every seventh day for seven weeks after death. The *Yi King* apparently refers to a seven-day period in the phrase, "The seventh day returns again." The importance which the ancient Chinese attached to numerical relations reminds us of the speculations of Pythagoras, who held that number was the foundation of the universe. The use of the trigrams and hexagrams in divination illustrates the magical character ascribed to numbers by the Chinese. The invention of the trigrams is ascribed to the mythical Fuhsi who is supposed to have lived more than three thousand years before the Christian Era. Out of the eight trigrams were developed the sixty-four hexagrams which are the subject of the speculations of the *Yi King*. Their significance was first interpreted by King Wen about the year 1122 B.C. In fact the trigrams were evolved naturally out of the manipulations of a whole and a broken line. The *Wu Chi* or unlimited, i.e. the Absolute, was represented by a whole line. In it we see represented the Unity that underlies all diversity. The whole line dividing itself produces duality or plurality. In these two, the whole and the broken line we have represented the dual forces of nature. By placing the whole and the broken lines each over itself and each over the other we produce four pairs. Continuing the process in an arrangement of three lines in a group we find that there are eight possible permutations. These are the eight trigrams, the common representation of which is as follows:

≡ ≣ ☰ ☲ ☳ ☴ ☵ ☶

A French Jesuit missionary in China, having read Leibnitz's paper on a binary system of numerical notation, was struck by the similarity between that and the Chinese system of whole and broken lines.[16] Leibnitz used zero and

[16] Attention was called to this again in recent years by Paul Carus in his *Chinese Philosophy*.

unity, but if one uses a broken line instead of zero and a straight line for unity, it is evident that numerical notation is just as possible with one system as with the other. Père Bouvet the missionary, wrote to Leibnitz and called attention to the similarity and suggested that in the trigrams and hexagrams we have nothing more than a binary system of numerical notation. Since the Chinese do ascribe the invention of numbers to Fuhsi, it is not impossible that the trigrams which he is supposed to have invented may have had originally an arithmetical significance. It is certain, however, that since the twelfth century B.C. they with the hexagrams have been used for purposes of divination only.

THE YIN YANG PHILOSOPHY

About the time that King Wen began to write his treatise on the hexagrams, that is to say, in the twelfth century B.C. a change began to manifest itself in the religious ritual of the Chinese. The Earth was regarded with more reverence than theretofore and placed almost on an equality with Heaven in worship. A sort of dualism began to be established. The founder of the Chou Dynasty, addressing the army, spoke of Heaven and Earth as the Father and Mother of all created beings. This tendency towards dualism in religion was the accompaniment of a dualism in philosophy which seems to have originated about that time. The whole and the broken lines of the trigrams may have suggested it. They were at least used to illustrate it. The whole line represented unity, strength, light, the male principle. The broken line represented plurality, weakness, darkness, and the female principle. The female principle is called *yin* and the male, *yang,* hence this philosophy is known as the *Yin Yang* philosophy. Instead of the whole line sometimes a circle is used to represent the primal Unity. This is divided by a curved line into two sections; one light, the other dark. Thus the *Wu Chi* or Absolute is represented as producing the dual forces of nature from which all things proceed. Within the light portion there is a dot of the black as an eye and similarly in the dark portion a white eye. Around the circle the eight trigrams are arranged in such a manner

as to place the three whole lines opposite the white portion, as emblematic of perfect strength, and the three broken
lines, emblem of greatest weakness, opposite the dark portion.[17] There is thus presented to us graphically a representation of the whole process of world evolution. The un-
created Absolute produces the dual principles which in
turn evolve the eight trigrams in which all the fortunes of
life, good and evil, and all the events of history may be
said to be typified.

There is a passage in the *Li Ki*, supposed to be apochry-
phal, which represents Confucius as saying:

> Man is the product of the attributes of Heaven and Earth by
> the interaction of the dual forces of Nature, a union of the animal
> and intelligent souls and the finest subtile matter of the five
> elements.

The passage was possibly interpolated when the classics
were recovered and reedited after their attempted destruction by the tyrant, Ch'in Shih Huang Ti, in the third century B.C. It may be regarded as representing the philosophy prevalent at the beginning of the Christian Era. The
theory of the existence in every man of an animal and an
intelligent soul is much older than the Christian Era, however, for in the days of Mencius (371–288 B.C.), man was
considered as having a "higher" and a "lower" nature.
There were philosophers of that period who taught the
duty of suppressing the desires because they belonged, as
was thought, to the lower nature. It was believed that by
so doing one could in some way strengthen his "higher
nature."

A philosopher, named Kao, said:

> What is not attained through words need not be sought in the
> mind: What is not attained through the mind need not be sought
> through the emotional nature.

The emotional nature, that is to say the desires and the
passions, are associated by the Buddhists with the "lower
nature" and Kao is regarded by some Chinese commentators as teaching a doctrine similar to that of the Buddhists,
although he knew nothing of the Buddha. Mencius denied

[17] See the diagram op. page 572.

Kao's first proposition. Mencius did not believe that all our knowledge comes from without. He admitted the truth of the second statement, that what is not attained through the mind need not be sought through the emotions. He made it the text for teaching the correct attitude towards the so-called "lower nature." "The will is superior to the emotions," he said, "therefore maintain a firm will, but do no violence to the emotions." He refused to join in a sweeping condemnation of the passions. They are natural and have a proper purpose to serve. Instead of crushing or suppressing them as Kao advocated, they ought to be controlled and directed to proper uses. He seemed to condemn both those who by unnatural suppression of the desires do violence to their natures and become abnormal and those also who by appeals to the emotions hope through some ecstasy of passion to find new truth. He illustrated this latter point by telling the story of a man who was dissatisfied with the slow growth of his grain and went into the field to help it grow by pulling each stalk up a little. The result was a destruction of the grain. "There are few," he said, "who do not try to help the grain to grow." He anticipated in a measure the teaching of Whittier in "The Brewing of the Soma":

> As in that child-world's early year,
> Each after age has striven
> By music, incense, vigils drear,
> And trance, to bring the skies more near,
> Or lift men up to heaven.

> And yet the past comes round again,
> And new doth old fulfill;
> In sensual transports wild as vain
> We brew in many a Christian fane
> The heathen soma still.

THE HERETICS

Mencius devoted some space in his writings to combating the teachings of other philosophers of his time whom he regarded as heretics. There was Yang Chu, a pessimist and a cynic who•said: [18]

[18] Translation by Legge. See *The Life and Works of Mencius.*

The virtuous and the sage die; the ruffian and the fool also lie. Alive, they were Yao and Shun; dead they were so much rotten bone. Alive they were Chieh and Chou; dead they were so much rotten bone. Who could know any difference between their rotten bones? While alive, therefore, let us hasten to make the best of life; what leisure have we to be thinking of anything after death?

Like the cynical author of Ecclesiastes he taught in effect that "there is one event to the righteous and the wicked" and that, as "a living dog is better than a dead lion," the best thing for one to do is to "go one's way, eat bread with joy and drink wine with a merry heart," . . . "for there is no work nor device nor knowledge, nor wisdom in the grave." Yang Chu has been called "the Epicurus of China" which is somewhat unfair to Epicurus. Mencius was horrified by the licentious teaching of this man which he thought was permeating society with disastrous results, and which, if not stopped, "would block up the paths of benevolence and righteousness."

Another popular philosopher, whom Mencius opposed, was Mo Ti, who held that the solution of the problems of human society was to be found in the practice of universal mutual love. If all should practice this mutual love, regarding the welfare of others with the same consideration as their own, there could be no crime, no disorder in the state, no war with other states. In substance Mo Ti's teaching was that of the Christian,—love for one's neighbor as for oneself. Mencius condemned the teaching as tending to throw society into disorder, for "to love all equally," he said, "would be to ignore the peculiar affection due to a father." It was a misinterpretation of Mo Tzu's teaching, however, who did not say that we were to love all *equally.*

Mencius here fell short of the teaching of his own master, Confucius, who held that the principle upon which one's relations with others was to be regulated was that of "reciprocity," "What you do not want done to yourself, that do not to others." Neither Confucius nor Mencius rose to the height attained by Lao Tzu. The Confucianists

Boddhi Dharma, Hindu, Founder in China of Ch'an Men or Zen Buddhist
Philosophical School: Died A.D. 529. From Sculpture, 1749.

oppose the teaching, "Return good for evil," saying "how then will you reward goodness? rather return good for good and justice for evil," but Lao Tzu said: "I am good to the good; I am good also to the bad. With the faithful I am faithful, but with the unfaithful I am also faithful."

After the time of Mencius there arose a philosopher, named Hsün Huang, who opposed the views of Mencius as to the natural goodness of human nature. He taught that man is naturally evil and becomes good only by education and training. In this, perhaps, he was not far from the position of modern science which teaches, not that man is evil by nature, but that he has evolved from lower orders and brings with him an inheritance of brute passions that must be held in check and guided by reason that he must,[19]

> Move upward, working out the beast,
> And let the ape and tiger die.

Because he took issue with the doctrine of Mencius, Hsün Tzu has been listed among the heretics, but Han Yü, in the ninth century of the Christian Era, sought to reconcile the views of the two philosophers.[20] Despite his reputation as a heretic, Hsün Tzu appears to have had considerable influence upon the development of philosophy in China.[21]

Among the heretical schools of philosophy we must place the Taoists and the Buddhists. The teachings of Lao Tzu and Chuang Tzu have already been set forth in brief in the chapter dealing with Taoism. Here we need merely to recall that the *Tao* of Lao Tzu is a conception that approaches in meaning the *nous* of Plato and the *logos* of Philo and the Neo-Platonists, and that the idealism of Chuang Tzu would have delighted the philosophers of the Eleatic School. As to Buddhism, although much has been said in the chapter dealing with this religion, it seems necessary to add a paragraph concerning the development of Buddhist philosophy in China. The Buddhist sects in China are distinguished one from another chiefly by their philosophical views. Buddhism, originating in India,

[19] So Tennyson wrote.
[20] Legge: *Life and Works of Mencius.*
[21] H. H. Dubs: *Hsün Tzu. the Moulder of Ancient Confucianism.*

started with a rich inheritance of philosophical conceptions. Its *nirvana,* the absorption of the individual consciousness in the universal, is a purely Brahmanic conception. *Karma* and its metempsychosis also were inherited. But after the death of the Buddha Hindu philosophers continued to speculate and each new school found adherents in the Buddhist church. The Southern School holding to the *hinayana* system is represented in China by but two sects. One, the *Chu,* holds to the reality of self and of the five attributes of personality;—form, perception, consciousness, action and knowledge. The other, the *Ch'eng Shih,* denies such reality.[22] The Northern School, following the *mahayana* teaching, has four sects in China that have put out some philosophical literature. The *Fa Hsiang* holds to the reality of the subject but denies the reality of the object. Self alone is real; the universe is an emanation of thought and is imaginary. The *San Lun* has had considerable influence in China. It denies reality both to subject and object. The *Hua Yen* is pantheistic. The *T'ien T'ai,* named for a beautiful range of hills in Chekiang, is a purely Chinese school, and characteristically adopts a middle ground between the idealists and realists. There are other sects but their tenets are not of much interest to philosophers.

Long before this development of Buddhist teaching took place in China, in the first century of the Christian Era, Wang Ch'ung (A.D. 27–97), a keen dialectician, subjected the teachings of his contemporaries to searching criticism. He even dared to ridicule Confucius and Mencius. He denied the existence of a soul at all, apart from the body. He held that the soul before one's birth was a part of the original vapor. A portion of this vapor condenses and becomes a constituent of the physical man. At death it is dissipated and returns to its original condition. This materialism shocked Confucianists and Taoists too, and, although Wang Ch'ung was a brilliant writer, he found but few followers.[23]

---

22 Wieger: *Bouddhisme Chinois.*
23 Vide A. Forke: ''Wang Ch'ung and Plato,'' in *Journal of China Branch of the Royal Asiatic Society,* vol. xxxi, No. 1.

POLITICAL PHILOSOPHERS

Confucius and Mencius accepted the philosophical conceptions of the ancients, as is evident from their writings and from the reports of their followers. But neither showed any fondness for metaphysical discussions. They gave their attention chiefly to social and political problems, as was natural and right in view of the decadent and disordered condition of their country. Although Mencius regarded himself as a loyal disciple of Confucius, it is not difficult to note a striking difference in his attitude and that of his master toward the problem with which they were both concerned, that of reforming the government. Confucius believed in reform from the top. As Plato had his philosopher-king, who was best fitted to rule, so Confucius had his *chüntzu* or prince, an ideal man by whose wisdom and character the state was to be saved. "As the wind blows, the grass bends." Given a perfect man as ruler, the people, in the opinion of Confucius, would voluntarily imitate his virtues. Mencius on the other hand held that "the people are the foundation of the state, that even the national altars are of secondary importance and that the monarch is the least important of all." True he did not expect the country to be ruled by a general assembly, but he declared that the voice of the people was to be listened to as the voice of God. In one other respect the two teachers greatly differed. Confucius had his face turned to the past. He was a legitimist. He admired the organization of the government under the Chou Dynasty. He wanted to see that house fully restored to power. Mencius, on the contrary, believed in the right of revolution. He looked to the future. He had lost all respect for the House of Chou and longed to see a new leader arise who could re-unite the country.

Shortly after the death of Mencius a new leader did arise and the unity of the state was re-established. But alas! it was not such a leader as Mencius had foretold. He had said: "The hearts of the people will turn to him who does not love to kill." Ch'in Shih Huang Ti who established the empire in 221 B.C. was not such a humane man, but quite otherwise. He was a cruel conqueror and an oppressive ruler, notwithstanding that he was a great organizer. Although his memory is execrated as that of a bloody tyrant, his system of government in most respects was that which persisted down to our own time.

In the first century of the Christian Era there arose a usurper, Wang Mang, whose character was a curious combination of contradictory traits. He had no hesitation in committing murder to attain the throne, yet he aimed at reforms that were designed to promote the welfare of the people. He sought to abolish slavery and to nationalize the land, saying:—"The land shall belong to the state: the slave shall belong to himself." He introduced also an income tax and established a state monopoly of the manufacture of intoxicating liquors. Most remarkable of his reforms was a system of price-fixing for grain, to protect the farmer and the consumer against the sharp practices of the middleman. He instituted state loans in aid of agriculture, too, and reformed the currency. These and other measures aroused all the propertied classes against himself and, lacking the support of the army, he perished.

This incident is mentioned because a somewhat similar attempt to establish a form of state socialism was made in the eleventh century by the celebrated philosopher, Wang An-shih, who is spoken of by the historian as a man of generous impulses, but one who lacked political experience. He aimed at increasing the wealth of the state and improving the condition of the common people. Misery, he said, was caused by seeking wealth without understanding the laws of economics. State loans in aid of agriculture and others in aid of commerce bore interest at the rate of two per cent a month. These loans secured upon the property of the borrowers drove them into bankruptcy. With all his desire to improve the condition of the people he simply made matters worse. Individual enterprise, too, was hindered by the interference of officials who were ignorant of the matters on which they gave advice. The historian, Ssu-ma Kuang, was chiefly responsible for Wang's removal from office and the restoration of the old order or disorder.

THE METAPHYSICIANS

As the T'ang Dynasty (A.D. 618–905) was noted for its poetry, so the Sung period (960–1278) was celebrated for its philosophy. Its extensive foreign commerce promoted intercourse with other nations. Its continuous warfare through three centuries with the Tartar tribes of the north deprived the Chinese of a great part of the empire and led eventually to the establishment of an alien dynasty. Myriads of Chinese were carried away captive to barbarian lands and myriads of barbarians invaded and settled in China. There was thus an intermingling of races and a profound disturbance of social conditions. The impoverishment of the state led, as we have seen, to political experiments that aimed at increasing the wealth of the country, but speculation did not stop with economics and politics; it went deeper and took up fundamental problems. Nestorian Christianity was powerful in Cathay and had numerous followers in China. Buddhism with its many sects had become the most popular religion of the Chinese and stimulated discussion of philosophical problems, while Taoist magic and necromancy made a powerful appeal to the credulous and stirred the imagination of poet and artist. What was it they may have asked themselves, that made China tremble before the invading barbarians? Could it be a judgment of Heaven for abandonment of the teaching of the ancient sages? Some such thought may have passed through the minds of thoughtful men. At any rate in the eleventh century of our era a philosophical movement was inaugurated which turned the current of Chinese thought into new channels and became the dominant intellectual force of the empire. From its inception it was a protest against the heresies of Buddhism and Taoism and professedly an attempt to restore Confucianism to authority. In truth it was not Confucianism but a Neo-Confucianism that was set forth. But among a backward-looking people like the Chinese, who held the sages of antiquity in reverence and said in effect: "The former days were better than these," it was necessary, in order to get a new doctrine accepted, to show that it was not new but old, that it was the teaching of the sacred books, for so indeed is progress made every where in this human world of ours.

Chou Tun-i, a provincial official noted for his gentle character and his just administration, was the author in the eleventh century of several philosophical treatises. The most important of these dealt with the origin of the universe which was illustrated by a diagram. Chou found the basis of his theory in the *Yi King* or Book of Changes, which deals with the hexagrams. These as already intimated take their rise from the manipulation of the whole and the broken line. But these two forms find their origin in the single whole line, representing unity, which by division becomes multiple. In Chou's diagram the whole line is represented by the circle, the perfect line, without beginning or end. This Grand Unity, which underlies all the diversity of nature, the ancient Chinese called the *T'ai Chi* or "Great Ultimate." The philosopher Chou called it *Wu Chi* or "Without-Limit," i.e. the Infinite or Absolute. This is the immaterial principle of the universe. It is the origin and source of all things, but its manner of operation is twofold, active and passive, according to Chou Tun-i. Active, energizing, the *Yang* ether is produced: passive, inert, the *Yin* ether appears. But the *Yang* and the *Yin* are coexistent. Neither has priority over the other. Nor is it possible to separate the *Yin-Yang* ether from the infinite and immaterial *T'ai Chi*. They are co-eternal. They are distinct but inseparable. The continuous alternation of action and rest are indicated by a diagram of concentric circles. The innermost, all white, represents the Absolute, the others are each divided into light and dark semi-circles, so arranged that the light half of one is in contact with the dark portion of the next circle, thus suggesting the change from action to rest and vice versa. This alternation of movement and rest gives rise to the dualism of nature;— light and darkness, heat and cold, male and female, and the combinations of *Yang* and *Yin* in varying proportions produce the five elements;—water, fire, wood, metal and earth.

The philosopher, Chou Tun-i, had two pupils, the brothers

Ch'eng, who carried on his work after his death and left writings that had considerable influence upon the development of the Sung School of philosophy. But the greatest of all the thinkers of the age was Chu Hsi. He was born in 1130 and died in 1200. He came of a distinguished family, and was fortunate in having a father who was an earnest student. But the father died when his son was but fourteen years of age, not, however, before he had impressed upon the child the importance of study. The guardians appointed for the boy were for a time interested in Buddhism. Chu Hsi became at first an ardent student of the system and gave attention, too, to the teachings of the Taoists. Although he later became the protagonist of Confucianism, his study of the rival systems of thought were not without influence upon him. He took his doctor's degree at nineteen and at twenty-two received his first appointment to office. He was a conscientious magistrate and popular because of his efforts to promote the welfare of the common people. His duties as superintendent of education were those which he found most agreeable. But he was a scholar rather than an administrator and after seven years' experience in government service he was glad to retire for literary work. Subsequently in 1194 he was summoned to Court, but his advice was not relished. He was glad to return to his home in 1197 and three years later he died. He was a voluminous writer. He edited the works of the two Ch'engs, published treatises combating theories that to him appeared heretical, revised the great history of Ssu-ma Kuang and wrote commentaries on the analects of Confucius and the works of Mencius. His interpretation of the Classics became authoritative in all the colleges of the empire. His philosophical work was the crowning achievement of the Sung period and has moulded Chinese thought from that day to our own times.[24]

He rounded out and completed the work begun by Chou

---

[24] The best exposition of the Sung Philosophy will be found in the works of J. P. Bruce: *Chu Hsi and his Masters* and *Philosophy of Human Nature by Chu Hsi.*

Tun-i and the brothers, Ch'eng. The immaterial Principle
of the universe is inseparably attached to an all-pervading
ether. These two are co-eternal. The two modes of being
of the Principle, action and rest, result in two conditions
of the ether, the *Yang* and the *Yin,* and from these all
things proceed, for the alternation of *Yang* and *Yin* result
in a revolution of the ether. This acquires great velocity
which causes the grosser portion to be segregated at the
centre, where it becomes the earth. The rarer portions are
retained at the periphery and become the sky, the sun,
moon and stars. There they are perpetually revolving,
while the earth remains stationary at the center. The sky
is not a firmament, he said, but a revolving atmosphere.
In popular speech the heavens have nine layers. This, he
declared, was not true: there were merely nine whorls.
He attacked the anthropomorphism of his day which regarded the deity as a super-man, yet he equally opposed
the view that there is no ruler in heaven. The attributes
which he ascribes to the Supreme Ruler imply a recognition
of personality. The will of this divine being is the *Tao* or
Way of life. It is the moral order. The nature of each
created being is determined by the endowment conferred
upon it of the *Li* or divine Principle in association with
the *ch'i* or ether, and the moral character of a man will be
affected by the quality of the ether conferred. As to what
may be hoped for after death he held that one may not say
that the individual survives. The spiritual part ascends
and is dispersed: the animal soul descends and comes to an
end. Still Chu Hsi had to reconcile this teaching with the
worship of the dead required by the Classics. This he attempted by holding that in effect one's ancestors live in
their descendants and that we show our reverence for the
memory of our forebears in our recognition of the family
solidarity and by ancestor worship.

Chu Hsi found a keen critic of his teaching in Wang
Yang-ming, a philosopher of the Ming period, who was born
in 1472. He was a consistent idealist. In his view, nothing
exists apart from the mind. Yet he was an efficient magis-

trate and a practical man of affairs. His moral influence was acknowledged and in recent times his writings have acquired a new popularity.[25]

THE DRAMA

The T'ang Dynasty had its poets: the Sung its philosophers, but the Mongol Dynasty which overthrew the Sung Dynasty was distinguished by its development of the drama. The Chinese drama, however is much older than the Mongol period (A.D. 1260-1368). It had its beginnings in an unknown antiquity. Like the Grecian drama, it was originally a religious ceremony. One of the oldest portions of the *Shu King* tells us that the Director of Music in the reign of Shun (twenty-third century B.C.) describing his worship of the spirits, said: "I smite the musical stone: I gently strike it, and the various animals lead on one another to dance." The ceremony was probably similar to that at the beginning of a new year celebrated by the lamas in Peip'ing and elsewhere, in which the monks wear masks representing the heads of animals. We learn from the *Li Ki* or "Record of Rites," as well as from the "Analects of Confucius" and the commentary of Tso Ch'iu-ming on the "Spring and Autumn Annals," that in the ancient worship of God as well as in the worship of ancestors, companies of mimes were employed, who performed a dance or pantomime to the accompaniment of orchestral music. In the earliest period they brandished battle axes, shields, and ox tails. Later there were two companies: one representing the civil life, waved plumes of pheasant feathers and flutes upon which they played, the other the warrior mimes, brandished battle axes and shields. The sumptuary laws of the Chou Dynasty prescribed that the King was to have eight ranks of eight mimes; chiefs of states, six ranks of six each; high ministers, four ranks of four and scholars two ranks of two each. Confucius denounced the head of the Chi family for his presumption in employing eight ranks as

[25] For the philosophy of Wang Yang-ming see work by Fred'k Goodrich Henke.

the King did. During the late Manchu regime at the worship of God in the Temple of Heaven there were eight ranks of civil dancers of eight men each, holding plumes and wands,—the latter, no doubt being intended to represent flutes,—and the same number of warrior dancers with spears, who posed to the accompaniment of music. The *Li Ki* tells us that in the celebration of the *Wu*, a dance invented by King Wu to commemorate his overthrow of the dynasty of Shang, the celebrants represented in pantomime the courage of Wu in going to war with the Shang monarch, his march northward against the royal force, his victory, the return southward and the rewarding of his allies and, by a laying aside of the battle axes and shields, the restoration of peace. In addition to these dances in the temples to God and to the ancestors, there were popular *No* celebrations, which were of a religious character intended to ward off evil influences from the village whose inhabitants were celebrating. A prominent feature was a procession of masked dancers who engaged in all sorts of buffoonery as they marched along the streets, not unlike in character the processions one sees to-day in many places at the Lantern Festival. It is related of Confucius that when the people of his village celebrated such a festival he showed his interest in them by standing on the steps of his house to watch the procession as it passed. Such were perhaps the beginnings of theatrical representation in China. The secular drama, however, does not make its appearance in history until the reign of Ming Huang (A.D. 713–756) of the T'ang Dynasty. His was the court in which such evil was wrought by the celebrated beauty, Yang Kuei Fei. The most brilliant poets, painters and musicians in the empire were gathered there. The days were spent in successive rounds of pleasure. There was an enclosure in the palace grounds known as the Pear Garden, where the gentlemen and ladies of the court often gathered together for enjoyment. Li Po would write poems. His Majesty would set them to music. Then they would sing the verses to the accompaniment of the lute, and at times they acted plays. To this day the theatrical profession is known as the Pear Garden and the emperor, Hsüan Tsung, called Ming Huang, i.e. "The Brilliant Emperor," is the patron saint of the actor.

The drama continued its evolution during the Sung Dynasty (A.D. 960–1278). A recent work by Wang Kuo-wei gives a history of the Chinese Theatre under the Sung and Yüan Dynasties. He assigns 280 plays to the Sung period:[26] under the Chin, or Golden Horde, which ruled the north of China during a portion of the Sung period (A.D. 1115–1234) 690 were known. Five hundred of these were still extant at the beginning of the Ming Dynasty (A.D. 1368), but to-day no more than 116 can be found.

The Sung Dynasty in the south and the Golden Horde in the north were both swept away by the Mongols, and when Kublai Khan had established his sway over the whole land in the year 1279 art and literature had a new birth. The Mongols had their plays, however, before they came into China. At any rate their cousins, the Cathayans, who preceded the Golden Horde in the control of north China, had dramatic entertainments on festive occasions.[27] After the Mongols conquered China, they adopted Chinese culture and in exchange did much for the development of the Chinese drama. A number of collections have been made of the plays of the Mongol period, some during the Ming Dynasty and others more recently. During the reign of the Mings (1368–1644) the playwrights continued their work: some six hundred dramas of that period are still to be had. The Manchus also contributed their quota: over eight hundred plays of note were written during the period in which they ruled the empire. To-day under the influence of western European culture the theatre is undergoing a slow transformation, both in the character of the plays presented and in the stage setting.

The village theatre has been described in an earlier chapter:[28] in the cities there are buildings especially erected for theatrical purposes. Until recently there was no charge

[26] Zucher: *The Chinese Theatre.*
[27] Giles: *History of Chinese Literature.*
[28] Chapter vi.

for entering the building or witnessing the play, but one was expected to take a table and order tea and other refreshments. The stage as a rule was barren of scenery and the actor had to depend entirely upon his histrionic talents to give an appearance of reality to the character or scene that he was representing. Until the establishment of the republic no women were permitted upon the stage. Female parts were taken by men trained for the purpose. The orchestra sat upon the stage behind the actors and kept up a perfect din during the performance. A troupe should have fifty-six actors, divided into twenty classes, according to the parts taken. The actors are trained from childhood, and until recently were considered outcasts. To-day there is greater respect for the profession. The plays are generally of two kinds: historical, in which battle scenes are a prominent feature, and those dealing with affairs of common people in every day life. The historical plays deal with dramatic situations in the careers of such national heroes as Liu Pei, Chang Fei and Kuan Yü, the three friends who took the oath of friendship in the peach orchard during the wars of the Three Kingdoms in the third century of our era, or that of the usurper, Ts'ao Ts'ao, and the strategist, Chu Koliang, of the same period, or with the victories of Kuo Tzu-i, the general who saved the T'ang Dynasty after the notorious beauty, Yang Kuei Fei, had well-nigh ruined it, or with the wars between the Chinese and the Tartars in the Sung period, when the patriot Yo Fei was falsely accused and put to death. In other plays the hero is usually the young graduate who after many hardships wins his doctor's degree and marries the beautiful heroine, for in China it is not the brave but the learned who deserve the fair. Filial piety is also a favorite theme, by which is meant the self-sacrifice of son or daughter through devotion to parents. Since marriages are usually arranged by the parents of the bride and groom without regard to the desires of these young people, love-making in the drama is necessarily clandestine. Superstition also has its part. Scenes from the spirit world are represented in the glow of the red light. Not a few

Chinese plays have been translated into European languages. Some have been modified and adapted to the Western stage. "The Orphan of Chao," translated by Premaré, became the foundation for Voltaire's *L'Orphelin de la Chine*.

Filial piety is represented in the dramatized story of Mu-lan, the daughter of a Chinese general of the sixth century, who took her father's place at the head of his troops, when he was too ill to obey the summons of the Emperor, and who served as a soldier for twelve years without betraying her sex.

In the "Red Pear Blossom," a play of the Mongol period, we have a successful graduate eager to meet a noted beauty, Hsieh Chin-lien. His friend, the Prefect, with whom he is staying, persuades him that Chin-lien "Golden Lily," is married, but secretly arranges with the girl under an assumed name to enter the yamen garden with her maid, as though coming to admire the flowers, and unaware of the presence there of a young gentleman. The two young women pretend to be alarmed, but yield to his entreaty to sit down and have a cup of wine. The next day the Golden Lily repays his kindness with the gift of a pitcher of wine and a red flower in a vase. She appears later and has him guess in vain the name of the flower. Another day she disguises herself as a flower seller and when asked by the young man the name of the red flower, she pretends great fright, telling him that it is a witch's flower, and that her son had been killed by just such a blossom, presented by a vampire, the ghost of a dead maiden who had bewitched her son and carried him off to Hades. The young graduate is greatly alarmed and flees, but later returns when reassured by the Prefect who makes due explanation.

Virtue always has its due reward in the Chinese drama. A sort of Chinese Cinderella is represented in a popular play. Her father, an upright mandarin, had been accused unjustly of defalcation and dies in prison. His only child, a daughter, is taken into the home of a wealthy merchant, whose property had been saved to him by the just decision of the mandarin. In this home the girl is treated most unkindly by the merchant's wife, who is jealous. During her husband's absence she sells the girl as a slave to the new magistrate, who after a time becomes acquainted with the young woman's sad story, restores her to liberty and marries her to his son.

Farces are common on the Chinese stage. The subjects are sometimes the hen-pecked husband, sometimes the fickle-minded widow, and occasionally the outlandish European as he appears to the Chinese.

FICTION

If under the head of fiction we must include all the parables invented to illustrate a theory or enforce a truth, and all the legends and fairy tales that have been handed down orally from generation to generation, all the wild imaginings of travellers and all the stories of miracles wrought by monks or magicians, then we shall have to say that fiction in China as elsewhere is well nigh as old as the language in which the tale is told. Story telling is a fine art, but it is in Asia and particularly in eastern Asia that the vagabond story-teller is still a welcome guest. The Princess Scheherazade was not more successful in charming the Sultan with her thousand tales than is the story teller in charming the crowd which he gathers on a street corner in Peking of a summer's evening when he recites the heroic deeds of the knights of old, or his own imagined adventures, or improvises tales of witches and fox maidens, of gods and demons, of necromancy and reincarnation.

Fiction very early found its way into Chinese literature. Chuang Tzu invented parables to illustrate his philosophical speculations. The stories illustrated in the paintings of Ku K'ai-chih were written in the third century of our era. During the T'ang period there were some charming allegories and some keen satires written. Fiction was employed also during the Sung period for political purposes. It was during the rule of the Mongols, however, that the Chinese novel made its appearance. It has ever since main-

Tiao Ch'an, a heroine of the novel, "The Three Kingdoms," accomplishes the destruction of the Tyrant, Tung Cho, by arousing his jealousy of Lü Pu. Period of novel A.D. Third Century, time of author, perhaps the Fourteenth Century.

tained its popularity.[29] The *San Kuo Chih Yen I* or "Story of the Three Kingdoms," is one of the most popular of historical novels, based upon the history of the struggles of the three kingdoms into which China was divided in the third century of our era. The novel was written by Lo Kuan-chung in the thirteenth century. Another rivalling it in interest is the *Lieh Kuo Chuan,* a story of the feudal age or period of the Chou Dynasty. It was written during the Ming period (A.D. 1368–1644). The most remarkable novel in Chinese, typical in every respect, accurately reflecting the life of a mandarin's family under the old regime, is the *Hung Lou Meng,* which is a thrilling love story colored by Buddhist faith and Taoist magic. It was written during the seventeenth century and is ascribed by some to Ts'ao Hsüeh-ch'in. It introduces some four hundred characters and the tale is drawn out to the length of some four thousand pages.[30] The scholars of the old regime refused to recognize plays and novels as belonging to real literature. Consequently the authorship of some of the most noted was not acknowledged. But there are six works of fiction that are given special recognition because of their excellent style. These six are: the historical novel, *San Kuo Chih Yen, The Hung Lou Meng, The Hsi Yu Chi, The Hsi Hsiang Chi, The Shui Hu Chuan,* and the *Ch'in P'ing Mei.* Two of these have been mentioned. The *Hsi Yu Chi* is a novel based upon the experiences of Hsüan Chuang, a Buddhist monk who visited India in the seventh century. He gave an account of his journey overland and his adventures by the way, which suggested to the novelist this very amusing tale that since the thirteenth century, when it was written, has tickled the literary palates of the Chinese scholars. The *Hsi Hsiang Chi* is a novel of the Mongol period that has been dramatized. It is still one of the most popular plays on the Chinese stage. The title translated is "Story of the West Hall." Chinese buildings are built around courts. The room on the west side is called the *Hsi Hsiang.* The tale is a love story of a young

---

[29] See H. A. Giles; *History of Chinese Literature.*
[30] Ibid. and A. Wylie: *Notes on Chinese Literature.*

student who is stopping for a time at a Buddhist temple, to which there come for worship, a lady with her daughter and her maid. The student and the daughter become enamored of one another. The mother opposes the union, but is outwitted by the aid of the maid. The *Shui Hu Chuan* is a popular collection of tales of robbers of the thirteenth century. It must be remembered that rebels or revolutionists to the government in power in China are always designated as "robbers." This was true of the revolutionists of 1911 as it was also of the T'aip'ings. The robbers are therefore often the champions of the people and the people sympathize with the attacks upon the oppressive mandarins.

The *Ch'in P'ing Mei* is a novel of the Ming period. It was placed under the ban by the Manchu government as being immoral. Nevertheless an imperial prince had it translated into the Manchu language. It pictures the dissolute manners of the court at K'aifeng during the twelfth century, about the time that the Tartars forced the Chinese to move their capital to the south. The novel to-day occupies a higher place than formerly in the estimation of scholars and is not infrequently employed for political propaganda.

A form of short story in which the Chinese are perhaps unrivalled is one in which the supernatural is the dominating feature. Such are the tales in the *Liao Chai Chih I;* tales of Taoist magic, of fox girls (that is to say, vampires that assume the appearance of beautiful young women and inveigle young men, whom they carry off with them to the spirit world), tales of ghostly visitants, of metempsychosis, of necromancy and witchcraft. The author of the *Liao Chai Chih I* was P'u Sung-ling, of the seventeenth century. He failed to take his Master's degree and thus never qualified for the civil service. He took his revenge in his writings by his ironical references to the mandarinate. A large part of his collection of stories has been translated by H. A. Giles.[31] Pere Wieger has made a collection of similar stories from a variety of Chinese sources which he has translated into French.[32]

[31] *Strange Stories from a Chinese Studio:* London, 1880.
[32] *Folk-lore Chinois Moderne:* Hochienfu, 1909.

OTHERS FORMS OF LITERATURE

It is impossible in a single chapter to do justice to all forms of literary activity in China. There is no field that has not been cultivated to some extent. Lexicography, astronomy, mathematics, geography, agriculture, medicine, divination, antiquities and the fine arts, religion, political science and education have all furnished themes for the writer. As the mass of literature has accumulated from age to age the government has had selections made from the most noteworthy works and published in huge collections. One of the earliest was made in the sixth century. Some of these collections professed to give the complete text of celebrated works which were no longer available except in private libraries or in government collections inaccessible to the public. Of encyclopedias the most famous is that prepared during the reign of the Manchu Emperor, K'anghsi (A.D. 1662–1723), known as the *T'u Shu Chi Ch'eng*, consisting of 1628 volumes of some 200 pages each. The Manchu rulers were noted for their patronage of literature and the Imperial Library preserved for the world many rare works of inestimable value. Some of these were in manuscript. The collection was divided into four categories: Classics, History, Philosophy and Miscellaneous Works. Much of this has now been published in form available to the ordinary reader.

Present day literature is profoundly affected by foreign influences. Christian missionaries are responsible for much of this, but more, perhaps, is due to the education abroad of many young Chinese; some in Japan, others in the United States and in Europe. The effect is to be seen chiefly in political and philosophical works, but also in fiction. American and Russian schools of thought probably have most disciples.

CHAPTER XVIII

EARLY FOREIGN INTERCOURSE

Be kind to the stranger who comes from afar.—Tseng Tzu.

In 327 B.C. Alexander the Great introduced Grecian influence into Central Asia where the Greco-Bactrian kingdom was subsequently established. He extended his conquests also into the Punjaub in northern India, a region which after his death came under the rule of Sandrokottos, or Chandragupta, as he was known in India, who maintained close relations with Seleucus in Syria. Through this channel a stream of Grecian influence flowed for a considerable period into India. The grandson of Chandragupta was Ashoka, the royal patron of Buddhism, whose conversion was to that religion what that of Constantine was to Christianity. Buddhism became the state religion of the Punjaub and Ashoka an ardent propandist who sent missionaries of the swastika into surrounding countries. Buddhism became established in Central Asia about 250 B.C. Before the time of Ashoka there was no sculptured image of the Buddha used in India. Greek artists were employed to supply the need.

THE INFLUENCE OF GREECE

But in 170 B.C. the Punjaub was invaded by the Bactrians, and their kingdom later was overthrown by the Indo-Scythians on A.D. 25. The Indo-Scythians in turn accepted Chinese suzerainty in A.D. 229.

Before this last mentioned date a new school of sculpture had sprung up in Gandhara which was even more decidedly Grecian than that of Ashoka. The artist used the Greek

Apollo as his model for the image of the Buddha. He was handicapped by the requirement that the urna be placed between the eyes, and by the demand for abnormally long ear-lobes, these being marks of Buddhahood. He marred the image by complying with these requirements, but he refused to represent the Buddha as a shaven-pated monk. Hence we still have the very un-Buddhistic curly locks. The drapery, too, is Grecian rather than Indian. Modern images, of course, are poor copies, for they are made by artisans, not by artists. Still if one visits a Buddhist temple anywhere in China to-day he can easily trace the features of the Apollo in the image of the Sakya Buddha.

Chinese expeditions were sent into Central Asia as early as the second century B.C., and it was quite possible for the knowledge of Buddhism to have been carried to the Chinese capital at that time. It was not, however, until A.D. 65 that the religion was officially introduced and an image of the Buddha installed in the imperial palace.

It is not alone in the images of the Buddha that the influence of Greek art is seen in China. The excavations of Sir Aurel Stein in Chinese Turkestan have uncovered the ruins of ancient Buddhist temples whose frescoes are undoubtedly in the Greek style.[1] And the same characteristics are to be found in the heroic statues of the Lung Men caves, in Honan Province, which were photographed and described by the late Edouard Chavannes.[2] Traces of the same influence are to be found also in the paintings of the Northern Wei period (A.D. 386–532) found in certain caves of north China, and in the sepulchral images of the T'ang period (A.D. 620–907), many of which have been recovered through excavations made by railway builders in recent years in Honan Province.

This Greek influence, however, was indirect. It accompanied an Indian religion. There was never any direct communication between China and ancient Greece. As already mentioned in an earlier chapter, the Buddhist missionaries to China came and went for 600 years. Dur-

[1] See "Sand Buried Ruins of Khotan" and "Desert Cathay."
[2] In his "Mission Archeologique en Chine."

ing that long period India exerted considerable influence in China, not only in religion and art but also in science, mathematics in particular, and in philosophy.

COMMERCE WITH ROME

Trade with the Chinese was known to the elder Pliny, who speaks of the silk, furs and iron brought from that country to Rome.[3] When the Emperor Wu of the Han Dynasty sent Chang Ch'ien into central Asia, in the second century B.C., he became acquainted with Parthia; and subsequently, in the first century A.D., the Chinese General, Pan Ch'ao, sent a subordinate, Kan Ying, into Parthia with instructions to visit the Roman Empire, or at least that portion of it which had become known to China, the province of Syria. Kan Ying reached the head of the Persian Gulf, but was deterred from making the voyage beyond that point by the tales told him of the hardships and dangers to be encountered.

Trade, however, was carried on between the Roman and the Chinese through the Parthians. The trade in those days was conducted by land. The route taken was across Turkestan and over the Pamirs through central Asia, approximately along the route taken now by the Russian Central Asian Railway, to Persia and thence to the Tigris at Ctesiphon. There the road divided. One route led to the head of the Persian Gulf and then by sea around Arabia to the head of the Gulf of Suez at Rekem, Solomon's Eziongeber, and from there by land to Petra and Gaza. From Gaza part of the trade was carried to Alexandria, and a part up the coast to Antioch, the capital of the Roman Orient.

The second route from Ctesiphon went to Zeugma, on the Euphrates, which was crossed by a bridge of boats, and thence over the desert to Tadmor, or Palmyra. The trade consisted in part of silk, iron, skins and hides from China, in exchange for precious stones, jewelry, glass, tex-

[3] In his Natural History.

tiles—especially those dyed at Tyre—cloth-of-gold and medicines.[4] The Parthians were the brokers in this trade and collected toll from both sides. But in A.D. 165 the Parthian war broke out, during the reign of Marcus Aurelius. This interrupted the traffic. The Roman merchants then sought an alternative route to China. They sent a commercial commission by sea, which reached the southern extremity of Indo China in 166, and made its way either by the Mekong or Salween into western China, and then to the Chinese capital at Loyang, on the Yellow River. The southern coast had been annexed by China in 110 B.C., but the Chinese control was weak, and no attempt had been made by China to develop commerce by sea. A second mission reached Nanking in A.D. 226 when that city was the capital of the Kingdom of Wu, one of the three kingdoms into which China at that time was divided.

THE ARABS IN CHINA

Trade began at Canton about A.D. 300. It was for centuries controlled by the Arabs. They, with a number of Hindu traders, were segregated in one-quarter of the city and ruled through their own headman. It is not true, as stated by some writers, that they ruled themselves in accordance with their own laws.[5] The Chinese found it a convenient way of dealing with aliens, who could not speak Chinese and whose customs differed from their own, to make one of the foreigners responsible for good order among them. But it was Chinese authority that was represented and Chinese law that was enforced. For slight offenses the culprits were condemned to be beaten with the bamboo. As a concession to them they were allowed to be whipped with a rattan instead of the bamboo, and three blows of the rattan were reckoned as equivalent to one with the bamboo.[6] This choice of a headman to enforce Chinese

---

[4] See Hirth's "China and the Roman Orient," a work of rare value long out of print.

[5] J. W. Foster in "American Diplomacy in the Orient," p. 89.

[6] Shou Shan Ko, Ts'ung Shu—Ping Chou K'o T'an. II:3.

orders was similar to the method by which Spain afterwards ruled the Chinese in the Philippines. The Dutch adopted a similar arrangement in Java. After the Arabs became Mohammedans they established a mosque in Canton. This was said to have been founded by a maternal uncle of Mohammed, about 628, but the tradition is unreliable. His grave is still shown at Canton. The Arabs, after the Mohammedan conquest of Persia, also maintained relations with the Chinese court by the overland route.

RELATIONS WITH JAPAN

During the Northern Wei Dynasty (A.D. 386–532) Buddhism spread into Korea, and in 595 Korea sent a Buddhist monk to Japan as instructor to the Japanese Prince Imperial. At the request of the Japanese he brought a number of Chinese artisans to Japan, and Chinese civilization was thus introduced into the islands. In A.D. 631, Japan sent an embassy to China. This was the beginning of political intercourse between the two countries.

The Japanese for centuries looked up to China as a pupil to a teacher. Their art and architecture, their laws and literature, political organization and religion, were almost wholly derived from China. But the Japanese are not mere imitators. They assimilate what they borrow from others and give it a touch which makes it their own. It appears to have been a custom among them to announce to the Chinese Government the accession of a new monarch and to accept investment from China.[7]

During the reign of the Mongols the Japanese lost their regard for China. Kublai Khan fitted out a great naval expedition for the conquest of the islands. This armada was destroyed by a mighty storm and by the prowess of the Japanese. But with the advent of the Ming Dynasty, in 1368, the relations between the two countries were somewhat improved. Some friction, however, resulted from the

[7] Chinese History of the Ming Dynasty. See also Wieger's "Textes Historique," pp. 2011 and 2022.

piratical attacks upon Chinese coast towns by Japanese free-booters. The Emperor of China demanded of the Japanese ruler that he arrest and punish them. He did so, and sent twenty of them to the Chinese court, together with an offering of tribute. The Chinese emperor thanked him, and sent the pirates to Ningpo, where they were put to death by being thrown into a cauldron of boiling water.[8] The Chinese always regarded presents as tribute, and enrolled as vassals all nations that sent embassies. In the case of the Japanese, however, it is asserted in the histories that China supplied Japan with its official calendar—a sign of vassalage, and that in 1409, when Japan announced the death of the Mikado, China sent an ambassador who conferred a posthumous name upon the dead monarch and invested his successor.

THE FIRST CHRISTIAN MISSIONARIES

In the track of the Mohammedans, came from Persia the first Christian missionaries, the Nestorians, who reached the Chinese capital in A.D. 635. A stone tablet, discovered at Hsianfu in A.D. 1625 bears an inscription stating that it was erected in A.D. 781 as a monument to these missionaries. They were well received. They translated their sacred books and established many churches. But when the Buddhists under later reigns began to be persecuted, Christian as well as Buddhist monks and nuns were compelled to take up secular occupations. The churches, however, continued to exist, and were protected by the Mongol Dynasty. But their teachers were not apparently of very good character, for Kublai Khan requested the Polos to have the Pope send out Roman Catholic missionaries. The Nestorian churches were no doubt eventually merged into those of the Roman faith.

CONTROL OF THE TRADE ROUTES

In the tenth, eleventh, and twelfth centuries the seaborne trade was greatly encouraged by the Chinese Govern-

[8] Chinese History of the Ming Dynasty. Also Wieger's ''Textes Historique,'' pp. 2020 and 2022.

ment, which derived a large revenue from the duties ŏn imports. Canton, Ch'üanchou (near modern Amoy), Foo-chow, Ningpo, and Shanghai all participated in this trade. But after the conquest of the greater part of Asia by the Mongols the orderly government maintained by them led to a revival of trade by land. Constantinople became the European entrepôt for oriental goods. The Arabs still controlled the Indian Ocean, and Alexandria in Egypt was a store-house for the luxuries of India and China. Under these circumstances the European nations vied with one another to obtain control of the overland trade. The ficti-tious will of Peter the Great, which is said to be responsible in a large degree for the advance of Russia across Asia, declares that the nation that controls the trade of the Far East will rule the markets of Europe. The statement, by whomever made, seems based upon a careful observation of history. When the lucrative trade with China was enriching Constantinople, Venice and Genoa struggled with one another to control the degenerate government on the Bosphorus.

In 1204 Venice succeeded in converting the fourth cru-sade into an attack upon Constantinople, where, by the aid of France, she was able to replace the Greek ruler with a Latin emperor in the person of Baldwin, although his power was limited by that of the Doge of Venice, who was called "Lord of one-fourth and one-half of the Roman Empire." It was during the Venetian control of Constan-tinople that the Polo brothers engaged in commerce there and went from there to the Crimea and thence, in A.D. 1260, to Bokhara and on to Karakorum, the capital of the Mongol emperors. The very next year the Genoese suc-ceeded in driving the Venetians out of Constantinople and in re-establishing a Greek dynasty there.

The Venetians, driven out of Constantinople, made Acre, on the east coast of the Mediterranean, a starting point for the overland journey of their caravans. In the fourteenth and fifteenth centuries the Ottoman Turks rose to power, and destroyed the peace which the Mongols had pre-served in Asia. Trade was interrupted, and eventually

Constantinople fell into Turkish hands. Before this last calamity had happened, the Venetians, finding the overland traffic impossible, entered into alliance with the Sultan of Egypt and formed a combination with the Arab traders. Then the merchant of Venice became the arbiter of the exchanges of Europe. But many cities in Europe became jealous of Venice and planned to obtain a share of the oriental trade. The old rival, Genoa, produced a vigorous young navigator, Christopher Columbus, who tried to convince the merchants of various countries that by sailing due west over the Atlantic one could reach Marco Polo's Cipango (Japan) and Cathay (China). He found the Portuguese deeply interested in another plan, which was to get to the Far East by circumnavigation of Africa. This was the plan which Prince Henry the Navigator had bequeathed to them. He had begun his explorations in 1415, but died in 1463 before the Cape had been reached. In 1487 Bartholomew Diaz reached the Cape of Storms, whose name was afterward changed to the Cape of Good Hope. Ten years later Vasco da Gama circumnavigated the continent of Africa, and in 1498 reached India. Although they were hospitably received in India they kidnaped the natives, and were soon engaged in wars of conquest marked by great violence and cruelty. Thus they built up a vast empire in the east, and absolutely destroyed every vestige of the flourishing commerce of the Arabs. Nevertheless, the Arabs left their imprint upon China. They introduced Mohammedanism into the south-eastern ports and into Turkestan in the north-west. The Emperor Ming Huan of the T'ang Dynasty, in the middle of the eighth century, brought in a force of Arab mercenary troops to the number of about 4000. These remained in the heart of China, married Chinese wives, and settled colonies of Mohammedans in most of the large cities of central China. To-day there are some fifteen million Mohammedans in the country. There are fifteen mosques in Peking, and numerous others in the commercial capitals of the country.

In 1511 the Portuguese attacked Malacca without provocation and captured it. The Malay Sultan appealed to his overlord, the Emperor at Peking, but he did not recover his capital. He retained a portion of his kingdom, however, and his descendants still rule over it from Johore under the protection of the British government.

In 1516 the Portuguese made a visit to China to prospect. The next year they sent four of their own vessels and four Malay ships from Malacca to the island of San Chuan, whose name resembled so closely the Portuguese for St. John that the place became known to Europeans as St. John's Island. From this place they were permitted to send two vessels to Canton to trade. One of them carried an envoy from the King of Portugal, named Thomé Pires, who asked permission to visit Peking. The reply from Peking was that Portugal ought first to restore to Malacca the territory taken from the Sultan.

On this visit the Portuguese behaved very circumspectly, so that the charges made against them by the jealous Arabs seemed to be without foundation. In 1520, therefore, word came that Pires might proceed to Peking. He arrived there in January, 1521, but in 1522 he was sent back in chains, and died in prison at Canton in 1523.

This severe treatment was due to the fact that after the envoy's departure for Peking there arrived at St. John's Island a second fleet of Portuguese vessels, whose commander in utter disregard of Chinese sovereignty, proceeded to build a fort and attempted to exercise jurisdiction over the inhabitants. Officers and crews alike behaved with great insolence and cruelty. It was charged that they were kidnaping women and girls. These acts confirmed the earlier reports of the Arabs that the Portuguese were bent on conquest. The Chinese retaliated upon the envoy. The Portuguese continued to come, however, and gradually established considerable colonies at Ningpo, Foochow, and Ch'üanchou (near modern Amoy). Their licentiousness and cruelty became so unbearable that in 1545 an imperial edict from Peking directed that they should be attacked wherever found, on sea or land. A massacre at Ningpo that year destroyed the colony there, and that at Ch'üan-chou in 1549 was likewise exterminated. A few survivors escaped. These gathered at Lampacao, a small island near Macao. A few years later they aided the Chinese in suppressing piracy along the coast, and in 1557 obtained permission to build some drying sheds at Macao. This grew into a Portuguese settlement. The Chinese, however, continued to exercise control over the place until 1848. The Portuguese, in recognition of Chinese sovereignty, had paid rent until that year, when they drove out the Chinese authorities and claimed ownership. This was not recognized by China until 1887. Macao was for many years the only port at which Europeans and Americans were allowed to reside.

There, too, the Portuguese maintained their reputation for cruelty. During the early part of the nineteenth century the port was notorious for the coolie traffic. Tens of thousands of Chinese were lured from their homes by false promises. Others were kidnaped. They were held in barracoons until a shipload had been assembled. Then they were packed in foul quarters in the hold, where many died, and shipped to Peru and Cuba, where they were virtually sold into slavery. American and British vessels were forbidden by their governments to engage in the business, and in 1871 an appeal by the coolies in Peru to the American Minister there led to an exposure of the infamy and to the suppression of the traffic.

Not all the Portuguese were vicious. In 1552 St. Francis Xavier, "the Apostle to the Indies," arrived at St. John's Island, intending to begin missionary work in China. He had just met with remarkable success in Japan. But he was stricken with fever immediately after his arrival at St. John's Island, and died without setting foot in China. He was followed in 1584 by Ricci, whose work was continued by Verbiest, Adam Schaal, and others of the Society of Jesus. These men acquired great influence at the Court

In Peking, but lost it when a dispute arose between the
Jesuits and other Catholic orders over the toleration by
the former of the worship of ancestors by Chinese converts.

In 1580 Philip II of Spain united Portugal to his crown.
Philip was having trouble with his Dutch subjects. They
had been accustomed to buying at Lisbon such oriental
products as they needed, but since they were at war with
Philip that port was closed against them. Thereupon, they
proceeded to take possession of the Portuguese empire in
the Far East. Nothing remains to Portugal to-day but
Macao, in China, the half of the island of Timor, and
Goa on the west coast of India, which is still the capital
of the Portuguese possessions in the east.

THE DUTCH AND CHINESE

Despite the success of the Dutch in their contest with
the Portuguese, and the favorable position which they had
secured in Japan, they made but little headway in their
endeavors to build up a trade with China. Their first
vessel arrived at Canton in 1604, but they failed then, and
repeatedly in later efforts, to supplant the Portuguese
there. They took possession of Formosa and the Pescadores, but were driven out by Koxinga. They performed
the kotow at Peking, which other Europeans refused to
do, but it won them nothing save the privilege of carrying
tribute to Peking once in eight years, and thus having their
countrymen, the liberty-loving Netherlanders, listed as
vassals of the Chinese. It was not until 1762 that they
were allowed to establish a hong at Canton.

SPAIN AND CHINA

The Spanish possession of the Philippines brought them
of necessity into communication with the Chinese, who for
centuries have had colonies in those islands. Their prosperity there excited the jealousy of the Spaniards. Ef-

forts were made to keep the Chinese out by terrorizing them. Twenty thousand, it is asserted, were massacred by the Spaniards in 1603, and twenty-two thousand more in 1639. But they continued to come. A head tax levied in later years scarcely checked the immigration. Most of the Chinese in the Philippines have come from the vicinity of Amoy. Our purchase of the islands has brought to the American Consulate at Amoy and the Legation at Peking a number of important diplomatic questions growing out of the presence in Fukien Province of Chinese residents of the Philippines who claim citizenship in the islands and the protection of the American government.

THE ARRIVAL OF THE BRITISH

The first British vessel reached China in 1637. Captain Weddell had taken the precaution to obtain a permit to trade there from the Portuguese authorities at Goa, but the jealous Portuguese at Macao declined to recognize it as valid, and proceeded to put difficulties in the way. Weddell was fired upon by the Chinese at the Bogue, but replied so forcibly as to put the forts out of business for a time. He proceeded to Canton as though he had been firing a salute, loaded with sugar and ginger and sailed away. Subsequent efforts of the British were unsuccessful until, in 1670, they opened trade at Amoy and in Formosa. In 1644 the Ming Dynasty was overthrown by the Manchus, but the latter did not succeed in conquering southern China until 1685. That year all the ports of China were thrown open to foreign trade by the Manchus, who had not yet learned to distrust the Europeans. The British did not at once take advantage of the opening; it was not until 1689 that the British East India Company sent another vessel to Canton. From that time to the present the British have held the foremost place in China's foreign trade, and, generally speaking, have taken the lead both in the promotion of commercial enterprises and in the settlement of diplomatic questions.

When the Manchus threw open the ports of China to foreign trade they were but slightly acquainted with the character of Europeans, and did not apparently anticipate any friction with them. This liberal attitude soon changed. The policy of the Mings was revived, and foreign traders were allowed access at the port of Canton only. The seamen of the 17th and 18th centuries were not over-scrupulous. There was a great deal of lawlessness. Kidnaping and slave-dealing were not uncommon, and smuggling was connived at by customs authorities in Europe as well as in China.

Shaw's Journals record that many of the British vessels, owned in India, "carried on a smuggling trade with the Dutch settlements in and about Malacca, and with the natives, whom they supplied with opium, clothing and fire-arms, etc., in return for which they received pepper, block tin and spices." [9] These, with articles from India, were carried to China and sold. "The establishments of the Swedes and Danes" were principally supported, so the journals state, "by the smuggling trade they carried on in the channel and upon the coasts of Britain." [10]

The British trade was a monopoly of the East India Company until 1834. But the captains and officers in the service of the company were allowed to engage in private trade and given certain cargo space in the vessels. This they filled, so Shaw tells us, "with fine teas, cassia, Nankin cloths, porcelain, etc., a considerable part of which, on their entering the English Channel, is disposed of to smugglers, between whom and the custom house officers there was always a clear understanding." [11] It was not remarkable, therefore, that in China too there was smuggling with connivance of the customs officials. It was opium exported from India that was especially compelled to seek illicit channels for introduction into China.

The poppy plant was introduced by the Arabs in the 8th century A.D. A decoction of its seeds was used in

[9] Journals of Major Samuel Shaw, p. 169.
[10] Ibid., p. 171.
[11] Ibid., p. 173.

medicine for a soporific. In the 10th century the exhila-
rating effects of the drink were sung by the Chinese poets
of the Sung Dynasty. It was not until the 15th century
that the opium began to be imported as a medicine. In
the 16th century it was produced in India and China, but
its uses were medicinal only. In 1620 tobacco was introduced into China from the Philippines. Imperial edicts
forbidding its use were powerless to prevent smoking. In
its preparation certain drugs were used; among them was
opium. Thus a taste for opium was cultivated. In time
the tobacco was omitted and the opium was smoked alone.
The habit spread rapidly, and was soon recognized as a
social evil. In 1729 an imperial edict prescribed severe
penalties for those who sold it, and later the death penalty
was prescribed for those who smoked; but the law was too
severe and became a dead letter. For a time the drug continued to be imported for medicinal purposes and paid
a light import duty, but smoking opium was made contraband. The difficulty of distinguishing between opium for
medicinal purposes and opium for smoking finally led to
the prohibition of the import altogether.

In the early years of British trade the ships of the East
India Company engaged in the traffic, but after the more
stringent edicts of 1800 the company's ships were forbidden
to accept cargoes of the drug. Other British vessels, however, continued the business, in which many merchants of
other nationalities also engaged. Americans were interested in it from 1810 onwards. Before the first war between China and Great Britain it made up an appreciable
part of our imports into China, and constituted from one-
fourth to one-third of the total imports from all countries.
Much of the opium handled by the Americans was brought
from Turkey. Britons were forbidden to deal in Turkish
opium, which competed with that from India. It is necessary to say, however, that the American government never
countenanced the trade, and its officers repeatedly warned
Americans that those engaging in it would have no protection from their government. There were always, of

course, large numbers of British and American merchants who refused to have anything to do with the evil traffic.

The opium was brought in foreign vessels to the China coast in the vicinity of Canton, and sold for cash to Chinese smugglers, who bribed their own customs officers to permit them to land it. This contraband traffic and the friction created by it became one of the causes that led to the first war between China and Great Britain.

This, however, was only one of a number of causes contributing to the disturbance of friendly relations between the two powers. The Chinese were arrogant. They regarded themselves as the only civilized people on earth, and looked upon all others as barbarians. The Europeans and Americans, on the other hand, considered themselves superior to the Chinese, and were satisfied that the European way of doing things was the only right way. The refusal of the Emperor to receive foreign envoys without the kotow, and the assumption of China that all other nations were her tributaries, angered the western world. Petty restrictions imposed by the Chinese upon foreign residents, the bankruptcy of Chinese firms that were in debt to European merchants for loans contracted in violation of Chinese law, the prohibition to deal with any firms outside the co-hong, and the extra-legal charges imposed by officials —all these things helped to create an atmosphere of distrust and bitterness, which could be cleared only by the lightning of war.

THE RUSSIAN ADVANCE IN THE ORIENT

The year 1689, in which the British East India Company succeeded in establishing itself in Canton, was also the year in which the first treaty between China and a European power was signed. That was the treaty of Nerchinsk between Russia and China, by whose terms the Russians were compelled to evacuate the valley of the Amur and agree to make the Yablonoi Mountains the boundary between Siberia and Manchuria.

The story of Russia's advance across Siberia is a thrilling one, rivaling that of our own pioneers who pushed the western frontier over the Alleghenies, across the Mississippi, and beyond the Sierras to the coast of the Pacific. In Moscow, next to the Kremlin, the most noted place is the Kitai Gorod—i.e., the "Chinese City." China to the Russians is still Kitai, just as to Marco Polo it was Cathay, another form of the same word. The history of the Kitai Gorod reaches far back into the past, to a time when the Grand Dukes of Moscow were subjects of the Mongols and received their investiture from the Grand Khan. It was in 1535 that Helena, mother of Ivan the Terrible, surrounded the Kitai Gorod with its own stone wall. Even then its shops and ware-houses were stored with the precious treasures of the East.

But Russia's relations with China began still earlier. In 1340, during the Mongol Dynasty, made famous by Kublai Khan, Russian imperial guards were employed by the emperors of China. It was Sophie Paleologus, niece of the last emperor of Christian Constantinople, who was unwilling to be subject to the Mongols, and who pushed her husband, Ivan III, into the daring revolt that put an end to Tartar dominion over Russia. The first Russian embassy to China was sent in 1567, but was no more successful in its efforts to establish relations with Peking than that of Portugal which preceded it but a few years.

The history of Asiatic Russia gathers about three great names; those of Yermak, Khabaroff, and Muravieff. On the first of September, 1581, at that period the Russian New Year's Day, Yermak, an ex-pirate with a price upon his head, led a band of adventurers over the Urals to explore the wilderness, subdue the savages, and enrich his employers, the Stroganoffs, with the stores of furs to be obtained. He subdued the tribes in the valley of the Ob, captured Sibir, the capital of a Mongol chieftain, and gave its name to the surrounding region, which became Siberia, a name extended to most of Asiatic Russia. The great Tzar pardoned his former offenses, and his memory to-day is held in honor by Russia's millions. He perished in the struggle with the Mongols, but his successors pushed on their explorations, and in fifty-five years from the beginning of Yermak's work, i.e., in 1636, they reached the Pacific. In 1644 when the Manchus were attacking Peking, the Russians entered the beautiful valley of the Amur. It was left for Khabaroff to colonize the valley. He entered it in 1650, although it was already occupied by subjects of the Manchu Emperor of China. In 1657 he reached the mouth of the Ussuri, and built a fort on the bluff at whose base the waters of the Ussuri mingle with those of the Amur. To-day this bluff is occupied by a city which bears his name, Khabaroffsk. Here he was attacked by the Chinese. Numerous engagements followed, and eventually the Russians, poorly supported by the Tzar's government, had to withdraw from the Amur Valley and agree, in the treaty of Nerchinsk in 1689, to fix the boundary at the water-shed which shuts in the valley on the north. This remarkable treaty is the longest lived treaty on record. Although slightly modified in 1727 and 1768 it formed the basis of Russia's relations with China until superseded by the treaty of Tientsin in 1858.

It is of interest for another reason also. In it for the first time China recognized the equality of a foreign state. It is sometimes said that it granted Russia extraterritorial jurisdiction in China. This is incorrect. The significance of the articles dealing with the punishment of offenses committed by the subjects of either power in the territority of the other is their mutuality. "Subjects of either nationality who pass the frontier for private business and commit crimes of violence to property and life are to be arrested and sent to the frontier, to be handed over to the chief local authority of their own country to be punished." They are recognized as under the protection of their own government, but that government cannot exercise jurisdiction over them until the offender is returned to its own territory.

Muravieff, the third great name in Siberian history, was that of a man entirely different in character from the two explorers. He was a young military officer who had distinguished himself in the war with Turkey, but in his dealings with China he displayed remarkable diplomatic, rather than military, qualities.

Sent to the Far East in 1854, during the Crimean War, to prevent the seizure of Kamtchatka by the British and French, by his tact he managed to preserve friendly relations with the Chinese, while using the Amur River, without Chinese permission, for the transport of troops and supplies. The Chinese were fully occupied in the suppression of the Taiping Rebellion. They could not afford to go to war with Russia. Moreover the British and French were pressing China with demands that led to the war of 1858 and 1860, and Muravieff utilized to his own advantage the ill feeling of China towards Britain and France. To Chinese protests he replied by referring them to the representative of Russia in China, who, with the representative of the United States, was watching developments around Canton and Shanghai. In the end he obtained for Russia without any military action, or even the threat of force, the cession of the left bank of the Amur and the maritime province east of the Ussuri. This gave Vladivostok to the Tzar.

THE BEGINNING OF AMERICAN RELATIONS

Our commerce with China began immediately after the close of the war of the revolution. The treaty of peace with Great Britain was signed in 1783. In February, 1784, the good ship, *Empress of China,* sailed from New York for Canton, where it arrived on August 28th. The vessel was commanded by Captain Green, but the venture was in charge of Major Samuel Shaw,[12] who became later the first official representative of the United States in China. He was a young man who had enlisted in the revolutionary army as soon as he came of age, in October, 1775. He was commissioned a Lieutenant of Artillery, and fought

[12] The Journal of Major Samuel Shaw, with a life of the author by Josiah Quincy, is authority for the statements relating to Shaw that are made in this chapter.

in every important engagement of the war. At its close he found himself a major, but penniless and in debt. When he offered his services to certain merchants of New York as supercargo for a shipment to China his offer was promptly accepted. The cargo was chiefly ginseng, a mild tonic for which the Chinese still have an appetite. Shaw dilated in his report upon the advantage which the Americans had over European competition in that "the otherwise useless produce of our mountains and forests" (i.e., ginseng) would suffice in a considerable degree to procure for us the "elegant luxury," tea.

It was French friendship that gave most assistance to the young American in initiating his enterprise. In the Straits of Sunda, at Java Head, he fell in with two French war-ships which had been loaned by the king to French merchants. The French officers invited him to accompany them, and the three vessels sailed together to Macao. Association in the war of the revolution had created strong ties between the peoples of the two countries. Shaw's journal contains the following entry concerning his arrival at Canton:

From Macao we proceeded towards Canton, and on the morning of the 28 (August) on opening the shipping at Whangpoa (14 miles below Canton), we saluted them with 13 guns, which were returned by the vessels of each nation. At eight o'clock we came to anchor, and again complimented the shipping with 13 guns.

Previously to our coming to anchor, the French ships sent two boats, with anchors and cables, under an officer, who assisted us in getting into a good berth, and staid on board until we were moored. The Danish sent an officer to compliment; the Dutch sent a boat to assist; and the English an officer "to welcome your flag to this part of the world."

. . . .

The behavior of the gentlemen on board the respective ships was perfectly polite and agreeable. On board the English it was impossible to avoid speaking of the late war. They allowed it to have been a great mistake on the part of their nation— were happy it was over—glad to see us in this part of the world—hoped all prejudices would be laid aside, and added that, let England and America be united, they might bid defiance to all the world.

On Shaw's return to the United States, in 1785, he found his former chief, General Knox, serving as Minister of War, and by him was offered a post as Secretary in the War Office, which he accepted for a few months. But he was induced to write a report of his voyage to the Minister for Foreign Affairs, the Honorable John Jay, and through him received the thanks of Congress. A few months later Congress elected him Consul to China, without salary. At the same time he was, of course, permitted to engage in trade. Thus he undertook his second voyage, in 1786, under more favorable auspices than the first. It is interesting to note that during these years immediately following the Revolution, we did not have a War Department, but a War Office—that instead of a Department of State and a Secretary of State we had an Office of Foreign Affairs and a Minister for Foreign Affairs. It is even more noteworthy that it was not the President who appointed Major Shaw to be Consul, but that the Congress elected him to that post.

The things which we wanted from China in those early days were silk, tea, and nankeens. Nankeens are heavy, unbleached cotton piece-goods made in the vicinity of Nanking. Silk and tea are still two of the largest items among our imports from China, but the cotton piece-goods trade has reversed its current. We now sell cotton cloth to China instead of buying such stuffs in China. This change has been brought about by the invention of the cotton gin and the power loom. China still uses her hand-looms, however, and the native cloth still commands a limited market there, because of its weight and strength; but the great factories that are being built will eventually destroy altogether the cottage industries. To-day there are 3,200,000 spindles in Chinese factories driven by steam, and power looms in their proportion are weaving cotton cloth.

In the days of Shaw the trade was conducted in sailing vessels. The forests of Maine furnished the timber for the wooden ships that were built in New England. The American "clipper" ship was famous the world over. At the commencement of our civil war in 1860 the American tonnage in the China trade had almost overtaken the British, but in the construction of iron vessels we could not compete so easily. When the Great World War broke out, in 1914, our carrying trade with China was almost nil. During the war our ship-building programme gave us a new mercantile marine, but it is doubtful that these vessels can be operated profitably without a subsidy, seeing that American seamen command so much higher wages than those of Europe or Asia. In 1914 our share of the tonnage in the China trade was less than one per cent, and in the foreign trade of China it was about seven per cent of the total. The situation improved considerably during the war, but the conditions were abnormal. American tonnage increased to five per cent and our share of the foreign trade of China to thirteen per cent of the total. Recent legislation by the Congress will doubtless encourage American trade with the Orient, by removing certain handicaps under which American companies have had to operate in China in competition with those of Europe.

American relations with China cannot be discussed without mention of the work of American missionaries. They are found both in Roman Catholic and in Protestant missions, but chiefly in the latter. The first Protestant missionary to China arrived there in 1807. He was a British subject, but he went out in an American vessel because of the unwillingness of the British East India Company to give him transportation. Subsequently the company recognized the value of his work and took him into its employ as translator. From the time of Robert Morrison to the present British and American missionaries have coöperated very zealously in their work. The Americans have done the larger part of the educational and medical missionary work, and they have also been interested in various other philanthropic enterprises. A British subject connected with an American mission prepared the first Chinese font of metal type which made possible the cheap production of books and newspapers. There is no Chinese alphabet, and since each word has its own symbol there are some thirteen thousand characters in common use. A case of Chinese type, therefore, occupies a small room. It was the arrangement of the case in such a manner as to make possible the ready finding of a character that was the chief difficulty to be overcome. Prior to this invention Chinese books were printed from wooden blocks, each page having its own block. There has been, it is true, a limited use of movable wooden type since the tenth century A.D. These usually represent characters in constant demand for perparing forms for public documents. The celebrated *Peking Gazette,* the oldest daily paper in the world, which dated from the eighth century A.D. was cut on tablets of wax from which the impressions were taken.

The introduction of movable metal type and the process of stereotyping has greatly increased the production and circulation of literature. In 1887 there were but three or four daily newspapers in China. In 1914 there were forty dailies in Peking alone. The work of the missionaries has had much to do also with the social and political reforms that have taken place in recent years.

CHAPTER XIX

OPENING THE GATES OF CHINA

There is no greater evil than thinking lightly of the foe.—Lao Tzu.

The irritating restrictions to which the foreign merchants at Canton had to submit, and the heavy burden of taxation borne by the trade there, led the British to attempt to open some other port, but all such attempts were unsuccessful. The co-hong which held the monopoly of trade at Canton wanted no rivals, and the officials who squeezed the co-hong were quite as determined as the co-hong to keep all gates closed save that at Canton only.

MACARTNEY'S EMBASSY

The British Government then undertook to open negotiations with the Court at Peking. In 1792 the Earl of Macartney was appointed ambassador to undertake this task, and arrived on August 5, 1793 at Taku. No expense had been spared in fitting out the embassy. Six hundred cases of choice presents were carried to Peking for the emperor. The Chinese were equally lavish in their entertainment of the mission. They are said to have spent $850,000 for this purpose.

By the Chinese these rich presents were regarded as tribute, and over the boats which conveyed the embassy and its treasures to Peking there floated flags bearing in Chinese the words "Tribute Bearers from England." Macartney knew that the inscriptions were there, but, as he did not read Chinese, he assumed that his ignorance would be taken for granted. On the other hand the Chinese knew that he had interpreters who could, and probably would, read the inscriptions. To the Chinese along the river the sight of this huge fleet of boats bearing tribute was proof of the greatness of China and the power of the Son of Heaven at Peking. From Peking the embassy had to make its way to the imperial hunting lodge at Jehol, beyond the Great Wall and distant four days' journey from the capital. Meantime, there had been much discussion concerning the kotow. The Chinese wondered whether the British would perform this obeisance or not; the British debated among themselves as to the propriety of making it. When the Earl was told that he must kotow he offered to do so, provided an officer of equal rank with himself would kotow to the portrait of the King of England which he carried with him. The official account of the embassy states that a compromise was reached, and that Macartney was received upon his bending one knee, as he did on approaching his own sovereign. Rockhill, however, in his account of "Diplomatic Audiences at the Court of China," presents evidence to support the statement of the Chinese that the British Ambassador did perform the three kneelings and nine head-knockings. Anderson, who was a member of the mission but was not present at the audience, stated that the ceremonial followed was kept a profound secret. The humiliation experienced, if such obeisance really was made, won nothing for the British. The Emperor handed the Earl a haughty reply to King George, and rather plainly intimated that it was time for the embassy to be going. The burdens upon trade were not lightened, but on the contrary were increased, and further friction was created by disputes over jurisdiction.

The British and the Europeans had several times attempted, but without success, to assert extraterritorial jurisdiction over their subjects in China. The Chinese from the beginning had always claimed territorial jurisdiction over alien residents.

Fighting within the territorial waters of China between British and Americans during the war of 1812 was another source of trouble, and was protested against by the Chinese Government.

All the old annoyances were continued, and in 1816 the British Government decided to make a second attempt to improve the situation. There was a new Emperor at Peking, Chiach'ing, a smaller minded man than his father, Ch'ienlung, and even more arrogant. Lord Amherst was the British envoy. He was very rudely treated by the Chinese. All the way from Taku to T'ungchou he was annoyed by their insistent demand that he should promise to kotow. Several members of the mission advised him to comply. But the opportunity to do so was not given. It was a custom of the Chinese Court to hold audiences at daylight, or even a little before daylight. After the Boxer troubles of 1900–1901, as a concession to Western customs the Empress Dowager, although still receiving Chinese officers at daylight, used to grant audiences to the diplomatic representatives at nine o'clock in the morning.

In Amherst's time, however, the old rule obtained, and when he reached T'ungchou, the terminus of the river journey, he was hurried to Peking during the night, traveling in a palanquin, and from Peking to the Summer Palace ten miles further, making a night journey of twenty-two miles in this uncomfortable fashion. Immediately upon his arrival, at five o'clock in the morning, he was summoned to audience. He refused, saying that his uniform and letters of credence had not yet arrived. He complained, too, that he was ill. The Emperor sent his physician, who reported that the ambassador was feigning illness. The Emperor in anger ordered him back to T'ungchou. Back to T'ungchou he was taken, and home to England without having accomplished anything.

CHINESE ARROGANCE

This attitude of the Chinese toward Western Powers is quite easy to explain now, but then it seemed as inexplicable as it was intolerable. All the nations around China, save one, Russia, were small and weak and had received their civilization from China. The Arabs, Portuguese, British and Dutch, moreover, had all come to Canton by sea, and were believed to be inhabitants of small outlying islands. Great Britain, although without her consent, had been inscribed among the tributaries; why should she be treated with more consideration than other tributaries? Russia had been treated as an equal, it is true, but Russia was manifestly a great power, stretching along the whole northern frontier of China.

As for the kotow, from the days of Themistocles to the present the European has refused to perform the humiliating obeisance demanded by Asiatic courts. Napoleon, however, held that the Chinese were quite right in demanding that aliens comply with the requirements of the court, that otherwise a foreigner is treated with more respect than a prince of the blood. He declared, too, that the claim of an ambassador to be the personal representative of his sovereign was an unreasonable one, since any messenger might carry a letter from one monarch to another. But Napoleon's views were not generally shared by European rulers. As for the Americans, their views were well expressed by Minister Ward, who, when told he must kotow refused saying: "No, I kneel only to God and woman."

The Chinese had finally to abandon both the claim to superiority and the demand for the kotow. When the Emperor Tungchih attained his majority, in 1873, and the diplomatic corps was received in audience, it was agreed after much discussion that the Ministers should bow three times before His Majesty. This they did, although the audience was not a success, since the diplomats were received in the hall where tributaries had audience. It was not until after the settlement of the Boxer troubles, in 1901, that the question of ceremony at imperial audiences was satisfactorily adjusted. But in the days of Macartney that was more than a hundred years in the future.

THE BREAKING POINT

The British East India Company's charter expired in 1834, and its monopoly of British trade at Canton came to an end. The company had given notice to the Chinese authorities that its operations were about to cease. The Chinese had replied that it would be necessary to appoint some one as *t'ai-pan* of the British merchants. By a *t'ai-pan* the Chinese meant a commercial man, representative of the British merchants, such as Chinese merchants had in Java or the Philippines, such as in the old days the Arabs had at Canton—a merchant and not a government official. They wanted one merchant selected to whom the Chinese could communicate the orders of the Government for all. But the British assumed that what was wanted and needed was an official representative of the British Government, of the sort which we call consular, one who could not only look after trade but exercise jurisdiction over British subjects. Accordingly Lord Napier and two others were appointed superintendents of British trade in China, and instructed, after due consideration of the subject, to set up a court to have jurisdiction over British subjects. Lord Napier was head of the Commission. All this was done without consulting the Chinese and without notifying them.

Lord Napier was instructed to avoid friction, but in the same document was given commands which would of necessity be found to create friction. He was required by his instructions to proceed directly to Canton, and to notify the Viceroy by letter of his arrival; but the Chinese regulations in force did not allow any foreigner to visit Canton without a permit, nor any communications to be made to officials except through the hong merchants, and all such communications had to be couched in the form of petitions. Lord Napier, of course, would not send his letter through merchants. He held himself to be of rank equal to that of a Viceroy, and he would not petition. He went to Canton without a permit; his letter was not received, and the merchants were punished for not preventing his coming. He was ordered back to Macao and refused to go. British trade then was stopped. British merchants were shut up in their hongs and all Chinese were forbidden to serve them or to supply them with food. British war-ships came for their protection. The people were alarmed, and finally, to relieve the merchants, Napier went back to Macao, and died almost immediately after his arrival there.

His associates and successors were better acquainted with the situation. They had formerly been connected with the East India Company and had lived some years in China. They were more circumspect therefore. But their passive attitude only postponed the inevitable conflict, for it strengthened, rather than weakened, the Chinese self-confidence, and made the position of the foreign merchant the more unendurable. The Chinese were filled with self-conceit because of their experience with weaker neighbors. They knew nothing of the strength of Europe, and their contempt for the foe was their undoing.

The claims of the East and the West were wholly irreconcilable. War seemed the only solution of the problem, and war came. It is known generally as the "Opium War," and opium was the immediate cause of the rupture between Great Britain and China. The opium question, however, as already said, was but one of the many causes leading to war.

Opium smuggling had increased rapidly. Foreigners of many nationalities were engaged in it; British, American, Portuguese and others. The Emperor was determined to put a stop to opium smoking and end the illicit traffic in the drug. Commissioner Lin, a man of iron will, arrived in Canton in March, 1839, with full power to investigate and to act. It did not take him long to make his investigation. In one week after his arrival he issued stringent orders to all foreign residents of Canton to deliver up all the opium in their possession within three days. Delay led to the shutting of all foreign traders in their hongs, cut off from all food and service and surrounded by a large force of troops. The demand of the British Superintendent for passports for the British was vain. He was compelled to deliver the opium, over twenty thousand chests, all of which was destroyed. The British immediately began preparations for war. It took time to send despatches to London; there was no telegraph in those days. A fleet was sent out and blockaded Canton in June, 1840. The war lasted two years. The Chinese were defeated everywhere, but the Chinese troops showed no lack of courage. Their equipment and their methods were obsolete. The British were impressed by the desperation of the Manchu garrisons at Chapu and Chinkiang. When they realized their defeat they killed their wives and children and then committed suicide. The treaty of peace was signed at Nanking on August 29, 1842. By that treaty the obnoxious monopoly of the co-hong at Canton was abolished. That city and four others were opened to foreign residence and trade. Consuls were allowed to reside at these ports. A reasonable tariff was promised. Twenty-one million dollars were to be paid as indemnity, of which six millions were for the opium that had been destroyed, and Hongkong was ceded to Great Britain.

But the opium question remained unsettled. The Chinese would not agree to legalize the traffic. During the negotiations at Nanking the British introduced the topic, and suggested that it would be well to allow the import of the drug under a heavy duty, and thus obtain a revenue from it. The Chinese asked the British why they did not forbid the production of opium in India. Sir Henry Pottinger replied that it would not be consistent with the constitution of Great Britain, and that, even if they did exercise so arbitrary a control over the tillers of the soil in India, it would not prevent the coming of the drug to China; that, if India did not produce it, other countries would—a rather lame excuse for an evil trade. He reminded them that, if they would only be virtuous, they would neither use the drug nor permit it to be smuggled.

The next year a treaty of commerce was signed which provided the promised tariff on imports and exports, and stipulated for a measure of extraterritoriality. This last, however, was more definitely provided for in the American treaty of 1844.

The tariff was made specific, but was based upon a general charge of five per cent ad valorem. A few articles paid a somewhat higher duty, and bread-stuffs and bullion were put upon the free list. This fastening of a treaty tariff upon China was an encroachment upon her sovereignty. The low rate adopted, too, was an injustice that has been perpetuated to our own day, one that is making very difficult the financial readjustment needed. The Boxer folly and the political troubles that have afflicted the country since 1911 have plunged the nation into debt; but if China enjoyed tariff autonomy these debts might easily be met. This was one of the subjects dealt with by the Washington Conference.

THE FIRST AMERICAN TREATY WITH CHINA

The war between Great Britain and China was watched with great interest by the American Government, and, as soon as the Congress assembled after news of the treaty of Nanking was received, that is to say in December, 1842, the President recommended that an appropriation be made for a commission to negotiate a treaty between the United States and China. It was Daniel Webster, Secretary of State, who first called attention to the desirability of such action. Caleb Cushing was the man selected as Commissioner. He was well received by the Chinese, and within six months after his arrival in China had signed a treaty which in some respects was an improvement upon that of the British. But it was the British that had opened the way for American action. Foster, in his "American Diplomacy in the Orient," calls attention to the curious style of the letter addressed by President Tyler to the Emperor of China.[1] Webster had resigned the Secretaryship of State, and this letter was evidently drafted by some subordinate in the Department who thought that the Chinese

[1] Op. cit., p. 81.

Emperor was to be treated in the same manner as the chieftain of a tribe of American Indians. To the Americans the Chinese were wild barbarians. This was shown, not only by the letter mentioned, but in the preparation of the copy of the treaty which was sent to Peking after the exchange of ratifications. Many years later, in 1901, during the settlement of the Boxer troubles, the American Minister appointed me to be a member of an international committee to examine the archives at the Chinese Foreign Office and arrange for their protection. The Chinese Government had fled when the capital was captured, and there had been much looting in the city. It was important that the records of the Foreign Office should be preserved.

On entering the Hall of Archives we found the whole lot of documents piled in a heap on the floor, as though it had been intended to set them afire. In the midst of the pile was the Chinese Government's copy of our first treaty. It was bound in purple plush, like an old-fashioned family album, and the seal attached was of solid silver, a replica of the great seal of the United States, obverse and reverse. It was fastened to the document by a gold cord. It was undoubtedly put up in this garish fashion in the belief that it would appeal to the supposed barbarous tastes of the Chinese.

But if Americans looked upon the Chinese as barbarians the latter returned the compliment with interest. When the yamen of the Canton Viceroy was seized by the British, during their second war with China, they found copies of the official reports made by the Chinese commissioner who negotiated with Cushing. In one of these reports he refers to Cushing in very disparaging terms as the ''Barbarian envoy,'' and told how his ''stupid ignorance'' had to be dispelled.[2] The two peoples have come to understand one another much better since then, and to appreciate the good features of each other's civilization.

The American treaty contained three important provisions not found in the British treaty. It was expressly provided that the Americans who should engage in the

[2] Ibid., p. 90.

ENTRANCE TO THE TSUNGLI YAMEN, PEIPING.

HALL OF AUDIENCE AT THE SUMMER PALACE.

opium traffic should receive no protection from the American Government. The treaty also contained a stipulation permitting revision at the end of twelve years, a very important one as it later appeared, when the Chinese resisted all attempts at revision. The third was more important than either of the other two. It was the stipulation relating to the extraterritorial jurisdiction to be exercised by the United States over its citizens in China. This question will be treated more fully elsewhere. In the previous chapter I have pointed out the mistake made by some writers, who assume that the surrender by the Chinese of territorial jurisdiction was readily made, and that the Arabs enjoyed a somewhat similar privilege in the ninth century of the Christian era.

THE SECOND WAR WITH GREAT BRITAIN

The treaties of 1842, '43 and '44 did not accomplish all that the Powers had expected. The Chinese had been defeated, but they were just as unwilling as ever to have any dealings with Western peoples. The ancient Chinese had tried to keep out the Mongols by building a brick wall across north China; their descendants tried to keep the Europeans at a distance by passive resistance, by delays, by all sorts of obstructive tactics, and more actively by evading treaty provisions.

The treaty powers sent out their commissioners to care for the interests of their citizens, but the Chinese provided no channel of communication with them. There was a Commissioner of Foreign Affairs at Canton, it is true, but, as was later discovered, his duty was to prevent any intercourse, if possible, and to hinder and obstruct communication. It was the Manchu officials, rather than the Chinese merchants, who were opposed to intercourse. The latter have always been eager to trade, and, as a rule, they have been very honorable in their dealings.

The American treaty, as already said, provided for revision at the end of twelve years, and Great Britain enjoyed favored nation treatment. The American treaty was due for revision in 1856, but all attempts even to discuss the question were evaded by the Chinese. When appeal was made to Peking the American commissioners were referred to the Chinese mandarin charged with the conduct of foreign affairs who resided at Canton. When this officer at Canton was asked for an interview he invariably replied that he would appoint an auspicious day at some time in the future, when he was not busy. But that auspicious day never arrived.

Disrespect shown to the British flag led to a second appeal to arms in the autumn of 1856. Canton was captured on October 29th. Search of the Viceroy's yamen discovered his correspondence with Peking, from which it was learned that it was the Court at Peking that was really responsible for the hostile attitude toward Western powers. It became necessary, then, to bring home to the Peking Court a realization of their own weakness, and the folly of deluding themselves with the fancy that procrastination could ever save them from a final accounting. It was not until the forts at Taku had been taken and Tientsin was captured that the Manchus at Peking were sufficiently alarmed to enter into negotiations. The French had a grievance in the torture and murder of a French missionary in Kuangsi Province, by a local magistrate who had escaped all punishment for his crime. The French, therefore, joined the British in the attack upon the Taku Forts, and the Anglo-French forces marched into Tientsin on May 30, 1858. The Chinese at once agreed to the revision of the British and French treaties. The Americans took advantage of the situation to negotiate a revision of theirs, and the Russians also entered into a new treaty.

OPIUM IN THE TREATIES OF 1858

William B. Reed was the American envoy who negotiated our treaty of 1858. He had instructions to support the Chinese in their attitude towards the opium traffic, and to renew the provisions of our treaty of 1844 in regard to that trade. In violation of these instructions he omitted the provision of our first treaty in regard to opium, and urged Lord Elgin, of the British embassy to try to have the trade legalized. Morse well says that Reed must be classed with those who have betrayed a great cause.[3]

Arrangements had been made to exchange ratifications the following year (1859), and for this purpose Mr. J. E. Ward was sent out by the American Government. The Russians had followed the old route of communication with Peking via Kiakhta, and had no difficulty in exchanging the ratification in the Chinese capital. The British treaty stipulated that ratifications should be exchanged at Peking. The American and French treaties did not specify the place, but each had a favored nation clause under which claim could be made for the same privilege. In the meantime the Chinese had rebuilt and strengthened the forts at Taku. Upon the arrival there of the American, British and French envoys, they were requested to land a few miles to the north, at Peitang, from which point they would be conveyed to Peking. The British and French declined to go to Peitang, and insisted on going up the Haiho to Tientsin. The American envoy went to Peitang, as requested, and was carried to Peking. There he was told that he could have no audience of the Emperor unless he would kotow, and it was upon this occasion that he made the reply already quoted: "I kneel only to God and woman." He was taken back to Peitang and exchanged ratifications there.

While he was upon his way to Peking the British and French attacked the forts at Taku and were beaten off with considerable loss. During the engagement Commander Tatnall of the American frigate, *Powhatan,* ordered a small steamer that accompanied him to tow several British launches into action. "Blood is thicker than water," he exclaimed. His action, however, was an embarrassment to the American Minister. The British and French had to

[3] International Relations of the Chinese Empire, I: p. 554.

draw off and refit. They came back the next year (1860) in stronger force, captured the forts, took Tientsin and marched to Peking. In vain the Peking Government strove to stop their advance, offering repeatedly to negotiate with them at other points on the way. The treachery of the Chinese in arresting British and French representatives who were within the Chinese lines under a flag of truce, and the torture and murder of several of these, hardened the resolution of the envoys. They seized the celebrated summer palace of the Emperor at Yuan Ming Yuan, looted and burned it, looted and destroyed a number of summer palaces belonging to imperial princes, and finally negotiated peace in the capital itself.

The Emperor, Hsienfeng, a dissipated man, the Empress and the Princess Yi, who was the secondary consort and the mother of the Emperor's only son, fled together to the hunting lodge at Jehol. There the Emperor died in the summer of 1861, being but thirty years of age.

Before leaving the capital Hsienfeng had appointed his brother, Prince Kung, plenipotentiary to make peace with the British and French. The envoys had been demanding day by day the return of the prisoners taken in violation of a flag of truce. Prince Kung had pleaded that peace should first be made, but he had had the survivors among the prisoners removed from the vile prison of the Board of Punishments to a pleasant little temple in the northern part of Peking, where they were at least more comfortable than they had been. Among them was Harry Parkes, the interpreter of the British mission, afterwards known as Sir Harry Parkes, one of the most vigorous ministers the British ever had at Peking. His escape from death was a very narrow one. After the flight of the Court, a mandate bearing the imperial seal was sent back to Prince Kung directing him to put the prisoners to death. But a private message from a courtier arrived at the same time, telling him the contents of the mandate and that the Princess Yi had written it. Prince Kung knew her bitter animosity to the Europeans, and he also knew that the execution of the prisoners would bring severe punishment upon

China. Accordingly he neglected to read the mandate until he had set the prisoners free, when he reported that the order had come too late.

Lord Elgin, the British envoy, entered Peking in state on October 24, 1860. The ratifications of the treaty of 1858 were exchanged in the yamen of the Board of Rites. At the same time a convention was signed by which the indemnity demanded of China in the treaty of 1858 was increased from Tls. 4,000,000 to Tls. 8,000,000. In addition to the ten new ports whose opening was provided for in the treaty, the city of Tientsin was included, and the Peninsula of Kowloon, opposite Hongkong, was ceded to Great Britain. The French entered Peking on the 25th of October, and after exchange of ratifications also secured a convention that increased their indemnity from Tls. 2,000,000 to Tls. 8,000,000.

The treaties of 1858, with the amendments made by the conventions of 1860, secured equal privileges for the four powers that had been negotiating; the United States, Great Britain, France, and Russia, for each had the favored nation clause in its treaty. These treaties, it may be said, really opened the gates of China. They forced upon her a recognition of western powers as being upon an equality with herself, and not her vassals. They provided for the residence of diplomatic representatives at Peking, and the establishment there of a Foreign Office with which these representatives might communicate.[4]

Among other provisions of note, one placed opium upon the tariff list, and so legalized that infamous trade, while another guaranteed freedom of religion and the privilege of religious propaganda by Christian missionaries, throughout the country.

The American treaty contained one very unusual clause. Article I provides that "If any other nation should act unjustly or oppressively, the United States will exert their good offices on being informed of the case, to bring about

---

[4] Theretofore all intercourse with foreign states had been conducted through the Li Fan Yuan, or Bureau of Dependencies, which did not even have the rank of a Ministry.

an amicable arrangement of the question, thus showing their friendly feelings.''

The Chinese have several times availed themselves of the good offices, both of our Government and of American statesmen not connected with the executive branch of the government. This provision of the treaty of 1858 was recalled with considerable interest when appeal was made to the American Commissioners at Paris in 1919 for the exercise of their good offices to prevent the transfer to Japan of the former German rights in the Province of Shantung.

The Russians, in addition to the treaty of Tientsin in 1858, had induced the Chinese a month earlier (May 29, 1858) to sign the treaty of Aigun, which made the left bank of the Amur as far as the mouth of the Ussuri the boundary between the two countries, and left the maritime province east of the Ussuri in joint possession of the two countries until its ownership could be definitely settled. Both nations were to enjoy the right to navigate the Amur, Sungari and Ussuri Rivers. The Russians used their good offices in behalf of China during the advance of the Anglo-French forces upon Peking. Thus they were able finally to persuade the Chinese to cede the maritime Province of Siberia to Russia. This was done in a treaty signed November 14, 1860. It had been but a short time since Russia herself had been at war with Great Britain and France in the Crimea, so that it was not surprising that Russia and China should have been drawn together.

CHAPTER XX

THE APOTHEOSIS OF AN AMERICAN

The plain man is the basic clod
From which we grow the demigod;
And in the average man is curled
The hero stuff that rules the world.

Foss.

The Chinese in their conflict with the British and French were handicapped by a great rebellion, which began in southwestern China in 1850, and spread during the following decade over most of the provinces in the southern half of the empire. Its ravages, indeed, extended along the Grand Canal as far north as the suburbs of Tientsin.

The man who was in a great degree instrumental in its suppression was an American, Frederick Townsend Ward, of Salem, Massachusetts.

THE SHRINE OF GENERAL WARD

At the China New Year in 1900 I went for a house-boat trip into the country southwest of Shanghai, and arrived one day at the gate of Sungkiang. This was the headquarters of General Ward during his military operations, and there he was buried. I enquired for his grave and was guided to it. In the south-eastern part of the city there is an open space of considerable extent. This was his drill ground. Beside it there is a little temple, and within the temple court-yard is his grave. The temple is of brick with a tile roof. The principal hall is built just in front of the tomb. Within the hall is an altar, the inscription over which tells the visitor that it is dedicated to the spirit of General Ward. The temple was in charge of a care-taker who lived there. It was kept in good con-

451

dition, and on the altar were the remains of the incense and candles which, with other offerings, had been sacrificed to the dead warrior at the New Year.

A Yankee sailor boy, a soldier in the Chinese imperial army, a saint in the Confucian calendar—such in epitome is the history of Frederick Townsend Ward. The love of adventure was in his blood, and the rattle of musketry to his ears was as the peal of an organ to a priest. Yet he was not fond of killing. He went unarmed into battle, carrying simply a slender walking stick with which to direct his troops. In this habit he was imitated by his British successor, the celebrated Major Charles George Gordon of the Royal Engineers, who is sometimes given improperly all the credit for the suppression of the Taiping Rebellion.

Ward was born in Salem in 1831. He made an effort to get into West Point, but failed. At fifteen years of age he went to sea. He was with Garibaldi in South America. At twenty he sailed from San Francisco for China. On his arrival in Shanghai in 1851, the fanatical leader of the Taiping Rebellion and his iconoclastic followers had just taken possession of the city of Yunganchou, in the province of Kuangsi, but were not yet thought of as in any way dangerous or worthy of serious attention. Ward found employment on a coasting steamer running out of Shanghai. In 1859 he had become an officer on the Chinese merchant steamer, *Confucius*. By this time the Taiping leader, Hung Hsiu-ch'üan, had created mighty armies, had declared himself emperor, had established his capital in the ancient city of Nanking, and had shaken the Manchu empire to its foundations.

THE ORIGIN OF THE REBELLION

Hung Hsiu-ch'üan was a curious character. Probably he was an epileptic. There is much in his career to remind one of Mohammed. He was born in 1813, about thirty miles north of Canton. His family, however, was not

Cantonese, but had come from the north. His father was a farmer. Hsiu-ch'üan was a student; he had entered the examinations several times but had failed to pass. When he was twenty years of age he had come into touch with Christian missionaries at Canton, but at that time had not been favorably impressed by them. Four years later, in 1837, he had been taken ill after another failure in the examinations, and had seen strange visions. Another decade passed; he went once more to Canton for the examinations and failed again. Then he went to call upon an American missionary, the Rev. Issachar Roberts. From him he received instruction in Christianity, but before he was ready for baptism he left the mission and went home. There he organized a society called the *Shang Ti Hui*, or Society of the Supreme God. He soon gathered a band of some thousands, devoted to the worship of one God, and intolerant of all forms of idolatry. Great zeal was shown in destroying idols and demolishing temples. This, of course, brought conflict with the authorities, for one cannot destroy the property of others without violating the law.

Rebellions are common enough in China. The history of the Manchu Dynasty is a history of a continuous succession of rebellions. During the twenty-six years of my own residence in China I do not remember one in which there was not, somewhere in that vast country, an uprising against the constituted authorities. The attacks of the *Shang Ti Hui*, therefore, upon the officials who sought to punish them for destruction of property, did not at first attract much attention. The society was but one more of those rebellious organizations which had kept Kuangsi in turmoil for several decades.

In 1850 Hung Hsiu-ch'üan was living in Lienchu, in the county known as Kueihsien, in Kuangsi. He appears to have been sincere in his acceptance of Christian doctrine, and his followers were well disciplined and attentive to religious affairs. Their strong faith added, of course, to their value as soldiers, and their attacks in large numbers upon temples made military measures a necessity upon the part of the authorities. Like Cromwell's troops they went out in unwavering confidence that the Lord of Hosts was with them, and their courage was irresistible. In 1851 they moved to Yunganchou, and there they were besieged by imperial troops in February, 1852. In April Hung cut his way out, and with a force of about ten thousand men he started on his journey northward.

TAIPING SUCCESS

He had no artillery, therefore he failed to take the provincial capital, Kueilin, which closed its gates against him. He marched around it and continued moving north, living upon the country as he went. In June he was more successful in Hunan Province, where several cities fell into his hands. By September he was at Ch'angsha, the capital of Hunan, but from it he was turned away by walls that he could not breach. There, however, he captured a lot of boats, with which his army moved down the Siang River. At its mouth the city of Yochow was taken. There was a government arsenal there which supplied them with guns and abundant ammunition, with which they moved down the Yangtze River. Before the end of the year Hung had captured Hanyang, and in January, 1853, the city of Wuchang, the viceregal capital of Hupei and Hunan. There they fitted out a powerful fleet. City after city along the Yangtze fell before them. On March 19, 1853, they stormed and captured Nanking, the ancient capital of the empire. Twenty thousand Manchus, resident there, were massacred; men, women and children. There the "Heavenly King," as the leader called himself, made his capital. There he lived the remainder of his life—eleven years—and from his palace there ruled a great portion of the empire.

It was while at Ch'angsha, in Hunan, that he first assumed the imperial title. He called his state the *"Taiping T'ien Kuo,"* or "Heavenly Kingdom of Great Peace," and himself the "Heavenly King of Great Peace." His fanaticism was shown in the position which he claimed for himself. He was not content, as Mohammed was, to be simply a prophet of God. He claimed to be the third person of the Trinity. God was the Heavenly Father, Jesus Christ was the Celestial Elder Brother, and Hung Hsiu-ch'üan was the Divine Younger Brother. He had his own version of the New Testament, and a hymn book also that was used in the religious services. Sunday was observed as a day of rest, and all troops had to parade for worship. In the beginning the movement was, perhaps, a sincere attempt at a religious reformation. The massacres that stained its record, to the zealous converts no doubt seemed justified by the examples given by the Israelites in their conquest of Canaan. But with success came volunteers of a less sincere and more adventurous character. The Christian missionaries at the beginning felt encouraged by the movement, thinking that Christianity was about to become the religion of the State under a new dynasty; but investigation showed that it was a bastard Christianity. I talked many years ago with Rev. Griffith John, who had visited the Taiping leader at Nanking in the days of his power. He said that the visit quickly disillusioned him. The Taiping King had simply become another oriental monarch, living in self-indulgence, surrounded by a harem of more than eighty women, and supported by the looting of the empire. There was no organized civil government, and apparently there was no constructive programme. It seemed altogether a negative and a destructive movement. The military forces were well organized and well disciplined, but a movement which had begun as a religious crusade was ending in nothing but plunder, outrage and debauchery. However inefficient the Manchu Government might be—and it was inefficient—the flabby, slimy iniquity at Nanking, a leech sucking the life blood of the nation, could do nothing to better conditions. It was but a vile parasite to be crushed and destroyed. The men who assisted in this work performed a real service for the people of China.

The military forces, as just said, maintained a fair degree

of discipline, but it was merely a discipline that preserved a good fighting machine. It did nothing to check pillage or promote peaceful industry. The leaders for the most part were loyal to their chief, and some of them developed real military ability. One of them, however, the Eastern Prince, began in 1856 also to have visions, in imitation of the "Heavenly King." But such imitation was not considered flattery by the chief. He had a monopoly of visions. Accordingly two other princes were entrusted with the duty of putting the Eastern Prince out of the way. This they did very expeditiously. Assassination, murder, massacre, every infamy marked the advance of these armies over the country. Villages were razed. Families were broken up and scattered. The people fled in terror. Years afterward I walked over the ruins of many of these deserted villages. A nurse in our family, sitting in the Garden at Shanghai, fell into conversation with another Chinese woman, who was discovered to be her own sister, lost as a child during one of these panics.

To the loyal Chinese these Taipings were known as "Long-haired Robbers." This was because they refused to shave the head and wear the queue, the token of submission to the Manchu Government.

THE ATTITUDE OF THE WESTERN POWERS

There was a disposition for a time in the United States and Great Britain to recognize the new dynasty. Mr. McLane, the American Commissioner to China in 1855, was authorized to do so, if, after investigation, he should think it advisable. Strict neutrality was maintained for some years by the Western Powers. But every investigation led to but one conclusion. What the Rev. Griffith John had found, all found—there was nothing in the movement to encourage hope that the Taipings would ever be able to establish an orderly government.

When Nanking was captured in 1853 there was, of course, a great deal of anxiety among the Americans and

Europeans in Shanghai, who did not know how soon their own homes might be destroyed. They accordingly organized a volunteer defense corps, and dug a moat on the west side of the International Settlement, connecting the creeks that bounded this settlement on the north and south. The Huangpu River is on the east side, so that this arrangement caused the settlement to be entirely surrounded by water.

Secret societies have flourished in China from ancient times, and generally, though not always they are of a political character. The success of the Taipings encouraged these revolutionary secret societies. One of the best known is that called the Triad, whose members are often called Chinese Masons. Their lodge and ritual have points of similarity to those of the Free Masons. A branch of this organization, called the "Little Sword Society" captured the native city of Shanghai in 1853. It was then a walled city of some 50,000 inhabitants, separated from the French Concession by a narrow moat. These "Small Swords" claimed to be allied to the Taipings, but the "Heavenly King," after investigation, refused to have anything to do with them, declaring that they were "too immoral." Thus the Taipings lost their only chance of acquiring a sea-port, with the opportunity which that would have given of obtaining supplies from abroad.

The Imperialists, in their attacks upon the "Small Swords," invaded the International Settlement on one occasion, and came into contact with the Foreign Volunteers, who drove them out. This indicates plainly that at that time the Western Powers had no more sympathy with the Manchus than with the rebels.

In 1859 when Ward made his first offer to aid the Imperial forces, he was arrested and brought before the American Consul, charged with violating the neutrality of the United States. He tried to clear himself by declaring that he had taken Chinese nationality, but, as that claim was a manifest absurdity at the time, he was locked up on board the American naval vessel *Chesapeake*.

Not long afterwards, being allowed on deck for exercise, he leaped overboard and swam ashore. He entered into a contract with a Chinese banking firm, Taki (or Tachi), to capture the city of Sungkiang, in return for which he was to receive Tls. 30,000. He enlisted a hundred sailors of various nationalities, and made the attempt, but failed. Returning to Shanghai, he discharged this nondescript force and substituted one hundred Filipinos and two American lieutenants. With this small force he succeeded in driving out the Taipings and capturing the city of Sungkiang. After this success he increased his force and attempted to take the city of Tsingpu. Again he failed, for the rebels also had European officers there and their force was stronger than Ward's. Ward, too, was wounded. He realized then that it would be necessary to organize and drill a large body of troops. This, when his wounds were healed, he proceeded to do. The troops thus drilled, because of their successes, became known later as the "Ever-Victorious Army."

Ward was a natural leader. He had great influence over his men, and was admired and trusted by them. His success in holding Sungkiang against a severe attack by the Taipings, and his victories over the rebels in repeated engagements, finally brought the British and American Governments to his support. China in recognition of his services gave him a commission as Colonel. With a large Chinese army under his command, braced by his own well-drilled troops and supported by the foreign authorities at Shanghai, he soon had the country cleared of rebels within a radius of thirty miles around that port. The Chinese generals in the Imperial army at that time were men of much more than ordinary ability. Tseng Kuo-fan, a Hunan man, was generalissimo, and his chief lieutenant was a rising young man of Anhui Prov-

[1] For life of Ward, see Historical Collections of the Essex Institute, Vol. XLIV, "Frederick Townsend Ward," by Rob't S. Rantoul.

ince, afterwards known all over the world as the Premier, Li Hung-chang. They were true patriots, who made the welfare of the State their chief concern. Ward continued his successes until, on the 21st of September, 1862, in the attack on Tzeki (Tzuchi), about ten miles from Ningpo, when attempting to scale the city wall, he was shot and mortally wounded. He was highly esteemed by his Chinese associates, and his death was greatly deplored.

POSTHUMOUS HONORS CONFERRED

The Imperial Government, upon learning of his death, at once issued an edict directing that certain honors should be conferred upon him. He was given posthumous promotion to the rank of Brigadier General, and two temples were ordered to be erected to his memory, one at Ningpo, near which city he was killed, and the other at Sungkiang, the place of his burial. When the American Chargé d'Affaires at Peking learned of this decree he went to the Foreign Office and suggested that, as Americans did not erect temples for the worship of the dead, it would be better simply to raise a stone monument at Ward's grave. But the Chinese conformed to their own custom and honored the dead warrior in their own way.

In 1901, while I was serving as a Secretary in the Legation at Peking, it became my duty, in response to a request from the Essex Institute at Salem, to get a copy of the imperial edict just mentioned and translate it. The Foreign Office at once turned up the records and sent a copy of the edict.

SUCCESSORS TO WARD

The first attempts to find a satisfactory commander for the Ever-Victorious Army after Ward's death were not successful; but on March 25, 1863, Major Charles George Gordon, of the British Royal Engineers, was permitted by his government to take the post. There was considerable feeling in the army against having a British commander. But they followed Gordon for a time and he led them to victory. Subsequently, however, many mutinied. About half the army quit before the capture of Soochow, in December, 1863. But Gordon was a good officer and a successful general. He filled up the ranks with prisoners captured from the Taipings. The morale of the rebels had already been destroyed by Ward's victories, and from this time on to the end their fall was rapid. Gordon was a high-minded man and could not get on with the Chinese. He had promised clemency to the Taiping leaders at Soochow if they surrendered. After they had done so the Chinese commander, Li Hung-chang, ordered their execution. This so enraged Gordon that he was disposed to resign. He remained in command, however, until the fall of Changchow, in May, 1864, and left the service in the following month.

THE END OF THE REBELLION

The war continued more than a year after his resignation, but the Ever-Victorious Army was disbanded, and the military operations of the last year were conducted by the Chinese themselves. The walls of Nanking were breached in July, 1865, and the city was taken by storm. On the 30th day of June preceding, the Taiping King had already committed suicide. In August the last remnants of the rebel army were captured and scattered.

While I was living in Nanking in the closing decade of the last century, I had occasion often to pass a small Buddhist convent in the western part of the city, where one of the ladies of the "Heavenly King's" harem was still living in seclusion. She had taken the vows of a nun.

Gordon was honored, both by the Chinese and by his own government. He was a man cast in heroic mould, and fell a martyr to his trust in others and his devotion to a cause that he regarded as a cause of peace and righteousness.

Ward and Gordon were of wholly different stamp.

strongly contrasting with one another. Born on opposite shores of the Atlantic, widely sundered in heritage and training, their graves, too, are separated by the breadth of the earth. Yet their lives touched for a brief moment and flowed in one channel. Ward was slain by Chinese fanaticism. Gordon, abandoned in Khartum, fell before the fanaticism of the Mahdi. Both gave their lives for the welfare of an alien race, and lie buried under foreign skies. The memory of one is preserved by a monument of bronze, erected by his own people in far Khartum; that of the other by a temple and altar, and the incense and sacrifices offered by a pagan people to his spirit.

CHAPTER XXI

BURLINGAME AND ORIENTAL IMMIGRATION

It is an accepted maxim of international law that every sovereign nation has the power, as inherent in its sovereignty and essential to self-preservation, to forbid the entrance of foreigners within its dominions, or to admit them only in such cases and upon such conditions as it may see fit to prescribe.—Vattel.

China's defeat in the two wars fought with Great Britain compelled her to allow British and other powers to send diplomatic representatives to reside in Peking. But she yielded with a bad grace, and her Court had as little intercourse as possible with these representatives of states that she regarded as barbarous. For some years she ignored all suggestions that she should reciprocate by sending Chinese envoys to the Western world.

It was Mr.—afterwards Sir—Robert Hart who persuaded the Chinese Foreign Office to modify its policy in this regard. Hart had come as Acting Inspector General of Customs from Shanghai to Peking in 1862, and in 1863 had obtained the substantive appointment to that office, in which his tact and his loyalty to the interests of his Chinese employers won their confidence and regard.

THE MARITIME CUSTOMS SERVICE

To explain Hart's position it is necessary to give a brief account of the origin of the Maritime Customs Service, of which he was the chief executive officer. It was the Taiping Rebellion that made possible the reorganization of the customs under the supervision of Europeans. While rebel forces were in occupation of Shanghai and the Western powers were maintaining strict neutrality, the Chinese customs authorities were unable to function at that port. The Consuls of the United States and Great Britain allowed their nationals to give bonds for the payment of duties at some future date. This action was disavowed by their governments. The Chinese Customs Taotai, who had taken refuge in the foreign settlement, was then persuaded to agree to the establishment of a commission composed of one American, one British subject, and one Frenchman, to superintend the collection of duties at the port. Subsequently it was found to be a more efficient method to place the office under one head. Mr. Lay, of the British Consular Service, was selected. The control was gradually extended to other ports where the officers of the imperial government had been unable to act; and after the second war with Great Britain, when the customs revenues were pledged by treaty for the payment by China of the indemnities exacted by Great Britain and France, the Chinese Government, in 1861, appointed Lay to be Inspector General of the Imperial Maritime Customs. In 1863 he was succeeded, as already said, by Robert Hart. Hart also came from the British Consular Service. It is to his wisdom and executive ability that China to-day owes the Maritime Customs which so satisfactorily serves the Republic. During the more than sixty years of its supervision of the foreign trade of China, it has in addition to the collection of duties done much to promote the welfare of the country. It has surveyed the coasts and rivers, built light-houses, buoyed the channels, established a postal system, protected the health of the ports, and established a bureau of statistics whose records supply us with the only reliable data on many subjects related to commerce and social conditions. Its school of languages, opened at Peking in 1862, and designed to educate men for interpreters, was the nucleus from which the national university developed.

A DIPLOMATIC SERVICE

Sir Robert had frequently urged the government to establish legations and consulates. On his return from leave of absence in 1867 he took up the matter again. At this time the American Minister in Peking was Anson Burlingame. He had been appointed in 1861, and had arrived in Peking in July, 1862. He was genial and tactful and a man of sanguine temperament. Chinese and Europeans were alike drawn to him, and when the Chinese Minister for Foreign Affairs learned, in 1867, that Mr. Burlingame was about to resign his post, he was requested by the Chinese Government to accept appointment as the ambassador from China to the governments of the Western world.

Accordingly on the 25th of February, 1868, he set sail from Shanghai for San Francisco, accompanied by one Manchu and one Chinese officer, both of high rank, by one British and one French Secretary, and by some thirty Chinese secretaries and attachés.[1] He was well received in the United States, but his fervent oratory there aroused expectations in the breasts of his hearers that were impossible of fulfillment in the then near future. The Chinese Government, in sending the mission abroad, wanted such representation made of the actual conditions in their country as would make the Western powers more tolerant and less disposed to press China to adopt in hasty fashion the inventions and methods of the West. Mr. Burlingame, however, saw in his appointment an evidence of great progress. His mind dwelt only upon the tremendous changes that were sure to follow eventually in the wake of this movement. He failed to note the obstacles in the immediate foreground because his gaze was fixed upon the attractive future in perspective.

From the United States the embassy proceeded to Great Britain, France, Germany and Russia. The promise to avoid undue pressure upon China was given by the American, British and German Governments. The French made no engagements in regard to the matter. All these governments called attention to the unwillingness of the Chinese Emperor to give audiences to Western diplomatic representatives, and the British and French sovereigns re-

[1] See Morse, International Relations of the Chinese Empire, Vol. II, Chap. IX.

ceived the mission only on the distinct understanding that the young Emperor, T'ungchih, would give audience to their ministers as soon as he attained his majority. In St. Petersburg Mr. Burlingame was taken ill. He died there in February, 1870, and the other members of the mission returned to China.

Mr. Burlingame has been rather severely criticised for his roseate descriptions of the conditions in China, which, in his view, indicated impending changes of great moment that were to modernize that hoary empire. But, after all is said, the spirit of hopefulness that animated him was better than the pessimism of his critics. The cabinets of the Western world needed the corrective of his opinions. They had looked too long on the dark side of the shield; they needed to view the situation from another angle and to give due consideration to Chinese sentiment if they were to deal fairly with China. If in Burlingame's over-sanguine anticipation of results he failed to see the difficulties of the immediate future, he nevertheless succeeded in the chief purpose of his mission; he brought about in the West a better feeling towards China, and he prepared the way for the appointment of Chinese diplomatic representatives abroad.

THE TREATY OF 1868

While in Washington, Burlingame negotiated with the American Government a new treaty, which in its final article—Article VIII—gave to the Chinese Government the assurance that the United States disclaimed "Any intention to intervene in the domestic administration of China in regard to the construction of railroads, telegraphs, or other material internal improvements." This met very fully the request of the Chinese that the powers would refrain from pressing China unduly to modernize the country. The first article recognizes China's right of eminent domain in the areas set aside at the open ports for foreign residence and trade. This may very properly be considered the beginning of American interest in the preservation of China's territorial integrity. Article II recognized China's right to regulate her internal trade, and Article III provided for the opening of Chinese consulates in the United States.

The most striking provision of the treaty, however, is that of Article V, the first sentence of which reads as follows:

The United States of America and the Emperor of China cordially recognize the inherent and inalienable right of man to change his home and allegiance, and also the mutual advantage of the free migration and emigration of their citizens and subjects respectively from one country to the other, for purposes of curiosity, of trade, or as permanent residents.

Equally interesting is a sentence in Article VI, which declares that:

Chinese subjects visiting or residing in the United States shall enjoy the same privileges, immunities and exemptions in respect to travel or residence as may be enjoyed by the citizens or subjects of the most favored nation.

It was distinctly stated, however, that nothing in this article was to confer naturalization upon Americans in China or upon Chinese in the United States.

The provisions just quoted were in entire harmony with the policy which the American Government had followed up to that time. Our country was to be an asylum for the oppressed of all nations. We welcomed with open arms immigrants from all lands. The American Government had for years been urging upon European statesmen the recognition of an inherent right in man to change his home and allegiance. Secretary Seward and Ambassador Burlingame were but urging upon China that which they had pressed upon Europe. China, in agreeing to these provisions, was abrogating an age-old statute of the empire, which forbade Chinese to go abroad.

At the time this treaty was negotiated there was, no doubt, a great demand for labor upon the Pacific coast of the United States, which accounts for the encouragement given by the American Government to Chinese immigration, a policy so opposed to present practice. Despite Chinese statutes to the contrary there had been a great deal of voluntary emigration from the southern provinces of China to the East Indies, and there had also developed a barbarous coolie traffic, by which tens of thousands of Chinese, who had been deceived into signing contracts or who had been kidnaped, had been forced into involuntary servitude in certain American countries, as stated in an earlier chapter. American legislation had forbidden American vessels to engage in this cruel business. The treaty under consideration, therefore, in providing for Chinese immigration into the United States, declared that both the high contracting parties reprobated "any other than an entirely voluntary emigration."

The Chinese had been coming to the United States in considerable numbers ever since the discovery of gold in California, whose Chinese name is "The Old Gold Mountains." Besides engaging in mining, they did much of the agricultural work of California, and had been successfully employed in railway building and in other enterprises, there and in other states.

In 1868, the year in which the Burlingame treaty was negotiated, there were already some 60,000 Chinese in the United States. The largest number admitted in any one year was 39,579 in 1882. The average annual immigration over a period of thirty years was a little more than 9000. The largest number at any one time in the country was 107,488 in 1890.

The Chinese were slow to ratify the treaty of 1868. Ratifications were exchanged in November, 1869, and the treaty was not proclaimed in the United States until February, 1870.

EXCLUSION OF CHINESE

Agitation against its provisions as to Chinese immigration began shortly afterwards. It was recognized generally that the Chinese were industrious, thrifty and law-abiding, and that the Chinese merchant was honorable in his dealings. The agitation was chiefly against the coolies engaged in manual labor. They had been accustomed to small wages at home, and their standard of living was a low one, one which white men could not accept. They crowded themselves together in the tenements of San Francisco and other cities in insanitary quarters, and were regarded as a menace, both to the welfare of the white laborer and to the health of the community.

These facts were published on the street corners by Dennis Kearney and others with so much success that the Congress, in 1876, appointed a commission to investigate the situation. That commission reported in 1877, and in the following year a bill was passed forbidding the immigration of Chinese laborers. President Hayes promptly vetoed it as a violation of our obligations under the treaty. But in 1880 a commission headed by President Angell, of the University of Michigan, went to Peking to endeavor to obtain China's consent to a modification of the treaty. The Chinese generously agreed to the request of the American Government, and entered into a new treaty whose first article provides that:

Whenever in the opinion of the Government of the United States, the coming of Chinese laborers to the United States, or their residence therein, affects or threatens to affect the interests of that country, or to endanger the good order of the said country or of any locality within the territory thereof, the Government of China agrees that the Government of the United States may regulate, limit or suspend such coming or residence, but may not absolutely prohibit it.

Pursuant to this agreement, the Congress in 1882 passed a bill suspending Chinese immigration for twenty years. This President Arthur vetoed, on the ground that it violated the spirit of the treaty of 1880, which clearly agreed that the limitation or suspension of immigration should be "reasonable." He held that twenty years was an unreasonably long period. Yielding to the President's argument Congress then reduced the period to ten years.

But neither the treaty of 1880 nor the legislation of 1882 satisfied the leaders of the anti-Chinese agitation, and in 1888 the government sought a new treaty with China which aimed at a virtual prohibition of Chinese labor immigration. During the negotiations the campaign preceding a national election had already begun. The two great parties were struggling to obtain the suffrages of the Pacific coast states, and Congress hurriedly passed a bill in glaring violation of the provisions of the treaty of 1880, absolutely prohibiting the immigration of Chinese laborers. President Cleveland, for party's sake, allowed it to become a law.

The situation was rectified in 1894 by a new treaty, which permitted the exclusion of Chinese laborers for ten years. Chinese self-respect was wounded by this agreement. Six months before the termination of the treaty in 1904, to prevent its automatic renewal, China, in accordance with its provisions, gave due notice to the American Government that it would not be renewed.

The American Legation at Peking, under instruction from the Department of State, began at once to hold conversations with the Chinese Foreign Office looking toward the negotiation of a new treaty. Various drafts and counter-drafts were submitted as possible substitutes for the obnoxious clauses of the old treaty. The writer was present at these conferences. The American Minister, Hon. W. W. Rockhill, found it impossible to persuade the Chinese Premier, Prince Ch'ing, to agree to any proposal that would at all satisfy the Department of State. Prince Ch'ing and his associates of the Foreign Office were always urbane. There was no doubt as to their friendly disposition toward the American Government and its representatives. They had not forgotten Minister Rockhill's services in the Boxer negotiations of 1901, but to agree to any further humiliation in the matter of Chinese immigration into the United States was a sacrifice of dignity and self-respect which they were determined to avoid. Prince Ch'ing was strengthened in his resolution by the action of the Chinese at Shanghai, Canton and elsewhere, in boycotting American trade.

The boycott was suggested by Chinese in San Francisco and other American cities. It is a favorite weapon in China. Through several months in 1904 and 1905 American trade suffered considerably. The Chinese Government did not authorize the boycott. On the contrary, at the request of the American Minister, they issued proclamations against it. Nevertheless, it was a plain revelation to the Peking authorities of the sentiment of the Chinese people. The negotiations for a new treaty failed. The boycott, too, was abandoned, and Congress passed a law making permanent the exclusion of Chinese laborers from the United States. China refused to make herself a party to such proceeding, and quickly ignored it. One result of the legislation has been a gradual reduction of the number of Chinese residents in our country. From 107,488 in 1890, the number dwindled to 71,531 in 1910, and to 61,631 in 1920. Of these 18,532 were born in the United States and are therefore American citizens. The U. S. Census for 1930 reports the number of Chinese in the United States as 74,594. That is a gain of 13,315 over 1920. That indicates an increase of about 2 per cent. per annum. Of the total probably not less than 30,000 were born in the United States.

JAPANESE IMMIGRATION

Another result of the anti-Chinese agitation has been an increase of Japanese residents. When the first restrictions upon Chinese immigration were permitted by the treaty of 1880, there were but 148 Japanese in the United States. In 1890 there were 2039. The census for 1920 gave the total number in the United States as 111,010, of whom 29,170 were reported to have been born in the United States. The U. S. Census for 1930 gives the number of Japanese in our country as 138,834, an increase of 27,824 over the returns of 1920. This indicates an annual increase during the decade of about 2.5 per cent. The more rapid increase of Japanese than of Chinese may be charged to two factors:— (1) the large number of old people among the Chinese and (2) the greater proportion of women among the Japanese. There are 72,000 Japanese women, but 15,000 only of Chinese. Probably not less than 50,000 Japanese are American born and therefore American citizens. The agitation against Oriental immigration to-day, therefore, is directed mainly against the Japanese, but in a lesser degree against Chinese and Hindus also. Early in the present century the demand for the exclusion of Japanese labor began to be heard. To prevent the enactment of an exclusion law, Japan sanctioned an oral agreement between the Japanese Ambassador and the Secretary of State, in which Japan voluntarily bound herself not to issue passports for the United States to laborers. This is known as the "Gentleman's Agreement." It is not a signed agreement; it is an oral promise which Japan is in honor bound to keep. There is, however, in the Department of State an unsigned memorandum of the conversations. In signing the new commercial treaty of 1911 between the United States and Japan the Japanese Ambassador added to the treaty the following statement:

In proceeding this day to the signature of the Treaty of Commerce and Navigation between Japan and the United States, the undersigned, Japanese Ambassador in Washington, duly authorized by his Government, has the honor to declare that the Imperial Japanese Government are fully prepared to maintain with equal effectiveness the limitation and control which they have for the past three years exercised in regulation of the emigration of laborers to the United States.

This is the only approach to an immigration convention between Japan and the United States, and this is merely a unilateral declaration of policy. This statement was made useless by the Act of Congress of 1924, which provides that "No alien ineligible to citizenship shall be admitted to the United States unless such alien is admissible as a non-quota immigrant" of one or another of certain specified classes. This effectually debars Japanese of the labor classes, for Japanese aliens are ineligible to citizenship.

The treaty of commerce and navigation of 1911 makes no restriction upon the incoming of Japanese. The provisions are entirely reciprocal. They grant to the Japanese in the United States all that Americans are granted in Japan. Article I reads as follows:

The citizens and subjects of each of the High Contracting Parties shall have liberty to enter, travel and reside in the territories of the other to carry on trade, wholesale and retail, to own or lease and occupy houses, manufactories, warehouses and shops, to employ agents of their choice, to lease land for residential and commercial purposes, and generally to do anything incident to or necessary for trade, upon the same terms as native citizens or subjects, submitting themselves to the laws and regulations there established.

It will be noted that the treaty gives Americans the right to reside in Japan and Japanese a right to reside in the United States for one purpose—*"to carry on trade."* There is no comma following the phrase, ''reside in the territories of the other,'' so that the words which follow it, ''to carry on trade,'' define the purpose of residence. The writer, who was connected with the Department of State during the negotiation of the treaty, knows that this interpretation was that put upon the clause by the American Government. The treaty does not forbid residence for other purposes, but no American could claim that the treaty gives him a right to live in Japan for the purpose of carrying on agriculture. The same is true of Japanese who come to the United States. Agriculture has to do with production; commerce with exchange. The treaty is a treaty of ''commerce and navigation,'' and therefore, deals specifically with these things. It does not limit residence in Japan to those Americans who are there for purposes of trade, but it is intended to define the rights of those who are there for that purpose. And reciprocally this is true also of Japanese in the United States. It should be noted, too, that the article gives the right to own homes, but not the right to own land. The right to lease land is granted provided it is leased for residential and commercial purposes. There is no grant of a right to lease land for agricultural purposes. Such leasing is not forbidden by the treaty, but the treaty is silent upon the question.

RECENT LEGISLATION

This matter of the owning or leasing of land by Orientals for agricultural purposes has become a very serious one in certain states of the Union. It is this which is responsible for much of the present-day agitation against Oriental immigration.

In 1913 the increase of land holdings by Japanese in California led to state legislation limiting land ownership by aliens to those who were eligible to naturalization under the laws of the United States. Orientals who are neither white nor black are ineligible to naturalization. *Leases* of land to aliens not eligible to naturalization were permitted, but were to be limited to three years' duration. But, inasmuch as there are many minor children of Oriental parentage who are native-born American citizens, it has been possible for lands to be purchased in the names of such children, and occupied by their parents as guardians of such minor children. In 1920 attempt was made to deprive the Oriental parents of this natural right to guardianship over their children. The courts, of course, decided against the constitutionality of such legislation.

Even the law limiting ownership of land by aliens to those who are eligible to citizenship can scarcely accomplish the purpose for which it was intended, because there are already in the state of California many Orientals who are native-born Americans, and therefore, held to be American citizens who can, and no doubt will, form land-owning companies, that can purchase or lease all the land that their race may require for agricultural purposes.

The situation in 1916 had become so critical along the Pacific Coast that when a new bill, restricting immigration, was introduced into Congress, attempt was made to incorporate in its text a reference to the "Gentleman's Agreement." The intent was to provide for the exclusion of Japanese laborers in case the "Agreement" should be terminated. The proposed clause would have exempted from the provisions of the law any country that voluntarily refused passports to laborers, but only so long as the restriction was enforced. The Japanese Ambassador at first made no objection to this phraseology, and of course, he did not claim the right to object to any phraseology; but in the following year, 1917, he did intimate to the Department of State that any attempt to make the Gentleman's Agreement a part of the law of the land was contrary to the spirit and purpose of the "Agreement," which was to leave the matter entirely to the voluntary action of the Japanese Government. Various attempts were made to modify the phraseology so as to meet the Japanese objection, and at the same time provide for the exclusion of certain Oriental laborers who were not excluded, either by the Chinese Exclusion Act or by the "Gentleman's Agreement." Finally, a very cumbersome substitute was accepted which excluded immigrants coming from regions bounded by certain meridians of longitude and parallels of latitude.

In the legislatures of a number of north-western states, in 1917, bills were introduced patterned after the California law, but at the request of the Department of State they were abandoned. Since the nation was engaged in war, the Government at Washington thought it an inopportune time to offend the sensibilities of those who were associated with us in the prosecution of the war. But with the coming of peace the agitation has been revived.

REASONS FOR EXCLUSION

The causes for the agitation against Oriental immigration are chiefly of two sorts, racial and economic.

However unreasonable race prejudice may be, it is folly to close one's eyes and pretend that it does not exist. There are men in every race who rise above it, but among the masses it is still potent. The Chinese and Japanese feel a racial antipathy to the European. That I have experienced during a long residence in the Far East. On the other hand the white man regards all colored races as inferior. This race prejudice is an inheritance of the ages, a primitive passion, and primitive passions are still the most powerful forces in human society. The zoning ordinances of certain California cities, which restrict the residence of Orientals to certain districts, have their origin in part in this feeling. Difference of color, difference of language, difference of religion, strange dress, peculiar customs and curious diet, all tend to awaken a feeling of hostility in the breast of the ordinary man, who is the center of his own little world and regards his practices as the hall-mark of civilization.

The zoning ordinances do have sometimes another side, and a better reason for their adoption. The Oriental laborer has been so poorly paid in his own land, as already said, that he has been forced to adopt a very low standard of living. He comes into the United States with his habits pretty well fixed, and is disposed to live—as he has been accustomed to live—in somewhat crowded and insanitary conditions. This, of course, is not true of well-to-do Orientals, whose homes are as clean and attractive as those of their western neighbors.

Mention of the low standard of living suggests at once the economic reason for exclusion. It is the menace of cheap labor, which, if allowed unrestricted entrance to our country, would force American manual laborers to accept wages that are insufficient for the maintenance of an American standard of living.

The plants which we cultivate for food must be protected from competition with the wild, or uncultivated, plants which we call weeds. The more highly developed the plant, the more carefully must it be protected. Otherwise it will degenerate and return toward the wild state in which it originated. Only as a wild plant can it enter into a struggle with wild plants. Now, our civilization is a highly developed and delicate plant, which cannot enter into unrestricted competition with certain other, more hardy, forms of civilization. Restrictive legislation is necessary for its protection.

Conditions in the Orient are improving, it is true, and possibly the time may come when economic conditions East and West may become so nearly alike as to require no such legislation. That condition, however, ought to be brought about by a leveling up in the Orient, not by a leveling down in the West.

LABOR AND WAGES IN THE ORIENT

The hope of such a change is shown in the modification of conditions now going on. Contact with the West in the open cities of China and in the ports of Japan has led to the introduction of western industrialism, with all its evils as well as its blessings. Huge factories have been built, new channels for labor created, and a consequent improvement in wages brought about. This has been accompanied by a partial development of the natural resources of the two countries. These are particularly abundant in China. This alone has benefited labor. Where such changes are going on the standards of living have risen.

Wages in silver in the coast cities of China are from two to four times what they were forty years ago, although they are still miserably inadequate. While wages have increased the cost of living also has increased. The improvement, therefore, is not so great as appears at first glance.

Unskilled labor, which in 1889 in Nanking earned 150 brass cash a day—at that time the equivalent of 14 cents in silver—in 1922 was paid 30 cents in silver (16 cents in American money). But the 150 cash in 1889 purchased seven and one-half pounds of rice, and the 30 cents in 1922 bought thirteen and one-half pounds of rice. This means that wages improved in thirty-three years by the value of six pounds of rice per diem—a gain of 80 per cent. This remarkable improvement, however, was due in large measure to the change which in thirty-three years came to Nanking. In 1889 Nanking was a closed city. Western influence was only beginning to penetrate. To-day it is an open port, where the new industrial system is already established with all the changes which steam and electricity, railways, steamships, and factory life can produce.

Conditions in Shanghai, which has been opened to foreign residence and trade since 1843, furnish a better index to the effects of intercourse with the West than those of an interior city can. In the China Year Book for 1928 there is a chapter by Geo. E. Sokolsky on prices in Shanghai, which gives us some very interesting facts. The lowest living wage there, he says, is 40 cents silver a day, yet there were mill operatives receiving but 22 cents silver a day, about U. S. $0.10 at the low valuation of the Chinese dollar in September, 1928. The Commercial Press at Shanghai made 40 cents a day its minimum wage and Japanese mills averaged 59 cents a day, excluding the wages of foremen. The British American Tobacco Company made an allowance for rice in addition to wages when the price exceeded $8.00 silver a picul, and the Commercial Press also added a sum to wages if rice cost more than $9.00 a picul. If the price of this article was over $9 but less than $14, those receiving $15 a month wages were given a bonus of $2 a month, those whose wages were from $15 to $20 received $1 and those whose pay was from $20 to $40 received no bonus. But, if the price rose above $14 a picul, the wages of the first class mentioned were increased by $3.50 a month, those of the second class by $2.50 and those of the third class $1.00 a month.*

"The years 1925-1931 have been years of great social and political upheaval. There have been strikes and lock-outs, anti-foreign propaganda, communist activity, civil war and depreciation of currency due to issue of paper money. Agriculture has been neglected and all industry disorganized. The price of rice has risen at times to as much as $22 a picul. The wages and prices of the past six years must therefore be considered as abnormal.

"We can better gauge the rate of progress if we take the decade 1912-1921. The wages of unskilled labor in Shanghai on an average increased from $0.30 a day to $0.35, a gain of nearly 17 per cent. Skilled artisans in some instances increased their wages from $0.50 a day to $1.00.* The World War affected conditions to some degree.

* These figures are all for silver unless otherwise mentioned.

"A recent study * of wages and prices in Peking during the period 1900–1925 showed that wages had doubled there during that time, but that the cost of living had also greatly increased so that the real gain to the worker was no more than 8 per cent for the unskilled laborer and 12 per cent for the skilled.

"This rise in the cost of living must be kept constantly in mind in any discussion of the improvement in wages. Sokolsky in the study to which reference has been made, takes the prices of 1913 as 100 and discovers that the increase in the price of rice by the end of 1926 was 91 per cent. The index number for other food was 194.9 and the average for all necessaries was represented by 186.3.

"Labor conditions in China since 1920 have been greatly influenced by the organization of labor unions. The old-time guilds were formed of masters as well as journeymen and apprentices, but the unions have been organized under Russian communist influences and have not only been limited, as elsewhere in the modern industrial world, to employees, but schooled in a radical hostility to employers that has worked injury to themselves. Exorbitant demands for unreasonable increases of wages have led to lockouts and anti-capitalistic outrages have aroused the hatred of the conservative classes who have wreaked vengeance upon the workers in wholesale massacres."

It seems worth while to compare conditions in China with those prevailing in Japan. Official statistics show that in thirty-three gainful occupations in Japan in 1917 the index number of wages was 181.1, the wages of 1900 being taken as 100. But during that same period the advance in the cost of living was also rapid. The index number for rice was 171, and the average for eight staples was 175.1. This would indicate an improvement in 17 years of about 6 per cent. But from an American standpoint the wages are still pitifully small. This will be seen when they are given in terms of American dollars and cents. In 1917 the most highly paid artisans in Japan,

* *Peking, a Social Survey;* by Sidney D. Gamble and Jno. S. Burgess.

according to official statistics, were the brick-layers, who were receiving $0.61 a day. The next were stone-cutters, receiving $0.55 a day. The most poorly paid were women in sericulture and those engaged in farm labor—$0.17 a day. The average of skilled artisans was $0.47, and the average in thirty-three occupations, skilled and unskilled, was $0.30. The condition of women and children employed in the factories, according to a trustworthy American observer,* was most deplorable.

Labor unions in Japan, whose membership had gradually increased to 260,348 in 1928, have brought about some improvement in wages for men, but have done very little for women workers. The average wages for male workers in factories in 1924 was Yen 1.75, in 1925, Yen 1.74, but in 1926, Yen 2.34 a day, which at the market rate of exchange amounted in U. S. money to $0.75¼, $0.71 and $1.07 respectively. But the wages for women operatives remained stationary at Yen 0.96, which at the varying rate of exchange amounted to U. S. $0.41 for 1924.

The Financial and Economic Annual of Japan gives the index number for the average wages of six women workers in factories as 101.4 for 1929. The average wage in U. S. money was $0.49. The average wage a day for five skilled artisans was Yen 2.34 or $1.166. The index number was 103.4. The prices of 1900 being taken as 100.

Some slight improvement has been made in the laws relating to factories. The maximum number of hours for a day's labor is fixed at 11, unless two days are allowed off each month. When an operative is employed over six hours he must be allowed a recess of half an hour. If employed ten hours or more, an hour's recess must be allowed. The average day in factories in 1925 was 10.34 hours. In weaving and dyeing concerns a worker's day was 11.27 hours and in filatures, 12.27. These facts and figures relating to Japan are taken from the **Japan Year Book** for 1928.

The Japanese themselves realize the importance of pro-

* *Modern Japan,* by Amos S. Hershey and Susanne Hershey, pp. 161-168.

tecting their own laborers from competition, for they do not permit the immigration of Chinese manual workers, since that would intensify the struggle for existence. Yet the difference between wage levels in the two countries is negligible. There ought not then to be any objection upon the part of the Japanese Government to the efforts of the United States to protect American labor. Japan, in fact, makes no objection, and for that reason voluntarily refuses passports to laborers. But Japan does not want the United States to enact a law excluding Japanese labor.

Why do we treat China in one way and Japan in another? The answer is simple; Japan has grown to be a mighty military power. The difference in our treatment of the two peoples is discreditable to us. We could have excluded Chinese labor without mentioning the people by name, and thus we should have avoided offending their sensibilities.

A POSSIBLE SOLUTION OF THE PROBLEM

The treaty obligations created by Minister Burlingame and Secretary Seward were the obstacles to an easy solution of the problem when it first presented itself. Out of this complicated situation a condition has arisen which is far from satisfactory. Strict justice would require that the law of exclusion should be general, shutting out all labor immigration from whatever region, if it comes from a country whose wages level and standard of living for laborers are widely different from those of our own land. Such a law seems to be impossible of enactment at present, and we have in recent legislation sought an amelioration of the general problem by admitting from any country in any one year a number not greater than three per cent of those now here who have immigrated from such country. This legislation, however, leaves unaffected the laws excluding Orientals and the "Gentleman's Agreement." [1]

In the opinion of the writer justice would seem to require

[1] Nullified by the Immigration Act of 1924, which provided that, with certain exceptions, "no alien ineligible to citizenship" should be admitted.

two things: (1) for the protection of our own people a general law forbidding all Oriental labor immigration; and (2) for the welfare of the Orientals who are now lawfully here, a law permitting their naturalization, so that they may be absorbed in our citizenship, and not be driven to segregate themselves, as they do now. Their present treatment forces them to close association with their own people, to the preservation of their native language and customs, and the training of their children, whom we call American citizens, to a foreign allegiance. The policy urged would do away with much of the ill feeling which now exists on both sides, and would promote a rapid Americanization of the Orientals now here. Naturalization is a matter wholly within the control of Congress, so that the legislation recommended is quite possible.

CHAPTER XXII

SPHERES OF INTEREST

As men rejoice when they divide the spoil.—Isaiah.

The essential principle of peace is the actual equality of nations in all matters of right or privilege.—Woodrow Wilson.

In 1894 Japan declared war upon China. The excuse was the situation in Korea. The cause was probably a complex one. First there was the desire of Ito to suppress the liberal agitation that was disturbing his government at home, and which had twice in five months led to a dissolution of parliament and a new election. Foreign war unites the factions at home; that is a commonplace of political philosophy. Secondly, there was perhaps the desire of the militarists to use the splendid war machine which, with the aid of German officers, they had built up, the war machine that was to prove to the Western world Japan's worthiness to stand alongside any of the great powers—the war machine that was to convince these powers that Japan could no longer be treated as an inferior state, but could and would make a tariff to suit herself—could and would exercise jurisdiction over the strangers within her gates. And lastly there was the old, old cause, the lust for power, the ambition to become the arbiter of affairs in the Orient, the desire, too, to glorify the state and extend its territorial boundaries.

KOREA'S RELATIONSHIP TO CHINA

Korea seems to have been connected with China since a colonization of the peninsula by Chinese in the twelfth

482

century B.C. Sometimes it had been a tributary state, sometimes a province of the empire, sometimes a vassal in revolt, but it had never been tributary to Japan. It is separated from Japan by a narrow strait, and has several times tempted Japanese aggression. Hideyoshi tried to subdue it, and was defeated by the skillful strategy and superior seamanship of a Korean admiral.[1] The relation of Korea to China puzzled Western diplomats. ''How,'' they asked, ''can Korea be tributary to China, and at the same time be permitted by China to make treaties with foreign powers and receive foreign envoys?'' From the oriental viewpoint there was no inconsistency. Mr. Rockhill likened the relationship to that sustained by a younger to an elder brother in a Chinese family. He is independent in the management of most affairs, but he owes a certain reverence to his elder brother.[2] When asked if Korea was free to enter into treaty relations with other powers China replied that she was. In fact, the Chinese government urged the United States to make a treaty with Korea, and gave assistance to that end in 1882.

Yet in 1887, when the first Korean Minister to the United States was about to present his credentials, the Chinese Minister endeavored to prevent such action except through the agency of the Chinese Legation. This, of course, the American government would not permit. It was this anomalous character of the relationship between China and Korea that made easy a war between China and Japan. Japan accepted the western theory and practice in international relationship. China clung to her belief that Korea was a vassal state, yet free to please herself in her foreign intercourse. We seem to-day to be approaching the Chinese theory, since various states in the British Empire are insisting upon the right to independent action in their relations with their neighbors, while at the same time retaining their places in that empire.

[1] See ''The Influence of the Sea on the Political History of Japan,'' by Admiral Ballard, pp. 44-67.
[2] China's Intercourse with Korea, p. 3.

OUTBREAK OF WAR

The statement made by some writers [3] that the immediate cause of the war between China and Japan was a breach by China of the Tientsin Treaty of 1885 is incorrect. Both powers had agreed in that treaty not to send troops into Korea without first giving notice one to another. The King of Korea appealed to China, her overlord, for assistance in suppressing a rebellion. China responded by sending a small force, but first notified Japan of intention to do so.[4] Japan, although uninvited, also sent a force—larger than that of China.

China, however, in notifying Japan of her intention to send assistance to Korea, said: "Such action is in harmony with our constant practice to protect our tributary states." To this Japan replied that she "had never recognized Korea as a state tributary to China."

Korea in the meantime had put down the rebellion unaided by either China or Japan. Japan proposed to China that they should together reform the Korean administration. China declined on the ground that she did not interfere in the internal affairs of her vassal states. Japan then gave notice that she would undertake the task alone. War was the result. Foreign residents of China and Japan who knew the real character of the two armies never had the slightest doubt about the outcome. China, a huge empire of between 300 and 400 millions of people, and covering a vast continental area, formed a group of provinces loosely held together by the corrupt, and inefficient government of a degenerate foreign dynasty. The people were parochial in their patriotism, divided by dialects and local prejudices, and were hindered in coöperation by lack of railways or other inland communications. The Chinese army existed chiefly on paper and, except for Viceroy Li's army in the north, was equipped with spears and muzzle-loading muskets. The fleet made a better showing. The

[3] McLaren's "Political History of Japan," p. 230.
[4] Morse's "International Relations of the Chinese Empire, Vol. III, pp. 21, 22.

only important naval engagement resulted in the withdrawal of the Japanese. But the ammunition of the Chinese was nearly exhausted, thanks to a corrupt government, and the day following the battle they sought refuge at Weihaiwei.

Japan was a small nation of less than fifty millions, occupying a compact group of islands ruled by a virile and progressive government. The people were thoroughly patriotic and knit together in their devotion to the Mikado. The strife of political partisanship was forgotten in the united clamor for war. The army and navy worked together as parts of one well-oiled machine. Victory perched upon the Japanese banners from the start. China was humiliated, and on April 17, 1895, agreed in the Treaty of Peace to recognize the complete independence of Korea.

MURDER OF KOREAN QUEEN

But the declaration of Korea's complete independence and autonomy did not put an end to Japan's efforts to reform the corrupt administration of Korea. There were two parties there. That of the Queen, who was a much stronger character than the King, was opposed to Japanese tutelage. Her father-in-law, who had once been Regent during the minority of his son, was more favorable to Japan. Moreover he disliked his daughter-in-law. The Japanese Minister was Viscount Miura. He unfortunately allowed himself to give support to a plot for the removal of the Queen. On the 8th of October, 1895, a large party of Japanese and Koreans surrounded the palace of the Queen, forced their way past the guards, murdered the Queen, wrapped her body in a blanket, saturated it with kerosene and burned it in the court-yard.[5] The Japanese Minister denied all knowledge of the crime. For some days the report of the murder was declared to be false. The Queen was said to be alive but in hiding. The pro-Japanese party took possession of the Government, but public opinion

[5] Hulbert's "Passing of Korea," Chap. IX, p. 139.

demanded an investigation of the crime. The evidence of Miura's complicity was convincing. He was recalled by his government and brought to trial. The court found that he had taken part in planning the assassination but that there was no evidence of his participation in the murder. As a representative of the Japanese Government he could not well be punished;[6] but he returned to private life. While Japan could not well punish her own chosen representative, however, there does not seem to be any good reason for rewarding him, unless she approved of his action. Yet when the horrified world had forgotten the murder, the Japanese Government, in 1910, made Miura a Privy Councillor, an exalted post which he retained until his death in 1925.[7]

The terms of peace between China and Japan included the cession of Formosa, the Pescadores and the southern part of Manchuria, known as the Liaotung Peninsula, together with the payment of an indemnity of two hundred million taels.

RUSSIA, FRANCE AND GERMANY INTERVENE

Before the signature of the treaty the Chinese negotiator, Li Hung-chang, apparently had received assurance from Russia that any cession of territory on the mainland would be protested. For her protest she probably had been promised certain compensation by China. Russia persuaded France and Germany to join her in this action, which, in May, 1895, took the form of a joint note recommending Japan, for the sake of the peace of the Far East, to restore South Manchuria to China. Japan had no option but to comply. She received an additional thirty million taels for the retrocession, but the offensive advice of the three powers was neither forgotten nor forgiven. She bided her time.

Russia received compensation the following year, when,

[6] See Mackenzie's "Tragedy of Korea," pp. 263-268. Official report of the trial.
[7] Japan Year Book.

at the coronation of the Tsar, the Chinese envoy, Li Hung-chang, agreed to a secret alliance between Russia and China for the protection of their respective territories against aggression by a third power. When the need for action came, however, in the war of 1904, China declined to observe the treaty and maintained neutrality.

During this visit of Li to Russia he also signed an agreement permitting Russia to biuld the Chinese Eastern Railway, across Northern Manchuria to Vladivostok, thus avoiding the long detour around the bend of the Amur River.

In the autumn of 1897 some brigands in Shantung raided and looted a village in the south-western part of that province, and killed a number of people, among whom were two Germans. This gave opportunity for a dramatic presentation of Germany's claim. A portion of the fleet rushed to the Bay of Kiaochow, landed blue-jackets, drove off the Chinese troops from the forts at Tsingtao, and seized that little fishing village. Demand was made for the punishment of the murderers and for compensation to the families of the victims. But in addition the Germans asked for the removal of the Governor of the Province who, according to Chinese theory, was responsible for good order within his jurisdiction. A large indemnity, too, was demanded for the German mission, with which to build mission houses and churches.

This was in November, 1897. Before March, 1898, Germany had decided to demand the lease of the Bay, having in the meantime obtained, as it seems, the consent of Russia, who in the secret treaty of 1896 had been promised a lease of the place. The lease of Kiaochow Bay for 99 years was signed on March 6, 1898, and carried with it the right to build certain railways, to work mines in a specified region, and an option on all public works in the province of Shantung requiring foreign capital or skilled labor.

This was followed immediately by a demand from Russia for corresponding privileges in South Manchuria. A convention, signed on March 27, 1898, granted Russia a lease for 25 years of the Kuantung Peninsula, which is the southern portion of that territory from which Russia had just forced Japan. With this lease was granted the right to build a railway to connect Port Arthur and Dalny (now Dairen) with the Chinese Eastern Railway. Two weeks later, on April 10th, France demanded her compensation— a lease for 99 years of the bay known as Kuangchou Wan, on the southern coast of China, and a concession for a railway from Tongking into Yünnan. The lease was signed on the 27th of May following.

The growl of the Russian Bear had awakened the British Lion, so that on June 9th and July 1, 1898, Great Britain had demanded and obtained a lease of the hinterland of Kowloon opposite Hongkong, and the port of Weihaiwei in Shantung opposite Port Arthur, which had just been leased to Russia. The former enlarged Hongkong colony from 29 to 405 square miles; the latter lease was to terminate when Russia should surrender Port Arthur and Dalny. There was a lull of a few months, but in March, 1899, Italy demanded the lease of Sanmen Bay, in Chekiang. This demand China refused. Instead of yielding preparations were made for war.

SPHERES OF INTEREST

Prior to the signing of the various leases mentioned, France on March 15, 1897, had asked of China an assurance that the Island of Hainan would never be alienated or ceded by China to any other foreign power. China replied that she had no intention of alienating it at all.

This led, on February 11, 1898, to a similar exchange of notes between Great Britain and China regarding the non-alienation of territory in the Yangtze Valley, and on April 4th of the same year, to a request from France respecting the non-alienation of territory in the three south-western provinces of China. On the 26th of the same month Japan and China exchanged notes concerning alienation of territory in the province of Fukien, opposite Formosa. In the following year, April 28, 1899, Russia

GATE OF RUSSIAN LEGATION, PEIPING.

EAST GATE OF LEGATION QUARTER, PEIPING.

and Great Britain entered into an agreement respecting their spheres of interest in China. Great Britain was not to seek for her subjects any railway concessions north of the Great Wall, and Russia was to avoid asking for railway grants in the Yangtze Valley.

Russia two months later, in an exchange of notes with China, secured an option on railway construction northwards or north-eastwards from Peking, provided foreign capital should be needed for the building of such lines.

In the matter of the notes relating to non-alienation of territory, China may be considered as having made a diplomatic blunder, in that she did not take her stand firmly upon her sovereign rights, and refuse to give any such assurances as were asked or to discuss the matter at all. In her reply she appears to have tacitly admitted a right on the part of the powers concerned to exact pledges from her. In this subtle way the several powers mentioned each laid the basis for a claim to a sphere of interest in China.

The Chinese people were greatly incensed by the aggressive policy of the Western powers thus indicated. Sir Charles Beresford visited China during the period in which these demands were made. After his return to Europe he published a volume called "The Break-up of China." It looked indeed for a time as though the old empire would fall to pieces. The Chinese newspapers were filled with denunciation of the Europeans, who, it was said, were about to "Slice China as a ripe melon."

THE AMERICAN ATTITUDE

Apologists for Japan's action at the Paris Peace Conference regarding Kiaochow Leased Territory have held that the American people were inconsistent in opposing the Shantung clauses of the Treaty of Versailles, since they said nothing about the seizure of the place by Germany, which was the original offense. But the critics forget that before the news of Germany's lease of Kiaochow was

made known, in March, 1898, the United States was in a
state of intense excitement over the destruction of the
U. S. warship *Maine,* which had been blown up in the
harbor of Havana on the 15th of February preceding.
The people were clamoring for war with Spain, which
was declared shortly afterwards, and in view of that approaching conflict it would have been the height of unwisdom to have incensed the German Government by
protesting its actions in China.

Nevertheless, the situation was one that was not over-
looked by Secretary Hay. Not long after the treaty of
peace with Spain was ratified, the Secretary, in September,
1899, addressed a note to each of the powers concerned
in the leases of Chinese territory, and in the establishment in that country of spheres of interest. In these notes
he asked the adherence of these governments to a policy
of equality of treatment for the commerce and navigation
of all nations, in such leased territories and spheres of
interest. This policy has been termed the policy of the
Open Door.

What Secretary Hay asked specifically was:

First (that each of the interested powers) Will in no way
interfere with any treaty port or any vested interest within any
so-called "Sphere of interest" or leased territory it may have in
China.

Second, That the Chinese tariff of the time being shall apply
to all merchandise landed or shipped to all such ports as are
within said "sphere of interest" (unless they be free ports), no
matter to what nationality it may belong, and that duties so
levied shall be collected by the Chinese Government.   •

Third, That it will levy no higher harbor dues on vessels of
another nationality frequenting any port in such "sphere" than
shall be levied on vessels of its own nationality, and no higher
railroad charges over lines built, controlled or operated within
its "sphere" on merchandise belonging to citizens or subjects of
other nationalities transported through such "sphere" than shall
be levied on similar merchandise belonging to its own nationals
transported over equal distances.

The governments addressed were those of Great Britain,
France, Germany, Italy, Russia and Japan. All declared

their adherence to the policy thus outlined. There are two things to be particularly remembered with respect to Secretary Hay's note: (1) It recognizes the existence of "spheres of interest" in China, although the phrase is put within quotation points. It does not protest against the claims to such "spheres," nor against the methods by which the leases of territory were obtained. It accepts a situation which seemed to him already existing. (2) No account was taken, in the correspondence, of China's feelings or desires in regard to the establishment of "so-called spheres of interest," neither was China asked to pledge herself to maintain an open door policy. The Chinese government seems to have been treated as negligible. Perhaps this was due to the feeling then prevailing throughout the western world that China was about to break to pieces. The Secretary was interested chiefly in the protection of American commerce, and sought to prevent the erection of tariff barriers in the "spheres of influence" less favorable to American trade than the existing Chinese treaty tariff.

His recognition of the spheres of interest was made still more evident when, in 1900, the American navy desired to lease a coaling station in the Samsah Inlet, in Fukien, within the sphere of interest claimed by Japan. Before mentioning the desire to China, he instructed the American Minister in Japan to ascertain whether the Japanese Government would make objection to the negotiation with China of such a lease. To this the Japanese Government, on December 10, 1900, replied declining to accede to the proposal. This action of Secretary Hay, moreover, was taken after the Boxer rising had shown how China viewed the whole policy of "spheres of interest."

THE BOXER RISING

It is sometimes stated incorrectly that the seizure by the Germans of Kiaochow Bay, which led to the policy of spheres of interest, was an act of reprisal for an attack by Boxers upon foreign missionaries, in other words that it was a punishment of China for tolerating Boxerism. This is an exact reversal of the facts regarding the rise of the Boxers. It was the seizure of Kiaochow and the leases of other ports that followed, together with the declaration of spheres of interest, that caused the Boxer rising. The murder of two German missionaries was a crime committed by ordinary brigands, of whom there are plenty at all times in China. It was not the result of any anti-foreign or anti-Christian movement. A whole village was attacked. It was the misfortune of the missionaries that they were staying there when the attack occurred. The murder of aliens has sometimes happened in our own land, yet no demand for the lease of a bay, the removal of a governor of a state, or the grant of railway and mining concessions in reprisal has ever been made by the government of the nation to which such aliens have belonged. It was the weakness of China that made possible such aggression there.

The first effect of the forced leases of territory to European powers, and their claims to various spheres of interest in China, was an earnest attempt by the liberal minded Chinese to bring about a reform of the Government. The young Emperor, Kuanghsü, had taken the reins into his own hands in 1889. One of his tutors, Wen T'un-ho, was known as a progressive man, and the Emperor, although a weakling, was disposed to follow his tutor's advice. There were three men whose writings had great influence upon the mind of the sovereign. Chang Chihtung, the Viceroy at Hankow, a liberal conservative, had published at the close of the Japanese war a small volume called "Learn," in which he urged the introduction of Western education, which he recognized as the source of Western power, and which, with Western industries and Western military organization, had given Japan the victory. Western religion he held to be unnecessary to China, and republicanism he regarded as dangerous.

The second writer was K'ang Yu-wei, a brilliant scholar but inexperienced in statecraft. He was an enthusiast who, on being recommended to the Emperor by his tutor, was called to Court, and for three months dazed the empire by a rapid succession of edicts which the young Emperor was induced to issue, and which aimed at the immediate transformation of China. The educational system was to be changed. The army was to be reorganized. Railways were to be built and mines to be opened. Useless offices were abolished and ultra-conservative officials were cashiered. Every one of the proposed changes was practicable and looked toward the modernization of the state, but the pace was too swift and the method employed lacked tact. It is noteworthy that the woman who halted the course of reform and turned back the tide of progress, was herself four years later issuing decrees of exactly the same tenor, in a vain effort to save the falling dynasty.

The third man to whom I have referred was Liang Ch'i-ch'ao, the foremost scholar of China in his day and one of the wisest of her statesmen. In 1898 he was editing a newspaper whose brilliant style and trenchant criticisms gave it a remarkably large circulation and great influence. It was the organ of the reformers. But there were two parties at Court, one composed largely of young men devoted to the Emperor, the other made up of older and more experienced men who supported the Empress Dowager. The Manchu Princes very generally sided with the Dowager, and were opposed to any movement that seemed to threaten their prerogatives, but there were a few progressive men among them.

Suddenly in 1898, on the morning of the autumnal sacrifice to Confucius, the officials leaving the sacred courts to return to their homes were startled by the report of a *coup-d'etat* at Peking.

In 1903 I was a guest at a birthday entertainment given by His Excellency Hu Yü-fen, a Cabinet Minister. The principal court of his palace had been converted into a theatre, and a famous troupe of players had been brought from Shanghai to entertain the guests. As I sat watching the play Mr. Hu seated himself beside me and asked if

I knew who the actors were. I answered that I did not. He then said: "These are the players who smuggled Liang Ch'i-ch'ao and T'an Tzu-t'ung into the palace of the Emperor five years ago." The story has been told in various forms. As gathered from various sources it seems to be as follows:

The Shanghai company, playing in Peking, received an invitation to play in the palace. They went, of course, and filled an engagement lasting several days. They went in and out the gates of the Forbidden City, repeatedly passing from their inn to the Court theatre and back again. The young reformers had some important message to convey to the Emperor. They were allowed to join the company and so pass in unobserved. The young Emperor between the acts was accustomed to visiting the green room, and thus came into conversation with the two messengers. It was probably the rumor of the *coup-d'etat* that was being planned by the party of the Empress Dowager that disturbed them, and apparently they suggested the course to be taken, which was to anticipate the action of the conservatives and strike first. At a subsequent meeting one night Yuan Shih-k'ai was summoned from Tientsin. He was known to be a liberal and, it was presumed, would support the Emperor. According to the account given me he was commanded by the Emperor to arrest and execute Jung-lu, the commander of the principal army of the empire, with headquarters at Tientsin, and bring that force to Peking to surround the palace of the Empress Dowager so as to prevent her interference with the government. Jung-lu was a childhood playmate of the Empress Dowager, and was the young officer of the Banner Corps who had saved her from assassination at the hands of court intriguers when she was returning from Jehol after her husband, the Emperor Hsienfeng, had died there in 1861. Jung-lu was a staunch friend of Her Majesty, and there was no way of getting the army for the protection of the Emperor except by his removal. Yuan, too, was the man chiefly responsible for the reorganization and general improvement of the army that was in progress, and was the very man therefore to head the troops.

But, unknown to the Emperor, Yuan Shih-k'ai and Jung-lu were sworn brothers; that is to say, they had entered into a blood covenant and were bound by a solemn oath to protect one another. Yuan listened to the orders of His Majesty and dissembled his real feelings. He appeared to fall in with the plot, but early the following morning, instead of waiting for the imperial warrant and the green arrow, which gave its possessor the power of life and death, he hurriedly left the city and returned to Tientsin. When a court officer arrived at his quarters with the Emperor's command he was not to be found. The Emperor then sent for T'an and gave to him the death warrant, written on yellow satin, and the green arrow, and directed him to go at once to Tientsin and find Yuan. If Yuan should refuse to carry out the orders then T'an was to execute them. "On no account lose sight of Yuan Shih-k'ai," was the last warning word of the Emperor. T'an went to Tientsin, found Yuan and delivered the message. "Very well," said Yuan, "let us go to Jung-lu's yamen." On reaching the gate Yuan told T'an to wait there, lest, while he went in one way, Jung-lu should come out by another. When Yuan saw Jung-lu he showed him the warrant and the green arrow, but was true to his oath. He allowed Jung-lu to get out by the back door, and spent some time in the yamen keeping T'an waiting. Jung-lu obtained a locomotive and car and rushed to Peking, then to the palace of the Empress Dowager, where, falling upon his knees in the doorway, he shouted: *"Chiu ming, Chiu ming"* (Save life, save life!) The Dowager appeared, asked the cause of the outcry and, upon learning of the plot, sent for the Emperor. "Boy," said she, "what is the meaning of this?" Then, snatching the seals away from him, she had him carried off to an island in the Western Park, where he was confined until the capture of Peking by the allied forces in 1900. The next day after his incarceration he was forced to sign a decree declaring that he was too ill to rule, and begging the Empress Dowager to resume the regency.

In the meantime T'an, at the gate of Jung-lu's yamen, waited for sometime for Yuan to appear. Then he remembered the Emperor's parting warning. It was too late. As he sought to enter the courtyard he met Yuan coming out. The latter said: "Jung-lu is not in his yamen; I have looked everywhere for him." T'an knew that he had been betrayed. He hurried over to the British settlement and explained the situation to K'ang Yu-wei and Liang Ch'i-ch'ao, who were staying there. They begged him to accompany them as they boarded the China Merchants' Steamer *Anping* for Shanghai. T'an refused, saying that he had disobeyed the Emperor and would return to Peking. He was a highly educated young man, son of the Governor of the Province of Hupei; but that did not save him. The next morning he and ten other young reformers were beheaded in the Vegetable Market Place of Peking—the common execution ground.

Friends in Tientsin telegraphed to Shanghai that the reform leaders, K'ang and Liang, were on a steamer bound for that port. The news of the coup at Peking, too, was spread abroad, and the reactionaries at the Capital sent orders to the Taotai at Shanghai to arrest the reformers upon their arrival. The steamer would land at the Chinese wharf, and the native police were in waiting there.

At the time I was serving as Vice Consul General at Shanghai. There was great excitement in the settlement. The British Consul General obtained a launch and went down the river to meet the incoming steamer. At Woosung he halted the vessel, which had a European as captain, and was received on board. He urged the two fugitives to accompany him, which they did. Then, ordering the launch to cross the river to the P. & O. steamer lying there, he put them on board and they escaped to Hongkong.

This failure of the reform movement drove many to join the secret societies that were conspiring for the overthrow of the dynasty. China is the paradise of secret societies. One of them was the *I Ho Tuan*, or *I ho Ch'üan*. It was known by both names. The former means "The Patriotic United Trainband"; the latter is "The Patriotic United Fists." In both names the purpose of the society is evident. It was a patriotic union for the defense of the State; but the use of the word "Fist," and the peculiar calisthenic exercises in which the members indulged, led the first translators of the term to call it a society of boxers. But it had nothing to do with boxing.

The aim of the society, when originally established, was the overthrow of the Manchu Dynasty, which the people held responsible for the misfortune which had fallen upon the country, particularly the aggressions of Western powers. The earliest placards put out by them show this beyond all question.

But the Empress Dowager and her reactionary supporters were shrewd enough to convince the leaders, either by bribery or otherwise, that the foreigners were to blame, and thus persuade them to turn their weapons against the hated intruders.

The Boxers met usually in Buddhist temples. There they were trained in the performance of certain physical and spiritual exercises that were to work enchantment and make them immune to foreign bullets. Strict observance of the prescribed régime was necessary. Any neglect would break the charm. If any fell in battle that would be proof of his sin.

By such training as this a wonderful morale was developed. Many were duped into the belief that by these arts they were made bullet-proof. The Empress Dowager, herself, appears to have believed that such a force was invulnerable and would be able to drive the foreigners into the sea. She had been taught that all these foreigners were barbarians, coming from small islands in the sea, and that they could easily be overwhelmed and expelled from the country. Her best advisers knew that this belief was unfounded, and deplored the folly of engaging in a war upon the rest of the world, but this advice was thrust aside for that of ignorant princes, superstition mongers and fakirs.

Following upon the seizure of Kiaochow by the Germans, and the demands of various powers for leases and spheres of interest, there came through 1898 a series of anti-foreign outbreaks in all parts of China, and rebellion against the dynasty in the south and west. In the autumn several of the powers sent guards to Peking to protect their legations. They remained through the winter, when Peking was almost inaccessible, and were sent away in the following spring. But in 1899 the disorders continued throughout the whole empire, taking more and more the form of an anti-foreign, rather than anti-dynastic, movement. The demands of Italy, backed by war-ships and the support of Great Britain, Germany and France,[8] and the development of German plans in Shantung, led to troop concentrations by China and a spasmodic effort to raise additional revenues for the war chest. The feeling in Shantung was especially bitter. The murder of a British missionary there in December brought about the removal of the Governor, Yü-hsien, and the appointment of Yuan Shih-K'ai in his stead. This was a fortunate change for Shantung, but Yü-hsien was received with honor by the Empress Dowager and given the Governorship of Shansi, where by his orders in 1900 fifty-four missionaries were put to death in his yamen.

From September, 1899, onwards the aims of the Boxers appear to have been consistently anti-foreign. Their attacks were directed against foreigners of all nationalities, and against Chinese Christians and all Chinese who sympathized with Europeans or favored the use of European inventions or any goods of foreign origin. Such Chinese were stigmatized as "Secondary devils." In May, 1900, legation guards were again sent to Peking. This small force of 458 officers and men, aided by 75 volunteers from the legations and missions and a few armed Chinese con-

[8] Morse's International Relations of the Chinese Empire, Vol. III, p. 124.

verts, held the legations in the south-eastern part of Peking and the Roman Catholic mission premises in the north-western part, through a siege of 55 days, during most of which period they were under rifle and shell fire. They were thus instrumental in saving the lives of a thousand foreigners and three thousand Chinese Christians.

Communication with Peking was broken on June 10, 1900. The same day Admiral Seymour, with detachments from the British, American, German and other war-ships numbering a little more than 2000 men, started from Tientsin for Peking to rescue the legations. They crossed the river at Yangtsun unopposed by the Chinese troops there, who numbered 4000 and who were decidedly friendly. As yet the Government was not openly supporting the anti-foreign movement. But as fast as Seymour's force advanced Boxers tore up the railway track before him and behind him. They showed wonderful courage, these fanatical bands, marching up against machine guns in the belief that they could not be killed.

Admiral Seymour never reached Peking. He had to build a railway as he advanced, and the number of wounded daily increased. On June 16th he was compelled to turn back to Tientsin, repairing the railway as he retreated. In the meantime the Admirals at Taku decided to take the forts at the mouth of the Hai Ho. The demand on June 16th for their surrender was resisted by the Chinese, and they were captured on the morning of the 17th. The American Admiral refused to take part in this attack, holding that the United States was not at war with China and that such action would endanger the lives of the foreigners in the interior and cause a union of Chinese forces against Seymour's column.

In this attitude he was supported by the American Government. His judgment seems to have been confirmed by the result, for immediately the Chinese declared war on the foreigners, and Seymour's little column was harassed, not only by Boxers, but by regular troops. The Legations, too, were on June 19th, given twenty-four hours in which to leave the city, which it was impossible for them to do under the circumstances. Baron von Kettler, the German Minister, was killed on the 20th, on his way to the Foreign Office, and on June 24th, the Empress Dowager issued a barbarous decree for the extermination of the foreigners wherever found. The Viceroys of the southern and central provinces refused to execute this foolish and wicked decree. They were joined by Yuan Shih-k'ai, Governor of Shantung, and by Tuan-fang, Acting Governor of Shensi. The latter sent the missionaries in his province under guard to Hankow. Jung-lu, the close friend of the Dowager Empress and once her most trusted adviser, in vain tried to stem the tide of folly. He informed the Viceroys in the south of the real situation. Thus all China, save three provinces, withdrew support from Peking.

This attitude of Jung-lu was not understood at the time by the Europeans in China. They knew him simply as the friend of the Empress Dowager, and clamored for his head when peace negotiations were begun, but better counsels prevailed. He called at the American Legation after peace was restored, and told us that we should one day learn that he had opposed the war and had done what he could to save foreigners from attack. This now we know to be the truth.

There are five other names that deserve to be held in honor by Americans and Europeans. Yüan-chang and Hsü Ching-cheng, in telegraphing the decree of June 24th which ordered the extermination of foreigners, had deliberately altered the word "slay" to "protect," and were sawn asunder in punishment of their daring disobedience. The son of the former told me the story of his father's martyrdom. Three other heroes were Li-shan, Lien-yüan, and Hsü Jung-i, who were put to death for opposing the declaration of war. Well does Kipling say:

> Not in the camp his victory lies,
>   Nor triumph in the market place,
> Who is his nation's sacrifice
>   To turn the judgment from his race.

Such courageous characters as these, and the endurance

of thousands of Chinese Christians who refused to recant in the presence of death and who sealed their faith with their blood, give us a better understanding of the Chinese than the cruel decrees of a selfish ruler or the barbarity of a frenzied mob.

PEACE NEGOTIATIONS

The summer of 1900 had harvested the sowing of 1898 and '99. The policy of spheres of interest had been met by the folly of Boxerism and the awful massacres perpetrated in Chihli, Shansi and Honan.

Secretary Hay comprehended the situation as apparently he had not understood it in 1899. Before the relieving force had captured Tientsin or started thence for Peking he seems to have made up his mind to two courses; first, to refuse to hold the Chinese people responsible for the wickedness of the Peking Court, and, secondly, to temper as far as possible the demands that would be made by an outraged world for reprisals.

It was well-known that the Emperor, the legitimate ruler of China, had had no sympathy with the reactionary movement headed by the Empress Dowager, and the consistent attitude of the American Department of State was that the Chinese Government had been temporarily overpowered by the Boxer element.

In reply to a telegram from the French Government dated July 2d, proposing that the powers should agree to maintain the territorial *status quo* in China, Secretary Hay replied in a circular communication to the seven principal powers, declaring the policy of the United States. This, he said, "is to seek a solution which may bring about permanent safety and peace to China, preserve Chinese territorial and administrative entity, protect all rights guaranteed to friendly powers by treaty and international law, and safe guard for the world the principle of equal and impartial trade with all parts of the Chinese Empire." The powers addressed agreed in this declaration of policy.

By this the Open Door came to mean much more than equality of opportunity in certain spheres of interest. Its scope was enlarged and included pledges to abstain from seizure of Chinese territory and from interference with Chinese administration.

The American Minister, Mr. Conger, who had shared with other Ministers and with the military commanders the anxiety and responsibility of protecting the foreign community in Peking during the siege, was given leave of absence for a few months, and Mr. Rockhill was sent out as a special commissioner to represent the United States in the peace negotiations. He knew China, and appreciated the many good qualities of Chinese character. He was well qualified, therefore, to carry out the moderating policy which Secretary Hay desired to have adopted. His influence throughout the negotiations was exercised in behalf of clemency, the reduction as far as possible of demands for death sentences, and the lightening of the burden of punitive indemnities to be put upon China. But even after the powers had been induced to agree upon a lump sum to be divided among themselves, it still remained so large as to create financial difficulties for the Chinese Government and hinder the execution of the reforms so greatly needed.

The settlement of the Boxer troubles by the protocol of 1901 was nevertheless a lenient one for China. It gave the old empire a new lease of life, and the pledges of the powers to respect its territorial integrity and avoid interference with its administration would, it was hoped, prevent further foreign aggression.

ADHERENTS OF THE OPEN DOOR POLICY

Spheres of interest, however, still remained. As we have seen, in the December following Secretary Hay's note of July 3, 1900, he had recognized Japan's sphere of interest in Fukien, when approaching that power in regard to the lease of a bay on China's coast for a coaling station.

But it follows that in so doing he could not have recognized any right in the possession of Japan inconsistent with the pledges just given "to respect China's territorial integrity and administrative entity."

The principle of the Open Door Policy as thus amended was re-affirmed by Great Britain and Germany on October 16, 1900, in an agreement in which these two powers declared that they would uphold for "all Chinese territory" a policy of equality of opportunity for the trade of all nations, and that they would not take advantage of the circumstances then existing to obtain for themselves any territorial advantage, but would seek to maintain undiminished the territorial conditions of the Chinese Empire.

The protocol in settlement of the Boxer troubles had scarcely been signed when the world was startled by the news of the Anglo-Japanese alliance of January 30, 1902. This was doubtless prompted by Russian aggressive movements in the Manchurian provinces of China. The policy of the Open Door was again emphatically reaffirmed, the two powers expressly declaring that they were "Specially interested in maintaining the independence and territorial integrity of the empire of China and the empire of Korea, and in securing equal opportunities in those countries for the commerce and industry of all nations."

Further support to the policy was given by the agreement of June 10, 1907, between Russia and Japan. Additional emphasis was given to these pledges in the Root-Takahira notes of November 30, 1908, declaring the common policy of the United States and Japan in the region of the Pacific Ocean, including a determination "to preserve the common interest of all powers in China by supporting by all pacific means at their disposal the independence and integrity of China and the principle of equal opportunity for commerce and industries of all nations in that empire."

Yet all these declarations apparently are to be interpreted in a Pickwickian sense, for when China entered into a contract on May 17, 1916, with Messrs. Siems & Carey, a firm of American engineers associated with the

American International Corporation, for the construction
of 1500 miles of railway, afterwards reduced to 1100 miles,
to be selected from a list of proposed lines, the firm found
itself blocked at every turn by the claims of various governments to options on railway building in the districts
concerned. One of the first proposals was for a line to
be built from Fengcheng in Shansi to Ninghsia in Kansuh.
The Russian government objected to the construction of
such a line on the ground that it extended through a region
reserved for Russian enterprise. Yet the agreement to
which the Russian government referred had no relation
to lines north-west or west of Peking, but only lines to be
built northwards or north-eastwards from Peking. At
that time the secret agreement of 1910 between Russia and
Japan giving the former a free hand in western Inner
Mongolia was unknown to other governments and had never
been recognized by China. These claims were formally
abandoned by the Soviet government in 1924. The next
line considered by the Siems-Carey firm was to be built
from Chuchow, on the Canton-Hankow Railway in Hunan
Province, to Yamchow on the southern coast of Kuangtung.
To this the French Government objected that the construction of the proposed line would violate the secret
understanding of September 26, 1914, embodied in an
exchange of notes between the French Minister in Peking
and the Chinese Minister for Foreign Affairs. This arrangement granted to French citizens an option on railway and mining enterprise in the province of Kuangsi,
through which the proposed line was to be built. The
Ministry in 1916 apparently was ignorant of the existence of such an agreement, and the American Government was disposed to question the value of an option of
which no public notice had been given. The American
engineers then undertook the survey of a line from Chou-
chiak'ou in Honan, via Siangyang in Hupei, into the
province of Szechuen. The survey disclosed a route into
Szechuen presenting fewer engineering difficulties, it was
claimed, than that to be taken by the Hankow-Szechuen
branch of the Hukuang Railways, contract for which was

signed in 1911 with the Four-Power Group. The British Government objected to the Siems & Carey project, on the ground that some years ago a Viceroy of Wuchang promised a British Consul General at Hankow that British capitalists should have a first option on lines to be built in the province of Hupei, which was to be crossed by the proposed line. Yet the central government had no record of any such agreement. Finally, the engineering company was to be employed in the improvement of the Grand Canal, under a contract between the Chinese Government and the American International Corporation which was to provide a loan for the purpose.

But the Grand Canal crosses Shantung Province, and the Japanese Government claimed to be heirs of all the rights formerly belonging to Germany in that province, among which was an option on all public works that should require foreign capital or foreign skilled labor. The American Government had declined to recognize that Germany had a monopoly of such enterprises in Shantung, and the German Government itself had declared that it did not claim a monopoly nor any exclusive rights in Shantung.[9] The Chinese Government, as bound by the convention with Germany, notified that power of its desire to make a loan for the improvement of the Canal, and the German Government, then engaged in the World War, declared that it had no interest in the undertaking. The American International Corporation, however, to silence objection, granted Japanese capitalists an interest in the enterprise to an amount of five-twelfths of the proposed loan. The loan, for six million dollars at seven per cent, has not yet been issued.

SPECIAL INTERESTS

Thus it will be seen that the pledges to maintain an open door, with equality of opportunity for the economic activity of the nationals of all countries, are to be interpreted as qualified by the special interests of the various

[9] Count von Bülow to the Reichstag, March 3, 1902.

powers in the regions where they claim to possess spheres of interest. In the correspondence between the United States and Russia, regarding the open door in Manchuria, Russia declared, on February 9, 1902: "There is no thought of attacking the principle of the open door *as that principle is understood by the Imperial Government of Russia*" [10] (italics are mine). Subsequent events would seem to have indicated that Russia did not understand that principle as some others did.

Generally speaking it may be said that the powers pledged to the Open Door Policy understood that pledge to mean these things:

(1) The territorial integrity and administrative entity of China are not to be impaired.

(2) Except in certain spheres of interest there is to be perfect equality of opportunity for the economic enterprise of the citizens of all nations.

(3) Within the spheres of interest, other conditions being equal, the power interested is to enjoy a preference in furnishing capital and skill for railway building, mining and other public works.

(4) No higher customs duties or tonnage dues are to be levied in a leased territory than are levied by the Chinese law, and no preference in regard to these is to be enjoyed by the power holding the lease of the port.

(5) No discrimination in freight rates is to be permitted on railways in China leased or operated by a foreign power or company.

This last item has not always been strictly observed. While regulations relating to freight shipments over such railroads have been expressed in phraseology apparently applicable alike to all shippers, they are sometimes so drawn as to provide a real discrimination in favor of the shippers of the lessee nationality. Thus petroleum shipped east or south over the Chinese Eastern Railway—i.e., Russian petroleum, paid one rate, but petroleum shipped north or west—i.e., American petroleum, paid a higher rate for the same distance.

[10] Foreign Relations of the U. S., 1902, p. 929.

So in 1914 the South Manchurian Railway Administration (Japanese) gave a special rate to merchandise shipped direct from Japan through Dairen or Port Arthur to points north of Mukden. The British and American Governments objected that their merchandise was not shipped through Japan. The regulation was amended to read: "all merchandise shipped from a foreign port through Dairen or Port Arthur direct to points nórth of Mukden" should enjoy the special rate. The protesting governments insisted that this too violated the Open Door Policy, since their goods were not shipped direct to points north of Mukden, but were transhipped at Shanghai, which is not a foreign port as related to Mukden. Then the rule was again amended to cover shipments from Shanghai in *Japanese* steamers, which also showed discrimination. Newchwang, too, complained of discrimination against that port, a complaint subsequently adjusted.

That the policy of the Open Door was to be interpreted in some way in harmony with the existence of special interests enjoyed by certain powers is indicated also in the Lansing-Ishii notes.[10a] These notes, signed on November 2, 1917, declare that:

Territorial propinquity creates special relations between countries, and, consequently, the Government of the United States recognizes that Japan has special interests in China, particularly in that part to which her possessions are contiguous.

The notes furthermore declare that

The territorial sovereignty of China, nevertheless remains unimpaired, and the Government of the United States has every confidence in the repeated assurances of the Imperial Japanese Government that, while geographical position gives Japan such special interests, they have no desire to discriminate against the trade of other nations or to disregard the commercial rights heretofore granted by China in treaties with other powers.

A further declaration is made in the note of opposition to the acquisition by any power of any special rights or privileges that would affect the independence or territorial

[10a] Subsequent events and mutual agreement between Japan and the United States led to the cancellation of these notes on April 14, 1923.

integrity of China. Adherence is given, too, to the policy of the Open Door, and equality of opportunity for commerce and industry in China.

The special interest of Japan, therefore, is not such an interest as abridges the commercial rights of other nations, or affects the sovereignty or independence of China. It can be no more than that interest which every nation has in the peace and prosperity of its neighbors. Moreover, the rule which gives Japan a special interest in China gives a special interest in China to Great Britain, France and Russia, all of which have territories contiguous to China. It gives a special interest in China also to the United States, which enjoys propinquity in its possession of the Philippines. By the same rule China has a special interest in Russian, British, French and Japanese possessions that join her own. The notes, therefore, scarcely do more than affirm the obvious, and the logical deduction from their statements merely makes more formal and definite the recognition of spheres of interest for Great Britain, France, Russia and Japan in regions contiguous to their own possession, a recognition already granted by implication in the notes of Secretary Hay.

It is true, however, that Japan endeavored to substitute in the notes the phrase ''special influence'' for ''special interest,'' but the American Government would not consent.

Willoughby quotes Cobbett as saying:

A sphere of influence so far as it can be said to possess a definite meaning, indicates a region, generally inhabited by races of inferior civilization, over which a State seeks, by compact with some other State or States that might otherwise compete with it, to secure to itself an exclusive right of making future acquisitions of territory (whether by annexation or by the establishment of protectorates), and, generally, also, the direction and control of the native inhabitants.[11]

Commenting on this Willoughby says: ''It will clearly

[11] W. W. Willoughby, ''Foreign Rights and Interests in China,'' p. 271.

appear that, as thus defined, the term Sphere of Influence has no application in China.''

It is true that official documents have avoided the use of the term "Sphere of Influence," but it is often used in popular speech in the Far East as synonymous with "Sphere of Interest." The desire of the Japanese to substitute the phrase "Special Influence" for "Special Interest" in the Ishii note is very significant, and when one reviews the history of China's relations with foreign powers, he cannot avoid the conclusion that "Spheres of Influence" as well as "Spheres of Interest" have been sought. The brief summary given in the first chapter of China's loss of territory indicates this very clearly.

French enterprise in the Indo-Chinese Peninsula was first directed to the acquisition of a position of influence in the councils of the State, by assistance to be given in the settlement of a dynastic question. A war, in 1858–62, to secure redress for the murder of French missionaries, obtained possession of three provinces, and led to a protectorate over Cambodia to replace that of Siam and Annam. In 1867 pretext was given for annexation of more territory in Cochin China. The Mekong proving to be of little value for navigation, attempt was made to navigate the Red River. The refusal of the Annamese to give consent led to war. China gave aid to her vassal but could not save her, and she unwillingly passed under the protection of France. Burmah, long a tributary of China, passed in very much the same way into the possession of Great Britain, although, sending a tribute mission to Peking as late as 1895.

The annexation of the northern provinces of India which formerly were included in the Chinese Empire was effected in similar fashion. Intervention to restore peace between certain provinces gave Britain an influence in them which was exercised first as arbitrator and then as protector. The present movement to deny China's sovereignty in Outer Tibet and make Britain arbitrator of differences between China and her vassal must be judged in the light of past history. The same is true of Russian influence in Urga. Japanese activity in Manchuria must be judged by the course taken by her government in its relations with Korea. In the Russo-Japanese war the Emperor of Korea declared his neutrality, but Japan paid no more attention to that than Germany did to the neutrality of Belgium. Japanese troops made a highway of Korea. Japan forced Korea into an unwilling alliance, and promised to respect her independence and territorial integrity. To this she was pledged by the treaty of alliance with Great Britain, but before the treaty of peace with Russia was signed Great Britain agreed to a revision of the treaty, in August, 1905. In this revised treaty Britain recognizes Japan's possession of paramount political, military and economic interests in Korea. Despite Japan's promise to the Emperor of Korea, he was compelled by forceful measures, in November, 1905, to sign away his independence and accept Japan's suzerainty. The Emperor in his despair appealed repeatedly to the United States to exercise its good offices, as promised in our treaty of 1882, but the American Government closed its ears. A special mission was sent to Washington, but reception of it by the Department of State was postponed until the protectorate was declared, when the Koreans were informed that it was too late.[12] There are several treaties, it seems, that have been considered mere "scraps of paper." We were the first power to withdraw our legation from Seoul. Still Korea retained a moiety of her sovereignty, but Japan's influence waxed, and in 1910 Korea was annexed to the Empire.

There is, therefore, good ground for thinking that Britain has looked upon Tibet, Russia upon Mongolia, and Japan upon Manchuria and Eastern Inner Mongolia as their respective Spheres of Influence.

THE WASHINGTON CONFERENCE

The importance of the Washington Conference to China can scarcely be overestimated. For the first time the

[12] Hulbert's "Passing of Korea," p. 222.

powers having interests in China invited the Chinese Government to become a party to an agreement relating to the Open Door and Equality of Commercial Opportunity in their country. This agreement is the only one that binds all the nine powers in one treaty to respect the sovereignty, independence, and the territorial and administrative integrity of China, and to maintain the policy of the Open Door. It binds China to avoid discrimination in the treatment of the subjects and citizens of the contracting States, and it pledges the powers other than China to withhold support from any arrangement purporting "to establish in favor of their interests any general superiority of rights with respect to commercial or economic development in any designated region of China." This is aimed directly at "Spheres of Interest." [13] Another article pledges the powers to withhold support from agreements *among their nationals* designed to create "Spheres of Influence." [14] The question naturally arises; have they bound the *Governments* not to claim Spheres of Influence?

RECENT CLAIMS TO SPHERES OF INTEREST

In the discussion of the Lansing-Ishii Notes, it was suggested that they tended to support the policy of Spheres of Interest. This was indicated in the correspondence between the Governments interested in the formation of the new International Consortium. The Inter-Bank Agreement by which the Consortium was established was signed on October 15, 1920. Its aim was to prevent the injury to China which would follow upon a general recognition of Spheres of Interest. This purpose is set forth in the preamble to the Agreement, and the matters with which it is concerned are stated as follows in its second article:

This agreement relates to existing and future loan agreements which involve the issue for subscription by the public of loans to the Chinese Government or to Chinese Government Departments or to provinces of China or to companies or corporations

[13] Nine-Power Treaty, Article III.
[14] Ibid., Article IV.

owned or controlled by or on behalf of the Chinese Government
or any Chinese Provincial Government or to any party if the
transaction in question is guaranteed by the Chinese Government
or Chinese Provincial Government but does not relate to agreements for loans to be floated in China.

It was thus intended to pool all options held by the
nationals of the Governments concerned and to provide for
an equal participation by such nationals in all future loan
contracts, if such participation should be desired.

The Japanese Government, however, while desiring that
its bankers should share in the enterprise, desired to except
from its operation the regions of Manchuria and Eastern
Inner Mongolia, since loans affecting these regions were
calculated "to create a serious impediment to the security
of the economic life and national defence of Japan."
Reference was made to the "very special relations which
Japan enjoys geographically and historically with the regions referred to, and which have been recognized by Great
Britain, the United States, France and Russia on many
occasions." In this connection the Lansing-Ishii notes were
recalled.

The American and British Governments declined to give
assent to this statement by Japan as showing a desire upon
Japan's part to exclude three of the four banking groups
from a share in the development of an important part of
the Chinese Republic. In the spring of 1920 Mr. Lamont
of the firm of J. P. Morgan and Co. went out to Japan
to consult with the Japanese Group and an agreement was
finally reached by which only extensions or branches of
existing railway lines or enterprises upon which substantial
progress had been made were to be excepted from the operation of the Agreement.

More recently, on May 18, 1928, as the Nationalist armies
approached Peking, the Japanese Government addressed
a warning both to the Peking and the Nanking authorities, in which it was declared that Japan attached the
"utmost importance to the maintenance of peace and order
in Manchuria" and was prepared to prevent the occurrence
of any disturbance of the peace and order there. The

Japanese Government stated further that, if the situation should become menacing, they might possibly be constrained to take appropriate and effective steps to maintain peace and order in Manchuria. The Peking Government replied very promptly, denying that Japan had any right to take steps to preserve the peace in Chinese territory.

This declaration on the part of Japan and others of similar import seemed to indicate a determination upon her part to place Manchuria under her protection, and many comments recalled the measures that were taken by Japan in Korea before the annexation of that state to the Japanese Empire. The suspicion that Japan might be contemplating the assumption of a protectorate over Manchuria was strengthened by the warning given on August 9, 1928, to the Military Governor of Manchuria by a representative of the Japanese Government that Japan disapproved of the proposed union of Manchuria with the Nationalist state. The events of 1931 and '32 in Manchuria tend to confirm one's suspicions as to Japanese aims in that region.

As for Russian claims to a sphere of interest in Outer Mongolia, that was formally abandoned by the Treaty between China and the Russian Union of Soviet Socialist Republics of May 31, 1924, which expressly recognizes Outer Mongolia as a part of the Republic of China and invalidates the Treaty of November 5, 1921, between the Moscow Government and the so-called Mongolian People's Revolutionary Government which the Russians had set up at Urga. The Russian troops were nominally withdrawn from Urga by March 6, 1925, but no successor has been chosen to the Hutukhtu who died in 1924, and Russian influences seem still to prevail there.

CHAPTER XXIII

THE ERA OF REFORM

No man putteth new wine into old bottles, else the new wine will burst the bottles.—Luke v:37.

The Master said, ''What is necessary is to make names correct.''—Analects of Confucius, xiii:3.

On the 7th of January, 1902, I stood on the balcony of a silk shop facing the *Ch'ien Men Ta Chieh,* or ''Great Front Gate Street,'' in Peking. It is the principal business street of the Outer City, commonly called the ''Chinese City,'' to distinguish it from the larger enclosure to the north, called the Tartar City.

The Manchu Court, after an exile of a year and a half, was returning to the Capital. When the American contingent of the forces sent to relieve the Legations had, in August, 1900, seized the *Ch'ien Men,* or ''Front Gate'' of the Capital, and had begun firing on the palace in the Forbidden City, the Empress Dowager and her courtiers had hastily fled out the back gate of the Forbidden City, across the northern part of the Tartar City and, accompanied by a frightened multitude and cursing guards, made their way through the north-western gate into the open country. The streets were filled with surging masses fleeing pell-mell in terror. It is said that the imperial guards killed more people getting out of the city than the allied forces did coming in.

The Empress Dowager had taken the precaution to have the Emperor accompany her. Her niece, the Empress, was also provided a place. The two imperial concubines, reputed to have held progressive views and to have had much influence with the Emperor, were left behind. The body of one was found in a well in the Forbidden

514

City. Some assert that she was thrown into the well by command of Her Imperial Majesty, the Empress Dowager. Others say she was a suicide. Her sister, the remaining concubine, was rescued from amidst the flying mob by an imperial prince, who conducted her to a place of safety and sent her on to join the Court. The Court had rested one night at the Summer Palace, and then by slow marches had made its way to the city of Hsianfu, the capital of Shensi, and anciently the capital of China, situated in the far north-west, a month's journey from Peking. After her return the Empress Dowager, referring to this experience, with pathos in her voice, said she had fled in such haste that she had had no time to comb her hair, and had had no breakfast that day save a hard-boiled egg.

THE RETURN OF THE COURT

Now, after eighteen months' waiting for the restoration of peace, she was returning to her palace. It was a bitterly cold day. A north-west wind was blowing. The streets were filled with germ-laden dust that penetrated one's eyes, nostrils, ears and lungs. The inhabitants of the city said: "The dragon is soaring in the clouds because the Emperor is abroad." The dragon is the emblem of imperial power. It also represents the power that rules the winds. Two lines of a Christian hymn would express very well the Chinese idea of the dragon:

> His chariot of wrath the deep thunder clouds form,
> And dark is his path on the wings of the storm.

It was a common tradition that if the Emperor at any time left his palace there would be a high wind accompanying him.

From the semi-lune which formerly concealed the "Front Gate" of the Tartar City, clear across the Chinese city to the Yungting Gate, a mile to the south, the street had been cleared of all booths and stalls. The roadway had been swept and then covered with yellow earth, yellow being the imperial color. Every shop and home on the street was closed and shutters put up over the windows. Every cross street was cut off by blue curtains, for no common eye must gaze upon majesty as it rides by. Only the imperial guard, drawn up on either side the way, was permitted upon the street. Princess, dukes and other nobles were with their several banner corps. From early morn until two o'clock in the afternoon the patient soldiers waited in their ranks in biting wind and suffocating dust, without food or drink.

It had been a long journey from Hsianfu to Peking. At the slow rate of imperial travel it had occupied some six weeks. The progress of the Court, with its thousands of servants and guards had been as great a calamity to the districts through which it passed as a swarm of locusts. Orders to respect private property and to pay for supplies were issued, but only to be ignored by rapacious underlings. This was one of the chief reasons that Chinese Emperors in recent times so seldom left the Capital. The Ministers and high officials would do all in their power to dissuade His Majesty from making a visit to any province where they had friends or relatives, knowing well how the people would suffer. As it was in England in the 14th century, so it was in China in the 20th. Green tells us that royal journeys in the days of Edward III beggared the people, who were fain to hide or eat their supplies to save them from the purveyors of the Court, who bought at fair market prices but never paid for anything.

We watched upon the balcony hour after hour, and, when we grew too cold, we would go into the shop and warm our hands at a charcoal brazier whose fumes filled the room and gave one a headache. When the atmosphere of the room became too stifling we would return to the balcony to get a breath of air. We were a party of Americans and Europeans from the legations, graciously permitted by the Chinese Government, in violation of ancient custom, to look down upon Imperial Majesty on this eventful day of re-entry into Peking. But we found that, despite all orders and precedents, the people of Peking were just as eager and determined as we to see the procession. Above the comb of every roof, now and again we saw long rows of heads appear and disappear, and myriads of dark eyes gazing curiously down over the tiles into the street. The gilded sign-boards of a thousand trades rattled in the wind. Near at hand rose the massive grey walls of the Tartar City. The roof-tree of the unfinished tower at the Ch'ien Men bore witness to the devastation wrought by the Boxer folly. Beyond the lofty city wall rose the Twin Pagodas, built in the days of Kublai Khan, and we could not but think of the many centuries that had passed since Marco Polo mingled with the courtiers of Peking, and of all the changes wrought by those centuries to this ancient city.

The Court had returned by way of the Yellow River valley to Kaifengfu and thence northward to Paotingfu, the old capital of Chihli Province. The railway which had been torn up by the Boxers was once more in operation from Paoting to Peking. For the first time in her life the Empress Dowager rode on a railway train. She was startled by the whistle of the train as it approached a crossing, and sent word to the engineer that thereafter he should not blow the whistle without first notifying her. The allied armies, on rebuilding the railways, had brought them into the city, cutting great gaps in the sacred walls for this purpose. Prior to the Boxer rising this had been forbidden, and now that their Majesties were returning, the existence of railway tracks through the walls was ignored. Instead of riding in a comfortable coach to the Ch'ien Men, the Court descended from the train at the old terminus, Machiapu, five miles away, and made the journey in palanquins and carts or on horseback, facing the bitter wind. Such is conservatism.

About two o'clock in the afternoon an alarm was given. A horde of eunuchs on shaggy, unkempt ponies came dashing by. These eunuchs, in their crimson robes covered with huge medallions of green and yellow, and wearing black caps with red feathers attached, looked like so many circus clowns. Behind them came the imperial herald crying the approach of the Court. Immediately the soldiers fell upon their knees and bowed their heads toward the ground. Next into view came the Imperial Guard followed by a group of military officers on horseback, Yuan Shih-k'ai in his yellow jacket riding in their midst. Close behind were the imperial standards, great triangular flags of yellow satin on each of which was embroidered the blue dragon trying to swallow a red sun. Beside the banners were the yellow umbrellas, emblems of power, upon whose flounces also were embroidered the imperial arms.

Behind these emblems, borne swiftly along by eight bearers, rode the Emperor in his yellow satin palanquin, which was lined with blue silk. He sat upon his feet and gazed straight ahead, like the Buddha on his lotus throne. Following the Emperor came the Empress Dowager with her guards. She was more human in her actions—pulled aside the curtains of her chair and waved her handkerchief toward the ladies on the balcony in token of friendly feeling. It was difficult to realize that a few months before she had been trying to destroy these legation folk with shot and shell.

After the Empress Dowager there came the Empress in her yellow chair, the imperial concubine and the ladies-in-waiting in their carts, and princes, dukes and other noblemen on their horses or in green chairs, with officers and attendants of various ranks bringing up the rear. It was a wonderful exhibition of barbaric splendor. The motley group of attendants, the lack of order, the wild riding, the gorgeous colors, the quaint costumes, the ancient emblems all united to make it like a scene from the Arabian Nights. It was the last pageant of its kind. It marked the end of an era.

The next time the Emperor went forth was to worship at the Temple of Heaven. He went escorted by modern troops, who stood and presented arms instead of groveling in the dust before him.

CHARACTER OF THE REFORM

With the return of the Court to Peking a very earnest movement for reform began. Edict followed edict with feverish haste. But the new wine was being poured into old wine-skins. The ferment extended throughout the empire. Manchu institutions could not stand the strain. In one brief decade the wine-skins were destined to burst, the Manchu Dynasty to disappear.

In one of the edicts issued by the Empress Dowager she quoted the saying of Confucius that the one thing needful was to correct the terms, or names, by which things were being called. Confucius was aiming his remark at an unfilial son and usurper. He meant that he would call things by their right names. With the Empress Dowager it meant that some of her reforms got no further than a change of names. Old offices were given new names and dedicated to new uses, but the corruption and inefficiency remained as before. The title, *Tsungli Yamen,* was an abridgment of the name by which the Foreign Office had been called. The full title when translated was "Office for the General Direction of the Affairs of Various Countries." This was changed to *Wai Chiao Pu,* or "Ministry of Foreign Relations." The *Hu Pu,* or "Board of Population," a name reminiscent of a time when its chief function was to take the census and collect poll tax and land tax, became the "Ministry of Finance." Other offices, too, were given new names. Seeing that changing the name did not always change the character of the institution some critics were disposed to pooh-pooh the whole reform movement. They called it a sham, and said that reform existed only on paper. But that was an unjust criticism. Had there been no real spirit of reform in the air, there would have been no ferment, and nominal changes might have sufficed. In that case no explosion could have occurred; the dynasty might have survived. But the people demanded real change. There was pretense, to be sure; there were insincere reformers. But there were others desperately in earnest. The old and new struggled together. Some really new institutions were created to meet the new situation. There was a Ministry of the Interior, with a national police force under its control. There was a Ministry of Commerce, a Ministry of Posts and Communications, a Ministry of Education, and multitudes of bureaus designed to aid in the modernization of the country. But vested interests are not easily destroyed. There were too many parasites who were unwilling to surrender their sinecures for the sake of the general good. They opposed the reforms because their craft was in danger. Men were puzzled by what they saw. The hypercritical saw only inconsistency. Others marveled at the rapidity of the changes being made and saw only progress.

We had been told repeatedly in the years before the Boxer crisis that the Chinese could never reform; that their institutions had become hardened and fixed, had not changed since the days of Confucius, had lost all their plasticity and could not be modified. The statement was untrue, for Chinese history records many crises which had introduced great changes and turned the current of national life into new channels. Future history, no doubt, will set down the year 1902 as the beginning of a new era in China, one that was to inaugurate other great social and political changes. For, in spite of pessimistic prophets, China began to change again but not as the Manchus designed. They started a movement which soon got beyond their control and whose outcome we cannot even yet foretell.

EDUCATIONAL REFORM

The failure of the Boxer rising, coming so soon after China's defeat by Japan, convinced even so pronounced a conservative as the Empress Dowager that China had to have a new system of education, if the nation was ever to develop the strength necessary to withstand the aggressions of the powers.

Even before she left Hsianfu to return to Peking she issued an edict requiring the officials of the empire to

HER IMPERIAL MAJESTY, THE EMPRESS DOWAGER
OF CHINA.

THE VICEROY CHANG CHIH-TUNG.

acquaint themselves with international law and political science, and giving them six months within which to complete the task. That, of course, was neither practical nor practicable. But immediately after her return to Peking she appointed a commission to draft a public school system. The two commissioners were Chang Chih-tung, the Viceroy at Wuchang, author of the little book called ''Learn'' which has already been mentioned, and Chang Po-hsi, the Minister of Education and one of the foremost scholars of China.

THE OLD SYSTEM

Prior to this there had been no public school system in China. Education was a private matter. The wealthy kept tutors for their children. In the villages and city wards the neighbors, under the leadership of their elders, clubbed together to maintain schools, each family paying the teacher a few hundred cash a month for each child sent. In this way one boy in ten, perhaps, learned enough characters to be able to keep his accounts. One in a thousand, it may be, could read a book or newspaper editorial understandingly. The only interest of the State in education was manifested in the holding of examinations for the civil and military services of the empire. The system of civil service examinations in vogue up to 1900 was at least a thousand years old, while in simpler form it had existed from very ancient times.

For the military examination little was required beyond physical culture and skill in horsemanship and archery. A slight acquaintance with the written characters of the Chinese language was desirable, but would not necessarily close the door to promotion. A well-known Major General in Peking under the Empire and the Republic could neither read nor write.

For the civil service the examination was very stiff, but was not calculated to determine a man's fitness for office. One had to know the written language and be very familiar with the Chinese classics, and with the history and literature of his country, to pass such an examination. Once a year the County Magistrate held an examination in his yamen of the young men who wanted to compete for admission to the civil service. The most promising students were selected to enter an examination the next year at the prefectural capital. The best of these were given the degree of *Hsiu Ts'ai*, commonly reckoned by Europeans as a B.A. degree. This degree qualified the holder to enter the lists the third year at the provincial capital, where thousands were gathered in the great examination halls. I have known as many as 27,000 to attend the examinations at Nanking. Three times for twenty-four hours each time the student was fastened in a cell, unable to communicate with anyone else, and while there required to write a thesis or a poem upon an assigned subject. The paper when finished was enclosed in an envelope which was marked with a cipher. Another envelope with the same cipher contained the student's name. This was designed to secure impartiality in the marking of the papers. But no matter how good the papers, the number who could be allowed to pass was strictly limited, and of these a fixed proportion had to be Manchus. Out of 27,000 not more than three hundred could obtain the degree of *Chü Jen*. These the following year would assemble at Peking for the metropolitan examination, where out of some 6000 candidates about three hundred would secure the degree of *Tsin Shih,* and one-third of these, at a subsequent palace examination, would be given the title of Hanlin and admitted to the National Academy. From these men were selected the historiographers who compiled the dynastic history.

The chief purpose of the examination, therefore, was to prepare men to serve the State, and nearly all the officials, from District (or County) Magistrate to the Prime Minister obtained their appointments originally through this method.

THE NEW SYSTEM

The edict of 1902 changed all this. At the beginning of 1904 the two commissioners, in a report that filled eight volumes, submitted a scheme for a public school system, based upon that in operation in Japan, which in turn was derived from that of the United States.

The system, as submitted and approved, had this serious defect. It made no provision for the education of girls except that it allowed their admission to the lowest grade primary. This defect was corrected to some extent by the activity of the women of China, who showed unexpected resourcefulness in their efforts to establish schools in their own homes or to establish free schools for the daughters of the poor. It was the Viceroy Tuan-fang who urged this upon the attention of the Empress Dowager, and the latter was quick to respond to the suggestion, for she had acquired her education for the most part after entering the palace. She directed the Princess Imperial to open a school in her own palace for daughters of the nobility and higher officials. This example was followed by many other princesses and wealthy women, and the example of Peking was followed in other cities, until many of the provincial governments themselves assumed the responsibility. This reform incidentally led to another, the abandonment of foot-binding by great numbers of Chinese. The Empress Dowager was quick to seize the opportunity given by the opening of schools for girls to have a rule made that no girl with bound feet would be admitted. The desire for education had more influence upon the practice than all the imperial edicts that had previously been issued.

The school system has been slightly modified since by the Republic. To-day the curriculum requires four years for the lower primary grade, two for the Higher Primary, three for the Junior Middle, four for the Senior Middle and five for the University. From the Junior Middle School one can, if he so desires, pass either to a Vocational School or to a Rural Normal School. From the Senior Middle School he may enter a Normal School or the University, and from the University he may enter the Graduate School.

It is true that before the Boxer troubles spasmodic efforts to establish colleges of the modern type had been made by various provincial governments, but they had not met with much success. They were not connected with any system of elementary education which could prepare students for their courses, and as long as the old system of examinations remained, with its chance of official preferment, the new colleges did not attract the best students. Even after the adoption of the new school system it was decided to retain for a time the old method of competing for degrees, reducing from year to year the number of degrees to be allowed, so making more gradual the transition to the new system. But after an experience of a year and a half this was found to be inadvisable, for as long as the old avenue to honor stood open few could be induced to try the more difficult path of modern education. On September 1, 1905, therefore, an imperial edict appeared abolishing forever the age-old but outgrown system of literary examinations. The effect was seen immediately in all parts of the empire. Great zeal was shown in the establishment of schools of the new order. Special funds for their support were provided by new provincial taxes, and these funds were increased by gifts of the wealthy and by popular subscriptions. In many places temples and other public buildings belonging to the community were taken over for the use of the schools. In other places village funds whose proceeds had theretofore been devoted to popular sports, to theatrical exhibitions or religious celebrations were directed to the more beneficial purpose of popular education. The great difficulty was to provide teachers. This is still a difficulty, although the normal schools now provide a goodly number from year to year. The demand for Western education led to a great increase in the number of students going abroad. This movement was aided by the action of the American Government, which in 1908 decided to return to China a portion of the Boxer indemnity. Up to the time of the entrance of China into the world war the indemnity was being paid in monthly installments, of which a definite proportion was handed back to China. The total to be thus returned was more than twelve million dollars, together with the interest accruing thereon. The Chinese Government, to show its appreciation of this action, informed the American Government in 1908 that the funds would be used to educate students in the United States. To carry out this plan the Tsing Hua College was established in Peking, where a constant group of some 500 students, chosen by competitive examination, is prepared for entrance to American universities. There are some twenty Chinese and twenty American teachers engaged in this work, and the government has given the school the confiscated grounds and buildings formerly belonging to an imperial prince who was a Boxer leader. This was an act of poetic justice, for education is the best antidote to Boxerism. These grounds adjoin the Yuan Ming Yuan, or Imperial Summer Palace, destroyed by the British and French in 1860. The college has recently added these historic grounds to its campus.

The disturbances that attended the revolution of 1911 and 1912, and the civil war which has been almost continuous since 1916, have greatly retarded the development of the school system. The latest statistics available show that there were in 1917, 122,286 schools, with an attendance of 4,075,338 students. This is to say that of perhaps 40 million children of school age there are only a few more than one in ten in government schools. Of these four millions the girls number but 177,273.[1] Since these statistics were compiled the education of girls has been receiving attention from the Government, and the national university at Peking has opened its doors to women. Many girls, however, are educated at home and in religious schools. The American missionaries have done a great educational work in China. The missionaries of other countries also have established schools, and all these together have supplemented the work of the public schools in a very effective manner.

RECENT DEVELOPMENTS

After the establishment of the Republic the National Board of Education adopted an alphabet, or more properly,

[1] Commercial Handbook of China. Julean Arnold. Vol. 2, p. 412.

a syllabary, for the writing of Chinese, but its imprac-
ticability was soon made manifest. Greater promise of popular education is found in the great Mass Education movement. This originated during the World War when illiterate Chinese with the allied forces in France made
frequent requests of James Yen, a graduate of the University of Virginia, to write letters for them to be sent
to their homes. He conceived the plan of teaching them
a number of characters sufficient to convey in simple
language the news of their welfare. After the War, this
plan was taken up in various parts of China and volunteer
teachers were enlisted to give the necessary instruction.
A thousand characters were chosen. Neighborhood meetings were held and those who learned the thousand characters were pledged to teach others. Thus thousands who
a short time since were illiterate can now read the papers
and books that use these characters. More recently a
second thousand of commonly used characters have been
chosen to add to the written language of those who desire it.

The disturbed condition of the country, the waste of
funds in civil war and the consequent poverty of the Government have retarded all progress in education. Excellent
plans have been adopted, but, in the main, the programme
is still very largely a paper one. The National Conference
in 1930 advocated a plan whereby elementary education
was to be given to 40,000,000 pupils within a period of
twenty years. Missionaries are still doing a great part of
the educational work, but the Government requires the
registration of all schools of higher learning, including private institutions, and forbids compulsory attendance at
religious services in such schools. It also forbids religious
instruction in any elementary schools. For pupils from
Christian families the missionaries hold religious services
outside school hours. Voluntary attendance on such services in the higher schools seems to be quite satisfactory.

MILITARY REORGANIZATION

One of the earliest reforms to be undertaken was that
of the army. Dr. Wu T'ing-fang once asked an Ameri-

can friend what reform should be undertaken by China
first of all. The friend replied: "Why, the educational,
of course." "Oh no," said the Minister, "While we are
getting the children educated you Western men will come
and take our country away from us. The first thing to
do is to build up an army."

There was much reason in this statement. Japan had
won the recognition of the European powers, not by her
educational system nor by improved administration, but
by the creation of a great army and navy and the waging
of successful war. On the other hand China's military
weakness had invited aggressive encroachment upon her
sovereign rights and led to the loss of some of her best
ports.

For centuries the Chinese had been taught to despise
the military art. I have already quoted a common proverb
which says, "Nails are not made of good iron nor soldiers
of good men." In China this once was true. Nails were
hammered out of scrap iron, and soldiers gathered from
the human scrap-heap. Before the war with Japan the
Chinese army, for the most part, was a rabble. To a considerable extent it existed on paper only. When the
inspector was about to visit a camp he sent notice in advance, so that the commanding officer would have time
to send out into the highways and hedges and, for a few
cents a day, line up a sufficient number of idle men to
fill the ranks. A military jacket was loaned to each one
and a musket or spear placed in his hands. He could
then stand up and be counted. After the inspection many
were discharged, and the monthly pay of the missing
found its way into the pockets of the officers.

Often prior to the war between China and Japan I
watched the drilling of the troops. Every fifth man carried
a long bamboo spear decorated with a red pennon. The
rest were armed with muzzle-loading muskets. When these
had fired their guns they would fall back a few paces to
give place to the spearmen, who rushed forward with
blood-curdling yells and brandished their weapons to hold
off the enemy until the muskets were re-loaded. The

Manchu banner men formed a separate organization. They were descendants of the conquerers of China, and prided themselves on their horsemanship and archery, but they were as unfit for modern warfare as the bowmen that followed the Black Prince would have been.

Before the war of 1894 with Japan there were some modern troops in China, but they were very few. The army that was led against the Japanese was a conglomeration of provincial levies, some with one equipment and some with another, all utterly unfit for real service. By 1900, when the Boxer rising occurred, some improvement had been made, but each Viceroy had his own army, and these armies were organized upon different models and carried rifles of various patterns.

The defeat of these troops and the Boxers in 1900 reinforced the lesson taught by the war with Japan, and convinced the authorities that their attitude towards the military had to be changed. Christian nations had taught the Chinese that the art of war was not to be despised, and that without a powerful army China was in danger of losing its independence. Systematic efforts were made to develop the martial spirit. Military training became compulsory in the public schools. Sons of the nobles and high officials were encouraged to take up the military career, and a special school for cadets of such families was opened in Peking. The whole army was reorganized upon a new basis. It was made national, no longer a collection of provincial forces, and it was placed under the direct control of a general staff at Peking. Moreover the rabble was excluded. Every recruit was required to bring evidence of the respectability of his family and had to be able to read and write. He was given a regular course of instruction, had to take notes and pass examination upon the lectures given, and was thoroughly and constantly drilled in the manual of arms and required to take daily exercise in the gymnasium. He was smartly dressed, fairly well paid and kept under strict discipline.

The result was shown in the annual maneuvers, which received very favorable comment from European critics.

TSING HUA COLLEGE, PEIPING — SUPPORTED BY THE RETURNED BOXER INDEMNITY.

BARRICADE, NEAR AMERICAN LEGATION DURING BOXER RISING.

The Washington Conference adopted a resolution advising China to reduce the forces under her warring *tu chüns*, or military governors. This action to some, however, appears rather ludicrous for two reasons. In the first place the Peking Government has shown itself powerless to control these warring factions. Repeated orders to halt their movements have been ignored. The exhortation is useless. Secondly, the total strength of the combined armies of China, if we accept the maximum estimate of a million, gives her but one soldier to every 400 of the population, while some of the powers that criticised are supporting in time of peace one soldier to 40 of the population, and others one to 217. It is a pity to see China wasting her strength in suicidal conflict, but Western aggression has made impressive the truth that "When a strong man armed keepeth his palace his goods are in peace."

The importance of this truth was emphasized during the conflict between China and Japan in 1931-32. China's unpreparedness compelled her to stand upon the defensive and trust for security to treaties and covenants rather than to naval and military strength. The result was disaster for China.

China's naval and aviation forces are negligible. She has a large army, but the greater part appears to be poorly drilled and inadequately equipped. At the meeting in 1929 of the conference upon disbandment, the total number of officers and men in the army was given as 1,800,000. This included forces that at times have been arrayed against the Nanking Government. The figures given are elastic, for in the continuous civil strife, the shifting of factions may lead to an increase of an army and its defeat may cause disintegration.

The expenditure for military purposes in 1929 was $209,536,969.49 (silver), nearly $98,000,000 in U. S. money, at the rate of exchange for that year. The budget for 1931-32 proposed to spend on military affairs $406,617,220. Though nearly twice the amount for 1929, it yet amounted to but about $100,000,000 in American money owing to the fall in the exchange value of silver.

JURIDICAL REFORM

Scarcely any reform initiated at the time was more important than that of the penal code and the courts. The chief reason influencing the government in the matter was the enjoyment by the foreign powers of a right of extraterritorial jurisdiction over their nationals in China. In 1902 a Commission on Juridical Reform was established by imperial edict, at the head of which the Empress Dowager appointed Dr. Wu T'ing-fang, so long the Chinese Minister in Washington, who had studied law in London and was familiar with Western codes, and Shen Chia-pen, the greatest authority at that time on Chinese law. Their report was made and adopted in 1905. It pointed out very truthfully that, while the criminal code of China was more severe than those of the West, the situation had earlier been just the reverse; that Western nations in recent times had modified their laws and made them more humane, and that Europeans and Americans now were unwilling to submit themselves to the severer laws of China. The memorialists referred to the exercise by foreign states of extraterritorial jurisdiction in China as an encroachment upon the sovereignty of China, and quoted the treaty of 1903 with the United States, and treaties with certain other powers also, as promising to surrender their extraterritorial jurisdiction whenever China should reform her code and courts.

EXTRATERRITORIALITY

Writers upon the subject of extraterritoriality usually find its origin in the relations between Turkey and the European states; but the privileges granted to the Christian Powers of Europe by the victorious Mohammed II cannot be regarded as a confession of weakness on his part. Rather his grant of jurisdiction should be looked upon as a formal recognition of a principle that was of very general application, and a practice whose roots strike far into the past, when sovereignty was regarded as personal and having nothing to do with geographical boundaries.

Hall's observation that "to the Oriental mind a personal law is more familiar and appears more natural than a territorial law"[2] was true rather of the Near East than of the Far East. China apparently arrived at the conception of sovereignty as territorial long before Europe did. Indeed the practice of the West is not even now consistent with its theory of sovereignty as territorial, for many Western nations insist still upon a claim to the military service of foreign born children of their subjects, although these children claim citizenship in the land of their birth.

It was feudalism that introduced into Europe the principle and practice of authority limited by territorial boundaries. With the fall of Rome these territorial lords became independent, but continued to regard themselves as rulers of territory rather than peoples.

China many centuries before Christ reached this conception of sovereignty as territorial by a very similar experience. The Chou Dynasty in 1122 B.C. divided the empire among feudal lords, who in return rendered military service to the Emperor. Their jurisdiction was limited by the boundaries of their territories. They gradually became independent of the central state, made war one upon another, and established treaties with one another in which they recognized the territorial sovereignty one of another, provided for extradition and arranged for interchange of commodities. When one of these states, in 249 B.C., swallowed up all the others, it carried over into the new empire the conception of sovereignty as territorial, and this conception persisted into recent times. The Manchus allowed the peoples of their dependencies to govern themselves by their own laws, but always and only upon the recognition of China as sovereign. European nations at the time of their first intercourse with China held confused notions upon the subject of sovereignty, generally insisting on territorial jurisdiction themselves but also at

2 Hall's "Foreign Jurisdiction of the British Crown," p. 133.

times attempting to exercise jurisdiction over their own people in other lands. The British Parliament in 1773 empowered the king to erect a supreme court at Calcutta, without seeking the consent of the titular ruler [3] In China, as a rule, they were compelled to allow the local government to exercise jurisdiction over their subjects, but often they resisted its authority and endeavored to supplant it. It was only after defeat in war that China consented to surrender jurisdiction. The humiliation, however, is one that has rankled in the breasts of the Chinese ever since. Thus the movement of 1902 to revise the code with a view to the abolition of extraterritoriality was a very natural one.

REVISION OF THE CRIMINAL CODE

In May, 1905, the commissioners made a partial report to the throne which was approved. This report recommended the abolition of certain cruel forms of punishment and the substitution of others more humane. Briefly, the sentence to a "lingering death," or "the death of a thousands cuts," was abolished. Decapitation was substituted, and it was forbidden to expose the head after execution, as had been customary in certain cases. Branding, beating with the bamboo, and wearing of the cangue, or wooden collar, were also abolished. Instead of these penalties imprisonment at hard labor was substituted. Such imprisonment, too, replaced the old sentences to exile within the limits of one's native province and deportation to the frontiers with military servitude.

Torture of criminals and witnesses, once very common, was forbidden, except in the case of a criminal convicted of a capital offense. The old law, as stated in another chapter,[4] required confession of guilt before execution, and if the hardened criminal would not confess he could be persuaded by torture to do so.

Since the establishment of the Republic the reform has been carried much further. Torture is now forbidden in

[3] Westlake, "Private International Law," p. 96 (139).
[4] Chapter VII.

all cases. A Provisional criminal code drawn up and published in 1923 which was based upon the continental practice in Europe, and a civil code as well as a code of procedure were also published in the same year. Since the establishment of the Nationalist Government at Nanking, these codes have been revised.

NEW PRISONS

The Manchu reform also included the building of modern prisons. Quite a number of these have already been completed. One of the first was that erected by the Viceroy, Yuan Shih-k'ai, at Tientsin. It is a model prison, clean, sanitary and well-managed, with night schools for the younger inmates, who are taught reading, writing and elementary mathematics, and with workshops where all are required to labor at certain trades, such as cabinet-making, tailoring, embroidery and black-smithing. Moral instruction is given daily by an officer who corresponds in his functions somewhat to a Western chaplain.

LAW SCHOOLS AND LAW COURTS

The need of properly trained judges led at once to the establishment of law schools, and with the development of the public school system and the education of many students abroad the improvement of the courts ought to be manifest. The troubles that have afflicted the country in recent years, however, have checked progress in this direction.

A beginning has been made in the establishment of the new courts, and these are no longer under the control of the administrative officers. The Manchu Government adopted the principle of a separation of the functions of the executive and judicial branches of the government, and to these the Republic has added a third branch, the legislative. There will be courts of first instance in all county towns, with appeal to the provincial high courts, and from there to the supreme court at the capital. In many places this reform still exists only in theory. The old courts still function. Men and money are lacking for the changes needed.

THE ATTITUDE OF THE FOREIGN POWERS

Despite the efforts of China to reform her codes and courts, some of the powers are still unwilling to place their citizens and subjects under the jurisdiction of Chinese courts.

In 1906 the United States greatly improved the administration of justice in its extraterritorial courts in China by creating a United States Court for China. This sits generally at Shanghai, but also makes periodical visits to other cities. But the best possible administration of justice in such courts leaves something to be desired. The various nations represented in China have different codes and different methods of procedure. Persons guilty of identical offenses are punished severely in one court and leniently in another. In 1901 two Chinese, two Americans, one Englishman, and a Dane were engaged in a case of robbery and murder at T'ungchou, near Peking. The two Chinese were beheaded within twenty-four hours. The two Americans sent to Tientsin for trial, were sentenced to four years in the penitentiary at Fort Leavenworth. The Consul did not have power of life and death. The Englishman was held for the next session of the British court at Tientsin, a delay of six months. The witnesses neglected to appear and he was discharged. The Danish Government had no arrangements for trial and the Dane was discharged.

These foreign courts, moreover, cannot compel the attendance of witnesses of another nationality, and this sometimes makes judgment difficult. The consular courts are often far from the scene of the crime, and Chinese will suffer in silence rather than take the long journey from home necessary to the laying of complaint before a foreign court.

For these and other reasons the Chinese at the Washington Conference urged the withdrawal of these courts by the powers represented at that conference. After some discussion it was resolved to constitute a commission to visit China to study the situation at first hand and recommend measures to be taken with a view to the eventual restoration to China of that territorial jurisdiction which should belong to her as a sovereign state in the modern world. It is not improbable that some arrangement will be made for the gradual transfer of jurisdiction, similar to that adopted in Siam by the British, French and American treaties with that state.

COMMISSION ON EXTRATERRITORIALITY

In accordance with the resolution, adopted by the Washington Conference on December 10, 1921, an international commission to inquire into the practice of extraterritorial jurisdiction in China met in Peking on January 12, 1926. Several months were spent in the investigation. The last session of the Commission was held on September 16, 1926, at which time a joint report was signed by all members. The report was published near the close of the year by the American Government. It points out the most serious objections to the present methods employed by the non-Chinese powers in the exercise of their jurisdiction in China. Among these are the multiplicity of courts, diversity of laws, lack of jurisdiction by the foreign courts over plaintiffs and witnesses of other than their own nationality, the inaccessibility of the courts in many cases, especially of the courts of appeal, and want of legislation to enable the courts to enforce reasonable regulations of local Chinese governments, such as those relating to traffic, license fees and other taxation.

The Commission found that there were more than 254,000 persons in China in 1925 enjoying extraterritorial status, ninety-eight per cent of whom were Japanese.

An examination of the laws of China disclosed the fact that, while the efforts of the Chinese during recent years to evolve a judicial system and draft laws deserving appreciation had resulted in a body of substantive law.

with the general principles of which the Commission was satisfied, still it was necessary to note that most of the laws had never received the sanction of parliament as required by the constitution. Many were merely mandates of the President or orders of the Minister of Justice, neither of whom had legislative power.

It was discovered, moreover, that since 1917 Canton had not recognized the authority of the central government, and that various military commanders had repeatedly assumed legislative and judicial functions.

A committee of the Commission made a tour of the country to inspect the workings of the courts and to examine the character of the Chinese prisons. According to the report there were but 139 modern courts of all kinds, although there were 1,800 large cities, and that for these courts there were no more than 1,293 officials. The new prisons, although quite modern in their construction and management, were but seventy-four in number. There were still some 1,600 prisons of the old type so severely condemned by Caleb Cushing when he negotiated our first treaty with China.

The Commission made a number of recommendations of a very practical and practicable character. When these are complied with, the Commission thought that the powers concerned would be warranted in surrendering their extra-territorial privileges.

When the Nationalist Party took over the government in 1928, its officers exerted themselves to fulfill the conditions demanded by the Commission. Dr. Tyau in his work, "Two Years of Nationalist China," records the progress made. The 139 modern courts of law of 1926 have become 423. It is hoped by the Government to increase this number to 3431 by 1935. The modern prisons have been increased to 79. 215 more are to be built by 1935, if the Government's plans are carried out.

In April 1929 the Chinese Minister for Foreign Affairs, Hon. C. T. Wang, entered into correspondence with various governments, asking for the abrogation of the extra-territorial clauses of their treaties. Since that time the matter has been continuously agitated. On February 12, 1931, Mr. Wang, in an address to press representatives, said:

"Of the twenty-five nations now in treaty relations with China, ten are without extraterritorial rights, six have agreed to relinquish such rights under certain conditions; treaties with three others have expired, and there are but six whose treaties have still a few years to run." *

Among those that are without extraterritorial rights are Austria, Germany and Russia. Among those whose treaties have not yet expired are the United States, Great Britain and France. The British treaty will expire in 1932, the American in 1933. The Japanese treaty expired in 1926, but the negotiations that have since taken place between China and Japan have not yet (May 1932) resulted in a new treaty. China insists upon the termination of extraterritorial jurisdiction; Japan has offered a compromise which has been rejected. The American and British governments expressed a willingness to agree to a gradual abandonment of their extraterritorial rights, but no definite plan had been adopted at the time of this writing. On May 4, 1931, the Minister for Foreign Affairs of China made a unilateral declaration, denouncing the treaties of extraterritoriality, to take effect January 1, 1932. Since that declaration was made, military aggression by Japan has caused the Nationalist Government of China to postpone the abrogation of the treaty provisions in question.

One of the most serious problems growing out of the agitation is that relating to the future government of Shanghai. That city, one of the most important commercial centers of the world, ranks third in the amount of its shipping. It covers an area of 345 square miles and has a population of 3,183,567. It is under the control of three municipal governments; those of the International Settlement, the French Concession and the Chinese area outside the settlements. Foreign residents number 49,393. Of the Chinese, who make up the remainder, 971,397 live in the

* *Chinese Affairs,* Feb. 15, 1931.

International Settlement and 421,885 in the French Concession.

When the Municipal Council of the International Settlement learned that British and American extraterritorial rights were likely to be abandoned in the near future, it invited the Hon. Mr. Justice Feetham, C.M.G. of the Supreme Court of the Union of South Africa to visit Shanghai, make a study of conditions and recommend some constructive scheme, which, while giving full consideration to the aspirations of the Chinese people, would at the same time afford reasonably adequate protection to the great commercial and business interests which have been developed at Shanghai. His conclusion was that, as to the rendition of the settlements, there ought to be a period of transition and that the length of such period was a question, not of years but of decades. As to the abolition of extraterritorial rights, he held that the continued control of the International Settlement by the Municipal Council was impossible without the enjoyment of extraterritoriality.

During Justice Feetham's visit a change in the administration of justice in Shanghai was made. Before the Chinese Revolution a so-called Mixed Court (a Chinese court with foreign assessors) had heard all cases in which Chinese were defendants or accused. During the political chaos that followed upon the overthrow of the Manchus, the Municipal Council took control of the court. It was returned to the Chinese Government in February 1930 under an agreement between China and the Powers interested. This agreement established a temporary arrangement, to last three years, which allowed China to substitute a "Special District Court" for the former Mixed Court. Foreign assessors were not to be used. Certain conditions were made by the Powers and accepted by China, which were to relieve the distrust of the Settlement residents. Justice Feetham found that these conditions were not always carefully observed, and that the court at times allowed itself to be coerced by political leaders at Nanking. This fact has increased the unwillingness of foreign residents to surrender their extraterritorial rights.

CURRENCY REFORM

An attempt was also made to reform the currency. In our commercial treaty of 1903 China had agreed to establish a uniform currency, so necessary to the promotion of commerce. The United States was interested also in stabilizing the ratio between gold and silver. The fluctuations at that time were rapid and great. Accordingly in January, 1904, the American Government sent Professor Jeremiah W. Jenks to China to study the situation. He spent some months there and recommended a gold exchange system similar to that in use in the Philippines. But his advice was not accepted by China.

I have already spoken of the confusion that exists in China due to the variety of monies in use, the different standards of weight and fineness used in the valuation of silver, the many kinds of dollars in circulation, and the unwillingness of the people to accept a token coinage. The proposed reform, therefore, was one of great importance, but it remains still unaccomplished. In 1905 an imperial edict appeared authorizing the minting of a silver and copper currency, to be uniform throughout the empire, but the edict was not carried into effect. In 1910 the Chinese Government requested the American Government to arrange with American bankers for a loan of fifty million taels for the purpose of currency reform. A group of American bankers was willing to make the loan, but this group of bankers had already entered into an agreement with certain British, French and German groups of bankers to share all business obtained in China. The Chinese Government, after some correspondence, consented to such an arrangement, and the negotiations were conducted, therefore, with the Four-Power Group, as it was called. A coinage system was arranged, the dollar being the unit, and minting regulations as to weight and fineness were adopted. The Chinese Government, in applying to the United States, had promised the appointment of an American financial adviser. When the matter came up in the negotiations considerable jealousy developed at once among the four powers that were supporting these groups, each unwilling that either of the others should have the advisorship.

CURRENCY REFORM POSTPONED

It was finally agreed that the office should go to some small state not represented in the negotiations. Mr. Vissering, President of the Java Bank of Amsterdam, was chosen. His experience with monetary affairs in the Dutch East Indies qualified him in an especial manner for the post. A contract was drawn up and initialed, but Mr. Vissering desired some assurance regarding his rank *vis-à-vis* the diplomatic representatives at Peking, and while this matter was being adjusted the revolution of 1911 broke out and the proposed reform was pushed aside.

During the negotiations the amount of the proposed loan had been increased from fifty million taels to fifty million gold dollars, in order to include a sum needed for financial readjustment in the Manchurian provinces. An advance of four hundred thousand pounds was made for this purpose before the conclusion of the negotiations. This loan of four hundred thousand pounds was extended from time to time for six-month periods; but in June, 1917, the American Group surrendered its interest in the proposed currency loan, and obtained a settlement of its share in the advance. The American Government, however, at once reminded China that the application for a loan for currency reform had been made originally to the Government of the United States, not to any particular group of American bankers, and the Chinese Government was requested to take note that American interest in the proposed loan was not abandoned. The action of the American Group will be more easily

understood when it is remembered that these banks had
been interested in the Chinese Reorganization loan of 1913,
but had withdrawn from the six-power group that was
negotiating that loan because the administration of President Wilson had declined to continue the support which
the preceding administration had given to these negotiations. The same banks were also interested in the loan
which was made in 1911 for the Hukuang Railways. That
interest is still retained. After the surrender by the
American banks of their interest in the currency loan the
Japanese asked for a share in the proposed loan and, it is
understood, were allowed participation. But nothing came
of the negotiations. In 1928 Dr. Kemmerer of Princeton
University was invited by the Government to visit China
and recommend measures looking to monetary reform as
well as to advice on fiscal and financial affairs. In November 1929 he reported a "Project Law for the gradual Introduction of a Gold Standard Currency."

He advised that it should be introduced province by
province. The plan did not propose a minting of gold
coins, but a silver currency to be maintained at parity with
gold. He recommended a gold unit to be called a Sun to
contain 60.1866 centigrams of pure gold, equal to forty
cents U. S. currency, which was about the value of the
Chinese dollar at that time. The silver coins were to be
as follows:—1 sun, 50 cents and 20 cents. The nickel
coins:—10 cents and 5 cents; and the copper coins, 1 cent,
1/2 cent and 1/5 cent.

A gold standard trust fund was to be created to the
amount of 35% of the value of the coins in circulation.
Moreover by the mechanism of buying or selling exchange
drafts, as required, the parity was to be maintained.

On January 15, 1930 the Minister of Finance issued
instructions to the Maritime Customs, directing that all
duties on *imports* should be collected on a gold basis and
that after February 1, 1930 the use of the Hai Kuan Tael
was to be discontinued and the new gold unit, recommended
by Dr. Kemmerer employed instead. Payment of such
duties could be made in dollars, taels or other currency

at the rate of exchange with the gold unit, which would be announced from time to time.

Disunion and civil strife, followed in the autumn of 1931 by the conflict with Japan, hampered all constructive efforts and these adverse conditions were accentuated by the fall of silver exchange, which reduced the value of the Customs Tael from U. S. $0.71 in 1928 to $0.46 in 1930 and to the $0.35 in 1931.

To assist the project for the adoption of a gold standard, the State Council in May 1930 decided to place an embargo upon the export of gold and the import of silver coins. Accordingly the Executive Yuan directed the Ministry of Finance to instruct the Maritime Customs to enforce the ban.

The Central Bank was established in 1928. It is a government institution, but certain public bodies participate in its supervision. It has a capital of $20,000,000.

ABOLITION OF SLAVERY

One great social reform was accomplished before the Manchus lost the throne. That was the abolition of slavery by an imperial edict of 1910. Slavery in China was an inheritance from a very ancient past, and its abolition was attended by many difficulties. A Chinese proverb says: "Old customs may not be broken." Vested interests in all lands are of course arrayed against reform.

In China under the old Manchu code the people were divided into four classes: banner-men, free Chinese subjects, out-castes, and slaves. To these we may add a fifth, the aborigines of the south and west, who were governed by their own chieftains.

The banner-men included the descendants of the Manchus, Mongols and Chinese who were associated in the Manchu conquest of 1644. They enjoyed special privileges. They drew pensions, were required to bear arms, and were forbidden to engage in trade. Prior to the legal reform of 1905 they were subject only to the jurisdiction of the Manchu code. The free Chinese made up the mass of the inhabitants, the farmers, artisans and merchants, as well as a majority of the gentry and officials. The out-castes were Chinese subjects engaged in degrading occupations which subjected them to certain disabilities. These were the actors, beggars, chair-bearers, barbers, lictors and prostitutes. Besides these there were the *to min*, a despised class of pariahs of unknown origin, in Chekiang Province. The disabilities of the last were removed in 1903, and attempts have been made at various times to improve the condition of others. Up to the close of the Manchu rule, however, they were excluded from the civil service examinations and were not allowed to hold office until after three generations of ancestors had pursued honorable callings.

Slaves were of three sorts: (1) household servants sold into slavery by their parents or guardians, and descendants of such slaves; (2) serfs attached to the estates of Manchu nobles. These serfs were descendants of the former owners of the land who, at the time of the Manchu conquest, surrendered themselves and their property to some Manchu lord in return for his protection, and (3) criminals sentenced to military servitude in punishment for crime. In this class descendants of such criminals were included. They suffered for the sins of their fathers.

Besides these there was a class known as *pao i*, who were retainers of the Manchu nobles, and who were bound to render suit and service, but they were not slaves in the ordinary sense of that word. They were admitted to the examinations and often held office.

The edict of 1910 was not wholly satisfactory. It set free the slaves of the Chinese, but the Manchus would not consent to free the serfs from their obligation to cultivate the soil. They were, however, given the status of hired laborers and could no longer be tried by the old slave code. But they were restricted in their movements. They were required to remain on the land. The *pao i*, too, were held to their duties. Further purchase and sale of men and women was absolutely forbidden, but, to provide for the relief of distress in time of famine, parents were allowed to bind out their children for a term of years. Such children could be redeemed if parents should be able later to repay the debt, and in any case they were to be set free at twenty-five years of age.

Concubinage was frowned upon but not absolutely forbidden. The *purchase* of a concubine was, however, not allowed. If a man took a concubine he was required to marry her according to legal forms duly witnessed.

Since the establishment of the Republic, of course, no form of slavery is tolerated by the law, but slavery and serfdom still exist in Mongolia. A conference on Mongolian Affairs, held at Nanking in May and June 1930 adopted a resolution to emancipate all slaves. It will take a considerable period of time to make this resolution effective among a primitive, nomadic people.

THE ANTI-OPIUM REFORM

An earlier chapter has already told of the introduction of the poppy into China by the Arabs in the 8th century. Mention was made, too, of the subsequent import of opium for medicinal purposes and the beginning of opium smoking. After the Chinese Government, in the treaties of 1858, had agreed to legalize the traffic, the production of opium in China soon outstripped the import of the foreign drug. The demoralizing effects of the vice of opium smoking can be appreciated only by those who have lived in close association with the Chinese, and witnessed the degradation and misery caused by it. The Empress Dowager, in 1906, made a heroic effort to suppress the vice and return to the early attitude of the dynasty toward the traffic. The import of opium in 1906 was 54,475 piculs, or 7,263,333 lbs. The native production no one knew, but a moderate estimate based upon the reports of observers in all parts of the country placed it at 175,000 piculs, or 23,333,333 lbs., more than three times the import.

The income to the government from the taxes on the native and imported drug was about Tls. 20,000,000 a year, i.e., about U. S. $15,000,000. Yet the government deliberately determined to sacrifice this revenue in order to rid the country of the awful curse. On September 20th of the year mentioned an edict appeared outlining a programme for the progressive decrease, during a period of ten years, of the production of opium, by a corresponding decrease in the acreage of poppy culture. At the same time measures were to be taken for the gradual suppression of opium smoking. Briefly these measures were (1) to register all opium smokers under 60 years of age, with the amount consumed daily by each; (2) to register all opium dealers and the amount of their sales, and forbid all sales except to licensed smokers and only to the amount of the daily consumption allowed; (3) the smoker's allowance was to be reduced at each renewal of the license; (4) the dealer's license to sell limited the amount to be sold and reduced it year by year; (5) all opium smoking dens were to be closed within six months. It is regrettable to have to note that the foreign settlements at the ports of China were among the last to close these dens. Municipal revenues from licenses were at stake.

For a time the Chinese made remarkable progress in the reform. To succeed in this attempted reform it was necessary to have the assistance of other powers. There was danger that the abandonment of opium smoking might be followed by the use of morphia. The treaty powers were therefore asked, in 1907, to agree to the prohibition, except under a physician's certificate, of all imports of morphia and of hypodermic syringes used for its injection. The powers agreed. It was useless, too, to forbid poppy culture unless the import of foreign opium could be checked. The British Government was approached and promptly gave its assistance by arranging for an annual reduction of 5100 piculs in the import, which would extinguish the trade in ten years or less.

But China made more rapid progress than was anticipated. *Gradual* reduction of poppy culture was found to be impracticable; some growers would profit at the expense of others. The governors of certain provinces prohibited any cultivation at all of the plant. This resulted in 1911 in a revision of the agreement with Great Britain, excluding foreign opium altogether from those provinces where poppy culture had ceased. In this way in a very short time a large part of the empire was closed to the import. The dealers in Shanghai made a great noise and tried to insist upon importation. For a time four provinces were left open to the traffic. Subsequently these also were closed, and a considerable amount of opium was left in the hands of the merchants.

Before this situation disclosed itself the American Government became directly interested in the reform. Opium smoking was common among the Chinese in the Philippines, and our government wanted to have the vice suppressed. Proposal was made to the powers interested in Far Eastern affairs that a commission should meet at Shanghai to study the question and recommend measures to be taken to aid the crusade.

One man, Dr. Hamilton Wright, more than any other, was responsible for the energy with which the matter was pushed. The International Commission met at Shanghai on February 1st, 1909, and on the 26th of that month unanimously adopted nine resolutions. Briefly they recognized the sincerity of China's efforts to effect this reform, and recommended the governments represented each to take measures to suppress the vice in its own territories. It urged them to prohibit the use of opium for any but medicinal purposes, and to prevent the shipment of the drug to any country that prohibited the import. It called attention also to the grave danger arising from the distribution and use of morphia. The governments concerned were asked to close all opium dens in their settlements in China, and apply to their citizens and subjects in China their domestic pharmacy laws. This last would make it possible to punish in the extraterritorial courts in China those foreigners who were obstructing the reform.

The American Government was quick to adopt the legislation recommended and, following up the measures already taken, requested the government of the Netherlands to invite the powers concerned to an international conference at The Hague. This conference met in December,

1911, and was attended by representatives of twelve powers. On January 23d, 1912, the conference adopted a convention designed to secure the legislation needed to bring about the suppression of the abuse of opium, morphia, cocaine and other habit-forming drugs. But since there were but twelve powers signing the convention some of these were unwilling to ratify it unless the governments of the world generally should also agree to support the movement. Accordingly the American Government at once asked and obtained the cooperation of all other American republics. A second conference met at the Hague on July 1, 1913, when it was learned that there were still several European and Asiatic governments that had not signed the convention. This caused further delay. A third conference was then called for 1914, and met at The Hague on June 15th. . It then appeared that 44 out of the 46 governments invited had signed the convention. Turkey and Serbia alone refused. Of those signing only eleven had ratified. A protocol was then drawn up and left at The Hague, which provided that any power signing it could put the convention into force for itself after December 31st, 1914. The United States, China, the Netherlands, and one or two other powers signed at once. But the Great World War broke out immediately afterwards and the proposed reform was forgotten. In the meantime the Chinese revolution of 1911, while aiding the movement in one way, seriously hindered it in others. The republic was, if anything, more determined than the empire to stamp out the curse of opium smoking. In some provinces men were put to death for opium smoking. But in other places, where military operations were in progress, the enforcement of the law was relaxed. Civil war has been almost continuous since 1913, and some of the military leaders, indifferent to everything but the immediate success of their cause, have encouraged the production of opium in order to raise the revenues needed for the support of the armies. Such action has been encouraged, too, by the great amount of smuggling of opium and morphia from neighboring countries.

In 1915 the official trade returns of the Japanese Government showed an import into that country of 358,543 ounces of morphia from Great Britain, two-thirds of the entire out-put of the British manufactories. Yet Japan has stringent laws regulating the sale of morphia to her own people. Japanese traders were charged with shipping large quantities of the drug into China through Japanese post-offices in that country, which, because of Japan's enjoyment of extraterritorial jurisdiction over her subjects in China, could not be searched by Chinese customs authorities. The Statistical Secretary of the Customs, a British subject, estimated the amount of morphia, thus smuggled in that year into China as worth one million pounds sterling.

When the attention of the British Anti-opium Society was called to this condition of affairs they secured the passage through parliament of an act, ostensibly a war-time measure, to prevent the export of morphia. The Japanese Government then permitted the introduction of poppy planting into Korea. Large quantities of opium were smuggled into Manchuria. Morphia, too, is said to have been manufactured by certain Japanese firms. Japanese papers published at Dairen carried a standing advertisement of a well-known firm in which opium and morphia were offered to the trade. For years past the Japanese Government has maintained an opium monopoly in Formosa to supply the addicts there with the drug. On taking over the former German leased territory in Kiaochow a similar arrangement was made there. The farmer of this monopoly, it was estimated, cleared a million yen in 1918. The Japanese Government controlled the customs there and the railway from Tsingtao to Tsinan. Large quantities of opium found their way into the interior of Shantung. Numerous Japanese drug-stores were found to be little better than opium shops in disguise, and many Japanese pedlars in Shantung and Manchuria sold hypodermic injections of morphia at from three to five cents a piece. They also sold the syringes, which are likewise contraband.

High-minded Japanese were shocked by this situation,

and by the callousness of their government, and urged that
something be done to remove the scandal.

The question came up at Paris in the Peace Conference,
with the result that a clause was inserted in the treaty
binding all the signatories to carry out the Convention of
1912. After ratification of that treaty the Japanese Government took certain measures to relieve itself of responsibility in connections with the illegal traffic. Arrangements were made to reduce gradually the sales of the
monopoly in Kiaochow, so that in five years the traffic
would cease. In the Liaotung Peninsula of Manchuria, if
action has been taken, as reported in the press, the situation would not seem to be much improved, since the
monopoly was reported to have been turned over to the
Municipality at Dairen.

The conditions prevailing at present in regard to the
traffic are far from satisfactory. The poppy cultivation in
India increased in 1921 from 144,000 to 204,000 acres,
according to a report to the *Times* of London by Dr.
Collins, one of the British delegates to the anti-opium conferences. The same authority stated that the annual export
of morphia from Great Britain to Japan had grown to
the enormous amount of 880,000 ounces in 1920. Most of
this passed through the United States. Recent legislation
by the Congress was designed to check this traffic through
our country. If we add to this the amount of opium and
morphia smuggled into China from Hongkong, Macao, Indo
China, Formosa and elsewhere, the total will be appalling.
In this smuggling no doubt large numbers of Chinese are
themselves engaged, and the callousness of other governments does not excuse the action of the Chinese authorities
who are tolerating open production in violation of law,
but it does in a measure explain it. Since the signing of
the treaty of Versailles the control of the question has
passed into the hands of the Council of the League of
Nations, in which our government has no voice. But the
American Government has been too long interested in the
reform to be indifferent to its success. It is disturbing to

learn that at a recent meeting of the Council of the League a proposal to "limit the production of opium to the demand for medicinal uses," while accepted in principle, was nullified by reservations on the part of producing powers, who appear more concerned for their revenues than for the promotion of the reform. Eight nations that are interested in the production and distribution of opium for smoking held a conference at Geneva which met on November 3, 1924. Although they professed to be aiming on grounds of humanity at the suppression of opium smoking with the least possible delay, they nevertheless established a legalized traffic in the drug. China, alone, of the eight nations refused to sign the agreement.

On November 17, 1924, a second conference was assembled, to which all the signatories of the Hague Convention of 1912 had been invited to send delegates. The discussion was marked by considerable acrimony. After an adjournment over the Christmas holidays the delegates reassembled on January 19, 1925. The American delegation urged that the manufacture and distribution of smoking opium should be entirely suppressed within a period of ten years. The powers interested in the traffic offered to agree to its suppression at the end of fifteen years from the date at which China should be found to have so far reduced its production of opium as to remove the danger of smuggling of the drug from China to other Far Eastern countries. The proposal seemed unethical and illogical. Opium is being produced in large quantities in China under the protection of military forces that are engaged in civil war, but in violation of Chinese law, which the central government is too weak to enforce. Failing an agreement, the American delegation withdrew from the conference on February 6, 1925. This was followed by the withdrawal of China. Subsequently, the conference adopted the first article of the American proposal, relating to the production and distribution of opium and coca leaves, but with a provision that made it of no real effect since it permitted any signatory to declare at the time of signature under what limitations the assent was given.

The Chinese Government has been unable to enforce its legislation for the suppression of opium production, and the hopes, raised in other countries by the Geneva convention of July 1931 designed to suppress the drug habit, were destroyed by the action of the Bangkok Conference in November of the same year. Radical measures for the prevention of opium smoking were declared to be impracticable as long as the illicit traffic in the drug continued on the then enormous scale. The real reason for the failure of the Conference was the desire of the interested nations to retain the enormous revenues derived from the vice.

CONSTITUTIONAL REFORM

In the summer of 1905 I stood on the platform of the railway station in Peking, whither I had gone to bid goodbye to the members of an imperial commission, which had just been appointed to visit Western countries to study and report upon constitutional methods of government. The two principal members of the commission were Duke Tse, a member of the imperial family, and Tuan-fang, the Viceroy of Nanking, both Manchus. There were also a number of Chinese on the commission. As I drew near the car of Duke Tse there was a sudden explosion; the side of the car was blown out, four or five persons were killed and a number of others badly injured. An investigation showed that a revolutionist had carried an infernal machine into the car, and, as he passed through the narrow corridor, had run against one of the servants of Duke Tse, who was trying to get out. The box containing the infernal machine fell to the floor and exploded. The revolutionist and the servant were among the killed. The departure of the commission was postponed for a time, but its members left later in the summer, and after visiting the United States and various countries of Europe returned to Peking in August, 1906. They immediately made their report to the throne recommending the preparation of the country for the introduction of representative government.

On the 1st of September, 1906, an imperial edict appeared approving of the recommendations of the commission. The edict recited the fact that all nations now were in free communication one with another, and that the laws and customs of one affected those of others; that other countries had constitutional government, and that the welfare of China demanded that she should do likewise; that an examination of the situation showed that China's lack of prosperity was due to a lack of cooperation between the throne and the people; and that, while the supreme authority remained vested in the Crown, it was right that the people should participate in the government. The decree announced furthermore that a period of preparation would be necessary before a parliament could be established. This period was subsequently fixed at ten years but afterwards shortened to seven. In 1907, as a measure of preparation, self-governing societies were organized to train the people in the duties of citizenship. The first municipal election, too, was held that year at Tientsin, Yuan Shih-k'ai's capital. That city became during his viceroyship a sort of political experiment station. The next year, 1908, arrangements were made for the election of provincial assemblies.

DEATH OF THE EMPEROR AND EMPRESS DOWAGER

In the autumn, however, political reforms were forgotten in the official mourning ceremonies that followed the death of the Empress Dowager and the Emperor, within twenty-four hours of each other, one on November 14th, the other on the 15th. Which died first is not certainly known to the public, but officially the Emperor was the first to pass away, giving the Empress Dowager opportunity to appoint P'u-yi, the Emperor's nephew, successor to the throne. This was in accordance with an agreement made in 1903 at the reconciliation of the two court factions; that of the Emperor and that of the Dowager. It was decided then that the Emperor's brother, Prince Ch'un, should marry the daughter of Jung-lu, the faithful supporter of the Dowager, her early playmate and the young Banner-man who had saved her in 1861 from the hand of the assassin. The arrangement announced at the time of the marriage as already stated,[5] was that, if a son should be born, he should be made the continuator of two lines, that of the Emperor T'ungchih, who died in 1875, and that of Kuanghsü, the then reigning sovereign. This was intended to correct the abnormal situation created by the selection of Kuanghsü, a cousin of T'ungchih, as successor to the latter. It is impossible, according to the Confucian teaching, for a man to worship the spirit of a relative of the same generation with himself. T'ungchih and Kuanghsü were first cousins. Through all the years since 1875 the dead emperor T'ungchih has been without a continuator of the line. Now, in a case of this sort, a man who has two lines to keep up must have two wives, for he must raise up descendants in two lines. This is the only case under the old Chinese law in which bigamy was made legal. Concubinage has a legal standing, but except in a case like that just described no man may have more than one wife. P'u-yi was proclaimed Emperor under the title of Hsüant'ung. He was four years of age in 1909 when his reign period began. He was married in December, 1922, when he was seventeen years of age.

DEGRADATION OF YUAN SHIH-K'AI

In September, 1908, some weeks before the death of the Dowager, a garden party had been arranged at the Summer Palace to which the Diplomatic Corps had been invited. A day or two before the date fixed for it, it was called off by the serious illness of Her Imperial Majesty. One day while she was very ill it was rumored that she was dead. A eunuch rushed into the presence of the Emperor saying: "The Old Buddha is dead." This was a common nickname for the Empress Dowager. Immediately the Emperor drew a sheet of paper from his desk and wrote a warrant for

[5] See Chapter IV.

the arrest and execution of Yuan Shih-k'ai. The Emperor had never forgotten nor forgiven his betrayal by Yuan in 1898. He had just sealed the document when the eunuch came running in again saying: "Oh, she's alive again." The Emperor thrust the document into the desk, where a few weeks later it was found by his widow after he and the Dowager had both passed away. She at once sent for Prince Ch'un, the father of P'u-yi. Prince Ch'un was Regent. The Empress said to him: "Here are your brother's commands; what will you do?" The Empress also cherished bitter feelings against Yuan. But someone gave him warning. He fled from Peking to Tientsin. While he was living in safety there in the British Settlement Prince Ch'ing made his peace with the Regent, and it was agreed that he might retire to his home. Accordingly he wrote that he had a sore foot and could no longer discharge the duties of his office, and begged to be allowed to retire. He went to his home in the province of Honan.

MOURNING PERIOD

In accordance with Manchu custom the whole empire mourned for one hundred days. No Chinese was allowed during that period to shave his head. In the braided queue he wore a white cord, instead of a red or black one, white being the color of mourning. All sign-boards over shop doors which had red or gilt coloring were changed to blue and white. No feasting was allowed; no marriages celebrated. Music was forbidden. In the spring of 1909 the remains of the Emperor were carried by 128 bearers from the capital to the imperial cemetery 85 miles southwest of Peking, known as the Western Tombs. The vault and temple constructed there for his tomb appeared very mean in contrast to those of the great emperors who had preceded him upon the throne. The building was still unfinished, indeed, at the time of the revolution.

The remains of the Empress Dowager, Tzuhsi, were kept in a hall reserved for that purpose at the foot of the Prospect Hill, until the autumn of 1909, a year after her death, when they were borne with great ceremony to the magnificent mausoleum which she had built for herself at the Eastern Tombs, 90 miles north-east of Peking.

Thrice the great empire of China has been ruled by a woman. All have been strong characters, but all guilty of great cruelties. Tzuhsi was perhaps the greatest of them all. She was the daughter of a Manchu Colonel of the Bordered Blue Banner Corps. Taken into the harem of the Emperor Hsienfeng in 1852, as a concubine of the fourth rank, she had become the mother of the only son of that Emperor, and was promoted from one rank to another until, at the death of her husband, she was known as the Princess Yi, mentioned in an earlier chapter. After her husband's death she became one of the regents, and was raised to the rank of secondary Empress Dowager, or, as more commonly called, the ''Western Empress Dowager,'' the east being the side of greatest honor. There she eclipsed her superior in rank, the Eastern Empress, with whom, however, she maintained a strong friendship. The words Tzuhsi are but two syllables of the long title that was conferred upon her, two syllables at a time, during her life.[6] She was a masterful woman with strong common sense, but lacking acquaintance with the world. She was a gracious hostess, but when her will was crossed she was cruel as the grave. She wasted the revenues of the empire upon her pleasures. The funds raised for the building of a navy she appropriated to the creation of a summer palace at Wan Shou Shan, adjoining the Yuan Ming Yuan Park that had been destroyed by the British and French in 1860. Like Athaliah of old she had no scruples about killing those who stood in her way, and, like Athaliah, she seized the kingdom. For nearly half a century she ruled the empire,

---

[6] The title in full was ''Tzu-Hsi, Tuan-Yu, K'ang-I, Chaô-Yü, Chuang-Ch'eng, Shou-Kung, Ch'in-Hsien, Ch'ung-Hsi, Sheng Mu.'' Its meaning is: ''The Holy Mother, Compassionate and Fortunate, Upright Protector, Reposeful and Firm, Glorious and Happy, Grave and Sincere, Long-Lived and Reverent, August and Gracious, Noble and Brilliant.''

and to her perhaps, more than to any other one person, the Manchu Dynasty owed its downfall. Her memory will be preserved, indeed, but not by the fragrant balsam of affection. It will be preserved by the bitter myrrh of hatred and unending regret.

CHAPTER XXIV

SETTING UP THE REPUBLIC

God said: "I am tired of Kings—
I suffer them no more.
Up to my ears the morning brings
The outrage of the poor.

Behold mine angel, Freedom!
Choose him to be your king.
He shall cut pathways east and west,
And fend you with his wing.

Emerson.

The people are the foundation of the State; the national altars are second in importance; the monarch is the least important of all.—Mencius (350 B. C.).

The death of the Emperor Kuanghsü and that of the Empress Dowager Tzuhsi, within a few days of each other, halted the programme of reform for a few months; but the provincial assemblies, elected by the people, met in their several capitals in October, 1909. Dr. Morrison, the correspondent of the *Times,* of London, visited a number of these assemblies and reported that their meetings were conducted with dignity, and that the members showed real capacity for legislative work. The assemblies did not possess legislative power, however; they were merely deliberative. But they recommended various measures to the provincial authorities which were of real importance to the people.

THE NATIONAL ASSEMBLY

A year later, October, 1910, the first national assembly met at Peking. It consisted of a single chamber and one half of its members were appointed by the Throne. It also had deliberative powers only. It represented very fairly the various elements of the population; Manchus, Mongols and Chinese. There were 16 imperial princes and dukes, 10 other Manchu nobles, 14 from the dependencies, 6 representatives of the imperial clan other than nobles, 32 officials from different departments of the government, 10 noted scholars, 10 of the largest tax payers, and 100 representatives elected by the provincial assemblies. There were two Presidents—one Manchu, Prince P'u-lun, and one Chinese, Sun Chia-nai. Despite the large representation of the Manchus and the official classes, the Assembly from the start showed itself hostile to the Government's programme. It demanded an immediate grant of power to legislate. Petitions to this effect had been presented before the death of the Empress Dowager, to which that willful woman had replied by reminding the petitioners that the constitution was being granted from above, not forced upon the Throne by the people. She affirmed the sacredness of the sovereign, who was possessed of all authority, although he desired to exercise it in accordance with constitutional forms. It will be noted that in this declaration she was following the example set by the Japanese Mikado in his grant of a constitution.[1] In fact the Empress Dowager expressly declared that the powers of the sovereign under the new dispensation were to be like those of the rulers of Japan and Russia. All laws were to be subject to his approval and all officials were to be appointed by him. He alone could convoke and dissolve parliaments. He was to remain the commander-in-chief of the army and navy. The expenses of the imperial household were to be taken from the treasury without any supervision by the parliament.

An assembly of this sort, as Maclaren has pointed out with respect to Japan, is "the most dangerous political institution that can be created in any country."[2] In Japan the Diet still labors under such limitations as were pro·

[1] Ito, in his commentary on the Constitution of Japan, Chapter I, page 2, said that the mention in the Constitution of certain provisions concerning the sovereign did not in any way imply that any new opinion was set forth; that, on the contrary, the original national polity was more strongly confirmed than ever.

[2] Maclaren's Political History of Japan, p. 151.

posed by the Empress Dowager to China, but Japan had only recently emerged from feudalism when the constitution was granted. The people are still submissive to their lords and are trained to worship the sovereign. There has as yet been but slight chance for the development of a strong popular party in opposition to the Throne. There is a liberal party headed by a few strong men, but it has not been able to remove the handicap just described. In China, on the other hand, there have been several institutions of a democratic character that have helped to prepare the people for political life. There moreover the existence of a foreign dynasty has been provocative of criticism, and has .made possible the organization of secret societies aiming at revolution. Such a programme as that outlined by the Dowager was, therefore, one sure to be taken advantage of by the enemies of the Manchus. The ferment began at once.

The Prince Regent, father of the baby emperor, was not a brilliant man. Neither was he tactful. Prince P'u-lun, the Manchu President, urged him to yield to the inevitable, to get credit for liberal views and save the dynasty, but his efforts were unavailing. The only concession which the Regent would make was to shorten the period of preparation, so that a real parliament possessed of legislative powers might meet in 1913 instead of 1917. The edict to this effect was issued on Nov. 2, 1910. It did not satisfy the radicals, who clamored for legislative power at once. On the 30th of November they put through a resolution asking that the cabinet be made responsible to the assembly, but the Regent rejected it. After a stormy session the assembly adjourned on Jan. 11th, 1911. Before the time for the next meeting had arrived the revolution had begun, and the dynasty was tottering to its fall.

RAILWAYS AND REVOLUTION

In May, 1911, the Chinese Government entered into a contract with the four-power group of bankers for a loan with which to build the Hukuang Railways. The lines were so called because they were to be constructed through the provinces of Hupei and Hunan, which collectively formed the Viceroyalty of the Hukuang, or the "Lake Plain." One line was to extend southwards from Hankow to the northern boundary of Kuangtung Province, where it was to connect with the railway being built by a Chinese company northwards from Canton. The other was to be built westwards from Hankow, across the eastern boundary of Szechuen Province, where it was to connect with a line to be built by a Szechuen company to Chengtu, the capital of that province. The banking group was at first composed of British and French bankers only, when the line southward from Hankow was that under consideration. But Germans offered China more attractive terms, which led to the incorporation of a German group and the inclusion of the line westward from Hankow. The Americans, however, had been given a promise in 1903 and again in 1904, that, in case the latter line should be built with foreign capital, British and American companies would be consulted.[3] In 1909, therefore, the American Government reminded China of this promise, and an American group was admitted to participation in 1910. Inasmuch as the Szechuen company had made very little progress in the construction of the proposed line from Kueichoufu to Chengtufu, the Peking Government decided to take over that section and increase the four-power loan from four million, the sum mentioned in the original contract, to six million pounds sterling. The final contract for this amount was signed on May 20th, 1911. The Szechuen Railway Company had raised eleven million taels, of which some seven millions had been lost in rubber speculation by the President of the company. Nothing had been accomplished except the construction of twenty or thirty miles of earth-work. When the news reached Chengtu that the Ministry of Communications had signed an agreement with foreign bankers for the building of the Szechuen Railway, the shareholders of the provincial company held

[3] See MacMurray's Treaties and Conventions with and Concerning China, pp. 885 and 886.

a meeting, on August 4th, and asked for reimbursement of their outlay. They declared that they had no objection to the loan, nor to the pledging of provincial taxes, but asked just treatment for themselves. The Minister of Communications, Sheng Hsüan-huai, proposed to give them four million taels' worth of shares in the new enterprise. This offer was rejected; the company demanded eleven million taels, or interest on that amount, and refused to take bonds. The Minister pointed out that seven millions had been lost, and that there remained but four millions. The company rejoined that the President who had misappropriated the seven millions had been appointed by the Peking Government, which was therefore responsible. Indignation meetings were held in various cities of Szechuen, and appeals were telegraphed to officials in Peking and to the Szechuen Guild in that city. The members of the guild held a meeting, and sent a deputation to wait upon the Prince Regent. The latter failed to realize the gravity of the situation, and stubbornly refused to yield or to compromise. On the 18th of August the shareholders met again, and gave the Government fifteen days within which to agree to the company's demands. During this period riots occurred in various cities of Szechuen, and officers of the imperial government were attacked. The company was supported in its demands by the provincial legislature. The ultimatum of the Szechuen people expired September 2. On the 4th of the month another meeting of the shareholders was held. Threats were made that the company would pay themselves by seizing the provincial taxes. The legislature prepared to resist the national government by organizing a force of militia. On the 6th of September an edict of the Prince Regent was received by the Viceroy directing him to suppress the disturbances. A meeting of the shareholders had been called for that day, and 600 men were assembled in a hall waiting for their leaders, who had been arrested by the Viceroy and were being held by him in his yamen. The excitement increased from day to day, and on the 9th of September a mob of armed men gathered in front of the Viceroy's yamen demanding an interview with that official. Subordinates appeared and told the leaders of the mob that the Viceroy would receive them if they would surrender their arms. They did so, and were immediately attacked by the Viceroy's guards, who massacred the defenseless people without mercy. This was the match that fired the train. The resulting explosion overturned the throne of the Manchus. The province of Szechuen at once flew to arms. Solemn pledges were taken by the leaders to stand by one another. Provision was made for the support of the families of all who might be killed in the conflict, and the names of such patriots were to be inscribed on a roll of honor. Thus far the professional revolutionists had had nothing to do with the movement. Dr. Sun was not in China, and General Huang Hsing had taken no part.

Members of the revolutionary secret societies, however, are found everywhere in China, and they were quick to take advantage of the situation. On October 8th, 1911, an explosion occurred in a house in the British Concession at Hankow. Investigation by the police discovered that it was headquarters of a revolutionary group engaged in making bombs. These were arrested and turned over to the Chinese authorities. The Viceroy at Wuchang, across the river from Hankow, promptly executed them on the 9th and was decorated by the Regent with the yellow jacket. The next night his yamen was in flames, and his own troops mutinied under the leadership of their Colonel, Li Yuan-hung, who was afterwards twice made President of China. Jui-cheng, the Viceroy, fled to a man-of-war in the river and was carried to Shanghai. He was deprived of his yellow jacket before he had worn it and was ordered to suppress the mutiny, but a few days later he died of chagrin in Shanghai.

In the meantime a large body of troops had been sent from Hupei Province to Szechuen to suppress the rebellion there. Tuan-fang, the liberal Manchu statesman who had been a member of the constitutional commission that was sent abroad in 1905, was ordered to take command of this force. He was not a military officer, but he was a Manchu, and was therefore presumed to be qualified for the post, for all Manchus were required to bear arms. Some weeks were consumed in making the arduous journey through the Yangtze gorges. Shortly after he reached Chungking, in Szechuen, his troops received word of the mutiny at Wuchang and revolted in sympathy with their comrades. Tuan-fang was helpless. A foreign educated physician exchanged sedan chairs with him, and on November 20 in disguise he attempted to escape from the city, but his troops held the city gates. He was recognized, taken prisoner, and after having his ears struck off was murdered. His head was carried triumphantly by two of his soldiers to Hankow, where they claimed the reward which the revolutionists had put upon the heads of Manchus. He was a scholar rather than a soldier, and should have been an archaeologist. His collection of antiques was remarkable and his judgment in such matters was widely acknowledged. He was a man of quiet habits and refined tastes, liberal minded and large hearted. To him very largely was due the programme of political reform introduced in 1905, and to him especially the women of China owe a debt of gratitude because of his efforts to introduce education for girls. He was innocent of the offenses which made the Manchus hated, but he suffered vicariously for the sins of his people.

Early in October, 1911, the annual military maneuvers ·were to have been held in the north. In anticipation of that event the Imperial Guard was drawn up one day on the plain north of Peking to be reviewed by the Regent. After the usual military movements, the Guard paraded before the Prince and was presented with a new silk flag. The standard-bearer received it from his hands and stepped backward to take his place in the ranks, caught his heel, stumbled and fell, dragging the beautiful dragon banner in the dust. The Prince, it is said, turned pale; perhaps in anger, perhaps in fear. It was an evil omen, but no one at that time recognized the nature of the calamity overhanging the Throne.

After the mutiny at Wuchang on October 10th the revolution spread rapidly. Hankow was captured and burned, and Hanyang with its arsenal was also taken. The provinces south of the Yangtze one by one seceded from the empire and set up independent governments. Strange to say the province of Kuangtung, of which Canton was the capital, was the last of the southern provinces to join the revolution, and did not do so until near the close of the year. Four of the south-western provinces entered into a federation with their capital at Wuchang, and with Colonel Li Yuan-hung as President. Somewhat later another group of provinces formed a union with headquarters at Shanghai.

THE REVOLUTION IN THE NORTH

Shantung, north of the Yangtze, seceded, and later returned to allegiance. There were uprisings at Taiyuan, in Shansi, and at Hsian, in Shensi, in both of which places the revolution was stained by the cruel massacre in cold blood of defenseless Manchus, men, women and children. Great assistance was given to the revolution by the National Assembly, which opened its second session on October 22. It renewed at once the demand of the preceding year for real legislative power, and added to this a demand for the prohibition of the appointment of princes of the blood to office, which meant the removal of the Premier, Prince Ch'ing. A renewal was also made of the demand that the Cabinet should be responsible to the Assembly. This programme was supported by the general officers of the northern army, who signed a round robin submitting to the Assembly the draft of a constitution in nineteen articles. Under this the Manchus were to retain the throne, but were to surrender all real power. Legislation was to be the function of the National Assembly alone. The Emperor could do nothing but promulgate laws, and this was to be an obligation of the throne. The constitution could be amended only by the Assembly. Even the executive power was taken away. The premier was to be elected by the Assembly, and the throne was compelled to appoint the man so chosen. The premier was to select the cabinet, whose members were then to be appointed by the Emperor. If the Government of the day should be defeated in the Assembly, one of two courses had to be taken; either the Cabinet had to be dismissed or the Assembly be dissolved; and no Cabinet could dissolve two Assemblies in succession. The military power was left nominally to the Emperor, but the army could not be employed to suppress internal disturbances except under special rules to be enacted by the Assembly. In foreign affairs, too, the Assembly was to be the deciding factor, since no treaty was to be binding until sanctioned by it. Financial control was secured by requiring all expenditures to be in accordance with the budget. Even appropriations for the imperial household were to be under the control of the Assembly. If the Assembly refused to appropriate for the budget, it was not allowable to do as is done in Japan, i.e., proceed according to the latest preceding budget. It will be seen that this outline embodied the best features of the British and French constitutions.

On November 2d, 1911, the Assembly adopted this constitution, and on the 3d passed a resolution requiring the Regent to take oath to observe it. That oath was to be taken in the most solemn manner possible, that is to say, the Regent was to take the oath in the Temple of Imperial Ancestors, thus calling the spirits of his ancestors to bear witness to it. He did this on November 26th but despite this complete surrender, on December 6th the Assembly compelled him to resign the regency.

YUAN RETURNS TO POWER

Prior to the adoption of this constitution, the Regent had made several attempts to bring Yuan Shih-k'ai back into office. It will be recalled that he had been allowed to retire in 1908, on the pretext of having a sore foot, but in reality to escape execution at the hands of the Regent. Now the Regent remembered that Yuan had built up the northern army and was its idol. He hoped by obtaining

Yuan's assistance to stem the tide of revolution which threatened to engulf the dynasty. Yuan, on being invited to return to power, declined politely, pleading that his foot was not yet well. But a gentleman who was in his confidence called at the Legation and assured us that Yuan would come when his conditions were accepted. This gentleman added very significantly; "He will come, but later we are going to have a republic, and Yuan will be President."

Repeatedly the Regent urged him to remember all the favors that he had received from the dynasty and come to its assistance. Yuan's conditions were that he should be made commander-in-chief of the army and navy, and that the funds in possession of the Court should be placed at his disposal for the support of the troops. These conditions were accepted. On November 4th an edict appeared appointing Yuan Premier. Still he declined. He wanted, no doubt, to be elected by the Assembly in accordance with the new constitution. This was done on the 7th. The election was confirmed by the Throne on the 9th. He declined again, but on the 15th he accepted. For several days before this acceptance Peking was in a panic. No one knew what would happen. The revolutionists were powerful even in the capital. Wild rumors were in circulation and tens of thousands fled from the city by all the gates; multitudes on foot, others on donkeys or in carts, chairs or other conveyances. The trains were packed; even the roofs of freight cars were covered. Yuan's acceptance relieved the tension, and after a time the city renewed its wonted appearance.

INTERESTING LEGISLATION

The National Assembly did not confine its attention to political problems, despite their absorbing character. It was an interesting experience to sit in the gallery and listen to the debates upon various topics. Not long after the reassembling in October a bill was introduced to abolish the wearing of the queue. As is pretty well known by most people now the queue was introduced by the Manchus, who, when they conquered China in 1644 compelled the Chinese men to shave their heads and wear the queue in token of their submission. At the same time another edict appeared requiring the women to unbind their feet. The men obeyed very promptly. The women never did obey, and none but a few could be induced by missionaries or reformers to avoid crippling their children, until the educational reforms of 1904 were introduced by the Empress Dowager.

The wearing of the queue was not only unsanitary, but, viewed historically, it was a badge of subjection, and therefore offensive to men who were struggling to destroy Manchu supremacy. Much oratory was expended in support of the bill mentioned, and few members of the Assembly ventured to oppose it. Among the latter was an old gentleman who closed a rather vehement speech with the remark: "I had rather lose my head than my queue." He sat down. The ballot was taken and the bill was carried by a large majority. The old gentleman then arose in a very dignified manner, gathered up his papers and stalked out of the house in indignant protest. As he passed down the aisle I noticed that his head was bald save for a short, thin queue six or eight inches long, hanging just above his neck. But the locks of Samson were not more dear to that hero than this little wisp of hair to this loyal subject of the Son-of-Heaven.

Another topic which came up for discussion much later was that of official dress. Manchu law prescribed in minutest detail the official dress of every man and woman according to their class. Now that China was being modernized it was perhaps not unnatural that the introduction of Western political institutions should be accompanied by Western costumes. So a bill was submitted and carried prescribing the sort of dress to be worn by officers of the government—the business suit, the morning frock coat, the informal dinner jacket and the swallow-tail; starched shirts, collars, neckties, silk hats, bowler hats and shoes. Patterns for all these were supplied. The change in the appearance of the Assembly was startling. The members of the National Assembly in 1911 and 1912 were clothed in silk and satin robes of brilliant colors. They presented a very attractive picture. The parliament of 1913 appeared in the new Western costume, black frock coats and dark trousers, a solemn and depressing sight. The change was the more distressing because the patterns were not understood by some of the tailors in the interior cities. Trousers of black satin and frock coats that touched the ankles seemed ludicrous to Western eyes, although to a man from Mars probably they would appear no uglier than those that copied the fashion plates.

A similar tendency to abandon old customs for new is seen in all the relations and activities of life in China. It is seen, too, in other lands. The picturesque is being exchanged for the commonplace and ugly. The beauty of Peking is being marred by European architecture, and the dignity and gentleness of the passing generation is being replaced by a rude counterfeit of European manners. Why should the world be of one costume, creed and custom? It is an aid to commercialism, to be sure, to standardize our clothing, furniture and architecture, our political institutions and our social and religious rites. But commercialism needs to be checked, not encouraged. This dull uniformity adds nothing to the beauty of the world or the joy of life. On the contrary it greatly lessens these. There ought to be a society for the preservation of native cultures to offset this drift toward a deadly sameness. We are all idolaters, and bow down to the gods of use and wont. What is strange to us we consider barbaric, and we think ours the only right way of doing things. But, to quote the moral of Kipling's poem,

> There are nine and sixty ways
> Of constructing tribal lays,
> And every single one of them is right.

Fortunately the resolutions of the parliament have had but little effect on the country generally. A reaction, it is hoped, will some day set in, and the best things of the old civilization be preserved.

A more thrilling episode in the legislation of the National Assembly was one impeaching the Minister of Communications for his denial of justice to the Szechuen Railway Company. His death was demanded by the Assembly, but he found refuge in one of the Legations, and was aided by foreign friends in escaping to Tientsin and Tsingtao.

When the new premier, Yuan Shih-k'ai, arrived in Peking he called at the various legations. He was in robust health and apparently in the best of spirits. He wore the usual dress of a Chinese civil official; satin gown and jacket, court beads and peacock plumes. In his conversation at the American Legation he was very frank, giving it as his opinion that a limited monarchy was better suited to China's condition than a republic. In the light of subsequent events this statement became important. While he was speaking the Military Attaché of the Legation came in wearing his uniform. Yuan, who had known him for some years, shook his hand and said: "I like to see a man in military uniform. You can believe everything a man says in that dress, but in this costume," pointing to his own Chinese gown, "you can't believe anything one says."

He left Peking almost immediately to take command of the imperial army near Hankow. That city was recaptured after some severe fighting, and Hanyang, separated from Hankow by the Han River, was taken shortly afterwards. General Huang Hsing was in command of the revolutionists in the latter city, but, according to reports received in Peking, ran away before the attack began. His subsequent record at Nanking justifies the belief that the report was correct.

The capture of these two cities by the imperialists was offset by the loss of Nanking at about the same time.

ABDICATION OF THE MANCHUS

Leaving his forces in possession of Hankow and Hanyang, Yuan returned to Peking and demanded additional funds for the prosecution of the war. They were not to be had. The Chinese Government then sought a foreign loan. The American Government suggested to that of Great Britain that the bankers of the two countries be advised not to make such a loan. None was available. Yuan then advised the Court that it would be necessary to negotiate a peace with the revolutionists. Tong Shao-yi left Peking on December 9th to represent the Imperial Government in such negotiations. He went first to Hankow, and on the 13th had an interview with Li Yuan-hung in Wuchang, where the latter served as President of a federation of several provinces. From Wuchang, Tong went to Shanghai, and there on the 18th met certain representatives of other revolting provinces, among them Dr. Wu T'ing-fang, formerly the Chinese Minister in the United States. Tong and Wu were both Cantonese. The revolutionists presented their proposals, which were to the effect that there should be an armistice and that the imperial troops should withdraw 100 li, that the Emperor should abdicate, that a republic should be established, and that an annual pension should be paid to the imperial family. Tong was reported as favoring the acceptance of these terms. He telegraphed them to Peking but secured no response, and on the 23d of December the conference adjourned. Yuan presented his resignation to the Throne on December 28th but it was not accepted. He then advocated the abdication of the dynasty. Dr. Sun Yat-sen, returning from abroad, arrived in Shanghai on the 27th of December, and on the 29th was elected President by representatives of the revolting provinces, except Chekiang, which protested. On New Year's Day, 1912, he took the oath of office at Nanking, at the tomb of Hung-wu, the founder of the Ming Dynasty. It was rather strange to find a republican President taking his oath at the tomb of an emperor; but the Mings were the latest Chinese rulers of China, and the Chinese had again come into their own.

It had been proposed on December 28th, in a decree of the Emperor, that the form of government should be left to a national assembly to be elected later. This had been accepted by the republicans on the 29th of December. But, with the election of Sun as President of a republic in the south, the country for a short period was divided. The southern provinces set up their capital at Nanking, adopted the Western calendar, and drew up a provisional constitution, under which, in fact, the republic functioned until October 10, 1923.

On January 17th we were startled by the report that Yuan had been assassinated. He was attacked as he was returning home from the palace. Two bombs were thrown, one of which killed the captain of his guard and wounded several cavalrymen. One of Yuan's carriage horses also was killed, but he himself escaped unhurt. Opinions differed as to the meaning of the attack. Some thought the bomb had been thrown by revolutionists; others believed the monarchists were responsible, for the monarchists were charging Yuan with treachery to the dynasty. Yuan continued to negotiate with the southern government, and finally came to an agreement with them on February 7th, 1912. In accordance with this arrangement the Empress Lungyü, Regent and foster-mother of the boy Emperor, abdicated the throne on February 12th. At the same time she commissioned Yuan Shih-kai to establish a republic. She gave as a reason for this surrender of the throne the desire to avoid further bloodshed.

The agreement with the republicans provided that the Emperor should retain his title as long as he lived, and should receive a pension of four million taels a year. This generous treatment of the imperial family was well deserved, seeing that by far the larger part of the empire was still loyal to the Manchus. The Chinese, however, have always treated with honor their fallen imperial houses, out of respect for the great men and wise rulers that they have produced. In Peking there is a temple erected by the Manchus to the virtuous rulers of former dynasties. The lineal descendant and representative of the emperors of the Sung Dynasty (A.D. 960-1278) lives in Kuangtung Province and still worships there the spirits of his ancestors. His brother, a graduate of Columbia University, is the well-known president of a technical college. The representative of the Mongol Dynasty (A.D. 1260-1368), a duke who is descended from the great Kublai Khan, lives in Peking, as does also the Marquis Chu who represents the Ming Dynasty (A.D. 1368-1644), and keeps up the worship at the celebrated tombs north of the capital.

BIRTH OF THE REPUBLIC

Other conditions of the agreement between Peking and Nanking were of considerable interest. Yuan was to be chosen President, and the southern government, with Sun at its head, was to withdraw. The Emperor, although retaining his own title, was not to grant any new titles of nobility, but those having titles were permitted to retain them. Under the Manchus the imperial family consisted of four ranks of princes, four grades of imperial dukes, and four of imperial nobles. These titles diminished by one degree as they passed from father to son, so that after twelve generations the descendants of a prince became commoners, unless by their own services to the state any of them should have merited promotion.

Outside the imperial clan there were eight families of iron-crowned princes, whose titles of prince were perpetual and did not diminish in degree from one generation to another. These were descendants of those Manchu princes who assisted in the conquest of China. The family of Confucius and the descendants of the Taoist Pope also transmit their titles without change.

In addition to the nobles of the imperial clan and the eight princely families, there were nine ranks of nobility composed of distinguished men and their descendants, upon whom titles were conferred for services to the state. Some of these descended unchanged for a number of generations mentioned in the patent, but all eventually diminished by one degree as they passed from father to son, unless such son earned promotion by his own services. Usually the first five of these nine titles are translated by the five

YUAN SHIH-K'AI—FIRST PRESIDENT OF ALL CHINA.

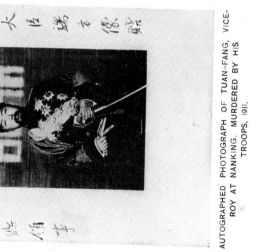

AUTOGRAPHED PHOTOGRAPH OF TUAN-FANG, VICE-ROY AT NANKING. MURDERED BY HIS TROOPS, 1911.

titles known in European heraldry; duke, marquis, earl, viscount, and baron. It is evident from what has been said that, since no new titles are to be granted, the titled nobility of China will gradually disappear, with the exception of those whose rank is hereditary forever.

The greatest sufferers by the overthrow of the Manchu dynasty are certain Manchu commoners, the bannermen, who, born to the profession of arms and the inheritance of a pension, have had no profession or calling upon which to depend for a livelihood. There were eight banners, distinguished by their colors. The highest in rank was the yellow banner with the white border, the second the plain yellow, the third the plain white, the fourth the white with red border, the fifth the plain red, the sixth the red with white border, the seventh the plain blue, and the eighth the blue with white border. Each banner contained three divisions; Manchu, Mongol, and Chinese. The Chinese bannermen were descendants of those who aided the Manchus in the conquest of their country. The pensions paid these bannermen varied according to rank from a tael (about seventy cents)* a month and a dole of rice, for a private, to Tls. 10,000 and something more than ten thousand bushels of rice each year to a prince of the first rank.[4] There were allowances also to cavalrymen for their horses, and special pensions for widows and spinsters, as well as allowances for weddings and funerals. The bannermen were also provided with houses, and in some of the colonies located at various strategic points they were provided with land. When the monthly stipend in silver and the rations of rice were stopped by the revolution many were left in danger of starvation. One of the first subjects discussed by the republican parliament was the measures to be taken for the relief of these people.

THE PROVISIONAL GOVERNMENT

It was the intention of the republicans at Nanking to make that city the capital, and they requested Yuan to

4 Ta Ch'ing Hui Tien, Book 249.

* In 1912.

come there to take the oath of office. A deputation was
sent to Peking to convey the request, and arrived there
on February 26th. They were received with great honor,
and escorted by Yuan's representatives to their quarters
in the Nobles' College. On passing from the station into
the Tartar City they were driven through the central gate
of the curtain wall of the Ch'ien Men, a gate previously
used only by the Emperor. Since they were representatives
of the sovereign people it seemed proper for them to use
the sovereign's gate, but superstition declared that such a
profanation of the sacred structure would bring bad luck
to the city. The circulation of such a warning prepared
the city for the fulfillment on February 29th. That evening the Premier, Yuan Shih-k'ai, entertained the leaders
of the southern delegation at dinner in the Foreign Office.
Suddenly in the midst of the feast the sound of a gun was
heard. Instantly the soldiers on guard around the building
fired their rifles in a mutinous riot. The electric lights
went out and the guests were left in darkness. The first
place attacked by the soldiers was the Nobles' College. The
members of the delegation who were not at the dinner
scrambled over the back wall of the compound into the
grounds of the Young Men's Christian Association, where
they were safe. Then there began a systematic looting of
the banks, silk-shops, and other large commercial establishments. Fires broke out in various parts of the city, and
for three days Peking was in a panic. The signal gun
that was fired sent a shell over the city, which passed
between the home of the American Minister and that of
the surgeon of the American Guard, struck the ground
sidewise, and glanced upward through a tent occupied by
several American marines, hit the ceiling of the verandah
of the guard barracks, and fell sidewise upon the floor
without exploding. Luckily no one was hurt. In two
minutes our guard was in possession of the tower over
the Ch'ien Men, the principal gate of the city, and held
it during the troubled times that followed for two years
or more. The Chinese authorities requested the diplomatic
corps to take charge of the capital and restore order. The

guards of the various legations totaled 2000 or more. In addition to these there were foreign railway guards at Tientsin and other points between Peking and the sea. But the ministers of the various powers declined to assume responsibility for order. They did, however, permit the guards to march to and fro through the streets. This had a quieting effect and helped to relieve the fears of the people. A portion of the 16th U. S. Infantry at Tientsin was brought up to strengthen our guard and to give protection to the various American missions in different parts of the city.

The soldiers engaged in pillage belonged to the 3d Division. They looted very thoroughly, and on the evening of the second day seized three trains on the Peking-Hankow Railway and departed with their treasure. The third day a number of innocent people, poking in the ashes of the burned shops, picked up various articles that had escaped destruction. These unfortunates were promptly arrested and executed. The republicans in the south were disposed to charge Yuan with having staged the mutiny for his own purposes. At any rate the delegation was convinced that it would be necessary to retain Peking as capital in order to keep the north quiet. It was agreed therefore that Yuan should take the oath of office in Peking as provisional President on March 10th. The ceremony was a simple one, held in the banquet hall of the Foreign Office. The guests were arranged around three sides of the hall. The President elect was escorted into the room by a few military officers, and took his place on the vacant north side. He was in the uniform of a general. He removed his cap, read his oath, and handed the document to the head of the Nanking delegation. He then received representatives of all branches of the government and of the non-Chinese citizens of the Republic. The most picturesque were the Tibetans, in purple gowns and yellow jackets with official hats. To them the President gave brilliant scarfs, in accordance with Tibetan custom.

THE PARLIAMENT

The reunion of the north and south under a republican government was followed immediately by the election of a new National Assembly. This, too, was of a provisional character. It met at Peking on the 29th of April. On May 7th it was decided that the permanent parliament should consist of two houses; a senate representing the provinces, dependencies and certain institutions, and the house of representatives, to be chosen from districts smaller than the provinces, much as the American House of Representatives is chosen.

This two-chamber parliament was duly elected, and met in the spring of 1913.

THE REORGANIZATION LOAN

In the meantime the new government was struggling with financial problems. It was estimated that the two armies north and south, still under arms, totaled about a million men. It was very desirable to reduce this force as soon as possible, and the cabinet hoped to get rid of the expense of supporting some 700,000 men. This could not be done until the soldiers were paid, and there would be no paying until a loan was negotiated. Application was made to the four-power group of bankers shortly after the abdication of the Manchus, and advances were made to meet immediate needs. The day before his inauguration Yuan had given these bankers a firm option on the requirements of the government for the succeeding four months and an option on the reorganization loan, if offered at terms as favorable as could be obtained elsewhere. Yet four days after his inauguration the premier Tong Shao-yi had made a loan contract with an outside group. The real reason for this breach of contract undoubtedly was the unwillingness of the Chinese to submit to supervision by representatives of the lenders in the expenditure of the loan. There was strong opposition, too, to the demand of the bankers for the reorganization, under foreign management, of the salt gabelle, which was to be security for the reorganization loan. The outside group of bankers was no doubt encouraged by the Russian Government, which wanted representation for its bankers in the proposed reorganization loan. Japan also was pressing for admission. The result was that Russian and Japanese interests were admitted on June 21st, when the four-power became a six-power group. There were many difficulties encountered, and the negotiations dragged through all of 1912 and the spring of 1913 before the loan agreement was finally signed. In the mean time the Republican administration at Washington, which had inaugurated "Dollar Diplomacy," was replaced on March 4th, 1913, by a Democratic Government. The American Group asked the new administration whether it desired to continue the policy of the Taft administration with regard to this loan. The American bankers, it should be remembered, had declined the invitation of British and French bankers to join in the loan for the Canton-Hankow Railway when it was first under consideration, and they had subsequently joined in forming the four-power group at the request of the American Government. They were unwilling to continue in the six-power group unless the new administration would request it. This, on March 13th, 1913, President Wilson declined to do. The Americans therefore withdrew, and the loan, as finally negotiated, was made by a five-power group. This withdrawal of the Americans was regretted by the Chinese, several of whose high officials expressed the opinion that the presence of the Americans in the group was on the whole favorable to Chinese interests. The action of the Washington Government was apparently based upon misinformation. Five years later President Wilson reversed his policy, and invited the members of the original American group, together with certain other banks, to undertake the formation of a new international consortium to undertake loans in aid of China. This new consortium is still laboring with the Chinese problem, but has as yet made no important loan.

Before the conclusion of the loan negotiations, on Feb
ruary 22d, 1913, the Chinese capital was startled to find
the flag over the entrance to the Forbidden City flying at
half-mast. Public interest for months had been concerned
with the problems of the new republic, and the rivalries
and jealousies of foreign powers shown in the loan negotiations. The inhabitants of the palace had been well-nigh
forgotten. The Empress Lungyü, after signing the edict
of abdication, had shut herself up and spent her days in
sorrow and tears. Her heart was broken. Her health had
given way and death had come, no doubt, as relief. During the remainder of February and throughout the month
of March the palace was in deep mourning. The city
generally shared in this mourning. Three days, March
18th, 19th, and 20th, were set aside for public obsequies.
An altar supporting the portrait of the dead empress was
erected in the gateway of the T'ai Ho Court, before which
the people of Peking paid their respects. During these
three days from early morning until night the inhabitants
of the capital passed in and out of the gates, in solemn,
orderly procession, to show their reverence for one who,
though so unhappy herself, had done so much to promote
the peace and happiness of the country. On April 3d her
coffin, covered by a richly embroidered canopy, was carried
through the city, followed by a long funeral train composed
of men carrying honorary umbrellas and others bearing
trays of rich gifts. There were camels and horses, too,
laden with furs, silks, and other tribute offerings to the
spirit of the dead. A special railway car had been prepared, which carried the remains and the funeral offerings
to the Western Imperial Cemetery, to the tomb which was
being completed there for her late husband.

It is a wonderfully beautiful valley in which the Western
Cemetery is located. The inclosure is ten miles north and
south and five miles east and west, guarded on the north
by a lofty, precipitous mountain range that slopes gradually down in a horse-shoe curve on the east and west. The
valley lies open to the warm influences of the south, as
required by geomantic rules, and is shaded by ash and

oak and elm, with groves of dark cypress around the tombs and temples. The crimson walls and golden colored tiles of the mausolea in the midst of these groves make a beau-;iful picture. As I stood on a slight elevation one autumn afternoon, and saw the purple mountains in the distance, and the mellow light of the sun streaming through the hazy atmosphere, shedding a halo of glory on the tomb of Yungcheng, the first of the emperors buried there, there came to my mind these lines of Shirley's hymn:

> The glories of our earthly state
>   Are shadows, not substantial things.
> There is no armor against fate;
>   Death lays his icy hand on kings.
> Sceptre and crown must tumble down,
>   And in the dust be equal made
> With the poor crooked scythe and spade.

In the midst of all this beauty sleeps the ill-starred monarch Kuanghsü, and beside him his unhappy Empress Lungyü. Yet all this grandeur can do nothing to win them honor, nor can it diminish by a single jot the deep and lasting ignominy of a reign that lost an empire.

RECOGNITION OF THE REPUBLIC

Although the Chinese Government regretted the withdrawal of the American group from the loan negotiations, the motives animating the American Government were greatly appreciated. President Wilson had spoken of the terms of the loan as "touching very nearly the administrative independence of China." He had objected, too, to the pledging of particular taxes, "some of them antiquated and burdensome," and their administration by foreign agents. The Chinese saw in these expressions an evidence of American friendship. The Minister of Foreign Affairs telegraphed to Washington expressing the hope that the United States would give the Chinese Republic early recognition. It had fallen to the author in February, 1913, again to take charge of the legation, and under all the circumstances it seemed to him that such recognition would be a good thing. The legation therefore recommended it. On April 7th we were instructed that, when the National Assembly had been convened with a quorum, and had organized for business by the election of officers, we should deliver to President Yuan a message from President Wilson recognizing the new republic. The new parliament met on April 8th, and the organization of the two houses was completed on April 30th. On May 2d President Yuan arranged a rather elaborate ceremony for the reception of President Wilson's message. The city was decorated with flags and there was great rejoicing. May 8th was set aside as a national holiday in celebration of the event, and on that day representatives of the National Chamber of Commerce, the guilds of Peking, and the universities and public schools formed a procession, each person carrying in one hand a Chinese flag and in the other an American flag, and came to the legation to express the gratitude of the people for the recognition given by the United States.

CONSTITUTION MAKING

One of the first tasks performed by the parliament was the selection of a committee to draft a permanent constitution. This committee chose as its place of meeting the *Ch'i Nien Tien*, the pavilion at the Temple of Heaven where prayer was made by the emperors of old for a fruitful year. It is the circular building with a triple roof of blue tiles erected on the uppermost of the three terraces that form the marble altar in the northern section of the Temple of Heaven. Without doubt it is the most beautiful building in Peking, and its holy associations made it a fitting place for the deliberations of the committee. But the work of the committee was never completed. Almost at the beginning it was seen that the views of the President and those of the majority party in the parliament were at variance. The committee wanted to make the presidency an office simply for the execution of the will of the parliament, a position similar to that of the French President. The cabinet was to be headed by a premier responsible to the parliament. The provinces, too, were to have a large measure of autonomy. President Yuan, on the other hand, wanted a strongly centralized form of government, and was determined not to be a mere figure-head. He wanted all the powers of the American President, together with the right to appoint the governors of the provinces. Yuan had been outwitted in the elections, but would not submit to the rule of the majority. His attempts to bribe and coerce led the more radical members of parliament to plot insurrection. This broke out in the early summer in the Yangtze Valley, but was put down by Yuan without much difficulty. His resort to martial law in Peking, and to secret tribunals and summary executions, terrorized many of his opponents and for a time silenced them. It was finally agreed that the articles of the constitution dealing with the election of a President should first be adopted, and such an election held without delay, after which other articles could be taken up and dealt with more leisurely. One reason for adopting this arrangement was that the European powers would not recognize the Republic until a President had been duly elected.

ELECTION AND INAUGURATION

On October 6th the parliament met to elect a President. There was a good deal of disorder, and attempts were made by Yuan's supporters to intimidate the opposition. Soldiers in civilian dress surrounded the parliament house, hustled and threatened the members, while detectives at the doors prevented any attempts to leave the house and break up the quorum. The session lasted from 8 A.M. to 8 P.M., and finally on the third ballot Yuan was elected. The following day Li Yuan-hung was elected Vice President. The inauguration ceremonies were held in the T'ai Ho Tien, the largest hall in the old imperial palace. It is built in the center of an enormous courtyard, where at New Year's receptions under the imperial régime the princes and nobles of all ranks gathered to kotow to the Emperor. The hall itself is about 150 feet long, 75 feet wide, and 75 feet high, erected on a white marble terrace. The walls are vermilion, the windows covered with carved lattices, and the bracket cornices painted in the five Chinese colors. The tiles are of golden color and glazed. The ceiling, supported by huge pillars of teak covered with red lacquer and gold, is paneled, and each panel decorated with the imperial arms. In this old hall, which once echoed to the tread of emperors, where even imperial princes prostrated themselves before the august Son of Heaven, there, standing upon the dais before which in other days he was wont to kotow, Yuan Shih-kai took the solemn oath to administer the government of the republic in accordance with the constitution. It is regrettable to be compelled to say that he did not keep that oath.

CHAPTER XXV

THE STRUGGLE FOR DEMOCRACY

Heaven hears and sees as the people hear and see.
Kao-yao, B.C. 2255.

These are the ends for which the associated peoples of the world are fighting and which must be conceded them before there can be peace. . . . (2) The settlement of every question, whether of territory, of sovereignty, of economic arrangement, or of political relationship upon the basis of the free acceptance of that settlement by the people immediately concerned.—Woodrow Wilson.

Immediately after his inauguration as President, Yuan Shih-k'ai set to work systematically to destroy the parliament. Charges were made against many of the leaders of the liberal party that they had been involved in the insurrection of the preceding summer. Orders were issued for their arrest. Many, remembering the summary executions of the summer, fled from Peking. A quorum was wanting in either house, and after some weeks of waiting the members dispersed. The President thereupon organized a new national assembly, or Council of State, whose membership was entirely within the control of himself and those attached to his fortunes. Then there began a skillfully conducted propaganda to make it appear that the people of China were calling upon Yuan to make himself emperor. With feigned indignation he put the prize away from him, until after repeated entreaties, all concocted by his subordinates, with pretended reluctance he consented to accept the crown. It was duly announced that the empire would be proclaimed upon the first of January, 1916. A few weeks in advance of that date the imperial Japanese Government, which, it might be supposed, would be the last to defend the republic, gave warning to Yuan that he could not be allowed to make himself emperor. That was

581

a staggering blow. To yield to the threat was to lose face. To proceed with his plans was to bring disaster upon himself and the country. To add to his confusion the southern provinces, which had for a time sullenly submitted to the usurper, suddenly rose in insurrection. The anxiety of Yuan brought on the return of an old disease and this, added to chagrin, caused his death in June, 1916. The real reason, of course, for Japan's opposition to Yuan's ambition, was not love of the republic but hostility to Yuan, whose work in Korea in opposition to Japan's plans in 1883–94 had never been forgotten nor forgiven.

Yuan Shih-k'ai had many admirable traits of character. Where his judgment was not clouded by personal interests he was a man of clear vision and swift decision—a man with the courage of his convictions. He was loyal to his friends and generous to a fault in his treatment of them, but he was remorselessly cruel in his punishment of his enemies. He admired strength, and believed that a strong government was necessary to the peace of China. It was in part, perhaps, the strength of character shown by the Empress Dowager that caused him to prefer her to the weak Emperor, Kuanghsü. Yet his sympathies, as shown by his course as Governor and Viceroy, were with progress rather than reaction, and he did not hesitate to resist the Boxer folly, even though he risked the favor of the Dowager Empress in so doing. As has been shown already, he was not at all scrupulous as to the methods employed to attain his ends, but in his last great offense he permitted his ambition to blind him to the real situation. He laid his hand upon the ark of liberty and perished. Whether he intended, when first chosen President, to play the part of a Napoleon and make himself emperor, is doubted by some, who think he was pushed on by his family and friends. As he lay in his coffin his old-time friend and companion, Hsü Shih-ch'ang, recently President of China, turned to the son of the dead man, it is reported, and said: "You see what you have done to your father." But Yuan was too strong a character to be warped from his chosen path by the entreaties of others. It must be believed, rather, that the entreaties merely reinforced his own secret desires. Among Americans and Europeans in China there were many who admired him, and who still share his belief that the government of the strong man is what China needs. He was succeeded in the presidency by Li Yuan-hung, the Vice President, a loyal republican who had refused to be bribed by a princely title to support the ambitious plans of his predecessor.

THE SHANTUNG QUESTION

In 1914, while Yuan Shih-k'ai was still President, the Great World War had broken out. The American Government at once consulted with the belligerents, proposing that arrangements be made to circumscribe the area of hostilities in the Far East. China, on August 3, 1914, asked the belligerents to undertake not to engage in hostilities, either in Chinese territory and marginal waters, or in the adjacent leased territories.

These measures were justified by the fact that the powers holding these leases were at war, one with another, and by the existence in the treaty ports of China of various foreign settlements, some under international control and others governed exclusively by one or another of the belligerents. Both Great Britain and Germany replied to the overtures of the American Government, expressing a willingness to maintain the status quo in the Far East. Germany offered to engage not to attack British colonies or warships or commerce in the Far East, in return for corresponding promises on the part of Great Britain. But before the arrangement could be completed Japan had decided to act. Early in August, Japan had offered to come to the assistance of Great Britain, but Great Britain declined the offer, since she was looking forward to some such arrangement as that contemplated by the American plan, and was desirous of keeping the war out of the Far East. Japan, on August 13, 1914, expressed to

China her displeasure at the latter's appeal to the good offices of the United States in support of her request for the neutralization of her coast. Japan by that date had already informed the British Government of her intention to join in the war against Germany, and had given assurance that she would respect the neutrality and territorial integrity of China.

China at the beginning of the war had at once taken up with Germany the question of the return of the Kiaochow leased territory, but before these negotiations were completed Japan had issued her ultimatum to Germany. A member of President Yuan's cabinet is reported to have stated that China then offered to join Japan in the recovery of the territory, but was rebuffed by Japan. This seems improbable, but, if true, China showed great weakness in not insisting upon joint action. The British Government did insist on participation in the attack. Japan's fleet was mobilized on August 12th. Her ultimatum to Germany was issued on the 15th. Germany made no reply, and on August 23d Japan declared war. Shortly thereafter, Japan notified China that military necessity required the occupation of Chinese districts outside the leased territory of Kiaochow. Great Britain, however, recognized no such necessity, and landed her force at Laoshan Bay, inside the leased territory out of reach of the guns of the German forts. Japan proceeded to Lungkou, on the north side of the Shantung Peninsula, about 100 miles from the nearest point in the leased territory, landed troops, seized the post and telegraph offices, constructed a military railway from Lungkou to Weihsien on the Shantung Railway, a distance of about 75 miles and billeted her troops upon the Chinese peasants. Supplies for the army were seized for which the Japanese paid in military notes. They were charged by the Chinese with showing great harshness and cruelty in their treatment of the peasants. These charges were confirmed by reports of American residents in Shantung.

The Chinese Government at that time was at peace with all the belligerents, and protested against the violation of its neutrality. The protest was unheeded. On September 3d, following a precedent set in 1904 during the Russo-Japanese war in an analogous situation in Manchuria, the Chinese Government established a zone of belligerency between Lungkou and Kiaochow leased territory. Japan paid no attention to the boundaries of this zone, but proceded to Weihsien and seized the railway station there. China protested again, and pointed out that the railway had not been in German military occupation, but under the protection of. China. Japan gave no heed to this protest, but moved her troops over the railway to Tsinan, the capital of Shantung, 254 miles from the port of Tsingtao, and took possession of the whole length of the railway. China made another protest, which also went unheeded. The forts at Tsingtao surrendered on November 7, 1914, to the Japanese and British forces, and on the 16th of that month the victorious armies entered the city. There being no further need for the occupation by Japan of districts outside the leased territory, China, in December, 1914, took up with Japan the matter of withdrawing her troops from those districts, and that of the abolition of the zone of belligerency. Japan objected, although she had not limited her military operations to that zone. On January 7, 1915, China gave official notice to Great Britain and Japan that the zone was abolished. Japan replied protesting that this was an unfriendly action, since China had not waited for Japan's reply to her request made in December for the withdrawal of her troops. The Japanese note added:

We cannot acquiesce therein under any circumstances. The Imperial Government deems it necessary to declare that, even if your Government actually cancels the communications concerning the creation of a war zone, the Imperial Government would not

permit the movement and actions of their troops within a necessary period to be affected or restricted by such act of cancellation.[1]

THE TWENTY-ONE DEMANDS

On January 18, 1915, Japan followed up the protest
by a presentation of the Twenty-one Demands. These demands were divided into five groups. The first related
to the province of Shantung, in which the territory formerly leased to Germany is situated. It required China to
assent to any arrangement which Japan might thereafter
make with Germany respecting the disposition of the
former German rights in Shantung. It also required China
to promise not to cede or lease any territory in Shantung,
or islands along its coast, to a third power, and asked the
right to build a railway from Chefoo or Lungkou to connect with the Shantung Railway, which had just been
seized by Japan. More cities in Shantung were to be
opened to foreign residence and trade.

The second group demanded that China acknowledge
Japan's predominant position in South Manchuria and
Eastern Inner Mongolia, and required China to extend the
lease of the Kuantung Peninsula, which by the original
agreement with Russia was to expire in 1923, to a ninety-
nine year period, to end in 1997, and that of the South
Manchurian Railway from 1928 to 2002. It also required
China to extend the fifteen-year lease of the Mukden-
Antung line to ninety-nine years, to end in 2007, and to
give a ninety-nine year lease to the Kirin-Ch'angch'un
line. Japanese were to have a right to own or lease land
in South Manchuria and Eastern Inner Mongolia, both
for commercial and agricultural purposes. Demand was
made also for certain mining privileges, and China was
to ask and obtain Japan's consent before granting to a
third power the right to build a railway, or to make a loan
to build a railway, in either region mentioned, or to make

[1] MacMurray's Treaties and Agreements with and Concerning
China, Vol. II, p. 1158.

any loan whatever secured upon the taxes of Eastern Inner Mongolia or South Manchuria.

The Japanese were also to be first consulted in case any political, financial, or military advisers or instructors were to be engaged for either of the districts mentioned.

The third group required China to consent to the conversion of its greatest iron mining and smelting concern, the Han-Yeh-P'ing Company, into a joint Sino-Japanese enterprise, and aimed to pledge China not to allow the company to dispose of any interest in this property without Japan's consent, and not to permit any mines in the neighborhood of those owned by the company to be worked by any other persons.

The fourth group pledged the Chinese Government not to cede or lease to a third power any harbor, bay or island along the coast of China.

The fifth demanded that China employ Japanese as advisers to the central government in political, financial, and military affairs. This was the course taken by Japan in Korea when preparing for the establishment of a protectorate over that country. Japanese hospitals, churches and schools were to have the right to own land in the interior of China. This group also demanded police rights in China for Japanese in certain districts, and pledged China either to buy fifty per cent or more of her munitions from Japan, or to establish a Sino-Japanese arsenal which was to use Japanese material and employ Japanese technical experts. It also asked certain railway privileges, and sought to prevent any contracts for industrial enterprise in Fukien Province with foreign capital without Japan's consent.[2]

Most of the demands, as is easily seen, were an encroachment upon the sovereignty of China. No sovereign independent state, except after humiliating defeat in war, will allow another power to dictate to it in such matters as those concerned in these demands. Yet these demands were made of China, not after an armed conflict but in

[2] For the official text of the demands see MacMurray's Treaties and Agreements with and concerning China, Vol. II, pp. 1231-1234.

a time of peace between the two countries. It was, however, a time of war in Europe, when the world's eyes were directed elsewhere, and the nations were, most of them, too busy to protest. It was, as a Japanese publicist said: "the opportunity of a thousand years."

The presentation of the demands was made in an unusual manner. Instead of handing them to the Minister for Foreign Affairs, the Japanese Minister at Peking placed them directly in the hands of President Yuan Shih-k'ai, which emphasized the affront; and, in so doing, Minister Hioki warned the President against making the demands known to other powers, on pain of serious consequences to China. At the same time Yuan was reminded that Japan was not favorable to his government but could be made so by proper action. Notwithstanding the effort of Japan to keep the demands secret, they quickly became known. On February 3, 1915, the Japanese Foreign Office issued an authoritative statement, declaring that the demands involved no violation of the territorial integrity of China and no impairment of foreign rights there. On the 11th of the same month, the representative of the Associated Press in Peking telegraphed to New York a translation of the demands which was almost literally correct. The Associated Press refused to publish them because the Japanese Embassy denied the truth of the report. The correspondent was asked to confirm his report. He was so indignant that he offered his resignation and was replaced. Prior to this, on February 8th, the Japanese Government had communicated to the powers interested in the Far East a memorandum, purporting to give the list of the demands, but in reality one containing merely a brief outline of eleven of the first fourteen, and omitting altogether those of Group V. Even of the eleven communicated those which were of most concern to other nations were so modified as to conceal their most offensive features.

In view of the dispute as to the character of these demands the Chinese Government, on February 17th, made known the complete text. This led Japan, on February

22d, to issue a supplementary statement containing seven of the missing ten demands, and to explain that these were not demands but *requests*. In presenting them to President Yuan, however, Minister Hioki made no such distinction, and as late as April 2, 1915, the Japanese Legation at Peking officially informed the Chinese Foreign Office that the Japanese Government recognized no such distinction, and would insist upon Group V equally with the others.

The negotiations dragged along for five months. On April 26th, the Japanese submitted a revised list, numbering twenty-four demands instead of twenty-one, but less offensive in some respects than the original twenty-one. The increase to twenty-four was made by separating those relating to South Manchuria from those concerned with Eastern Inner Mongolia. The last-mentioned region was one in which it was more difficult than in South Manchuria to grant the privileges asked. In presenting the revised demands, the Japanese Minister stated that, if the Chinese Government would agree to the revised list without modification, Japan would promise to restore the Kiaochow Leased Territory to China at an opportune time in the future. With respect to some of the demands China had yielded during the progress of the negotiations, but on May 1st seemed less disposed than ever to agree to others, and even made counter demands upon Japan. Briefly they were as follows:

1. Unconditional restitution to China of the leased territory of Kiachow.

2. Agreement by Japan to the participation of China in the peace conference between Japan and Germany.

3. The Japanese Government to bear the damages incident to hostilities in China between Japan and Germany.

4. Immediate removal of all the Japanese military establishments connected with hostilities between Germany and Japan, and the prompt withdrawal of Japanese troops from within China's neutral territory.

The courage shown in making these demands was admirable; one may question the wisdom. Japan replied on

May 7th with an ultimatum, requiring China within fifty-one hours to agree to the amended articles of the first four groups and one article of the amended Group V, failing which Japan would take such action as she might deem necessary to meet the situation. At the same time Japanese reservists in Mukden were ordered to report at their stations, and Japanese residents at Peking, Hankow and Canton instructed to seek places of safety. A Japanese war ship was sent to Chingwantao.

The note embodying the ultimatum agreed to withdraw and reserve for future consideration all the demands of Group V except the one relating to Fukien Province. The promise to return Kiaochow Leased Territory still held good.

China for centuries had been taught the foolishness of war. The military art had been neglected. Military officers were despised by civil officials. The Confucian classics taught in the schools emphasized the doctrine that if the government is just it will meet with just treatment. But here was a situation for which such teaching made no provision. China was helpless and had to submit. On May 25th, two treaties were signed. That relating to the province of Shantung yielded the demands, except that the item relating to the alienation of territory was embodied in an exchange of notes, and provided that no territory or island along the coast would be leased or ceded "to any foreign power"—not merely to a "third power." This treaty was accompanied also by another exchange of notes, which provided that when the territory of Kiaochow at the close of the war should be left to the free disposal of Japan, this power would restore it to China upon four conditions:

1. The whole bay to be open to foreign residence and trade.

2. A concession under the exclusive jurisdiction of Japan to be established at some place there to be chosen by Japan.

3. Another settlement, if desired, to be set aside for other foreign residents.

FORTIFICATION AT ENTRANCE TO BRITISH LEGATION.

AMERICAN MINISTER'S RESIDENCE.

4. Disposition of public properties to be arranged by China and Japan.

The second treaty, relating to South Manchuria and Eastern Inner Mongolia, omitted the preamble of the draft which was to recognize Japan's predominant position in those regions. It granted practically all that was asked respecting South Manchuria, except the lease of the Kirin-Ch'angch'un Railway for ninety-nine years. Instead China agreed to revise the then existing agreement relating to the loan for that line. This was done on October 12, 1917. The loan is to run for thirty years, and during that period the South Manchurian Railway Company is to operate the line. In the phraseology finally adopted the notes relating to loans for railway building and other purposes, and the employment of advisers, are made permissive, not mandatory; but this counts for little where a weak power is being coerced by a strong one.

With respect to Eastern Inner Mongolia nothing was granted, save that China agreed to open certain cities and towns to foreign residence and trade, and promised that, if any foreign capital should be needed for railways there, or any foreign capital borrowed on the security of the taxes of that region, negotiations would be opened first with Japanese capitalists.

The demands of Group III were divested in the main of those features to which China and other powers had objected. China was pledged not to object to the cooperation of Japanese capitalists in the Han-Yeh-P'ing enterprise, and promised not to confiscate the property nor convert it into a state enterprise without Japan's consent. Japan's claim to such pledges is based upon the existence of a large loan to the company by Japanese capitalists.

The demands of Group IV, pledging China not to alienate to any other power than Japan any harbor or island along the coast of China was not mentioned in the treaty. To have done so would have given Japan as a sphere of interest the whole coast of China, if precedents set in 1898 were to be followed. All the items of Group V *[8] were

[8] Abandoned at the Washington Conference.

reserved for later negotiations, except number 6, which in the revised form required China to promise that no nation would be permitted to construct a dockyard, a coaling station, or a naval base on the coast of Fukien. China was herself forbidden to construct such works for her own defense with any foreign capital other than Japanese. The demand was complied with in an exchange of notes. This demand was no doubt due in part to a rumor that the Bethlehem Steel Corporation had entered into a contract with the Chinese Government to construct such a naval station at Mamoi on the Fukien coast. No such contract existed,[3] but the rumor, coupled with the enquiry made by Secretary Hay in 1900, asking Japan's consent to the establishment on that coast of an American coaling station, not unnaturally created some anxiety in Japan.[4]

AMERICAN INTERESTS IN THE TWENTY-ONE DEMANDS

The demands as finally revised and agreed to were less serious than they were as originally presented. This will be seen from the review just made. Nevertheless the agreements embodied in the treaties and notes signed on May 25, 1915, seemed to affect rather gravely the sovereignty and administrative integrity of China, and to impair the treaty rights of other powers.

The American Government, on March 13, 1915, presented to the Japanese Ambassador a memorandum reviewing American policy in the Far East, and the pledges given by Japan and other powers to maintain the Open Door in China. The Secretary of State pointed out the conflict between American treaty rights and the privileges which Japan was seeking for herself. Again on May 13th, shortly before the signing of the treaties, the American Government addressed identical notes to China and Japan, refusing to recognize any agreement or undertaking impairing the treaty rights of the United States and its citizens in

3 See MacMurray, op. cit., p. 1236.
4 See Chapter XXII ante.

China, the political or territorial integrity of the Republic of China, or the Open Door Policy.[5]

THE SECRET TREATIES OF 1917 AND 1918

Examination of the treaty of May 25, 1915, relating to Shantung, and of the notes attached to it, will show that while Japan promised to return the leased territory to China, no mention was made of any intent to return the Shantung Railway. This important railway, whose port facilities are the finest in north China, and whose extensions as planned will make it one of the most important channels of communication in China, has been ever since the seizure by Japan the item most difficult of adjustment in the negotiations between China and Japan for the settlement of the Shantung question. Based upon the fiction that Germany had held the railway in military occupation—a statement which seems to be contrary to fact—the Japanese occupied the whole line with their troops. The Chinese protested in vain, as has been shown. Their efforts to have the troops withdrawn resulted in their own humiliation by the treaties which they were forced to sign on May 25, 1915. Military occupation led to an attempt by the Japanese to establish a civil administration along the railway. On October 1, 1917, an imperial ordinance was promulgated establishing such civil administration for the leased territory and the "railway zone." The existence of a railway zone in Shantung was another convenient fiction. No such zone was known to the agreements with Germany. One article of the Convention of March 6, 1898, concerning the lease of Kiaochow Bay stipulated that German subjects might develop mines within 30 *li* (ten miles) on either side of the railway, but this concession did not carry with it any jurisdiction over the territory concerned, and the right to mine in such territory was expressly surrendered in 1911, in exchange for the grant of specific mining areas in four districts.

[5] MacMurray, op. cit., p. 1236.

The Chinese Government promptly protested against the encroachment upon its sovereignty. The American Government, in December, 1917, communicated with Japan, making enquiry concerning the reported establishment of civil government, saying it was loath to believe that such aggression had taken place. Japan replied that there had been a misapprehension—that the phrase "civil administration" did not imply *domestic* administration. This statement seemed to be somewhat disingenuous. This civil administration in the spring of 1918 attempted to take a census of American missionaries, who declined to acknowledge its authority. Despite China's protest the civil administration continued to function until the autumn of 1918. In order to quiet the agitation of the people of Shantung China signed a secret treaty with Japan on September 24th of that year, agreeing to surrender the whole railway line to a Sino-Japanese company still to be formed, and which was to police the line with Chinese police under Japanese officers, in return for which concession Japan was to withdraw her troops, except a consular guard at Tsinan, and abolish the civil administration.

Before the establishment of the civil administration along the railway, Japan had taken certain other measures designed to strengthen her position in Shantung. In January, 1917, the under-sea warfare had become more and more severe. Both Great Britain and France were negotiating with Japan in an endeavor to obtain the assistance of the Japanese navy in removing this menace. Japan was willing to give this assistance provided her allies would agree to support her claims at the Peace Conference to the former German rights in Shantung and the islands in the Pacific, north of the equator which had formerly belonged to Germany.

The situation became still more critical when Germany, on January 31, 1917, notified the American Government that after February 1st of that year, all vessels, neutral as well as belligerent, found within a defined zone around Great Britain, France and Italy and in the eastern Mediterranean would be sunk. To obtain the assistance needed to overcome this menace Great Britain, in an exchange of notes with Japan, dated February 16, 1917, agreed as requested to support Japan's claims. However, the *quid pro quo* mentioned in the notes was not naval assistance, but a support by Japan of British claims to the former German islands south of the equator. For some reason it was not thought desirable to have it appear that the naval assistance of an ally could be had only upon the terms mentioned. That the real *quid pro quo* was the sorely needed naval assistance was disclosed to the American delegation to the Peace Conference on January 18, 1919, by a member of the British delegation. This was confirmed later by the British Premier, Lloyd George, at a meeting of the Council of Three on April 22d, when he explained that Great Britain was bound to support the claims of Japan, saying that when this engagement was made the submarine campaign was very formidable, that there was a shortage of torpedo boat destroyers in the Mediterranean, that Japanese help was urgently required, and that the Japanese had asked for this arrangement to be made. Great Britain was hard pressed and had agreed. France also exchanged secret notes with Japan, dated March 1, 1917, promising her support, in return for which Japan was to give support to an effort to induce China to break off diplomatic relations with Germany, deport Germans from China, and sequestrate their property.

Japan, it was alleged in Peking,[6] had for two years opposed the efforts of Great Britain and France to induce China to enter the war, on the side of the allies. This, if true, explains the insertion in the exchange of notes with France, of the clause just mentioned. Russia gave her promise to support Japan's claims in another secret note, dated March 5th and Italy subsequently bound herself by an oral promise. All these secret agreements were kept from the knowledge of the United States, even after its entrance into the war, and were not disclosed until the

[6] Putnam Weale's "The Fight for the Republic in China," pp. 231-239.

meeting of the Peace Conference. Having secured the
support of Great Britain, France, Russia and Italy, the
Government of Japan next sought to obtain from the
United States such a recognition of its special interests in
China as would weaken American opposition to Japan's
ambitions in Shantung and Manchuria, and perhaps pave
the way to support of them by the United States at the
Peace Conference. Such recognition was obtained in the
Lansing-Ishii notes of November 2, 1917, already discussed
elsewhere.[7] These notes obtained from the American Government a recognition of Japan's special interest in China,
particularly in the regions contiguous to Japanese territory.

CHINA IN THE WAR

The American Government having received Germany's
note of January 31, 1917, threatening destruction to all
vessels, neutral or belligerent, found after February 1st
within certain zones, Secretary Lansing, on February 3d
at the direction of the President announced the severance
of all diplomatic relations with Germany, and the following
day urged the other neutral nations of the world to take
similar action. China responded promptly on February
9th by sending a warning to Germany of her intention to
sever relations if Germany should carry out her threat
against neutral commerce. At the same time the Chinese
Government assured the United States of her sympathy
with our government in the action taken. Germany did
not reply to China until March 10th, the very day on
which the President of China recommended to Parliament
the severance of relations. This action was directly due
to the sinking a few days earlier of the French steamship
Athos, with the loss of the lives of 500 Chinese who were
on their way to France as a labor battalion.

The Chinese Parliament responded promptly on March
12th to the suggestion of President Li, by a vote approving
the proposed breaking off of diplomatic relations with

[7] See Chapter XXII.

Germany. This was done on March 14th. Then there commenced a strange contest. The Premier, Tuan Chi-Jui, who was also Minister of War, was for an immediate declaration of war, but a large party in parliament believed it unnecessary to go to war, particularly since China was in a very poor state of defense. A more potent reason for withholding the declaration of war was the fear that the premier was bent on building up a strong army to overawe parliament, rather than to make war on Germany. This fear was due to the known attitude of Premier Tuan, who held the view that China needed a strong central government, and who did not sympathize with the ruling party in parliament, whose draft of a constitution, almost completed, provided a very large measure of autonomy for the provinces. The suspicion concerning the premier's aims was strengthened by the appearance of Japanese agents who were reported to be making a large loan to the premier and his party. The President, Li Yuan-hung, was in favor of an immediate declaration of war, but he sympathized with the views of the majority party in parliament in the matter of the constitution. The party opposed to the war was supported by Dr. Sun Yat-sen, who addressed a telegram to Lloyd George, protesting against the effort being made to induce China to declare war on Germany. Dr. Sun was born near Macao and had spent most of his life outside of China, and he showed in this telegram how far he was from understanding the real feelings of the Chinese people. The premier was supported by the military governors of the northern provinces, who met in Peking and adopted a resolution advocating the immediate declaration of war. While parliament was still debating the question, on May 10, 1917, a great mob surrounded the chamber of the House of Representatives, hustled the members as they passed in, hooted and jeered and yelled for war. It was soon discovered that the greater part of the mob was composed of soldiers disguised in civilian dress and sent there by the premier. After some hours the President obtained a troop of cavalry which dispersed the rioters. Parliament refused to be coerced.

The cabinet, disgusted with the premier's action, resigned. On May 19th parliament refused to declare war until the cabinet was reorganized. Premier Tuan was forced to resign. The military governors of the northern provinces met at Tientsin, on June 1st, and again attempted to coerce the government into a declaration of war. The President tried to obtain military support for himself and for the protection of parliament. He purchased a supply of arms which were allowed to fall into the hands of the opposing party. In his extremity the President turned to a military officer of the old Manchu régime, General Chang Hsün, who was stationed midway between Tientsin and Nanking with some 40,000 troops under his command. Since the downfall of the Manchu Dynasty he had been supporting the Republic, but chiefly because of his devotion to his former chief, Yuan Shih-k'ai. He was not identified with either party to the dispute concerning the provisions of the proposed constitution or that relating to the declaration of war. Presumably President Li thought that, being unprejudiced, General Chang would be able to serve as mediator in the dispute and find a satisfactory solution of the difficulty. The solution he found was far from being what was expected, but it did for a moment bring the opposing forces into harmony in a most unexpected and dramatic fashion. He compelled the President to dissolve parliament, although the President, under the provisional constitution then in force, had no such authority. A majority of the parliament fled to Canton and set up a government there, claiming to be the only lawful government of China.

General Chang entered Peking with a small force of troops on July 1st, but instead of attempting to compose the dispute between the factions for and against war, issued a forged proclamation in the name of the President, re-establishing the Manchu monarchy. In the middle of the night he dragged the little boy emperor out of his bed and set him upon the throne of his ancestors. The effect next morning was magical. All factions throughout the country at once united against Chang and the Manchus. The ex-premier himself headed the forces against Peking. The restored empire was never recognized anywhere outside the walls of Peking, and in six days it had surrendered again to the Republic. President Li, however, was so chagrined by the result of his efforts that he resigned, and was succeeded by the Vice-President, Feng Kuo-chang. General Tuan Chi-Jui was restored to the premiership, and on August 14 the Peking Government declared war upon Germany and Austria. There was no parliament in the north to approve or disapprove, but the exiled parliament at Canton was not to be outdone by Peking, and also declared war. There was, therefore, no real division of sentiment between north and south on the question of republicanism versus monarchism, nor on that of war against the Central European powers.

China's part in the war was not of great importance, it is true, but it enabled the allied and associated powers to rid the Far East of German intrigue and to cut off from Germany certain supplies. German and Austrian subjects were expelled from China and repatriated. German and Austrian vessels interned in Chinese ports were seized and chartered to several of the powers at war with Germany. The United States obtained two of them, and also entered into a contract with the Chinese Government dockyard at Shanghai to build four vessels for the American shipping board. The vessels were built and delivered according to contract. China's action also aided in the control of the situation in Siberia and the check upon German intrigue there with the Russian Union of Soviet Socialistic Republics.

CHINA AT THE PEACE CONFERENCE

China, being one of the belligerents, appointed a delegation to attend the Peace Conference at Paris. Great wisdom was shown in the selection of the delegation, for, although the struggle between the northern and southern provinces over the constitutional question was still going on, the newly elected President, Hsü Shih-ch'ang determined to have both parties represented at Paris, and appointed members of the Canton Government as well as of the recognized Government at Peking.

One of the first subjects that came before the Conference was the disposition to be made of the former German colonies. This brought the Shantung question immediately to the front. On January 27, 1919, the Japanese delegation laid before the Council of Ten Japan's claim to the transfer direct to her of all the rights formerly enjoyed by Germany in the province of Shantung, as well as the ownership of the islands in the Pacific north of the equator formerly belonging to Germany. China, as a belligerent and the possessor of the sovereignty of Shantung, objected, stating that in her declaration of war against Germany she had abrogated all treaties and conventions between Germany and herself, and had extinguished all German rights in Shantung. The Japanese quoted the treaties of 1915 between the Chinese and themselves. China pointed out that these treaties had been extorted from her by force. The discussion came up several times in the Council during the spring of 1919, but without decision. Telegrams poured in from China protesting against the attitude of Japan. Among these were telegrams addressed to the American delegation from the provincial assembly of Shantung, from the provincial chamber of commerce of that province, from the provincial educational association, and from prominent citizens of the province headed by Duke K'ung, the lineal descendant of Confucius and the representative of that family. They had a show of right to make this appeal to the United States, inasmuch as the treaty between the United States and China of 1858 provides that "If any other nation should act unjustly or oppressively the United States will exert their good offices, on being informed of the case, to bring about an amicable arrangement of the question." The American delegation did exert itself to bring about an amicable adjustment of the question. At one of the meetings of the Council Baron Makino, for the Japanese delegation, had said that Japan was in actual possession of the leased territory, that it had been taken from Germany by conquest, and that before returning it to China it was necessary that Japan should obtain the right of free disposal from Germany. President Wilson in reply pointed out that the Council was dealing with territories formerly German without consulting Germany at all. The situation became more acute after the discussion of Italian claims along the Dalmatian coast. In that discussion President Wilson took the position that the private understanding between Italy on the one hand and Great Britain and France on the other, known as the Pact of London, was no longer applicable to the situation, since other powers had subsequently been brought into the war with no knowledge of that pact, and since the Austro-Hungarian Empire, at whose expense the pact was to be kept, was no longer in existence. He appealed in a public letter to the people of Italy to take a more generous attitude towards the people of the new state on the eastern shore of the Adriatic. The Italian delegation in protest left the Conference and went home, where their attitude was indorsed by the Italian people. There was discontent, too, in other quarters, and the Japanese intimated that if the former German rights in Shantung were not transferred to them they would refuse to sign the treaty of peace. The situation was critical. President Wilson, in regard to the treaties extorted from China in 1915 by Japan, took a position similar to that which he had taken toward the Pact of London. Lloyd George stated that Great Britain was bound in regard to the Japanese claim in the same way as toward the Italian claim. President Wilson tried repeatedly, but in vain, to persuade the Japanese to modify their attitude. He proposed that all these rights be transferred to the Five Powers as trustees, to be subsequently returned by them to China. But to this also the Japanese were unwilling to agree.

On April 22d, it was agreed to refer to the experts on Far Eastern matters the question whether it would be better for China to have the provisions of the treaty of 1915 respecting Shantung carried out, or simply to have transferred to Japan the rights formerly enjoyed by Germany in the province of Shantung. The experts reported that either alternative presented serious disadvantages for China, but that of the two the least objectionable was to have Japan succeed simply to the rights formerly enjoyed by Germany.

The author, who was a member of the committee that made this report, supplemented it with a letter addressed to President Wilson, in which he stated his objections to the adoption of either course.

The Council of Three actually adopted the alternative reported by the committee to be the less objectionable of the two proposed. The Chinese delegation protested, and refused to sign the Treaty of Versailles. Subsequently they signed the treaty of peace with Austria, and by virtue of that act, which was ratified by the Chinese Government, China became a member of the League of Nations.

CHINA AT THE WASHINGTON CONFERENCE

The Shantung question, however, remained unsettled. The action of the Chinese delegation in refusing to sign the Treaty of Versailles was universally approved in China. The students and merchants there inaugurated a boycott of Japanese trade, as a concrete expression of their hostility to Japan's course of action. This resulted in considerable loss to Japanese merchants. The Japanese made repeated efforts to negotiate the Shantung Question with China. China consistently refused, insisting that the way to restore Kiaochow Leased Territory was to withdraw Japanese forces.

In 1921 the representatives of British dominions met in London in the early summer, in a Council of the Empire. The Anglo-Japanese Treaty of Alliance was about to expire, and the question of its renewal was brought under consideration. There was a divergence of opinion as to the advisability of renewing it. One argument against the renewal was that American opinion was hostile to it. As revised at the close of the Russo-Japanese war, in August, 1905, it provided that:

> If by reason of unprovoked attack or aggressive action, wherever arising, on the part of any other power or powers, either Contracting Party should be involved in war in defense of its territorial rights or special interests . . . the other Contracting Party will at once come to the assistance of its ally, and will conduct the war in common and make peace in mutual agreement with it.

This meant that, if unhappily war should break out between Japan and the United States, Great Britain would be bound to join Japan, unthinkable as that may be, because when nations go to war it is almost invariably claimed by both parties to the conflict that the attack was "unprovoked."

In 1911 the British Government obtained a revision of the treaty of alliance, by adding a provision relieving either Contracting Party of the obligation to go to war with a country with which it had entered into a treaty of general arbitration. Following up this arrangement a treaty of arbitration with the United States was negotiated, but the Senate of the United States failed to ratify it. In 1916 a treaty providing a method of investigating any questions that might arise between the two countries, and stipulating for a period of delay before appeal to arms, was entered into by the United States and Great Britain; but it is not a treaty of general arbitration. The Anglo-Japanese Alliance therefore remained, in the eyes of many Americans, "A stone of stumbling and a rock of offense."

The Council of the Empire, it was reported, had decided that a conference of the three powers; Great Britain, the United States, and Japan, upon Far Eastern matters, ought to be held at London; and the British Government was considering the matter of issuing invitations for such a conference, when the American Government, which had decided to propose a conference of the five principal military powers of the world on Limitation of Armament, learned of the British proposal, and modified its own plans to include the subject of Far Eastern Affairs. This was the more necessary since the questions are so closely related. Four other powers, all interested in Far Eastern matters, were then added to the list of the invited.

This Conference met at Washington on November 12, 1921, and concluded its labors on February 6, 1922. The Shantung Question could not be brought directly before this Conference with any hope of settling it, because, of the nine powers represented there, seven were bound by the Treaty of Versailles.

But Japan and China arranged that their delegates to the Washington Conference should at the same time confer together upon this subject. The American and British Governments appointed each an observer, to sit in these meetings and employ their good offices in endeavors to adjust any differences that might arise. The negotiations lasted nearly ten weeks, the results being reported from time to time at the plenary sessions of the Conference. These negotiations resulted in a treaty between the two powers, signed on February 4, 1922, which, although not formally acknowledged to be the work of the Conference was nevertheless one of its most noteworthy achievements. The treaty in brief provided that within certain stated periods after ratification, the leased territory on the one hand, and the railway on the other, were to be returned to the administration of China; that the option formerly held by Germany on public works in the province of Shantung was to be given up by Japan, that the mines were to become a joint Sino-Japanese concern, that the port of Tsingtao was to be open to foreign residence and trade and be governed by China, alone, and not by a foreign municipality, as is the case at Shanghai and other treaty ports, and that all vested interests were to be respected.

With regard to vested interests, it is to be noted that the leasing of the territory to Germany did not dispossess the owners of private property except as expropriated by the German Government or voluntarily sold by the proprietors. The city of Tsingtao covered 4650 acres while under German administration, and of this area only 310

acres were privately owned. The remainder was held by
the German Government after expropriation and leased
by that Government to lot holders. The Japanese, after
taking possession, expropriated an additional 852 acres
lying north of the city and disposed of this in part to
their own people. They also disposed by public sale of
the government lands in the city, nearly all of which was
taken by Japanese. The Japanese will therefore retain
their commercial interests in Tsingtao, which during their
occupation have become very large. Among other vested
interests must be classed the manufacture of salt, which
the Japanese have developed very extensively. The salt
industry, however, is a government monopoly in China,
and by engaging in this business the Japanese were en-
croaching upon the rights of China and depriving that
Government of a portion of its revenue. In the settlement
made it is stipulated that China shall purchase these Japanese interests for a fair compensation, and shall permit
an export of salt to Japan upon reasonable terms. The
Shantung salt is more highly prized in China than any
other because of its purity.

The cables from Tsingtao which had been given to Japan
by the Treaty of Versailles are acknowledged to belong
to China, with the exception of those portions which have
been taken to connect Tsingtao with Sasebo. This cable
will go to Japan.

Agreement upon the several articles of the Treaty was
reached without much difficulty except in the case of those
dealing with the Shantung Railway. In 1918 China had
agreed in a secret treaty with Japan that the railway
should become the property of a Sino-Japanese company,
but the agreement was never ratified by the Chinese parliament. The Treaty of Versailles gave the line entirely to
Japan, and Japan was debited with some fifty-four million
marks (gold) on her claim against Germany, this being
its value at the time of its seizure as estimated by the
reparations commission. China, however, never signed the
Versailles Treaty, so that the disposition of the line lacked
validity.

The Japanese at Washington urged that the arrangement of 1918 be carried out, that is to say, that the line become a Sino-Japanese concern, but China refused to consent, asking instead that it be recognized as belonging to her and that she be allowed to compensate Japan for the transfer. After much discussion, Japan agreed to sell out to China, the latter to pay the amount estimated by the reparations commission as the value of the railway when seized, plus such amounts as Japan had expended for extensions and permanent improvements. This was agreed to, but, when China offered to pay cash, Japan declined to accept it, and insisted that China borrow from Japanese bankers the sum needed for the redemption of the line and allow the loan to run for several decades. The properties of the railway and its revenues were to be security for the loan, and during its continuance a Japanese was to be Traffic Manager. A traffic manager in China is a very important person; he wields great power. He can control the policy of the railway to a great extent and, if he so desires, he can by manipulation of rates and by assignment of cars discriminate in favor of the trade of his own countrymen. Such discrimination in the matter of freight shipments is not unknown in China. To have a loan secured by the railway, running for a long term of years during which the lenders might to a considerable degree control the line in their own interest, did not seem an acceptable arrangement to the Chinese delegation.

After weeks of debate a solution of the difficulty was found. It was agreed that China should give treasury notes in payment, secured upon the railway and its revenues, and running for fifteen years. China is to have the option of paying all or any part after five years, and pending the payment of the loan in full the Chinese Government is to select and appoint a Japanese as Traffic Manager and another Japanese as Associate Chief Accountant, both of whom shall be under the control of a Chinese Managing Director and removable by him for cause.

Since the Japanese so readily agreed upon other matters, it is rather unfortunate that they did not continue to manifest a magnanimous spirit by accepting payment at once in cash, and thus end without further delay their lien upon the province.

The stipulations of the Treaty respecting the Leased Territory, the mines and public property, have been already carried out. The Leased Territory of Kiaochow was transferred to China on December 5, 1922.

Other matters concerning China dealt with by the Conference were embodied in a treaty signed by the representatives of the nine powers. Mention has already been made of the manner in which this Conference dealt with the questions of "Spheres of Interest" and "Spheres of Influence."[8]

TARIFF REVISION

Among other questions dealt with by the Conference is that of Tariff Revision. Although in the First Article of the Nine-Power Treaty the powers other than China solemnly agreed to respect the "sovereignty, the independence, and the territorial and administrative integrity of China," they were unwilling in the Treaty on Tariff Revision to restore to China her tariff autonomy. The inconsistency was recognized by Senator Underwood, the American Commissioner, who reported to the Conference the work of the sub-committee. "It may seem an anomaly to the people of the world," he said, "that this Conference, after declaring that they recognize the sovereignty and territorial integrity of China, should engage in a compact with China about a domestic matter that is a part of her sovereignty."

At the close of the first war with Great Britain, in 1842, China, beaten in that conflict, was compelled by treaty to limit her duties on imports and exports to five per cent ad valorem. These duties had been made specific by agreements with the several powers. Since prices vary continually the specific duties were no longer

[8] See Chapter XXII.

as much as five per cent, and the Treaty provided for a commission to revise the schedule and bring them up to an effective five per cent.

China, however, pointed out that the rate, 'five per cent ad valorem, is too low and asked that it be raised. The question had been brought up during the negotiations of the American, British, and Japanese commercial treaties in 1902 and 1903, and in these treaties it was stipulated that the duty on imports and exports might be increased provided that China would abolish *likin*. *Likin* is a duty on internal transit, first introduced during the Taiping Rebellion (1853–1866) to finance the operations of the Imperial Government for the suppression of that disturbance. It has been retained and extended as a profitable source of revenue for provincial treasuries, but it is a serious obstacle to trade. The word *likin* means one per mille, but the tax in these days amounts on an average to about two and a half per cent. Foreign merchants avoid its collection by a payment at the port of a commutation transit tax of two and one-half per cent, but goods not provided with certificates to this effect are levied upon repeatedly as they are shipped from province to province, and, even when provided with certificates, the goods are held for examination, causing many vexatious delays. The opening of packages at various stations is also apt to result in damage and sometimes in loss. It has been the urgent desire of merchants, both Chinese and foreign, that this hindrance to the free movement of goods should be removed.

The British and American treaties of 1902 and 1903 respectively agreed that in lieu of *likin* a surtax might be levied upon imports and exports. The surtax on imports was to be seven and one-half per cent, making the total tax twelve and a half per cent ad valorem. The duty upon exports was to be raised to seven and a half per cent by a surtax of two and a half per cent. The Japanese treaty specified no definite rate of increase. The arrangement was never consummated, however, because certain other powers were unwilling to agree to the surtaxes unless compensated therefor by the grant of special favors.

THE SPECIAL CONFERENCE

But a better spirit prevailed at the Washington Conference of 1921–22. The nine powers represented at that conference agreed that within three months after the Tariff Treaty should come into force a Special Conference should meet in China to prepare the way for the abolition of *likin* and the fulfillment of the other conditions stipulated in the commercial treaties of 1902 and 1903. These were treaties of the United States, Great Britain and Japan with China, making abolition of *likin* a condition of an increase in the duties upon imports and exports.

The calling of a Special Conference was made necessary by the disturbed condition of China. It was not certain that the Peking Government could abolish *likin* throughout the country, since its authority was disputed in several provinces. An investigation had therefore to be made and a course of procedure outlined. The Special Conference was to have authority not only to prepare for the abolition of *likin* and the increase thereafter in the rates of duty to be levied, but also to grant an immediate surtax upon imports of two and one-half per cent. on ordinary goods and five per cent. upon luxuries even before *likin* should be abolished. This of itself, it was thought, would give China a very considerable increase in revenue.

An attempt was made to earmark this expected increase for the repayment of foreign loans not otherwise secured. To this China strenuously objected that, as a sovereign state, she could not permit others to dictate how she should use her revenues. Eventually, however, the Chinese delegates agreed that the Special Conference might decide the purposes for which and the *conditions* under which the surtax might be levied, but the repayment of foreign loans was not definitely stated to be one of the purposes. The word "conditions" was a euphemism to cover a demand by certain delegates that the surtax was to be granted provided the proceeds should be deposited in the banks of more than one nationality and not, as was then being done with the customs receipts, placed entirely with the Hongkong and Shanghai Banking Corporation, a British institution.

Unfortunately for China, France, one of the nine powers that negotiated the Treaty, withheld her ratification of the Tariff Treaty until August, 1925, which greatly delayed the promised relief.

UNIFORMITY OF DUTIES

An important change intended to be wrought by the Tariff Treaty was the abolition of the reduction heretofore allowed in duties on imports and exports carried over the land frontiers. This reduction has amounted to one-third in most instances, but has varied somewhat on different frontiers. On the Burmese boundary the duty on imports into China was reduced by three-tenths and that on exports from China by four-tenths.

The practice was first sanctioned in the treaty of 1881 between China and Russia. The overland trade between the two countries was very large, and there being no Trans-Siberian Railway at that time, the trade was handicapped by the expense of transportation by camels across Mongolia and by cart and boat through Siberia. The reduction was intended to lessen in some degree the disadvantages of the land trade as compared with the sea-borne commerce. The precedent was used by Great Britain, France and Japan to obtain similar reductions over their frontiers that touch China. But the building of railways has greatly changed conditions, and, although some opposition was manifested, the Washington Conference finally agreed that these reductions should be abolished.

On the whole the Tariff Treaty, although inconsistently withholding assent to China's reasonable request for tariff autonomy, was distinctly advantageous to that country.

OTHER AGREEMENTS AT WASHINGTON

The Conference agreed also to a withdrawal of their post-offices from China in January, 1923, for the sale to

China of wireless stations there, with certain exceptions, and for an investigation of the new Chinese codes and courts with a view to the eventual surrender to China of the extraterritorial privileges of foreign residents.

The Chinese delegation requested that the treaties and notes growing out of the Twenty-one Demands be considered, pleading that since they were signed under duress they ought to be canceled. Baron Shidehara's reply to the Chinese request has already been quoted.[9] The demand, he said, would establish a dangerous precedent affecting the stability of international relations everywhere. Unanimity being indispensable, as a rule, in international decisions, it was impossible for the Conference to deal with this question. But the Japanese announced that they would abandon their option on loans for railway building and other purposes in South Manchuria and Eastern Inner Mongolia, and would no longer insist upon the preference granted in favor of the appointment of Japanese as advisers. They also withdrew from further consideration the demands under Group V, which in 1915 had been reserved for future negotiation. These were the demands most seriously affecting the sovereignty of China. This renunciation of acquired rights was a fine action, and won well deserved praise for the delegation.

The question of the Twenty-one Demands was raised in a more acute form by the resolution of the Chinese House of Representatives, adopted November 1, 1922, unanimously requesting the Government to secure an abrogation of the treaties growing out of these Demands. To a foreign observer the time seemed most inopportune to raise such a question, when China was torn by internal dissension, and was too weak in a military sense to defend herself in case such provocative action were to lead to a conflict of arms. But the reason for introducing the resolution was, no doubt, that under the original agreement with Russia the lease of the ports of Dairen and Port Arthur was to expire in 1923. The extension of the lease which Japan

[9] See Chapter I.

had obtained was secured by the threat implied in the
ultimatum of 1915.

THE PEKING CONFERENCE

All the powers interested except France ratified the
Tariff Treaty very promptly. France delayed for more than
three years, but on August 5, 1925 gave her approval. The
Chinese Government then called the Special Conference,
provided for in the Treaty, to meet at Peking on October
26, 1925. Two days before the time of meeting, China's
National Tariff Law was promulgated, providing for
a graduated scale of import duties with a minimum of seven
and one-half per cent. *ad valorem* and a maximum of forty
per cent., except that wine and tobacco and articles, similar to those under government monopoly, were to be subject to special treatment. The manufacture and distribution of salt is controlled by the Government and importation of salt, therefore, is forbidden. The duties upon wines
and tobaccos were to vary from fifty to eighty per cent.
ad valorem. The promulgation of this law was in anticipation of the procedure that the Chinese Government had
determined upon for the Conference. The Tariff Treaty
did not specifically authorize the Special Conference to discuss the question of tariff autonomy, but merely to prepare
the way for the abolition of *likin* and the levying of certain surtaxes and to consider interim provisions to be applied prior to the abolition of *likin* and the fulfillment of
the other conditions laid down in the treaties of 1902 and
1903 already mentioned. But China had decided to make
a demand for tariff autonomy as a right inherent in sovereignty.

The Special Conference met as arranged and was attended by representatives of all the powers signatory to the
Washington Treaty, together with delegates from Norway,
Sweden, Denmark, Spain and Peru, invited in accordance
with the provisions of that Treaty.

The representatives of China, in presenting the proposals
of that Government, referred to the declaration made at

Washington by the eight non-Chinese powers, in the Treaty relating to Principles and Policies, that they would respect the sovereignty, the independence and the territorial and administrative integrity of China.

Relying upon this declaration, the Chinese Government asked the powers that were participating in the Peking Conference to declare formally to the Government of the Republic of China their respect for its tariff autonomy and agree to the removal of all the tariff restrictions contained in the treaties then existing. The acknowledgment of China's tariff autonomy was not to be conditioned upon her abolition of *likin* or upon any other *quid pro quo*. Nevertheless in the next article of China's proposals the abolition of *likin* was promised to take effect not later than January 1, 1929, simultaneously with the enforcement of the National Tariff Law, mentioned above.

The proposals of the Chinese Government were received sympathetically by the delegations of the treaty powers. They recognized China's need of increased revenue and acknowledged in principle that tariff autonomy was a right inherent in sovereignty. The British and Japanese intimated that a unified and stable government was a matter deserving attention. The French delegation stressed the need of financial rehabilitation and a number of delegations in their responses, the American in particular, touched upon the abolition of *likin* as one of the purposes for which the conference was called, and asked information as to the plan by which this reform was to be accomplished. While the abolition of *likin* was not made a condition of the recognition of China's tariff autonomy, it was plainly intimated that the two things were to be accomplished coincidently.

The American and the Japanese Governments each presented proposals differing from one another and from those of China in details, but both aiming at a practical solution of China's difficulties. The three plans were taken under consideration by the Conference and on November 19, the committee, charged with the drafting of articles dealing with tariff autonomy, adopted the following:

The Delegates of the Powers assembled at this Conference resolve to adopt the following proposed articles relating to tariff autonomy with a view to incorporating them together with other matters to be hereafter agreed upon in the treaty which is to be signed at this Conference.

The Contracting Powers other than China hereby recognize China's right to enjoy tariff autonomy, agree to remove the tariff restrictions which are contained in existing treaties between themselves respectively and China, and consent to the going into effect of the Chinese National Tariff Law, January 1, 1929.

The Government of the Republic of China declares that *likin* shall be abolished simultaneously with the enforcement of the Chinese National Tariff Law and further declares that the abolition of *likin* shall be effectively carried out by the first month of the eighteenth year of the Republic of China (January 1, 1929).

The articles indicate the sentiment that prevailed at the Conference, but they had not yet been incorporated in any treaty when the sittings of the Conference were suspended.

Aside from the question of tariff autonomy the most important matter discussed by the Conference was that of the surtaxes to be imposed on imports in the interim preceding the enforcement of the National Tariff Law. The Washington Treaty authorized the Special Conference "to consider the interim provisions to be applied prior to the abolition of *likin* and the fulfillment of the other conditions" laid down in the treaties of 1902 and 1903 and stipulated that the surtax should be "at a uniform rate of two and a half per cent. *ad valorem*" with an increase up to five per cent. for certain articles of luxury. China, however, asked for a much heavier surtax on imports so that a scientific and graduated schedule might become possible.

The consideration of this request developed much difference of opinion, and, in order to give China immediate relief, it was agreed on November 14 that the surtaxes allowed in the Washington treaty should be adopted for the time being. On March 25, 1926, a graduated tariff was approved which imposed surtaxes on imports ranging from two and one-half per cent. *ad valorem* on certain staples to thirty per cent. on various luxuries.

The objects for which the increased revenue derived

from the surtaxes should be appropriated was another topic that created much discussion. The proposal that appears to have met with most favor was that this increased revenue should be devoted to the following purposes in the order in which they are named:

(1) Compensation to the provinces for the loss of revenue from *likin,*

(2) Unsecured debts,

(3) Constructive undertakings, and

(4) Administrative expenses.

This would seem to make small provisions, if any, for the most pressing need of China, which was revenue for the central government that would enable it to suppress disorder and restore unity to the country.

The work of the Conference was greatly retarded and finally interrupted by civil strife. No treaty was signed, and the Conference suspended its sittings on July 3, 1926, awaiting a time when the restoration of a stable government in China should make possible the completion of the negotiations.

On July 25, 1928, the American Government signed a treaty with China, recognizing the tariff autonomy of the latter. The new import tariff went into effect February 1, 1929. Rates, revised in 1931 vary from 7½ to 50 per cent ad valorem.

PRESENT CONDITIONS IN CHINA

The internal condition of China is still far from satisfactory. Military Governors, each with an army under his command, are in possession of various districts upon which they fasten themselves like leeches, draining the revenues for their own enrichment and the support of their troops.

The original dispute between the northern and southern parties was a constitutional one. The more democratic south wanted local autonomy and a loose federation of provinces. The north, more accustomed to imperialism, wanted a centralized government. To this original dispute was added that relating to the status of the exiled parliament at Canton, and the legitimacy of the Government at Peking elected by the new parliament chosen in 1918. The President elected by the last-mentioned parliament was Hsü Shih-ch'ang, a typical Chinese gentleman of the old school. Amiable and conciliatory, he strove to reconcile the opposing parties but failed.

A FATEFUL YEAR

The year 1920, as we have seen, was a famine year. Two seasons of drought with failure of crops in the Yellow River Valley and adjoining districts had brought nineteen millions of people out of forty-eight in five provinces face to face with starvation. The American Red Cross, as usual, came to the rescue. The Chinese Government made a loan to aid in relief work and other funds were received from many sources. Many of the sufferers were put to work building high-ways or constructing the earth-work for proposed railways. The women and girls were given in-door occupations and thus the recipients of relief were made in part to earn what they received. But after all the total loss of life mounted into the millions.

Besides the horrors of famine, China had to endure the contemptuous disregard of her sovereignty and violation of her territories by Russian armies in Mongolia and by Japanese troops in Manchuria. But worse than all else was the distress and misery occasioned by a foolish fratricidal civil war.

THE CHIENTAO AFFAIR

The sending of Japanese troops into Manchuria was an act of reprisal for the burning by brigands on October 3 of the Japanese consulate at Hunchun, in the Chientao District. Large numbers of Koreans living in the region were suspected by the Japanese authorities of plotting against Japan. Canadian missionaries accused the Japanese troops of gross cruelty in the massacre without trial of thousands of innocent men and the burning of their homes and winter supplies of food, thus causing helpless women and children to perish of cold and hunger. General Sato, defending Japanese action, said: "I regret that Koreans are not alive to the fact that their real grievance is against these mischief-making missionaries." Japan has sometimes been unfortunate in that her "left hand," the Foreign Office, has been ignorant of what her "right hand," the Army has been doing.

THE CAPTURE OF URGA

February, 1920, saw the tragic end of Admiral Koltchak, executed at Irkutsk by the Social Revolutionaries there. His subordinates fled over the border into Mongolia. One of them, Baron Ungern von Sternberg, in October, 1920, attacked Urga, the capital of Outer Mongolia, and was driven off, but returned in February, 1921, and took the place with the aid of a large force of Mongols who were enraged against China by the oppression of "Little" Hsü, the General who had been in command, and who had deprived the Hutukhtu of his political power and of his liberty. Sternberg was charged with the summary execution of many Russian Communists, Jews and certain Chinese. But a few weeks later he himself was driven out by Russian Red troops and after his capture was put to death. The Russian troops established the People's Revolutionary Government which continued to hold the place until its evacuation by the Red Army in May, 1925. Russian influence is still all-powerful there.

CIVIL WAR

In March, 1920, President Hsü Shih-ch'ang renewed his efforts to bring about the unification of the country by a proclamation in which he appealed to the Cantonese faction to enter into negotiations to that end. But Dr. Sun and his party refused to recognize that Hsü Shih-ch'ang was President. They claimed to be the only "constitutional" government in China, despite the fact that according to the constitution the terms of office of all the members of its parliament had expired. Dr. Wu T'ing-fang said

that he had joined the Canton Government to preserve a
constitutional régime. But in April, 1920, the Canton
Government split into two factions. Dr. Sun, Dr. Wu
T'ing-fang and T'ong Shao-yi, finding themselves in the
minority, fled to Shanghai. The majority party charged
that they carried with them the seals and the funds of the
government. At Shanghai they claimed to be the Canton
Government and entered very cordially into communication with the Peking Government to arrange terms of reunion. The plan was an excellent one: Both parliaments
were to agree upon dates on which they would dissolve.
Not later than October 10, 1920, a new parliament was to
be elected. The election law was to be amended so as to
reduce the membership of the Senate by one-half and that
of the House by one-third. Both the Peking and Canton
governments were then to be abolished and a new President
elected.

The Canton Government, however, objected to any dealing with the three men at Shanghai as representative of
Canton. On the other hand the Anfu Party, then in possession of the Peking administration, protested against any
attempt to make arrangements for reunion through the
party in possession of Canton. This was a move directed
against General Wu P'ei-fu commanding a large army in
central China who was consulting with the Canton government in an effort to bring about the calling of a national
convention to adjust all differences between the North and
South. Such a universal desire for peace and reunion
ought to have made it possible to find a common ground
of agreement, but personal ambitions over-ruled all better
impulses and led to further civil war.

General Hsü Shu-tseng, better known as "Little Hsü,"
was the acknowledged leader of the Anfu Party. He was
the man who had suppressed the Hutukhtu's government
at Urga and created ill feeling among the Mongols. In the
summer of 1920 he was in Peking. His removal from office
was demanded by Ts'ao K'un, the Military Governor of
Chihli, and by Wu P'ei-fu, on the ground of malfeasance
in office. The President removed him. His arrest was

ordered, but he fled to the Japanese Legation where he was given asylum. Tuan Chih-jui, the Premier, belonged to the Anfu Party which indignantly demanded the removal of General Wu P'ei-fu and the reprimanding of Ts'ao K'un. General Wu, who had reached an understanding with the Canton Government, and knew that his rear was safe, then moved a part of his army towards Peking. On June 23, 1920, he met Ts'ao K'un and Chang Tso-lin, the Military Governor of Manchuria, in conference at Pao-tingfu. The three northern leaders agreed upon a programme in which they demanded that negotiations for peace should be conducted with all factions and not merely with three men at Shanghai.

On July 11, 1920, skirmishing began between the army of Wu P'ei-fu and that under the control of the Anfu Party. On the 13th the Premier demanded of the President that he dismiss General Wu and degrade Ts'ao K'un, otherwise he, the Premier, would seize the capital. But the fighting resulted in the complete defeat of Tuan Chih-jui, who resigned his office and retired to a Buddhist monastery to study philosophy. Chang Tso-lin had sent a force into Chihli, but it took no part in the fighting. He supported Wu P'ei-fu as against Tuan and the Anfu Party, but he did not approve the plan for a national convention. It was abandoned, and in October the new Government issued a call for the election of a new parliament, representative of the whole country, through which it was hoped a reunion might be effected.

In the meantime a change had taken place at Canton. The party of Dr. Sun captured the city and Dr. Sun returned there in November and set up a new government. This at once changed the attitude of Dr. Sun toward the project for reunion. He now proclaimed that before reunion could be achieved it would be necessary to summon a peace conference to discuss the legal questions involved. Thereupon in April, 1921, disregarding his former pretence of respect for the constitution and over-riding the protest of the military commander who had captured the city for him, he allowed a handful of members of the old parliament of 1913, whose mandate had long since expired, to elect him President. He then began to raise an army to invade the North. General Ch'en Chiung-ming, the commander of the Cantonese army, objected to this movement, but Dr. Sun was a typical opportunist. He had been a bitter foe of Tuan Chih-jui and then had joined him in war upon Wu P'ei-fu. He had been an enemy of Chang Tso-lin, but now he sought a partnership with him. Chang had frankly said that he did not think the constitution was suited to conditions in China, and Dr. Sun was pretending that his fight was one for the constitution. But "what is the constitution between friends!" The two men formed an alliance to crush Wu P'ei-fu. The forces gathered in the vicinity of Peking. The hope of Dr. Sun that an attack from the South would cause Wu to divide his forces was disappointed by the refusal of General Ch'en to attack. But in April, 1922, Sun persuaded a subordinate of General Wu in the province of Honan to create a mutiny. General Wu was prepared for this and directed the Christian General, Feng Yü-hsiang, to move from Shensi into Honan. He did so and quickly suppressed the mutiny. His forces were famous for the good discipline maintained and for their fighting quality. A portion of this force was moved toward Peking and participated in the victory that was won by General Wu. It was on this occasion that these troops of General Feng were reported to have gone into battle wearing arm bands with these words in Chinese: "Trust in God and show no mercy." Marshal Chang Tso-lin's troops were utterly routed.

After this victory General Wu sought to devise a plan for reunion that would find support throughout the country, north and south. Since the South did not recognize Hsü Shih-ch'ang as President, he suggested to the President that he should retire. He did so on June 2, 1922, and sought consolation in the study of Buddhist philosophy. Since Li Yüan-hung was a hero in the eyes of the South and had been President when the Cantonese party had left Peking, he was induced to return temporarily to the post of chief executive until an election could be held. For the purpose of securing an election that would suit the South, he summoned the parliament of 1913 to assemble at Peking. He also invited the principal supporter of Sun's government, Dr. Wu T'ing-fang, to come to Peking as acting Premier. But Dr. Wu was already at death's door. Grief-stricken over the condition of his country, he died on the 23d of June.

In the meantime General Ch'en Chiung-ming, in command of the Cantonese army, was outraged by Dr. Sun's unwillingness to meet General Wu's overtures. Sun Yat-sen, it seems, could never support any plan which did not originate with himself. He would not support Wu P'ei-fu even when Wu was doing the things which had been demanded by Sun, himself. The result was that General Ch'en seized Canton and sent Sun once more into exile. In his wrath Dr. Sun ordered his war vessels to bombard the city without giving the non-combatants a chance to escape. For this act of barbarism he was severely censured by the world.

The old parliament assembled in Peking on the first of August, 1922. The various parties that made up its membership then spent several months in moves and counter-moves for its control. Dr. Sun saw that he was not likely to be the choice for President and maneuvred to break the quorum. By suitable inducements he persuaded some two hundred members or more to leave Peking for Shanghai where he was staying. But they could do nothing there and stronger inducements persuaded them to return to Peking. In the summer of 1923, as the time for the election of a President drew near, Li Yuan-hung, who had been installed as a temporary chief executive, was advised to retire. He declined to do so before a President should be elected. Thereupon the "Christian General" Feng used forceful measures to compel him to leave the capital. The election was held as scheduled, on October 6, 1923. Ts'ao K'un, the Military Governor of Chihli, was elected President. He was inaugurated on October 10. His first measure was to insist upon the ratification of the new constitution which had been in the making since 1913. It contained all the provisions upon which the Kuo Min Tang in the years 1912-17 had insisted, but Dr. Sun was not appeased. He raised the cry of bribery and demanded the removal of President Ts'ao.

The rise of Ts'ao K'un from the humble condition of a peasant lad, peddling notions on the streets of Tientsin, to that of President of the Republic of China, was something that caught the imagination of thousands. Nowhere save in the United States could such a change be paralleled.

Dr. Sun once more consulted with Marshal Chang Tso-lin. Since they had been unable to subdue Wu P'ei-fu by force of arms, they decided to resort to less worthy measures. General Feng Yü-hsiang, the "Christian General," was flattered. Why should he remain in subordination to Wu P'ei-fu? He had the best army in the country. Financial inducements apparently again played an important rôle. Marshal Chang moved his forces towards Chihli, in October, 1924. Wu's army met them near Shanhaikuan. Wu depended upon the support of General Feng, who betrayed him in the critical moment of the battle. Wu P'ei-fu was overwhelmed. Feng seized Peking and imprisoned President Ts'ao, the man whom he had helped to elect. But it had not been Marshal Chang's intention, nor that of Dr. Sun, to have General Feng control Peking. The latter was induced to attend a conference at Tientsin. To this conference Chang Tso-lin, Tuan Chih-jui, Feng Yühsiang and Sun Yat-sen were invited. Before Sun's arrival, the three other leaders had agreed that Tuan should take the post of chief executive and be supported by Chang and Feng. This was done on November 10. Sun arrived in Peking on December 31, 1924, but he was quite ill. Tuan Chih-jui had already issued a call for a reorganization conference which met in February, 1925, but accomplished nothing. When Sun heard that the call had been issued, he made objection to the plan. Recalcitrant to the end, this stormy petrel of Oriental politics was always ready with a protest. He had fallen under Russian influence and wanted to have the delegates to the proposed conference chosen by the Soviet method. His illness increased in gravity and resulted in his death on March 12, 1925. In spite of his failings which were obvious, he was regarded by the Chinese everywhere as a great hero. An imposing mausoleum for his remains has been built at Nanking.

THE MANCHU EMPEROR

In the settlement made with the Manchu Government in 1912, it had been agreed that the Emperor should retain his title as long as he lived, be granted a palace in which to live and allowed a pension of four million taels a year. One of the first things that General Feng did, on seizing Peking, was to deprive the Emperor of his title, compel him to leave the capital and reduce his pension to $500,000 per annum. Two millions of the allowance formerly granted were to be set aside for the establishment of a factory for the employment of destitute Manchus. The ex-emperor removed to Tientsin, where he became plain Mr. Henry Pu. On November 14, 1931, under Japanese escort he went to Mukden (Shenyang) and on March 9, 1932 Japan made him ruler of Manchu Kuo with capital at Changchun, now Hsinching.

RUSSIAN INFLUENCE

As early as April, 1920, the Russian Union of Soviet Socialistic Republics attempted to enter into relations with China, offering in return for recognition to surrender all Russian concessions in China and various other treaty rights including extraterritorial jurisdiction. Conferences were initiated which resulted in suspension of payments on the Russian share of the Boxer Indemnity and the withdrawal of recognition from the representatives of the Russian Republic of the Kerensky régime, who were still in Peking and at the Chinese ports. Following upon these measures, the Chinese Government entered into an agreement on October 2, 1920, with the Russo-Asiatic Bank providing for a joint Chinese-Russian Board of Directors to control the Chinese Eastern Railway. There were to be five directors of each nationality, one of the Chinese to be

President with a casting vote. This placed the railway under Chinese control.

In 1921 China sent a mission to Moscow to study the situation there and in August, 1922, a representative of Russia, M. Joffe, arrived in China and proposed an agreement along the lines suggested in 1920. It was not until May 31, 1924, however, that Chinese recognition of the Russian Soviet Government was accorded. The agreement contained seven stipulations: Russians were to be employed on the Chinese Eastern Railway. The extraterritorial jurisdiction formerly enjoyed by Russia was surrendered. The public property of the Russian Government, except the concessions at Tientsin and Hankow, was to be turned over to the Soviet Government. Russian Church property was to be turned over to some person or organization to be designated by the Russian Soviet Government. The Russian share of the Boxer Indemnity was to be devoted by China to educational purposes, supervised by a joint committee as in the case of the American share. The Chinese Government should not recognize as valid any treaty or agreement between Russia and a third party, negotiated since the overthrow of the Tsarist régime and affecting the rights and interests of China. This referred to the agreement between the Russian Soviet Government and the Revolutionary Government of Outer Mongolia. The seventh stipulation was to the effect that the former Russian concessions at Tientsin and Hankow were not to be given to any other power.

A number of Russians found an asylum in China after the revolution of November, 1917. Some of these were employed by Marshal Chang Tso-lin and other military commanders in the northern provinces. After China's recognition of the Soviet Government Russian influence of a communistic character began to be felt at Peking. Such influence was evident at Canton at an earlier date. This was due to the pleasant relations established between Dr. Sun and the Rusian envoy, Joffe, in 1923. The effect of this intercourse was seen in the seizure of temples and other public properties by Dr. Sun in 1924, the organization of laborers and in legislation antagonistic to capitalistic interests. Dr. Sun had entered into an agreement with Joffe to accept political and military advisers in return for financial assistance from Russia together with arms and ammunition. In Peking, General Feng Yü-hsiang was maintaining close relations with Moscow and receiving from Russia arms and military advisers.

THE RETURN OF WU P'EI-FU

After his betrayal by the "Christian" General, Feng Yü-hsiang, in 1924, General Wu P'ei-fu returned to the Yangtze Valley where he reassembled his scattered forces and prepared to avenge the wrong that he had received. Feng was compelled to depend almost wholly upon Russia for munitions, which were brought to him overland across Mongolia. For this reason, if for no other, he had to maintain friendly relations with Moscow. Marshal Chang Tso-lin had no such need. He could obtain his supplies without difficulty and he had shown a bitter hostility to the recognition accorded Russia. Wu P'ei-fu was no less hostile to Communism, whether north or south of him. There was thus a ground of sympathy between Chang and Wu. But through the year 1925 they remained hostile. Chang, after his victory of 1924, had attempted to extend his control to Shanghai. In the autumn of 1925 he was forced to abandon that region by the military operations of General Sun Chuang-fang coming from the province of Chekiang. Sun Chuang-fang and Wu P'ei-fu were thus drawn together and eight provinces in the region of the Yangtze were brought to support the alliance. Chang withdrew his armies into Manchuria, November, 1925.

THE SHANGHAI RIOT

During a strike in a Japanese-owned mill in Shanghai in the spring of 1925, a Chinese operative was killed by a Japanese. This led to a bitter feeling against foreign resi-

dents and a demand by Chinese generally for the abolition
of the extraterritorial jurisdiction enjoyed by foreign powers. The agitation was conducted very largely by students
and laborers. On May 30, 1925, students haranguing the
crowds on the streets were told that they were obstructing
traffic and ordered to move on. Several who did not obey
were arrested and taken to the police station. A noisy crowd
gathered there, into which, after warning, the police fired.
Several students were killed and a larger number were
wounded. The men who gave the order to fire were British.
This involved the British with the Japanese as objects of
attack. The agitation spread to other ports, notably Hankow and Canton. On the 23d of June after a mass meeting
at the parade ground in Canton a procession was formed to
distribute hand bills. Passing the end of the bridge that
connects with the island of Shameen where the British and
French settlements are located, fifty-two Chinese were
killed and one hundred and seventeen wounded by a British
machine gun. The British claimed that the Chinese fired
the first shot. The Chinese commission, appointed to investigate the massacre, declared that the attack was unprovoked and the persons killed and wounded were unarmed.
An Anti-British boycott resulted which through the year
1926 inflicted great loss upon British trade.

The Japanese settled their mill strike in 1925 and paid
a solatium to the family of the man who was killed. Hostility to all foreign residents seemed to increase, however,
through 1925 and 1926. This strengthened the hands of the
Chinese delegates at the Tariff Conference in their demand
for tariff autonomy and emphasized the cry for the abolition of extraterritoriality.

The affair at Canton, moreover, strengthened the Nationalist Party there. The party was charged with Communism, and it is true that Russian advisers were prominent in the affairs of the party, but the platform put forth,
containing fourteen articles, had nothing in it of a communistic character.

THE DOWNFALL OF FENG YÜ-HSIANG

After the withdrawal of Chang Tso-lin's forces into Manchuria, Feng was called upon to suppress a rising against his authority headed by the Military Governor of Chihli. About the same time Chang had to face a serious rebellion among his troops led by General Kuo Sung-ling. The latter was apparently about to succeed when favorable action by Japan enabled Chang to recover himself. Kuo was captured and with his wife was put to death.

The revolt of Kuo was said to have been encouraged by Feng. Chang had already been estranged to a degree from Feng by his seeming attachment to the communists. This feeling was increased after the affair with Kuo, and Chang Tso-lin had more reason than ever to feel drawn towards his old enemy, Wu P'ei-fu.

Early in 1926 they formed an alliance, and declared war on Feng. The latter was handicapped by the action of the Diplomatic Corps which insisted upon a literal interpretation of the Treaty of 1901 which forbade the fortification of the mouth of the Hai Ho. This gave an advantage to Feng's foes.

Feng withdrew his forces from Peking in good order and turned the command over to his subordinates. These men who had once been under the orders of Wu now offered to make him President. With rare wisdom Wu P'ei-fu declined the bribe and preferred to keep faith with Chang. He demanded unconditional surrender, but the Kuo Min Chün, as Feng's army was called, moved northwards and late in 1926 returned into Shensi, its old camping ground.

Tuan Chih-jui was forced once more to quit Peking and the overthrow of the Government was that which interrupted the proceedings of the Tariff Conference and those of the Conference on Extraterritoriality.

THE CANTON INVASION OF THE YANGTZE VALLEY

The Communist Party having obtained control of the government at Canton through the operations of the so-called "Red" army, in the summer of 1926 made preparations for an advance northwards. The troops were apparently well drilled by their Russian instructors and were also well equipped. On September 3, 1926, they laid siege to the city of Wuchang, capital of the two Hukuang provinces. The neighboring cities of Hankow and Hanyang. just across Yangtze River, were taken without difficulty. Silver bullets were believed to have been more effectual than lead in their capture. Wuchang made a heroic defence, but fell on the 10th of October. Propaganda distributed by aeroplane probably hastened the surrender. The defection of one of Wu P'ei-fu's generals greatly crippled the northern army. Owing to its demoralization, the Cantonese were able to penetrate into Honan Province.

The advance of the Nationalist Army towards the Yangtze Valley was preceded by organization of the workers in various cities along the route into labor unions, who were promised increase of wages and better conditions of living as soon as the Nationalist forces should come into control. A wide distribution was made, too, of anti-foreign and anti-Christian propaganda. American and British missionaries were particularly denounced as agents of capitalistic countries. Russian political advisers were held responsible for this propaganda. At Changsha several million dollars had been invested by American philanthropists in a university, hospital, and other benevolent institutions. Even the students in the university, known as Yale-in-China, were induced by this propaganda to turn upon their instructors and compel them to leave the city.

At Hankow, it was reported that some 240,000 workers had been organized into unions. On the arrival of the Nationalist forces, these unions made a general demand for a large increase in wages, the result being that many establishments closed down, and tens of thousands of strikers were thrown out of employment.

British trade had been considerably damaged by the prevailing animosity shown towards Great Britain. Impelled, no doubt, by a desire to improve this condition of affairs, the British Government, on December 18, 1926, addressed a note to the various governments interested in China, proposing a conciliatory policy. They expressed a willingness to revise the unequal treaties as soon as a responsible government should be constituted in China. They proposed an immediate and unconditional grant of the surtaxes on imports at the rates that were under discussion in the Washington and Peking conferences, and they suggested also the carrying into effect of certain of the recommendations of the Commission on Extraterritoriality. The proposals did not meet with the approval of the powers. They were rejected by the Cantonese faction also, which in the meantime had established its capital at Wuchang on the Yangtze, opposite Hankow.

On January 26, 1927, the American Government made known its willingness to negotiate a revision of the obnoxious treaties as soon as a commission should be constituted that could speak for all China.

The Nationalist Party having expressed a willingness to treat with the powers separately, the British Government made further proposals both at Peking and at Wuchang on January 29, 1927. These were very liberal, including among others an expression of willingness to have British subjects in China placed under the jurisdiction of the modern Chinese courts and the new penal code, as well as to subject them to Chinese taxation. The right of British missionaries to own land in the interior of China was to be surrendered, and the missionaries were to be required to comply with Chinese school regulations in their educational work.

While these negotiations were pending, the anti-foreign agitation in China was increasing and the danger to British residents prompted their Government to despatch naval and military forces for their protection. Because of this action Eugene Chen, speaking for the Cantonese faction, refused to sign any agreement until this supposed threat of force was withdrawn.

On January 3, 1927, rioting broke out in the British concession at Hankow, and, although bluejackets were landed, they were forbidden to fire on the mob. The next day they were returned to their ships and the Nationalist troops were asked to restore order. They did so, but there began immediately an exodus of British subjects from that city, followed a little later by foreign residents of other nationalities. Hostility to foreigners increased and spread both up and down the river, and foreign colonies in the upper Yangtze Valley began to move to the coast.

The Nationalists had moved north in two divisions. The army that was following the coast reached Foochow about the middle of January. In view of the hostility to foreigners shown by this force, the American Government on January 12 advised American citizens to leave Fukien Province. On the 17th of the month anti-Christian mobs maltreated the missionaries at Foochow and sacked the churches and mission houses. Early in February this army was attacked by troops of the northern Government, and on the 7th of the month was driven back with severe losses. Notwithstanding this setback, the army quickly recovered its morale and seized Hangchow on the 16th of February.

As the Nationalist forces approached Shanghai, the foreign residents of that port together with the refugees flocking there from the interior were placed in great danger. The British Government with wise forethought had anticipated this condition of affairs and had landed several thousand troops, which were set to work constructing a line of barbed wire and sandbags for the defence of the international settlement. A few detachments of other nationalities assisted in this work, and the French constructed defence works for their settlement. Without this preparatory work it probably would have been impossible to protect the lives of the thousands of Americans and Europeans gathered there, or to defend their property from the looting soldiery.

Although the northern troops under Sun Chuang-fang had defeated the Nationalist forces at Yenchou, as stated above, they were not proof against southern propaganda. They were accordingly replaced by troops from Shantung belonging to the army of Chang Tsung-ch'ang. These men had a reputation for lack of discipline and for great brutality. They fell back towards Shanghai and, on March 20, yielded that city to the southern army without a struggle. The General in command, Pi Shou-chen, was subsequently beheaded for this alleged betrayal of the northern cause. Although repeated attempts were made both by the retreating and the advancing forces to enter the international settlement, the foreign forces there were able to prevent such an invasion.

On March 24, the Nationalist forces entered the city of Nanking. They did not, as a rule, molest the native inhabitants, but they systematically looted foreign houses and attacked foreign consuls and other foreign residents. Over four hundred of these were Americans. Seven foreigners were killed and a number wounded. About one hundred foreign houses were looted and several were burned. The Nationalist faction attempted to disclaim responsibility for the outrages at Nanking, but their commander in chief, General Chiang K'ai-shek, after investigation, discovered that their troops were the offenders and that the Political Committee at Wuchang, controlled by the Russians, had given secret orders, unknown to Chiang, authorizing the attacks.

After the capture of Nanking, the Nationalist army attempted to move north in three columns, but all three were defeated and thrown back to the south of the Yangtze. Only at Hankow were the Nationalists in possession of any important territory north of the great river, but the "Christian" General, Feng Yü-hsiang, holding the province of Shensi, was in alliance with them. In May, Feng was being held in check by the forces of Wu P'ei-fu in

Honan, and Marshal Chang Tso-lin was moving slowly towards Hankow.

On April 3d, rioters in the Japanese concession at Hankow were shot by Japanese bluejackets. This brought on further trouble between the Chinese and Japanese and led to a general evacuation of the Japanese at that port.

THE RIFT IN THE LUTE

Returning to the situation in central China, when General Chiang Kai-shek learned that the Political Committee at Hankow was responsible for the outrages at Nanking, he repudiated its authority and set up a separate government. Hostilities broke out between the two factions of the Kuo Min Tang and a strong demand was made by the conservatives for the expulsion of the Russian advisers from China. In the meantime the Northern forces had reached the Yangtze at Pukow in April, 1927, but in May were forced back to the Yellow River. This afforded General Chiang opportunity to get in touch with Marshal Feng Yü-hsiang, who was naturally opposed to Marshal Chang Tso-lin, the Peking Dictator, who had driven Feng from that capital in 1926. Chiang and Feng met at Hsüchou in June, 1927, and agreement was made for cooperation. Feng agreed to the expulsion of the Communists from Hankow, but insisted that, nevertheless, the left wing faction of the Kuo Min Tang had a right to representation in the councils of the party. The Russians left Hankow in July to return to their own country, but in November Borodin was back in China again, and Marshal Feng continued to employ Russian officers in his army.

In the summer of 1927 General Chiang attempted to move northwards, but conditions in his rear compelled a retreat. The disturbing Communists were attempting to recover control, but by November the Conservatives, who had established a government at Nanking, were able to occupy the Wuhan cities.

In the same month the Soviet Consulate at Shanghai was raided and in December the Nationalists broke off relations with Russia. An orgy of bloody persecution followed. Hundreds of alleged Communists were arrested and put to death without formal trial. On December 11, 1927, a rising of laborers at Canton was suppressed with great cruelty. Press reports stated that two hundred Chinese Communists were put to death and with them eight or nine Russians, one being the Russian Vice Consul. These barbarities continued during the early part of 1928. In February it was reported that seventeen hundred more Communists had been executed at Canton, and on June 8, 1928, that fourteen girls and three boys had suffered the extreme penalty for Communistic activity.

Since these Communists had been created by the activities of the Nationalists themselves and their Russian advisers, such heartless massacres seemed doubly cruel.

Madame Sun Yat-sen and the quondam Minister for Foreign Affairs, Mr. Eugene Chen, both protested the dismissal of the Russians and in the summer of 1927 sailed for Russia, where they were cordially received. During 1928 they continued to oppose the Conservatives whom they accused of having abandoned the principles and policies of Dr. Sun.

TROUBLE WITH JAPAN

Marshal Wu P'ei-fu, having lost control of Hankow in the autumn of 1926, remained for a time in Honan, but he refused to cooperate with Chang Tso-lin in the movement of the spring of 1927 to recover control of Nanking. Subsequently he went into retirement in Szechuen and took no part in the events of 1928. His removal and the retreat of the forces of Chang Tso-lin to the Yellow River left the way practically clear for the transfer of the Nationalist army from the Yangtze to the Yellow River valley. The cooperation of Feng Yü-hsiang with Chiang Kai-shek brought the best disciplined army in China to the assistance of the latter. These Northern troops had left a good record in Peking and would be less obnoxious to the people of the northern provinces than the troops from the South. The

Nationalists obtained also the support of Governor Yen Hsi-shan of Shansi, the Model Governor, whose troops were also northern men, near neighbors to the people of the capital. To these three armies a fourth was added when the Kuangsi men in Hankow, under General Pai Chung-hsi, threw in their lot with the army of the Conservatives.

General Chiang, having crushed the opposition in his rear and having secured these powerful allies, in April, 1928, began again the march northwards.

In the preceding year, when the Nationalists made their attempt to reach Peking, the Japanese had sent troops into Shantung to protect their interests there. These interests were quite extensive and important. It is estimated that the public property held by the Japanese Government there was worth not less than $31,000,000 and the private property of Japanese subjects, some $80,000,000. There are still some 18,000 Japanese living in the province. When the Nationalists had been compelled to fall back, the Japanese in the autumn of 1927 had withdrawn their forces. Now in 1928, as the Nationalist forces approached the capital of Shantung, the important city of Tsinan, the Japanese again sent troops for the protection of lives and property. When one recalls the unprovoked attacks upon the American, British and Japanese Consulates at Nanking in March, 1927, the looting of foreign homes, the assaults and murders committed, all being the crimes of Nationalist soldiers, one can hardly blame the Japanese for taking measures for the protection of their people at Tsinan.

The vanguard of the Nationalist army entered Tsinan on May 1, 1928. The Japanese had gathered their subjects into two protected areas in the foreign suburb. These were surrounded by sandbags and barbed wire.

It would have been wise for the Chinese, while protesting against the Japanese action, to have avoided a conflict by marching their troops around the city instead of taking them into the city, especially since General Chiang showed by his subsequent action that he desired to avoid a conflict.

On May 2, General Chiang informed the Japanese commander that he assumed responsibility for the good order of the city and suggested that the sandbags and barbed wire be removed because they evidenced distrust of his army. Accepting Chiang's assurances, the Japanese removed their defences. The next day Chinese soldiers looted a Japanese shop. A small guard of Japanese soldiers was sent to give protection. This enraged the Chinese who began firing upon the Japanese. The latter re-established their sandbag and barbed wire entanglements. For eight days the irregular firing kept up. It was not a fight, as has been represented, between a large Chinese army and a small Japanese force. The orders of the Chinese were to avoid a conflict, and General Chiang repeatedly attempted to stop the firing. He removed his troops as rapidly as possible from Tsinan, but there were mutinous and disorderly soldiers incited, no doubt, by false reports and filled with hatred, who disobeyed orders and kept up the fight. That outrages were committed by Chinese troops upon Japanese men and women seems beyond doubt, but equally barbarous cruelties appear to have been inflicted by Japanese upon Chinese, even upon the wounded in the hospital. The incident was settled by an exchange of notes on March 28, 1929, in which both governments expressed regret for the occurrence and made arrangement for the adjustment of losses.

Not content with the measures taken in regard to Shantung, Japan on May 18, 1928, as already stated, warned both Peking and Nanking that if the peace and order of Manchuria should be threatened by the civil war, she would possibly be constrained to take effective steps to avert disorder in that region. The further statement was made that, if Mongolia or Manchuria should be disturbed by the retreat of defeated troops of either army, Japan would prevent the entrance of such troops into either of the districts mentioned.

THE EVACUATION OF PEKING

The affair with Japan at Tsinan was not allowed by General Chiang to stay the march of his army northward.

Marshal Feng's force moved forward through Honan, followed by that of Pai Chung-hsi from Hankow, and Governor Yen Hsi-shan threatened the right flank of the Northern army. Chang Tsung-ch'ang and Sun Chuan-fang, operating under the Dictator, Chang Tso-lin, were forced backward. But Chang Tso-lin made a public announcement that he had no desire to quarrel with Nationalism, that he had come into Peking to check the spread of Red propaganda. This referred to the employment of Russian officers by Marshal Feng while he was in possession of Peking and Feng's close association with Russians charged with Communism. It is to be remembered, moreover, that Chang Tso-lin and Dr. Sun were allies at the time of the latter's death. On June 2, 1928, Marshal Chang Tso-lin announced that he would evacuate Peking for the sake of peace. He had already for a month or more been moving his Manchurian forces back to Mukden. Apparently there was some understanding between Chang and Chiang, as nothing was done to take advantage of the evacuation or to attack the retreating army. The withdrawal was made in excellent order and without alarming the residents of Peking. The Dictator left a small guard to maintain order and appointed a Committee of Safety to administer the Government until the Nationalists should assume charge. On June 3, 1928, he took train for Mukden. The next day, as his car was passing under the viaduct of the South Manchuria Railway just outside of Mukden, a mine was exploded which blew off the top of Marshal Chang's car and damaged an abutment of the viaduct. Marshal Chang and Governor Wu of the Amur Province were both so seriously wounded that they died the same day. An investigation of the crime was made, but the Japanese Government refused to make public the resulting report. On July 1, 1929, however, the Japanese War Office announced that Colonel Kawamoto would be punished for turning over the patrolling of the viaduct to Chinese guards, and further stated that General Muraoka had resigned the Manchurian command.

This by implication placed the blame upon the Chinese. Chang, however, had lost the favor of Japan by bringing Manchuria into the civil war against Japan's warning. His son and successor, Chang Hsueh-liang,* ignored a similar warning and lost the government of Manchuria. It is easy to believe, therefore, that Chang Tso-lin was killed by Japanese. It is incredible, moreover, that Chinese would be allowed to police the South Manchuria Railway viaduct. Another reason assigned for Japan's hostility to Chang was the latter's unwillingness to agree to a consolidation of railways in Manchuria.

CHANG TSO-LIN

Marshal Chang Tso-lin, at the time of his death, was between fifty and sixty years of age. He came into notice during the Russo-Japanese War, at which time he was the leader of a band of Hung Hutzus, or Red Beards, fighting on the side of Japan. After the War he was taken with his force into the service of the Chinese Government and in 1911 he was appointed Military Governor of Manchuria. He served Yüan Shih-k'ai while the latter was President and in the troubled period of 1917 he supported Tuan Chih-jui in the restoration of the Republic. He was charged by his enemies with being in the sleeve of Japan. It must be admitted that he preserved good order in his provinces and made them a place of refuge for Chinese driven from their homes by civil war. From the leadership of a band of outlaws he thus rose to a position of great power. For two years he was Dictator of China. His political activities brought him a fortune estimated at ninety million dollars (silver), nine millions of which his son and successor set apart for the promotion of education in Manchuria.

THE OCCUPATION OF PEKING

The Nationalists entered Peking on June 8, 1928, and were peacefully installed in control of the ancient capital. The householders put away the five-barrel flag of the Republic and replaced it with the Nationalist flag, a red

* This is the accepted transliteration of the name, but its owner prefers the spelling, Chang Hsiao-liang.

banner with a single white star in a blue field in the upper
corner next the staff. The city of Tientsin was also occupied without resistance, many of the Northern troops being
taken into the Nationalist army. The occupation of the
capital and adjacent regions was made easier by the use
of Northern troops for the most part. Peking was taken
over by Governor Yen of Shansi and Marshal Feng was
put in charge of southern Chihli.

CHANGING NAMES

Names are perhaps given too much importance by the
Chinese. Attention was called to this when speaking of
the reforms introduced by the Empress Dowager in 1902-07.
It is common to hear Chinese quote the saying of Confucius: "If names be incorrect, statements will not accord
with facts. If statements do not accord with facts, affairs
will remain incomplete. If affairs are not brought to completion, there will be a lack of order and harmony, and,
if order and harmony be lacking, justice will be arbitrary."
Therefore one of the first things to engage the attention
of the Nationalist leaders after Peking was occupied was
to change the name of Peking, which means "Northern
Capital" to Peip'ing, i.e. "Northern Peace," and declare
that the capital was removed to Nanking. At the same
time, the name of the province in which Peking is located,
Chihli, meaning "Direct Government," was altered to
Hopei, i.e. "North of the Ho," to correspond with that of
its neighbor, Honan, "South of the Ho." The Ho is the
Huang Ho or "Yellow River."

There are several good reasons for removing the capital
to Nanking. It is more centrally located than Peking and
more accessible to all parts of the Republic. Peking, moreover, is distasteful to the Chinese because by the Protocol
of 1901 the foreign legations there are permitted to fortify
the quarter of the city where they are located and to maintain legation guards and guards along the railway to the
sea. Another reason for disliking Peking is that it is
associated with the memory of Mongol and Manchu con-

querors and surrounded by the estates of the hereditary Manchu and Mongol nobility. More important is the fact that Japan is in practical control of Manchuria and holds also the Shantung Railway so that Peking could easily be isolated in case of trouble between the two countries.

Against these obvious reasons for changing the capital must be set one great disadvantage, that is, the cost of constructing a new capital at a time when the Government is hard pressed for funds. A Reconstruction Committee reported to the Central Executive Committee that the cost of building the capital at Nanking would be about fifty million dollars, silver. When one recalls that there are magnificent buildings in Peking, sufficient for all the needs of government, some of them buildings of great beauty and historic interest, one can not avoid the feeling that the removal of the capital was a serious mistake.

LOOTING THE DEAD

While these affairs were engaging the attention of the Nationalist Government, soldiers belonging to one of the defeated armies were discovered to have violated the Manchu Imperial Tombs about ninety-five miles east of Peking. There are two large cemeteries of the Manchu Dynasty, the one just mentioned and a second about eighty-five miles southwest of Peking. Each is a large park containing thousands of acres, protected from evil influences by lofty ranges of mountains on the north, the side of darkness. The tombs are huge vaults, each capable of holding several hundred persons. These vaults in the case of important personages are covered with earth in which groves of trees are planted, so that they have the appearance of miniature mountains. On the south side of the most important sepulchre there is erected a hall of sacrifice and a tower for the protection of the tablet that bears the posthumous name. These buildings are of beautiful architecture. The walls of the vaults are very thick and to break them open it was necessary to use powerful explosives. Thirteen were plundered. Among them were

the graves of the greatest of the Manchu rulers, Ch'ienlung
who reigned from A.D. 1736 to 1796, and Tzuhsi, the Empress Dowager, who was three times Regent of China, and
who died in 1908. The value of the loot taken, consisting
chiefly of gold, pearls, jade and other precious stones, was
variously estimated at from twenty to forty millions of
dollars. But even the lowest of these estimates is probably
extravagant. It has been the custom of the Chinese from
very ancient times to place treasure in the grave with the
dead. Pearls, jade and gold were particularly prized because of the power which they were supposed to possess
of preserving the corpse from decay.

THE NATIONAL GOVERNMENT

China is still called a republic, but the present Nationalist
Government is not republican as that word is commonly
understood in the West. It is oligarchical rather than
republican. The leaders declare that in accordance with
the plans of Dr. Sun there are three stages in the establishment of the new government: the military, the period of
tutelage, and that of representative government. It is their
belief that the military stage has been completed and that
they are now in the period of tutelage. After the people
shall have been duly educated for the responsibilities of
citizenship then they will be granted self-government in
a real parliament.

For the present the government is simply that of a
political party, the Kuo Min Tang. The party elects a
Central Executive Committee, which is the supreme authority when the party Congress is not in session. No one
can be admitted to the Kuo Min Tang who is not in sympathy with its aims and methods. All differences of opinion
must be discussed in the meetings of the Congress or at the
plenary sessions of the Executive Committee. Once a decision is taken the minority must abide by that decision; the
Government must not be embarrassed by opposition. All
this savours of Moscow. Russian influence is manifest, too,
in the organization of the administration.

The Central Executive Committee delegates to its Central Political Council the formation of policies and the general direction of the National Government, but the Political Council does not itself attempt to carry out these policies. They are executed by the State Council, now known as the "National Government Council." The Central Political Council of the Central Executive Committee, according to President Chiang Kai-shek, is the "highest legislative, directive and controlling organ in the Kuo Min Tang System of government."

The National Government Council consists of sixteen members, and forms a cabinet, composed of the President, the heads of the five *yüan* (courts), and certain other important administrative officers.

The division of government among five *yüan* is intended to carry out the will of Dr. Sun, who believed that he had made a discovery in political science; that there are not three, but five branches of government; executive, legislative, judicial, examination and control. Civil service examinations in most countries are regarded as a function of the executive. By "control," as is now interpreted by the Nationalist Party, two things are meant; auditing of accounts and impeachment. But auditing is generally considered a duty of the executive branch of government and impeachment is, strictly speaking, a judicial matter. Nevertheless in our own government, borrowed from that of Great Britain, we set up a special court for the impeachment of civil officers of the federal government; the Senate sitting as court and the House of Representatives acting as prosecutor.

The five *yüan* are the Administrative, the Legislative, Judicial, the Examination and the Control *Yüan*. Under the Administrative there are eleven ministries and four commissions. The ministries are, Interior, Foreign Affairs, War, Navy, Finance, Agriculture and Mining, Industries Commerce and Labor, Education, Communications (Post and Telegraph), Railways, and Public Health. The four commissions are concerned with Reconstruction,

Mongolian and Tibetan Affairs, Opium Suppression, and Famine Relief.

Shortly after the occupation of Peking, the military leaders, General Chiang, Marshal Feng, Governor Yen and others on July 6, 1928, paid a visit to the monastery, Pi Yün Ssu, in the hills west of Peking, to pay their respects to the remains of Dr. Sun, which had been guarded there since his death. Wreaths of flowers were placed upon the casket, offerings of food were made and an address to his spirit was read. Such reverence for the dead is common in China, as is well-known. On the 26th of May, 1929, the body of the dead leader was placed upon a railway train at Peip'ing and carried to Nanking. Relatives and high officials attended. Lion Hill at Nanking saluted with 101 guns and the foreign men of war in the river Yangtze each with 21 guns as the cortege crossed the river.

For three days the body lay in state and on June 1, escorted by the officers of the National Government and by the Diplomatic Corps as well as by a vast concourse of the people of all classes, it was carried to the beautiful and costly mausoleum that had been built for its reception on Purple Mountain. With marks of reverence and offerings of flowers it was laid in the vault and salvos of artillery from the fort and the river spoke the long farewell. It is now the custom at all government meetings to bow reverently before the portrait of Dr. Sun and the new school regulations require all pupils to do so. Even mission schools are compelled to hold a memorial service for Sun Yat-sen every Monday morning. Are we to think of this as the beginning of a new religious cult?

THE THREE PRINCIPLES

Corresponding to the three stages in the evolution of the new government are the Three Principles of Dr. Sun. A treatise dealing with these Principles seems to be the Bible of the new cult and to have for the Nationalist Party all the authority of inspired scripture. The first of these three Principles is Nationalism, and therefore the aim of the first period in the development of the state is the destruction of sectionalism and the establishment of national unity. Such a union is held to have been brought about by the military movement that led to the occupation of Peking. The second principle is Democracy and the second period is accordingly devoted to teaching the people their rights and duties as citizens of the future republic. The third principle is Economic Improvement. It aims at the promotion of the welfare of the people by such legislation as will raise the standard of living and lessen the evils of poverty. In the third period, which is still in the future, the people will take charge of the Government and conduct it in a manner to further popular interests.

Dr. Sun had real sympathy with the toilers of the world and seemed to look forward to some form of state socialism as promising to ameliorate their condition. He had been quickly won to Russian sovietism, that is to say, to a method of selecting representatives not by districts but by occupations. This would give the manual laborers opportunity to secure control of the government. He died holding this faith and a few days before his passing he wrote to the Russian Government to thank them for the advisers and other assistance sent, and promised that his followers would continue to work with Russia. The Kuo Ming Tang did so until the outrages at Nanking in 1927 caused a split in the party, when the Russian Advisers, as we have seen, were sent away. The Nanking Government, however, has not altogether abandoned Dr. Sun's programme. As we have already noted, it has enacted many laws in the interest of the manual workers. It also holds to the soviet method of election. The delegates to the Constitutional Convention held in May, 1931, were chosen in this manner.

RUSSIAN INTRIGUE

The discovery that the Russian advisers of the Nationalist faction, apparently with the knowledge and approval of the Moscow Government, were using the Chinese to further Bolshevist aims rather than to assist the Nationalist cause led to a widespread distrust of them. It was evident that the Moscow Government was aiding a movement against Peking while maintaining an embassy at that capital.

On the 5th of March, 1927, the *Pamiat Lénina,* a Russian vessel, was seized by the northern Government at Tsingtao, after search had disclosed that she was laden with propaganda intended to create an uprising against Peking. Among the persons arrested was Madame Borodin, wife of the Political adviser at Wuchang.

On the 6th of April, the premises of the Russian embassy were searched and important documents were seized. These gave evidence of the existence of an organization in Peking, apparently directed by the embassy, which aimed at the overthrow of the Peking Government. A number of arrests followed, fifteen of the accused being Russians. These persons were connected with the Russian Embassy and claimed diplomatic immunity. They were imprisoned four months before a preliminary hearing was given them. Nothing resulted from this hearing except the return of the prisoners to confinement. It was not until September 8, 1928, more than seventeen months after arrest, that they were allowed bail. On the thirteenth of that month the Procurator reported that fourteen were entitled to diplomatic immunity and that there was no evidence against the fifteenth. Such long detention of foreign residents without trial did not tend to dispose the Western Powers to surrender extraterritorial jurisdiction. It was to the credit of the Nationalist Government, however, that no more than three months were allowed to elapse after their occupation of Peking before the case was adjudicated.

The raid upon the Russian Embassy was protested by the Moscow Government. The Embassy was closed and diplomatic relations between the two countries were suspended.

RECONSTRUCTION

The unity achieved in 1928 by the coalition of the Kuo Ming Tang army with those of Feng and Yen did not last long.

The Government at Nanking set to work enthusiastically on the task of reconstruction and education, to which Dr. Sun's period of tutelage was to be devoted. Vast projects were broached and made subjects of legislation;—the building of a capital at Nanking which called for a large outlay for streets and public buildings; the extension of railways; the introduction of a new and uniform coinage; the reclamation of waste lands; the encouragement of emigration from congested districts to the border provinces; improved facilities for education, and government aid to commerce and industry. Unfortunately most of these excellent plans were still in the paper stage in 1932. Because of strife and division the building of the new political edifice had to be undertaken by men who labored with sword at hand.

NEW TREATIES

Some notable things were accomplished nevertheless. Attention has been called already to the successful insistence upon tariff autonomy, and to the large increase in the number of modern courts, established with a view to the early recovery of jurisdiction over foreign residents. The claims growing out of the attacks upon foreigners in Nanking in 1927 and the fighting between Chinese and Japanese troops at Tsinan in 1928 were all satisfactorily adjusted in 1929. August, 1929, saw the rendition of the Belgian concession at Tientsin and October that of Great Britain at Chinkiang.* Of considerable importance also were three new treaties with European states;—Poland, Greece and Czecho-Slovakia. These were signed in the summer and autumn of 1929 and each acknowledged China's complete sovereignty both as to tariff-making and to jurisdiction.

* The British concessions at Hankow and Kiukiang had been returned in 1927.

But, despite these creditable achievements, the year 1929 was one of renewed strife in many quarters.

DISBANDMENT CONFERENCE

In January and February, 1929, a conference was held at Nanking to consider plans for the disbandment of the armies that were consuming the resources of the state. There were not less than 1,800,000 men under arms. The conference agreed that the number should be reduced to 800,000, but very little was really done. A loan of $50,-000,000 was authorized to enable the Government to pay the soldiers and repatriate those who were to be discharged. A commission to supervise the disbandment was appointed and at a second meeting of the conference in August reported that 390,000 officers and men had been discharged and repatriated. Jealousy among the regional leaders sacrificed national welfare to personal ambition. General Feng and Governor Yen had entered into coalition with Chiang as equals, not as subordinates. Moreover the Kuo Min Tang in its earlier history had always insisted upon regional autonomy. But the conference on disbandment seemed to show a desire on the part of the group that was conducting the Nanking government to build a strongly centralized administration at that city and get rid of other regional leaders and their armies. Nanking was to control in all affairs; military, financial, and economic. All transportation and communication, commerce and industry were to be regulated by the central government. As we have already noted, even the large cities were to be deprived of self-government and be ruled from Nanking.

DISAFFECTION

This disposition of the Nanking leaders created considerable discontent in many quarters. A revolt broke out in Shantung at the end of January, 1929. In February

Hunan was the scene of trouble caused by the Kuangsi group, which removed the Governor of Hunan. Both these revolts were quickly suppressed. But General Feng Yü-hsiang was disillusioned by April and resigned the portfolio of the Ministry of War. The following month he was expelled from the party and a little later a warrant was issued for his arrest, but he had returned north and was protected by his friend, Yen Hsi-shan. Feng denounced the Nanking oligarchy for its ostentation, extravagance and nepotism and charged its members with graft and oppression. The charge of oppression seems to have been substantiated later by the accusation made by the philosopher Hu Shih, well-known in the United States and Europe, that the Government was violating fundamental human rights in its persecution of those who could not agree with it. Hu Shih himself was subsequently denounced as a traitor for criticising the Government.

The discontent continued to increase. In September, 1929, Chang Fa-kuei raised the standard of opposition to Nanking and moved his troops from Ichang to Kuangsi where his forces secured a foothold that was still in his possession throughout 1931. Ten members of the Central Executive Committee supported his action.

The situation grew more alarming in the following month. Fukien Province seceded from the Nanking-controlled territory, and war broke out in the Yellow River Valley, where General Feng's army seized the railway junction, Chengchou. General Chiang hastened to that region, provided with $15,000,000. With this he soon made peace, paying Feng's army $13,000,000 and sending the remainder to the forces of Chang Fa-kuei. But the relief was temporary only. In February, 1930, both Feng and Yen were arrayed against Nanking. A rival government was set up at Peip'ing, the name of which city was again changed for a few months and was called Peking. Fighting lasted from May, 1930, to the end of September. The North had the advantage for a time, but at the end of September Chang Hsueh-liang moved from Manchuria to intervene in the general interest of peace. He was received at Peip'ing without hostility and Yen retired to his own province, Shansi. Feng, receiving no aid from Yen, was compelled to surrender.

RUSSIAN COMPLICATIONS

Returning to May, 1929, we find Nanking's domestic troubles aggravated by Communist activity. On the 27th of that month the Communist Party of China held a meeting in the Russian Consulate in Harbin. The local authorities raided the consulate and secured documents, alleged by the Chinese to show that the Chinese Eastern Railway Administration was being used to further communistic activity in China and to promote factional strife and division among the Chinese people. Thirty-seven Russians were arrested and imprisoned. Russia retaliated by arresting a number of Chinese merchants in her territory. A war of words followed in which Russia threatened to withdraw her consuls from China and break connections between the Siberian Railway and the Chinese Eastern. Raids were made across the border by both parties and some fighting occurred. But on December 22, 1929, an agreement was reached at Khabarovsk between the representatives of the two countries, which provided for a settlement upon the basis of the treaty of May, 1924, which forbids the use of the railway for propaganda purposes and stipulates that neither party will permit within its territories the existence of any organization plotting against the welfare of the other. The Nanking Government, not entirely satisfied with the terms of the Khabarovsk agreement as to the management of the railway, has repeatedly but unsuccessfully attempted to reopen the question.

CONTRASTING ACTIVITIES

While the Nanking Government was engaged in a very serious struggle with the northern group in 1930 a force of irregulars, alleged to be Communists, took advantage of the opportunity to raid Changsha. Looting on a large scale followed. The Japanese consulate was destroyed and missionaries were robbed. Through a great part of central China brigands pillaged without restraint and numbers of Chinese as well as foreign residents were kidnapped and held for ransom. The authority of Nanking was reduced to a minimum. Its Government controlled no more than the province of Chekiang (General Chiang's home) with portions of Kiangsu, Anhui, Hupei, and Shantung and the city of Canton. Added to the misery thus created there came definite news of the appalling character of the famine which had been ravaging the provinces of Shensi and Kansu. It was this last item of news, no doubt, that induced the Government to propose the establishment of a Famine Relief Fund. The proposal was that each province should set aside for this purpose 2 per cent of its annual budget until $200,000 should be thus reserved for every million of the population of the province and that a similar appropriation be made by the central Government until a total of $50,000,000 should be accumulated. But the plan, however admirable on paper, was not to be realized while the country remained in such a disorderly condition.

In contrast to these discouraging events mention must be made of the meeting at Nanking in the spring of 1930 of the National Educational Conference attended by more than ninety delegates, and the organization of a National Quarantine Service, which did excellent work in inoculating thousands against cholera and in taking measures to prevent an outbreak of bubonic plague in Manchuria. With the aid of an American company some progress was made in aviation; in addition to routes already open new ones were projected for the carrying of mail and passengers. Laws relating to municipal and county government were adopted and further plans were proposed for strengthening the power of Nanking. Chief of these was a suggestion favorably entertained to divide the provinces into smaller units so as to make some sixty or seventy instead of the twenty-eight now existing. The appointment of the governors of these provinces would increase the power of the central Government and lessen that of Nanking's rival regional rulers.

The agreement for the rendition by Great Britain of Weihaiwei was signed in April, 1930, and the territory was turned back to China on October 1, the same year.

The Fourth Plenary Session of the Central Executive Committee met at Nanking on November 12, 1930 and decided that a National People's Convention should be called to meet May 5, 1931. Certain officers of the Government announced that a Provisional Constitution was to be adopted by the People's Convention. Dr. Wang Chung-hui, President of the Judicial Yüan, denied this, saying that the adoption of a constitution at such a time would be premature. Hu Han-min, President of the Legislative Yüan, on January 10, 1931, announced that the purpose of the Convention was to secure popular approval for the Nationalist programme and to consider such matters as would tend to consolidate the nation and promote needed reconstruction.

But, before the Convention assembled, it was evident that the party was divided upon the question of adopting a provisional constitution. Those opposed declared that the proposal was made in the interest of General Chiang who aimed at being made a dictator. This he hotly denied, but when the Provisional Constitution was adopted it did greatly increase his powers, since it provided that the President was to appoint the heads of the five yüan.

The Government in January promulgated a law providing for the election of 520 delegates to the Convention. These delegates were elected by labor unions, peasants' unions, commercial associations, educational societies and professional associations. The elections appear to have gone off without friction except in Hankow and Shenyang (Mukden) where riots occurred. The rift in the party widened. Hu Han-min, who was apposed to the adoption of a constitution at the approaching convention resigned on March 2, and was placed under domiciliary arrest. The Cantonese in the Government almost to a man supported Hu Han-min. Among them were some of the strongest men in the party, Wang Chung-hui, Wang Ching-wei, Sun Fo (Son of Sun Yat-sen), and Tong Shao-yi, former Premier of the Republic. Pai Chung-hsi, Li Tsung-jen and other malcontents also joined the secessionists who assembled at Canton, where they set up a rival government on May 28, 1931. In retaliation for Nanking's treatment of Hu Han-min, the Cantonese drove out from their city the military officer representing Nanking and seized the military academy. Preparations were made for another civil war. The Customs receipts, except the portion reserved for payment of foreign indebtedness, were seized, although a few months earlier these same men had denounced Yen Hsi-shan's similar action at Tientsin as very wicked. They also re-introduced *likin,* the tax on inland transportation of goods which had already been abolished in accordance with the Government's agreement with foreign powers. These same Cantonese officials had given their assent to abolition when they were in the Nanking Government. A few weeks after their separation from Nanking their troops moved northward and occupied a city in southern Hunan.

On May 5, 1931, the People's Convention met with an attendance of 475 delegates and adopted a Provisional Constitution. The Constitution provided for the equality of all citizens before the law, irrespective of sex, race or religion, and furnished the usual safeguards for person and property. It assured encouragement to agriculture and industry and promised a form of labor insurance. This Constitution was to be the Organic Law until a majority of the provinces should reach the stage of constitutionalism. This was to be determined by the existence of autonomous government in all the counties of such provinces. When a majority of the provinces should reach that stage a National Congress was to be summoned to adopt a permanent constitution.

Shortly after the adjournment of the Convention, Gen-

eral Shih Yu-san raised the standard of revolt in the
Yellow River valley, and marched northward to the capture
of Paotingfu, about 85 miles southwest of Peip'ing. This
movement was perhaps designed to aid the Canton secessionists, but it was quickly suppressed. In the same
month General Chiang was engaged in an attempt to suppress once more the ever-recurring menace of the Communists in Kiangsi. Mr. Yang Chien of the National
Research Institute, made a personal investigation and submitted to the Government a report upon the strength of
Communism in south China. The report was startling in
the frank revelation it made of the seriousness of the
situation.*

TROUBLE WITH JAPAN

Ever since the presentation of the Twenty-one Demands
by Japan to China in 1915 there has been friction between
the two countries. The Chinese have steadfastly refused
to acknowledge the validity of the treaties extorted from
them in support of these demands. The American Government, too, notified both China and Japan in May, 1915,
that it would not recognize any treaty between them that
would impair American rights or the political or territorial
integrity of China. In 1919 at Paris, as the Minutes of the
Council of Three show, President Wilson informed the
Council and, at a later date, told the Japanese delegation
also, that nothing he had said was to be construed as a
recognition of the treaties of 1915 and 1918. In the same
year at Washington while the Peace Treaty was before the
Senate, he informed the Japanese Ambassador that his
assent to the Shantung clauses of that treaty had been
given upon the understanding that the Japanese Government would disregard the treaties of 1915 and 1918 in carrying out these clauses, and that non-compliance with that
understanding might oblige him to consider the necessity
of discontinuing his support of the articles.

One of these treaties, as shown elsewhere,† granted very

* Published in *Chinese Affairs*, July 15, 1931.
† Page 591.

valuable privileges to Japan in Manchuria and Mongolia. Among these was the extension of the lease to the Kuantung Peninsula and of that to the South Manchuria Railway. The lease to the peninsula would otherwise have expired in 1923 and the right of China to purchase the railway would have become exercisable in 1939. The desire to have these leases extended was no doubt the compelling motive that influenced Japan to resort in 1915 to such a questionable method of getting what she wanted.

Naturally the Chinese Government has not given hearty assistance to Japan in appropriating the benefits thus forcibly wrung from China. This is the foundation in part of the charge made by Japan that China does not observe her treaties. There is another treaty affecting Manchuria which the Japanese accuse China of ignoring, the treaty of December 22, 1905, in which China assented to the transfer of the Russian leases to Japan at the close of the Russo-Japanese War. Japan asserts that a secret clause to that treaty binds China not to build any main line railway in the neighborhood of the South Manchurian Railway and parallel to it or any branch line that would be prejudicial to the interest of the South Manchuria line. The Chinese Government denies that any such secret clause was signed. However that may be, the Chinese have built a railway from Chinchow to Tsitsihar which parallels in a general sense the South Manchuria line. Other railways, too, have been built by China that compete with branches of the South Manchuria Railway. On the other hand it is to be said that all these railways have been built with the assistance of Japan. Until 1931 Japan made but little objection because they were all feeders to a considerable amount to her commerce at Dairen. In 1931, however the progress being made in the construction of a new port at Hulutao, which would furnish an independent outlet to shipments over Chinese lines, gave Japan cause for alarm. The railway situation in Manchuria, therefore, must be set down as one of the causes of conflict of 1931 and 1932 between China and Japan.

THE WANPAOSHAN INCIDENT

There have been many minor causes of ill feeling between the two peoples. One was the quarrel in April, 1931, at Wanpaoshan between Koreans and Chinese over the construction of an irrigating canal which crossed Chinese property without permission. The Koreans, being Japanese subjects, were supported by Japan's police in Manchuria, although Japan has no treaty right to station police outside the Leased Territory. The ill feeling spread to Korea where riots resulted in the murder of 119 Chinese, the wounding of 370 others and the destruction of Chinese property to the value of more than $2,000,000. Chinese merchants in retaliation organized an anti-Japanese boycott. The Wanpaoshan affair was settled by diplomacy on August 5, 1931, but popular feeling was still excited.

JURISDICTION

Another source of friction was the question of the continuance of Japan's extraterritorial jurisdiction over her subjects in China. The treaty-right to such jurisdiction expired in 1926, and Japan had tried repeatedly without success to have it renewed. The latest occasion was during the negotiations in the spring of 1931. These, as already stated, were without result. When the Chinese Minister for Foreign Affairs announced on May 4 that all treaty clauses providing for extraterritorial jurisdiction would be abrogated from January 1, 1932, there was a great outcry by the Japanese that they had been flouted and had lost prestige.

But the prestige of Japan was no more injured than that of the United States, Great Britain or France, for these powers still had treaty-rights to jurisdiction that had not expired. The Japanese in Manchuria seemed to feel most deeply on the subject and organized a society for the protection of their interests.

THE MURDER OF NAKAMURA

While the flames of hostile feeling were thus being fed, Captain Nakamura of the Japanese army was murdered by Chinese militiamen at a small village near Taonan, Manchuria. This was on June 27, 1931. It was discovered upon examination that Captain Nakamura was traveling with a passport that falsely described him as an educator, intending to make exploration in the Hsingan Mountains. When Baron Shidehara, Minister for Foreign Affairs, learned this, he begged the military officers not to make public the connection of the murdered man with the army, but the army cried aloud to be avenged. On August 4 the Minister of War addressed a group of officers whom he told of the possibility of serious trouble in Manchuria and Mongolia and urged greater devotion on the part of his hearers. The Minister for Foreign Affairs rebuked him, saying that such speeches would give rise to more talk of the dual diplomacy of Japan, that is to say, the rumor that the Ministry of War frequently acted in foreign relations in opposition to the Foreign Office. On the 19th. of August a meeting of army officers joined in a petition to the Japanese Minister of War to take the matter out of the hands of the Foreign Office and vindicate the attitude of the army. On the 27th of August the *Japan Chronicle* reported that a proposed increase of the garrison in Korea was explained to the Imperial Diet by the Minister of War by saying that in case of trouble in Manchuria it would be easy to move troops from Korea without exciting comment. This appears to have been done, for on the night of the 18th of September the city of Shenyang (Mukden) was suddenly occupied and the arsenal seized.

THE UNDECLARED WAR

The immediate cause of this action was said by Japan to be the destruction by Chinese soldiers of a small bridge on the South Manchuria Railway. But the Japanese police the railway with their own troops and could easily have had the offenders brought before a Chinese court and had them punished. The vandalism, however dastardly, was not a crime committed by the Chinese Government and certainly was not of sufficient gravity to justify a military invasion. The excuse given was evidently a mere subterfuge, since the occupation of Manchuria, as has been indicated, was planned some months before the bridge was destroyed.

After the seizure of Shenyang, the Japanese Foreign Office explained to the world that the incident was a local one and would soon be settled. When the troops left the railway zone to occupy other districts, the Japanese Foreign Office assured the world that they would return to the zone just as soon as Japanese interests were safeguarded. But Japanese policy was not determined by the Foreign Office; the army was in charge and determined to vindicate its attitude. Its movements were not in the control of the Minister for Foreign Affairs. City after city was occupied until Manchuria was in Japanese possession. No declaration of war was made and up to the date of this publication the diplomatic and consular officers of each country were functioning as usual in the territories of the other.

APPEAL TO THE LEAGUE OF NATIONS

It was important for Japan's purpose that no declaration of war should be made, since the Covenant of the League of Nations provides that, ''Should any member of the League resort to war in disregard of its covenants under Articles XII, XIII, or XV, it shall *ipso facto* be deemed to have committed an act of war against all other members of the League.''

For the same reason, although attacked by Japan, China could not declare war without appearing to put herself in the position of a violator of the Covenant. The Chinese Government, therefore, directed the authorities in Manchuria to avoid resistance to Japan. At the same time she appealed to the Council of the League to take such action as it should deem wise and effectual to safeguard the peace, as stipulated in Article XI.

While the Council deliberated, the Japanese military authorities continued to strengthen their position. Chinese Government deposits in the banks in Manchuria were seized. The local governments were displaced by others under control of Japan. Japanese courts were set up and Japanese law enforced. All measures commonly taken by an invading force in time of war were taken by the Japanese military authorities and all Chinese who resisted were treated as brigands.

The aim of Japan seemed to be to take a course similar to that taken by her in 1894-1910 in Korea. Korea, once a dependency of China, was first definitely detached from China, and declared independent. Later it was forced into a relation of dependence upon Japan and finally was annexed to Japan. In similar fashion Japan prepared to set up an independent Manchuria, adopted for it a distinctive flag and made the former Emperor of China the head of the new state.

The Council of the League was after long delay induced to appoint a Commission to go out and investigate the situation at first hand and make report. But long before the Commission could reach Manchuria its occupation by Japan was an accomplished fact.

A VIOLATION OF TREATIES AND AGREEMENTS

Such occupation of a portion of the territory of China and the establishment there of an independent government was plainly not only an act of war, but was also in violation of all the numerous treaties and agreements signed by Japan promising to respect the territorial integrity of China.

THE OCCUPATION OF SHANGHAI

The aggressive action taken by Japan in Manchuria naturally aroused deep resentment throughout China. The Anti-Japanese Boycott Society in Shanghai was stirred to renewed activity. Forcible measures were taken to restrain Chinese merchants from dealing with Japanese. Japanese goods were seized wherever found in disregard of law and publicly destroyed. Japanese mills in Shanghai were compelled to shut down and thus some 60,000 Chinese were thrown out of employment to be added to the millions who were suffering already from flood and famine. One day an altercation between a Chinese and a Japanese led to a brawl in which a Japanese Buddhist monk was killed. In reprisal Japanese killed a couple of Chinese. Thereupon the Japanese Government sent some war vessels to Shanghai. They landed sailors in the settlement to protect their nationals, and the Admiral demanded of the Mayor of Greater Shanghai the dissolution of the Society that was responsible for the boycott. The Mayor responded by ordering the discontinuance of boycott activities by the Society. A peaceable settlement of the issue seemed possible. But no law or ordinance can compel people to buy where they do not want to buy. Neither can any agreement between governments prevent individuals from quarreling. Japanese accused Chinese of sniping. This furnished the excuse for the bombardment by Japan of an unfortified city in violation of the rules of war and that too without giving women and children an opportunity to escape. The Chinese military forces at hand stood upon the defensive and astonished the world by the heroism of that defense. Moreover this invasion of the heart of China by Japan brought all factions of China into union. Nanking, Canton, Chang Fa-kuei in Kuangsi and Feng Yü-hsiang in the north were all made to forget their personal ambitions and join in resisting their common foe.

Lao Tzu in his Tao Te Ching said :—''There is no greater misfortune than despising the enemy.'' This was the misfortune of the Japanese Admiral. He seemed to anticipate an easy occupation of Shanghai just as the army had so easily occupied Manchuria. The resistance was so firm that he was compelled to ask for reinforcements. These came and still no progress was made. Aerial bombardment laid waste several suburbs, yet despite the inferiority of

Chinese equipment the defense held out. Again and again reinforcements came, but it was not until the end of February'that a slight break appeared in the Chinese line. It has been explained already that Shanghai consists of three areas governed by three municipalities. The French Concession is the southernmost of the two foreign settlements. The International Settlement joins it on the north, but is itself divided into two parts by the Soochow Creek which flows through it. That portion of the International Settlement that lies north of the Soochow Creek is called Hongkew. It was in this section that most of the Japanese residents were living. There were about 13,000 of them. Extending like a bow around the two foreign settlements is the Chinese city of Shanghai.

The landing of foreign forces for the protection of the settlements has often been necessary in the past when the lives or property of foreign residents was endangered by Chinese mobs.

The Japanese, therefore, were but following precedent in landing sailors for the protection of their subjects and valuable interests in Hongkew. But when they made the settlements a base for warlike operations in attacks upon China, in a quarrel in which other foreign residents of Shanghai were not interested, they were acting without precedent and were endangering the lives of other foreigners, apparently without justification.

ACTION OF LEAGUE ASSEMBLY

As the indecisive struggle went on, Japan proposed to the Powers that joint international action should be taken to isolate each important port in China by a neutral zone to be established around it, thus separating it and its trade from the influences of the unending civil strife. But such a manifest infringement of China's sovereignty was promptly rejected to Japan's chagrin. The Council of the League having failed to improve the situation, China made appeal to the Assembly under Article XV of the Covenant. The Assembly responded on March 9 by requiring a cessation of hostilities and the withdrawal of Japan's forces from China. The Assembly also gave warning that no settlement of the trouble obtained by violation of the Pact of Paris (Kellogg Pact) that is to say, by the use of armed force would be recognized. A committee of nineteen was appointed with full power to act while the Assembly was not in session. This committee insisted upon a complete withdrawal of Japanese forces from positions outside the foreign settlements. The terms were accepted by both parties, but Japan qualified her acceptance by the statement that her troops would be withdrawn ''in the near future,'' and that the time would be determined by herself. The agreement was signed on May 5, 1932 in a hospital at Shanghai, where all the Commissioners were patients. The Chinese representative had been beaten by disgruntled students; the Japanese Commissioners with a number of compatriots had been attacked by a Korean revolutionist whose bomb killed two persons and wounded several.

The agreement reached at Shanghai took no note of the situation in Manchuria. A Commission, sent out by the Council of the League of Nations, entered Manchuria on April 2, 1932 to study conditions on the ground. No report of its findings had been published at the time of this writing. Japan's promise to the League Council to withdraw her troops into the Railway Zone has not been fulfilled. Men forget that in Japan the War Office is not obliged to keep promises made by the Foreign Office.

RENEWAL OF INTERNAL STRIFE

While the fighting was going on at Shanghai, Japanese vessels made an attack on Nanking. Thereupon the Chinese capital was removed to Honan, a city in the vicinity of the ancient capital, Loyang, whose name was at once given to Honan. In this secure position, far removed from the coast, the government would be safe from foreign attack. But when peace had been signed at Shanghai the rival factions, that had united to resist Japan, at once renewed their quarreling. The outlook is discouraging. Will history repeat itself?

CHAPTER XXVI

FOREIGN TRADE

Speed on the ship, but let her bear
No merchandise of sin,
No groaning cargo of despair,
Her roomy hold within;
No Lethean drug for eastern lands,
No poison draught for ours,
But honest fruits of toiling hands
And Nature's sun and showers.

Whittier.

Reference has been made elsewhere to the early trade of China with the West. China's exports to Rome via Parthia were chiefly silk, iron, furs, skins and hides. The imports from Rome were bright-colored textiles, precious stones and jewelry, drugs and glass. Some of the last-mentioned appears to have been in the form of imitation jewels, in the manufacture of which the Syrians seem to have been very skillful.[1] Glass making was not introduced into China until the 5th century A.D.[2] and prior to that date vessels of glass were considered very precious. Even at a later period the celebrated poet, Li Po (A.D. 702), as quoted by Hirth, represents the fairy princess, T'ai Chen, as drinking from a glass cup, implying that glass was a very precious article.[3]

But long before China's trade with Rome, in the 12th century B.C., she was trading in such articles as silk, furs, linen,[4] skins, silver, copper and iron, precious stones, pearls, ivory and gold.[5]

Iron manufacturing became a government monopoly in

[1] Hirth: ''China and the Roman Orient,'' p. 237.
[2] Ibid., and p. 232.
[3] Op. cit., p. 233.
[4] Dolichos and boehmeria.
[5] ''Tribute of Yü.''

645

the 7th century B.C. and remained for a long time under official control.[6] Hirth quotes Ma Tuan-lin as authority for the statement that in 110 B.C. there were forty districts in which government inspectors supervised the manufacture of iron. Pliny complained that in his day the Romans wasted money on silk and other Asiatic luxuries, with the result that the balance of trade against Rome in her commerce with the Orient amounted to between 55 and 100 million sesterces a year.[7] This would amount to from two to five millions of dollars, at a time when the purchasing power of money was much greater than now.

MEDIAEVAL TRADE

In the 9th and 10th centuries of the Christian Era the foreign trade of China was chiefly sea-borne, and the imports consisted of ivory, frankincense, tortoise shell, camphor, rhinoceros horns, copper, coral, amber, pearls, precious stones, ebony, spices, drugs, sapan-wood and colored cotton fabrics. The exports were porcelain, cotton piece goods, silk, gold and silver.[8] Tea is mentioned as a common drink in China by the Arab travelers who visited that country in the 9th century, but it does not appear to have figured in the exports at that period.[9] The duties paid on imports varied from 10 per cent on pearls and camphor to 30 and 40 per cent on other articles. The duties were paid in kind, and such stores as were not wanted by the Court were placed on the market.[10] Marco Polo in his day said that the import duty was 10 per cent as a rule, but that freight charges were from 30 to 44 per cent, so that the merchant had to "pay a good half of the value of his investment" for freight and duty.[11]

[6] Hirth's "Ancient History of China," p. 204.
[7] Hirth: "China and the Roman Orient," p. 226.
[8] See Hirth and Rockhill: "Chau Ju-Kua," p. 16–19, and Renaudot's translation of "Ancient Accounts of India and China by Two Mohammedan Travellers," p. 20.
[9] Renaudot, op. cit., p. 25.
[10] Chau Ju-Kua, pp. 19–21.
[11] Cordier's Yule's Marco Polo, II, p. 235.

The first British ship to reach China sought a cargo of sugar and ginger, as said in another chapter. Sugar was probably already an article of export in days of the Arab monopoly of trade. It is mentioned by the two Arab travelers, whose accounts Renaudot has translated, as an article of manufacture at that period, i.e., the 9th century A.D.

MODERN TRADE

From Shaw's journals we learn that the Europeans in his day had difficulty in selling goods to the Chinese to balance purchases, and had to make up the deficit by payments of silver in large quantity.[12] Some of the "country vessels" of the British, that is to say vessels owned by British subjects in India and sailing from that country, carried Indian products to the Dutch settlements in the East Indies, and loaded there with spices and block tin for China. These, with opium and cotton from India, to a certain extent replaced the shipments of silver.

Shaw, in his report to the Hon. John Jay, Secretary of the United States for Foreign Affairs, dated January, 1787, says:[13]

The English ships bring out from Europe lead and large quantities of cloth; which latter the company are obliged by their charter to export annually to China, for the encouragement of the home woolen manufacture. The remainder of their cargoes is made up of supplies for the company's establishments in India, and such European commodities as will suit the various markets upon the coast. After having disposed of these, they take on board cotton, with which, and their lead, and cloth, they proceed to China. The English derive considerable advantage from the permission granted to private ships, owned by their subjects in India, to trade with China. These vessels, besides the cotton, sandal-wood, putchock-root, ebony, opium, shark-fins and birds'-nests they bring from the coast, carry on a smuggling trade with the Dutch settlements in and about Malacca, and with the natives, whom they supply with opium,

12 Shaw's Journals, pp. 229 and 230. See Morse, "International Relations of the Chinese Empire," I, p. 79.
13 Shaw's Journals, pp. 342 and 343.

clothing, fire-arms, etc., in return for which they receive pepper, block-tin and spices. The net proceeds of these, with the silver and other articles they bring from India, are, to the amount of about one third, carried back in such merchandise as will suit the India markets; and the remainder, either in cash or transfers on the Chinese merchants, is paid into the company's treasury, for which they receive bills on the company in England, at the exchange of five shillings and sixpence sterling for a dollar, payable twelve months after sight. This fund has for a number of years rendered it unnecessary for the company to export from Europe any specie for carrying on their commerce with the Chinese.

With respect, however, to this advantage derived by the English from their subjects in India, as well as from their credit with the Chinese, it must be observed that both have been pushed as far as they would bear. Last year their ships depended greatly on the latter of these resources for their homeward cargoes, and the company have sent from England the present year upwards of three millions of dollars in specie alone.

It was this difficulty in maintaining a favorable trade balance that encouraged opium smuggling from India. Vessels of all nations engaged in it to a considerable extent, and in the end it resulted in a draining of silver away from China instead of the former import of treasure into that country. Morse in his "International Relations of the Chinese Empire"[14] states that "The English trade was fed to an increasing extent by opium, the proportion rising from one-sixth in 1818 to over one-half in 1833." Raw cotton from India formed one-fourth and English woolens one-eighth of British imports into China in 1833. Of the exports from China to Great Britain at that time 47 per cent was in tea, about 16 per cent in silk, and 21 per cent in hard cash.

Opium smugglers were at a great advantage, since they paid no duty on the import, and in addition received payment for the contraband drug in silver. With this they could buy such return cargoes as they liked. After 1858, however, opium was placed on the tariff list. The trade was legalized. Smuggling practically ceased. But production was undertaken in China on a large scale, and steadily

14 Op. cit., pp. 82 and 83.

increased until the reform measures of 1906. Now again opium is contraband. Smuggling is resumed. Foreign production of the drug is increased, and foreign powers, although signatories of the Anti-Opium Convention of 1912 and the Versailles Treaty of 1919, profit by the illicit trade. They shrug their shoulders and disclaim responsibility. Like Pilate of old they wash their hands in token of cleanliness, but the stains of opium are not easily removed.

Despite Major Shaw's optimistic outlook for a trade in ginseng with which to finance American purchases of silk, tea and nankeens,[15] American merchants found it necessary to carry specie to Canton to pay for three-fourths of their return cargoes. From 1830 onwards they substituted bills on London for specie.[16] Ginseng is still imported into China to the value of nearly three million taels a year, but more than half of this amount comes from Japan (including Korea). The amount credited to the United States in 1921 is insignificant, although much of the 859,194 taels worth, reported as coming from Hongkong, no doubt originated in our country.

During the sixteen years 1818-1833, thirty-seven American vessels a year, on an average, visited Canton. They carried imports estimated at an average value per annum of $6,100,185, of which $307,875 worth was in opium and $2,161,724 in other goods. The balance, $3,630,586 was in treasure. The average value of the exports each year from China to the United States during that period was $6,453,- 492.[17] In other words during that period we sold to China on an average two and a half million dollars worth of goods every year, and bought from China nearly six and a half millions worth.

CHINA'S FOREIGN TRADE TO-DAY

The foreign commerce of China has changed considerably during the past century. Tea and silk are still exported

---

[15] See Chap. XVIII.
[16] Morse, op. cit., I, p. 202.
[17] Morse, op. cit., p. 89.

in large quantities, but India and Japan have forged to the front in the tea trade, and there are several rivals competing in the production of silk. The Chinese have lost much of the silk trade by their lack of care in breeding and feeding silk-worms and in their reeling of the silk. Some improvement is now being undertaken in both these matters. The decline of the tea trade is also due to want of care in the growing and manufacture of that article. The dependence of these two trades upon a multitude of small farmers who produce silk and tea of varying qualities has made it difficult to accomplish any general improvement, but the attention of the government has been drawn to the matter by the merchants interested with the result that some effort is being made to educate the people in the proper care of silk-worms and the better production of silk and tea.

Cotton is still grown in China and nankeens are still manufactured, but the power looms of the West have reversed the current of trade, so that to-day cotton piece goods are imported into China in enormous quantities. China, however, is improving the quality of her cotton, and the power loom is being gradually introduced. Some of the factories erected are financed with European and American capital. These mills are supplying in part the demand of China for cotton yarn, and in a small measure the coarser varieties of cotton cloth needed. As greater experience comes in the promotion of corporate enterprise the Chinese themselves will be able to supply a larger and larger proportion of the cotton goods needed. For the present, however, they still find it profitable to establish small factories with cheap hand looms.

Other changes in the import and export trade of China are directly traceable to the advancement of the Western world in the physical sciences, particularly in the application of steam and electricity in the invention of labor-saving machinery and the development of the chemical industries. The total number of items in the import list of the Chinese Maritime Customs to-day is 467, and in the export list 303. Many of these items are articles which a hundred years ago were either unknown or but just coming into being. Others, though known, were unknown to the China trade, for in those days China was self-centered, sufficient unto herself and able to supply all her own needs, and Western men were either ignorant of China's resources or unable to develop a trade in any but a few items.

Among the imports to-day that were unknown a century ago may be mentioned aluminum, condensed milk, steam engines and all forms of steam-driven and electrical machinery, chemical dyes, gas engines, rubber goods, all railway apparatus, most of the present-day scientific apparatus, petroleum and its products, matches and motor cars.

But the most remarkable addition to the import list, a very recent one, is that of artificial silk. The patient silk worm, chewing mulberry leaves and spinning silk, it appears, is unable to compete economically with the man-made process of producing silk from wood pulp. Although the artificial product may not be equal to the natural in quality, it finds a demand in China, especially among the manufacturers of knitted goods, where combinations of silk and cotton are used.

The returns of trade made by the Maritime Customs of China for the years 1925-31 inclusive, would be very misleading if consideration should not be given to the effects of civil war during those years. The devastation wrought by marching armies, the interruption of transport, the imposition of exorbitant taxation and forced loans, strikes and lockouts and the involuntary idleness of the peasants greatly injured the market for foreign goods. This injury was aggravated by the decline in the gold value of the tael, since this increased to Chinese purchasers the cost of such articles. The value of the Hai Kuan Tael in 1925 averaged U. S. $0.84, in 1926, $0.76 and in 1930, $0.46. Such a decline in some cases gave an increase in the tael value of foreign imports even when there was a real decline in the quantity imported. Under ordinary circumstances the fall in exchange would tend to increase exports since a gold dollar could buy more than in the preceding years, of goods, priced in taels. But owing to the unfortunate condition of the country this advantage could not be fully realized.

IMPORTS

The gross value of China's import trade in 1930 was Hai Kuan Taels 1,309,800,000. This was an increase of 44 million taels over the value of the imports in 1929. The figures are deceptive as to quantity, however, since the low silver exchange greatly increased the cost to purchasers. The items in which American trade was most interested were:

	Hai Kuan Taels
Cotton goods	149,839,000
Raw Cotton	132,266,000
Kerosene	65,043,000
Tobacco	58,373,000
Machinery	44,283,000
Agricultural machinery	1,489,757
Wheat flour	31,926,000
Cigarettes	25,500,000
Paper	37,400,000
Sugar	86,000,000
Rice	121,000,000
Iron and Steel	57,000,000
Wool and Woolen goods	24,800,000
Artificial Silk	21,200,000
Hemp and Goods	20,000,000
Electrical goods	17,300,000
Aniline Dyes	14,300,000
Gasoline	12,400,000

The use of electricity is growing. This has led to the local manufacture of bulbs and fittings, dry batteries, and illuminated signs.

There was somewhat of a slump in the import of artificial silk. Floss and yarn fell from 144,442 piculs* in 1929 to 124,511 piculs in 1930. Piece goods from 2,866,582 pieces in 1929 to 2,511,348 in 1930.

The American share of the import trade was Hk. Tls. 231,653,000 as against Tls. 230,109,000 in 1929. But, owing

* A picul is equal to 133⅓ lbs. Av.

to the decline of silver exchange, the amount in gold dollars declined from $147,269,760 to $106,560,380.

EXPORTS

China's total export trade in 1930 was valued at Tae₁s 894,843,594, or U. S. $411,628,053. This was a loss in taels of 120,000,000 from the value for 1929. The low value of the tael ought to have encouraged foreign buying, but world-wide depression in business lessened the demand and civil war in China interrupted traffic and disorganized trade.

The first place in the list of exports is taken by beans and bean products, which were sent abroad to the value of Tls. 185,300,000. The second place was taken by silk and silk piece goods, valued at Tls. 123,700,000. Most of this was raw silk, worth Tls. 109,181,124. But there was a decline from the figures for 1929 for the shipments of raw silk.

It is noteworthy that while raw cotton was imported in 1930 to the value of Tls. 132,300,000, it was also exported to the value of Tls. 26,500,000. The American share of China's export trade in 1930 amounted to Hk. Tls. 131,-880,000, a decline from 1929 of nearly six million taels, but in U. S. dollars a falling off of 27,550,389. This was due to the fact that in 1929 the tael had an average value of 64 cents while in 1930 it was worth but 46 cents.

The items in the export trade in which the United States was chiefly interested were in the following items and amounts :—

	Pounds
Raw Silk	9,886,000
Wood Oil	126,300,000
Carpet wool	31,044,000
Egg Products	13,130,000
Tin	11,000,000
Waste Silk	4,350,000
Tea	7,080,000
Antimony	13,000,000
Perilla and Sesame	53,800,000
Peanuts, Shelled	3,050,000
Soy Oil	7,270,000

Goat skins, pieces, numbers 7,661,000. Furs were valued at U. S. $4,770,000. Sausage casings were worth U. S. $1,600,000. Rugs measured 3,165,000 sq. ft.*

It should be noted that machine-made goods that compete with imports from foreign lands are beginning to be exported in considerable quantity. Foreign capital as well as Chinese is invested in these factories. Chinese cheap labor is easily trained to the manipulation of machines. The coarser grades of cotton textiles are already competing with the products of Manchester and Japanese mills. The invasion of Manchuria in the autumn of 1931 led to a severe boycott by China of Japanese trade. The Japanese mills at Shanghai were compelled to close. The total value of factory products exported in 1930 was Tls. 75,557,605 and for the preceding year was Tls. 79,188,698.

The total value of the Foreign Trade of China for 1930, including both imports and exports, was Tls. 2,204,-000,000, or U. S. $1,013,840,000. The total revenue from the Maritime Customs was Tls. 180,619,758, an increase over that of 1929 of Tls. 27,789,665. The Tonnage Dues were Tls. 3,106,590 as against Tls. 3,177,265 for 1929.

AMERICAN SHIPPING

As long as commerce depended upon sailing vessels built of wood, Americans could compete very well with the rest of the world in shipbuilding. The forests of Maine and the shipyards of New England supplied all the tonnage we needed for our carrying trade, and the beautiful "clipper" was celebrated throughout the world. But during our Civil War iron steamships became common, the beautiful wooden sailing vessel had to yield place to the ugly but more useful steamer, and the United States with its high-priced labor could not build iron or steel vessels as cheaply as the shipyards of Britain. Thus it has come to pass that, while our commerce with the Far East has greatly in-

* These statistics are in part from the Chinese Maritime Customs Reports, but the itemized table is taken from "China Through the American Window," by Julean Arnold, the American Commercial Attaché in China.

creased during the past century, our interest in the shipping has greatly declined. In 1833 sixty-one American vessels with a tonnage of 26,621 visited Canton. This was above the average, however, for that period. But by 1852 no less than 47 per cent of all the foreign shipping clearing from Shanghai was American. The British regained the lead in 1858 and the American portion fell to twenty-five per cent.[19]

More recent legislation designed to protect American seamen by forbidding the employment on American vessels of men who cannot understand orders given in English failed of its purpose. Many American vessels were transferred to other flags. Our shipping engaged in the China trade in 1914 had already dwindled in the number of vessels engaged to less than one and a half per cent of the total number, and in tonnage to a trifle more than one per cent. In 1916, in spite of the opportunities given by the European war, it declined still further to nine-tenths of one per cent of the total tonnage. Our flag had almost entirely disappeared from the Pacific.

As the danger of our becoming involved in the war increased emergency legislation provided a great increase in our merchant marine, and our proportion of the carrying trade in the commerce with China increased from 799,913 tons in 1916 to 1,214,921 in 1918, and our percentage of the total rose again to a little more than one and a half per cent.[20] The report of the Chinese Maritime Customs for 1924 gives the entries of American vessels at Chinese ports as 6,435, with a tonnage of 6,359,589, and the percentage of our tonnage to the whole foreign tonnage four and one-half per cent. For 1927 the entries of American vessels were 4,844 with a tonnage of 5,570,000. Our share of the tonnage was nearly 4.8 per cent. The number of entries for 1928 was 6,377 with a tonnage of 6,364,102 and for 1929 the number of entries was 6,933 and the tonnage, 6,653,495. This seems to indicate an improvement, but our share of the total was but 4.3 per cent.

[19] Morse, ''International Relations of the Chinese Empire,'' Vol. I, pp. 89 and 343.
[20] Arnold, Commercial Handbook of China, Vol. I, p. 75.

Unless some form of subsidy is granted, it appears unlikely that we can maintain an American wage standard and compete with those who employ cheap Oriental labor and, in addition, receive subsidies in aid of navigation. Yet the disadvantages of having to depend upon others for shipping in time of war were clearly shown in 1917, and it seems incredible that the American people will consent to return to that condition.

Should we not learn wisdom from our neighbors, the Japanese, who are our chief competitors in the Pacific? That the Japanese Government is alive to the importance of a good merchant marine is shown by the subsidies granted to Japanese shipping companies. The Japan Year-Book for 1931 states that subsidies were allowed on many routes, including those to North and South America. Generally speaking, a vessel to be eligible for a subsidy must be under fifteen years of age, must be home-built and above 3,000 tons gross. Such vessels moreover, must have a speed of twelve knots or more an hour. For every one thousand miles traveled a qualified vessels on over-seas routes receives not more than fifty *sen* (25 cents*) per ton gross, with an addition of ten per cent for every knot per hour above twelve. The subsidy is decreased for vessels five years old by five per cent for every year above five, until the fifteen-year period is reached, when payment ceases.

Some of the largest and swiftest Japanese steamships are those plying between Japan and the west coast of the United States. These compete with American vessels, of course, and are aided in that competition by the subsidies received.†

THE OPEN CITIES

Although most of the important nations of the world are engaged in commerce with China, their citizens and

---

* The value of the Yen dropped in 1931 to U. S. $0.32, so that at the time of this writing the value of 50 *sen* was no more than 16 cents.

† The Mail Contract Bill passed by Congress of the U. S. in 1928 gives some assistance to American shipping on the Pacific.

subjects are permitted by treaty to reside and do business only in a limited number of Chinese cities, known commonly as "open ports," or "treaty ports." There is an exception to this rule; missionaries are allowed to live, travel and propagate their religion in all parts of the country. Not all open cities of China are treaty ports. Some were opened by the Chinese Government upon its own initiative. Most, however, have been forced open by the pressure of foreign powers, generally after a war in which China has been defeated. This reluctance upon China's part to the opening of the country to the residence of foreigners is not without justification.

In the early period of foreign intercourse the Chinese segregated the alien merchants in a quarter of Canton where they could be more easily controlled, and where they could follow their outlandish customs without offense to the sensibilities of Chinese aristocrats, who regarded themselves as far superior to the barbarians of the West. A similar arrangement is seen to-day in the zoning ordinances of some of our American cities.

After the first war with Great Britain and the establishment by foreign powers of extraterritorial jurisdiction over their nationals in China, the restriction of foreigners to residence and trade in a few ports became of great importance. It is evident that if foreigners are not to be subject to the control of the local authorities they should be kept near enough to their own consulates to be under the restraint of their national authorities. Ninety years ago five cities were opened. After the second war with Great Britain eight more were opened, and since that time the number has grown to about one hundred. Many of these, however, are of slight interest to any foreign power except Japan, and Japan apparently is influenced by other than purely commercial motives in asking for the opening of some of the towns in regions where she claims special interests.

It is not necessary here to give the names of all the open cities. A list of the most important, with their location, will be found in the Appendix, together with population and trade statistics. The open cities and towns may be grouped in five classes. The first class includes treaty ports with national settlements,* such as Canton, Hankow, Kiukiang, Chinkiang, Tientsin and Newchwang, where one or more foreign powers have each established a separate settlement under the government, either of its consular authorities, or that of the Consul and the national community. Before the recent World War there were five separate foreign muncipalities at Hankow and eight at Tientsin. Since the close of the war Germany and Austria have lost their concessions. Such a multiplication of municipal governments in communities of a few thousand people is not only wholly unnecessary, but is often a source of friction between the various foreign colonies. The second class is composed of those open ports where there are international settlements governed by municipal councils elected by the foreign residents. Such are Shanghai (except the French Concession) and Amoy. These international governments are in some respects under the supervision of the Consular Corps of the port concerned and of the Diplomatic Representatives at Peking. The regulations adopted by the Council must have the approval of these foreign authorities, and in case of suit against the municipality the Court of Consuls has jurisdiction.

The third class may be said to be made up of those ports which have long been open to foreign residence and trade, but where, for various reasons, no separate foreign settlement has been established. The foreigners may gather in one quarter, usually but not always outside the city walls, but no area has been set aside by the Chinese Government for such residence, and there is therefore no regularly established foreign municipal control. The few Europeans and Americans gathered in such places generally coöperate in matters relating to the safety and comfort of the community. They assess themselves for such purposes as road-

* The British national concessions at Hankow, Kiukiang, Amoy and Chinkiang have been surrendered and those of other nations elsewhere have in some instances been given up, but this does not mean that the ports are closed or that foreign colonies have deserted them.

building, lighting, street cleaning, and the employment of night watchmen, but the only representatives of foreign jurisdiction are the Consuls located there, some of whom are frequently chosen from among the merchants of the nationalities concerned. Such ports are Foochow and Chefoo.

The fourth class includes the towns which China has of her own volition thrown open to foreign residence and trade. This has generally been done to forestall a demand by some foreign power. The advantage to China in so doing is that the area set aside for foreign residence is retained under the municipal control of the Chinese authorities. The foreign Consuls located at such places look after the protection of their national interests but do not interfere in the local government. Such places are Tsinan in Shantung and Yochow in Hunan.

The fifth class is composed of ports situated in leased territories, such as Dairen and Porth Arthur in Manchuria, Weihaiwei* in Shantung, Kuangchowwan in Kuangtung and formerly Tsingtao in Shantung. The last-mentioned is in the territory of Kiaochow, once leased to Germany but in 1923 was returned to the government of China by Japan. These ports in leased territories are governed by the lessee power. Other foreign powers are not permitted the exercise of extraterritorial jurisdiction within the boundaries of such territories.

ENTRANCE AND CLEARANCE OF SHIPPING

To enter a Chinese port pilotage is not compulsory, but pilots are available. Scales of fees are fixed and easily obtainable.[21] Vessels are moored in accordance with the orders of the Harbor Master. Any violation of his orders will prevent loading, unloading or clearance of the vessel

* Weihaiwei leased territory was returned to China on October 1, 1930.

[21] For Shanghai see Arnold, "Commercial Handbook of China," Vol. II, p. 152. On March 5, 1931, the National Government promulgated new regulations which require all candidates for a pilot's license to pass examination and after March 5, 1933 will exclude from the calling all who are not citizens of the Republic of China.

until the orders are obeyed. Vessels moored by their own anchors pay no mooring charges, but those made fast to fixed moorings pay a small fee. All vessels pay wharfage dues, which in Shanghai are 2 per cent of the duty. Every harbor has its own special regulations to prevent obstruction of the channel, the disposal of garbage and refuse, the landing of explosives and other dangerous goods, the use of whistles and sirens, and other matters affecting the welfare of the port.

In China, as in other foreign countries, the master of an American vessel, on arriving in port, deposits his ship's papers with his Consul, and when evidence is presented to show that all disputes between Master and crew have been settled, all dues and duties paid, and other port regulations complied with, clearance is granted and the ship's papers returned to its master.

The tonnage dues payable to the Chinese Government [22] vary from one mace per ton register, for vessels under 150 tons, to four mace per ton for those over that limit. A mace, in 1930, was equivalent to U. S. $0.046. In addition to the tonnage dues special taxes are levied in certain ports to cover the cost of harbor improvements. In Shanghai three per cent of the customs duty on cargo is added for the support of the river conservancy work. In Tientsin, to pay for the dredging of the Taku Bar, a tax is levied of four per cent of the customs duties on cargo, and an additional tax of ten taels cents a ton on the shipping that crosses the bar. On the tonnage of ships that remain outside five tael cents a ton is levied, or ten tael cents a ton on all cargo discharged or loaded.[23] At various other ports similar surtaxes are levied for the support of conservancy work.

THE TARIFF

The Chinese Government levies duties on exports as well as imports. The rate was formerly fixed by treaty at five

[22] Ibid., Vol. II, p. 151.
[23] Arnold, "Commercial Handbook of China," Vol. II, p. 314.

per cent ad valorem, as stated elsewhere.[24] Now that the Treaty Tariff has been abrogated, the National Government has promulgated new Tariff Lists, as stated elsewhere. The import of certain articles is prohibited. Among these are opium, morphia—except when certified to be for medical purposes—and salt. The import of arms and munitions of war of all descriptions is forbidden, except at the requisition of the Chinese Government or for sale to persons duly authorized by the Government. The regulation covers sporting and ammunition, but reputable persons can usually obtain the necessary permit from the Chinese authorities.

Goods imported at one port which have paid duty may be shipped to another open port without additional payment of duty, provided they are accompanied by an exemption certificate which will be issued upon application by the Customs.

Goods re-exported after payment of import duty, if shipped within three years in their original packages and with original markings, may claim a refund of the customs duties paid. If the original packing is destroyed no refund can be claimed, but the goods may be exported free of export duty.[25]

Goods shipped from the port of entry to any place other than a treaty port, and goods brought from the interior to a treaty port are liable to the payment of likin,* which, as said elsewhere, is a tax on goods in transit. This obstruction to free trade in the interior of China has been the source of much complaint. The annoyance caused by detention and examination of goods and frequent collections of likin is avoidable to some extent by the payment of a commutation transit tax. For imports going inland the commutation tax amounts to a half import duty on dutiable goods and two and one-half per cent ad valorem on duty-free goods. This payment is made at the place of import, and a transit pass is issued which accompanies the

[24] Chapters XIX and XXV.

[25] Arnold, op. cit., Vol. II, p. 87.

* The National Government abolished likin by an order dated December 15, 1930, to take effect January 1, 1931, but the order does not appear to find observance in all parts of the country.

goods to destination. For exports the properly certified foreign firm obtains at the Custom House a blank pass, which is sent with his agent into the interior. In accordance with its terms the buyer is enabled to bring goods to the port of shipment without payment of likin. Before shipment abroad the half duty and export duty are paid at the port. Foreign governments usually hold that the payment of the commutation transit tax should exempt the goods from all other taxation after reaching destination, but the Chinese local authorities frequently levy octroi at the city gates or impose a destination tax in some other form. The text of Article XI of the Japanese Commercial Treaty of 1896 provides as follows:

It shall be at the option of any Japanese subject desiring to convey duly imported articles to an inland market to clear his goods of all transit duties by payment of a commutation transit tax or duty equal to one-half of the import duty in respect of dutiable articles and two and one-half per cent upon the value in respect of duty free articles; and on payment thereof a certificate shall be issued which shall exempt the goods from all further inland charges whatsoever.

The phrase "All further inland charges whatsoever" would seem at first glance to sustain the contention of foreigners, but the Chinese hold with considerable show of reason that the likin from which exemption is claimed is a tax on goods in transit, and that nothing else was under consideration in the drafting of the article, so that the exemption cannot be made to apply to taxes levied after the arrival of goods at destination.

TARIFF REVISION

Although the tariff was fixed at five per cent ad valorem by the treaties, the duties in the schedule were as a rule converted into specific duties. Since prices are continually changing the specific duty occasionally represented a rate quite other than five per cent. For this reason the schedule was several times revised. The first occasion was in 1858. The export duties remained practically unchanged since that date until China recently acquired tariff autonomy.

Many Chinese statesmen recognized the unwisdom of a tax upon exports, but the duty on exports is still levied, although its abolition is being considered. Japan in 1858 adopted a similar practice, but the export duty there was abandoned in 1878.

In 1901, after the Boxer troubles, which placed a heavy indemnity upon China, the treaty powers agreed to another revision of the import duties in order to bring them up to an effective five per cent ad valorem. This revision was accomplished in 1902, and the new specific schedule was appended to our révised treaty of 1903. By 1917 prices again had so far altered that another revision was made, and, since many powers were then at war and prices abnormal, it was agreed that a further revision should be had two years after the close of the War. In 1921, however, the Washington Conference was called to consider Pacific and Far Eastern Questions, as well as those relating to Limitation of Armament. The revision was, therefore, postponed. At the Washington Conference China urged her claims to tariff autonomy and asked that, if the powers there represented would not agree to an immediate restoration of tariff autonomy, arrangements might be made for such return to her of her sovereign right at some definite date in the future. But China was in a disturbed condition, and the commercial powers of the West were selfish. The request was not granted, but a treaty dealing with the tariff was signed by all the nine powers represented. That treaty promised an immediate revision of the tariff schedule to make the duties correspond to the requirements of the earlier treaties, and held out the hope of an increase in the rate, the abolition of likin, and the abolition of the reduction allowed in duties on goods imported over the land frontiers. The revision to bring the duties up to an effective five per cent ad valorem was completed in 1922. The new schedule went into effect January 17, 1923. This could be done without waiting for the ratification of the Washington Treaty, since the old treaties have fixed that rate. But the more important provisions of the Washington Treaty could not be carried out until all the powers signatory had ratified it. The last of the signatories gave its assent in August, 1925, and a conference to arrange for tariff revision met at Peking in the October following, but failed to reach agreement. After the Nationalist forces occupied Peking, the United States, through its Minister in Peking, Hon. Jno. V. A. MacMurray, entered into a treaty with the new Government of China, abrogating all provisions of former treaties that had deprived China of tariff autonomy. The American Government, however, reserved the right to favored nation treatment. The new tariff schedule went into effect on February 1, 1929. It has since been revised. In 1931 the schedule for imports contained 647 items. Most duties had been made specific, but in some cases they were still ad valorem, varying from five per cent on ores and seven and a half per cent on aluminum to twenty-eight and thirty on certain groceries and fifty per cent on certain tobacco products and various liquors.

CONSULAR FUNCTIONS

Goods shipped to the United States, whether from China or elsewhere, must be accompanied by an invoice certified by the consul at the port of shipment. This is necessary to enable the customs authorities in the United States to keep informed as to the prices of articles imported, and thus make a correct estimate of the duty. Only shipments of less than one hundred dollars value, or personal effects accompanying a passenger, are exempt from this requirement. The certifying of invoices is, therefore, one of the most important functions of the consul. He must keep himself acquainted with the state of the market, the fluctuations of prices and exchange. In the case of certain kinds of goods he is required, moreover, to see that they are disinfected and certify to that fact. He must know, too, that the vessel departing for an American port is in proper sanitary condition and grant it a bill of health. When epidemics occur these must be promptly reported to the American Government and, if quarantine regulations are in force, he must see that they are observed by American vessels or those departing for the United States.

All Americans in China are registered at the consulates. Marriages, births and deaths are recorded, passports issued, and certificates granted to Chinese students, merchants, travelers and officials departing for the United States, to assure our immigration authorities that such persons do not belong to the classes of Chinese excluded from the United States. The consul must also report regularly to the Department of State upon the condition of trade in his district.

The United States has eighteen consulates in China, not including that at Hongkong, which is a British Crown Colony. All China is divided into districts. Each district, with all Americans and American interests therein, is under the supervision of one of the consulates.

Owing to the enjoyment by the United States of extraterritorial jurisdiction over American citizens in China, the consuls there are charged with judicial functions. All cases of a criminal character involving offenses which under American law are punishable with a fine of one hundred dollars, or imprisonment for sixty days, or both, are tried by the consul. More serious cases are tried by the United States Court for China, and even in the cases of less importance appeals lie from the consular courts to the United States Court for China. From the decisions of the latter appeals lie to the United States Circuit Court of Appeals of the Ninth Judicial Circuit—California.

Cases of Americans against Chinese are tried in Chinese courts by Chinese law, but the American Government is represented by a consular officer who sits as an assessor,* with the right to question and cross-question witnesses and to protest if need be against the procedure or decision of the court. Appeals lie to the higher authorities of China, who review the case in conference with the superior consular authorities.

* As stated in Chapter XXIII the use of foreign assessors in the Chinese District Court at Shanghai has been abandoned. The same will be true elsewhere when extraterritorial jurisdiction is surrendered.

TRADE-MARKS, COPYRIGHTS AND PATENTS

Various unsuccessful attempts have been made in the past by American and other foreign representatives in China to obtain protection there for trade-marks, copyrights and patents. The importance of such protection is easily seen. In our treaty of 1903 China agreed to give the protection needed, except that in the case of copyrights the protection was granted only to books, maps, prints and engravings especially prepared for the use and education of the Chinese people.

This qualification, inserted at the request of the Chinese Commissioners, was designed to enable Chinese schools to obtain American text books at the mere cost of re-printing with a slight change of form. The Nationalist Government is disposed to be more just. It recently issued regulations for copyright to an author for life and to his heirs for thirty years after the author's death. Penalty for infraction $50 to $500.

New Provisional Regulations for the protection of trade-marks were promulgated in May, 1930. Registration is to be made with the Ministry of Industry, Commerce and Labor, both for copyright and for trade marks. This arrangement, of course, does not protect such industrial property against infringement in China by non-Chinese, if the latter enjoy extraterritoriality. To secure such protection the American Government has entered into a number of treaties with other powers to give mutual protection in their extraterritorial courts in China to trade-marks, copyrights and patents.[26]

Infringement of trade-marks has been only too common in the past in the Far East. Since the masses of the people are unable to read a European language, it is easy to make a colorable imitation of a trade-mark without copying

[26] Such treaties exist between the United States and the following countries: Belgium, France, Germany, Great Britain, Italy, Japan, the Netherlands, Russia and Sweden. Russia and Germany, however, no longer enjoy extraterritorial jurisdiction.

exactly the printed legend. Counterfeit goods, bearing such a mark, similar to a well-known and popular brand, can take advantage of the reputation of the genuine goods to circulate alongside them. Communication is difficult in most provinces of China and years may pass before the owner of the genuine mark can learn that the reputation of his goods is being injured by the counterfeit. If suit be brought, the counterfeiter may deny intent to infringe and claim that the marks are unlike.

NEW LEGISLATION

When those nations that still exercise consular jurisdiction in China are compelled to surrender that right, all foreign firms in China and all foreign residents, except diplomatic representatives, will become subject to Chinese law and to the jurisdiction of Chinese courts. The National Government has been busily engaged in preparing for that day. There has been much legislation since 1928, some of it is of interest to foreign business men. Among laws which have not been mentioned in preceding chapters are the following:

The law governing Chambers of Commerce, the Company Law, the Law relating to Negotiable Instruments, the Stock Exchange Law, and others relating to Insurance Societies, Maritime Trade, regulating Electrical Industries, supervising Public Utilities, and providing for Arbitration in Civil Suits. A recent enactment adopted on June 6, 1931, provides for a Business Tax. It is to be levied upon all sorts of business enterprises except agricultural, and excepting also banks and factories organized as limited share companies, since these are liable, the one to Income Tax and the other to the Factory Tax.

THE CHINA TRADE ACT OF 1922

Formerly American merchants in China were handicapped to a degree by the want of any federal incorporation law, and by the exemption from income taxes enjoyed by their competitors in trade. This handicap has now been removed by the China Trade Act, approved September 19th, 1922. This provides for the appointment of a Registrar, who must be an officer of the Department of Commerce and whose office shall be in China. Companies incorporated under this act have their head offices in the District of Columbia. A majority of the incorporators and directors must be American citizens, and one must be a resident of the District of Columbia. The duration of the corporation is not to exceed twenty-five years, but may be extended from one period to another by the Secretary of Commerce. Such companies may engage in general trade and other forms of business enterprise except banking and insurance.

An important provision amends the Revenue Act of 1921 so as to exempt from income tax "an amount equal to the proportion of the net income derived from sources within China which the par value of the shares of stock of the Corporation owned on the last day of the taxable year by individual citizens of the United States or China, resident in China, bears to the par value of the whole number of the shares of stock of the corporation outstanding on such date." [27]

[27] The Act further provides that the amount exempted shall not exceed the amount of a special dividend certified under another paragraph which reads as follows:

"Such credit shall not be allowed unless the Secretary of Commerce has certified to the Commissioner (1) the amount which, during the year ending on the date of filing the return, the corporation has distributed as a special dividend to or for the benefit of such individuals as on the last day of the taxable year were citizens of the United States or China, resident in China, and owned shares of stock of the corporation, (2) that such special dividend was in addition to all other amounts, payable or to be payable to such individuals or for their benefit, by reason of their interest in the corporation, and (3) that such distribution has been made to or for the benefit of such individuals in proportion to the par value of the shares of stock of the corporation owned by each; except that if the corporation has more than one class of stock, the certificate shall contain a statement that the articles of incorporation provide a method for the apportionment of such special dividend among such individuals, and that the amount certified has been distributed in accordance with the method so provided."

This Act, the writer believes, will take rank with that of 1906 creating the U. S. Court for China, in the importance which it has for the advancement of American interests for China.

MINING

The investment of foreign capital in mining and manufacturing enterprises in China is provided for by treaty and by Chinese legislation; but the mining regulations formerly adopted by the Chinese Government were not of a character to encourage such investment. With a very natural desire to protect her own interests China forbade the holding by foreigners of more than fifty per cent of the shares of any mining corporation.

Such corporations were placed under the control of the Provincial Industrial Bureau of the province concerned.[28] These provisions were not of a sort to induce foreign capitalists to invest in large amounts except in places where special mining grants have been made by treaties upon terms not affected by these regulations.* The new mining law adopted by the Nationalist Government "provides that all iron, copper and petroleum mines as well as anthracite coal mines suitable for metallurgical purposes shall be state-owned." In accordance with this provision, the Government announced in March, 1931, a plan for state development of coal, gold, oil and copper mines. Nevertheless there is provision made in the Mining Law for the protection of private undertakings. Concessions may be granted to individuals who are Chinese citizens for the exploitation of state-owned mines. Moreover concessions obtained before the promulgation of the Law are regarded as having been acquired in accordance with the Law.

MANUFACTURING

Although manufacturing in a small way, with steam-driven machinery, was begun by foreigners in China soon after the opening of the free ports in 1842, it was not until 1895 that express permission to do so was granted by

[28] "China Year Book," 1922-23, p. 131.
* *Chinese Affairs*, March 15, 1931.

treaty. The Peace Treaty between China and Japan of that year provides in Article XI that

> Japanese subjects shall be free to engage in all kinds of manufacturing industries in all the open cities, towns and ports of China, and shall be at liberty to import into China all kinds of machinery, paying only the stipulated import duty thereon.

This provision was expanded the following year in a protocol appended to the Japanese Commercial Treaty of 1896. Article III of that protocol says:

> The Government of Japan concedes the right of the Chinese Government to impose upon articles manufactured by Japanese subjects in China such a tax as may seem expedient, provided that the said tax shall not differ from or exceed the tax paid by Chinese subjects; and provided that the Chinese Government shall, when the Japanese Government so desires, immediately provide sites for the formation of special Japanese settlements in Shanghai, Tientsin, Amoy and Hankow.

Under this provision the building of factories and the use of steam-driven machinery received quite an impetus. Other countries than Japan claimed favored nation treatment. But it was after the settlement of the Boxer troubles that foreign enterprise in this direction became most noticeable. The British Commercial Treaty of 1902 and our own of 1903, containing substantially the same provisions relating to the subject, sought to obtain in exchange for a surtax on import duties still more favorable treatment for "products of foreign type turned out by machinery in China." Such goods, whether manufactured by foreigners or by Chinese, were to be granted a rebate of the import duty and of two-thirds of the surtax on raw materials brought from abroad used in such manufacture, and of all duties paid on Chinese raw material used, and be free of all export duty, coast trade duty and export surtax. But these provisions have never gone into effect, because the treaty powers, other than the United States, Great Britain and Japan, have never agreed to the increase in duties on imports. Moreover China's recovery of tariff autonomy has nullified all such treaty arrangements.

The investment of foreign and Chinese capital in such

enterprises, however, has not needed the proposed additional encouragement. China is a great reservoir of cheap and fairly efficient labor. The Chinese workman soon learns to use foreign machinery, and bids fair to become a dangerous rival of the Western operative.

The transformation that is thus taking place in China is not advantageous to American trade. For a time there will be a demand for foreign machinery, and manufacturers of machinery will profit thereby, but the use of such machinery must in the long run reduce our export of articles of the type being manufactured by it. It is bringing cheap Oriental labor into competition with our own more highly paid labor. As stated above, the competition at present is to be found only in coarser types of products, but as skill increases it is likely to affect the finer sorts.

It is not alone the foreigner in China who is investing funds in these enterprises; many of the share-holders in foreign companies are Chinese. It will be noted that our Trade Act of 1922 specifically provides for such shareholders in American companies. There are also a number of large enterprises that are entirely Chinese.[29]

The change which China is undergoing through the substitution of machinery for handicraft is one which was bound to come, and China, with a territory as large as our own and with national resources similar to our own in quantity and kind, is likely in the future to become one of our chief competitors in the markets of the world.

[29] For statistics for factories see ''China Year Book,'' 1925.

IMPORTANT DATES IN CHINESE HISTORY

B.C. 2356. Probable date of accession of Yao, the first ruler mentioned in the Book of History.

2205. Traditional date of the founding of the Hsia Dynasty.

1766. Founding of the Shang Dynasty.

1122. Founding of the Chou Dynasty.

841. Historical period commences.

605. Traditional date of birth of Lao Tzu.

551. Birth of Confucius.

479. Death of Confucius.

372. Birth of Mencius.

249. End of the Chou Dynasty.

212. Confucian classics burned.

204. Great Wall completed.

A.D. 65. Buddhism introduced.

618. Mohammedanism introduced.

635. First Christian missionaries (Nestorian) arrived at the capital.

1275. Marco Polo reached Peking.

1516. Portuguese first arrived in China.

1552. St. Francis Xavier died at St. John's Island.

1557. Portuguese settle at Macao.

1601. Ricci reaches Peking.

1637. First British vessel arrives at Canton.

1644. Russians first enter the valley of the Amur.

1644. Manchus capture Peking.

1689. First Treaty between Russia and China.

1689. British establish a trading post at Canton.

1720. Chinese Co-hong (Monopoly) organized at Canton.

1729. First edict against opium smoking.

1733. Chinese send embassy to St. Petersburg.

1784. August 28, first American vessel, "Empress of China," arrives at Canton.

1793. Macartney's Embassy (British) arrives at Peking.

1796. Edict against opium smoking.

1800. Edict forbids import of opium.

1807. Robert Morrison, first Protestant missionary, reaches Canton.

1816. Amherst embassy arrives at Peking.

1834. British East India Company's monopoly ended.

1839. Commissioner Lin seizes and destroys opium at Canton.
1840. British blockade Canton.
1842. Anglo-Chinese Treaty of Nanking signed, August 29.
1843. British Commercial Treaty signed, October 8.
1843. Shanghai opened, November 17.
1844. First American Treaty with China, signed July 3.
1849. Portuguese expelled Chinese Customs from Macao, March 5.
1849. Governor Amaral assassinated, August 22.
1851. Taiping Rebellion began.
1853. Nanking captured by Taipings.
1854. Agreement for foreign administration of Customs at Shanghai, June 29.
1856. Affair of the lorcha "Arrow" at Canton, October 8.
1857. Canton captured by British and French, December 29.
1858. Tientsin Treaties, American, British, French and Russian, signed in June.
1859. Americans and Russians ratify treaties of 1858.
1859. British and French suffer defeat at Taku, June 25.
1859. Frederick T. Ward enters service of the Chinese against the Taipings.
1860. British and French take Peking, October 13.
1860. British Convention signed at Peking, October 24, French, October 25.
1860. Ward captures Sungkiang, July 17.
1861. Robert Hart in temporary charge of Customs, June 30.
1862. Ward killed in battle at Tzuchi, September 21.
1863. Robert Hart appointed Inspector General of Customs.
1863. Colonel Gordon assumed command of Ward's army, March 25.
1864. Gordon disbands his forces, May 31.
1864. Nanking recovered by Imperial army and Taipings dispersed
1866. Mohammedan rebellion in Ili.
1867. General Tso opens campaign against rebels.
1867. American war ship visits Korea in January.
1867. French annex three provinces of Cochin China, in June.
1867. Burlingame commissioned by China as envoy to western powers, December 31.
1868. Burlingame Treaty in re Chinese Immigration signed, Washington, July 28.
1868. American war ship visits Korea.
1870. Burlingame died at St. Petersburg, February 23.
1870. Tientsin Massacre, June 21.

1871. Russians occupy Kuldja.
1871. American naval expedition to Korea, May-July.
1871. Cable to Shanghai opened, June 3.
1873. Diplomatic Corps received in audience for first time, June 29.
1875. January 12, Kuanghsü proclaimed emperor.
1875. Augustus R. Margary, British diplomatic officer, murdered in Yunnan by Chinese, February 21.
1875. Coolie traffic at Macao suppressed.
1876. Japanese naval expedition to Korea in January.
1876. Japanese-Korean Treaty signed, February 26.
1876. Great famine begins in Shansi.
1876. Chefoo Treaty (British) signed September 13.
1876. Railway between Shanghai and Woosung begun.
1876. Chinese protest against building of the railway.
1877. Chinese purchase and destroy the railway.
1877. First Chinese envoy sent to London.
1878. Mohammedan rebellion suppressed, January 2.
1878. First Chinese envoy to the United States received, October 28.
1878. Kaiping coal mine opened.
1878. Russia asked to restore Kuldja to China, July.
1878. Customs Post Office established, December.
1880. American-Chinese Immigration Treaty, signed November 17.
1880. American Commercial Treaty, signed November 17.
1880. Telegraph land lines sanctioned, November.
1881. Russia surrenders Kuldja and Ili, Treaty signed February 24.
1881. The "Chinese Rocket" (locomotive) made first trip, June 9, from Kaiping Colliery to canal.
1881. Shanghai-Tientsin telegraph opened, December 1.
1882. American Treaty with Korea signed, May 22.
1883. Annam becomes French protectorate, August 25.
1884. Franco-Chinese war over Annam.
1884. Chinese and Japanese troops fight in streets of Seoul, December 5.
1885. Chinese-Japanese Convention regarding Korea signed at Tientsin, April 18.
1885. Franco-Chinese Treaty of Peace signed at Tientsin, June 9.
1886. Franco-Chinese Convention in re frontier trade, signed April 25.
1886. Anglo-Chinese Convention in re Burmah and Tibet, signed July 24.
1887. New Franco-Chinese Convention in re frontier trade, June 26.

1887.   Portuguese-Chinese Treaty, yields Macao to Portugal, December 1.
1888.   Railway opened from Tongshan to Tientsin, August.
1890.   Anglo-Chinese Convention concerning Sikkim and Tibet, March 17.
1890.   Hanyang Iron Works opened, November 27.
1891.   Anti-Missionary Riots in Yangtze Valley, May-June.
1894.   Anglo-Chinese Convention in re Burmah and Tibet, March 1.
1894.   American-Chinese Treaty prohibiting immigration of Chinese laborers for ten years, March 17.
1894.   Tonghak Rebellion in Korea, March-May.
1894.   China and Japan declare war, August 1.
1894.   Battle of the Yalu, September 17.
1895.   Li Hung-chang arrives at Shimonoseki to negotiate peace.
1895.   Peace Treaty with Japan signed, April 17.
1895.   Franco-Chinese Convention regarding frontier trade, June 20.
1895.   Russia, France and Germany advise Japan to retrocede the Liaotung Peninsula, April.
1896.   Russo-Chinese Agreement regarding the Chinese Eastern Railway, September 8.
1897.   Declaration as to non-alienation of Hainan, March 15.
1897.   Two German missionaries murdered in Shantung, November 1.
1897.   Germans seize Tsingtao, November 14.
1898.   Declaration as to non-alienation of Yangtze Valley, February 11.
1898.   Promise to Great Britain as to Inspectorate General of Customs, February 13.
1898.   Lease of Kiaochow to Germany for ninety-nine years, March 6.
1898.   Lease of Kuantung Peninsula to Russia for twenty-five years, March 27.
1898.   Declaration as to non-alienation of southern provinces.
1898.   American contract for Hankow-Canton Railway.
1898.   French seize Kuangchouwan, April 22.
1898.   Declaration as to non-alienation of Fukien, April 26.
1898.   Anglo-Chinese Convention for lease of Kowloon hinterland, June 9.
1898.   Anglo-Chinese Convention for lease of Weihaiwei, July 1.
1898.   Empress Dowager seizes government, imprisons Emperor, September 22.

1899. Anglo-Russian agreement as to interests in Manchuria and the Yangtze region, April 29.
1899. Boxer Society organized in May.
1899. Secretary Hay sends out notes on Open Door, September 6.
1900. Legation Guards sent to Peking, May 31.
1900. Admiral Seymour leaves Tientsin for Peking, June 10.
1900. Japanese Secretary Sugiyama murdered, June 11.
1900. Forts at Taku captured by allied forces, June 17.
1900. China declares war, June 20.
1900. Baron von Ketteler murdered, June 20.
1900. Allied forces enter Peking, August 14.
1901. Peace signed at Peking, September 7.
1902. Court returns to Peking, January 7.
1902. Anglo-Japanese Alliance signed January 30.
1902. British Commercial Treaty, September 5.
1903. American and Japanese commercial treaties signed, October 8.
1903. Great Britain sends expedition to Tibet, July.
1904. Japan declares war on Russia, February 8.
1904. China denounces Immigration Treaty with the United States.
1904. British forces enter Lhasa, August 3.
1905. President Roosevelt suggests that Russia and Japan make peace, June 8.
1905. Anglo-Japanese Treaty of Alliance revised, August 12.
1905. Russia and Japan sign peace treaty at Portsmouth, N. H., September 5.
1905. China accedes to transfer to Japan of Russian rights in Manchuria, December 22.
1906. Anglo-Chinese Treaty concerning Tibet, April 27.
1906. Imperial Edict in preparation for constitutional government, September 1.
1906. Imperial Edict introducing anti-opium reform, November 21.
1906. Edict raises rank of Confucius in pantheon, December 30.
1907. First municipal elections under new order.
1907. Anglo-Russian agreement touching Tibet, August 31.
1908. Death of the Emperor, Kuanghsü, November 14.
1908. Death of the Empress Dowager, Tzu-hsi, November 15.
1909. Opium Commission meets at Shanghai, January 1.
1909. Provincial assemblies meet in October.
1910. Provisional National Assembly meets, October 3.

1911. Four-Power Group signs contract for Hukuang Railways, May 20.

1911. October 10, Outbreak of Revolution at Wuchang.

1911. Outer Mongolia declares independence, Hutukhtu crowned Emperor, December 28.

1912. Sun Yat-sen inaugurated President of southern provinces, January 1.

1912. Manchus abdicate, February 12.

1912. Yüan Shih-kai inaugurated Provisional President of China, March 10.

1913. Empress Lungyü dies, February 21.

1913. The United States recognizes the Chinese Republic, May 2.

1913. Yüan Shih-kai inaugurated President of China, October 10.

1914. Japan demands from Germany surrender of Kiao-chow, August 15.

1914. Japan and Great Britain capture Tsingtao, November 7.

1915. Japan presents to China Twenty-one Demands, January 18.

1915. China signs Treaties growing out of twenty-one demands, May 25.

1915. Yüan plans to make himself an emperor; Japan objects, December.

1916. Insurrection in southern provinces; Yüan dies, June 6.

1917. The American Government invites China to break relations with Germany, February 4.

1917. China agrees to American proposal, February 9.

1917. Secret agreement between Japan and Great Britain concerning Shantung, February 16.

1917. Secret agreement with France as to same, March 1.

1917. Secret agreement with Russia as to same, March 5.

1917. China breaks relations with Germany, March 14.

1917. China declares war on Germany, August 14.

1917. The Lansing-Ishii Notes signed, November 2.

1918. Secret agreements between China and Japan relating to Shantung, signed September 24 and 28.

1919. Chinese Delegation to Peace Conference declines to sign Treaty of Versailles, June 28.

1920. Recognition of Russian representatives withdrawn by China, September 23.

1922. Treaty between China and Japan relating to Shantung signed at Washington, February 4.

1922. Nine-power Treaty relating to territorial integrity

and independence of China signed at Washington, February 6.

1924. Russian Union of Soviet Socialistic Republics recognized. Treaty signed May 31.

1925. Sun Yat-sen died at Peking, March 12.

1925. Riot at Shanghai, May 30. Killing of Chinese by police leads to boycott of British trade.

1925. Boycott extends. Riot at Hankow, June 8.

1925. Public meeting at Canton to protest police action at Shanghai. Results in riot, June 23. Many Chinese killed.

1925. Conference on Treaty Tariff Revision met at Peking, October 26.

1926. Conference on Extraterritoriality opened at Peking, January 12.

1926. July 3, Tariff Conference at Peking suspended its sittings.

1926. September 16, Commission on Extraterritoriality adjourned.

1926. October 10, Wuchang on the Yangtze surrenders to Nationalists.

1926. December 18, British Government addresses note to the Powers proposing common policy towards China.

1927. January 3, Anti-British riot at Hankow. British bluejackets landed.

1927. January 4, Nationalist troops occupy British Concession at Hankow.

1927. January 17, Anti-Christian mobs sack churches and maltreat missionaries at Foochow.

1927. January 26, American Government declares its policy in relation to China.

1927. January 27, British troops landed at Shanghai.

1927. February 1, American Government announces that naval forces in China will be increased to give protection to Americans there.

1927. February 17, Nationalists capture Hangchow.

1927. March 5, Russian vessel, the *Pamiat Lenina,* is seized by the Peking Government.

1927. March 20, Nationalists capture native city of Shanghai.

1927. March 24, Nationalists take Nanking, attack foreign consuls and other foreign residents, kill seven and wound a number, loot and burn foreign residences.

1927. April 6, Soviet bank at Peking adjoining Russian Embassy is raided by Chinese police and important documents seized.

1927. April 9, Russian Chargé d'Affaires withdrawn from Peking.

1927. April 11, The United States, Great Britain, France, Italy and Japan send identical notes of protest concerning Nanking outrage.

1927. November 7, Russian Soviet Consulate at Shanghai raided by a mob.

1927. November 17, The Nanking faction of the Nationalist Party having defeated the Communist faction, occupied the Wuhan cities.

1927. December 11, Uprising of laborers at Canton is suppressed with execution of several hundred Chinese and eight or nine Russians, including Russian Vice Consul.

1927. December 15, Nationalist Government withdraws recognition from Russian Soviet Government.

1928. March 30, Nationalist Government apologizes to American Government for outrages of March, 1927, at Nanking against the American Consul and other American citizens.

1928. April, Early in this month the Nationalist army in alliance with two northern armies moved towards Peking.

1928. May 1, Vanguard of Nationalist forces under General Chiang Kai-shek enters Tsinan.

1928. May 3, Hostilities break out between Nationalist soldiers and Japanese troops in Tsinan. Hostilities continue eight days.

1928. May 18, Japan warns Peking and Nanking governments that no disorders will be permitted in Manchuria.

1928. June 4, Marshal Chang Tso-lin killed by bomb explosion while on train returning to Mukden.

1928. June 8, Nationalist forces under Governor Yen Hsi-shan of Shansi occupy Peking without fighting.

1928. July 25, United States signs treaty recognizing China's autonomy in matter of import and export tariffs.

1928. August 10, Japan warns Chang Hsueh-liang not to raise the Nationalist flag in Manchuria.

1928. August 19, China settles with Great Britain for outrages of March 1927.

1928. August 27, Briand-Kellogg Pact renouncing war signed at Paris.

1928. October 16, France accepts China's apology for outrage of 1927 at Nanking.

1928. October 18, China settles with Italy for outrage of March 1927.

1929. March 28, Japan and China settle for clash at Tsinan, May, 1928.

1929. May 2, China settles with Japan for outrage at Nanking, 1927.

1929. May 27, Chinese police raid a Communist meeting in Russian Consulate at Harbin.

1929. June 1, State burial of remains of Sun Yat-sen at Nanking.

1929. September 23, Clash between Chinese and Japanese police at Tiehling.

1929. November   , First report of Kemmerer Commission on Monetary Reform.

1929. December 22, Khabarovsk Agreement in matter of Raid on Russian Consulate, May 27.

1930. February 7, Central Government declares certain features of Khabarovsk Agreement to be *ultra vires*.

1930. February 17, China and Diplomatic Corps agree on Provisional Court for Shanghai.

1930. August   , China complains to Japan of latter's Post Offices retained in Manchuria in violation of Washington Treaty.

1930. October 1, Weihaiwei returned by Great Britain to China.

1931. April-August, Riots in Manchuria and Korea over Wanpaoshan Lease.

1931. April 20, National Conference on Aviation meets at Nanking.

1931. May 5, People's Constitutional Convention assembles at Nanking.

1931. May 12, Provisional Constitution adopted.

1931. August 5, Japan and China agree upon settlement of Wanpaoshan affair.

1931. July and August, Floods in Yangtze, Yellow and Huai Rivers bring disaster to sixteen provinces and forty millions of people.

1931. September 19, Japan without declaration of war seizes Shenyang (Mukden) and arsenal. Same day seize Antung, Newchwang and other places.

1931. September 19, China appeals to League of Nations.

1931. September 22, League Council urges Japan and China to refrain from acts that may aggravate situation. Same day Japan seizes Liaoyuan.

1931. September 28, Japan sets up Japanese courts in Manchuria.

1931. October 7, Japan seizes provincial funds of Kirin.

1932. January 3, Japan occupies Chinchow.

1932. January 28, Japan without declaration of war bombards unfortified city of Shanghai.

1932. March 2, Chinese army retreats in good order to take up a new position.

1932. March 9, ex-Emperor Pu-yi installed as head of an independent government of Manchuria.

1932. March 10, Assembly of League of Nations agrees upon a three-point proposal for settlement of Chino-Japanese affair.

BIBLIOGRAPHY

Note.—Despite the length of this list, the author has not aimed at making it exhaustive. He has selected the works of various periods, which, in his judgment are likely to furnish the most accurate information upon the subjects touched upon in this volume.

ABEEL, DAVID, "Journal of Residence in China and the Neighboring Countries." New York, 1836.

ABEL, CLARKE, "Narrative of a Journey in the Interior of China." London, 1818.

ANDREWS, ROY C., "Camps and Trails in China." New York, 1919.

ARNOLD, JULEAN, "Commercial Handbook of China," two vols. Washington, 1919.

AUBER, PETER, "China; an Outline of its Government, Laws and Policy." London, 1834.

BABER, E. COLBORNE, "Travels and Researches in West China." London, 1882.

BAKER, RAY STANNARD, "Woodrow Wilson and World Settlement." New York, 1922.

BALL, C. J., "Chinese and Sumerian." Oxford, 1913.

BALL, JAMES DYER, "Things Chinese." New York, 1904.

—— "The Chinese at Home." London, 1912.

BARD, EMILE, "Chinese Life in Town and Country," translated from the French by H. Twitchell. New York, 1905.

BARROW, SIR JOHN, "Travels in China." Philadelphia, 1805.

—— "Life of the Earl of Macartney." London, 1807.

BAU, MINGCHIEN JOSHUA, "The Foreign Relations of China." Chicago, 1921.

BEAL, SAMUEL, "A Catena of Buddhist Scriptures from the Chinese." London, 1871.

—— "Buddhism in China. London, 1884.

—— "The Life of Hiuen Tsiang." London, 1888.

BLAKESLEE, GEORGE H., "China and the Far East," Clark University Lectures. New York, 1910.

681

BLAKESLEE, GEORGE H., "Recent Developments in China," Clark University Lectures. New York, 1913.

BINYON, LAURENCE, "The Flight of the Dragon" (Chinese Art). London, 1911.

—— "Painting in the Far East." London, 1913.

BLAND, J. O. P. AND BACKHOUSE, E., "China under the Empress Dowager." Philadelphia, 1910.

—— "Annals and Memoirs of the Court of Peking." London, 1914.

BLAND, J. O. P., "Life of Li Hung-chang." London, 1917.

—— "Recent Events and Present Policies in China." London, 1912.

BREDON, JULIET, "Sir Robert Hart." London, 1909.

—— "Peking, a historical and intimate description of its chief places of interest." Shanghai, 1920.

BRETSCHNEIDER, E., "Botanicon Sinicum" in three parts. Shanghai, 1895.

—— "Archaeological and Historical Researches on Peking and its Environs" (pamphlet). Shanghai, 1876.

BUSHELL, S. W., "Chinese Art," two volumes. London, 1910.

BUSS, KATE, "The Chinese Drama." Boston, 1922.

CALIFORNIA, STATE BOARD OF CONTROL OF, "California and the Oriental." Sacramento, 1920.

CAMPBELL, CHAS. W., "China"; one of the Peace Handbooks, H. M. Stationer's Office. London, 1920.

CARUS, PAUL, "Lao-Tze's Tao-Teh-King." Chicago, 1898.

—— "Chinese Philosophy." Chicago, 1902.

CHAVANNES, EDOUARD, "La Sculpture sur Pierre en Chine." Paris, 1893.

—— "Les Mémoires Historiques de Se-ma Ts'ien," five vols. Paris, 1895–1905.

—— "Mission Archéologique en Chine." Paris, 1909–13.

—— "Les Documents Chinois découverts par Aurel Stein dans les Sables du Turkestan." Oxford, 1913.

CHINESE GOVERNMENT, Reports of the Maritime Customs; Statistical Series, Quarterly Returns and Annual Reports.

—— Reports of Maritime Customs; Decennial Reports.

—— Reports of the Maritime Customs; Special Series.

—— "Opium," Historical Note by Jos. Edkins, D.D. 1889.

—— "Medical Reports," issued at irregular intervals.

—— "Silk." 1881.

—— "Chinese Music." 1884.

—— "Medicines Exported from Hankow."

CHINESE GOVERNMENT, "Tea." 1888.

—— "Law of the Organization of the Judiciary" (English translation published by Ministry of Justice).

—— "Provisional Regulations of the High Courts and their Subordinate Courts of the Chinese Republic" (English Translation).

—— "Regulations of the Arbitration Court of the Chinese Republic" (English Translation).

—— "Rules for the Government and Administration of Prisons in China" (English Translation).

—— "Provisional Regulations for the Detention Houses" (English Translation).

—— "Commercial Associations Ordinance of the Chinese Republic" (English Translation).

—— Ministry of Communications. "Modern Transportation and Communication in China."

—— "The China-Japanese Negotiations; Official Statement. Peking, 1915.

—— "Conversations between Chinese and Japanese Delegations." Washington, 1923.

CLARK, ROBERT S. and ARTHUR SOWERBY, "Through Shen-Kan." London, 1912.

CLEMENTS, PAUL H., "The Boxer Rebellion." New York, 1915.

CLOUD, F. D., "Hangchow, the 'City of Heaven'; Soochow 'the Beautiful.'" Shanghai, 1906.

COLQUHOUN, A. R., "Amongst the Shans." New York, 1885.

COLTMAN, ROBERT, "The Chinese, their Present and Future." Philadelphia, 1891.

CONGER, SARAH PIKE, "Letters from China." Chicago, 1909.

CORDIER, HENRI, "Histoire des relations de la Chine avec les puissances occidentales, 1860–1900," three vols. Paris, 1901.

—— "Yule's Travels of Marco Polo," two vols. New York, 1903.

—— "Histoire générale de la Chine et de ses relations avec les pays étrangers depuis les temps les plus anciens jusqua le chute de la dynastie Mandchoue," four vols. Paris, 1920.

CRANMER-BYNG, "The Book of Odes" (Translation). London, 1920.

—— "The Lute of Jade" (Translation). New York, 1909.

CURTIN, JEREMIAH, "History of the Mongols." Boston, 1908.

DAVIS, SIR JNO. F., "China during the War and since the Peace," two vols. London, 1852.

DAVIS, SIR JNO. F., "Chinese Poetry." London, 1870.
DAVIES, HENRY R., "Yunnan the Link between India and the Yangtze." Cambridge, 1909.
DE LACOUPERIE, "The Western Origin of the Early Chinese Civilization." London, 1894.
DE LABOULAYE, "Les Chemins de Fer de Chine." Paris, 1911.
DE GROOT, J. J. M., "The Religious System of China," twelve volumes planned, five completed; publication began Leyden, 1892.
DENNETT, TYLER, "Americans in Eastern Asia." New York, 1922.
DER LING, THE PRINCESS, "Two Years in the Forbidden City." New York, 1912.
DEWEY, JOHN, "China, Japan and the United States of America." New York, 1921.
DICKINS AND STANLEY LANE-POOLE, "Life of Sir Harry Parkes." London and New York, 1894.
DOOLITTLE, JUSTUS, "Social Life of the Chinese," two vols.
DOUGLAS, ROBT. K., "Society in China." London, 1901.
—— "Confucianism and Taouism." London, 1889.
—— "Chinese Stories." London, 1893.
DU BOSE, H. C., "Dragon, Image and Demon." New York, 1887.
DU HALDE, JEAN BAPTISTE, "Description géographique, historique, etc. de I'empire de la Chine." La Haye, 1736.
EDKINS, JOSEPH, "Chinese Buddhism." London, 1890.
—— "Religion in China." London, 1893.
EITEL, ERNEST J., "Feng-shui." Hongkong, 1873.
—— "Buddhism; its Historical, Theoretical and Popular Aspects." Hongkong, 1884.
FERGUSON, JNO. C., "Outlines of Chinese Art." Chicago, 1919.
FORTUNE, R., "Three Years' Wanderings in the Northern Provinces of China." London, 1847.
—— "A Journey to the Tea Countries." London, 1852.
FOSTER, JNO. W., "American Diplomacy in the Orient." Boston, 1903.
FIELDE, ADELE M., "A Corner of Cathay." New York, 1894.
—— "Pagoda Shadows." New York, 1887.
GAILLARD, LOUIS, "Croix et Swastika en Chine." Shanghai, 1893.
GALLAGHER, PATRICK, "America's Aims and Asia's Aspirations." New York, 1920.
GILES, HERBERT A., "Gems of Chinese Literature." London, 1884.
—— "Chinese Literature." New York, 1901.

GILES, HERBERT A., "Chinese Poetry." London, 1898.
—— "Strange Stories from a Chinese Studio." London, 1880.
—— "Chuang Tzu." London, 1889.
—— "China and the Manchus." Cambridge, 1912.
—— "The Civilization of China." New York, 1911.
GAUTIER, JUDITH, "Chinese Lyrics," translated from French by Jas. Whitall. New York, 1918.
GULLAND, W., "Chinese Porcelain." London, 1918.
GUNDRY, RICHARD S., "China Present and Past." London, 1895.
GRAY, JOHN HENRY, "China; a History of the Laws, Manners and Customs of the People." London, 1878.
GUTZLAFF, CHAS., "History of China," two vols. London, 1834.
GILMOUR, JAMES, "Among the Mongols." London, 1888.
—— "More about the Mongols." London.
HEADLAND, ISAAC T., "Home Life in China." New York, 1914.
—— "Court Life in China." New York and Chicago, 1909.
HENRY, B. C., "Ling Nam, or Interior Views of Southern China." London, 1886.
HERTSLET, "China Treaties," two vols. London.
HINCKLEY, FRANK E., "American Consular Jurisdiction in the Orient." Washington, 1906.
HIRTH, FREDERIC, "China and the Roman Orient." Shanghai, 1885.
—— "Ancient History of China." New York, 1911.
HIRTH & ROCKHILL, "Chau-Ju-kua" (Chinese and Arab Trade in 12th and 13th Centuries). St. Petersburg, 1911.
HOLDICH, "Tibet the Mysterious." London, 1906.
HORNBECK, STANLEY K., "Contemporary Politics in the Far East." New York, 1916.
HUC, M., Travels in Tartary, Thibet and China." Reprint, Chicago, 1898.
—— "The Chinese Empire." London, 1855.
HULBERT, H. B., "The Passing of Korea." New York, 1906.
HUNTINGTON, ELLSWORTH, "The Pulse of Asia." Boston and New York, 1907.
—— "Civilization and Climate." New Haven, 1922.
HUNTINGTON & VISHER, "Climatic Changes." New Haven, 1922.
HOSIE, ALEXANDER, "Three Years in Western China." London, 1897.
—— "Manchuria." London, 1901. Boston and Tokyo, 1910.
—— "On the Trail of the Opium Poppy." London, 1914.
IDES, EVERT YSBRANDSZOON, "Three Years' Travels from Moscow overland to China." London, 1706.

686 *Bibliography*

JAPANESE GOVERNMENT, "Imperial Government Railways Official Guide," vol. I. "Manchuria and Chosen."
JAMES, SIR HENRY E. M., "The Long White Mountain." London, 1888.
KENT, PERCY H., "The Passing of the Manchus." London, 1912.
KING, F. H., "Farmers of Forty Centuries." Madison, 1911.
KOCH, WALDEMAR, "Die Industrialisierung Chinas." Berlin, 1910.
KU HUNG-MING, "Letters from a Viceroy's Yamen." Shanghai, 1901.
LANDON, PERRCEVAL, "The Opening of Tibet." New York, 1906.
LANNING, GEORGE, "Old Forces in New China." London, 1912.
LANSING, ROBERT, "The Peace Negotiations." Boston and New York, 1921.
LATOURETTE, KENNETH SCOTT. "The Development of China," New York, 1929.
LAUFER, BERTHOLD, "Chinese Pottery of the Han Dynasty." Leiden, 1909.
LEAVENWORTH, CHAS., "The Arrow War with China." London, 1901.
—— "The Loochoo Islands." Shanghai, 1905.
LEGGE, JAMES, "The Chinese Classics" (text and translation), seven vols. London, 1861–1893.
—— "The Religions of China." New York, 1881.
—— "The Texts of Taoism," two vols. Oxford, 1891 (Sacred Bks. of East).
—— "A Record of Buddhistic Kingdoms" (travels of Fa-hien). Oxford, 1886.
LEONG, V. K. and TAO, L. K., "Village and Town Life in China." London, 1915.
LESDAIN, COUNT DE, "From Peking to Sikkim." London, 1908.
LI, UN-BING, "Outlines of Chinese History." Shanghai, 1914.
LITTLE, ALICIA H. A. (Mrs. Archibald Little), "Intimate China." London, 1899.
—— "The Land of the Blue Gown." London, 1902.
LITTLE, ARCHIBALD, J., "Mt Omi and Beyond." London, 1901.
—— "Through the Yangtze Gorges." London, 1898.
—— "Gleanings from Fifty Years in China." London, 1910.
LOCKHART, WILLIAM, "The Medical Missionary in China." London, 1861.
MACGOWAN, JOHN, "The Imperial History of China." Shanghai, 1906.
—— "Side-lights on Chinese Life." London, 1907.

MAC MURRAY, JOHN V. A., "Treaties and Agreements with and concerning China," two vols. New York, 1921.

MACKENZIE, "The Tragedy of Korea." London, 1908.

MARGARY, AUGUSTUS RAYMOND, "Journey from Shanghai to Bhamo" from his journals. London, 1876.

MARTENS, FREDERICK H. and WILHELM, R., "The Chinese Fairy Book." New York, 1921.

MARTIN, W. A. P., "A Cycle of Cathay." London, 1896.

—— "The Lore of Cathay." New York, 1901.

—— "The Awakening of China." New York, 1907.

MAYERS, WILLIAM FREDERICK, "The Chinese Reader's Manual." Shanghai, 1874.

—— "The Chinese Government." Shanghai, 1897.

McCORMICK, FREDERICK, "The Tragedy of Russia in Pacific Asia." New York, 1907, two vols.

—— "The Flowery Republic." London, 1913.

MICHIE, ALEXANDER, "The Englishman in China" (Career of Sir R. Alcock). Edinburgh, 1900.

MILLARD, THOMAS F., "America and the Far Eastern Question." New York, 1909.

—— "Our Eastern Question." New York, 1915.

—— "Democracy and the Eastern Question." New York, 1919.

MISSION BOOK CO., "China Mission Year Book." Shanghai.

MORRISON, GEORGE E., "An Australian in China." London, 1902.

MORSE, H. B., "The Trade and Administration of the Chinese Empire." Shanghai, 1908.

—— "The Gilds of China." London, 1909.

—— "The International Relations of the Chinese Empire," three vols. London, 1910–1918.

MOULE, ARTHUR EVANS, "New China and Old." London, 1892.

MÜNSTERBERG, "Chinesische Kunst-Geschichte," two vols. Esslingen, 1910.

NEVIUS, J. L., "China and the Chinese." New York, 1869.

OLEARIUS, A., "The Voyages and Travels of the Ambassadors, sent by Frederick, Duke of Holstein," etc. (translated by John Davies). London, 1662.

OSBECK, PETER, "A Voyage to China and the East Indies." London, 1771.

OLIPHANT, LAURENCE, "A Narrative of the Earl of Elgin's Mission to China and Japan." London, 1860.

OVERLACH, T. W., "Foreign Financial Control in China." New York, 1919.

OSSENDOWSKI, FERDINAND, "Beasts, Men and Gods." New York, 1922.

PARKER, E. H., "A Thousand Years of the Tartars." Shanghai, 1895.

—— "China Past and Present." London, 1903.

—— "Ancient China Simplified." London, 1908.

—— "China, Her History, Diplomacy and Commerce," New Edition. London, 1919.

PELLIOT, PAUL, "Les Grottes de Touen-Houang." Paris, 1914.

PERRY-AYSCOUGH & OTTER-BARRY, "With the Russians in Mongolia." London, 1914.

PIGGOTT, SIR FRANCIS, "Exterritoriality." London, 1892.

POTT, F. L. HAWKS, "The Outbreak in China." New York, 1900.

—— "A Sketch of Chinese History." Shanghai, 1903.

—— "The Emergency in China." New York, 1913.

PUMPELLY, RAPHAEL, "Across America and Asia." New York, 1871.

—— "Explorations in Turkestan, Expedition of 1904." Washington, 1908.

QUINCY, JOSIAH, "The Journals of Major Samuel Shaw." Boston, 1847.

REINSCH, PAUL S., "An American Diplomat in China." New York, 1922.

RENAUDOT, EUSEBIUS, "Ancient Accounts of India and China by Two Mohammedan Travellers, who went to those parts in the 9th Century." London, 1733.

RICHARD, L., "Comprehensive Geography of China" (translated from the French by M. Kennelly). Shanghai, 1908.

RICHARD, TIMOTHY, "Forty-five Years in China." New York, 1916.

RICHTHOFEN, BARON F., "Letters." Shanghai, Reprint, 1903.

—— "China." Berlin, 1912.

ROCKHILL, W. W., "The Land of the Lamas." New York, 1891.

—— "The Dalai Lamas of Lhasa and their Relations with the Manchu Emperors of China." Leyden, 1910.

—— "Diplomatic Audiences at the Court of China." London, 1905.

—— "China's Intercourse with Korea." London, 1905.

—— "The 1910 Census of China." New York, 1912.

—— "See Hirth & Rockhill.

ROSS, E. A., "The Changing Chinese." London, 1911.

ROSS, JOHN, "The Manchus." London, 1880.

—— "The Origin of the Chinese People." Edinburgh and London, 1916.

REID, GILBERT, "China Captive and Free." New York, 1921.

ROCHER, EMILIE, "La Province Chinoise du Yünnan," two vols. Paris, 1880.

RUSSELL, BERTRAND, "The Problem of China." New York, 1922.

SCHOFF, WILFRED H., "Parthian Stations by Isidore of Charax." Philadelphia, 1914.

SHIGEYOSHI, OBATA, "The Works of Li Po" (Translation of Li Po's verses). New York, 1922.

SMITH, ARTHUR H., "Chinese Proverbs." Shanghai, 1888.

—— "Chinese Characteristics." Chicago, 1894.

—— "Village Life in China." New York, 1899.

—— "China in Convulsion," two vols. New York, 1901.

SOOTHILL, WILLIAM EDWARD, "The Analects of Confucius." Yokohama, 1910.

—— "The Three Religions of China." London, 1913.

SPALDING, WILLIAM F., "Eastern Exchange, Currency and Finance." London, 1917.

STAUNTON, SIR GEORGE, "Macartney's Embassy to China," three vols. London, 1797.

—— (Translation of the Penal Code of China) "The Ta Tsing Leu Lee." London, 1810.

STEIN, SIR AUREL, "Sand-buried Ruins of Khotan." London, 1903.

—— "Ruins of Desert Cathay." London, 1912.

—— "Serindia." Oxford, 1921.

TREDWELL, WINIFRED R., "Chinese Art Motives Interpreted." New York, 1915.

TYAU, M. T. Z., "The Legal Obligations arising out of Treaty Relations between China and other States." New York, 1917.

—— "China's New Constitution and International Problems." New York, 1918.

—— "China Awakened." New York, 1922.

U. S. GOVERNMENT, "Foreign Relations of the United States." Washington, Annual vols.

—— Department of Labor, "Treaty, Laws and Rules governing the Admission of Chinese." Washington, 1914.

—— Official Report of the Washington Conference on the Limitation of Armament and on Pacific and Far Eastern Questions. Washington, 1922.

VON STRAUSS, VICTOR, "Lao Tse's Tao Te King." Leipzig, 1870.

WADDELL, L. A., "The Buddhism of Tibet." London, 1895.

WALEY, ARTHUR, "A Hundred and Seventy Chinese Poems." New York, 1922.

WALEY, ARTHUR, "More Translations from the Chinese." New York, 1919.

WAGEL, S. R., "Chinese Currency and Banking." Shanghai, 1915.

WEALE, PUTNAM (B. S. Simpson), "The Fight for the Republic in China." New York, 1912.

WIEGER, LEON, "Folklore Chinois Moderne." Hochienfu, 1909.

—— "Bouddhisme Chinois." Hochienfu, 1910.

—— "Le Canon Taoiste." Hochienfu, 1911.

—— "Les Vies Chinoisis du Buddha." Hochienfu, 1909.

—— "Les Pères du Système Taoiste." Hochienfu, 1913.

—— "Textes Historiques." Hochienfu, 1903, three vols.

—— "Textes Philosophiques." Hochienfu, 1906.

—— "Moral Tenets and Customs in China." Hochienfu, 1913.

WERNER, E. T. C., "China of the Chinese." New York, 1920.

—— "Descriptive Sociology." London, 1870.

WILLIAMS, FRED. W., "Anson Burlingame and the First Chinese Mission to Foreign Powers." New York, 1912.

—— "The Life and Letters of Samuel Wells Williams." New York, 1889.

WILLIAMS, ROSE S., "Keramic Wares of the Sung Dynasty." New York, 1914.

WILLIAMS, S. WELLS, "The Middle Kingdom," two vols. New York, 1883.

WILLIS, BAILEY WITH ELIOT BLACKWELDER AND R. H. SARGENT, "Researches in China." Washington, 1907–13.

WILSON, ERNEST H., "A Naturalist in Western China." London, 1913.

WILLOUGHBY, W. W., "Foreign Rights and Interests in China." Baltimore, 1920.

—— "China at the Conference" (Washington Conference). Baltimore, 1922.

WOODBRIDGE, SAMUEL I., "China's Only Hope" (translation of Chang Chih-tung's 'Learn'). Chicago, 1900.

WOODHEAD, H. G. W., "The China Year Book." Tientsin. Annual issue.

YETTS, W. PERCEVAL, "Symbolism in Chinese Art." Leyden, 1912.

YOUNGHUSBAND, SIR F., "India and Tibet." London, 1910.

YULE, HENRY, "Cathay and the Way Thither." New Edition by Cordier, London, 1916.

—— "The Book of Ser Marco Polo." See Cordier.

ZABEL, RUDOLF, "Deutschland in China." 1902.

RECENT PUBLICATIONS

ARNOLD, JULEAN H., "Some Bigger Issues in China's Problems," Shanghai, 1928.

BEAL, SAMUEL, "Fo So Hsing Tsan King, a Life of Buddha, Sacred Books of the East," Volume XIX, Oxford, 1883.

BONNARD, ABEL, "In China 1920–21," London, 1926.

BRUCE, J. P., "Philosophy of Human Nature," by Chu Hsi. Translation, London, 1922.

—— "Chu Hsi and His Masters," London, 1923.

CANTLIE AND JONES, "Sun Yat-sen and the Awakening of China," Chicago, 1912.

CLYDE, PAUL HIBBERT, "International Rivalries in Manchuria," 1689–1922, Ohio State University, Columbus, 1928.

DAVIDS, T. W. RHYS, "Buddhist Suttas. Sacred Books of the East," Volume XI, Oxford, 1881.

DER LING, PRINCESS, "The Old Buddha," New York, 1928.

DENNIS, ALFRED L. P., "Adventures in American Diplomacy," New York, 1928.

DE ROSNY, LEON, "Chan-hai-king," Paris, 1891.

DINGLE, E. J., " China's Revolution," London, 1912.

FENOLLOSA, ERNEST, "Epochs of Chinese and Japanese Art," London, 1912.

GAMBLE, SYDNEY D. AND BURGESS, JNO. S., "Peking, a Social Survey," New York, 1921.

GILBERT, RODNEY Y., "What's Wrong with China?" London, 1926.

GILES, LIONEL, "Confucius," London, 1920.

——, "Musings of a Chinese Mystic," London, 1920.

GOODNOW, FRANK J., "China, an Analysis," Baltimore, 1926.

GOWEN, H. H. AND HALL, JOSEF, "Outline History of China," New Edition, Boston, 1926.

HAIL, WILLIAM JAMES, "Tseng Kuo-fan and the T'aip'ing Rebellion," Yale University, New Haven, 1927.

HARRIS, NORMAN DWIGHT, "Europe and the East," Boston and New York, 1926.

HARRISON, MARGARET, "Asia Reborn," New York, 1928.

HEDLEY, JOHN, " Tramps in Dark Mongolia," London, 1910.

HENKE, FREDERICK G., "The Philosophy of Wang Yang-ming," Translation, London and Chicago, 1916.

HIRTH, FREDERIC, "Scraps from a Collector's Note Book," New York, 1905.

HUNTINGTON, ELLSWORTH, "The Character of Races," New York and London, 1924.

692 *Bibliography*

Hsu Shu-hsi, "China and her Political Entity," New York, 1926.
Kansas, Sidney, "U. S. Immigration, Exclusion and Deportation," Washington, 1927.
Kihachi Imai and Motosaburo Matsutani, "Ideals of the Shinran Followers," Tokyo, 1918.
King-Hall, Stephen, "Western Civilization and the Far East," New York, 1924.
MacNair, Harley F., "Modern Chinese History," Selected Readings, Shanghai, 1923.
—— "China's New Nationalism," Shanghai, 1925.
Monroe, Paul. "China, A Nation in Evolution," Chautauqua, 1928.
Müller, Max, "The Dhammapada, Sacred Books of the East," Volume X, Oxford, 1881.
Mah, Ngui-wing, "Foreign Jurisdiction in China," New York, 1924.
Norton, Henry Kittredge, "China and the Powers," New York, 1927.
Paleologue, M., "L'Art Chinois, Paris, 1887.
Petrucci, Raphael, "Chinese Painters," New York, 1920.
Pick, Eugene, "China in the Grip of the Reds," Shanghai, 1927.
Rantoul, Robt. S., "Frederick Townsend Ward," Salem, Mass., 1908, and Addenda, 1908.
Rin-Chen Lha-Mo, "We Tibetans," London, 1926.
Rockhill, W. W., "The 1910 Census of the Population of China," New York, 1912.
Saunders, Kenneth, "Gotama Buddha," New York, 1920.
—— "Epochs in Buddhist History," Chicago, 1924.
Segalen, Victor, "Mission Archéologique en Chine," Paris, 1923–24.
Sforza, Comte Carlo, "*L'Enigme Chinoise*," Paris, 1928.
T'ang Leang-li, "China in Revolt," London, 1927.
Teichman, Eric, "Travels in North-West China," Cambridge University Press, 1921.
—— "Travels in Eastern Tibet," Cambridge University Press, 1922.
Treat, Payson J., "The Far East," New York, 1928.
U. S. Government, "Report of the Commission on Extraterritoriality," Washington, 1926.
Vinacke, Harold M., "A History of the Far East in Modern Times," New York, 1928.
Waley, Arthur, "An Introduction to the Study of Chinese Art," London, 1923.

WARNER, LANGDON, "Japanese Sculpture of the Suiko Period,"
  Yale University Press, 1923.
WEALE, PUTNAM, "Why China Sees Red," New York, 1925.
WERNER, E. T. C., "Myths and Legends of China," London, 1922.
WILLIAMS, E. T., "A Short History of China," New York, 1928.
WILLOUGHBY, W. W., "Foreign Rights and Interests in China,"
  New Edition, Baltimore, 1927.
YETTS, PERCIVAL AND OTHERS, "Chinese Art," London, 1925.
ZÜCHER, "The Chinese Theatre," Boston, 1925.

PERIODICAL PUBLICATIONS

China Weekly Review,	Shanghai.
Chinese Affairs,	Nanking.
Chinese Recorder,	Shanghai.
Current History,	New York.
North China Herald,	Shanghai.
Maritime Customs Reports,	Shanghai.
The China Year Book,	Tientsin and London.
The Japan Year Book,	Tokyo.
The N. Y. Times,	New York.
The Educational Review,	Shanghai.
The Chinese Social and Political Science Review,	Peip'ing.
China Monthly Trade Report,	U. S. Department of Commerce.

ADDITIONAL BIBLIOGRAPHY

ABEND, HALLETT, "Tortured China." New York, 1930.

ARNOLD, JULEAN, "China through the American Window." Shanghai, 1932.

CHAPMAN, H. OWEN, "The Chinese Revolution, 1926-27." London, 1928.

GODSHALL, WILSON LEON, "Tsingtau under Three Flags." Shanghai, 1929.

HOLCOMBE, ARTHUR N., "The Chinese Revolution." Cambridge, Mass., 1930.

ICHIHASHI, YAMATO, "The Washington Conference and After." Stanford Univ., 1928.

KING, PAUL, "Weighed in China's Balance." London, 1928.

KINNEY, HENRY W., "Manchuria To-day." Dairen, 1930.

LATOURETTE, K. S., "A History of Christian Missions in China." New York, 1929.

LATTIMORE, OWEN, "Manchuria, a Cradle of Conflict." New York, 1932.

MAY, HERBERT L., "A Survey of Smoking Conditions in the Far East." New York, 1927.

MASPERO, HENRI, "La Chine Antique." Paris, 1927.

MORSE, H. B. and MACNAIR, HARLEY F., "International Relations of the Far East." New York, 1931.

STEIGER, GEORGE NYE, "China and the Occident." New Haven, 1927.

SION, JULES, "Asie des Moussons." Paris, 1928.

TYAU, M. T. Z., "Two Years of Nationalist China." Shanghai, 1930.

YOUNG, C. WALTER, "Japan's Special Position in Manchuria." London, 1931.

WU CHAO-CHÜ, "The Nationalist Programme for China." Shanghai, 1929.

SOME REVIEW ARTICLES, PAMPHLETS AND REPRINTS

BUCH, JOHN LOSSING, "Agriculture and the Future of China," in *Annals of American Academy of Political and Social Science,* Nov. 1930.

BURGESS, J. S., "Guilds," in same number.

GAMBLE, SIDNEY D., "A Family Budget in Peip'ing," in same number.

WILLIAMS, E. T., "Japan's Interest in Manchuria," *Univ. of Calif. Chronicle,* January 1932.

APPENDIX

CHINA: Area, 4,431,702 square miles. Population, 473,658,451
Capital, Nanking;† population, 561,443

Provinces	Area in Sq. Mi.	Population	Capital
Heilungkiang	....	....	Tsitsihar
			(Lungkiang)
Kirin	448,957	32,000,000	Kirin (Yungchi)
Liaoning			Mukden
(Shengking)	....	....	(Shenyang)
Jehol*	....	....	Chengte
Chihli (Hopei)	115,830	29,252,000	Tientsin
Shansi	81,853	10,000,000	Taiyuan (Yangchu)
Shensi	75,290	8,800,000	Hsian (Changan)
Kansu	125,483	5,000,000	Lanchow (Kaolan)
Sinkiang			
(Turkestan)	550,000	2,491,000	Tihua
Shantung	55,984	38,000,000	Tsinan (Licheng)
Honan	67,954	25,600,000	Kaifeng
Kiangsu	38,610	35,873,246	Tantu
Anhui	54,826	21,715,396	Anking (Huaining)
Hupei	71,428	27,105,969	Wuchang
Kiangsi	69,428	24,467,000	Nanchang
Hunan	83,398	31,591,211	Changsha
Szechuen	218,533	76,613,000	Chengtu
Chekiang	36,680	20,632,701	Hangchow
			(Hang Hsien)
Fukien	46,332	12,157,741	Foochow (Minhou)
Kuangtung	100,000	30,000,000	Canton (Puyun)
Kuangsi	77,220	12,258,580	Nanning (Yungning)
Kueichou	67,182	9,000,000	Kueiyang
Yunnan	146,714	11,020,607	Yunnan (Kunming)
Chahar*	....	1,900,000	Kalgan (Wanchuan)
Suiyüan*	....	645,000	Suiyüancheng
			(Kueisui)
Ninghsia*	....	435,000	Ninghsia
Mongolia	1,200,000	600,000	Urga
Tibet	....	....	Lhasa
Chinghai			
(Kokonor)	700,000	6,500,000	Hsining
Hsikang*	....	....	Kangting
Totals	4,431,702	473,658,451	

†Since Japan's attack upon Shanghai, Loyang in Honan Province has become a temporary capital.

* The new provinces, Jehol, Chahar, Suiyüan and Ninghsia are all carved out of Mongolia and the areas of these provinces are included in the 1,200,000 square miles of Mongolia; Chinghai and Hsikang are carved out of Tibet and their areas and populations are included in the figures given for Tibet.

PRINCIPAL OPEN CITIES AND TOWNS

Name	Location	Population	Total Trade 1930, Hk. Taels[1]
Aigun	Heilungkiang	38,112	37,176
Sansing [2]	Kirin	1,400	6,445
Manchouli, (Lui Hsien).	Heilungkiang	11,300	
Harbin	Kirin	262,969	4,079,794
Suifenho	Kirin	4,300	
Hunchun	Kirin	39,000	
Lungchingtsun .	Kirin	3,638	142,650
Antung	Liaoning (Shengking)	92,469	4,134,059
Tatungkou	Liaoning (Shengking)	4,900	55,007
Dairen	Kuantung, Leased Ter.	205,761	12,334,348
Newchwang (Yingkou) ..	Liaoning	106,086	3,406,599
Chinwangtao ..	Hopei (Chihli)	20,020	1,001,908
Tientsin	Hopei (Chihli)	1,388,747	13,225,647
Weihaiwei	Shantung	44,643	175,019
Lungkou	Shantung	11,524	739,274
Chefoo	Shantung	130,575	
Tsingtao	Shantung	367,410	9,181,070
Chungking	Szechuen	635,000	1,241,932
Wanhsien	Szechuen	207,837	283,974
Changsha	Hunan	606,972	747,183
Yochow	Hunan	4,200	594,147
Ichang	Hupei	107,980	241,517
Shasi	Hupei	95,843	369,731
Hankow	Hupei	777,993	7,496,548
Kiukiang	Kiangsi	80,217	1,121,363
Wuhu	Anhui	130,706	1,118,726
Nanking	Kiangsu	561,443	694,541
Chinkiang	Kiangsu	172,000	1,711,443
Shanghai	Kiangan	3,124,212	86,643,483
Soochow	Kiangsu	260,000	230,003
Hangchow (Hang Hsien).	Chekiang	506,930	333,748
Ningpo	Chekiang	212,518	799,831
Wenchow	Chekiang	678,376	209,752
Santuao	Fukien	9,000	146,832
Foochow	Fukien	314,345	1,527,065
Amoy	Fukien	164,984	3,456,993

[1] The figures are from the Maritime Customs Report of China, a tael being equal to U. S. $0.46.

[2] The ports are listed in the order given in the Customs Reports, beginning with those in northern Manchuria.

PRINCIPAL OPEN CITIES AND TOWNS—*Continued*

Name	Location	Population	Total Trade 1930, Hk. Taels
Swatow	Kuangtung	161,087	4,917,865
Canton	Kuangtung	812,241	9,743,560
Kongmoon	Kuangtung	81,874	1,194,822
Samshui	Kuangtung	8,840	427,495
Kiungchow	Kuangtung (Hainan)	45,751	557,761
Pakhoi	Kuangtung	35,000	14,566
Wuchow	Kuangsi	83,494	1,249,601
Nanning	Kuangsi	73,412	30,974
Lungchow	Kuangsi	13,000	7,651
Mengtze	Yünnan	38,562	1,663,957
Szemao	Yünnan	13,736	7,517
Tengyueh	Yünnan	19,000	212,646
Kowloon	Kuangtung		935,370
*Kowloon Railway Stations	Kuangtung		361,577

* Kowloon, opposite Hongkong is leased to Great Britain, but the railway to Canton maintains its own Customs station.

RAILWAYS [1]

All lines standard gage (4 ft. 8½ in.) and Government-owned unless otherwise stated.

Name	Mileage

1. Peking-Mukden (Ching-Feng) 526
   Branches:
   1. Peking-Tungchow (Tunghsien) 14
   2. Fengtai-Lukouchiao 4
   3. Tangho-Chinwangtao 6
   4. Lienshan-Hulutao Harbor 7
   5. Koupangtze-Yingkow (Newchwang) 57
   6. Chinhsien (Chinchou)—Peipiano 36
2. Peking-Hankow Railway 755
   Branches:
   1. Liangsiang-Tuli ...... ⎫   ⎧ 12
   2. Liuliho-Choukueichuang ⎬ to local coal mines... ⎨ 10
   3. Kaoyihsien-Lincheng... ⎭   ⎩ 10
   4. Kaopeitien-Siling (Imperial Tombs) 26
3. Tientsin-Pukow Railway 627
   Northern Section, German-built, 392 miles to Hanchuang.
   Southern Section, British-built, 237 miles Hanchuang to Pukow.

[1] Information regarding railways from China Year Book and Arnold's Commercial Handbook.

Name	Mileage
Branches of Northern Section:	
1. Chentangchwang–Liangwangchwang	16
2. Lincheng–Tsaochwang	19
3. Yenchowfu–Tsiningchow	19½
4. Lokou–Huangtaichiao	5½
5. Tuliu–Pauto–Techow–Grand Canal	2½
4. Peking–Suiyuan–Paotochen Railway	507
Branch: Peking–Mentaokao	16½
5. Shanghai–Nanking Railway	193
Branch: Shanghai–Woosung	10
6. Shanghai–Hangchow–Ningpo Railway	171
Shanghai–Hangchow, 118 miles	
Hangchow–Ningpo, 53 miles	
Branch: Junction with Shanghai–Nanking	8
7. Cheng–Tai Railway	151
From Shihchiaochuang on Peking-Hankow line to Taiyuanfu in Shansi (Metre-gage)	
8. Taokow–Chinghua Railway (Government)	93
From coal mines at Chinghuachen in Shansi to Taokow where water connection is made with Tientsin, crosses Peking–Hankow line at Sinsiang.	
Branch: Yiuchiafen–Taoching	1
9. Lung–Hai Railway (includes old Pien-Lo line, Kaifengfu to Honanfu, 115 miles). Total to Sanchow	1270
Planned to extend from Haichow on the sea-coast via Hsüchow in Kiangsu, Kaifeng in Honan and Hsian in Shensi to Lanchow in Kansu (about 533 miles completed between Hsüchow and Tungkuan), crosses Peking–Hankow line at Chengchow, Honan.	
10. Kirin–Changchun Railway	80
Operated as a branch of the South Manchuria Railway.	
11. Chuchow–Pinghsiang	65
From Chuchow, Hunan on Kankow–Canton line to coal mines at Pingshiang, Kiangsi.	
12. Canton–Kowloon	111
The southern section, 22 miles, from Shum Chun to Kowloon is British.	
13. Changchow–Amoy	18
14. Ssupingkai–Taonan	265
Completed as far as Taonan, operated as branch of S. Manchuria, from Ssupingkai.	
14A. Taonan–Angangki	141.7

Name	Mileage
23. Sunning Railway (Private)	63½
From Samkaphoi via Sunning to Kongmoon.	
24. Swatow-Chaochowfu (Private)	26½
25. Tayeh Mines Railway (Private)	17
Narrow gage from Huangchou on the Yangtze to the Tayeh iron mines.	
26. Tai-Tsao Railway (Private)	27
From Yihsien coal mines to Taierhchuang on Grand Canal.	
27. Hulun-Hailun .... (est.)	100
28. Tahushan-Tungliao-Taonan .... (est.)	330
29. Shenyang (Mukden)-Hailungchen Kirin ..... (est.)	260
30. Kirin-Tunhua .... (est.)	100

TELEGRAPHS

Lines of wire	104,484 miles
Offices	1,155
Wireless offices	64

TELEPHONES

Government-owned	54,783
Company-owned	12,958
Total	67,741

HIGHWAYS

Motor Roads	20,973 miles
Under Construction	5,005 "
Other possible for motor traffic	13,837 "
Motor Vehicles	27,985

AVIATION

Number of Companies	2
Number of Planes	100
Routes	2,500 miles

STEAMSHIP COMPANIES

Over Seas Mail Lines

Name	Ports	Flag
1. Nippon Yusen Kaisha	Seattle, Los Angeles, and San Francisco to Japan, Shanghai, Hongkong and Philippines. Japan to China and Europe; Japan to China and Australia; Japan to China, India and Africa; Japan to China and South America.	Japanese
2. Hamburg-American	Hamburg to Far East	German
3. Canadian Pacific	Vancouver to Japan, Shanghai and Hongkong. .	British
4. Peninsular Oriental	London to Hongkong, Shanghai, and Japan......	British
5. Messageries Maritimes	Marseilles to Hongkong, Shanghai and Japan..	French
6. Osaka Shosen Kaisha	Kobe to Tientsin, Shanghai to Europe and America via Suez; and Japan to Pacific Coast of U. S.	Japanese
7. Norddeutscher Lloyd	Bremen to Far East	German
8. The Robert Dollar Co.	San Francisco and Seattle to Japan and China and around the world.	American and British

STEAMSHIP COMPANIES—*Continued*

Name	Ports	Flag
9. Oregon-Oriental	Portland to Far East	American
10. Mitsu Bussan Kaisha	San Francisco to Japan and China	Japanese
11. Ben Line	Great Britain to China	British
12. British India S. N. Co.	India and China	British
13. China Mutual S. N. Co.	China and European Ports	British
14. East Asiatic Co.	China and European Ports	Danish
15. Glen Line	Great Britain and China	British
16. Lloyd Triestino	Mediterranean Ports and China	Italian
17. Holland-Oost Azie Lijn	Europe and China	Netherlands
18. Canadian Government Merchant Marine	Victoria, B. C. and Far East	Canadian
19. China Import and Export Lumber Co.	Pacific Coast Ports of U. S. to China	American
20. Dairen Kisen Kaisha	Japan and China	Japanese
21. Java-China-Japan Lijn	Amsterdam to East Indies and China	Dutch
22. Nisshin Kisen Kaisha	Japan and China	Japanese
23. Ocean Steamship Co.	Seattle to Far East	American
24. Oceanic and Oriental SS. Co.	San Francisco to Far East	American
25. Oregon Oriental Line	Portland, Oregon, to Far East	American
26. Pacific Steam Navigation Co.	Seattle to Far East	American
27. Rickmers Linie	Hamburg to Far East	German
28. Standard Oil Co.	New York to Far East	American

NOTE.—This list is not complete, but it is believed that the companies having most frequent sailings are included.

Companies Operating Mainly or Exclusively in the Far East

Name	Flag	Name	Flag	Name	Flag
Asiatic Petroleum Co.	British	Dairen Kisen Kaisha	Japanese	Mitsui Bussan Kaisha	Japanese
China Government SS. Administration	Chinese	Douglas SS. Co.	British	Ningshao S. N. Co.	Chinese
China Merchants S. N. Co.	Chinese	Harada SS. Co.	Japanese	Nisshin Kisen Kaisha	Japanese
China Navigation Co.	British	Hongkong, Canton & Macao Steamboat Co.	British	Philippines SS. Co.	American
China Siam S. Nav. Co.	Chinese	Hoong On SS. Co.	British	San Peh S. N. Co.	Chinese
China Engineering & Mining Co.	British	Indo-China S. N. Co.	British	South Manchuria Railway Co.	Japanese
Compagnie Asiatique de Navigation	French	Java-China-Japan Line	Dutch	Straits SS. Co.	British
		Kawasaki Kisen Kaisha	Japanese	Taito S. N. Co.	Japanese
		Kwong Line	Chinese	Tien Hsin SS. Co.	Chinese
		Messageries Cantonaises	French		

NOTE.—For this list the author is indebted to the China Year Book.

DISTANCES ALONG THE COAST (Nautical Miles)

	Shanghai	Woosung	Gutzlaff	Foochow	Amoy	Swatow	Hongkong
Woosung	14						
Gutzlaff	66	52					
Foochow	420	406	354				
Amoy	620	606	554	200			
Swatow (from Shanghai direct 673)	755	741	689	335	135		
Hongkong (from Shanghai direct 826)	908	894	842	488	288	153	
Canton (from Shanghai direct 909)	991	977	925	571	371	236	83

	Shanghai	Tsingtao	Weihaiwei	Chefoo	Taku	Tientsin
Tsingtao	390					
Weihaiwei	492 (direct)	270				
Chefoo (from Shanghai direct 511)	532	310	40			
Taku	725	503	233	193		
Tientsin (from Shanghai direct 740)	776	554	284	241	51	
Peking (by rail via Nanking from Shanghai, 909, via Hankow by Yangtze River and rail 1350)	862	640	370	327	137	86

	Miles
Shanghai to Dairen	567
" to Newchwang	701

	Miles
Shanghai to Vladivostok	995
" to Nagasaki	412

	Miles
Shanghai to Kobe	755
" to Yokohama	1101

DISTANCES ON THE YANGTZE RIVER

Shanghai to	Shanghai	Kiangyin	Chinkiang	Nanking	Wuhu	Tatung	Anking	Kiukiang	Hankow	Shasi	Ichang
Kiangyin	95										
Chinkiang	156	61									
Nanking	201	106	45								
Wuhu	256	161	100	55							
Tatung	318	223	162	117	62						
Anking	364	269	208	163	108	46					
Kiukiang	453	358	297	252	197	135	89				
Hankow	595	500	439	394	339	277	231	142			
Shasi	882	787	726	681	626	564	518	429	287		
Ichang	965	870	809	764	709	647	601	512	370	83	
Chungking	1427	1332	1271	1226	1171	1109	1063	974	832	545	462

NOTE.—For the above tables the author is indebted to the China Yearbook.

DISTANCE BY RAILWAY

Peking to Tientsin.............	86 Miles
" to Tsinanfu..............	306
" via Tsinanfu to Tsingtao........	562
" via Tientsin to Nanking........	716
" via Nanking to Shanghai........	909

Peking to Great Wall at Nankou......	30 Miles
" to Kalgan............	104
" to Hankow..........	755
" to Mukden...........	525

AMERICAN CONSULATES IN CHINA

Shanghai in Kiangsu Province
Nanking in Kiangsu Province
Hankow in Hupei Province
Chungking in Szechuen Province
Changsha in Hunan Province
Tsingtao in Shantung Province
Tsinan in Shantung Province

Chefoo in Shantung Province
Tientsin in Chihli Province
Kalgan Chihli
Harbin in Kirin Province
Mukden in Shengking Province
Antung in Shengking Province
Foochow in Fukien Province

Amoy in Fukien Province
Swatow in Kuangtung Province
Canton in Kuangtung Province
Yünnanfu in Yünnan Province
Peking in Chihli (vice consul attached to the Legation)[1]

IN ADJACENT TERRITORIES

Hongkong (British Colony), Saigon (Indochina), Dairen (Japanese Leased Territory)

[1] Peking is not an open city, but by tolerance of China many foreigners are permitted to do business there.

Foreign Population of China
(From the Customs Returns for 1930)

Nationality	Firms	Persons
American	566	6,875
Austrian	17	244
Belgian	24	527
British	1,027	13,015
Czecho-Slovak	29	560
Danish	39	638
Dutch	33	652
Finnish	3	287
French	186	8,575
German	207	3,006
Italian	51	713
Japanese	4,633	255,686
Mexican	.....	4
Norwegian	20	280
Polish [1]	36	1,526
Portuguese	150	2,330
Russian	1,073	65,361
Spanish	24	327
Swedish	10	192
Swiss	46	354
Others	15	783
Total	8,189	361,940

Foreign Mission Statistics

(Condensed from China Year Book, 1931)

I. *Protestant*

Foreign Missionaries	6,346	Hospitals	323
Colleges and Middle		Communicants	
Schools	11,024	(1922)	402,539

Chinese Force

Ordained Chinese..	1,965	Teachers	10,848
Evangelists	11,256	Total Chinese employed	24,732

II. *Roman Catholic*

Bishops	76	Lay Brothers, European	314
European Priests..	1,975	Lay Brothers, Chinese	466
Native Priests	1,369	Nuns, European...	1,327
Christians	2,486,841	Nuns, Chinese	2,641

III. *Y. M. C. A.*

Stations 40

Members 41,570

BANKING IN CHINA

I. *European and American Banks*

Name	Head Office	Number of Branches
American Express Company..	Shanghai	4 (Agencies)
American Oriental Banking Corporation	Shanghai	2 (Affiliations)
Banque Belge pour l'Etranger	Brussels	3
Banque de l'Indo Chine......	Paris	7
Chartered Bank of India, Australia and China	London	6
Deutsch-Asiatische Bank	Berlin	5
Equitable Eastern Banking Corporation	New York	1
Far Eastern Bank of Harbin	Harbin	6
Far Eastern Jewish Bank of Commerce	Harbin	
Far Eastern Mutual Credit Corporation	Harbin	
Hongkong and Shanghai Banking Corporation	Hongkong	9
Italian Bank for China......	Shanghai	1
Jewish People's Bank	Harbin	
Mercantile Bank of India, Ltd.	London	2
National City Bank	New York	8
Nederlandsche Handel Maatschappij	Amsterdam ...	2
Nederlandsch-Indische Handelsbank	Amsterdam ...	4
P. and O. Banking Corporation	London	3
Philippine National Bank....	Manila	1
Raven Trust Co.	Shanghai	

II. *Japanese Banks*

Name	Head Office	Number of Branches
Antung Jitsugo	Antung	19
Bank of Chosen	Seoul	18
Bank of Taiwan	Taipeh, Formosa	8
Bank of Tsinan	Licheng	1
China and Southern.........	Taipeh	1
Changchun Industrial Bank..	Hsinching	
Cheng Hsin	Newchwang ...	
Dairen Commercial Bank.....	Dairen	
Fankiatun Bank ....:.......	Fankiatun	
Great Eastern Bank.........	Peip'ing	3
Harbin Bank	Harbin	
Hsi Chen	Antung	
Industrial and Commercial Bank	Liaoyang	
Japan China Bank	Tiehling	
Japanese Bank of Manchuria.	Dairen	13
Kaiyuan Bank	Kaiyuan	
Kirin Bank	Yungchi	
Kyoiko Bank	Dairen	
Manchuria Investment Bank..	Shenyang	
Mitsubishi Bank, Ltd.	Tokyo	1
Mitsui Bank, Ltd.	Tokyo	1
Mukden, Shokusan	Shenyang	
Ni-Itaka Bank, Ltd.	Taihoku	2
Peace Bank	Yungchi	1
Ryojun	Port Arthur ..	
Seiryu Ginko	Dairen	14
South Manchuria Bank......	Anshan	
Sumitomo Bank, Ltd.	Osaka	2
Szepingkai Bank	Szepingkai ...	
Ta Chang	Liaoyang	
Tientsin Bank	Tientsin	1
Yokohama Specie Bank, Ltd..	Yokohoma	13

III. *Chinese Banks*

Name	Head Office
(a) Government Banks:	
Central Bank	Shanghai
Bank of China	Peip'ing
Bank of Communications	"
(b)[1] Private Banks:	
Chung Hua Savings	Peip'ing
Commercial Guarantee Bank of Chihli	"
Industrial Development Bank of China	"
The National Industrial Bank of China	Tientsin
Chung Fu Union Bank	"
The Continental Bank	"
Fengtien Industrial	Shenyang
Harbin Commercial Bank	Harbin
National Commercial Bank	Shanghai
Shanghai Commercial & Savings Bank	"
Ningpo Commercial Bank	"
Yung Hung Banking Cor	"
Chung Hwa Commercial & Savings Bank	"
Commercial Bank of China	"
Kiangsu Bank	"
Tung Lai Bank	Tsingtao
Young Brothers Banking Cor	Chungking
Shantung Commercial Bank	Licheng
Industrial & Commercial Bank	"
The Hunan Provincial Bank	Changsha
Wei Fung Commercial Bank	Hankow
Chung Yuen Industrial Bank	"
Chekiang Industrial Bank	Hanghsien
Taoyih Banking Cor	"
Chekiang Chu Feng Bank	"
Amoy Commercial Bank	Amoy
Fu Tien Bank	Kunming

[1] This list is far from complete, but it is believed that all important banks are included.

THE PRESS IN CHINA

NOTE.—The number of periodical publications in China is very great. There are over eight hundred listed, of which all but a very few are daily newspapers in the vernacular. The following list is believed to include those in which the readers of this volume are likely to be interested.

PEIP'ING:

The Peking Leader (English Daily) (Chinese-owned).
Le Journal de Pekin (French Daily).
Shun Tien Shih Pao (Chinese Daily) (Japanese-owned) and 68 other dailies in Chinese in Peking.
The Chinese Social and Political Science Review (English Monthly) (Chinese-owned).
Tsing Hua Journal (English Monthly), and 36 other periodicals; weeklies, fortnightlies and monthlies.

TIENTSIN:

The Peking and Tientsin Times (English Daily).
The North China Star (English Daily) (American-owned).
North China Daily Mail (Evening, English Daily).
The China Advertiser (English Daily) (owned by Japanese).
Tientsin Jih Pao (Chinese Daily).
China Illustrated Review (English Weekly).
And ten other daily papers and eighteen weeklies and monthlies in Chinese.

DAIREN:

The Manchurian Daily News (English Daily) (Japanese-owned).
The Light of Manchuria (English Monthly) (Japanese-owned).

HARBIN:

Harbin Observer (English Daily).
Novosti Jisny (Russian Daily).
Tung Ya Jih Pao (Chinese Daily).
And seven other Chinese dailies and one other Russian daily.

SHANGHAI:

North China Daily News (English Daily).
North China Sunday News (English Weekly).
North China Herald (Weekly).
Shanghai Evening Post and Mercury (American Daily).
China Press (English Daily) (American Management).
Journal de Shanghai (French Daily).
The China Weekly Review (American-owned Weekly).
Capital & Trade (American-owned Weekly).
China Digest (American-owned Weekly).

The China Critic (Chinese-owned Weekly).
The Chinese Nation (Chinese-owned Weekly).
Shanghai Times (English Daily).
The Sunday Times (English Weekly).
Far Eastern Review (English Monthly) (American-owned).
China Weekly Review (English Weekly) (American-owned).
Chinese Recorder (English Monthly) (American-owned).
China Far East Finance and Commerce (English Weekly).
British Chamber of Commerce Journal (English Monthly).
Sin Wen Pao (Chinese Daily).
Shanghai Journal of Commerce (Chinese Daily).
Shun Pao (Chinese Daily).
Shih Pao ("Eastern Times")—(Chinese Daily).
The Universal Gazette (Chinese Daily).
And seven other Chinese dailies.
The Bankers' Weekly (Chinese Weekly).
The Eastern Magazine (Chinese Monthly).
China Journal of Science and Arts (Monthly).
And fifty-five other publications of varying periodicity.

HANKOW:
Central China Post (English Daily).
Hankow Chung Hsi Pao (Chinese Daily).
Hankow Sin Wen Pao (Chinese Daily).
Hankow Herald (Daily, American).
And eleven other Chinese dailies, and five Chinese weeklies.

CANTON:
The Canton Gazette (Chinese-owned Daily).
The Canton Times (English Daily).
Seventy-two Guilds Press (Chinese Daily).
And thirty-nine other Chinese dailies, and fifty-two other
Chinese publications of varying periodicity.

HONGKONG:
Hongkong Daily Press (English Daily).
South China Morning Post (English Daily).
Hongkong Telegraph (English Daily—Evening).
China Mail (English Daily—Evening).

NANKING:
Chinese Affairs (Weekly).

TSINGTAO:
Tsingtao Times (Daily, British).

EXCHANGE FLUCTUATIONS

NOTE.—The money of China consists of: (1) brass cash, each worth about one-twentieth of a cent, U. S. currency; (2) of copper coins, each worth about a half-cent, and (3) of a silver dollar and its fractions, the dollar being of the weight and fineness of a Mexican dollar and equivalent to about U. S. $0.55 in exchange transactions. There is also a great deal of silver bullion used, whose value is estimated in taels. The tael is not coined, and it varies in weight and fineness in different parts of the country. The customs tael, used in levying and collecting duties on imports and exports is theoretically of a fineness of 1000 and a weight of 583.3 grains. There is no such silver in current use, so that it follows that in paying duties the sum due must be converted into the local currency. Generally speaking this is a double process; the customs taels are changed into local taels and these into local dollars, the commonly used currency. Since the Chinese currency is not based upon a gold standard, its value in the currencies of the western world changes from day to day, sometimes with very disastrous results to trade. The following table records the value of the customs tael in the monies of Europe, America and Japan and its relation to the Chinese dollar during the years, 1912–1927. The table is taken from the Maritime Customs Report.

Year	U. S. Money $	British s. d.	French Frc.	German Mks.	Indian Rup.	Japanese Yen	Russian Roub.	Hong-kong $
1912	0.74	$3\ 0\frac{5}{8}$	3.85	3.12	2.27	1.49	1.45	1.52
1913	0.73	$3\ 0\frac{1}{4}$	3.81	3.08	2.25	1.47	1.44	1.51
1914	0.67	$2\ 8\frac{3}{4}$	3.45	2.79	2.04	1.34	1.36	1.47
1915	0.62	$2\ 7\frac{7}{8}$	3.39	2.67[1]	1.95	1.25	1.63[1]	1.41
1916	0.79	$3\ 3\frac{13}{16}$	4.63	3.68	2.46	1.54	2.52[1]	1.54
1917	1.03	$4\ 3\frac{13}{16}$	5.94	4.78[1]	3.11	1.98	5.08[1]	1.63
1918	1.26	$5\ 3\frac{7}{16}$	7.11	....	3.55	2.37	....	1.61
1919	1.39	$6\ 4$	10.12	....	3.54	2.72	....	1.68
1920	1.24	$6\ 9\frac{1}{2}$	17.79	....	3.34	2.38	....	1.58
1921	0.76	$3\ 11\frac{7}{16}$	10.29	....	2.92	1.57	....	1.50
1922	0.85	$3\ 9$	10.23	....	2.87	1.72	....	1.49
1923	0.80	$3\ 5\frac{3}{4}$	13.16	....	2.55	1.63	....	1.51
1924	0.81	$3\ 7\frac{15}{16}$	15.60	....	2.53	1.95	....	1.53
1925	0.84	$3\ 5$	17.92	....	2.31	2.04	....	1.48
1926	0.76	$3\ 1$	23.85	....	2.08	1.58	....	1.42
1927	0.69	$2\ 9$	17.46	2.89	1.88	1.44	....	1.40
1928	0.71	$2\ 11\frac{1}{8}$	18.13	2.98	1.95	1.53	....	1.42
1929	0.64	$2\ 7\frac{13}{16}$	16.43	2.70	1.77	1.38	....	1.38
1930	0.46	$1\ 10\frac{11}{16}$	11.71	1.93	1.27	0.92	....	1.36

[1] Shanghai customs' rate.

The Shanghai tael contains 565.65 grains of silver and is reckoned as 944 fine 111.40 Shanghai taels are equivalent to 100 Haikuan or customs taels.

The Kuping Tael is the treasury tael at Peking, 575.8 grains of silver 1000 fine. Of this money of account it takes 101.642 taels to equal 100 Haikuan taels, and 100 Kuping taels are equivalent to 109.60 Shanghai taels.

The Tientsin tael weighs 557.4 grains and is 992 fine. 105.215 Tientsin taels equal 100 Haikuan taels.

The Hankow tael weighs 554.7 grains and is 967 fine.

CURRENCY TABLE

10 Hsien = 1 Wei
10 Wei = 1 Hu
10 Hu = 1 Ssu
10 Ssu = 1 Hao
10 Hao = 1 Li (Cash)
10 Li = 1 Fen (Candareen)
10 Fen = 1 Ch'ien (Mace)
10 Ch'ien = 1 Liang (Tael)

TABLE OF CHINESE WEIGHTS

1 Tael or *Liang* = 583.3 grains (1⅓ oz. Avoirdupois) 37.783 grammes.

16 Taels = one Catty (1⅓ lbs. Avoirdupois), Chinese name *Chin*.

100 Catties = one Picul or *Tan* (133⅓ lbs. Avoirdupois) 60.453 Kilos.

NOTE.—These equivalents are fixed by treaty with foreign powers and are legal in all dealings affecting foreign trade, but they are not generally accepted throughout the country. There are many *liang, chin,* and *tan;* even in the same city different trades have different standards. The Manchu Government before its downfall adopted a system of weights and measures which it endeavored to make uniform throughout the empire, but local custom was too powerful. The Republic has not been any more successful, but when China shall have recovered from the present strife and division, it is probable that the standards will be gradually adopted by all sections.

MEASURES OF CAPACITY

Measures of capacity vary quite as much as those of weight. The unit is the Shih, which in the measurement of tribute contains 6292 cubic inches. This is divided in Chinese official calculations into a quadrillion parts according to the table, which, like nearly all Chinese tables, is a decimal one. For practical purposes it is necessary only to use the following:

10 Ch'ao = 1 Shao
10 Shao = 1 Ko
10 Ko = 1 Sheng (pint)
10 Sheng = 1 Tou
10 Tou = 1 Shih

The *sheng* approximates an American pint or a French litre· the *tou* is frequently called a peck by foreigners in China.

MEASURES OF LENGTH

By treaty the foot is fixed at 14.1 inches English, or 0.358 metre. In common use it varies according to trade; the carpenter's foot in many places is 12.5 inches English, the tailor's foot nearly 14 inches.

10 Fen = 1 Ts'un (inch)
10 Ts'un = 1 Ch'ih (foot)
10 Ch'ih = 1 Chang
5 Ch'ih = 1 Pu or Kung
1800 Ch'ih or 360 Pu = 1 Li (⅓ of a mile approximately)

MEASURES OF AREA

The common unit for the measurement of land is the *mou*, which varies in different parts of the country, but for rough calculations may be taken as about ⅙ of an acre. The *mou* is divided decimally.

10 Hsien	=	1 Wei
10 Wei	=	1 Hu
10 Hu	=	1 Ssu
10 Ssu	=	1 Hao
10 Hao	=	1 Li
10 Li	=	1 Fen
10 Fen	=	1 Mou
100 Mou	=	1 Ch'ing

25 square ch'ih (feet)	=	1 Square Pu or Kung
240 Square Pu	=	1 Mou

HOLIDAYS COMMONLY OBSERVED *

Since the establishment of the Republic the Western Calendar has been made official, but the people generally throughout the country continue to observe the holidays according to the ancient lunar calendar. According to the latter the year begins with the first day of the new moon after the sun enters the constellation of Aquarius. Thus it may fall as early as January 21 and as late as February 19.

The Chinese are not acquainted with a weekly division of time except as they have come into contact with western people. In Peking, in the open ports and in some of the provincial capitals Sunday is now observed as a holiday in public offices and in the schools, but shops do not close as a rule. Other holidays are as follows:

January 1, Official New Year's.

Old China New Year's Day, variable, shops close 3 to 15 days.

First Moon 15th day, lunar calendar, Feast of Lanterns.

March 21, Vernal Equinox, worship of Confucius.

Third Moon, 1st to 15th, lunar calendar, Ch'ing Ming Festival. (Worship of ancestors at grave.)

Fifth Moon, 5th day, lunar calendar, Dragon Boat Festival. (Accounts to be settled.)

Seventh Moon, 7th day, lunar calendar Festival of the Herd Boy and Weaver Girl.

Seventh Moon, 15th day, lunar calendar, All Souls Feast.

Eighth Moon, 15th day, lunar calendar, Moon's Birthday. (Settlement of Accounts.)

September 21, Autumnal Equinox, Worship of Confucius.

October 10, Anniversary of Revolution, National Holiday.

Ninth Moon, 9th day, lunar calendar, Ascending the Heights.

Winter Solstice, Worship of Ancestors in Temple or Home.

* See also page 721.

Twelfth Moon, 23rd day, lunar calendar, God of Furnace reports to Heaven.

Twelfth Moon, 30th day, lunar calendar, God of Furnace returns, (Settlement of all accounts).

Foreign banks and business houses in the ports of China usually observe their several national holidays.

METEOROLOGICAL

The Roman Catholic Mission (Society of Jesus) at Shanghai for many decades past has kept a careful record of meteorological phenomena. By correspondence with observers in other parts of the Far East the station at Shanghai has been able to make a study of Chinese meteorology and publish valuable forecasts of the weather. Among the stations along the coast of Asia are those at Vladivostok, Newchwang, Shanhaikuan, Tientsin, Taku, Chefoo, Weihaiwei, Tsingtao, Tokyo, Hankow, Chinkiang, Woosung, Shanghai, Gutzlaff, Chenhai (Ningpo), Wenchow, Santuao, Foochow, Taihoku (Formosa), Amoy, Swatow, and at various places in Japan.

MEAN TEMPERATURE AND HUMIDITY AT SHANGHAI AND HONGKONG

Month	Shanghai (Averages of 34 yrs.)		Hongkong[1] (Averages of 24 yrs.)		
	Temperature	Humidity	Temperature	Maximum	Humidity
January.....	37.4° F.	80	60° F.	79.3	74
February.....	39	79	58	79.1	76
March.......	46.2	79	62.7	82.1	83
April........	56	80	70.2	88.6	85
May.........	64.2	80	76.8	91.5	83
June........	74.8	84	80.7	93.6	83
July........	79.6	84	81.8	94	82
August......	79.5	84	81.3	97	83
September....	72.3	84	80.4	94	77
October......	63.2	80	76.3	93.8	71
November....	52	77	69.2	85.6	65
December....	41.6	76	62.7	81.9	66
Average....	58.8° F.	80	71.6° F.	....	77

[1] The report of the Hongkong Observatory for Hongkong for 35 years varies slightly from this.

NOTE.—The highest recorded temperature at Shanghai was 102.9 Far. in 1892 and 1894. During a period of forty years the thermometer at Shanghai reached 100 F. eighteen times and four times reached 102.

The above table based upon the reports of the Observatory at Sicawei, Shanghai, is taken from the China Year Book for 1916.

Mean Barometric Pressure[1]

(Reduced to Freezing-point and Sea-level)

Month	Shang-hai	Hong-kong	Foo-chow	Chung-king	Chefoo	Peking
January	30.33	30.16	30.26	30.22	30.20	30.37
February	30.28	30.14	30.24	30.12	30.27	30.21
March	30.17	30.06	30.14	30.06	30.17	30.22
April	30.00	29.96	30.00	29.96	30.04	30.05
May	29.87	29.86	29.91	29.81	29.85	29.87
June	29.74	29.76	29.78	29.69	29.67	29.67
July	29.69	29.73	29.73	29.64	29.59	29.66
August	29.73	29.74	29.75	29.72	29.63	29.79
September	29.91	29.84	29.86	30.00	29.82	29.85
October	30.11	29.99	30.02	30.10	30.03	30.14
November	30.24	30.11	30.16	30.19	30.15	30.33
December	30.31	30.19	30.26	30.32	30.17	30.35
Average	30.03	29.96	30.00	29.97	29.96	30.04

[1] Report of Siccawei Observatory, from China Year Book, 1923. The following meteorological tables are from the same year book.

Rainfall

(Monthly Average)

Month	Shanghai (1873–1902) Inches	Hongkong (1884–1907) Inches
January	2.15	1.41
February	2.29	1.70
March	3.21	2.95
April	3.59	5.66
May	3.60	12.75 (48.84 max.)
June	6.66	16.43 (34.37 max.)
July	5.10	12.37 (28.23 max.)
August	5.94	14.29 (27.86 max.)
September	4.72	9.47 (30.60 max.)
October	3.31	4.53
November	1.85	1.51
December	1.18	1.06
Mean Annual	43.60	84.13

METEOROLOGY OF PEKING, 1921

Month	Barometer	Mean Temperature, ° F.	Average Maximum, ° F.	Average Minimum, ° F.	Rainfall, Inches
January....	30.26	27.0	37.9	17.4	0.02
February...	30.12	31.8	44.3	21.2	
March.....	30.04	40.7	51.5	30.0	0.16
April.......	29.88	55.8	66.9	44.2	0.02
May.......	29.69	67.9	78.8	55.6	1.39
June.......	29.61	74.8	86.4	63.7	1.75
July.......	29.57	81.5	90.0	70.5	3.89
August.....	29.60	75.9	86.2	68.5	2.45
September..	29.82	70.0	82.6	59.0	0.35
October....	29.96	56.5	68.4	45.1	0.04
November..	30.07	39.1	40.3	23.9	
December..	30.09	29.1	40.6	22.1	

CLIMATE OF TIENTSIN

Tientsin is the port of Peking, 86 miles distant, on the Hai Ho, about 30 miles from the sea. Its proximity to the region of the Yellow River Valley which suffers from periodical visitations of drought and flood makes the following tables relating to rainfall and temperature of considerable interest.

RAINFALL

The average rain and snow-fall in Tientsin for 30 years has been 19.55 inches. The figures by years are as follows:

Year	Inches	Year	Inches	Year	Inches
1892	21.40	1902	9.99	1912	31.32
1893	22.44	1903	15.95	1913	15.43
1894	30.50	1904	23.61	1914	26.57
1895	14.44	1905	19.48	1915	19.22
1896	23.57	1906	15.64	1916	21.61
1897	24.36	1907	16.25	1917	16.32
1898	15.88	1908	26.30	1918	19.93
1899	12.42	1909	14.65	1919	20.00
1900	12.35	1910	17.81	1920	11.06
1901	23.17	1911	25.71	1921	19.15

Temperature

The highest and lowest temperatures (Fahr.) at Tientsin during 20 years beginning in 1902 have been as follows:

Year	Maximum	Minimum	Year	Maximum	Minimum
1902	113.0	13.0	1912	100.0	4.0
1903	102.0	10.0	1913	103.0	2.0
1904	102.0	8.0	1914	104.0	2.0
1905	102.0	12.0	1915	100.0	−4.0
1906	105.0	5.0	1916	104.0	−4.0
1907	104.0	12.0	1917	105.0	0.0
1908	104.0	4.0	1918	105.0	7.0
1909	107.0	2.0	1919	107.0	−4.0
1910	103.0	2.0	1920	108.0	5.0
1911	96.0	−4.0	1921	102.0	1.0

It will be of interest to compare the meteorological reports from the Yangtze Valley and from South China with that from Peking for 1921.

Meteorology of Hankow, 1921

Month	Barometer, Inches	Temperature, °F., Maximum	Temperature, °F., Minimum	Temperature, °F., Mean	Rainfall, Inches
January...	30.378	60	15	37.5	0.52
February..	29.964	83	30	56.5	1.07
March....	30.037	86	30	58	4.10
April......	30.037	83	38	60.5	14.02
May......	29.817	92	61	76.5	7.45
June......	29.705	98	64	81	18.16
July......	29.723	103	73	88	3.02
August....	29.688	103	67	85	5.92
September.	30.003	88.5	58	73.25	7.74
October...	29.833	82	52	67	4.35
November.	30.145	76	40	58	0.50
December..	30.205	65	34	49.5	0.83

METEOROLOGY OF CHUNGKING, 1921

Month	Barometer, Inches	Temperature, ° F., Maximum	Temperature, ° F., Minimum	Temperature, ° F., Mean	Rainfall, Inches
January...	29.96	52.5	43	47.5	0.26
February..	29.55	59.4	46.4	52	0.42
March....	29.47	64.9	50.5	56.1	2.04
April......	29.27	75.6	61.3	68.7	4.02
May......	29.16	79.3	69.1	73.9	8.23
June......	29.94	83.9	72.7	77.7	11.16
July......	28.77	89.2	77.5	84.7	8.83
August....	29.08	86.0	75.9	79.3	10.28
September.	29.33	74.5	70.7	74.3	4.45
October...	29.47	67.8	62.8	64.6	3.37
November.	29.62	62.6	55.9	59.4	0.93
December..	29.59	56.9	51.6	53.6	0.93

METEOROLOGY OF CANTON, 1921

Month	Barometer, Inches	Temperature, ° F., Maximum	Temperature, ° F., Minimum	Temperature, ° F., Mean	Rainfall, Inches
January...	30.27	63	48	54	0.54
February..	30.16	68	52	59	1.56
March....	30.05	70.2	57.9	63.3	2.39
April......	30.01	78.7	66.7	71.3	1.45
May......	30.21	86.2	76.3	77.5	16.42
June......	29.63	88.2	75	81.3	9.28
July......	29.79	90.7	77.2	83.1	11.18
August....	29.69	89.3	78.4	84.2	7.81
September.	29.91	87.4	73.6	77.2	12.67
October...	30.03	85.7	67.6	75.6	0.20
November.	30.16	78.4	58.8	66.9	0.54
December..	30.20	71.4	55.6	62.3	0.39

Mean Annual Barometric Pressure

Shanghai	Hongkong[1]	Foochow	Chungking	Chefoo	Peking
30.03	29.96	30	29.97	29.96	30.04

Average Rainfall During 35 Years

Shanghai	Hongkong [1]	Peking
44.1 inches	84.13 inches	25 inches

[1] The report of the Hongkong Observatory gives for that port as the mean of 35 years barometric pressure, 29.844, rainfall, 83.83.

Mortality Statistics

(Shanghai)

Mortality has ranged from 24.6 per mille in 1891 to 11.2 in 1905 among the foreign residents of Shanghai. Including Chinese and non-residents visiting the port, the figures were 34.6 per mille in 1902 when cholera prevailed to 12.1 in 1906, of which 1.5 were from zymotic diseases. In 1907 the mortality was 17.9 and in 1908, 15.9.

Official Holidays

Under the present Nationalist Government the following are official holidays and commemoration days:—(Solar Calendar)

January 1, Anniversary of the Founding of the Chinese Republic (southern) 1912.

March 12, Anniversary of death of Dr. Sun Yat-sen.

March 29, Anniversary of Martyrdom of 72 Patriots, Flowers Hill, Canton, 1911.

May 5, Anniversary of inauguration of Dr. Sun in 1921 as President of the Canton Government.

May 9, National Humiliation Day, commemorating the Twenty One Demands made by Japan in 1915.

July 9, Commemorating start of expedition against the North in 1926.

October 10, Anniversary of the Chinese Revolution of 1911.

November 12, Birthday of Dr. Sun Yat-sen.

New Standards of Weights and Measures

(From China Year Book, 1931)

Weight, Government Scale

1 Kung Ssu equals	1 Milligramme		
10 Kung Ssu equal	1 Kung Hao	or	1 Centigramme
10 Kung Hao "	1 Kung Li	"	1 Decigramme
10 Kung Li "	1 Kung Fen	"	1 Gramme
10 Kung Fen "	1 Kung Ch'ien	"	1 Decagramme
10 Kung Ch'ien "	1 Kung Liang	"	1 Hectogramme
10 Kung Liang "	1 Kung Chin	"	1 Kilogramme
10 Kung Chin "	1 Kung Heng	"	1 Myriagramme
10 Kung Heng "	1 Kung Shih	"	1 Quintal
10 Kung Shih "	1 Kung Tun	"	1 Tonne

Market Scale

10 Shih Ssu equal	1 Shih Hao
10 Shih Hao "	1 Shih Li
10 Shih Li "	1 Shih Fen
10 Shih Fen "	1 Shih Ch'ien
10 Shih Ch'ien "	1 Shih Liang or 31¼ Grammes
16 Shih Liang "	1 Shih Chin or ½ Kung Chin or 500 Grammes or on Ku P'ing (Treasury) Scale, 13 Liang 4 Ch'ien
100 Shih Chin "	1 Shih Tan

Capacity, Government Scale

1 Kung Ts'o equals	1 Millilitre		
10 Kung Ts'o equal	1 Kung Shao	or	1 Centilitre
10 Kung Shao "	1 Kung Ho	"	1 Decilitre
10 Kung Ho "	1 Kung Sheng	"	1 Litre
10 Kung Sheng "	1 Kung Tou	"	1 Decalitre
10 Kung Tou "	1 Kung Shih	"	1 Hectolitre
10 Kung Shih "	1 Kung P'ing	"	1 Kilolitre

Market Scale

1 Kung Sheng equals 0.966 Sheng of Old Standard. The Old Standard Sheng contained 1.0354688 Litres.

Appendix   722a

LENGTH, GOVERNMENT SCALE

1 Kung Li equals	1 Millimetre		
10 Kung Li equal	1 Kung Fen	or	1 Centimetre
10 Kung Fen "	1 Kung Ts'un	"	1 Decimetre
10 Kung Ts'un "	1 Kung Ch'ih	"	1 Metre
10 Kung Ch'ih "	1 Kung Chang	"	1 Decametre
10 Kung Chang "	1 Kung Ying	"	1 Hectometre
10 Kung Ying "	1 Kung Li	"	1 Kilometre

MARKET SCALE

10 Shih Hao equal 1 Shih Li
10 Shih Li " 1 Shih Fen
10 Shih Fen " 1 Shih Ts'un
10 Shih Ts'un " 1 Shih Ch'ih or ⅓ Kung Ch'ih or 1.4
Ch'ih Old Standard
10 Shih Ch'ih " 1 Shih Chang
10 Shih Chang " 1 Shih Ying
10 Shih Ying " 1 Shih Li

AREA, GOVERNMENT SCALE

1 Kung Li equals 1 Centiare
10 Kung Li equal 1 Kung Fen
10 Kung Fen " 1 Kung Mou or 1 Are or 10 Sq. Kung
Ch'ih
100 Kung Mou " 1 Kung Ch'ing or 1 Hectare

MARKET SCALE

10 Shih Hao equal 1 Shih Li
10 Shih Li " 1 Shih Fen
10 Shih Fen " 1 Shih Mou or 6,000 Sq. Shih Ch'ih
100 Shih Mou " 1 Shih Chang

INDEX

Actors, social status of, 134–135
"Admonitions," painting, 355–356
Agricultural implements, 109–110
Agricultural products, variety of, 7, 97–107
Agriculture, importance of, 86 ff., 113–117, 126
Alchemy, origin and spread of, 327–333
All Souls, feast of, 217–219
Almanac, the Chinese, 77, 207–208
Altai Mountain System, the, 19–20
Altyn Tagh, the, 20
America, beginning of trade relations with, 431–435; treaties with, 443–445, 446, 449, 465–467, 468–469. See United States
American Government, attitude of, toward opium trade, 427–428, 444–445, 449–450, 544–545, 547–548, toward leased territory in China, 489–491, 501–502, toward currency loan, 537–540, toward Shantung question, 583–584, 592–593, 600–602
American International Corporation, railway construction by, blocked, 503–504
American Presbyterian Mission attacked by mob, 120
American Red Cross, relief administered by, 159–160, 616
Americans in China, regulations concerning, 665–667

Amherst's mission to China, 438
Amidhism, religion of, 296–297
Ancestor worship, 64–66, 253 ff.
Anfu Party, 618–619
Angell, President, commission headed by, 468
Anglo-Japanese Treaty of Alliance, 503, 595–596, 602–603
Animal resources, 7, 9, 10, 91, 108, 109
Annam, former dependency, 6, 7
Anti-opium reform, 542–549. See also Opium
Arabs, early trade with, 417–418, 420; Mohammedanism introduced by, 418, 419, 421, poppy plant introduced by, 426
Army, 526–529; unpreparedness of the, 484–485
Arnold, Julean, cited on use of hand-looms, 181
Art, early Chinese, 339–345; a renaissance, 345–347; Buddhist influence on, 347–349, 352, 354, 360, 361–362; Taoist emblems in, 349; Confucian emblems in, 350, wood carving, 350–351, sculpture, 351–354; painting, 354–357; technique, 358–359; rival schools of, 359–362; T'ang Dynasty painting, 362–364; Sung Dynasty painting, 365–366; Yuan, Ming, and Ch'ing Dynasty painting, 366–368
Arthur, President, cited on Chinese immigration, 468
Artisan guilds, 189–193, 194
Assemblies, provincial, 555